Library of Congress Cataloging in Publication Data

Kearns, George, comp.
   Literature of the world.

   SUMMARY: An anthology for the high school
student of poetry, short stories, essays, and
plays from various countries and periods.

   1. Literature—Collections. 1. Literature—
Collections I. Title.
PN6014.K34 1974   808.8   73–7987
ISBN 0-07-033437-4

    14 15 16   98 97

Send all inquiries to:
Glencoe/McGraw-Hill
21600 Oxnard Street, Suite 500
Woodland Hills, CA 91367

Editorial Development: Linda Richmond
Editing and Styling: Linda Epstein
Text Design: John Keithley and Carol Boyar
Cover Art: Florence Noa
Production: Peter Guilmette and John Sabella

Literature of the World

Second Edition

Edited by *George Kearns*

 **Glencoe McGraw-Hill**

New York, New York   Columbus, Ohio   Woodland Hills, California   Peoria, Illinois

Acknowledgments

The editor wishes to thank the following for permission to reprint material included in this anthology:

George Allen & Unwin Ltd., for "The String Game" from *Specimens of Bushman Folklore.*

Chatto & Windus for "Dreaming in the Shanghai Restaurant" from *Addictions* by D. J. Enright. Reprinted by permission of Chatto & Windus, the publishers.

The Clarendon Press for "The Capital," "Cold Up North," and "Lament of the Brazen Camels" from *The Poems of Li Ho* translated by J. D. Frodsham, copyright 1970. Reprinted by permission of the Clarendon Press, Oxford.

Coward-McCann for "On My Style" from *The Difficulty of Being* by Jean Cocteau, translated by Elizabeth Sprigge. English copyright © 1967 by Elizabeth Sprigge.

The John Day Company for "With the Army at the North Frontier" by Li I from *The White Pony*, edited by Robert Payne, The John Day Company, New York, 1947.

The Devin-Adair Company for "The End of a Good Man" from *The Man Who Invented Sin* by Sean O'Faolain. Copyright 1948 by The Devin-Adair Company. Reprinted by permission of The Devin-Adair Company.

Dodd, Mead & Company, Inc. for "Street Cries" from *The Sceptred Flute* by Sarojini Naidu. Copyright 1917, 1928 by Dodd, Mead & Company. Copyright renewed 1945, 1956 by Sarojini Naidu.

Doubleday & Company, Inc. for "The Guest" by Albert Camus from *Voices from France* by Miriam Morton. Copyright © 1969 by Miriam Morton; for eleven haiku from *An Introduction to Haiku* by Harold G. Henderson. Copyright © 1958 by Harold G. Henderson; for "Friends in San Rosario" from *Roads of Destiny* by O. Henry. Copyright © 1909 by Doubleday & Company, Inc. All reprinted by permission of Doubleday & Company, Inc.

E. P. Dutton & Co., Inc. for "Hands" from the book *This Is Moscow Speaking* by Yuli Daniel (Nikolai Arzhak). Translated by Stuart Hood, Harold Shukman & John Richardson. Copyright © 1965 by Institut Littéraire S.A.R.L. Paris. Copyright 1968 in the English translation by Harvil Press, London and E. P. Dutton & Co., Inc., New York; for "The Nefarious War" from *The Works of Li Po* translated by Shigeyoshi Obata. Copyright 1922, 1950 by E. P. Dutton & Co., Inc. Both reprinted by permission of the publishers.

John Farquharson Ltd. for "The Actor" by Stan Barstow.

Farrar, Straus & Giroux, Inc., for "Two Memories of Sido" from *Earthly Paradise* by Colette, copyright © 1966 by Farrar, Straus & Giroux, Inc.; for "The Snake and the Crocodile" from

Contents

Unit Three
Fables & Legends

Unit Four
Drama

Unit Five
Poetry

POEMS ABOUT DEATH

POEMS ABOUT NATURE

POEMS ABOUT ANIMALS

POEMS OF DELIGHTS

POEMS OF COMEDY AND SATIRE

AFRICAN AND INDIAN SONGS AND CEREMONIES

CONCRETE POEMS

Unit Six
A Diversity of Cultures

Unit Seven
Personal Experience

Unit Eight
No Man Is an Island

Preface

The aim of this second edition of *Literature of the World* is to offer a collection of the very best literature of both the Western and non-Western worlds. In the process of selecting individual pieces, the editor has sought to provide material which is truly representative of the culture from which it comes. In addition to recognized landmarks of world literature, the reader will also find many pieces which are presented here for the first time. In many instances, these selections have been specially translated for this volume. These selections have been included because they are typical products of the cultures which produced them.

The selections have been grouped in eight teaching units. The first two units—STORIES AND TALES FROM THE PAST and STORIES OF THE TWENTIETH-CENTURY—are devoted exclusively to the short story, a genre which has always been popular with the world's writers. The works in these two units exhibit a wide range of literary themes and styles. Taken together, these two units illustrate the evolution of the short story from medieval sources to the present day.

FABLES AND LEGENDS, the third unit, is new to this edition. It is designed to acquaint the student with material which has had a wide-ranging effect on world literature and culture. In their subject matter, the selections are typical of the areas from which they originated.

DRAMA, the fourth unit, contains three complete plays. One is representative of the Japanese achievement in this art form. Another is of Nigerian origin. The highlight of the unit is Bertolt Brecht's masterpiece *Galileo*.

POETRY, the fifth unit, includes a wide range of poems representative of various authors, periods, and styles. To demonstrate that poets throughout the world have been continuously concerned with similar subjects, the selections are grouped in eleven separate thematic subunits.

The three remaining units—A DIVERSITY OF CULTURES, PERSONAL EXPERIENCE, and NO MAN IS AN ISLAND—are also thematic in nature. The first two are new to this edition. Each contains a generous assortment of literary genres. Each unit is structured to enable the student to grasp the central notion that literary artists throughout the world have a great deal in common and that they share a common goal: to make the human experience intelligible.

Those familiar with the first edition will be immediately aware of the substantial revision which this volume represents. Of the 146 selections included in this edition, ninety are completely new. In addition, greater emphasis has been placed on the inclusion of the works of major non-American writers. Such significant authors as Anton Chekhov, Isak Dinesen, Heinrich Böll, Sean O'Faolain, Charles Baudelaire, Albert Camus, and Bertolt Brecht are well represented. Readers will also notice that the greater majority of the new selections are of recent origin and that several have been taken from the emerging literature of the African continent.

In addition to the general introductions which precede each unit, each of the selections in this edition is accompanied by an explanatory note which is designed to whet the reader's appetite and to provide necessary background information. These notes concentrate on literary and historical concerns. Biographical information on individual authors will be found in a separate section at the end of the book. The discussion questions not only emphasize literary analysis but also attempt to assist the student in placing the work in the context of the unit in which it appears and in the broader context of the specific national culture it represents.

In this edition the illustration program is closely coordinated with the content of the selections. Each illustration is representative of fine art, and the specific pieces are drawn from a variety of Western and non-Western sources. Each unit is introduced by a reproduction which in itself makes a statement about the unit's content. Mini-galleries composed of content-connected reproductions accompany many units. The purpose of the illustration program is to expose the student to a sampling of world art and to suggest that painters and sculptors consistently deal with the same basic ideas as literary artists.

The editor wishes to thank the many teachers who have contributed suggestions for improvement which have been incorporated into this edition. A special word of thanks is due to Ms. Mary McKeown, principal of the American School in Chicago. Ms. McKeown and members of her staff—Ms. Laurie Muelder, Ms. Fanny Segalla, and Mr. Tom Kennelly—read and reacted to the overall plan and to the developing manuscript at various stages. Their comments and reactions were helpful, pertinent, and very much appreciated.

Finally, the editor hopes that this collection of world literature will make some small contribution to the noble purpose of broadening the student's understanding of the world's human community. It is about this goal that the 1970 Nobel Prize winner in literature, Aleksandr I. Solzhenitsyn of the Soviet Union, spoke so eloquently in the acceptance speech which he wrote but never delivered:

> The only salvation of humanity lies in everyone concerning himself with everything everywhere: the peoples of the East cannot be totally indifferent to what takes place in the West; and the peoples of the West cannot be totally indifferent to what takes place in the East. And literature, one of the most delicate and responsive instruments of human existence, has been the first to take hold of, to assimilate, to seize upon this feeling of the growing unity of humanity.

Dom
Der Reiter
Presse– und Informationsamt der Bundesregierung

Unit One Stories & Tales from the Past

There is no such thing as a completely new story. This may seem like a strange statement, for we know that thousands of "new" stories appear every year in books, magazines, and plays, in movies, and on television. Surely a few of these must be original?

The answer is both yes and no. The most important kind of originality of a work of fiction usually springs from the way a writer treats his subject. The basic plot—or narrative pattern—is probably not new; in fact it has probably been used for centuries.

To understand this is to find an exciting insight into the world of fiction. Certain narrative patterns are repeated over and over again, but *not* because writers are lazy, or dishonest, or unimaginative. They are repeated because both writers and readers find that these basic stories relate to our human experience at a very deep level of our consciousness.

Let us look at one specific example. Probably no basic story is more widely used than that of a journey or quest. In a quest story the hero departs from home, passes through dangers and adventures, then returns with riches or happiness or experience.

As you read the stories on the following pages you will find this theme transformed over and over again. In the opening unit it can be seen very clearly in the tales by Boccaccio and Cervantes. In these two stories especially, the theme of journey/quest is obvious. But sometimes writers use it in ways which are not so easy to see. Kafka's short fable "My Destination" page 121 treats the quest with a modern irony and bewilderment.

In the Japanese play "The Dwarf Trees" (page 185) there is a double journey or quest: first, by the Emperor of Japan, who wanders about the countryside in disguise; second, by the hero of the play, who journeys to the Emperor's Court where he regains his lost fortune.

Look, too, at Yeats's poem "An Irish Airman" (page 236). On first reading it, you may not consciously connect the poem with the narrative pattern of the quest because it is a lyric poem and the narrative is implied, not stated. But on a closer look the theme is clearly there: the airman has left the safety of his home to seek his "fate" and a new kind of "delight" to satisfy his restless spirit.

Probably very few writers sit down to write saying to themselves something like, "Now I am going to use the narrative pattern of the journey or quest." Rather, the pattern comes to them instinctively for the very reason that it corresponds so deeply to human experience. In a sense every man's life is a journey or quest, even though his adventures may seem much more ordinary than those of Don Quixote or Odysseus or Sir Galahad. The decisions we must make, the dangers we must face in an ordinary life, are just as great as are meetings with ogres and dragons.

A leading student of myth and literature, Joseph Campbell, says in his book *The Hero With a Thousand Faces*, that stories from all times and cultures "will be always the one, shape-shifting yet marvelously constant story that we find, together with a challengingly persistent suggestion of more remaining to be experienced than will ever be known or told." He then goes on to say: "The latest incarnation of Oedipus, the continual romance of the Beauty and the Beast, stand this afternoon on the corner of Forty-second Street and Fifth Avenue, waiting for the traffic light to change."

The art of storytelling, then, is more than a form of entertainment, even though we expect a good story to be entertaining. It is also a way for men to express their sense of the mystery of experience. It is also a way for us to give shape or meaning to experience. Of the stories in the following section some are comic, some are tragic, and some are romantic; and many are mixtures of these three modes. But all of these stories have two things in common: each was intended to be an amusement, a diversion; and at the same time each was meant to bring some kind of order into the chaos of life, even if that order takes the form of a question rather than a clear answer.

This tale by the great French storyteller, de Maupassant, may remind the reader of the work of Edgar Allan Poe. Like Poe's "The Cask of Amontillado" and "The Tell-Tale Heart," this story explores a haunted mind. Through an atmosphere of hallucination, and through the revealing voice of the speaker, de Maupassant takes us into a world of uncertain reality. There are two stories here, and they overlap like a double exposure on a piece of film. One is the story that the speaker wants to tell; the other is the story that he tries to hide, even from himself. By the time the reader comes to the final paragraph, he knows more about the speaker than the speaker knows about himself. This ironic double vision gives the story its significance. To the speaker the events represent the unfathomable mystery that has victimized him; to the reader they show the pit of despair the speaker has dug for himself.

Guy de Maupassant

Who Knows?

Thank God! At last I shall write what happened! But can I? Do I dare? It is so fantastic, so inexplicable, so incomprehensible, so mad!

If I were not sure of what I saw, sure that there was no flaw in my reasoning, no error in my conclusions, no gap in the inflexible sequence of my observations, I should believe myself simply subject to hallucinations, the victim of a strange vision. After all, who knows?

Today I am in a sanatorium,[1] but I entered voluntarily, out of prudence, or was it fear? One man alone knows my story, the house doctor. Now I shall set it all down, I don't know quite why. Perhaps to unburden myself of the thing inside me that haunts me like some dreadful nightmare. Anyhow, here it is.

I have always been a recluse, a dreamer, a kind of philosopher, detached and kindly, satisfied with little, harboring no bitterness against men and no grudge against heaven. I have always lived alone, because a kind of uneasiness seizes me in the presence of others. How can I explain it? I cannot. It's not that I shun society. I enjoy chatting or dining with my friends but when I feel them near me for any length of time, even the most initimate, I get bored, tired, unnerved, and feel a growing, obsessive desire to have them leave me to myself, to be alone.

1 sanatorium *Here, an establishment for treating nervous or mental diseases.*

This desire is more than a need, it is an irresistible necessity. And if I were to be forced to remain with people, if I had to give lengthy attention to their conversation, something would happen. What? Ah! Who knows? Possibly only a fainting spell? Of course, probably only a fainting spell.

I am so fond of being alone that I cannot even endure the nearness of others sleeping under my roof; I cannot live in Paris because living there is for me a constant agony. I die inside, and for me it is both physical and nervous torture to sense this huge swarming crowd, breathing around me even in their sleep. Ah! The sleep of others is even more painful to me than their speech. And I can never rest, when I know or feel that there are other beings, on the other side of the wall, who suffer this nightly suspension of consciousness.

Why am I this way? Who knows? Perhaps the reason is quite simple: I tire very quickly of anything outside myself. There are many people like me.

There are two kinds of people. Those who need others, who are distracted, amused, soothed by company, while loneliness assails, exhausts, and destroys them, as would the ascent of a terrible glacier or the crossing of the desert. And those who, on the contrary, are worried, bored, irritated, and cramped, by contact with others, while solitude gives them peace and rest in the freedom and fantasy of their thoughts.

It is, in fact, a recognized psychological phenomenon. The former are meant to live the life of the extrovert; the latter, that of the introvert. In my own case, my attention to outward things is brief and quickly exhausted, and, when it reaches its limits, I am conscious of an unbearable physical and mental discomfort.

The result has been that I am, or rather was, very much attached to inanimate objects, which take on for me the importance of human beings, and that my house has, or rather had, become a world in which I lived a lonely but active life, surrounded by things, furniture, and ornaments that I knew and loved like friends. I had gradually filled my life with them, and embellished it with them, and felt content and satisfied, happy as in the arms of a loving woman whose familiar caress has become a calm and gentle need.

I had had this house built in a beautiful garden that separated it from the roads, not far from a town, where I could enjoy the social amenities, of which I felt the need from time to time. All my servants slept in a building at the far end of a walled kitchen garden. In the silence of my house, hidden as it was and buried under the foliage of tall trees, the enveloping darkness of the nights was so restful and welcome that I always put off going to bed for several hours, so that I might enjoy it longer.

That evening *Sigurd*[2] had been given at the local theater. It was the first time I had heard this beautiful fairy play with music and I had thoroughly enjoyed it.

I was returning home on foot, at a lively pace, with scraps of melody running in my head, and entrancing scenes still vivid in my mind. It was dark, pitch black; I could hardly see the road, and several times I nearly fell headlong into the ditch. From the tollhouse to my place is a little more than half a mile or about twenty minutes' slow walking. It was one o'clock in the morning, one or one-thirty; the sky suddenly cleared a little before me and the crescent moon appeared, the melancholy crescent of the waning moon. The moon in its first quarter, when it rises at four or five in the evening, is bright, with cheerful, silvery light, but in the last quarter, when it rises after midnight, it is a dull copper color, and ominous—a real witches' Sabbath[3] moon. All night walkers must have noted this. This first quarter's crescent, even when slender as a thread, sheds a faint but cheerful gleam, which lifts the heart, and throws clearly defined shadows on the ground; the last quarter's crescent sheds a fitful light that casts almost no shadow.

2 Sigurd *A play based on the legend of Siegfried.*
3 Witches' Sabbath *A midnight meeting of witches and magicians held on Halloween and at other times, such as Walpurgis Night.*

The dark silhouette of my garden loomed ahead and for some reason I felt rather hesitant at the idea of going in. I slackened my pace. The night was very mild. The great mass of trees looked like a tomb, in which my house lay buried.

I opened my garden gate and went down the long driveway leading to the house. The rows of sycamores, arched overhead, made a lofty tunnel that flowed by dense clusters of green and wound around the lawn on which flower beds in the lightening darkness formed oval patches of no particular color.

Nearing the house, I felt curiously uneasy. I paused. There was not a sound, not a breath of air stirring in the leaves. "What's wrong with me?" I thought. For ten years I had been coming home like this without ever feeling nervous. I was not afraid. I have never been afraid of the dark. The sight of a man, a burglar or a thief, would merely have thrown me into a rage, and I would have jumped on him without a moment's hesitation. Besides, I was armed. I had my revolver. But I did not put my hand on it, because I wanted to resist the fear stirring within me.

What was it? A foreboding? The mysterious premonition that grips a man's mind at the approach of the supernatural? Perhaps. Who knows?

As I went on, I felt shivers running down my spine, and when I was close to the wall of my great shuttered house, I felt that I must wait a few minutes before opening the door and entering. So I sat down on a garden seat under the drawing-room windows. I stayed there, trembling, leaning my head against the wall, staring into the blackness of the foliage. During those first moments I noticed nothing unusual around me. I was aware of a buzzing in my ears, but I often hear that. I sometimes think I can hear trains passing, bells ringing, or crowds tramping.

But soon the humming became more distinct, more definite, more recognizable. I had been wrong. It was not the usual throbbing of my arteries that caused these noises in my ears, but a definite, though confused, noise that was coming, no doubt about it, from inside my house.

I could hear it through the wall, a continuous noise, no, more a rustling than a noise, a faint stirring of things, as of many objects being moved about, as if someone were shifting all my furniture and dragging it about.

Naturally, for some time I thought I must be mistaken. But, having put my ear against a shutter to hear the strange noises in my house more clearly, I was quite firmly convinced that something abnormal and inexplicable was going on inside. I was not afraid, but, I was—how shall I say?—bewildered and astonished. I did not cock my revolver, suspecting—and how right I was!—that it would be of no use. I waited.

I waited a long while, unable to come to a decision, with my mind perfectly clear but deeply disturbed. I waited motionless, listening to the growing noise, which kept gaining in intensity until it finally rose to an impatient, angry rumble.

Then, suddenly, ashamed of my cowardice, I seized my bunch of keys, chose the one I needed, thrust it into the lock, turned it twice, and, pushing in the door with all my strength, I sent it crashing against the wall inside.

The bang echoed like a gunshot, and the crash was answered by a fearful uproar from cellar to attic. It was so sudden, so terrifying, so deafening that I stepped back several paces, and, although I realized it was useless, I drew my revolver from its holster.

I still waited, but not for long. I could now distinguish an extraordinary sound of tramping, not of human feet or shoes, but of crutches, wooden stumps, iron stumps that rang out like cymbals.

Suddenly, on the threshold of the front door I saw an armchair, my big reading chair, come strutting out. It moved off into the garden. It was followed by others from the drawing room; next came the low sofas crawling along like crocodiles on their stumpy legs, then all the rest of my chairs, leaping like goats, and the little footstools hopping along like rabbits.

Imagine my feelings! I slipped into a flower bed where I crouched, my eyes glued on this exodus of my furniture. It all came out, one piece after another, quickly or slowly, according to shape and weight. My piano, a concert grand, galloped past like a runaway horse, with a faint jangle of music still inside it; the smaller objects, brushes, cut glass, goblets, slid over the gravel like ants, gleaming like glowworms in the moonlight. The carpets and hangings crawled away, with all the oozing elasticity of devil fish.[4] Then I saw my desk appear, a rare eighteenth-century collector's item, containing all my letters and the whole painful record of my heart's spent passion. And in it were also my photographs.

Suddenly I was no longer afraid, I threw myself upon it, I grappled it as one grapples with a thief in flight, but it pursued its irresistible course, and in spite of my utmost efforts, I could not even slow it up. As I wrestled like a madman with this terrible force, I fell to the ground in the struggle. Then it rolled me over and over, dragging me through the gravel, and the other furniture close on its heels had already begun to tread on me, trampling and bruising my legs, then, when I let go, the others swept over my body like a cavalry charge over an unhorsed soldier.

At last, mad with terror, I managed to drag myself out of the main path and I hid again in the trees, watching the disappearance of the smallest, tiniest, humblest pieces I had ever owned.

Presently I heard, in the distance, inside my house, now as sonorous as it was empty, a terrific din of doors being shut. They banged from attic to basement, until at last the hall door, which I myself had left open in my mad flight, slammed shut with a bang.

I fled at a run toward the town and did not recover my composure until I got to the streets and met some people coming home late. I rang the bell of a hotel where I was known. I had dusted off my clothes, and I explained that I had lost my keys, including the key of the kitchen garden where my servants slept in a separate house, behind the garden wall that protected my fruit and vegetables from thieves.

I buried myself in the bed they gave me, but I couldn't sleep, so I waited for daylight, listening to the violent beating of my heart. I had given orders for my servants to be informed at dawn, and my valet knocked at my door at seven in the morning.

He looked upset.

"A terrible thing happened last night, sir," he said.

"What?"

"All your furniture has been stolen, sir, everything, down to the smallest things."

This news cheered me. Why? Who knows? I was calm, sure that I could conceal my feelings and never tell anyone what I had seen. I would hide it, bury it in my mind like some ghastly secret. I answered:

"Then they are the same people who stole my keys. The police must be informed immediately. I'm getting up and will be with you in a few moments."

The inquiry lasted five months. Not even the smallest of my ornaments or the slightest trace of the thieves was ever found. Good God! If I had told what I knew—if I had told—they would have put away, not the thieves, but me, the man who could have seen such a thing!

Of course, I knew how to keep my mouth shut. But I did not furnish my house again. It was no good. It would only have happened again. I never wanted to go back to it again. I never did. In fact, I never saw it again.

I went to a hotel in Paris and consulted doctors about my state of nerves, which had been worrying me since that dreadful night.

4 devil fish *A kind of octopus.*

They prescribed travel and I took their advice. I began with a trip to Italy. The sun did me good. For six months I wandered from Genoa to Venice, from Venice to Florence, from Florence to Rome, from Rome to Naples. Next I toured Sicily, that land of such wonderful scenery and monuments, relics left by the Greeks and Normans. I crossed to Africa and traveled at my leisure through the great desert, so yellow and calm, where still camels, gazelles, and nomadic Arabs roam, where, in the clear, dry air no obsession can persist by night or day.

I returned to France via Marseilles, and in spite of the gaiety of Provence[5] the diminished intensity of the sunlight depressed me. On my return to the continent, I had the odd feeling of a patient who thinks he is cured but who is warned by a dull pain that the source of illness has not been eradicated.

I went back to Paris, but after a month I was bored. It was autumn, and I wanted to tour Normandy,[6] which was new ground to me, before winter set in.

I began with Rouen,[7] of course, and for a week I wandered about, intrigued, delighted, and thrilled in this medieval town, the amazing museum of rare Gothic monuments.

Then, one afternoon, about four o'clock, as I was walking down an extraordinary street, along which flowed an inky black stream, my attention, previously centered on the strange and ancient appearance of the houses, was caught suddenly by a row of secondhand furniture shops.

They had, indeed, chosen the right spot, these seedy junk dealers in this fantastic alley of houses overlooking this sinister stream, under pointed roofs of tile or slate on which the weather vanes of a vanished age still creaked. Stacked in the rear of the dark shops could be seen carved chests, china from Rouen, Nevers, and Moustiers, statues, some painted, others carved in wood, crucifixes, Madonnas, saints, church ornaments, vestments, copes,[8] even chalices and an old gilded wooden tabernacle now vacated by God. What extraor-

dinary storerooms in these great, lofty houses, packed from cellar to attic with all sorts of objects whose usefulness was really at an end, and that had outlived their natural owners, their century, their period, their fashion, to be bought as curios by later generations.

My passion for antiques revived in this collector's paradise. I went from shop to shop, crossing in two strides the bridge made of four rotten planks thrown over the stinking flow of the stream. Then—God have mercy! —I felt my heart in my throat! I saw one of my finest wardrobes[9] at the edge of a vault crammed with junk and that looked like the entrance to the catacombs of some cemetery of old furniture. I drew near, trembling all over, trembling to such an extent that I did not dare touch it. I put out my hand, then I hesitated. But it *was* mine—a unique Louis XIII,[10] unmistakable to anyone who had ever seen it. Suddenly, peering farther along toward the darker interior of this gallery, I noticed three of my petit-point[11] chairs, and, farther off, my two Henry II tables, which were so rare that people came from Paris to see them.

Imagine, just imagine my state of mind!

Then I went forward, dazed and gripped by emotion, but I persisted, for I am no coward. I went on as a knight of the Dark Ages would have penetrated a magic circle. As I advanced, I found all my belongings, my tapestries, my weapons, everything, except the desk containing my letters, which I could not discover anywhere.

And so I continued, descending to dark corridors to climb up again to the upper stories. I was alone. I called but there was no answer. I was alone; there was no one in this huge, winding labyrinth of a building.

Night came on and I had to sit down in the dark on one of my own chairs, for I wouldn't go away. From time to time I called out, "Hello! Anybody there?"

I must have been there for more than an

---

5 Provence *Historical region of southeast France.*
6 Normandy *Historical region of northwest France.*
7 Rouen *A manufacturing city, the capital of Normandy.*
8 copes *Embroidered capes worn by priests during certain ceremonies.*
9 wardrobes *Large trunks.*
10 Louis XIII *A piece of furniture from the reign of Louis XIII of France (1610–1643).*
11 petit-point *Hand embroidery used in upholstering.*

hour when I heard footsteps, light, slow steps; I could not tell where they were coming from. I nearly ran away, but, pulling myself together, I called out again and saw a light in the next room.

"Who's there?" said a voice.

I answered, "A customer."

The answer came: "It's rather late; we're closed."

I retorted, "I've been waiting for more than an hour."

"You could have come back tomorrow."

"No. Tomorrow, I am leaving Rouen."

I did not dare go to him and he did not come to me. All this time I saw the reflection of his candle shining on a tapestry in which two angels were hovering over the dead on a battlefield. That, too, belonged to me. I said:

"Well! Are you coming?"

He replied, "I'm waiting for you."

I got up and went toward him.

In the center of a large room stood a very short man, very short and very fat, phenomenally, hideously fat.

He had a sparse beard, straggling, ill-kept, dirty yellow beard, and not a hair on his head, not one! As he held his candle raised at arm's length in order to see me, the dome of his bald head looked like a miniature moon shining in this huge room stacked with old furniture. His face was wrinkled and bloated, his eyes mere slits.

I bargained for three of my chairs, paid a large sum for them, then and there, giving him merely the number of my suite at the hotel. They were to be delivered the next day before 9 A.M.

Then I left. He saw me to the door quite politely.

I went straight to the police station, where I told the inspector of the theft of my furniture and the discovery I had just made.

He got in touch immediately by telegraph with the magistrate who had first investigated the theft at my home, and asked me to wait for the answer. An hour later it was received and completely confirmed my story.

"I'll have him arrested and questioned at once," he said, "for he might become suspicious and move your belongings. You had best have your dinner and come back in two hours. I'll have him here and interrogate him in your presence."

"Fine! And thank you very much."

I had dinner at my hotel, and my appetite was better than I should have thought possible. I was rather pleased. My man was caught.

Two hours later I was back at the police station, where the officer was waiting for me.

"Well, sir," he said, seeing me approach. "We didn't find your man. My men couldn't lay their hands on him."

I felt faint.

"But—you have found the house?" I asked.

"Of course. It will be watched until he comes back. But he has disappeared."

"Disappeared?"

"Yes. He usually spends the evening with his neighbor, a queer old hag, a widow called Madame Bidoin, a second-hand dealer like himself. She hasn't seen him this evening and couldn't help us. We shall have to wait until tomorrow."

I left. The streets of Rouen now seemed sinister and threatening, with the disturbing effect of a haunted house.

I slept badly, plagued by nightmares whenever I dozed.

Since I did not want to seem too worried or impatient, I waited until ten o'clock the next morning before going back to the police.

The dealer had not returned. His shop was still closed.

The inspector said, "I have taken the necessary steps. The prosecutor has been informed. We'll go together to the shop, have it opened, and you can show me what belongs to you."

We took a cab. Officers were stationed, along with a locksmith, in front of the shop door, which had been opened.

When I entered, I saw that my wardrobe, my chairs, my tables, and all my household effects were gone. And the night before I had not been able to take a single step without bumping into one of my possessions! The superintendent, surprised, looked at me, with suspicion at first.

"Well, sir," I said, "the disappearance of my furniture coincides strangely with the disappearance of the dealer."

He smiled.

"That's true. You were wrong to buy and pay for your own belongings, yesterday. It tipped him off."

I replied, "What I can't understand is that all the space occupied by my things is now filled with other pieces."

"Oh," said the superintendent, "he had all night, and accomplices, no doubt. This building must communicate with the neighboring houses. Don't fear, sir, I'll see to this business myself. The thief will not escape us for long, we've got his hideout."

My heart was pounding so violently I thought it would burst.

I stayed on for two weeks in Rouen. The man never came back. Unbelievable! God knows nobody could outwit or trap a man like that!

Then on the following morning I received this strange letter from my gardener, who had been acting as caretaker for my house, which had remained unoccupied since the robbery.

Dear Sir:

I beg to inform you that last night something happened, which we can't explain, nor the police either. All the furniture has come back; all of it, even the smallest bits. The house is now just as it was the night of the robbery. It's enough to make you doubt your sanity! It all happened the night of Friday and in the early hours of Saturday. The paths are cut up as if everything had been dragged from the garden gate to the door. It was just the same the day it all disappeared.

I await your return and remain,
Your respectful servant,
Philippe Raudin

No, no, never! I will not return there!

I took the letter to the chief inspector in Rouen.

"Now that's a very clever way of making restitution. Let's play possum. We'll catch our man one of these days."

But they didn't catch him. No! They never caught him, and now I am as terrified of him as if a wild animal were loose on my track.

Disappeared, escaped, this monster with the bald head like a full moon! They'll never catch him. He'll never go back to his shop. Why should he? I am the only one who can find him and I refuse to.

I won't, I won't!

And if he does go back, if he returns to his shop, who can prove that my furniture was ever there? There is only my word against his, and I have a feeling it is becoming suspect.

No! My life was getting impossible. And I couldn't keep the secret of what I had seen. I could not go on living normally with the fear that this horror might begin again.

I went and consulted the doctor who is director of this sanatorium and told him the whole story.

After questioning me thoroughly, he said:

"My dear sir, would you be willing to stay here a while?"

"Of course, Doctor."

"You have means?"

"Yes, Doctor."

"Would you like a private apartment?"

"Yes, Doctor."

"Would you like your friends to come and see you?"

"No, no. No one. The man from Rouen might venture to pursue me here to get even with me."

I have been alone, completely alone here for three months. My mind is almost at ease. I am afraid of only one thing—supposing the antiquary[12] went mad—and was sent to this asylum—Even prisons aren't safe!

Claire Noyes/TRANSLATOR

12 antiquary *One who collects or studies antiquities.*

For Discussion

1 How would you describe the speaker of this story? When he says that he is "sure" of what he saw, and "sure" that there is no gap in his reasoning, whom does he seem to be trying to convince? He asks himself, "Why am I this way?" and then answers, "I tire quickly of anything outside myself." Is this a good answer to his own question? Where else do you find him revealing aspects of himself which he does not understand, or does not want to reveal?

2 Does the weird, galloping escape of the furniture suggest what is happening within the speaker's mind? Why does he say that he will not furnish his house again because the furniture will only make another escape? How does the dark, empty house reflect its owner, who cannot bear to have people near him?

3 Why does all the furniture return to the house after the speaker buys some of it back from the dealer? Why does he fear this person? The speaker ends his story by saying, "Even prisons aren't safe!" What meaning can you find in this statement?

4 What seems to be the cause of the speaker's trouble? Has he committed a crime, or offended anyone? Where does he always seek the cause of his trouble, and where do you think he should look? Is there any suggestion that he will ever be "cured"?

One of the great themes of literature, from the Greek tragedies to the modern Theater of the Absurd, is the difference between appearance and reality. In "The Beggar" Chekhov presents a humorous example of the way in which reality can turn out to be illusion.

Anton Chekhov

The Beggar

"Kind sir, have pity; turn your attention to a poor, hungry man! For three days I have had nothing to eat; I haven't five kopecks[1] for a lodging. I swear it before God. For eight years I was a village schoolteacher and then I lost my place through intrigues. I fell a victim to calumny. It is a year now since I have had any work——"

The lawyer Skvortsoff looked at the ragged, fawn-colored overcoat of the applicant, at his dull, drunken eyes, at the red spot on either cheek, and it seemed to him as if he had seen this man somewhere before.

"I have now had an offer of a position in the province of Kaluga," the beggar went on, "but I haven't the money to get there. Help me kindly; I am ashamed to ask, but—I am obliged to by circumstances."

Skvortsoff's eyes fell on the man's overshoes, one of which was high and the other low, and he suddenly remembered something.

"Look here, it seems to me I met you day before yesterday in Sadovaya Street," he said, "but you told me then that you were a student who had been expelled, and not a village schoolteacher. Do you remember?"

"No-no, that can't be so," mumbled the beggar, taken aback. "I am a village schoolteacher, and if you like I can show you my papers."

"Never mind lying! You called yourself a student and even told me what you had been expelled for. Don't you remember?"

Skvortsoff flushed and turned away from the ragged creature with an expression of disgust.

"This is dishonesty, my dear sir!" he cried angrily. "This is swindling! I shall send the police for you! Even if you are poor and hungry, that does not give you any right to lie brazenly and shamelessly!"

The poor man caught hold of the door han-

1 kopecks *Russian coins of little value; 100 make a ruble.*

dle and looked furtively round the entrance hall, like a detected thief.

"I—I am not lying——" he muttered. "I can show you my papers."

"Who would believe you?" Skvortsoff continued indignantly. "Don't you know that it's a low, dirty trick to exploit the sympathy which society feels for village schoolteachers and students? It's revolting."

Skvortsoff lost his temper and began to scold the beggar unmercifully. The impudent lying of the ragamuffin offended what he, Skvortsoff, most prized in himself: his kindness, his tender heart, his compassion for all unhappy things. That lie, an attempt to take advantage of the pity of its "subject," seemed to him to profane the charity which he liked to extend to the poor out of the purity of his heart. At first the ragged man continued to protest innocence, but soon he grew silent and hung his head in confusion.

"Sir!" he said, laying his hand on his heart, "the fact is I—was lying! I am neither a student nor a schoolteacher. All that was a fiction. Formerly I sang in a Russian choir and was sent away for drunkenness. But what else can I do? I can't get along without lying. No one will give me anything when I tell the truth. With truth a man would starve to death or die of cold for lack of a lodging. You reason justly, I understand you, but—what can I do?"

"What can you do? You ask what you can do?" cried Skvortsoff, coming close to him. "Work! That's what you can do! You must work!"

"Work—yes, I know that myself; but where can I find work?"

"Rot! You're young and healthy and strong; you could always find work if you only wanted to, but you're lazy and spoiled and drunken! You smell like a barroom. You're rotten and false to the core, and all you can do is to lie. When you consent to lower yourself to work, you want a job in an office or in a choir or in a billiard parlor—any employment for which you can get money without doing anything! How would you like to try your hand at manual labor? No, you'd never be a porter or a factory hand; you're a man of pretensions, you are!"

"You judge harshly," cried the beggar with a bitter laugh.

"Where can I find manual labor? It's too late for me to be a clerk because in trade one has to begin as a boy; no one would ever take me for a porter because they couldn't order me about; no factory would have me because for that one has to know a trade, and I know none."

"Nonsense! You always find some excuse! How would you like to chop wood for me?"

"I wouldn't refuse to do that, but in these days even skilled woodcutters find themselves sitting without bread."

"Huh! You loafers all talk that way. As soon as an offer is made you, you refuse it! Will you come and chop wood for me?"

"Yes, sir; I will."

"Very well; we'll soon find out. Splendid— we'll see——"

Skvortsoff hastened along, rubbing his hands, not without a feeling of malice, and called his cook out of the kitchen.

"Here, Olga," he said, "take this gentleman into the woodshed and let him chop wood."

The tattered scarecrow shrugged his shoulders as if in perplexity, and went irresolutely after the cook. It was obvious from his gait that he had not consented to go and chop wood because he was hungry and wanted work, but simply from pride and shame, because he had been trapped by his own words. It was obvious, too, that his strength had been undermined by vodka and that he was unhealthy and did not feel the slightest inclination for toil.

Skvortsoff hurried into the dining room. From its windows one could see the woodshed and everything that went on in the yard. Standing at the window, Skvortsoff saw the cook and the beggar come out into the yard by the back door and make their way across the dirty snow to the shed. Olga glared wrathfully at her companion, shoved him aside with her elbow, unlocked the shed, and angrily banged the door.

"We probably interrupted the woman over her coffee," thought Skvortsoff. "What an ill-tempered creature!"

Next he saw the false teacher, false student seat himself on a log and become lost in thought with his red cheeks resting on his fists. The woman flung down an ax at his feet, spat angrily, and judging from the expression of her lips, began to scold him. The beggar irresolutely pulled a log of wood toward him, set it up between his feet, and tapped it feebly with the ax. The log wavered and fell down. The beggar again pulled it to him, blew on his freezing hands, and tapped it with his ax cautiously, as if afraid of hitting his overshoe or of cutting off his finger. The stick of wood again fell to the ground.

Skvortsoff's anger had vanished and he now began to feel a little sorry and ashamed of himself for having set a spoiled, drunken, perchance sick man to work at menial labor in the cold.

"Well, never mind," he thought, going into his study from the dining room. "I did it for his own good."

An hour later Olga came in and announced that the wood had all been chopped.

"Good! Give him half a ruble,"[2] said Skvortsoff. "If he wants to he can come back and cut wood on the first day of each month. We can always find work for him."

On the first of the month the beggar made his appearance again and earned half a ruble, although he could barely stand on his legs. From that day on he often appeared in the yard and every time work was found for him. Now he would shovel snow, now put the woodshed in order, now beat the dust out of rugs and mattresses. Every time he received from twenty to forty kopecks, and once, even a pair of old trousers were sent out to him.

When Skvortsoff moved into another house he hired him to help in the packing and hauling of the furniture. This time the poor fellow was sober, gloomy, and silent. He hardly touched the furniture, and walked behind the wagons hanging his head, not even making a pretense of appearing busy. He only shivered in the cold and became embarrassed when the carters jeered at him for his idleness, his feebleness, and his tattered, fancy overcoat. After the moving was over Skvortsoff sent for him.

"Well, I see that my words have taken effect," he said, handing him a ruble. "Here's for your pains. I see you are sober and have no objection to work. What is your name?"

"Lushkoff."

"Well, Lushkoff, I can now offer you some other, cleaner employment. Can you write?"

"I can."

"Then take this letter to a friend of mine tomorrow and you will be given some copying to do. Work hard, don't drink, and remember what I have said to you. Good-by!"

Pleased at having put a man on the right path, Skvortsoff tapped Lushkoff kindly on the shoulder and even gave him his hand at parting. Lushkoff took the letter, and from that day forth came no more to the yard for work.

Two years went by. Then one evening, as Skvortsoff was standing by the ticket window of a theater paying for his seat, he noticed a little man beside him with a coat collar of curly fur and a worn sealskin cap. This little individual timidly asked the ticket seller for a seat in the gallery and paid for it in copper coins.

"Lushkoff, is that you?" cried Skvortsoff, recognizing in the little man his former wood-chopper. "How are you? What are you doing? How is everything with you?"

"All right. I work for the government now and get thirty-five rubles a month."

"Thank Heaven! That's fine! I am delighted for your sake. I am very, very glad, Lushkoff. You see, you are my godson, in a sense. I gave you a push along the right path, you know. Do you remember what a scolding I gave you, eh? I nearly had you

2 ruble *The chief monetary unit of Russia.*

sinking into the ground at my feet that day. Thank you, old man, for not forgetting my words."

"Thank you, too," said Lushkoff. "If I hadn't come to you then I might still have been calling myself a teacher or a student to this day. Yes, by flying to your protection I dragged myself out of a pit."

"I am very glad, indeed."

"Thank you for your kind words and deeds. You talked splendidly to me then. I am very grateful to you and to your cook. God bless that good and noble woman! You spoke finely then, and I shall be indebted to you to my dying day; but, strictly speaking, it was your cook, Olga, who saved me."

"How is that?"

"Like this. When I used to come to your house to chop wood she used to begin: 'Oh, you sot, you! Oh, you miserable creature! There's nothing for you but ruin.' And then she would sit down opposite me and grow sad, look into my face and weep. 'Oh, you unlucky man! There is no pleasure for you in this world and there will be none in the world to come. You drunkard! You will burn in hell. Oh, you unhappy one!' And so she would carry on, you know, in that strain. I can't tell you how much misery she suffered, how many tears she shed for my sake. But the chief thing was—she used to chop the wood for me. Do you know, sir, that I did not chop one single stick of wood for you? She did it all. Why this saved me, why I changed, why I stopped drinking at the sight of her I cannot explain. I only know that, owing to her words and noble deeds a change took place in my heart; she set me right and I shall never forget it. However, it is time to go now; there goes the bell."

Lushkoff bowed and entered the theater.

Marion Fell/TRANSLATOR

For Discussion

1 What is the difference between what Lushkoff appears to be and what he really is?

2 Does Skvortsoff genuinely want to reform Lushkoff? Or does he want to flatter his own vanity by creating Lushkoff in his own image?

3 Is Skvortsoff a villain? Does your attitude toward him change during the story? Does it change toward Lushkoff and Olga?

4 Compare the first description of Olga by Skvortsoff with the last description of her by Lushkoff. What is the difference?

5 Judging from your own experience, are there more Skvortsoffs in the world, or more Olgas?

6 Is money the only thing Lushkoff begs for? If not, what else does he need?

7 Why does Lushkoff say that he owes a deeper gratitude to Olga?

8 Good literature is often said to be "universal" in its meaning, that is, that it is not limited to the age in which it was written. This story was written in Russia in the time of the czars. What has it to do with the modern reader? Could it have happened in an American city today?

neath their rusty rifles, and that little General on his great black horse, in front of them all, alone.

The General made them carry straw into the church, and put his boys to sleep like a father. In the morning, before dawn, if they weren't up at the sound of the bugle, he rode into the church on his horse, swearing like a Turk. That was a man! And on the spot he ordered five or six of them to be shot. Pippo, the dwarf, Pizzannello, the first ones they laid hold of. The wood-cutter, while they were making him kneel against the cemetery wall, wept like a child because of certain words his mother had said to him, and because of the cry she had uttered when they tore him from her arms. From afar off, in the remotest alleys of the village as you sat behind your closed door, you could hear those gun-shots firing one after the other, like cannon-crackers at holiday time.

And then came the real judges, gentlemen in spectacles perched upon mules, done up with the journey, complaining still of their fatigue, while they were examining the accused in the refectory[7] of the monastery, sitting on one hip on their seats, and saying aha! every time they changed the side. A trial that would never come to an end. They took the guilty over away to the city, on foot, chained two by two, between two files of soldiers with cocked muskets. Their women followed them running down the long country roads, across the fallow land, through the cactus thickets and the vineyards and the golden-coloured wheat, tired out, limping, calling out their names every time the road made a bend and they could see the faces of the prisoners. At the city they shut them up in the great prison that was high and vast as a monastery, all pierced with iron-barred windows; and if the women wished to see their men, it was only on Mondays in presence of the warders, behind the iron grating. And the poor fellows got yellower and yellower in that everlasting shadow, never seeing the sun. Every Monday they were more taciturn, and

they hardly answered, they complained even less. Other days if the women roved in the square round the prison, the sentinels threatened them with their guns. And then never knowing what to do, where to find work in the town, nor how to earn bread. The bed in the stables cost two cents; the white bread they swallowed in a gulp did not fill their stomachs; and if they crouched down in the doorway of a church, to pass the night there, the police arrested them. One by one they went back home, first the wives, then the mothers. One good-looking lass lost herself in the town and was never heard of again. All the others belonging to the village had come back to do the same as they had done before. The gentry couldn't work their lands with their own hands, and the poor folks couldn't live without the gentry. So they made peace. The apothecary's orphan son stole Neli Pirru's wife, and it seemed to him a proper thing to do, to revenge himself on the one who had killed his father. And when the woman had qualms now and then, and was afraid that her husband when he came out of prison would cut her face, the apothecary's son replied, "Don't be afraid, he won't come out." Nowadays nobody thought of them; unless it was some mother, some old father, when their eyes wandered towards the plain where the city lay, or on Sundays when they saw the others talking over their affairs quietly with the gentry, in front of the club, with their caps in their hands; and they convinced themselves that rags must suffer in a wind.

The case lasted three years, no less; three years of prison without ever seeing the sun. So that the accused seemed like so many dead men out of the tomb, every time they were conducted fettered to the court. Whoever could manage it had come down from the village, witnesses, relatives, people full of curiosity, like a holiday, to see their fellow villagers, after such a long time, crowded together in the chicken-coop of the prisoner's dock—and real chickens you became, inside there! And Neli Pirru had to see the apothe-

7 refectory *A dining hall.*

Two thousand years ago, the Roman patriot Cicero was tempted to join a revolution against a dictatorial government. He wanted to restore the liberties of the Roman Republic, and yet the question of revolution made him pause. He wrote to his friend Atticus, "How can we guarantee that a new government will not turn into a new tyranny?"

We live in an age of revolution, and Verga's "Liberty," written almost a century ago, remains strangely timely. In many countries the common man has been frustrated to find that a change of leaders has made no essential change in his own way of life.

The story is set in Sicily and, according to the author, is based on an actual incident that took place in 1860 when Garibaldi, the General of the story, was fighting for the freedom and national integrity of Italy. The peasants of a small town, fired by the cry of "liberty," take the law into their own hands and begin to revenge themselves on the landowners, the *hat-folk* (for wearing a hat was a mark of social position). The peasants find, to their bewilderment, that the kind of liberty they expected to have has slipped from their hands.

Giovanni Verga

Liberty

They unfurled a red-white-and-green handkerchief from the church-tower, they rang the bells in a frenzy, and they began to shout in the village square, "Hurray for Liberty!"

Like the sea in storm. The crowd foamed and swayed in front of the club of the gentry, and outside the Town Hall, and on the steps of the church—a sea of white stocking-caps,[1] axes and sickles glittering. Then they burst into the little street.

"Your turn first, baron! You who have had folks cudgelled by your estate-keepers!"

At the head of all the people a witch, with her old hair sticking up, armed with nothing but her nails. "Your turn, priest of the devil! for you've sucked the soul out of us!" "Your

turn now, rich glutton, you're not going to escape no matter how fat you are with the blood of the poor!" "Your turn, police-sergeant; you who never took the law on anybody except poor folks who'd got nothing!" "Your turn, estate-keepers, who sold your own flesh and your neighbour's flesh for twenty cents a day!"

And blood smoked and went drunk. Sickles, hands, rags, stones, everything red with blood! *The gentry!* The *hat-folks!* Kill them all! Kill them all! Down with the *hat-folks!*

Don Antonio was slipping home by the short cuts. The first blow made him fall with his bleeding face against the causeway. "Why? Why are you killing me?" "You as

1 stocking-caps *Long, knitted, cone-shaped caps with a tassel or pompon; worn especially for* *winter sports. Wearing a stocking-cap shows a person of lower social position, such as a peasant.*

well, the devil can have you!" A lame brat picked up the filthy hat and spat inside it. "Down with the hats! Hurray for Liberty! You, take that!" Then for his Reverence who used to preach hell for anybody who stole a bit of bread. He was just coming back from saying mass, with the consecrated Host inside his fat belly. "Don't kill me, I am in mortal sin!" Neighbour Lucia being the mortal sin; Neighbour Lucia whose father had sold her to the priest when she was fourteen years old, at the time of the famine winter, and she had ever since been filling the streets and the Refuge with hungry brats. If such dog's-meat had been worth anything that day they'd have been able to stuff themselves with it, as they hacked it to pieces with their hatchets in the doorways of the houses and on the cobble-stones of the street. Like the wolf when he falls famished on a flock of sheep, and never thinks of filling his belly, but just slaughters right and left with rage —Milady's[2] son, who had run to see what was happening—the apothecary,[3] while he was locking up shop as fast as he could— Don Paolo, who was coming home from the vineyard riding on his ass, with his lean saddle-bags behind him. And he was wearing into the bargain a little old cap that his daughter had embroidered for him long ago, before the vines had taken the disease. His wife saw him fall in front of the street-door, as she and her five children were waiting for him and for the handful of stuff for the soup which he had got in his saddle-bags. "Paolo! Paolo!" The first fellow caught him in the shoulder with a hatchet cut. Another was on him with a sickle, and disembowelled him as he was reaching with his bleeding arm for the knocker.

But the worst was when the lawyer's son, a lad of eleven, blond as gold, fell no one knows how, overthrown in the crowd. His father had raised himself two or three times before he dragged himself aside into the filth, to die, calling to him: "Neddu! Neddu!" Neddu fled in terror, mouth and eyes wide open, unable to make a sound. They knocked him down; he also raised himself on one knee, like his father; the torrent passed over him; somebody put his great boot on the boy's cheek and smashed it in; nevertheless the lad still begged for mercy with his hands. He didn't want to die, no, not in the way he had seen his father killed; it broke his heart! The woodcutter out of pity gave him a great blow with the axe, using both hands, as if he had had to fell a fifty-year-old oak-tree— and he trembled like a leaf. Somebody shouted, "Bah, he'd have been another lawyer!"

No matter! Now they had their hands red with such blood, they'd got to spill the rest of it. All of 'em! All the *hats!* It was no longer hunger, beatings, swindling which made their anger boil up again. It was innocent blood. The women most ferocious of all, waving their fleshless arms, squealing in falsetto, with rage, the tender flesh showing under the rags of their clothing. "You who came praying to the good God in a silk frock!" "You who thought yourself contaminated if you knelt beside poor folks! Take that! Take that!" In the houses, on the staircases, inside the alcoves, a tearing of silk and of fine linen. Oh the earrings upon bleeding faces, oh the golden rings upon hands that tried to ward off the hatchet-strokes!

The baroness had had the great door barricaded: beams, wagons, full casks piled against it, and the estate-keepers firing from the windows to sell their lives dear. The crowd bowed its head to the gun-fire, because it had no weapons to respond with. Because in those days it was death-penalty for having fire-arms in your possession. Hurray for Liberty! And they burst in the great doors. Then into the courtyard, up the steps, dislodging the wounded. They left the estate-keepers for the time. They would settle them later. First they wanted the flesh of the baroness, flesh made of partridges and good wine. She ran from room to room with her baby at her breast, all dishevelled—and the rooms were many. The crowd was heard howling along the twistings of the passages, advancing like a river in flood. The oldest son, sixteen years of age, also with fair white flesh still, was crying: "Mamà! Mamà!" At the first rush they sent the door down on top of him. He clung to the legs which trod him down. He cried no more. His mother had taken refuge on the balcony, clasping her baby close, shutting its mouth with her hand so that it should not cry, mad. The other son wanted to defend her with his body, glaring, as if he had a hundred hands, clutching all those axes by the blades. They separated them in a flash. One man seized her by the hair, another by her hips, another by her dress, lifting her above the balcony rail. The charcoal-man tore the infant baby from her arms. The other brother saw nothing but red and black. They trampled him down, they ground his bones with iron-shod heels; he had set his teeth in a hand which was squeezing his throat, and he never let go. Hatchets couldn't strike in the heap, they hovered flashing in the air.

And in that mad carnival of the month of July, above all the drunken howling of the fasting crowd, the bell of God kept on ringing frantically, until evening, with no midday, no ave-maria,[4] like in the land of the Turks. Then they began to disband, tired with the slaughter, quietly, slinkingly, every one fleeing from his companion. Before nightfall all doors were shut, in fear, and in every house the lamp was burning. Along the little streets no sound was heard save that of the dogs, which went prying in the corners, then a dry gnawing of bones, in the bright moonlight which washed over everything, and showed the wide-open big doors and the open windows of the deserted houses.

Day broke: a Sunday with nobody in the square, and no mass ringing. The sexton[5] had burrowed into his hiding hole; there were no more priests. The first-comers that began to gather on the sacred threshold looked one another in the face suspiciously; each one thinking of what his neighb... his conscience. Then, whe... number, they began to murm... without mass, and on a Su... The club of the *gentry* wa... and they didn't know where... masters' orders for the w... church tower still dangled t... green handkerchief, flaccid,... of July. And as the shade... outside the churchfront, the... all in one corner. Betwee... houses of the square, at the... row street that sloped steepl... could see the fields yellow... and the dark woods on the... Now they were going to sha... and woods among themselv... calculating to himself, on... much he should get for hi... looking askance at his nei... meant that everybody shou... —yon Nino Bestia and yon... have liked to make out tha... on the bossy tricks of the *h*... no surveyor to measure t... lawyer to put it on to paper,... be going at it tooth and... booze your share at the p... afterwards we've got to sta... again—thief here and thief... there was Liberty, anybod... eat enough for two ran the... in like those there *gentry!*... brandished his fist in the... grasped the axe.

The next day they hear... was coming to deal out ju... made folks tremble. They... of their own soldiers climb... ravine towards the village;... down rocks you could ha... all. But nobody stirred. Th... and tore their hair. And th... with long beards only sat... hill with their hands bet... watching those tired boys...

---

2 Milady *"My Lady"; refers to a rich or titled woman.*

3 apothecary *One who prepares and sells drugs or compounds for medicinal purposes.*

4 ave-maria *The ringing of the church bells at a certain time of the day.*

5 sexton *A church officer or employee who takes care of the church property and sometimes rings the bell for services and digs graves.*

6 Etna (or... *in Sicily.*

cary's lad face to face, the fellow who had become his relation underhand! They made them stand up one by one. "What is your name?" And each one answered for himself, name and surname and what he had done. The lawyers fenced away with their speeches, in wide, loose sleeves, getting besides themselves, foaming at the mouth, suddenly wiping themselves calm with a white pocket-handkerchief, and snuffing up a pinch of snuff.[8] The judges dozed behind the lenses of their spectacles, which froze your heart. Facing were seated twelve *gentry* in a row, tired, bored, yawning, scratching their beards or gabbling among themselves. For sure they were telling one another what a marvellous escape it had been for them that they weren't gentry of that village up there, when the folks had been making liberty. And those poor wretches opposite tried to read their faces. Then they went away to confabulate together, and the accused men waited white-faced, with their eyes fixed on the closed door. As they came in again, their foreman, the one who spoke with his hand on his stomach, was almost as pale as the prisoners, and he said, "On my honour and on my conscience———!"

The charcoal-man, while they were putting the handcuffs on him again, stammered: "Where are you taking me to? To the galleys? Oh, why? I never got so much as half a yard of land! If they'd told me what liberty was like———!"

D. H. Lawrence/TRANSLATOR

For Discussion

1 The trouble with political slogans is that they are meant to have the widest popular appeal, and so they are never well defined. In one sense the meaning of this story turns ironically on the cry *Liberty!* How did the peasants of this Italian village interpret it? How, in the light of events, were they mistaken?

2 Note that this story has no single or central character with whom the reader spends much time. If you had to describe the hero of this story, who or what would it be?

3 The mood of this story breaks sharply in the middle. Can you point out the paragraph where this change of mood takes place?

4 How do the people see the judges who come to try their fellow townsfolk? Why is it significant that these judges come from another place and are not citizens of the town? Who do the judges represent? That is, what interests do they protect?

5 In the last paragraph the charcoal-man leaves his final statement incomplete. What is the full implication of his fragmentary sentence?

6 Can you think of any political slogans or cries which are used today? How are they likely to be misunderstood? To bring about disappointment for those who believe in them?

8 snuff *A preparation of pulverized tobacco inhaled through the nostrils.*

In turning from Verga's "Liberty" to this tale by Boccaccio, we turn from a world of realism and disillusion to one of romantic fantasy. Boccaccio follows a pattern almost as old as the art of storytelling itself; the *Odyssey* is a classic example —a perilous journey which ends with the hero being restored to his kingdom and his faithful wife. In Boccaccio's tale both the hero and heroine live through dangers and coincidences before order is restored to their world. In a Romance, as in this story, order is often symbolized by a marriage, after which the hero and his bride live "happily ever after."

In this kind of story things always work out happily simply because the writer wants them to, not because they correspond to "real life." Dangerous events are not allowed to become tragic. It is a classic story-pattern which can be used crudely, as in many popular novels and movies; or beautifully, as in Shakespeare's *The Tempest*.

Emilia, through whom Boccaccio tells his story, knows exactly what a romantic tale is for: "I think that love affairs should end happily," she says, and proceeds to make up just such a story.

Giovanni Boccaccio

How Two Lovers Were Reunited

When it was Emilia's turn to tell a story, she said, "I think that love affairs should end happily, not in misery. And so that will be the theme of my story."

Not far off the shore of Sicily there is a small island called Lipari. There, not long ago, there lived a beautiful girl, the daughter of a rich family, and her name was Costanza. A young man also lived on the island, and his name was Martuccio. He was handsome, well-behaved, and a skilled craftsman. Now these two young people fell in love with each other, and Costanza was not happy when Martuccio was out of her sight.

Martuccio wanted to marry her, but her father refused permission because the boy was poor. Martuccio was inflamed with anger when he saw that he was rejected because he was not rich. So, together with some friends, he left the island of Lipari and said that he would never return until he had made his fortune.

He became a pirate and sailed the Barbary Coast.[1] His new life as a pirate brought him riches, and he would have done very well

1 Barbary Coast *Coastal region in North Africa, extending from Egypt to the Atlantic Ocean.*

except that he became too greedy. He and his friends amassed a great deal of money in a short time, but they were not content with what they had, and finally they were attacked by the Saracen[2] navy. After a sea-battle, Martuccio's ship was sunk and most of his crew was drowned. He, himself, was captured and taken to Tunis where he was put in prison. There he remained for many years.

The news of the sea-battle came to Lipari, and everyone said that Martuccio had drowned with the rest of his men. Costanza, whose heart had been broken when her lover had left the island, wept bitterly when she heard of his death, and she determined to end her own life. But she was not brave enough to kill herself violently, and so she thought of another way to die.

One night she stole out of her father's house and went down to the shore where she found a small fishing boat. The owner must not have been far away, for the boat still had its mast, sail and oars. She got into the boat and rowed out to sea—for everyone on that small island knew how to handle a boat. Then she hoisted the sail, threw away the oars and the rudder, and left herself to the mercy of the winds. The wind, she thought, would soon turn the boat over or drive it onto the rocks, and she would drown no matter how hard she tried to save herself. So she wrapped her head in her cloak and, weeping, lay down in the bottom of the boat.

But what she expected did not, in fact, happen. The wind that night was mild and the seas were calm. The little boat was carried across the sea and arrived on the shore of a town called Susa, about a hundred miles from Tunis. Costanza was still asleep. But it happened that just as the boat came to the shore a poor woman was working on the beach, hauling in the fishing nets which were drying in the sun. When she saw the little boat, with its sails still up, she thought that perhaps some fishermen had gone to sleep and did not know that their boat had come

to shore. She went over to the boat, and there she found the sleeping Costanza. The poor woman woke her up.

Costanza could see that the woman was a Christian, from the clothes she wore. Then the woman spoke to her in Italian, asking her how she had come there in such a small boat. When Costanza heard the woman speaking Italian, she was afraid that the wind had brought her back to Lipari, and she jumped up. But when she looked around, she could see that she was in a strange country. "Where am I?" she asked.

"This is Susa, on the Barbary Coast, my child," said the woman.

Costanza now saw that the Lord had not wished her to die, and she was frightened and ashamed. She knelt down in the boat and burst into tears. The poor woman was moved by her tears, and finally she persuaded Costanza to come with her to her hut. There the woman asked her to tell her story, and she gave her something to eat.

"Who are you," asked Costanza, "and how is it that you speak Italian?" When the woman explained that she, too, was Italian, and that she worked with Christian fishermen, Costanza, in spite of her sorrow, took it for a good omen, and she began to feel glad that she was still alive. She refused to give her name, or say where she was from, but she asked the poor woman to help her and keep her from danger.

Carapresa—for that was the woman's name —was a kindly person. So when she had finished bringing in her nets, she took her own cloak and wrapped Costanza in it, and brought her into the town of Susa.

"Costanza," she said, "I am going to take you to the house of a Saracen lady for whom I sometimes work. She is a wonderful person, very kind, and I am sure that she will take you in and treat you like a daughter. But you must be very good to her, and help her all you can, until the Lord brings you a new fate."

So Carapresa brought her to the house of

2   Saracen   *A member of a nomadic people of the deserts between Syria and Arabia.*

the Saracen lady, who was very old. And when the woman heard Costanza's story, she wept with pity. She kissed Costanza, took her by the hand, and brought her into the house where she lived with several other women. These women lived by embroidering silk, making designs on leather, and weaving baskets out of palm leaves. Within a few days Costanza began to learn these trades, and the women came to be very fond of her. Soon she was able to speak their language, for the women taught her.

Now while Costanza was living in Susa, and everyone back in Lipari gave her up for dead, there was a King in Tunis by the name of Mariabdela. A young Spaniard, however, was trying to win the throne of Tunis for himself. He gathered an army and marched against Tunis to capture it.

Martuccio was still in prison in Tunis, and he heard about the attack. By now he had learned the language of the Barbary Coast, and when he heard that the King was in danger, he said to one of the prison guards, "If I could obtain an audience with the King, I think I could give him some advice that would help him drive back these attackers."

The guard told the Chief Jailer, who brought the word to the King, and the King commanded that Martuccio be brought to him.

"What is this advice you have for me," said the King.

"Your Majesty," said Martuccio, "in battle your army depends more than anything else upon its archers. Well now, if you could find a way in battle to see that the enemy archers have no arrows and yet that your own archers have plenty of arrows, you would surely win."

"Yes," said the King, "if we could arrange that we would win for certain."

"Then," said Martuccio, "I shall tell Your Majesty how to do it. You must have the strings of the bows your archers use made very fine, very thin. Then you must have special arrows made which can fit only these

thin strings. You must do this in great secrecy, so that your enemy knows nothing of your plan. Now this is what I have in mind: when, in battle, your enemies' archers and your own have both shot all their arrows each side will have to pick up the arrows that have been shot at them. But your enemies will find that they cannot use your arrows, because the strings in their bows will be too thick. On the other hand, your archers will be able to use the arrows of the enemy. So your men will have arrows and your enemies will have none."

The King was impressed with Martuccio's plan, and followed it in every detail. And indeed, he won the war. As a reward, he gave Martuccio a position of importance, and Martuccio became wealthy.

Soon the whole country was talking about what had happened, and Costanza found that her lover, whom she had long thought dead, was alive. Her love for him revived and grew stronger than ever. Her hopes had been dead, but now they came to life. She told her friend, the Saracen lady, all of her past history, and that she wanted to go at once to Tunis so that she might see with her own eyes what she had heard through rumor. The lady agreed, and just as if Costanza were her own daughter, she travelled with her to Tunis where they stayed with one of the lady's relatives. They sent Carapresa on ahead of them to find out what she could about Martuccio. When Carapresa indeed told the lady that the rumor was true, she wished to be the one who told Martuccio that Costanza was in Tunis.

The Saracen lady then went to Martuccio's house, and said to him, "Martuccio, one of your servants from Lipari has come to my house and would like to speak with you there."

Martuccio, grateful to the Saracen lady, went to her house, where he found Costanza, who almost fainted from happiness. She could not control her feelings. At first she ran to him with open arms and threw herself upon him. Her joy was great, but she also remembered all the sorrow they had passed through. She could not speak, and she began to cry. Martuccio, also, was so overcome with amazement, that at first he could not speak. Then he sighed, and said, "Oh, my dear Costanza! Are you alive? Is it you? Long ago I heard that you had been drowned at sea. Back in Lipari they knew nothing about you."

Then he, too, began to cry, and embraced her and kissed her. After a while, Costanza told him everything that had happened to her, and of the kindness she had received from the Saracen lady. Then Martuccio went back to the King, told him the whole story, and said that he and Costanza wanted to be married under their own law. The King was amazed. He sent for Costanza, heard her story from her own lips, then said, "Indeed, you deserve this man. He should be your husband."

The King had rich presents brought and gave them to Martuccio and Costanza. Then Martuccio thanked the Saracen lady for all she had done, and rewarded her. The lady returned home, weeping for Costanza's happiness.

After a while the two lovers, together with Carapresa, sailed for home. How can I describe the welcome they received? There Martuccio and Costanza had a lavish wedding, and they lived forever after in peace and happiness.

George Kearns/TRANSLATOR

For Discussion

1 "Martuccio wanted to marry her, but her father refused permission because the boy was poor." This is one of the oldest and most familiar themes in romantic fiction— young lovers kept apart by family problems or prejudices. Sometimes the lovers belong to different nations, sometimes to different social classes: there are a thousand variations on the theme. What other works of literature can you think of which take shape around this basic problem?

2 The headnote to this selection states that in a story of this kind "Dangerous events are not allowed to become tragic." What are some points in this story where Boccaccio could have turned it into tragedy if he had wanted to?

3 What are some of the happenings in this story which would be completely improbable in "real life" but which we accept within the framework of the story? Why are you willing to accept these improbable events—if, indeed, you accept them? What other imaginative works (including movies, comic strips, television plays, as well as "literature") are based on improbable things happening?

4 Do you feel that you "know" the characters in this story as well as you know them in Chekhov's "The Beggar," for example? Does it matter?

5 With whom do you sympathize in this story? Why?

6 It is easy to dismiss a story like this by saying that it shows no deep social concern, or that it is contrived, or that it is "too good to be true." And yet stories built on this basic pattern are probably more common than any other kind of story. In one form or another they are the staple of fiction throughout the ages. Clearly they satisfy some deep need for many readers. Can you account for this?

In the preceding story by Boccaccio we have studied a classic tale of Romance. The trouble with Romance is that men often confuse it with reality, as did Cervantes' Don Quixote. This old Spanish gentleman's head is filled with romantic tales of knights, ladies, and evil enchanters. As he sets out alone to right the wrongs of the world, he is both noble and sad. Tall and gaunt, his eyes find romantic drama in a row of windmills, a barber's washbowl, and a flock of sheep. At his side rides his plump servant, Sancho Panza, puzzled by the contradiction between what he sees and what Don Quixote tells him he sees. Sancho's eyes provide one truth, but the romantic dreams of Don Quixote provide another. The following three episodes from Cervantes' great novel are typical of their adventures.

Don Quixote's vision is so noble and lofty that he is blind to the common reality around him. Sancho indeed sees things as they are, but he lacks the poetry and ideals without which our lives would be incomplete. Both visions are needed—the real and the ideal. Cervantes' stroke of genius was not so much in creating either Don Quixote or Sancho, but in bringing them together.

Miguel de Cervantes Saavedra

Some Adventures of Don Quixote

DON QUIXOTE AND SANCHO SET OUT ON THEIR ADVENTURES

Don Quixote persuaded a laborer, a neighbor of his named Sancho Panza, to join him on his adventures. This Sancho was a good man but not very bright. Don Quixote talked to him so much and made him so many promises that finally poor Sancho agreed to go along and serve him as squire. Don Quixote said that Sancho should be glad of the chance to serve him because upon one of their adventures they might easily conquer some island; and if that should happen, he would leave Sancho there as governor. In the light of this promise, and others like it, Sancho deserted his wife and children and became his neighbor's squire.

Next, Don Quixote set about raising money. Some things he sold, others he pawned—always making a bad bargain—until at last he had the sum he needed. Then he equipped himself with a shield, which he borrowed from a friend, and patched up his broken helmet as well as he could. Sancho, his squire, was informed of the day and hour on which they would set out so that he might prepare provisions for the journey. Don Quixote told him not to forget to bring saddlebags. Sancho agreed and added that he was going to bring along a very fine donkey, because he was not used to traveling on foot. The mention of the donkey made Don Quixote pause for a moment: he could not remember having heard of any instance in which a knight had been accompanied by a squire who rode on a donkey. But, in spite of this, he decided to let Sancho bring it and determined to provide him with a more noble mount as soon as he had a chance. After all, he was sure to meet with some discourteous knight whose horse he could take. He provided himself with shirts and everything else he could get his hands on. And when all these arrangements had been made, they set out upon their adventures: Sancho without saying goodbye to his wife and children, Don Quixote without bidding farewell to his housekeeper and niece. They left the town one evening without anyone seeing them, and rode so far in the night that by morning they felt sure no one could ever find them.

Sancho Panzo sat upon his donkey like a patriarch; he had his saddlebags, his leather bottle, and great hopes of becoming governor of the island his master had promised him.

"Your Honor, knight errant," said Sancho, "don't forget about that island you've promised me. I shall be a good governor, even if it is a very large island!"

Don Quixote replied: "Sancho Panza, my friend, you should know that the knights errant of old always appointed their squires to be governors of the islands or kingdoms they conquered. For my part, I shall honor this tradition. In fact, I shall improve upon it: some of those knights made their squires wait until they were very old. Then, after many hard days and worse nights of service, they would give them the title of Count, or perhaps at the most Marquis, of some unimportant valley or province. But if you live —and if I live!—it may very well happen that we shall not have to wait six days until I conquer a kingdom of such importance that it has other kingdoms beneath it. And you shall be crowned the king of one of them. Do not say impossible! For such surprising and unbelievable adventures befall a knight errant that I may easily give you more than I promise!"

"In that case," answered Sancho Panza, "if I were to become King—through the miracle of which Your Honor speaks—then my wife would be Queen and my children Princes."

"Do you doubt it?" asked Don Quixote.

"Yes, I do doubt it," said Sancho. "I believe that even if God rained crowns on the Earth, none of them would fit my wife's head. She would be a poor queen, sir. Yet I believe that with God's help she might make a good countess."

"Leave it to Heaven, Sancho," answered Don Quixote. "God will know what is best for her. As for yourself, do not humble yourself to accept less than the governorship of a province."

"No, sir, I shall not," answered Sancho, "not with a master like yourself. I know you will give me whatever is good for me, and as much as I can handle."

THE ADVENTURE OF THE WINDMILLS

Just then, as they rode across the plain, there appeared thirty or forty windmills. As soon as Don Quixote spied them, he said to his squire:

"Fortune has guided us better than we could have hoped for. Look there, friend Sancho Panza, and you will see more than thirty horrid giants! I shall do battle with them and kill them all. What we take from them will be the beginnings of our fortunes: for it is a good and holy fight in which I shall wipe from the face of the earth these evil creatures!"

"What giants?" asked Sancho Panza.

"Those giants right there!" answered his master. "The ones with the long arms. Some giants are said to have arms several miles long."

"But Your Honor," said Sancho, "what you are looking at are not giants. They are windmills, and what look like arms are merely sails which turn in the wind."

"It is obvious that you know nothing about adventures," said Don Quixote. "If you are afraid, then fly and say your prayers. In the meantime I shall engage these giants in fierce and unequal battle."

Having said this, he dug his spurs into the sides of his horse Rosinante and dashed off, paying no attention to Sancho, who kept shouting that the figures he was about to attack were windmills and not giants. But Don Quixote was so certain that they were giants that he did not hear Sancho's cries, nor, when he came near them, did he notice the true nature of his enemies. He cried out to them in a loud voice:

"Do not run away from me, you cowards, you hateful creatures! It is one lone knight who attacks you!"

Just then a small breeze came across the plain and caused the sails to start turning. When Don Quixote saw this he cried:

"Though you have more arms than the famous giant Briareus,[1] you shall soon pay for your evil deeds!"

Saying this, he dedicated himself to his lady, Dulcinea del Toboso,[2] that she might aid him in battle. Then he put up his shield, settled his lance in place, and set off on Rosinante at full gallop. He attacked the first windmill he came to, thrusting his lance into one of its sails. But the wind turned the sail with such strength that it shattered his lance and lifted both horse and rider into the air, tossing Don Quixote across the fields.

As fast as his donkey could trot, Sancho Panza came to the aid of his injured master. But when he arrived at Don Quixote's side, he found that the knight could not get up: such was the shock Rosinante had given him when they fell.

"God help us!" cried Sancho. "Didn't I tell Your Honor to be careful about what you were doing? Didn't I tell you they were windmills? And how could anyone miss it unless he had windmills in his head!"

"Be quiet, friend Sancho," replied Don Quixote. "The affairs of war are subject to change. Moreover, I believe—and it is a fact—that the evil magician Frestón—the same one who has robbed me of my house and all my books—has in fact changed those giants into windmills! He wants to rob me of the glory of conquering them. Yes, he hates me! But in the end, in the end, the power of his evil acts shall fall before the goodness of my sword!"

"God's will be done," said Sancho, and helped his master to get up and climb up on Rosinante, whose back was almost broken.

THE ADVENTURE OF THE ENCHANTED HELMET

Turning to the right, they set off on another road. They had not traveled far before Don Quixote spied a man on horseback. On his head, this man had something that shone like gold.

As soon as Don Quixote caught a glimpse of him, he turned to Sancho Panza and said: "It is my opinion, Sancho, that all the old sayings have a good deal of truth in them. After all, they are drawn from Experience, which is the Mother of Science. I am thinking in particular of the saying that *When one door shuts, another door opens.* Look: here is another adventure—and a better one. Un-

---

1 Briareus *In classic legend, a huge monster with 100 arms and 50 heads.*

2 Dulcinea del Toboso *This lady existed only in Don Quixote's imagination. He knew that the ancient knights all had beautiful ladies to whom they dedicated their noble deeds.*

less I am deceived, there comes towards us now a man wearing upon his head the Helmet of Mambrino.[3] As you know, I have sworn an oath about this very helmet."

"Look carefully before you speak, sir, and move carefully before you act," said Sancho. "If I were free to speak my mind, I could give you several reasons why you are mistaken."

"How can I be mistaken, faithless traitor?" cried Don Quixote. "Tell me, do you or do you not see that knight who is riding towards us on a light gray horse? Is he not wearing upon his head a helmet of gold?"

"What I see," said Sancho, "or perhaps I should say what I *perceive*—is a man riding a gray donkey just like mine. And he has something shining on his head."

"Well! It is the Helmet of Mambrino!" said Don Quixote. "Stand to one side and let me handle him alone. I shall save time by refusing to speak a single word—yet I shall bring this adventure to its end. And I shall soon have the helmet I have so long desired."

Now the truth of the matter about the helmet, the horse, and the horseman was this: There were two villages nearby. One of them was so small that it could afford neither a druggist's nor a barber shop. The other village, not far away, had both. The barber from the larger town took care of the smaller one, too. It happened that day that there was a sick man who had to be bled, and someone else who needed a shave. And so the barber was riding over to take care of them, and he was bringing along with him his brass bowl.

Now, just as the barber was riding along, it began to rain. He did not want to get his hat wet (it was probably a new one), and so he put the bowl over his head. Since the brass was polished, it could be seen from half a mile away. He was, as Sancho said, riding a gray donkey. And that is how Don Quixote came to believe that the barber was a knight on a gray horse and that he wore a golden helmet. Don Quixote found it easy to

adapt everything he saw to his own fancies about chivalry.

When Don Quixote saw the poor rider approach, he did not bother to speak to him, but he spurred Rosinante into a full gallop. He lowered his lance, meaning to spear the poor barber on it. Without slowing down, he shouted out:

"Defend yourself, base creature! Or surrender freely the helmet which is rightly mine!"

The barber, who had no idea what was going on, saw this phantom descending upon him. All he could do to avoid the lance was to let himself fall down off his donkey. As soon as he touched the ground, he got up and ran across the fields like the wind. The brass bowl was left lying on the ground.

Don Quixote was overjoyed to see the bowl, and said that the pagan had acted wisely. He ordered Sancho to pick up the helmet.

"Lord!" said Sancho, holding it in his hands, "What a fine brass bowl! This is worth a *real*[4] if it's worth a penny."

He handed it to his master, who put it on his head and kept turning it around and around, looking for the vizor. But there was no vizor.

"The pagan for whom this helmet was made had an enormous head," said Don Quixote. "The worst of it is that part of it is missing."

When Sancho heard the brass bowl referred to as a helmet, he had to laugh. But he remembered how angry his master could get, and so he stopped.

"Why are you laughing, Sancho?" asked Don Quixote.

"I am laughing," Sancho said, "to think how big the head of the pagan who owned it must have been. In fact, it's exactly like the kind of bowl a barber uses."

"Sancho, do you know what I think?" said Don Quixote. "I think this famous and enchanted helmet had fallen into the hands of someone who did not know what it was.

3 Helmet of Mambrino *A helmet of pure gold which made Mambrino, a legendary pagan king, invulnerable.*

4 real *The chief monetary unit of Spain at one time.*

This person, when he saw it was made of pure gold, took part of it and melted it down for money. He turned the rest of it into what—as you say—looks like a barber's bowl. Never mind. The fact that it has undergone a transformation does not bother me, for I know what it really is. As soon as I arrive at a town where there is a blacksmith, I shall have it repaired. It shall be as fine a helmet as the one that Vulcan, god of blacksmiths, gave to Mars, the god of War. In the meantime, I shall wear it as well as I can, for something is better than nothing. Moreover, it will protect my head from stones."

George Kearns/TRANSLATOR

For Discussion

**DON QUIXOTE AND SANCHO
SET OUT ON THEIR
ADVENTURES**

1 How does Don Quixote tempt Sancho to leave his wife and children and become a knight's squire? Does this indicate that for all his matter-of-fact qualities Sancho, too, has illusions?

2 When Don Quixote speaks of the "knights errant of old," what do we learn about his sense of reality? What happens to men who try to live in the past, or live out of books? How does Don Quixote see only what he wants to see? And what *does* he want to see?

**THE ADVENTURE OF THE
WINDMILLS**

1 There is a common saying which has its source in this episode from *Don Quixote*: "He is tilting at windmills." What does it mean? Is it unnatural for men to "tilt at windmills"?

2 If you had the power, would you confine Don Quixote to a sanatorium for treatment? Or would you allow him to lead his life as he wishes to?

3 If Don Quixote had suddenly found himself in a sanatorium, how would he have interpreted what had happened to him?

**THE ADVENTURE OF THE
ENCHANTED HELMET**

1 What is the difference between the way Sancho sees the barber's bowl and the way in which Don Quixote sees it? What is the value placed on it by each? How does the way each man sees the bowl reflect his own personality?

2 In this episode, can you interpret Don Quixote's victory as a defeat? How will strangers react to a man wearing a barber's bowl for a helmet?

A recurrent figure in fiction is that of the romantic rogue, the criminal who, because he is more dashing and high-spirited than his enemies, enlists our sympathies. This is the stuff from which movies about pirates and gangsters are made. Shake-speare's Falstaff is of this company.

In this story by the Russian poet and storyteller Pushkin, there is no question that the dashing bandit Kirdjali is a thief and murderer; and Pushkin makes no effort to "redeem" him at the end. It is obvious that Pushkin both condemns him and admires him at the same time.

Something of this same ambiguous figure, the romantic thief, appears in Montanelli's "His Excellency" (page 59).

Alexander Pushkin

Kirdjali

Kirdjali was a Bulgarian by birth. In Turkish, Kirdjali means a knight in armour, a bold fellow. I don't know his real name.

Kirdjali and his acts of banditry brought terror to the whole countryside. In order to give some idea of him I will tell about one of his exploits. One night he and his friend, Arnout, rode into a Bulgarian village. They set both ends of the village on fire and began to go into the huts. Kirdjali killed everyone in sight, and Arnout carried off their possessions. As they did this they both shouted: "Kirdjali! Kirdjali!" The villagers who were not killed ran away.

When Alexander Ipsilanti began his revolution to free Greece from Turkish rule, Kirdjali decided to join him. Kirdjali and his robbers weren't interested in the revolution, but they saw that the war gave them a good opportunity to get rich.

Ipsilanti himself was a brave man, but he did not have the qualities needed for leading such a daring revolt. He did not know how to handle or control the men who were fighting under him. They did not respect him or have confidence in him. After some disastrous defeats, Ipsilanti had to flee into exile, and he was replaced as leader of the revolution. During this period many of the finest young men in Greece were killed, for the Turks outnumbered them ten to one.

Kirdjali was a member of a regiment which found itself without leadership just before the great battle of Skoulana. But Kirdjali and his men had no need for a leader.

The battle of Skoulana was a defeat for the Greek revolutionists. Outnumbered, they turned and fled with the whole Turkish army after them. The next day the Turks attacked the Greeks again, using cold steel. The battle was fierce. The revolutionists had to re-treat behind the Russian lines. During the course of this battle Kirdjali was wounded.

So the revolt was over. The Turks were victorious. This left Kirdjali and his men behind the Russian lines in Turkish Bessarabia. There the Russians protected them and they led an idle life. They could be seen sitting in coffee houses with long pipes in their mouths, sipping coffee out of small cups. Their embroidered jackets and red-pointed slippers were beginning to wear out, but they still wore their tufted skull caps on the sides of their heads, and swords and pistols still protruded from their broad sashes. No one complained about them. It was impossible to imagine that these poor, peaceful-looking men were the notorious revolutionists, the companions of Kirdjali, and that he was among them.

The Turkish Pasha[1] found out that Kirdjali was in his territory, and under a treaty he had with the Russians, he demanded that the bandit be delivered to him.

The police began a search and finally captured Kirdjali in the house of a fugitive monk, where he was sitting in the dark having supper with seven of his companions. Kirdjali was arrested; he did not try to conceal the truth. He told the police that he was, indeed, Kirdjali.

"But," he added, "since I have come here I have not robbed anything from anyone—not even from a gypsy. I am a thief to the Turks, but I am a guest to you Russians. I have no money. I have lived by begging. Why, then, do you hand me over to my enemies?"

After that Kirdjali was silent and waited for the decision that was to determine his fate. He did not have to wait long. The authorities did not have to treat him as a romantic figure, and decided to turn him over to the Turkish Pasha.

A man of heart and intellect, at that time a young and unknown official, but now occupying an important position in the govern-ment, told me about Kirdjali's departure, which he witnessed:

A *karousta*—a low wicker cart drawn by horses—stood at the gates of the prison. The local people, in their picturesque clothes, some of the women carrying children, stood around the *karousta*. The men were silent, the women expected something exciting to happen.

The gate opened. Several policemen came out, followed by two soldiers who were leading Kirdjali in chains.

He appeared to be about thirty years old. His face was dark, his features regular and harsh. He was tall, broad-shouldered, and seemed to have an unusual physical strength. He wore a bright, many-coloured turban on the side of his head, and a broad sash around his slender waist. A long robe of thick, dark blue cloth and a pair of red slippers made up the rest of his costume. He looked proud and calm.

One of the officials, an old man in a worn-out uniform with its buttons hanging down, and with a pair of glasses pinching the purple knob he had for a nose, unrolled a piece of paper and snuffled as he read it aloud. From time to time he glanced haughtily at the chained Kirdjali, to whom the paper referred. Kirdjali listened with attention. The official finished his reading, folded up the paper, and then shouted at the people that they make way so the *karousta* could be brought up. Then Kirdjali turned to him and said a few words. His voice trembled, his face changed, he burst into tears and fell at the feet of the police official, clanking his chains. The police official, terrified, jumped back. The soldiers were about to pull Kirdjali to his feet, but he got up by his own strength, gathered his chains, stepped into the *karousta*, and cried, "Drive on!" A policeman took his seat beside him, the driver cracked his whip, and the *karousta* rolled away. My friend, the young official who told me the story, went up to the police officer, and asked, "What did Kirdjali say to you?"

1 Pasha *A man of high rank*
(as a former governor in Turkey).

The police officer smiled. "He asked me to look after his wife and child, who live in a Bulgarian village. He is afraid they may suffer because of him. People are so stupid!"

The story affected me deeply. I was sorry for poor Kirdjali. For a long time I heard nothing more about him. Then years later I met my friend, the young official. We began to talk about the past.

"What about Kirdjali," I asked. "Do you know what became of him?"

"Oh, yes, I do," he said, and he told me the following.

Kirdjali was taken before the Turkish Pasha, who condemned him to death. The execution was delayed: the Pasha wanted to wait until a holiday when he could hold a public execution. In the meantime Kirdjali was put in jail.

The prisoner was guarded by seven Turks (in their hearts just as much thieves as was Kirdjali). They respected him and, like all Orientals, listened with pleasure to his strange stories.

The guards and the prisoner became very friendly. One day Kirdjali said to them: "Brothers! My death is near. No one can escape his fate. I shall soon be leaving you. I want to leave you all something to remember me by."

The Turks listened carefully.

"Brothers," Kirdjali went on, "three years ago when I was a bandit, a friend of mine and I buried out in the woods a kettle full of money. Well, it looks like neither he nor I will ever get to use it. All right: take it and use it for yourselves."

The Turks almost went crazy. The question was: how would they find the sacred spot where the money was buried? They thought and thought and finally decided that Kirdjali would lead them to the place.

Night came. The Turks took the chains from the prisoner's feet, tied his hands with a rope, and left town with him—to the place out on the plains where the money was buried.

Kirdjali led them, going in one direction, from one hill to another. They walked on for a long time. At last Kirdjali stopped near a large stone, paced off twelve steps, stamped his foot on the ground, and said, "Here is the spot!"

Four of the Turks took out their great swords and began to dig. Three remained on guard. Kirdjali sat down on the stone and watched them work.

"Well, how long is it going to take you?" he asked. "Haven't you found it yet?"

"Not yet," said the Turks. They were digging so hard that the perspiration was falling from them like rain.

Kirdjali began to get impatient.

"What people!" he exclaimed. "They don't even know how to dig a hole. I would have finished the job in a few minutes. Children! Untie my hands and give me one of those swords."

The Turks held a conference. "Well, what harm is there?" they thought. "Let's untie his hands and let him work. He's only one and we are seven."

So the Turks untied his hands and gave him a sword.

At last Kirdjali was free and armed. How he must have felt at that moment! He began digging quickly, the guard helping him. Suddenly he plunged his sword into one of them, and leaving the blade stuck in the man's breast, snatched a couple of pistols from his belt.

The remaining six Turks, seeing Kirdjali armed with two pistols, ran off.

Kirdjali has resumed his life as a bandit. Not long ago he wrote to the Governor of the Province demanding a large sum of money. If the money wasn't paid, he would burn down the town and kill the Governor himself! And they paid him what he demanded.

That's Kirdjali!

George Kearns/TRANSLATOR

For Discussion

1 Some tales about romantic bandits make excuses for their central characters. Robin Hood, for example, "robs from the rich and gives to the poor." In other stories the outlaw has been forced into a life of crime by some injustice done him by society. Are there any such excuses to be made for Kirdjali? Does he do anything for which there is no good excuse?

2 Readers of fiction always enjoy stories about men who trick other people. We enjoy reading about people who triumph through the use of their wits, and this becomes one of the appeals of detective stories and spy stories. In what other selections you have read in this section did you find men coming out on top of a situation because they were clever?

3 Where and how does Pushkin enlist our sympathy for Kirdjali? At what point is the author's admiration for him most obvious?

4 For many years the American movie industry had a strong production code which insisted that every wrongdoer had to meet his just reward. If someone was a murderer, for example, he had to die or be sent to prison in the final reel. In this story Kirdjali escapes and remains free, as far as we know, to continue his career as a bandit. We can assume that he will go on murdering people. Does this make the story immoral in any way? Would you object to its being told to young children? Why, or why not?

Men often try to repay evil with evil, to demand "an eye for an eye." Such a concept of justice has caused discord among men and nations throughout history. Hatred becomes a chain from man to man, nation to nation. Neither has found it easy to follow the admonition to "turn the other cheek." Occasionally, as in this story, a man of great restraint and compassion manages to break the chain of vengeance.

Johann Peter Hebel

The Hussar

When, at the beginning of the French Revolution, the Prussians[1] made war against the French and rode through the province of Champagne,[2] no one imagined that the wind would change and that before long, in the year of 1806, the French would come to Prussia and return the uninvited visit. For not every Prussian behaved as befits an honorable soldier in an enemy country.

Thus, then, a Prussian hussar,[3] who was an evil person, invaded the house of a peaceable man, took from him all his money and much else of value, and finally even his pretty bed with the brand-new bedspread, and mistreated husband and wife. Their boy, eight years old, begged him on his knees at least to give back the bed to his parents. The hussar pushed him away harshly. Their daughter ran after him, caught hold of his cape, and implored him for mercy. But he seized her and threw her into the well in the courtyard, and got away with his loot.

Years afterward, he retired, settled in the city of Neisse in Silesia,[4] and thought little of the crime he had once committed, believing that the grass had grown over it long ago.

But what happened in the year of 1806? The French marched into Neisse, and one evening a young sergeant was quartered at the home of a good woman who attended him well. The sergeant was honorable, behaved decently, and seemed cheerful.

1 Prussians *People of Prussia, a former German state in northern and central present-day Germany.*

2 Champagne *A region of northeast France.*

3 hussar *A member of any of various European units originally* modeled on the Hungarian light cavalry of the fifteenth century.

4 Silesia *A former province in southeast Prussia.*

The next morning the sergeant did not come down to breakfast. The woman thought: "He's still asleep," and put his coffee in the oven to keep warm. After a while, when he still didn't come, she went up to his room to see whether he was all right, and softly pushed open the door.

There was the young man, awake and sitting up in bed, with his hands folded, and sighing as if he'd met with some great misfortune, or as if he had become homesick or some such thing. He did not notice that someone was in the room.

The woman went quietly to him and asked: "What has happened to you, sergeant, and why are you so sad?"

The young man looked at her with a tearful expression and said that the spread of the bed in which he'd spent the night had belonged to his parents in Champagne; they'd lost everything in the pillage fourteen years before and had become paupers, and all that was coming back to him now, and his heart was full of sorrow. For the sergeant was the son of the man who had been robbed in Champagne, and he still recognized the spread and the red initials that his mother had sewed on it.

The good woman was frightened and said she'd bought the bed-cover from a hussar who still lived in Neisse, and that she should not be blamed.

The Frenchman got up and had himself taken to the home of the hussar, and recognized the man.

"Do you recall," he said to the hussar, "how fourteen years ago you took away from an innocent man in Champagne all his possessions, even his bed, and took no pity when

an eight-year-old boy begged for mercy? And do you still remember my sister?"

At first the old wretch tried to make excuses, saying that in wartime, as everyone knows, not all things go as they should, and what one fellow leaves, another takes, so one might as well do the taking oneself. But when he saw that the sergeant really was the boy whose parents he had plundered and mistreated, and as he remembered the sister, the hussar's voice failed, in remorse and terror, and he fell on his shaking knees before the Frenchman unable to utter anything but "Forgive me." "But," he thought to himself, "this won't help much."

The gentle reader may think, gleefully: "Now the Frenchman will hack the hussar to pieces." But that would not tally with the truth. For when a man's heart is stirred and almost breaking in pain, he cannot take revenge. For vengeance is too small and contemptible, and he thinks: "We are in the hands of God," and he can't bring himself to repay evil with evil. Thus thought the Frenchman, too, and he said: "That you mistreated me, I forgive you. That you mistreated my parents and made them paupers, my parents will have to forgive you. That you threw my sister into the well, where she perished—may God forgive you that." With these words he went away without doing the hussar the slightest harm, and he became well again in his heart.

But the hussar felt afterward as though he'd stood before the Last Judgment and had been found wanting. He did not have one peaceful hour from that day on, and a quarter of a year later, it is said, he died.

Paul Pratt/TRANSLATOR

ℱo𝓇 𝒟iscussion

1 Like Verga's "Liberty" this is a story about revenge. In "Liberty" the peasants revenge themselves upon the land-owning class, and then society revenges itself upon the peasant-revolutionists. Do you find any true justification for revenge in either of the two stories?

2 In Dante's *Inferno* each sinner receives eternally a punishment which is appropriate to his sin. What is the hussar's

punishment in this story? Who delivers it? Is it appropriate to the crime?

3 Do you agree with the hussar's claim that during wartime ordinary human decency is suspended? What comment does the son's action make upon this statement?

4 Which of the two men in this story fits the image of the conquering soldier? Which of the two actually has the greater strength?

5 What does the author mean when he writes, "For vengeance is too small and contemptible"? If the son had killed the hussar would he have satisfied the demands of justice? Or would he only have added another evil to the evil already committed?

6 How do you think most men would have resolved the moral dilemma in which the son finds himself?

We have seen that there are several fictional patterns or figures which recur over and over again in literature. This is not to say that the authors who use these patterns lack originality, or even that they are always aware that they are following a pattern at all.

Rather, it suggests that certain fictional situations have a profound appeal to the imagination.

In this story Andreyev uses just such a standard figure: the clown whose heart is breaking. We find him in the popular opera *I Pagliacci*, in the films of Charlie Chaplin, and less obviously, in Shakespeare's *Hamlet*, whose hero cannot refrain from making bitter jokes in the face of tragedy and death.

Leonid Andreyev

Laughter

I

At 6:30 I was certain that she would come, and I was desperately happy. My coat was fastened only by the top button and fluttered in the cold wind; but I felt no cold. My head was proudly thrown back and my student's cap was cocked on the back of my head; my eyes with respect to the men they met were expressive of patronage and boldness, with respect to the women, of a seductive tenderness. Although she had been my only love for four whole days, I was so young, and my heart was so rich in love, that I could not remain perfectly indifferent to other women. My steps were quick, bold and free.

At 6:45 my coat was fastened by two buttons, and I looked only at the women, no longer with a seductive tenderness, but rather with disgust. I only wanted *one* woman—the others might go to the Devil; they only confused me, and, with their seeming resemblance to Her, gave to my movements an uncertain and jerky indecision.

At 6:55 I felt warm.

At 6:58 I felt cold.

As it struck 7:00 I was convinced that she would not come.

By 8:30 I presented the appearance of the most pitiful creature in the world. My coat was fastened with all its buttons, collar turned up, cap tilted over my nose, which was blue with cold; my hair was over my forehead, my mustache and eyelashes were whitening with rime, and my teeth gently chattered. From my shambling gait and bowed back, I might have been taken for a fairly hale old man returning from a party at the almshouse.

And She was the cause of all this—She! Oh, the Dev——! No, I won't. Perhaps She couldn't get away, or She's ill, or dead. She's dead!—and I swore.

II

"Eugenia Nikolaevna will be there tonight," one of my companions, a student, remarked to me, without the slightest *arrière pensée*.[1] He could not know that I had waited for her in the frost from seven to half-past eight.

"Indeed," I replied, as if in deep thought, but within my soul there leapt out, Oh, the Dev——! "There" meant at the Polozovs' evening party. Now the Polozovs were people with whom I was not upon visiting terms. But this evening I would be there.

"You fellows!" I shouted cheerfully. "Today is Christmas Day, when everybody enjoys himself. Let's do so too."

"But how?" one of them mournfully replied.

"And, where?" continued another.

"We'll dress up and go around to all the evening parties," I decided.

And these insensate individuals actually became cheerful. They shouted, leapt, and sang. They thanked me for my suggestion, and counted up the amount of "the ready" available. In the course of half an hour we had collected all the lonely, disconsolate students in town; and when we had recruited a cheerful dozen or so of leaping devils, we repaired to a hairdresser's—he was also a costumier—and let in there the cold, and youth, and laughter.

I wanted something somber and handsome, with a shade of elegant sadness; so I requested, "Give me the dress of a Spanish grandee."[2]

Apparently this grandee had been very tall, for I was altogether swallowed up in his dress, and felt as absolutely alone as though I had been in a wide, empty hall. Getting out of this costume, I asked for something else.

"Would you like to be a clown? Motley with bells?"

"A clown, indeed!" I exclaimed with contempt.

"Well, then, a bandit. Such a hat and dagger!"

Oh! dagger! Yes, that would suit my purpose. But unfortunately the bandit whose clothes they gave me had scarcely grown to full stature. Most probably he had been a corrupt youth of eight years. His little hat would not cover the back of my head, and I had to be dragged out of his velvet breeches as out of a trap. A page's dress would not do: it was all spotted like the pard. The monk's cowl was all in holes.

"Look sharp; it's late," said my companions, who were already dressed, trying to hurry me up.

There was but one costume left—that of a distinguished Chinese man. "Give me the Chinese man's," I said with a wave of my hand. And they gave it to me. It was the Devil knows what! I am not speaking of the costume itself. I pass over in silence those idiotic, flowered boots, which were too short for me, and reached only half-way to my knees; but in the remaining, by far the most essential part stuck out like two incomprehensible adjuncts on either side of my feet. I say nothing of the pink rag which covered my head like a wig, and was tied by threads to my ears, so that they protruded and stood up like a bat's. But the mask!

It was, if one may use the expression, a face *in the abstract*. It had nose, eyes, and mouth all right enough, and all in the proper places; but there was nothing human about it. A human being could not look so placid

1 arrière pensée *A hidden meaning.*

2 grandee *A Spanish or Portuguese nobleman of the first rank.*

—even in his coffin. It was expressive neither of sorrow, nor cheerfulness, nor surprise—it expressed absolutely nothing! It looked at you squarely, and placidly—and an uncontrollable laughter overwhelmed you. My companions rolled about on the sofas, sank impotently down on the chairs, and gesticulated.

"It will be the most original mask of the evening," they declared.

I was ready to weep; but no sooner did I glance in the mirror than I too was convulsed with laughter. Yes, it will be a most original mask!

"In no circumstances are we to take off our masks," said my companions on the way. "We'll give our word."

"Honor bright!"

III

Positively it was the most original mask. People followed me in crowds, turned me about, jostled me, pinched me. But when, harried, I turned on my persecutors in anger— uncontrollable laughter seized them. Wherever I went, a roaring cloud of laughter encompassed and pressed on me; it moved together with me, and I could not escape from this circle of mad mirth. Sometimes it seized even myself, and I shouted, sang, and danced till everything seemed to go around before me, as if I was drunk. But how remote everything was from me! And how solitary I was under that mask! At last they left me in peace. With anger and fear, with malice and tenderness intermingling, I looked at her.

"It's I."

Her long eyelashes were lifted slowly in surprise, and a whole sheaf of black rays flashed upon me, and a laugh, resonant, joyous, bright as the spring sunshine—a laugh answered me.

"Yes, it's I; I, I say," I insisted with a smile. "Why didn't you come this evening?"

But she only laughed, laughed joyously.

"I suffered so much; I felt so hurt," I said, imploring an answer.

But she only laughed. The black sheen of her eyes was extinguished, and still more brightly her smile lit up. It was the sun indeed, but burning, pitiless, cruel.

"What's the matter with you?"

"Is it really you?" she said, restraining herself. "How comical you are!"

My shoulders were bowed, and my head hung down—such despair was there in my pose. And while she, with the expiring afterglow of the smile upon her face, looked at the happy, young couples that hurried by us, I said, "It's not nice to laugh. Don't you feel that there's a living, suffering face behind my ridiculous mask—and can't you see that it was only for the opportunity it gave me of seeing you that I put it on? You gave me reason to hope for your love, and then so quickly, so cruelly deprived me of it. Why didn't you come?"

With a protest on her tender, smiling lips, she turned sharply to me, and a cruel laugh utterly overwhelmed her. Choking, almost weeping, covering her face with a fragrant lace handkerchief, she brought out with difficulty, "Look at yourself in the mirror behind you. Oh, how droll you are!"

Contracting my brows, clenching my teeth with pain, with a face grown cold, from which all the blood had fled, I looked at the mirror. There gazed back at me an idiotically placid, stolidly complacent, inhumanly immovable face. And I burst into an uncontrollable fit of laughter. And with the laughter not yet subsided, but already with the trembling of rising anger, with the madness of despair, I said—no, almost shouted, "You shouldn't laugh!"

And when she was quiet again, I went on speaking in a whisper of my love. I had never spoken so well, for I had never loved so strongly. I spoke of the tortures of expectation, of the venomous tears of mad jealousy and grief, of my own soul, which was all love. And I saw how her drooping eyelashes cast thick, dark shadows over her blanched cheeks. I saw how across their dull pallor the fire, bursting into flame, threw a red reflection, and how her whole pliant body involuntarily bent towards me.

She was dressed as the Goddess of Night, and was all mysterious, clad in a black, mist-like face, which twinkled with stars of brilliants.[3] She was as beautiful as a forgotten dream of far-off childhood. As I spoke, my eyes filled with tears, and my heart beat with gladness. And I perceived, I perceived at last, how a tender, piteous smile parted her lips, and her eyelashes were lifted all a-tremble. Slowly, timorously, but with infinite confidence, she turned her head towards me, and . . .

And such a shriek of laughter I had never heard!

"No, no, I can't," she almost groaned, and throwing back her head, she burst into a resonant cascade of laughter.

Oh, if but for a moment I could have had a human face! I bit my lips, tears rolled over my heated face; but it—that idiotic mask, on which everything was in its right place, nose, eyes, and lips—looked with a complacency stolidly horrible in its absurdity. And when I went out, swaying on my flowered feet, it was a long time before I got out of reach of that ringing laugh. It was as though a silvery stream of water were falling from an immense height, and breaking in cheerful song upon the hard rock.

IV

Scattered over the whole sleeping street, and rousing the stillness of the night with our lusty, excited voices, we walked home.

A companion said to me, "You've had a colossal success. I never saw people laugh so —Hey! what are you up to? Why are you tearing your mask? I say, you fellows, he's gone mad! Look, he's tearing his costume to pieces! By God! he's actually crying."

For Discussion

1 In the first sentence we find an unusual phrase, "desperately happy." Although at this point we do not know the narrator well, what does it suggest about him? How does it prepare us for his condition at the end of the story?

2 In the first paragraph we read that the narrator's coat was only fastened by one button. In the second paragraph we read that fifteen minutes later his coat was fastened by two buttons. What is the significance of this?

3 The narrator tells us, with no trace of self-humor, that he had known his beloved "for four whole days." What does this suggest about him? Is he in any way like Don Quixote? If so, how?

4 The story is divided into four short sections. Between each of these sections there are a few lines of white space indicating a brief gap in the action. What happens during each of these "white spaces"?

5 At the party the narrator is dressed in a clownish costume and wears the mask of an "abstract" human face. The woman he loves is dressed as the Goddess of Night. How do their costumes reflect their relationship?

6 Try to state the central irony of this story in a single sentence. The clue to this irony is in the final paragraph.

3 brilliants *Diamonds or other gems cut in a particular form with numerous facets so as to have special brilliance.*

O. Henry's story about life in an American frontier town is a variation of the tale of the city mouse and the country mouse. There are many versions of this fable, ancient and modern. Usually the simplicity and folk wisdom of country people are shown to be superior to the sophistication of city life.

O. Henry

Friends in San Rosario

The west-bound stopped at San Rosario on time at 8:20 A.M. A man with a thick black-leather wallet under his arm left the train and walked rapidly up the main street of the town. There were other passengers who also got off at San Rosario, but they either slouched limberly over to the railroad eating-house or the Silver Dollar saloon, or joined the groups of idlers about the station.

Indecision had no part in the movements of the man with the wallet. He was short in stature, but strongly built, with very light, closely trimmed hair, smooth, determined face, and aggressive, gold-rimmed nose glasses. He was well dressed in the prevailing Eastern style. His air denoted a quiet but conscious reserve force, if not actual authority.

After walking a distance of three squares he came to the center of the town's business area. Here another street of importance crossed the main one, forming the hub of San Rosario's life and commerce. Upon one corner stood the post-office. Upon another Rubensky's Clothing Emporium. The other two diagonally opposing corners were occupied by the town's two banks, the First National and the Stockmen's National. Into the First National Bank of San Rosario the newcomer walked, never slowing his brisk step until he stood at the cashier's window. The bank opened for business at nine, and the working force was already assembled, each member preparing his department for the day's business. The cashier was examining the mail when he noticed the stranger standing at his window.

"Bank doesn't open 'til nine," he remarked, curtly, but without feeling. He had had to make that statement so often to early birds since San Rosario adopted city banking hours.

"I am well aware of that," said the other man, in cool, brittle tones. "Will you kindly receive my card?"

The cashier drew the small, spotless parallelogram inside the bars of his wicket, and read:

J. F. C. NETTLEWICK
National Bank Examiner

"Oh—er—will you walk around inside, Mr. —er—Nettlewick. Your first visit—didn't know your business, of course. Walk right around, please."

The examiner was quickly inside the sacred precincts of the bank, where he was ponderously introduced to each employee in turn by Mr. Edlinger, the cashier—a middle-aged gentleman of deliberation, discretion, and method.

"I was kind of expecting Sam Turner round again, pretty soon," said Mr. Edlinger. "Sam's been examining us now for about four years. I guess you'll find us all right, though, considering the tightness in business. Not overly much money on hand, but able to stand the storms, sir, stand the storms."

"Mr. Turner and I have been ordered by the Comptroller to exchange districts," said the examiner, in his decisive, formal tones. "He is covering my old territory in southern Illinois and Indiana. I will take the cash first, please."

Perry Dorsey, the teller, was already arranging the cash on the counter for the examiner's inspection. He knew it was right to a cent, and he had nothing to fear, but he was nervous and flustered. So was every man in the bank. There was something so icy and swift, so impersonal and uncompromising about this man that his very presence seemed an accusation. He looked to be a man who would never make nor overlook an error.

Mr. Nettlewick first seized the currency, and with a rapid, almost juggling motion, counted it by packages. Then he spun the sponge cup toward him and verified the count by bills. His thin, white fingers flew like some expert musician's upon the keys of a piano. He dumped the gold upon the counter with a crash, and the coins whined and sang as they skimmed across the marble slab from the tips of his nimble digits. The air was full of fractional currency when he came to the halves and quarters. He counted the last nickel and dime. He had the scales brought, and he weighed every sack of silver in the vault. He questioned Dorsey concerning each of the cash memoranda—certain checks, charge slips, etc., carried over from the previous day's work—with unimpeachable courtesy, yet with something so mysteriously momentous in his frigid manner, that the teller was reduced to pink cheeks and a stammering tongue.

This newly imported examiner was so different from Sam Turner. It had been Sam's way to enter the bank with a shout, pass the cigars, and tell the latest stories he had picked up on his rounds. His customary greeting to Dorsey had been, "Hello, Perry! Haven't skipped out with the boodle yet, I see." Turner's way of counting the cash had been different too. He would finger the packages of bills in a tired kind of way, and then go into the vault and kick over a few sacks of silver, and the thing was done. Halves and quarters and dimes? Not for Sam Turner. "No chicken feed for me," he would say when they were set before him. "I'm not in the agricultural department." But, then, Turner was a Texan, an old friend of the bank's president, and had known Dorsey since he was a baby.

While the examiner was counting the cash, Major Thomas B. Kingman—known to everyone as "Major Tom"—the president of the First National, drove up to the side door with his old dun[1] horse and buggy, and came inside. He saw the examiner busy with the money, and, going into the little "pony corral," as he called it, in which his desk was railed off, he began to look over his letters.

Earlier, a little incident had occurred that

1 dun *A variable color averaging a nearly neutral, slightly brownish dark gray.*

even the sharp eyes of the examiner had failed to notice. When he had begun his work at the cash counter, Mr. Edlinger had winked significantly at Roy Wilson, the youthful bank messenger, and nodded his head slightly toward the front door. Roy understood, got his hat and walked leisurely out, with his collector's book under his arm. Once outside, he made a bee-line for the Stockmen's National. That bank was also getting ready to open. No customers had, as yet, presented themselves.

"Say, you people!" cried Roy, with the familiarity of youth and long acquaintance, "you want to get a move on you. There's a new bank examiner over at the First, and he's a stem-winder.[2] He's counting nickels on Perry, and he's got the whole outfit bluffed. Mr. Edlinger gave me the tip to let you know."

Mr. Buckley, president of the Stockmen's National—a stout, elderly man, looking like a farmer dressed for Sunday—heard Roy from his private office at the rear and called him.

"Has Major Kingman come down to the bank yet?" he asked of the boy.

"Yes, sir, he was just driving up as I left," said Roy.

"I want you to take him a note. Put it into his own hands as soon as you get back."

Mr. Buckley sat down and began to write.

Roy returned and handed to Major Kingman the envelope containing the note. The major read it, folded it, and slipped it into his vest pocket. He leaned back in his chair for a few moments as if he were meditating deeply, and then rose and went into the vault. He came out with the bulky, old-fashioned leather note case stamped on the back in gilt letters, "Bills Discounted." In this were the notes due the bank with their attached securities, and the major, in his rough way, dumped the lot upon his desk and began to sort them over.

By this time Nettlewick had finished his count of the cash. His pencil fluttered like a swallow over the sheet of paper on which he

had set his figures. He opened his black wallet, which seemed to be also a kind of secret memorandum book, made a few rapid figures in it, wheeled and transfixed Dorsey with the glare of his spectacles. That look seemed to say: "You're safe this time, but—"

"Cash all correct," snapped the examiner. He made a dash for the individual bookkeeper, and, for a few minutes there was a fluttering of ledger leaves and a sailing of balance sheets through the air.

"How often do you balance your passbooks?" he demanded, suddenly.

"Er—once a month," faltered the individual bookkeeper, wondering how many years they would give him.

"All right," said the examiner, turning and charging upon the general bookkeeper, who had the statements of his foreign banks and their reconcilement memoranda ready. Everything there was found to be all right. Then the stub book of the certificates of deposit. Flutter-flutter—zip—zip—check! All right. List of overdrafts, please. Thanks. H'm-m. Unsigned bills of the bank next. All right.

Then came the cashier's turn, and easygoing Mr. Edlinger rubbed his nose and polished his glasses nervously under the quick fire of questions concerning the circulation, undivided profits, bank real estate, and stock ownership.

Presently, Nettlewick was aware of a big man towering above him at his elbow—a man sixty years of age, rugged and hale, with a rough, grizzled beard, a mass of gray hair, and a pair of penetrating blue eyes that confronted the formidable glasses of the examiner without a flicker.

"Er—Major Kingman, our president—er—Mr. Nettlewick," said the cashier.

Two men of very different types shook hands. One was a finished product of the world of straight lines, conventional methods, and formal affairs. The other was something freer, wider, and nearer to nature. Tom Kingman had not been cut to any pattern. He had been mule-driver, cowboy, ranger, soldier, sheriff, prospector and cattleman.

2 stem-winder *Slang: a very meticulous person.*

Now, when he was bank president, his old comrades from the prairies, of the saddle, tent, and trail, found no change in him. He had made his fortune when Texas cattle were at the high tide of value, and had organized the First National Bank of San Rosario. In spite of his largeness of heart and sometimes unwise generosity toward his old friends, the bank had prospered, for Major Tom Kingman knew men as well as he knew cattle. Of late years the cattle business had known a depression, and the major's bank was one of the few whose losses had not been great.

"And now," said the examiner, briskly, pulling out his watch, "the last thing is the loans. We will take them up now, if you please."

He had gone through the First National at almost record-breaking speed—but thoroughly, as he did everything. The running order of the bank was smooth and clean, and that had facilitated his work. There was but one other bank in the town. He received from the Government a fee of twenty-five dollars for each bank that he examined. He should be able to go over those loans and discounts in half an hour. If so, he could examine the other bank immediately afterward, and catch the 11:45, the only other train that day in the direction he was working. Otherwise, he would have to spend the night and Sunday in this uninteresting Western town. That was why Mr. Nettlewick was rushing matters.

"Come with me, sir," said Major Kingman, in his deep voice, that united the Southern drawl with the rhythmic twang of the West. "We will go over them together. Nobody in the bank knows those notes as I do. Some of 'em are a little wobbly on their legs, and some are mavericks without extra many brands on their backs, but they'll most all pay out at the round-up."

The two sat down at the president's desk. First, the examiner went through the notes at lightning speed, and added up their total, finding it to agree with the amount of loans carried on the book of daily balances. Next,

he took up the larger loans, inquiring scrupulously into the condition of their endorsers or securities. The new examiner's mind seemed to course and turn and make unexpected dashes hither and thither like a bloodhound seeking a new trail. Finally he pushed aside all the notes except a few, which he arranged in a neat pile before him, and began a dry, formal little speech.

"I find, sir, the condition of your bank to be very good, considering the poor crops and the depression in the cattle interests of your state. The clerical work seems to be done accurately and punctually. Your past-due paper is moderate in amount, and promises only a small loss. I would recommend the calling in of your large loans, and the making of only sixty and ninety day or call loans until general business revives. And now, there is one thing more, and I will have finished with the bank. Here are six notes aggregating something like $40,000.00. They are secured, according to their faces, by various stocks, bonds, shares, etc., to the value of $70,000.00. Those securities are missing from the notes to which they should be attached. I suppose you have them in the safer vault. You will permit me to examine them."

Major Tom's light-blue eyes turned unflinchingly toward the examiner.

"No, sir," he said, in a low but steady tone: "those securities are neither in the safe nor the vault. I have taken them. You may hold me personally responsible for their absence."

Nettlewick felt a slight thrill. He had not expected this. He had struck a momentous trail when the hunt was drawing to a close.

"Ah!" said the examiner. He waited a moment, and then continued: "May I ask you to explain more definitely?"

"The securities were taken by me," repeated the major. "It was not for my own use, but to save an old friend in trouble. Come in here, sir, and we'll talk it over."

He led the examiner into the bank's private office at the rear, and closed the door. There was a desk, and a table, and half-a-dozen leather covered chairs. On the wall was the mounted head of a Texas steer with horns five feet from tip to tip. Opposite hung the major's old cavalry saber that he had carried at Shiloh[3] and Fort Pillow.[4]

Placing a chair for Nettlewick, the major seated himself by the window, from which he could see the post-office and the carved limestone front of the Stockmen's National. He did not speak at once, and Nettlewick felt, perhaps, that the ice should be broken by something so near its own temperature as the voice of official warning.

"Your statement," he began, "since you have failed to modify it, amounts, as you must know, to a very serious thing. You are aware, also, of what my duty must compel me to do. I shall have to go before the United States Commissioner and make——"

"I know, I know," said Major Tom, with a wave of his hand. "You don't suppose I'd run a bank without being posted on national banking laws and the revised statutes! Do your duty. I'm not asking any favors. But I spoke of my friend. I did want you to hear me tell you about Bob."

Nettlewick settled himself in his chair. There would be no leaving San Rosario for him that day. He would have to telegraph the Comptroller of the Currency; he would have to swear out a warrant before the United States Commissioner for the arrest of Major Kingman; perhaps he would be ordered to close the bank on account of the loss of the securities. It was not the first crime the examiner had unearthed. Once or twice the terrible upheaval of human emotions that his investigations had loosed had almost caused a ripple in his official calm. He had seen bank men kneel and plead and cry like women for a chance—an hour's time—the overlooking of a single error. One cashier had shot himself at his desk before him. None of them had taken it with the dignity and coolness of this stern old Westerner. Nettlewick felt he owed it to him at least to listen if he wished to talk. With his elbow

on the arm of his chair, and his square chin resting upon the fingers of his right hand, the bank examiner waited to hear the confession of the president of the First National Bank of San Rosario.

"When a man's your friend," began Major Tom, somewhat didactically, "for forty years, and tried by water, fire, earth, and cyclones, when you can do him a little favor you feel like doing it."

("Embezzle for him $70,000.00 worth of securities," thought the examiner.)

"We were cowboys together, Bob and I," continued the major, speaking slowly, and deliberately, and musingly, as if his thoughts were rather with the past than the critical present, "and we prospected together for gold and silver over Arizona, New Mexico, and a good part of California. We were both in the war of 'sixty-one, but in different commands. We've fought Indians and horse thieves side by side; we've starved for weeks in a cabin in the Arizona mountains, buried twenty feet deep in snow; we've ridden herd together when the wind blew so hard the lightning couldn't strike—well, Bob and I have been through some rough spells since the first time we met in the branding camp of the old Anchor-Bar ranch. And during that time we've found it necessary more than once to help each other out of tight places. In those days it was expected of a man to stick to his friend, and he didn't ask any credit for it. Probably the next day you'd need him to get at your back and help stand off a band of Apaches, or put a tourniquet on your leg above a rattlesnake bite and ride for whisky. So, after all, it was give and take, and if you didn't stand square with your pardner, why, you might be shy one when you needed him. But Bob was a man who was willing to go further than that. He never played a limit.

"Twenty years ago I was sheriff of this county and I made Bob my chief deputy. That was before the boom in cattle when we both made our stake. I was sheriff and collector, and it was a big thing for me then. I

3 Shiloh *The site of the battle of Shiloh in the Civil War; located in southwest Tennessee.*

4 Fort Pillow *Fort on Mississippi River, 40 miles north of Memphis, Tennessee; scene of Federal defeat on April 12, 1864.*

was married, and we had a boy and a girl—
a four and a six year old. There was a comfortable house next to the courthouse, furnished by the county, rent free, and I was sav-
ing some money. Bob did most of the office
work. Both of us had seen rough times and
plenty of rustling and danger, and I tell you
it was great to hear the rain and the sleet
dashing against the windows of nights and
be warm and safe and comfortable, and know
you could get up in the morning and be
shaved and have folks call you 'mister.' And
then, I had the finest wife and kids that ever
struck the range, and my old friend with me
enjoying the first fruits of prosperity and
white shirts, and I guess I was happy. Yes,
I was happy about that time."

The major sighed and glanced casually out
of the window. The bank examiner changed
his position, and leaned his chin upon his
other hand.

"One winter," continued the major, "the
money for the county taxes came pouring in
so fast that I didn't have time to take the
stuff to the bank for a week. I just shoved
the checks into a cigar box and the money
into a sack, and locked them in the big safe
that belonged in the sheriff's office.

"I had been overworked that week, and
was about sick, anyway. My nerves were out
of order, and my sleep at night didn't seem to
rest me. The doctor had some scientific
name for it, and I was taking medicine. And
so, added to the rest, I went to bed at night
with that money on my mind. Not that there
was much need of being worried, for the safe
was a good one, and nobody but Bob and I
knew the combination. On Friday night
there was about $6,500.00 cash in the bag.
On Saturday morning I went to the office as
usual. The safe was locked, and Bob was
writing at his desk. I opened the safe, and
the money was gone. I called Bob, and
roused everybody in the courthouse to announce the robbery. It struck me that Bob
took it pretty quiet, considering how much it
reflected upon both him and me.

"Two days went by and we never got a
clue. It couldn't have been burglars, for the
safe had been opened by the combination in
the proper way. People must have begun to
talk, for one afternoon in comes Alice—that's
my wife—and the boy and girl, and Alice
stamps her foot and her eyes flash, and she
cries out, 'The lying wretches—Tom, Tom!'
and I catch her in a faint, and bring her
'round little by little, and she lays her head
down and cries and cries for the first time
since she took Tom Kingman's name and fortunes. And Jack and Zilla—the youngsters—
they were always wild as tigers' cubs to rush
at Bob and climb all over him whenever they
were allowed to come to the courthouse—
they stood and kicked their little shoes, and
herded together like scared partridges. They
were having their first trip down into the
shadows of life. Bob was working at his
desk, and he got up and went out without a
word. The grand jury was in session then,
and the next morning Bob went before them
and confessed that he had stolen the money.
He said he lost it in a poker game. In fifteen
minutes they had found a true bill[5] and sent
me the warrant to arrest the man with whom
I'd been closer than a thousand brothers for
many a year.

"I did it, and then I said to Bob, pointing:
'There's my house, and here's my office, and
up there's Maine, and out that way is California, and over there is Florida—and that's
your range 'til court meets. You're in my
charge, and I take the responsibility. You be
here when you're wanted.'

" 'Thanks, Tom,' he said, kind of carelessly;
'I was sort of hoping you wouldn't lock me
up. Court meets next Monday, so, if you
don't object, I'll just loaf around the office
until then. I've got one favor to ask, if it
isn't too much. If you'd let the kids come
out in the yard once in a while and have a
romp I'd like it.'

" 'Why not?' I answered him. 'They're
welcome, and so are you. And come to my
house the same as ever.' You see, Mr. Net-

5   true bill   *A bill of indictment
endorsed by a grand jury as war-
ranting prosecution of the accused.*

tlewick, you can't make a friend of a thief, but neither can you make a thief of a friend, all at once."

The examiner made no answer. At that moment was heard the shrill whistle of a locomotive pulling into the depot. That was the train on the little, narrow-gauge road that struck into San Rosario from the south. The major cocked his ear and listened for a moment, and looked at his watch. The narrow-gauge was in on time—10:35. The major continued:

"So Bob hung around the office, reading the papers and smoking. I put another deputy to work in his place, and, after a while, the first excitement of the case wore off.

"One day when we were alone in the office Bob came over to where I was sitting. He was looking sort of grim and blue—the same look he used to get when he'd been watching for Indians all night or herd-riding.

"'Tom,' says he, 'it's harder than standing off redskins; it's harder than lying in the lava desert miles from water; but I'm going to stick it out to the end. You know that's my style. But if you'd tip me the smallest kind of sign—if you'd just say, "Bob I understand," why, it would make it lots easier.'

"I was surprised. 'I don't know what you mean, Bob,' I said. 'Of course, you know I'd do anything under the sun to help you that I could. But you've got me guessing.'

"'All right, Tom,' was all he said, and he went back to his newspaper and lit another cigar.

"It was the night before the court met when I found out what he meant. I went to bed that night with the same old, light-headed, nervous feeling come back upon me. I dropped off to sleep about midnight. When I woke I was standing half-dressed in one of the courthouse corridors. Bob was holding one of my arms, our family doctor the other and Alice was shaking me and half crying. She had sent for the doctor without my knowing it, and when he came they found me out of bed and missing, and had begun a search.

"'Sleep-walking,' said the doctor.

"All of us went back to the house, and the doctor told us some remarkable stories about the strange things people had done while in that condition. I was feeling rather chilly after my trip out, and, as my wife was out of the room at the time, I pulled open the door of an old wardrobe that stood in the room and dragged out a big quilt I had seen in there. With it tumbled out the bag of money for stealing which Bob was to be tried—and convicted—in the morning.

"'How the jumping rattlesnakes did that get there?' I yelled, and all hands must have seen how surprised I was. Bob knew in a flash.

"'You darned old snoozer,' he said, with the old-time look on his face, 'I saw you put it there. I watched you open the safe and take it out, and I followed you. I looked through the window and saw you hide it in that wardrobe.'

"'Then, you blankety-blank, flop-eared, sheep-headed coyote, what did you say you took it for?'

"'Because,' said Bob, simply, 'I didn't know you were asleep.'

"I saw him glance toward the door of the room where Jack and Zilla were, and I knew then what it meant to be a man's friend from Bob's point of view."

Major Tom paused, and again directed his glance out of the window. He saw someone in the Stockmen's National Bank reach and draw a yellow shade down the whole length of its plate-glass, big front window, although the position of the sun did not seem to warrant such a defensive movement against its rays.

Nettlewick sat up straight in his chair. He had listened patiently, but without consuming interest, to the major's story. It had impressed him as irrelevant to the situation, and it could certainly have no effect upon the consequences. Those Western people, he thought, had an exaggerated sentimentality. They were not businesslike. They needed to be protected from their friends. Evidently the major had concluded. And what he had said amounted to nothing.

"May I ask," said the examiner, "if you have anything further to say that bears directly upon the question of those abstracted securities?"

"Abstracted securities, sir!" Major Tom turned suddenly in his chair, his blue eyes flashing upon the examiner. "What do you mean, sir?"

He drew from his coat pocket a batch of folded papers held together by a rubber band, tossed them into Nettlewick's hands, and rose to his feet.

"You'll find those securities there, sir, every stock, bond, and share of 'em. I took them from the notes while you were counting the cash. Examine and compare them for yourself."

The major led the way back into the banking room. The examiner, astounded, perplexed, nettled, at sea, followed. He felt that he had been made the victim of something that was not exactly a hoax, but that left him in the shoes of one who had been played upon, used, and then discarded, without even an inkling of the game. Perhaps, also, his official position had been irreverently juggled with. But there was nothing he could take hold of. An official report of the matter would be an absurdity. And, somehow, he felt that he would never know anything more about the matter than he did then.

Frigidly, mechanically, Nettlewick examined the securities, found them to tally with the notes, gathered his black wallet, and rose to depart.

"I will say," he protested, turning the indignant glare of his glasses upon Major Kingman, "that your statements—your misleading statements, which you have not condescended to explain—do not appear to be quite the thing, regarded either as business or humor. I do not understand such motives or actions."

Major Tom looked down at him serenely and not unkindly.

"Son," he said, "there are plenty of things in the chaparral,[6] and on the prairies, and up the canyons that you don't understand. But I want to thank you for listening to a garrulous old man's prosy story. We old Texans love to talk about our adventures and our old comrades, and the homefolks have long ago learned to run when we begin with 'Once upon a time,' so we have to spin our yarns to the stranger within our gates."

The major smiled, but the examiner only bowed coldly, and abruptly quitted the bank. They saw him travel diagonally across the street in a straight line and enter the Stockmen's National Bank.

Major Tom sat down at his desk and drew from his vest pocket the note Roy had given him. He had read it once, but hurriedly, and now, with something like a twinkle in his eyes, he read it again. These were the words he read:

DEAR TOM:

I hear there's one of Uncle Sam's greyhounds going through you, and that means that we'll catch him inside a couple of hours, maybe. Now, I want you to do something for me. We've got just $2,200.00 in the bank, and the law requires that we have $20,000.00. I let Ross and Fisher have $18,000.00 late yesterday afternoon to buy up that Gibson bunch of cattle. They'll realize $40,000 in less than thirty days on the transaction, but that won't make my cash on hand look any prettier to that bank examiner. Now, I can't show him those notes, for they're just plain notes of hand without any security in sight, but you know very well that Pink Ross and Jim Fisher are two of the finest men God ever made, and they'll do the square thing. You remember Jim Fisher—he was the one who shot that faro[7] dealer in El Paso. I wired Sam Bradshaw's bank to send me $20,000.00, and it will get in on the narrow-gauge at 10:35. You can't let a bank examiner in to count $2,200 and close your doors. Tom, you hold that examiner. Hold him. Hold him if you have to rope him and sit on his head. Watch our front window after the narrow-gauge gets in, and when we've got

6 chaparral *A dense, impenetrable thicket of shrubs or dwarf trees.*

7 faro *A banking game in which players bet on cards drawn from a dealing box.*

the cash inside we'll pull down the shade for a signal. Don't turn him loose till then. I'm counting on you, Tom.

Your old Pard,
Bob Buckley,
Prest. Stockmen's National

The major began to tear the note into small pieces and throw them into his waste basket. He gave a satisfied little chuckle as he did so.

"Confounded old reckless cowpuncher!" he growled, contentedly, "that pays him some on account for what he tried to do for me in the sheriff's office twenty years ago."

For Discussion

1 An author often reveals his attitude toward a character through the details he chooses to describe him. By looking at the details describing J. F. C. Nettlewick, what can you say about O. Henry's attitude toward him? By the same method, what can you say about O. Henry's opinion of Major Tom Kingman? What do the names Nettlewick and Kingman suggest?

2 In this story O. Henry examines honesty from several points of view. How is Major Kingman honest? How is he dishonest? Which kind of honesty does O. Henry appear to admire?

3 Major Kingman's account of his relationship with Buckley creates a story within a story. What does the inner story—about Bob's loyalty—have to do with the story as a whole? Does Nettlewick understand the significance of Major Kingman's story?

4 O. Henry was famous, as was de Maupassant, for his "surprise endings." Is the ending of this story really a surprise, or could you see it coming? What clues, if any, did the author drop along the way?

5 How do Major Kingman and Bob Buckley represent the pioneer spirit? What is their attitude toward rules and authority? What does O. Henry suggest about the future of the pioneer spirit by making Kingman and Buckley bankers?

Another classic theme in literature is man's attempt to change or outwit his fate. Oedipus, in the Greek legend, left his home in Corinth in order to avoid a prophecy that he would kill his own father. Unknown to him, the man he thought was his father had adopted him when he was a baby. Along the road he met and killed a stranger who turned out to be his real father. In trying to escape his destiny, Oedipus had rushed headlong into it. Likewise, in the Old Testament, Jonah tried to avoid God's commandment that he should go to Nineveh. Trapped inside the whale, he found himself carried to Nineveh and faced with the very duty he had tried to escape.

"The Monkey's Paw" is a story in which gentle people tamper with fate's secrets and turn their quiet lives into a nightmare. They find that as they disturb the balance of destiny they must pay a severe price for every gift they receive. As in so many stories, we are faced with the question: is man's ignorance of his future a curse, or a blessing?

W. W. Jacobs

The Monkey's Paw

Without, the night was cold and wet, but in the small parlor of Lakesnam Villa the blinds were drawn and the fire burned brightly. Father and son were at chess, the former, who possessed ideas about the game involving radical changes, putting his king into such sharp and unnecessary perils that it even provoked comment from the white-haired old lady knitting placidly by the fire.

"Hark at the wind," said Mr. White, who, having seen a fatal mistake after it was too late, was amiably desirous of preventing his son from seeing it.

"I'm listening," said the latter, grimly surveying the board as he stretched out his hand. "Check."

"I should hardly think that he'd come tonight," said his father, with his hand poised over the board.

"Mate," replied the son.

"That's the worst of living so far out," bawled Mr. White, with sudden and unlooked-for violence; "of all the beastly, slushy, out-of-the-way places to live in, this is the worst. Pathway's a bog, and the road's a torrent. I don't know what people are thinking about. I suppose because only two houses on the road are let, they think it doesn't matter."

"Never mind, dear," said his wife soothingly; "perhaps you'll win the next one."

Mr. White looked up sharply, just in time

to intercept a knowing glance between mother and son. The words died away on his lips, and he hid a guilty grin in his thin gray beard.

"There he is," said Herbert White, as the gate banged to loudly and heavy footsteps came toward the door.

The old man rose with hospitable haste, and opening the door, was heard condoling with the new arrival. The new arrival also condoled with himself, so that Mrs. White said, "Tut, tut!" and coughed gently as her husband entered the room, followed by a tall burly man, beady of eye and rubicund[1] of visage.

"Sergeant-Major Morris," he said, introducing him.

The sergeant-major shook hands, and taking the proffered seat by the fire, watched contentedly while his host got out whisky and tumblers and stood a small copper kettle on the fire.

At the third glass his eyes got brighter, and he began to talk, the little family circle regarding with eager interest this visitor from distant parts, as he squared his broad shoulders in the chair and spoke of strange scenes and doughty deeds, of wars and plagues and strange peoples.

"Twenty-one years of it," said Mr. White, nodding at his wife and son. "When he went away he was a slip of a youth in the warehouse. Now look at him."

"He don't look to have taken much harm," said Mrs. White politely.

"I'd like to go to India myself," said the old man, "just to look round a bit, you know."

"Better where you are," said the sergeant-major, shaking his head. He put down the empty glass and, sighing softly, shook it again.

"I should like to see those old temples and fakirs[2] and jugglers," said the old man. "What was that you started telling me the other day about a monkey's paw or something, Morris?"

"Nothing," said the soldier hastily. "Leastways, nothing worth hearing."

"Monkey's paw?" said Mrs. White curiously.

"Well, it's just a bit of what you might call magic, perhaps," said the sergeant-major offhandedly.

His three listeners leaned forward eagerly. The visitor absent-mindedly put his empty glass to his lips and then set it down again. His host filled it for him.

"To look at," said the sergeant-major fumbling in his pocket, "it's just an ordinary little paw, dried to a mummy."

He took something out of his pocket and proffered it. Mrs. White drew back with a grimace, but her son, taking it, examined it curiously.

"And what is there special about it?" inquired Mr. White, as he took it from his son and, having examined it, placed it upon the table.

"It had a spell put on it by an old fakir," said the sergeant-major, "a very holy man. He wanted to show that fate ruled people's lives, and that those who interfered with it did so to their sorrow. He put a spell on it so that three separate men could each have three wishes from it."

His manner was so impressive that his hearers were conscious that their light laughter jarred somewhat.

"Well, why don't you have three, sir?" said Herbert White cleverly.

The soldier regarded him in the way that middle age is wont to regard presumptuous youth. "I have," he said quietly, and his blotchy face whitened.

"And did you really have the three wishes granted?" asked Mrs. White.

"I did," said the sergeant-major, and his glass tapped against his strong teeth.

"And has anybody else wished?" inquired the old lady.

"The first man had his three wishes, yes," was the reply. "I don't know what the first two were, but the third was for death. That's how I got the paw."

His tones were so grave that a hush fell upon the group.

---

1 rubicund *Ruddy; having a healthy reddish color.*
2 fakirs *Itinerant Hindu ascetics or wonder-workers.*

"If you've had your three wishes, it's no good to you now, then, Morris," said the old man at last. "What do you keep it for?"

The soldier shook his head. "Fancy, I suppose," he said slowly. "I did have some idea of selling it, but I don't think I will. It has caused enough mischief already. Besides, people won't buy. They think it's a fairy tale, some of them, and those who do think anything of it want to try it first and pay me afterward."

"If you could have another three wishes," said the old man, eyeing him keenly, "would you have them?"

"I don't know," said the other. "I don't know."

He took the paw, and dangling it between his front finger and thumb, suddenly threw it upon the fire. White, with a slight cry, stooped down and snatched it off.

"Better let it burn," said the soldier solemnly.

"If you don't want it, Morris," said the old man, "give it to me."

"I won't," said his friend doggedly. "I threw it on the fire. If you keep it, don't blame me for what happens. Pitch it on the fire again, like a sensible man."

The other shook his head and examined his new possession closely. "How do you do it?" he inquired.

"Hold it up in your right hand and wish aloud," said the sergeant-major, "but I warn you of the consequences."

"Sounds like the *Arabian Nights*," said Mrs. White, as she rose and began to set the supper. "Don't you think you might wish for four pairs of hands for me?"

Her husband drew the talisman[3] from his pocket and then all three burst into laughter as the sergeant-major, with a look of alarm on his face, caught him by the arm.

"If you must wish," he said gruffly, "wish for something sensible."

Mr. White dropped it back into his pocket, and placing chairs, motioned his friend to the table. In the business of supper the talisman was partly forgotten, and afterward the three sat listening in an enthralled fashion to a second installment of the soldier's adventures in India.

"If the tale about the monkey paw is not more truthful than those he has been telling us," said Herbert, as the door closed behind their guest, just in time for him to catch the last train, "we shan't make much out of it."

"Did you give him anything for it, father?" inquired Mrs. White, regarding her husband closely.

"A trifle," said he, coloring slightly. "He didn't want it, but I made him take it. And he pressed me again to throw it away."

"Likely," said Herbert, with pretended horror. "Why, we're going to be rich, and famous, and happy. Wish to be an emperor, father, to begin with; then you can't be henpecked."

He darted round the table, pursued by the maligned Mrs. White armed with an antimacassar.[4]

Mr. White took the paw from his pocket and eyed it dubiously. "I don't know what to wish for, and that's a fact," he said slowly. "It seems to me I've got all I want."

"If you only cleared the house, you'd be quite happy, wouldn't you?" said Herbert, with his hand on his shoulder. "Well, wish for two hundred pounds, then; that'll just do it."

His father, smiling shamefacedly at his own credulity, held up the talisman, as his son, with a solemn face somewhat marred by a wink at his mother, sat down at the piano and struck a few impressive chords.

"I wish for two hundred pounds," said the old man distinctly.

A fine crash from the piano greeted the words, interrupted by a shuddering cry from the old man. His wife and son ran toward him.

"It moved," he cried, with a glance of disgust at the object as it lay on the floor. "As I wished it twisted in my hands like a snake."

"Well, I don't see the money," said his son,

3 talisman *Something producing apparently magical or miraculous effects.*
4 antimacassar *A cover to protect the back or arms of furniture.*

as he picked it up and placed it on the table, "and I bet I never shall."

"It must have been your fancy, father," said his wife, regarding him anxiously.

He shook his head. "Never mind, though; there's no harm done, but it gave me a shock all the same."

They sat down by the fire again while the two men finished their pipes. Outside, the wind was higher than ever, and the old man started nervously at the sound of a door banging upstairs. A silence unusual and depressing settled upon all three, which lasted until the old couple rose to retire for the night.

"I expect you'll find the cash tied up in a big bag in the middle of your bed," said Herbert, as he bade them good night, "and something horrible squatting up on top of the wardrobe watching you as you pocket your ill-gotten gains."

II

In the brightness of the wintry sun next morning as it streamed over the breakfast table Herbert laughed at his fears. There was an air of prosaic wholesomeness about the room which it had lacked on the previous night, and the dirty, shriveled little paw was pitched on the sideboard with a carelessness which betokened no great belief in its virtues.

"I suppose all old soldiers are the same," said Mrs. White. "The idea of our listening to such nonsense! How could wishes be granted in these days? And if they could, how could two hundred pounds hurt you, father?"

"Might drop on his head from the sky," said the frivolous Herbert.

"Morris said the things happened so naturally," said his father, "that you might if you so wished attribute it to coincidence."

"Well, don't break into the money before I come back," said Herbert, rising from the table. "I'm afraid it'll turn you into a mean, avaricious man, and we'll have to disown you."

His mother laughed, and following him to the door, watched him down the road, and returning to the breakfast table, was very happy at the expense of her husband's credulity. All of which did not prevent her from scurrying to the door at the postman's knock, nor prevent her from referring somewhat shortly to retired sergeant-majors of bibulous habits when she found that the post brought a tailor's bill.

"Herbert will have some more of his funny remarks, I expect, when he comes home," she said, as they sat at dinner.

"I dare say," said Mr. White, pouring himself out some beer; "but for all that, the thing moved in my hand; that I'll swear to."

"You thought it did," said the old lady soothingly.

"I say it did," replied the other. "There was no thought about it; I had just—What's the matter?"

His wife made no reply. She was watching the mysterious movements of a man outside, who, peering in an undecided fashion at the house, appeared to be trying to make up his mind to enter. In mental connection with the two hundred pounds, she noticed that the stranger was well dressed and wore a silk hat of glossy newness. Three times he paused at the gate, and then walked on again. The fourth time he stood with his hand upon it, and then with sudden resolution flung it open and walked up the path. Mrs. White at the same moment placed her hands behind her, and hurriedly unfastening the strings of her apron, put that useful article of apparel beneath the cushion of her chair.

She brought the stranger, who seemed ill at ease, into the room. He gazed furtively at Mrs. White, and listened in a preoccupied fashion as the old lady apologized for the appearance of the room, and her husband's coat, a garment which he usually reserved for the garden. She then waited as patiently as her sex would permit for him to broach his business, but he was at first strangely silent.

"I—was asked to call," he said at last, and

stooped and picked a piece of cotton from his trousers. "I come from Maw and Meggins."

The old lady started. "Is anything the matter?" she asked breathlessly. "Has anything happened to Herbert? What is it? What is it?"

Her husband interposed. "There, there, mother," he said hastily. "Sit down, and don't jump to conclusions. You've not brought bad news, I'm sure, sir," and he eyed the other wistfully.

"I'm sorry——" began the visitor.

"Is he hurt?" demanded the mother.

The visitor bowed in assent. "Badly hurt," he said quietly, "but he is not in any pain."

"Oh, thank God!" said the old woman, clasping her hands. "Thank God for that! Thank——"

She broke off suddenly as the sinister meaning of the assurance dawned upon her and she saw the awful confirmation of her fears in the other's averted face. She caught her breath, and turning to her slower-witted husband, laid her trembling old hand upon his. There was a long silence.

"He was caught in the machinery," said the visitor at length, in a low voice.

"Caught in the machinery," repeated Mr. White, in a dazed fashion, "yes."

He sat staring blankly out at the window, and taking his wife's hand between his own, pressed it as he had been wont to do in their old courting days nearly forty years before.

"He was the only one left to us," he said, turning gently to the visitor. "It is hard."

The other coughed, and rising, walked slowly to the window. "The firm wished me to convey their sincere sympathy with you in your great loss," he said, without looking round. "I beg that you will understand I am only their servant and merely obeying orders."

There was no reply; the old woman's face was white, her eyes staring, and her breath inaudible; on the husband's face was a look such as his friend the sergeant-major might have carried into his first action.

"I was to say that Maw and Meggins disclaim all responsibility," continued the other. "They admit no liability at all, but in consideration of your son's services they wish to present you with a certain sum as compensation."

Mr. White dropped his wife's hand, and rising to his feet, gazed with a look of horror at his visitor. His dry lips shaped the words, "How much?"

"Two hundred pounds," was the answer.

Unconscious of his wife's shriek, the old man smiled faintly, put out his hands like a sightless man, and dropped, a senseless heap, to the floor.

III

In the huge new cemetery, some two miles distant, the old people buried their dead, and came back to a house steeped in shadow and silence. It was all over so quickly that at first they could hardly realize it, and remained in a state of expectation as though of something else to happen—something else which was to lighten this load, too heavy for old hearts to bear. But the days passed, and expectation gave place to resignation—the hopeless resignation of the old, sometimes miscalled apathy. Sometimes they hardly exchanged a word, for now they had nothing to talk about, and their days were long to weariness.

It was about a week after that that the old man, waking suddenly in the night, stretched out his hand and found himself alone. The room was in darkness, and the sound of subdued weeping came from the window. He raised himself in bed and listened.

"Come back," he said tenderly. "You will be cold."

"It is colder for my son," said the old woman, and wept afresh.

The sound of her sobs died away on his ears. The bed was warm, and his eyes heavy with sleep. He dozed fitfully, and then slept until a sudden wild cry from his wife awoke him with a start.

"The monkey's paw!" she cried wildly. "The monkey's paw!"

He started up in alarm. "Where? Where is it? What's the matter?"

She came stumbling across the room toward him. "I want it," she said quietly. "You've not destroyed it?"

"It's in the parlor, on the bracket,"[5] he replied, marveling. "Why?"

She cried and laughed together, and bending over, kissed his cheek.

"I only just thought of it," she said hysterically. "Why didn't I think of it before? Why didn't you think of it?"

"Think of what?" he questioned.

"The other two wishes," she replied rapidly. "We've only had one."

"Was not that enough?" he demanded fiercely.

"No," she cried triumphantly; "we'll have one more. Go down and get it quickly, and wish our boy alive again."

The man sat up in bed and flung the bedclothes from his quaking limbs. "Good God, you are mad!" he cried, aghast.

"Get it," she panted; "get it quickly, and wish—Oh, my boy, my boy!"

Her husband struck a match and lit the candle. "Get back to bed," he said unsteadily. "You don't know what you are saying."

"We had the first wish granted," said the old woman feverishly; "why not the second?"

"A coincidence," stammered the old man.

"Go and get it and wish," cried the old woman, and dragged him toward the door.

He went down in the darkness, and felt his way to the parlor, and then to the mantelpiece. The talisman was in its place, and a horrible fear that the unspoken wish might bring his mutilated son before him ere he could escape from the room seized upon him, and he caught his breath as he found that he had lost the direction of the door. His brow cold with sweat, he felt his way round the table, and groped along the wall until he found himself in the small passage with the unwholesome thing in his hand.

Even his wife's face seemed changed as he entered the room. It was white and expectant, and to his fears seemed to have an unnatural look upon it. He was afraid of her.

"Wish!" she cried, in a strong voice.

"It is foolish and wicked," he faltered.

"Wish!" repeated his wife.

He raised his hand. "I wish my son alive again."

The talisman fell to the floor, and he regarded it shudderingly. Then he sank trembling into a chair as the old woman, with burning eyes, walked to the window and raised the blind.

He sat until he was chilled with the cold, glancing occasionally at the figure of the old woman peering through the window. The candle end, which had burnt below the rim of the china candlestick, was throwing pulsating shadows on the ceiling and walls, until, with a flicker larger than the rest, it expired. The old man, with an unspeakable sense of relief at the failure of the talisman, crept back to his bed, and a minute or two afterward the old woman came silently and apathetically beside him.

Neither spoke, but both lay silently listening to the ticking of the clock. A stair creaked, and a squeaky mouse scurried noisily through the wall. The darkness was oppressive, and after lying for some time screwing up his courage, the husband took the box of matches, and striking one, went downstairs for a candle.

At the foot of the stairs the match went out, and he paused to strike another, and at the same moment a knock, so quiet and stealthy as to be scarcely audible, sounded on the front door.

The matches fell from his hand. He stood motionless, his breath suspended until the knock was repeated. Then he turned and fled swifty back to his room, and closed the door behind him. A third knock sounded through the house.

5 bracket *A short wall shelf.*

"What's that?" cried the old woman, starting up.

"A rat," said the old man, in shaking tones —"a rat. It passed me on the stairs."

His wife sat up in bed listening. A loud knock resounded through the house.

"It's Herbert!" she screamed. "It's Herbert!"

She ran to the door, but her husband was before her, and catching her by the arm, held her tightly.

"What are you going to do?" he whispered.

"It's my boy; it's Herbert!" she cried, struggling mechanically. "I forgot it was two miles away. What are you holding me for? Let go. I must open the door."

"For God's sake don't let it in," cried the old man, trembling.

"You're afraid of your own son," she cried, struggling. "Let me go. I'm coming, Herbert; I'm coming."

There was another knock, and another. The old woman with a sudden wrench broke free and ran from the room. Her husband followed to the landing, and called after her appealingly as she hurried downstairs. He heard the chain rattle back and the bottom bolt drawn slowly and stiffly from the socket. Then the old woman's voice, strained and panting.

"The bolt," she cried loudly. "Come down. I can't reach it."

But her husband was on his hands and knees groping wildly on the floor in search of the paw. If he could only find it before the thing outside got in. A perfect fusillade of knocks reverberated through the house, and he heard the scraping of a chair as his wife put it down in the passage against the door. He heard the creaking of the bolt as it came slowly back, and at the same moment he found the monkey's paw, and frantically breathed his third and last wish.

The knocking ceased suddenly, although the echoes of it were still in the house. He heard the chair drawn back and the door opened. A cold wind rushed up the staircase, and a long loud wail of disappointment and misery from his wife gave him courage to run down to her side, and then to the gate beyond. The street lamp flickering opposite shone on a quiet and deserted road.

For Discussion

1 What does the opening scene of the story reveal about the White family? What do Mr. White's chess tactics suggest about his personality? How does this prepare us for his role as the one who will test the powers of the monkey's paw?

2 Why does Sergeant-Major Morris keep his three wishes a secret?

3 What happens to Mrs. White during the course of the story? How does she change? How does Mr. White change?

Compare the way each of them feels toward the monkey's paw just after the fulfillment of the first wish.

4 Can the reader be sure that the monkey's paw brought about the fulfillment of the final two wishes? What evidence is there that the son actually arose from the grave? What evidence is there that he returned to the grave? Is it possible that he only appeared to Mr. and Mrs. White in their imaginations?

5 If you had a monkey's paw with similar powers, could you contrive a wish to outwit fate?

Louise Nevelson
Forgotten City
New York University Art Collection
Gift of Mrs. Anita Berliawsky

Unit Two
Stories of the Twentieth Century

There is no sharp break between modern fiction and stories written in earlier centuries. All stories seek to entertain at the same time that they give a shape to human experience, and all have roots in myth, folktales, and legends. Between modern stories and older stories the similarities are greater than the differences.

If, however, we were to attempt to define the special characteristics of modern fiction, we might point out two things:

1. An increase in realism, as opposed to fantasy and romance; and also a greater use of realistic detail. To take a sharply contrasting pair of stories: Boccaccio's "How Two Lovers Were Reunited" is a tale of wonders and adventures; but surely Boccaccio never wanted to deceive anyone into thinking that it "really happened." Giovanni Verga, on the other hand, added a footnote to his story "Liberty" which states: "This story is based on an actual incident in the revolution of 1860." And Verga uses enough detail to make the reader feel he is actually witnessing the events of the story:

One man seized her by the hair, another by the hips, another by her dress, lifting her above the balcony rail. . . . The other brother saw nothing but red and black. They trampled him down, they ground his bones with iron-shod heels; he had set his teeth in a hand let go. . . .

Of course one can find realistic details like this in the battle scenes of Homer's *Iliad*. What we are talking about here is a tendency, rather than a sharp distinction. *In general, modern fiction—that is, from the mid-nineteenth century to the present—has presented the reader with stories which could have happened and has tried to give an illusion of actuality by using colloquial speech and other forms of sharply observed detail.* To take some examples from stories in the following section:

Tight-corseted, he wore a monocle and false teeth ... his cheeks were clean-shaven, his trousers miraculously pressed. ...
(Montanelli, "His Excellency")

I followed her into the kitchen; we put the rest of the appetizers back into the refrigerator, and I crawled about on the floor looking for the top of the mayonnaise tube.
(Böll, "Like a Bad Dream")

In older, more heroic and poetic literatures, we are not likely to encounter anything as common as the top of a mayonnaise tube. But of course modern writers have abandoned larger-than-life heroes and kings. Their attention has turned to the common man, and toward the small-scale, prosaic details of his everyday life. Kings did not have to crawl about on kitchen floors looking for lost objects; the servants did that—offstage.

2. An increased interest in psychology. Once again, we are talking about a tendency. Writers of the past like Homer and Cervantes knew a great deal about the human mind, but they spent more time describing exterior, rather than interior, events. In much modern fiction there is very little incident, with a greater attention to minute stages of a character's mind. The narrative often comes to a complete halt while we study delicate shadings of psychological reaction to events, often in interior monologues:

I try to cast out these thoughts. For I am to serve the good. I must set about the destruction of evil.... I can do that: I shall be the supreme judge. But why the future tense? I am the supreme judge. ... What am I saying, what am I doing? But why ask?
(Kawalec, "I Kill Myself")

The modern author often assumes a detailed knowledge of what his characters are thinking about from moment to moment:

After a while she realized that he was observing her just as she was observing him. He was no longer just run to earth and crouching for a spring, but he was wondering, trying to know. At that she seemed to see herself with the eyes of the wild animal at bay in his dark hiding-place. ...
(Dinesen, "The Ring")

Shakespeare and Euripides, of course, have given us equally subtle accounts of their characters' thoughts. But in modern fiction and drama we often find that the psychological event is what the story is all about, to an extent that we do not find it so isolated in classical literature.

The violence of war devastates landscapes and makes jagged ruins of cities. Likewise, it uproots men from their normal lives and gives them opportunities to test themselves under pressure of death. Just such a chance—for heroism or for cowardice —is given to the central character of "His Excellency." This story takes place against the background of the Second World War. During the war, the Germans and the Italians fought side by side. At the end of the war, under the leadership of Marshal Badoglio, the Italian army turned against the Germans and joined the British and Americans. The characters in "His Excellency" are Italian prisoners of war who have been captured by the Nazis.

Indro Montanelli

His Excellency

There it is, lined up with the other sixty-four coffins from the Fossoli concentration camp, and the crowd has sprinkled it, like the others, with flowers. Among all these people gathered here in the silence of the Milan cathedral, surely I am not the only one to know. Yet there has been no protest. Truly, men are as lenient to the dead as they are harsh with the living. The coffin will now pass like the others between the reverent throngs, like the others it will be buried and, on June 22 of each year, will receive its quota of rhetoric spilled over the common grave. Fair enough. . . . Who are we to judge?

His Excellency, General Della Rovere, army corps commander, intimate friend of Badoglio's[1] and "technical adviser" to General Alexander, was locked up by the Germans in the San Vittore prison of Milan in the spring of 1944 when the Allied armies were still fighting their slow way up the Italian peninsula. He had been captured near Genoa while trying to land at night from an Allied submarine to take command of the resistance movement in the north. A soldier to his finger tips, he had impressed even Franz, the German warder, who would stand at attention when addressing him and had gone so far as to have a cot placed in his cell. So the Italian guard, Ceraso, informed me as he passed my spy hole with a rose in a glass, picked expressly for His Excellency. Later Ceraso returned to say that the General wished to see me, and, letting me out, escorted me to his cell.

"Cavalry officer" was written all over those arched legs, that slight build, and aristocratic profile. Tight-corseted, he wore a monocle

1 Badoglio *In 1943, after the fall of Mussolini, Field Marshal Pietro Badoglio became Premier of Italy. General Alexander was the British commander.*

and false teeth, and the thought struck me of how convincing, after all, is our racial destiny. What else could a man like that become if not a general? With steely grace he could give an order and make it sound like a plea, and even now, weeks after his capture, his cheeks were clean-shaven, his trousers miraculously pressed, while one could almost detect on his polished shoes a pair of invisible spurs.

"Montanelli, I presume?" he said with a slight drawl, polishing his monocle without giving me his hand. "I already knew of your presence here before landing. Badoglio in person had informed me. His Majesty's Government[2] is following your case with the utmost sympathy. Let it be understood, however, that the day you face the firing squad you will have done no more than your duty. Please stand at ease." Only at these last words did I realize that I was standing heels joined, thumbs touching the seams of my trousers just as the drill book says. "We are all on temporary duty here, right?" he continued, cleaning the nail of one little finger with the nail of the other. "An officer is at all times merely on temporary duty, he is a *novio de la muerte*, as the Spaniards say, a bridegroom of death." He smiled at me, paced leisurely up and down the cell flexing his slim, arched legs; then, stopping again before me, cleaned and replaced his monocle. "We two are very near our wedding day," he continued. "My sentence has already been pronounced. And yours?"

"Not yet, sir," I answered almost mortified.

"It will be," he went on. "You will have the honor of being shot in the chest, I hear. Splendid. There is no better proof of your conduct under interrogation. The Germans are rough in obtaining confessions but chivalrous toward those who abstain. Good. Your orders are to continue. In case of torture, if you feel you must utter a name—I cast no doubt on your spiritual endurance, but there is a limit to the physical—utter mine. I have nothing to lose. Actually, I

had nothing to hide even from my old friend, Marshal Kesselring,[3] when he questioned me. I did, however, explain that I hardly expected the British submarine captain to be such a fool as to answer the decoy signals of a German patrol boat. 'You trust the English?' Kesselring smiled. 'Why not? We even trusted the Germans once,' I smiled back. 'Sorry!' he said, 'I have no choice but to shoot you.' 'No hard feelings,' I concluded. But to come back to your case: when you are up for questioning again, stick to your line. After all, we have such a simple duty left: to die like gentlemen. What is your indictment?"

I explained my case fully. His Excellency listened with his eyes to the ground like a confessor, nodding approbation from time to time.

"A clear case," he concluded. "Captured in the performance of duty. It's a soldier's death. They absolutely *must* shoot you in the chest. It's strictly regulations. Let me know how things develop. You can go now."

That was the first day in all the six months since my arrest that I did not think of my wife locked in her cell in another wing of the building. Toward evening I begged Ceraso to sign me up for the barber the next day and in the meanwhile to bring me a comb. And that night, braving the cold, I took my trousers off before lying on my plank and hung them on the window bars hoping they would regain their shape.

On the following days, through my spy hole, I was able to observe His Excellency in his cell just across from mine. One by one, all the prisoners were called to report to him, and all came. In theory, our wing, the dreaded Fifth, was for "solitaries" and so it had been up till that time, but the prestige of His Excellency was obviously so great that the Italian warders felt they could stretch a point. On entering, his guests would stand at attention, even the Communists, and bow stiffly. Later, on leaving, they would walk with a prouder carriage. Number 215, who

2   His Majesty's Government *Victor Emmanuel III was king of Italy from 1900 to 1946.*
3   Marshal Kesselring   *The German commander.*

so often sobbed for his wife and children, after talking with the General fell silent, and even when caught smoking by Franz took his lashes without a whimper. Ceraso told me that almost all, after their talk, had asked, like me, for the barber, a comb, and a little soap. Even the warders now wore their caps straight and tried to speak correct Italian. The wing had never been so quiet, and when Müller came on inspection he praised the new discipline. For the first time he omitted calling us "anti-Fascist dogs" and "dirty Badoglian traitors," confining himself to an allusion to the "felonious King," at which we all looked at the ceiling pretending not to hear, while His Excellency, who was standing a little forward as befitted his rank, turned deliberately on his heels and reentered his cell. Müller snorted, but said nothing.

One morning Colonel P. and Colonel F. were taken. Asked if they had a last wish, they mentioned the General, who received them on his threshold, and that was the only time I ever saw him shake hands. Then, caressing with a slow gesture his silvery hair and adjusting his monocle, he smiled and said something to the two officers—something cordial and tender, I am sure. Suddenly, snapping to attention and fixing them coldly in the eyes, he gave them the military salute. P. and F. were pale as chalk, but smiling, and never had they looked so much like colonels as when they moved off, erect, with firm step, between the S.S. men.[4] We heard later that they had both cried, "Long live the King" as they fell.

That same afternoon I was taken down for questioning, and Müller warned me that this was my last chance and that if I did not speak up, etc. ... But I hardly heard, nor, though I kept my eyes glued to his, saw him. All I could see were the two pale faces of P. and F. and the marblelike face of His Excellency, and all I could hear was his drawling soft voice ... *"novio de la muerte* ... performance of duty ... death on the field. ..."* Müller gave me up without torture after two

hours. Even if he had tortured me, I believe I would not have uttered a word, not even the name of His Excellency, in front of whose cell, on my return, I begged Ceraso to let me stop.

Della Rovere was sitting on the edge of his cot. Putting down his book, he stared at me at length while I stood at attention. Then he said slowly: "Yes, indeed. I expected as much of you," and dismissed me with a gesture. But on the threshold he called me back. "Just a second!" and he rose to his feet. "There is a thing I still wish to say. A—uhm—difficult thing. I am, I wish to say, extremely satisfied with your conduct, Captain Montanelli. And I wish this good warder to listen well, for he will be our only surviving witness. Very, very satisfied.... A jolly good show, sir!" And that night, for the first time, I felt alone in the world, joyously alone with my beautiful bride, Death, forgetful of my wife and my mother, and for once my Country seemed to me a real and an important thing.

I never saw him again, but after the liberation I gathered the details of his end from one of the survivors of Fossoli.

His Excellency appeared very put out when suddenly, together with a crowd of other San Vittore inmates, he was packed into a boxcar train and shipped to the Fossoli concentration camp. During the journey he sat on the kit packs which his fellow prisoners had laid down as a seat for him and refused to rise even when Schultze came in for inspection. Schultze struck him, shrieking: *"Du bist ein Schwein, Bertoni!"*[5] But the General found it superfluous to explain that he was not Bertoni, but Della Rovere, a corps commander, friend of Badoglio's and technical adviser to Alexander. Without a twitch he picked up his monocle, luckily unbroken, replaced it, and remained seated. Schultze went out cursing.

At Fossoli, His Excellency no longer enjoyed the little favors he was used to. He was placed in a common shed and put to

4 S.S. men *The German storm troopers.*
5 "Du bist ein Schwein, Bertoni!" *German: "You are a pig, Bertoni!"*

work. His companions took turns in sparing him the more humiliating tasks like latrine duty, but never, of his own initiative, did he shirk a job, even though manual labor weighed heavily on him, for he was no longer young. Digging, or carrying bricks, often with a grimace of pain, he would keep a sharp eye open to see that no one gave a poor show, and at day's end he would reprimand those who needed it. To him, they were all officers and gentlemen, and such did they continue to feel under the flash of his monocle and the lash of his words. Desperately, heroically, he struggled to keep his nails spotless and his cheeks shaven. He never complained.

Neither then, nor later, was the motive for the June 22 massacre ever made clear. The order came from Milan, some said as a reprisal for something which had happened in Genoa. Lieutenant Dickermann read out the sixty-five names drawn by lot from those of the four hundred inmates lined up in a square. Among the first was the name Bertoni. No one stepped forward. "Bertoni!" roared Dickermann. "Ber-to-ni!" and he stared at the point where Della Rovere stood. Did Dickermann understand, or did he merely choose to humor a dying man? "*Gut, gut,*" he chuckled. "Della Rovere, *wie Sie wollen. . . .*"[6] All held their breath as they watched His Excellency slip his monocle into place and take three slow steps forward. "*General* Della Rovere, please!" he corrected, taking his place by the other doomed men. With the nail of his right forefinger he began to clean the nail of his left—both marvelously steady.

The sixty-five were manacled, blindfolded, and pushed against the wall. Only His Excellency refused to have his eyes covered and was humored. Then the machine guns were

set. His Excellency took a step forward. "Hold it! Stop!" cried Dickermann reaching for his revolver. His Excellency took another step. "Gentlemen!" he cried with a voice like a bugle. "In this supreme moment let our thoughts rise . . ." But Dickermann's "Fire!" and the opening crash of the guns cut him short. They all went down. But the General was the only one who did not squirm on the ground, and his monocle remained miraculously in its place. It was still on when they dropped him into the common trench, and he is still wearing it, I assume, there in his coffin.

That coffin which today, June 22, anniversary of the massacre, stands before me in the Milan cathedral, does not hold the body of the imaginary General Della Rovere—true! Merely the remains of the former jailbird Bertoni, a Genoese, by profession cardsharp and thief, who, when arrested by the Germans for some petty crime, offered to spy for them in prison by impersonating a non-existent general, and succeeded only too well. . . .

Does it really matter? Surely the Cardinal Archbishop did no wrong in blessing this body together with the others?

For, after all, Bertoni, the cardsharp, the thief, the spy, was indeed a general at the hour of death, and undoubtedly he died convinced that he was the friend of Badoglio's and "technical adviser" to Alexander. But for him, I would never have felt a hero for one night in my cell. . . . And P. and F. would not have walked to the firing squad as colonels should. . . . Because of him, those who lacked courage found it, and Number 215 stopped whimpering for his wife and children. . . .

Peace to his twisted soul.

Uguccione Ranieri/TRANSLATOR

---

6 "Gut, gut. Della Rovere, wie Sie wollen. . . ." *German:* "*Good, good. Della Rovere, if you prefer. . . .*"

For Discussion

1 The noble General Della Rovere turns out to be a cardsharp, Bertoni, whom the Germans have planted as a spy on his fellow Italians. What effect does the impersonation have on his own character? What does it have on the men he is supposed to betray? What attitude do the Germans take toward him? Why?

2 At his execution, why does the General refuse to plead for his life? Did the Germans make a mistake in executing him? Why do they execute him along with sixty-four other prisoners?

3 Notice that the author makes himself a character in his own story. Does Montanelli condemn Bertoni? Does he praise him? Does he make Bertoni a hero or a villain?

4 We usually disapprove of a person who pretends to be something other than what he is. What makes Bertoni's a special case? Did he have a right to be buried as a general, together with sixty-four martyrs?

64

The Artist's View

The twentieth century has produced many previously unknown and unheard of forces which have influenced and shaped modern man. The artists represented on these pages deal with typically twentieth-century phenomena and highlight the significance of each.

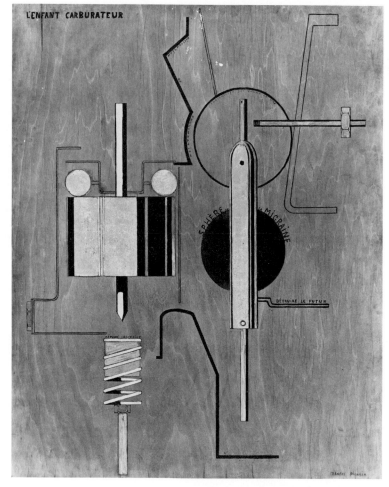

Using oil, pencil, and metallic paint on plywood, the artist comments on the stark mechanization of the current century.

Francis Picabia
The Child Carburetor
The Solomon R. Guggenheim
   Museum, New York

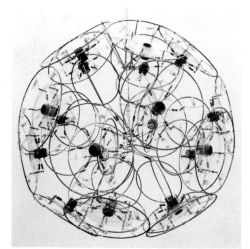

The complex arrangement of photoelectric cells and wire suggests the technological complexity of the modern world.

James Seawright
Photohedron
The Solomon R. Guggenheim
   Museum, New York
Gift, Theodoron Foundation

Modern man's preoccupation with building and construction is highlighted in this contemporary oil painting.

Fernand Léger
Les Constructeurs (reproduction from portfolio "Contrastes")
New York University Art Collection
Gift of Edward Albee

The starkness of the modern city and the constancy of change are captured in this drypoint sketch.

Armin Landeke
Rooftops, Fourteenth Street
Courtesy of The Brooklyn Museum
Dick S. Ramsay Fund

This lithograph suggests the more open and informal styles and conventions of the modern world, which contrast with the more controlled formality of the past.

Miguel Covarrubias
The Lindy Hop
Philadelphia Museum of Art,
Purchased: The Harrison Fund
Photograph by A. J. Wyatt, Staff Photographer

In this bronze statue, the sculptor reflects the groping loneliness which has to a large extent become a characteristic of modern man.

Max Ernst
Anxious Friend
The Solomon R. Guggenheim
   Museum, New York
Gift, Mr. and Mrs. Jean de Menil

This montage represents the artist's view of the pressures, contradictions and complexities of the current day.

Robert Rauschenberg
Visual Autobiography
The Solomon R. Guggenheim
   Museum, New York

Most serious modern literature presents a view of life in which man finds himself in grim, ironic, or absurd situations. This story, by one of the best modern French writers, is unusual because it is light, romantic, and has a happy ending, even if it's not the happy ending we expect.

Françoise Mallet-Joris

Air des Clochettes

No doubt Spring had had its eye on Max for some time: it sometimes rather enjoys leading ambitious young men a dance. At all events, when Max left the house, at about three o'clock, with the firm intention of meeting Miss Arabella Graham for tea, Spring—which had been lying in wait for him at the corner of the street—pounced so abruptly, with such a wealth of bright sunlight and intoxicating scents, that Max could scarcely breathe.

As everyone willingly recognised, Max was a sensible young man. Even now, when he was sallying forth to meet a girl who, in all probability, would soon become his wife, his thoughts were of strictly prosaic matters. Did his blue suit look a little too worn? What make was Arabella's car? Would they marry on terms of separate maintenance? So it is not so much to him as to the insidious Spring weather that we should ascribe the birth of this exotic notion: *Suppose, he told himself, I were to take a turn round the Botanical Garden while I'm waiting?* A fatal idea, since the Botanical Garden was Spring's quintessential domain; and indeed, no sooner had Max entered it than, by some magical metamorphosis, all his sensible ideas disappeared, like a lumbering herd of elephants in full retreat, leaving him alone and defenceless in this enchanted enclave.

The automatic sprinklers were revolving on the lawns, flinging out wide circles of glittering freshness. Small fair-haired children romped and tumbled and picked themselves up again with short, shrill cries like bird-calls.

Sitting there on a rustic bench, among all the mothers and nurses, this carefully dressed young man, with the solemn expression and stiff, rather awkward movements, might perhaps be considered a trifle ridiculous. But such a thought never entered his head. At the age of twenty-five, Max Péralbe, shortly to become engaged to the wealthy Arabella Graham, and a future lawyer of note, was discovering his first Spring.

"Seven francs, Monsieur, if you please," murmured the woman chair-attendant.

"That's quite reasonable, Madame."

"Ah, Monsieur, don't I know it! I have to scrape a living from this job, and I'm a war-widow, too."

She moved off with some dignity, leaving Max reflecting, in a mood of absurd enthusiasm, how he loved war-widows in the Botanical Garden on a fine afternoon. It was at this precise moment that he noticed a grey skirt about ten yards away from him. It was a very simple skirt, made—as far as he could judge—of some ordinary, unremarkable material, and embroidered in white round the hemline with a pattern of small hoops like those bordering the lawns: in short, a skirt such as he must have seen a thousand times before.

Yet on this May afternoon the skirt, and its owner's slender, pliant waist, struck him with the force of a revelation. Never in his life had Max felt so young, so exhilarated, and so cheerfully irrational. It was all due to the Botanical Garden, with its stretches of damp, green lawn, gleaming softly in the shade, and, above all, to this grey skirt and white blouse, bent so gracefully over what looked like a cheap paperback novel, under the shade of a majestic sycamore (*a variant of the maple; known also as the false plane*). Max recalled, not for the first time, that he had done well in botany at school. (But then, what had he not done well in, with the ruthless discipline that his mother imposed on him?) But to-day, unprecedentedly, all these hard-won achievements seemed somehow a barren tri-

umph. Had he not just discovered something his mother had never taught him—the joys of dreaming in the sunlight, in a garden, not too far from an attractive grey skirt?

Then he gave a tiny start. A child had just run up to the grey skirt, and a small, very grubby hand was tugging at her violently.

"Ma'mselle, what are those things that spin round and round as they fall?" he asked. He was a nice little boy, rather pale, and not too well dressed. But Max paid no real attention to him: he was so overwhelmed by the sense of relief that the word "Mademoiselle" had engendered in his own mind. So she wasn't married, then! And to complete the spell she now spoke, in an unforgettable voice, warm, disturbing, sweetly modulated. She said: "It's a seed, Emile, the seed of the plane-tree."

Max half rose from his park bench, a diffident yet (of course) attractive smile hovering on his lips. He would go over and correct this mistaken piece of information. Mademoiselle, he would say, that is not the plane-tree, but its pseudo-variant, the sycamore. She would be astonished at his knowledgability and they would thereupon launch into a long, passionate conversation about botany, with her raising her lovely eyes to his (what colour were they? So far he hadn't got near enough to see) and then, suddenly, clasping her hand, he would say—he would say—well, what? Twice already, in fact, her eyes *had* looked up at Max, with a certain mild surprise; twice Max had half-risen and then sat down again. Half-risen, because Spring, mischievous yet benevolent, gave him an encouraging push from behind on each occasion; subsided, because his legs were promptly turned to water by an appalling realisation, as potent in its way as the scent of trees and flowers all around him: Miss Arabella Graham was awaiting his arrival in Mrs. Page's drawing-room. Miss Arabella Graham was going to sing.

In the opinion of Mme Péralbe, Max's

mother, Miss Arabella Graham was the most eminently suitable fiancée, bride, and, above all, daughter-in-law that one could hope to find anywhere. Max had been of the same opinion; his views rarely differed from those expressed by his mother. Arabella would know exactly how to advance a rising young lawyer's interests; she would not only bring him a fortune, but help him to achieve a position in high society, get him into the fashionable swim. Max already visualised himself gliding along regally in his car, or receiving future clients in a luxurious suite of offices, while everywhere people whispered (how flattering to be thus recognised!): Look, there goes the famous Maître Péralbe!

At least, this was the kind of picture he normally conjured up when he thought about his plans for the future. But by some incomprehensible trick of fate, these images, summoned up now as reserves against the too-seductive Spring, firmly refused to take shape in his mind. What he recalled instead, all too readily, were Arabella's extraordinary height (she stood a good half-head taller than he did), her outdoor, not to say military complexion (what Mme Péralbe called a "good, healthy appearance"), and her frightful soprano voice—reedy, shrill, over-mannered—which issued so unexpectedly from that square, robust body, and which its owner was determined to make heard, at the slightest opportunity, singing the *Air des clochettes*[1] from Delibes' *Lakmé*. For the first time he considered this voice, not with his customary feeling of resignation, but with something approaching active intolerance. "I loathe the *Air des clochettes!*" he told himself.

Then, for the third time, he rose to his feet —only to subside once more—as the unknown girl got up from her chair and walked off, with a light, graceful gait, holding the little boy by the hand. Max's private guardian angel (a guardian angel equipped, in all likelihood, with detachable lace collar, pince-nez, and gold watch-chain, and even, perhaps, displaying that faint moustache and Bourbon

nose which were the imperious Mme Péralbe's most prominent features) now whispered in his ear: "Don't follow *her!* She's just an ordinary children's nurse—perhaps even a typist, or a factory worker. *Not* the kind of woman that should attract the famous Maître Péralbe."

But Maître Péralbe, intoxicated with Spring, replied: "This girl's *really* twenty, and Arabella's been twenty for the last seven years. This girl has violet-coloured eyes, the rarest shade in existence. If Arabella's eyes are of any particular colour at all I can only say I've never noticed it. When Arabella walks, she looks as though she's marching behind a column of troops. But there are girls who walk on air, and I never knew it!" So he set off in pursuit of the grey skirt with its plain white hooped hemline.

The grey skirt stopped in front of a small merry-go-round, and the child rushed on to it. Max stood some ten yards off, watching her tenderly. How pretty she was, sitting there on that little rustic bench! They had been engaged since the evening before. His jurisprudence all forgotten, Max was teaching Violet Eyes the names of flowers and trees. They were arguing (oh, very lovingly) about their plans for the future—plans which had nothing whatsoever in common with those he had conceived (so long ago, it seemed a century) regarding Arabella: schemes in which virtue and courage were the key qualities, schemes for a hard-working life crowned by slow, meritorious success. Had he not told his mother the previous evening, when she ventured to criticise his plan to marry this young working-class girl: "Love is worth more than all the riches in the world."

Now they were at their wedding, a modest but poetical ceremony in some small, ivy-clad, suburban church, and it was his blushing bride who leaned on his arm, with her grey skirt and violet eyes and the dear contralto voice that never sang, never would sing the *Air des clochettes*. Here they were in their small, comfortable apartment, with the curtains drawn and the lights switched on, and

1 Air des clochettes *"The Bell Song"; from the opera* Lakmé, *a showy soprano aria.*

she—the impeccable young housewife per-
sonified—was setting a steaming supper on
the dazzlingly white tablecloth, sweet recom-
pense after a hard day's work. And now, on
this fine afternoon, it was their son riding on
the merry-go-round, with such a dexterous
mastery of the hand-rings, and very soon his
father would go and make a fuss over him,
while Violet Eyes looked tenderly on. . . .

Time passed as though in a dream; and as
though in a dream he remembered Arabella,
who was waiting for him to arrive at Mrs.
Page's so that she could give her recital, and
who would still be waiting a good many
hours hence. No, he wouldn't waste any
time, or keep her dangling; he'd simply say:
"Arabella, find yourself another man, and live
for love." But she, in her despair, would
commit suicide next day, in the most tactful
possible manner, leaving her entire fortune
to him in her will.

As they went into the little open-air puppet
theatre, with its musty damp-mushroom
smell, they were an established, wealthy couple. Their son clapped his hands in delight.
The velvet curtain raised clouds of dust. A
gigantic crocodile was doing its best, in a
surly, lethargic way, to devour the innocent
puppet-hero. But what Max saw as he
watched the stage was his first client, a murderer whom he defended with such dash and
brilliance that from then on he was the one,
the only attorney in Paris. With a languid
gesture he waved away the crowds of journal-
ists before returning to their apartment in
the Bois. The car (a brand-new American
model) was waiting to take him and his wife
to some première. They said goodbye to
their children (two or three of them now,
dressed in the most fetching pyjamas and
romping about a spacious nursery) and finally
arrived at the Opéra. The Republican
Guards, sabres drawn, gave them a formal
salute. Everyone recognised them: they were
the handsomest couple in Paris. A loud whisper ran through the foyer: "Look, there's
Maître Péralbe and his wife—he's the one

who defended that famous case, and inherited
an enormous fortune—yes, some English-
woman, she was in love with him—oh look,
what a beautiful creature his wife is!"

There was clapping, applause. Why?
Presumably the performance was over. Max
drifted out with the other spectators, vaguely
surprised at no longer seeing his wife in a
gorgeous décolleté dress, and at hearing
little Emile exclaim, in his shrill little boy's
voice: "It wasn't a real crocodile, was it?"

She was walking across the Botanical Garden now, through the main entrance, then
into a dark and narrow street. Still wrapped
in his dream, Max followed them. She did
not turn round, but little Emile—doubtless
unaware that this strange man had been his
father for the last hour or so—showed ingenuous astonishment when he saw him still
trailing along ten yards in the rear. Street
succeeded street, each narrower than the last,
each more proof against the magic power of
the season. But Max failed to take the hint.
They were going home together to their
apartment. In a moment now——

Then, brutally torn out of his fantasy, he
stopped at the same moment as she did, and
watched her vanish into a red-brick apartment
building, and stood there outside, dazed, irre-
solute. Their home? Here? In this hideous
red-brick edifice, in this courtyard where no
sunshine ever penetrated, among these humble streets—soiled and worn, as though by
long over-use—with their dingy stores and
screaming children? As though suddenly
awakened from some Arabian Nights fairy-
tale, he stared around him. What he saw,
alas, stripped of the glamour which Spring
had shed about him, was a scene all too
similar to that which greeted his eyes every
day, in the apartment he shared with his
mother. "We must get out of this place,"
was her constant cry. "At all costs we must
get out——"

He tried to recall his earlier rapture, the
memory of two violet eyes that held the
promise of happiness and tranquility. Spring

was working in him still. He conjured up that melodious voice, the dreams he had nursed of an obscure, hard-working life. His own talent and energy would suffice to let him scale the heights. But there was still that dark presence by his side; he heard his dangerous guardian angel whisper, insinuatingly: "What? Live for years in a house like *that*? Especially when one gesture, one decision will enable you to start from the top of the ladder instead of painfully scaling it rung by rung? Think: years of drudgery, and financial troubles, and domestic rows blown up by your inability to make both ends meet. Years of wondering—as you wondered today—whether your blue suit isn't too shiny and worn. Years in which your wife gets old, and clients don't appear, and your stock of courage gets used up and cannot be redeemed. . . ."

Spring was still struggling, but more weakly now: in these streets it was deprived of its natural allies, the trees and the sunlight. But with a last effort its voice still reached Max's ears, a long sighing murmur like the wind: "Come on, Max, show a little courage! Look round you again, more closely this time. Remember the tranquil light in those violet eyes of hers. There is more reality in these little concrete balconies and poky, shabby apartments than in the finest house on earth that has not been won by one's own efforts. . . ."

But Max did not hear; he was far too busy being sorry for himself. The wretched victim of Violet Eyes, he was ending his days in this frightful red-brick apartment house, an embittered failure, looking back with poignant regret to the brilliant life which his genius would inevitably have won him had he not, one spring day, in a fit of madness. . . . Automatically he glanced at his watch. Five o'clock. Perhaps she was waiting for him still, the one who could, must, save him from this dreadful fate. He pictured her stamping impatiently (no longer did he tell himself what a soldier-like charm those feet possessed). He imagined his mother, a dignified figure, with that air of a slumming duchess which American women always found so impressive, but nevertheless suffering dreadfully: twisting a fold of her old black satin dress between her fingers, suffering a thousand deaths at the thought that the whole scaffolding of small deceits and innocent lies and heroic self-assertion that she had so laboriously built up round the heiress might come crashing down.

"Your poor mother!" the guardian angel murmured, with unctuous hypocrisy. "Your poor widowed mother, who sacrificed so much in order to give you a decent upbringing! Think how hurt she'd be, how much she'd suffer if this marriage didn't take place. Think how she's looking forward to riding in an American car. What's become of your filial devotion?" For a moment, leaning against the front window of the bakery, Max still hesitated. For a moment longer he glimpsed that grey skirt, those violet eyes, that light, buoyant step as she passed by him. Then, in a flash, the image faded, and Max, feeling as though he had suddenly recovered from a fit of insanity, flung himself into a taxi.

What on earth can have happened to me? he wondered, as he nervously begged the driver to hurry. *That was a close shave, and no mistake.*

Ten minutes later, a grey skirt appeared from the main entrance of a shabby, red-brick apartment house, and a pair of violet eyes glanced up and down the deserted street, with curiosity and, perhaps, some disappointment. A large American car was parked a short distance away. The grey skirt climbed into it.

"Take me home now, Albert," she said, in a soft, pleasant voice.

Albert obediently set the car in motion, his face, beneath the peaked and braided cap, a mask of sullen disapproval. He did not care for these lower-class districts. Two hours he had been kept hanging around, and not one suitable café in sight! What on earth had possessed Mademoiselle to come and visit this sick girl-friend of hers? To start with, one didn't have friends in this sort of area, it simply wasn't done. Mademoiselle simply didn't know how to behave. And look at the way she dressed! You'd take her for a typist, despite all her money. God, if he, Albert, had his fingers on some of that. . . . As he drove he, too, began to dream; so did Mademoiselle herself, ensconced in the back of the car. What a nice young man he'd been, she thought, the one who followed her. If only he'd had the courage to say something. . . . She sighed over this missed opportunity for at least five minutes before she forgot him.

Meanwhile at Mrs. Page's a lady was saying: "I ran across your son in the Botanical Garden, Madame Péralbe. Don't you think that's charming? Such a serious young man, and there he was daydreaming in the sunshine. . . ."

And Miss Arabella Graham went across to an imposing lady dressed in black satin, and murmured, through set, smiling lips: "Madame, your son is nothing but a lecher! He was following a girl in the street! I saw him. I never wish to set eyes on this—this person again. I have my dignity, Madame." And without listening to the dowager-like protestations that greeted this statement, she walked to the piano with her long, firm stride, while everyone applauded, and proceeded to render the *Air des clochettes*.

Peter Green/TRANSLATOR

For Discussion

1 This story is based on coincidences, at least partly. What are they? By definition a coincidence is improbable, but it can be believable. Do you find this story believable? Why or why not?

2 What kind of person is Max? How is his little walk through the city and into the Botanical Garden a voyage of self-discovery? What does he find out about himself? Does he act on this self-knowledge?

3 What, for Max, are the advantages and disadvantages of marrying Miss Arabella Graham?

4 What does Max see when he looks at the house where the Mademoiselle lives? How does it change his mind? Was he serious about her in the first place?

5 What is the final de Maupassant-like twist to the story? Is Arabella Graham being just or unjust to Max?

6 At the beginning of the story Max is engaged to Arabella Graham, and at the end of the story we can assume that they will not be married. Yet we suggested in the headnote to the story that it has a happy ending. You may disagree with this interpretation, but before you disagree, consider: How could his rejection by Arabella possibly work out happily for Max?

With most writers it is best not to mix their biographies with their writings. In the case of Jerzy Kosinski, it is hard to keep the two separate. As a child in Poland during the Second World War, he wandered through war-ravaged landscapes keeping himself alive any way he could. He suffered greatly and watched the war make ordinary people behave like animals. His books almost seem like emblems of the spiritual scars he received in childhood. No writer's world is darker or more pessimistic about human nature.

Kosinski's novels are not novels in the ordinary sense. They are usually a series of episodes held together by the author's own compulsions. He now lives in the United States and writes in English, though the Europe of his childhood continues to haunt his work.

Jerzy Kosinski

from Steps

There was a man at the university who had wronged me. I discovered he was of peasant stock and therefore privileged among those whom the Party[1] had pushed into the university for political reasons. I could not change the climate which favored him and thus saw no way of countering his enmity. It occurred to me that to blame the system was simply an excuse which prevented me from facing him.

At that time we were all required to join the para-military student defense corps. Every unit in turn had to guard the university arsenal, which was under the jurisdiction of the city garrison. We regularly had a two-day guard duty, which was organized along military lines: the guards' quarters occupied a wing of the university and were run like an army barracks. Telephone messages had to be recorded and acted upon as set forth in the military manuals, and instructions had to be followed with the utmost precision, since, as we were often warned, the city military commander might at any time declare a full-scale alert to test the efficiency of the student defense corps.

One day I observed this man reverently acknowledging instructions from the headquarters of the university arsenal, his knuckles tense and white as he gripped the telephone receiver. I looked at him closely again. I now had a plan.

By the time he was appointed guard commander for a weekend, I had already spent many hours practicing a brusque military voice, smart with clipped arrogance. On his

1 the Party *The Communist Party.*

first day of duty I telephoned him at midnight, and in the most urgent and authoritative tones announced I was the city garrison duty-officer and that I wished to speak directly to the guard commander. In my assumed voice I proceeded to inform him that an army exercise was in progress, and that in accordance with the plan, he was to muster the university unit and move through the park for a surprise attack on the city arsenal. Once there, his unit was to disarm the regular guards, force an entry and take over the building until the exercise was called off. I asked him to give the instructions back to me: he excitedly repeated my orders, obviously failing to register the omission of the daily password, which I could not give him.

When half an hour later I telephoned the post again, there was no answer: his unit had probably left to storm the arsenal.

On Monday all of us heard about what had happened. Exactly as I had intended, his unit had advanced and attacked the arsenal. In the garrison a full-scale alert had been set off, since it was assumed that there was either a mutinous invasion under way, a counterrevolution, or some secret regional exercise. The university unit was promptly rounded up and arrested; its commander was charged with armed insurrection.

During the court-martial he insisted that backed by the password he had acted under direct orders from the city's garrison. He clung pathetically to his story.

For Discussion

1 This story is told with great economy. The author tells us almost nothing about the country in which it takes place, and yet we understand the situation completely. What kind of nation or society is this?

2 In the first paragraph the narrator tells us that the man he hates is "of peasant stock and therefore privileged." Why is this?

3 What motives does the narrator have for his actions? Obviously, he wants to revenge himself on the man who wronged him, but his fury seems to extend beyond this single man. On what else does he take his revenge?

4 Does the narrator have any regrets for what he has done? Do you, the reader, feel that he was wrong? Why or why not?

The Soviet Union exercises a strict censorship over its writers. Officially approved literature and art is supposed to be optimistic and to create an atmosphere in which the citizens have no doubts about their work or their duties to the State.

Yuli Daniel's writings are not allowed to be published in his own country. Even so, he has been accused of treason because his stories have been published in Europe and America. From

this story one can see why his writing meets with official disapproval. Like de Maupassant's "Who Knows?" it is a monologue by a man with a haunted mind.

Yuli Daniel

Hands

You're an educated man, Sergey, you've got manners. So you don't ask questions, you keep quiet, not like our chaps at the factory —they ask me straight out: "Is it drink that's given you the shakes?" My hands, they mean. Think I didn't notice how you looked at them and turned away? And now, too, you keep trying to look past them. I realize it's because you're tactful, you don't want to embarrass me. But I don't mind, you can look as much as you like. It's not every day you see such a thing. And it's not drink, let me tell you. Actually, I don't drink much— when I do, it's more for company, or to mark an occasion like now with you. We couldn't meet again after all this time and not have a drink. I remember all about those days. How

we went on reconnaissance, and how you talked French to that White Guard,[1] and how we captured Yaroslavl[2] ... Remember that meeting you addressed? You took me by the hand—I happened to be next to you— and you said: "With these very hands" ... Come on, Sergey, pour us a drink or I might go to pieces. I've forgotten what they call these shakes, there's a medical word for it. But I've got it written down, I'll show you afterwards ... Anyway, I'll tell you how it happened. It was all because of an incident. But to take things in their right order: As soon as we were demobilized after the Civil War, in that victorious year 1921, I went back to my old factory. I got a grand welcome—you know how it was—a revolutionary

1 White Guard *The Menshevik Army, which fought against Lenin's Red Army (the Bolsheviks) in the Civil War of 1918– 1920.*

2 Yaroslavl *A city in the north-central region of Soviet Russia.*

hero ... And then I was a Party member, a politically conscious worker as they say. I used to straighten people out. There was a lot of talk in those days: "What have we been fighting for? Can't we manage better than this? No bread, nothing ..." I'd always cut them short. I was always firm. I never fell for that kind of Menshevik[3] muck. Go on, pour yourself a drink, don't wait for me. But hardly had I worked for a year when—bang—they summoned me to the Regional Committee. "Here you are, Malinin, here's your travel permit," they said. "The Party is mobilizing you, Vasily Malinin, into the ranks of the glorious Cheka, to fight against counterrevolution. We wish you success," they said, "in the struggle with the world bourgeoisie, and if you meet Comrade Dzerzhinsky, give him our greetings." "Well, I'm a Party man. I'm at the Party's orders," I said. I took the travel permit, dropped in at the factory to say goodbye to the chaps, and went off. As I went, I kept thinking of how I would mercilessly hunt down those counterrevolutionaries, so they shouldn't make a mess of our young Soviet regime. Well, I arrived, and I did see Felix Edmundovich Dzerzhinsky,[4] and gave him the message from the Regional Committee. He shook me by the hand and thanked me. Then he drew us all up in a row—about thirty of us Party members who had been mobilized—and he told us: "You can't build a house on a swamp. First you have to dry the swamp, and while you're doing that, you've got to destroy the vermin that's there. That's an iron necessity," he said. "And each of you must put his hand to it ..." He told it like a story or a fable but it was all quite clear. He looked very stern while he was saying it, he never smiled once. After that, they sorted us out, to know who was to go where. "How much schooling have you had?" they asked me. Well, you know how it was—my schooling was the German War, the Civil War, the factory—all I'd done before that was two years at the parish school ... So they assigned me to a Special Duties Section—or to put it plainly, the firing squad, the one that carries out executions. You wouldn't say it was a difficult job exactly, but it wasn't easy either. It affects your heart. It's one thing at the front, you understand: there it's either him or you. But here ... still, you get used to it of course. You follow your man across the yard and you say to yourself: "You've got to do it, Vasily, you've *got* to. If you don't finish him off now, the rat will do in our whole Soviet Republic." I got used to it. I drank a bit of course. They issued us with alcohol. All these stories about special rations—rolls and chocolate for the Cheka—they were nothing but bourgeois lies. Our rations were the ordinary soldier's rations—bread and gruel and salted fish. But they did issue us with alcohol. You couldn't do without it, you understand. Well anyway, that was how I worked for seven months, and then there was this incident. We were ordered to liquidate a group of priests. For counterrevolutionary propaganda. With intent. They'd been subverting their parishioners. On account of Tikhon,[5] I suppose. Or perhaps they were just against socialism—I don't know. Anyway, they were enemies. There were twelve of them. Our commander gave us the orders: "You, Malinin, take three," he said, "and you, Vlasenko, the next three, and you, Golovchiner, the next, and you ..." I can't remember what the fourth was called. He was a Lett,[6] he had a strange name, not like one of ours. He and Golovchiner went first. The arrangements were like this: the guardroom was in the middle—on one side of it was the room where the condemned were kept, and on the other was the yard. We took them one by one. When you finished with one in the yard, you and the chaps dragged him out of the way and you returned for the next. They had to be dragged out of the way because otherwise when you led the next one out and he saw the corpse he might struggle and try to break free, and give you no end of trouble—as was only natural,

---

3 Menshevik *A revolutionary group opposed by the Soviet government (the Bolsheviks).*
4 Dzerzhinsky *Head of Cheka, the Soviet Secret Police.*

5 Tikhon *A patriarch of the Russian Orthodox Church who had come into conflict with the government. He had been stripped of his powers and arrested.*

6 Lett *A person from Latvia, a region on the Baltic Sea which was annexed by the Soviet Union.*

of course. It's better when they keep quiet. Well, that day, Golovchiner and the Lett finished with theirs, and it came to my turn. I'd already had a drink by then. Not that I was afraid, or religious or anything like that. I'm a Party man, I'm hard, I don't believe in any of those gods or angels or archangels— but all the same I somehow didn't feel myself. It was easier for Golovchiner, he's a Jew, people say they don't have ikons,[7] I don't know if that's true—but I sat and drank, and all sorts of foolishness kept passing through my head: how my mother, when she was alive, used to take me to the village church, and how I'd kiss the hand of our parish priest, Father Vasily—he was an old man and he always used to joke with me and call me his namesake ... Well, anyway; I went to fetch the first one and took him out and finished him off. Then I came back and had a smoke, and did the second one. I came back and had a drink and I didn't feel too well, so I said to the chap: "Wait a minute, I'll be back." I put the Mauser[8] on the table, and went out. I must have had too much to drink, I thought. I'll stick my fingers in my throat and make myself sick, and have a wash, and I'll be all right. I did all that, but I still didn't feel better. All right, I said to myself, I'll finish the job and I'll go and have a sleep. I picked up the Mauser and went for the third one. The third one was young—a big, hefty, good-looking young priest. I led him along the corridor, and I noticed how he lifted the hem of his cassock —it was down to his heels—as he crossed the threshold, and somehow I felt sick, I couldn't understand what was happening to me. We came out into the yard. He stuck his beard in the air and looked at the sky. "Walk on, Father," I said, "don't look back. You prayed for heaven and you'll soon be there." I was just joking to keep my spirits up, why I don't know. It had never happened to me in my life before to talk to the condemned. Well, I let him walk three paces ahead, as we always did, and put the barrel of my gun be-

tween his shoulder blades and fired. You know what a Mauser shot is like—a crash like a cannon, and it kicks so that it nearly dislocates your arm. But when I looked— there was my shot priest turning round and walking back at me. It's true of course that every case is different: some people fall flat, others spin round, and a few start pacing, reeling like drunks. But this one was walking towards me with short steps, as though floating in his cassock, just as though I hadn't shot him. "Stop it, Father," I said, "halt!" and I shot him again—this time in the chest. But he tore his cassock open over his chest— he had a hairy, ugly chest—and walked straight on, shouting at the top of his voice: "Shoot at me! Antichrist! Kill me, your Christ!" I lost my head, I fired again and again. But he kept coming on! No wound, no blood, he was walking along and praying aloud: "Lord, you have stopped a bullet armed by evil hands. I accept to die for Your sake! ... No one can murder a living soul!" and something else of that sort ... I don't remember how many times I fired; all I know is I couldn't have missed, I was firing at point blank. There he stood before me, his eyes burning like a wolf's, his chest bare, and a kind of halo round his head—it occurred to me afterwards that he was standing against the sun and the sun was setting. "Your hands," he shouted, "your hands covered with blood! Look at your hands!" I threw the Mauser down and ran into the guard room, knocked someone over in the doorway and ran inside—the chaps were all looking at me as if I were mad, and laughing. I grabbed a rifle from the stack and yelled: "take me this minute to Dzerzhinsky or I'll bayonet the lot of you!" Well, they took the rifle away from me and they led me off quick march. I walked into his study and broke free from the chaps and I said to him, trembling all over and stuttering: "Shoot me, Felix Edmundovich," I said, "I can't kill a priest!" That's what I said, and fell down, and that's all I can remember. I came to myself in the hos-

7 ikons *Religious images.*
8 Mauser *A pistol.*

pital. The doctors said: "nervous shock." They looked after me well, I must say. I got treatment, and the place was clean, and the food was good considering the times. They cured me—all but my hands, you see how they won't keep still. I suppose that nervous shock went to my hands. I was sacked from the Cheka of course—those sort of hands are no use to them. Nor of course could I go back to minding a machine. So they made me factory storekeeper. Well, it's a useful job. I can't do any paper work, of course— can't fill any forms, because of my hands. They gave me an assistant for that, a good

sensible girl. That's how it is with me now. As for the priest, I discovered afterwards. There wasn't anything divine about it. It was just that, when I went to the washroom, the chaps took the bullets out of the cartridge clip and filled it with blanks. Just for a joke. Oh well, I'm not angry with them—they were young, and it wasn't pleasant for them either, so they thought this up. No, I'm not cross with them. It's just that my hands . . . they're no good for any work.

Stuart Hood, Harold Shukman, and John Richardson/TRANSLATORS

For Discussion

1 What is the situation? To whom is the narrator talking? Why does he trust him?
2 Do you have the feeling that he is telling this story for the first time, or that he has told it often? Why?
3 Does the narrator consider himself a loyal citizen? Is there any sign that he consciously opposes the government?

4 Do you think that a writer should be able to publish anything he writes, even if the government thinks it is harmful? What arguments can you give in favor of complete freedom of the press? What exceptions, if any, would you make?
5 In not allowing this story to be published, was the Russian government shortsighted? What defense could you make of it as a contribution to society?

"On a summer morning a hundred and fifty years ago . . ." The beginning of this story echoes the old formula "Once upon a time . . ." The opening phrase perfectly sets the tone for the rest of the tale: something halfway between psychological realism and a fairy tale. The fairy tale elements are reinforced throughout the story: there is a passing reference to Red Riding Hood and, even more important, there is the ring. For the magic ring, with its implications of a mystical circle, is a standard ingredient in folktales.

Isak Dinesen

The Ring

On a summer morning a hundred and fifty years ago a young Danish squire and his wife went out for a walk on their land. They had been married a week. It had not been easy for them to get married, for the wife's family was higher in rank and wealthier than the husband's. But the two young people, now twenty-four and nineteen years old, had been set on their purpose for ten years; in the end her haughty parents had had to give in to them.

They were wonderfully happy. The stolen meetings and secret, tearful love letters were now things of the past. To God and man they were one; they could walk arm in arm in broad daylight and drive in the same carriage, and they would walk and drive so till the end of their days. Their distant paradise had descended to earth and had proved, surprisingly, to be filled with the things of everyday life: with jesting and railleries, with breakfasts and suppers, with dogs, haymaking and sheep. Sigismund, the young husband, had promised himself that from now on there should be no stone in his bride's path, nor should any shadow fall across it. Lovisa, the wife, felt that now, every day and for the first time in her young life, she moved and breathed in perfect freedom because she could never have any secret from her husband.

To Lovisa—whom her husband called Lise—the rustic atmosphere of her new life was a matter of wonder and delight. Her husband's

fear that the existence he could offer her might not be good enough for her filled her heart with laughter. It was not a long time since she had played with dolls; as now she arranged her flowers she again lived through an enchanting and cherished experience: one was doing everything gravely and solicitously, and all the time one knew one was playing.

It was a lovely July morning. Little woolly clouds drifted high up in the sky, the air was full of sweet scents. Lise had on a white muslin frock and a large Italian straw hat. She and her husband took a path through the park; it wound on across the meadows, between small groves and groups of trees, to the sheep field. Sigismund was going to show his wife his sheep. For this reason she had not brought her small white dog, Bijou, with her, for he would yap at the lambs and frighten them, or he would annoy the sheep dogs. Sigismund prided himself on his sheep; he had studied sheepbreeding in Mecklenburg[1] and England, and had brought back with him Cotswold[2] rams by which to improve his Danish stock. While they walked he explained to Lise the great possibilities and difficulties of the plan.

She thought: "How clever he is, what a lot of things he knows!" and at the same time: "What an absurd person he is, with his sheep! What a baby he is! I am a hundred years older than he."

But when they arrived at the sheepfold the old sheepmaster Mathias met them with the sad news that one of the English lambs was dead and two were sick. Lise saw that her husband was grieved by the tidings; while he questioned Mathias on the matter she kept silent and only gently pressed his arm. A couple of boys were sent off to fetch the sick lambs, while the master and servant went into the details of the case. It took some time.

Lise began to gaze about her and to think of other things. Twice her own thoughts made her blush deeply and happily, like a red rose, then slowly her blush died away, and the two men were still talking about sheep.

A little while after their conversation caught her attention. It had turned to a sheep thief.

This thief during the last months had broken into the sheepfolds of the neighborhood like a wolf, had killed and dragged away his prey like a wolf and like a wolf had left no trace after him. Three nights ago the shepherd and his son on an estate ten miles away had caught him in the act. The thief had killed the man and knocked the boy senseless, and had managed to escape. There were men sent out to all sides to catch him, but nobody had seen him.

Lise wanted to hear more about the horrible event, and for her benefit old Mathias went through it once more. There had been a long fight in the sheep house, in many places the earthen floor was soaked with blood. In the fight the thief's left arm was broken; all the same, he had climbed a tall fence with a lamb on his back. Mathias added that he would like to string up the murderer with these two hands of his, and Lise nodded her head at him gravely in approval. She remembered Red Riding Hood's wolf, and felt a pleasant little thrill running down her spine.

Sigismund had his own lambs in his mind, but he was too happy in himself to wish anything in the universe ill. After a minute he said: "Poor devil."

Lise said: "How can you pity such a terrible man? Indeed Grandmama was right when she said that you were a revolutionary and a danger to society!" The thought of Grandmama, and of the tears of past days, again turned her mind away from the gruesome tale she had just heard.

The boys brought the sick lambs and the men began to examine them, lifting them up and trying to set them on their legs; they squeezed them here and there and made the little creatures whimper. Lise shrank from the show and her husband noticed her distress.

"You go home, my darling," he said, "this will take some time. But just walk ahead slowly, and I shall catch up with you."

1 Mecklenburg *A former state in northern Germany.*
2 Cotswold *An area of south-west central England.*

So she was turned away by an impatient husband to whom his sheep meant more than his wife. If any experience could be sweeter than to be dragged out by him to look at those same sheep, it would be this. She dropped her large summer hat with its blue ribbons on the grass and told him to carry it back for her, for she wanted to feel the summer air on her forehead and in her hair. She walked on very slowly, as he had told her to do, for she wished to obey him in everything. As she walked she felt a great new happiness in being altogether alone, even without Bijou. She could not remember that she had ever before in all her life been altogether alone. The landscape around her was still, as if full of promise, and it was hers. Even the swallows cruising in the air were hers for they belonged to him, and he was hers.

She followed the curving edge of the grove and after a minute or two found that she was out of sight to the men by the sheep house. What could now, she wondered, be sweeter than to walk along the path in the long flowering meadow grass, slowly, slowly, and to let her husband overtake her there? It would be sweeter still, she reflected, to steal into the grove and to be gone, to have vanished from the surface of the earth from him when, tired of the sheep and longing for her company, he should turn the bend of the path to catch up with her.

An idea struck her; she stood still to think it over.

A few days ago her husband had gone for a ride and she had not wanted to go with him, but had strolled about with Bijou in order to explore her domain. Bijou then, gamboling, had led her straight into the grove. As she had followed him, gently forcing her way into the shrubbery, she had suddenly come upon a glade in the midst of it, a narrow space like a small alcove with hangings of thick green and golden brocade, big enough to hold two or three people in it. She had felt at that moment that she had

come into the very heart of her new home. If today she could find the spot again she would stand perfectly still there, hidden from all the world. Sigismund would look for her in all directions; he would be unable to understand what had become of her and for a minute, for a short minute—or, perhaps, if she was firm and cruel enough, for five—he would realize what a void, what an unendurably sad and horrible place the universe would be when she was no longer in it. She gravely scrutinized the grove to find the right entrance to her hiding-place, then went in.

She took great care to make no noise at all, therefore advanced exceedingly slowly. When a twig caught the flounces of her ample skirt she loosened it softly from the muslin, so as not to crack it. Once a branch took hold of one of her long golden curls; she stood still, with her arms lifted, to free it. A little way into the grove the soil became moist; her light steps no longer made any sound upon it. With one hand she held her small handkerchief to her lips, as if to emphasize the secretness of her course. She found the spot she sought and bent down to divide the foliage and make a door to her sylvan closet. At this the hem of her dress caught her foot and she stopped to loosen it. As she rose she looked into the face of a man who was already in the shelter.

He stood up erect, two steps off. He must have watched her as she made her way straight toward him.

She took him in in one single glance. His face was bruised and scratched, his hands and wrists stained with dark filth. He was dressed in rags, barefooted, with tatters wound round his naked ankles. His arms hung down to his sides, his right hand clasped the hilt of a knife. He was about her own age. The man and the woman looked at each other.

This meeting in the wood from beginning to end passed without a word; what happened could only be rendered by pantomime. To the two actors in the pantomime it was

timeless; according to a clock it lasted four minutes.

She had never in her life been exposed to danger. It did not occur to her to sum up her position, or to work out the length of time it would take to call her husband or Mathias, whom at this moment she could hear shouting to his dogs. She beheld the man before her as she would have beheld a forest ghost: the apparition itself, not the sequels of it, changes the world to the human who faces it.

Although she did not take her eyes off the face before her she sensed that the alcove had been turned into a covert. On the ground a couple of sacks formed a couch; there were some gnawed bones by it. A fire must have been made here in the night, for there were cinders strewn on the forest floor.

After a while she realized that he was observing her just as she was observing him. He was no longer just run to earth and crouching for a spring, but he was wondering, trying to know. At that she seemed to see herself with the eyes of the wild animal at bay in his dark hiding-place: her silently approaching white figure, which might mean death.

He moved his right arm till it hung down straight before him between his legs. Without lifting the hand he bent the wrist and slowly raised the point of the knife till it pointed at her throat. The gesture was mad, unbelievable. He did not smile as he made it, but his nostrils distended, the corners of his mouth quivered a little. Then slowly he put the knife back in the sheath by his belt.

She had no object of value about her, only the wedding ring which her husband had set on her finger in church a week ago. She drew it off, and in this movement dropped her handkerchief. She reached out her hand with the ring toward him. She did not bargain for her life. She was fearless by nature, and the horror with which he inspired her was not fear of what he might do to her. She commanded him, she besought him to

vanish as he had come, to take a dreadful figure out of her life, so that it should never have been there. In the dumb movement her young form had the grave authoritativeness of a priestess conjuring down some monstrous being by a sacred sign.

He slowly reached out his hand to hers, his finger touched hers, and her hand was steady at the touch. But he did not take the ring. As she let it go it dropped to the ground as her handkerchief had done.

For a second the eyes of both followed it. It rolled a few inches toward him and stopped before his bare foot. In a hardly perceivable movement he kicked it away and again looked into her face. They remained like that, she knew not how long, but she felt that during that time something happened, things were changed.

He bent down and picked up her handkerchief. All the time gazing at her, he again drew his knife and wrapped the tiny bit of cambric round the blade. This was difficult for him to do because his left arm was broken. While he did it his face under the dirt and sun tan slowly grew whiter till it was almost phosphorescent. Fumbling with both hands, he once more stuck the knife into the sheath. Either the sheath was too big and had never fitted the knife, or the blade was much worn—it went in. For two or three more seconds his gaze rested on her face; then he lifted his own face a little, the strange radiance still upon it, and closed his eyes.

The movement was definitive and unconditional. In this one motion he did what she had begged him to do: he vanished and was gone. She was free.

She took a step backward, the immovable, blind face before her, then bent as she had done to enter the hiding-place, and glided away as noiselessly as she had come. Once outside the grove she stood still and looked round for the meadow path, found it and began to walk home.

Her husband had not yet rounded the

84

edge of the grove. Now he saw her and
helloed to her gaily; he came up quickly and
joined her.

The path here was so narrow that he kept
half behind her and did not touch her. He
began to explain to her what had been the
matter with the lambs. She walked a step
before him and thought: All is over.

After a while he noticed her silence, came
up beside her to look at her face and asked,
"What is the matter?"

She searched her mind for something to
say, and at last said: "I have lost my ring."

"What ring?" he asked her.

She answered, "My wedding ring."

As she heard her own voice pronounce the
words she conceived their meaning.

Her wedding ring. "With this ring"—
dropped by one and kicked away by another
—"with this ring I thee wed." With this
lost ring she had wedded herself to something. To what? To poverty, persecution,
total loneliness. To the sorrows and the sin-
fulness of this earth. "And what therefore
God has joined together let man not put
asunder."

"I will find you another ring," her husband
said. "You and I are the same as we were
on our wedding day; it will do as well. We
are husband and wife today too, as much as
yesterday, I suppose."

Her face was so still that he did not know
if she had heard what he said. It touched
him that she should take the loss of his ring
so to heart. He took her hand and kissed it.
It was cold, not quite the same hand as he
had last kissed. He stopped to make her
stop with him.

"Do you remember where you had the
ring on last?" he asked.

"No," she answered.

"Have you any idea," he asked, "where you
may have lost it?"

"No," she answered. "I have no idea."

For Discussion

1 One of the archetypal stories not too
deeply buried in "The Ring" is that of
the Fall of Adam and Eve and their ex-
pulsion from Paradise. We are told that
before their marriage Sigismund and Lise
lived in a "distant paradise." After marriage they had "descended to earth." At
the end of the story they are somewhat
in the position of Adam and Eve, no
longer living under any special protection
but having to face life and each other as
ordinary men and women. Reality, perhaps the modern equivalent of Sin, has
crept into their paradise.

The story is not a strict allegory, in
which each detail corresponds directly to
points on another map of meaning. But
there is a general correspondence. What
are some of the details which indicate
that the earthly paradise of Sigismund
and Lise is falling apart? That they are
becoming less innocent, growing up?
What details suggest that there is death
and evil in the world? Who or what
would correspond to the Serpent that
tempted Eve?

2 When the husband and wife hear that
there is a thief roaming around, he says
"Poor devil," and she says, "How can you
pity such a terrible man?" What does
this suggest about the difference between
them? How does Lise change in the
course of the story? How, at the end of
the story, could they be said to be closer
together, even though a secret stands between them?

3 Why does the thief choose to take Lise's
handkerchief and not her more valuable
ring?

4 Why does Lise keep her encounter with
the thief a secret from her husband?
She has, after all, done nothing to be
ashamed of. Or has she? What reasonable story could she have told her husband? Why does she refuse to tell him
anything about her encounter?

This story, set in modern Germany, can also be read as a reflection of the story of Adam and Eve. The temptation they faced is a common one in today's world, so common that many people think of it as "an ordinary business transaction."

Heinrich Böll

Like a Bad Dream

That evening we had invited the Zumpens over for dinner, nice people; it was through my father-in-law that we had got to know them: ever since we have been married he has helped me to meet people who can be useful to me in business, and Zumpen can be useful: he is chairman of a committee which places contracts for large housing projects, and I have married into the excavating business.

I was tense that evening, but Bertha, my wife, reassured me. "The fact," she said, "that he's coming at all is promising. Just try and get the conversation round to the contract. You know it's tomorrow they're going to be awarded."

I stood looking through the net curtains of the glass front door, waiting for Zumpen. I smoked, ground the cigarette butts under my foot, and shoved them under the mat. Next I took up a position at the bathroom window and stood there wondering why Zumpen had accepted the invitation; he couldn't be that interested in having dinner with us, and the fact that the big contract I was involved in was going to be awarded tomorrow must have made the whole thing as embarrassing to him as it was to me.

I thought about the contract too: it was a big one, I would make 20,000 marks[1] on the deal, and I wanted the money.

Bertha had decided what I was to wear: a dark jacket, trousers a shade lighter and a conservative tie. That's the kind of thing

1 mark   *Monetary unit of Germany.*

she learned at home, and at boarding school from the nuns. Also what to offer guests: when to pass the cognac, and when the vermouth, how to arrange dessert. It is comforting to have a wife who knows all about such things.

But Bertha was tense too: as she put her hands on my shoulders, they touched my neck, and I felt her thumbs damp and cold against it.

"It's going to be all right," she said, "you'll get the contract."

"Christ," I said, "it means 20,000 marks to me, and you know how we need the money."

"One should never," she said gently, "mention Christ's name in connection with money!"

A dark car drew up in front of our house, a make I didn't recognize, but it looked Italian. "Take it easy," Bertha whispered, "wait till they've rung, let them stand there for a couple of seconds, then walk slowly to the door and open it."

I watched Mr. and Mrs. Zumpen come up the steps: he is slender and tall, with graying temples, the kind of man who fifty years ago would have been known as a "ladies' man"; Mrs. Zumpen is one of those thin dark women who always make me think of lemons. I could tell from Zumpen's face that it was a frightful bore for him to have dinner with us.

Then the doorbell rang, and I waited one second, two seconds, walked slowly to the door and opened it.

"Well," I said, "how nice of you to come!"

Cognac glasses in hand, we went from room to room in our apartment, which the Zumpens wanted to see. Bertha stayed in the kitchen to squeeze some mayonnaise out of a tube onto the appetizers; she does this very nicely: hearts, loops, little houses. The Zumpens complimented us on our apartment; they exchanged smiles when they saw the big desk in my study, at that moment it seemed a bit too big even to me.

Zumpen admired a small rococo[2] cabinet, a wedding present from my grandmother, and a baroque[3] Madonna in our bedroom.

By the time we got back to the dining room, Bertha had dinner on the table; she had done this very nicely too, it was all so attractive yet so natural, and dinner was pleasant and relaxed. We talked about movies and books, about the recent elections, and Zumpen praised the assortment of cheeses, and Mrs. Zumpen praised the coffee and the pastries. Then we showed the Zumpens our honeymoon pictures: photographs of the Breton coast,[4] Spanish donkeys, and street scenes from Casablanca.[5]

After that we had some more cognac, and when I stood up to get the box with the photos of the time when we were engaged, Bertha gave me a sign, and I didn't get the box. For two minutes there was absolute silence, because we had nothing more to talk about, and we all thought about the contract; I thought of the 20,000 marks, and it struck me that I could deduct the bottle of cognac from my income tax. Zumpen looked at his watch and said: "Too bad, it's ten o'clock; we have to go. It's been such a pleasant evening!" And Mrs. Zumpen said: "It was really delightful, and I hope you'll come to us one evening."

"We would love to," Bertha said, and we stood around for another half-minute, all thinking again about the contract, and I felt Zumpen was waiting for me to take him aside and bring up the subject. But I didn't. Zumpen kissed Bertha's hand, and I went ahead, opened the doors, and held the car door open for Mrs. Zumpen down below.

"Why," said Bertha gently, "didn't you mention the contract to him? You know it's going to be awarded tomorrow."

"Well," I said, "I didn't know how to bring the conversation round to it."

"Now look," she said in a quiet voice, "you could have used any excuse to ask him into your study, that's where you should have talked to him. You must have noticed how interested he is in art. You ought to have

---

2 rococo *An artistic style, especially of the eighteenth century, characterized by fanciful, curved, spatial forms and ornaments of pierced shellwork.*

3 baroque *An artistic style, especially of the seventeenth century, characterized by elaborate and sometimes grotesque ornamentation.*

4 Breton coast *The coastline of Brittany, a region in northwest France.*

5 Casablanca *Seaport city on the west coast of Morocco.*

said: I have an eighteenth-century crucifix in there you might like to have a look at, and then . . ."

I said nothing, and she sighed and tied on her apron. I followed her into the kitchen; we put the rest of the appetizers back in the refrigerator, and I crawled about on the floor looking for the top of the mayonnaise tube. I put away the remains of the cognac, counted the cigars: Zumpen had smoked only one. I emptied the ashtrays, ate another pastry, and looked to see if there was any coffee left in the pot. When I went back to the kitchen, Bertha was standing there with the car key in her hand.

"What's up?" I asked.

"We have to go over there, of course," she said.

"Over where?"

"To the Zumpens," she said, "where do you think?"

"It's nearly half past ten."

"I don't care if it's midnight," Bertha said, "all I know is, there's 20,000 marks involved. Don't imagine they're squeamish."

She went into the bathroom to get ready, and I stood behind her watching her wipe her mouth and draw in new outlines, and for the first time I noticed how wide and primitive that mouth is. When she tightened the knot of my tie I could have kissed her, the way I always used to when she fixed my tie, but I didn't.

Downtown the cafés and restaurants were brightly lit. People were sitting outside on the terraces, and the light from the street lamps was caught in the silver ice-cream dishes and ice buckets. Bertha gave me an encouraging look; but she stayed in the car when we stopped in front of the Zumpen's house, and I pressed the bell at once and was surprised how quickly the door was opened. Mrs. Zumpen did not seem surprised to see me; she had on some black lounging pajamas with loose full trousers embroidered with yellow flowers, and this made me think more than ever of lemons.

"I beg your pardon," I said, "I would like to speak to your husband."

"He's gone out again," she said, "he'll be back in half an hour."

In the hall I saw a lot of Madonnas, gothic and baroque, even rococo Madonnas, if there is such a thing.

"I see," I said, "well then, if you don't mind, I'll come back in half an hour."

Bertha had bought an evening paper; she was reading it and smoking, and when I sat down beside her she said: "I think you could have talked about it to her too."

"But how do you know he wasn't there?"

"Because I know he is at the Gaffel Club playing chess, as he does every Wednesday evening at this time."

"You might have told me that earlier."

"Please try and understand," said Bertha, folding the newspaper. "I am trying to help you, I want you to find out for yourself how to deal with such things. All we had to do was call up Father and he would have settled the whole thing for you with one phone call, but I want you to get the contract on your own."

"All right," I said, "then what'll we do: wait here half an hour, or go up right away and have a talk with her?"

"We'd better go up right away," said Bertha.

We got out of the car and went up in the elevator together. "Life," said Bertha, "consists of making compromises and concessions."

Mrs. Zumpen was no more surprised now than she had been earlier, when I had come alone. She greeted us, and we followed her into her husband's study. Mrs. Zumpen brought some cognac, poured it out, and before I could say anything about the contract she pushed a yellow folder toward me: "Housing Project Fir Tree Haven," I read, and looked up in alarm at Mrs. Zumpen, at Bertha, but they both smiled, and Mrs. Zumpen said: "Open the folder," and I opened it; inside was another one, pink, and on this I read: "Housing Project Fir Tree Haven—Excavation Work." I opened this too, saw my estimate lying there on top of the pile; along the upper edge someone had written in red: "Lowest bid."

I could feel myself flushing with pleasure, my heart thumping, and I thought of the 20,000 marks.

I closed the file, and this time Bertha forgot to rebuke me.

"*Prost*,"[6] said Mrs. Zumpen with a smile, "let's drink to it then."

We drank, and I stood up and said: "It may seem rude of me, but perhaps you'll understand that I would like to go home now."

"I understand perfectly," said Mrs. Zumpen, "there's just one small item to be taken care of." She took the file, leafed through it, and said: "Your price per square meter is thirty pfennigs[7] below that of the next-lowest bidder. I suggest you raise your price by fifteen pfennigs: that way you'll still be the lowest and you'll have made an extra four thousand five hundred marks. Come on, do it now!" Bertha took her pen out of her purse and offered it to me, but I was in too much of a turmoil to write; I gave the file to Bertha and watched her alter the price with a steady hand, re-write the total, and hand the file back to Mrs. Zumpen.

"And now," said Mrs. Zumpen, "just one more little thing. Get out your check book and write a check for three thousand marks; it must be a cash check and endorsed by you."

She had said this to me, but it was Bertha who pulled our check book out of her purse and made out the check.

"It won't be covered," I said in a low voice.

"When the contract is awarded, there will be an advance, and then it will be covered," said Mrs. Zumpen.

Perhaps I failed to grasp what was happening at the time. As we went down in the elevator, Bertha said she was happy, but I said nothing.

Bertha chose a different way home, we drove through quiet residential districts, I saw lights in open windows, people sitting on balconies drinking wine; it was a clear, warm night.

"I suppose the check was for Zumpen?" was all I said, softly, and Bertha replied, just as softly: "Of course."

I looked at Bertha's small, brown hands on the steering wheel, so confident and quiet. Hands, I thought, that sign checks and squeeze mayonnaise tubes, and I looked higher—at her mouth, and still felt no desire to kiss it.

That evening I did not help Bertha put the car away in the garage, nor did I help her with the dishes. I poured myself a large cognac, went up to my study, and sat down at my desk, which was much too big for me. I was wondering about something. I got up, went into the bedroom and looked at the baroque Madonna, but even there I couldn't put my finger on the thing I was wondering about.

The ringing of the phone interrupted my thoughts; I lifted the receiver and was not surprised to hear Zumpen's voice.

"Your wife," he said, "made a slight mistake. She raised the price by twenty-five pfennigs instead of fifteen."

I thought for a moment and then said: "That wasn't a mistake, she did it with my consent."

He was silent for a second or two, then said with a laugh: "So you had already discussed the various possibilities?"

"Yes," I said.

"All right, then make out another check for a thousand."

"Five hundred," I said, and I thought: It's like a bad dream—that's what it's like.

"Eight hundred," he said, and I said with a laugh: "Six hundred," and I knew, although I had no experience to go on, that he

6 Prost *German: "to your health."*
7 pfennigs *A German coin of little value; 100 pfennigs equal a mark.*

would now say seven hundred and fifty, and when he did I said "Yes" and hung up.

It was not yet midnight when I went downstairs and over to the car to give Zumpen the check; he was alone and laughed as I reached in to hand him the folded check. When I walked slowly back into the house, there was no sign of Bertha; she didn't appear when I went back into my study; she didn't appear when I went downstairs again for a glass of milk from the refrigerator, and I knew what she was thinking; she was thinking: he has to get over it, and I have to leave him alone; this is something he has to understand.

But I never did understand. It is beyond understanding.

Leila Vennewitz/TRANSLATOR

For Discussion

1 If, as we suggested in the headnote to this story, it reflects the story of Adam and Eve, who or what is the Serpent? Who is the driving force in giving way to temptation—the man or the woman?

2 What is ironic about the fact that the narrator and his wife have an eighteenth-century crucifix in their apartment, and that the Zumpens have "a lot of Madonnas" in their hall?

3 The narrator begins by "wondering why Zumpen had accepted the invitation; he couldn't be that interested in having dinner with us." Why did Zumpen come to dinner?

4 What does this story have to say about a lot of "social" activity in the modern world? How "social" is it?

5 What does the story say about certain kinds of marriages? For what reasons do you think the narrator married Bertha?

6 "Mrs. Zumpen did not seem surprised to see me." Why not?

7 What is ironic about the narrator saying that he "sat down at my desk, which was much too big for me"?

8 Bertha says, "Life consists of making compromises and concessions." Even if you agree, would you interpret the remark in the same way Bertha does?

9 At what point in the story do you see most clearly that the narrator has a conscience? How strong is his conscience?

10 Everyone seems to have made money out of this deal, the narrator and his wife and the Zumpens. Who lost?

Increasingly, modern fiction has turned its attention away from the adventures of heroic and extraordinary men and looked at the lives of ordinary people, the kind of people we might meet every day. This naturalistic fiction can be dull if the writer gives us only a picture of life's surface, no matter how accurate that picture may be. In stories like "The Actor," however, the author goes beyond the surface to show us that the most ordinary slice of life is more complex than we may have suspected.

One of the pleasures of fiction is to read about things we never knew; another is to read about things we have known all along, but have forgotten. Even though we know that men like Albert are more complex than they appear, we often take them for granted.

The story takes place in a small city in modern England.

Stan Barstow

The Actor

He was a big man, without surplus flesh, and with an impassivity of face that hid extreme shyness, and which, allied with his striking build, made him look more than anything else, as he walked homewards in the early evening in fawn mackintosh and trilby hat, like a plain-clothes policeman going quietly and efficiently about his business, with trouble for someone at the end of it.

All his adult life people had been saying to him, "You should have been a policeman, Mr. Royston," or, more familiarly, "You've missed your way, Albert. You're cut out for a copper, lad." But he would smile in his quiet, patient way, as though no one had ever said it before, and almost always give exactly the same reply: "Nay, I'm all right. I like my bed at nights."

In reality he was a shop assistant and could be found, in white smock, on five and a half days of the week behind the counter of the Moorend branch grocery store of Cressley Industrial Co-operative Society, where he was assistant manager. He had been assistant manager for five years and seemed fated to occupy that position for many more years to come before the promotion earmarked for him would become fact. For the manager was of a settled disposition also, and still comparatively young and fit.

But Albert did not apparently worry. He did not apparently worry about anything;

but this again was the deception of his appearance. Quiet he might be, and stolid and settled in his ways; but no one but he had known the agony of shyness that was his wedding day; and no one but he had known the pure terror of the premature birth of his only child, when the dead baby he had longed for with so much secret yearning had almost cost the life of the one person without whom his own life would hardly have seemed possible—Alice, his wife.

So it was the measure of his misleading appearance and his ability to hide his feelings that no one ever guessed the truth, that no one was ever led from the belief that he was a taciturn man of unshakeable placidity. "You want to take a leaf out of Albert's book," they would say. "Take a lesson from him. Never worries, Albert doesn't."

Thus Albert, at the age of thirty-seven, on the eve of his small adventure.

Amateur drama was a popular pastime in Cressley and varied in standard from rather embarrassing to really quite good. Generally considered to be among the best of the local groups was the C.I.C.S. Players—the drama group of Cressley Industrial Co-operative Society. They restricted their activities to perhaps three productions a year and worked hard to achieve a professional finish. It was about the time of the casting for the Christmas production, perhaps the most important of the year, since at this time each group was shown in direct comparison with all the other bodies who joined together in the week-long Christmas Festival of Amateur Drama in the Co-operative Hall, that the rather fierce-looking lady from General Office who was said to be the backbone and mainstay of the C.I.C.S. Players, happened to visit the shop and seeing Albert on her way out as he towered over a diminutive woman customer, stopped abruptly and, waiting only till he was free, crossed over to him and said, "Tell me, have you ever acted?"

As it was the oddest thing anyone had ever asked him, Albert simply stared at the woman while a colleague said, "He's always acting, Albert is. Make a cat laugh, the antics he gets up to."

"Take no notice of him," Albert said. "He's kiddin'."

"What I mean," the lady said, "is, have you had any experience of dramatics?"

"Dramatics?" Albert said.

"Taking part in plays."

Albert gave a short laugh and shook his head.

"There's a chap coming from M.G.M. to see him next week," the facetious colleague said. "Cressley's answer to Alan Ladd."

Ignoring the irrepressible one, the lady continued her interrogation of Albert with: "Has anyone ever told you you look like a policeman?"

"I believe it has been mentioned," said Albert, wondering if the woman had nothing better to do than stand here asking him daft questions all morning.

She now looked Albert over in silence for some moments until, unable to bear her scrutiny for another second, he bent down and pretended to look for something under the counter. He had his head down there when she spoke again and he thought for a moment he had misheard her.

"Eh?" he said, straightening up.

"I said, would you be interested in a part in our new production? You know, the C.I.C.S. Players. We're doing R. Belton Wilkins's *The Son of the House* for the Christmas Festival and there's a part in it for a police constable. We've no one in the group who fits the role nearly so well as you."

"But I can't act," Albert said. "I've never done anything like that before."

"It's only a small part—about a page. You'd soon learn it. And you'd find it great fun to be part of a group effort. There's nothing quite like the thrill of the stage, you know."

"Aye, happen it's all right if you're that way inclined," Albert said, and was relieved to see a customer at the lady's elbow.

"Well, I won't keep you from your work," she said; "but think it over. We'd love to have you, and you'd never regret it. We start rehearsals next week. I'll pop in and see you again later. Think it over."

"Aye, aye," Albert said. "I'll think it over." Meaning that he would dismiss it from his mind for the nonsense it was as soon as she was gone. Acting! Him!

But he did not dismiss it from his mind. A part of his mind was occupied with it all morning as he attended to his customers; and at lunch-time, when the door had been locked, he went over to one of the young lady assistants from the opposite counter.

"You're mixed up with this acting thing, aren't you?"

"The Players?" the girl said. "Oh yes. It's grand fun. We're doing R. Belton Wilkins's latest West End[1] success for our next production."

"Aye," Albert said, "I've been hearin' so. I've had yon' woman on to me this morning."

"You mean Mrs. Bostock. I saw her talking to you. A real tartar, she is. Terrifically keen and efficient. I don't know what we'd do without her."

"She's been doin' a bit o' recruitin' this morning," Albert said. "Been on to me to take a part in this new play. Don't know what she's thinkin' about." All morning a new feeling had been growing in him and now he realized that he was pleased and flattered by Mrs. Bostock's approach, nonsense though it undoubtedly was. "I always thought you wanted these la-di-da chaps for play-actin'," he said; "not ord'nary chaps like me."

"I don't know," the girl said, unbuttoning her overall. "What part does she want you for?"

"The policeman."

"Well, there you are. Perfect type-casting. You look the part exactly."

"But they'd know straight away 'at I wasn't an actor, soon as I opened me mouth."

"They don't want to know you're an actor. They want to think you're a policeman."

"But I can't put it on."

"Policemen don't put it on, do they? You'd just have to be yourself and you'd be perfect."

"And I've no head for remembering lines," Albert said.

"How do you know if you've never tried?"

"Hmm," Albert said.

"Look," the girl said, "I'll bring my copy of the play back after dinner and you can have a look at the part. As far as I remember, it's not very long."

"Oh, don't bother," Albert said. "I'm not thinkin' o' doin' it."

"No bother," the girl said. "You just have a look at it and see."

That afternoon, in the intervals between attending to customers, Albert could be seen paying great attention to something slightly below the level of the counter; and when the shop had closed for the day he approached the girl who had lent him the book and said, "Will you be wantin' this tonight? I thought I might take it home an' have a look at it."

"It's getting you, then?"

"Well, I've read it about half-way through," Albert said, "an' I've got interested like. In the story, I mean. I'd like to see how it ends, if you can spare the book."

"You can borrow it," the girl said. "You'll find it very gripping near the end. It ran for over two years in London."

"You don't say so," Albert said. "That's a long time."

"Of course, we're only doing one performance," the girl said, "so you needn't get the wind up."

"What d'you think happened at the shop today?" Albert asked Alice after tea that evening.

Alice said she couldn't imagine.

"We had that Mrs. Bostock down from

1 West End *The western portion of London.*

General Office an' she asked me if I'd like a part in this new play they're getting up."

"You?" Alice said. "She asked you?"

"Aye, I knew it," Albert said. "I knew you'd think it was daft an' all.

"I don't think it's daft at all," Alice said. "I'm surprised, but I don't think it's daft. What part does she want you to play?"

"Guess," Albert said. "She took one look at me an' offered me the part."

Alice began to laugh. "Why not? Why ever shouldn't you?"

"Because," Albert said, "there's a difference in walkin' the streets lookin' like a bobby an' walkin' on to a stage an' reckonin' to be one. I don't think I could do it, not with maybe hundreds o' people watchin' me."

"Oh, I don't know. They tell me you forget the audience once you start saying your lines."

"Aye, an' supposin' you forget your lines? What then?"

"Well, you just have to learn them. And you have rehearsals and what not. I don't suppose it's a long part, is it?"

Albert fingered the book. "Only a page. I have it here."

"Oh, ho!" Alice said.

"Well, young Lucy Fryer would bring it for me, an' I started readin' it and got interested. It's a real good play, y'know. They ought to do it on the telly. It ran for two years in London."

Alice took the book and looked at the title. "Yes, I've heard of this."

"It's all about a young feller and his dad's ever so rich and dotes on the lad. Thinks the sun shines out of him; an' all the time this lad's a real nasty piece o' work. A proper nowter."[2]

"Where's the policeman's part?"

"In the second act. Here, let me show you. This lad an' his brother are havin' a row, see, because he's run some'dy down in his car and not stopped, because he was drunk. An' right in the middle of this I come in an'——"

"*You* come in?" Alice said. "I thought you weren't interested in the part?"

Albert looked sheepish. "I haven't said I am," he said. "I sort o' tried to imagine myself as I was reading it, that's all."

"I see," Alice said.

"Aye, that's all . . . What you lookin' at me for?"

"I'm just looking," Alice said.

It was two days later that Mrs. Bostock came in again.

"Well," she said with ferocious brightness, "did you think it over?"

"He's read the play, Mrs. Bostock," Lucy Fryer said, coming over. "I lent him my copy."

"Splendid, splendid."

"Yes, a very entertainin' play indeed," Albert said. "But I haven't said owt[3] about playin' that part. I don't think it's owt in my line, y'see. She thinks so, an' my missis; but I'm not sure."

"Nonsense," Mrs. Bostock said.

"Y'see I'm not the sort o' feller to show meself off in front of a lot o' people."

"Rubbish," Mrs. Bostock said.

"Oh, it's all right for you lot. You've done it all before. You're used to it."

"Come to rehearsal Monday evening," Mrs. Bostock commanded.

"Well, I don't know."

"My house, seven-thirty. I won't take no for an answer till you've seen us all and given it a try. Lucy will tell you the address." And she was gone.

"A bit forceful, isn't she?" Albert said.

"A tartar,"[4] Lucy said.

"Oh, heck," Albert said, "I don't like this at all."

But secretly now he was beginning to like it enormously.

At seven twenty-five on Monday evening he presented himself, dressed carefully in his best navy blue and shaved for the second time that day, at the front door of Mrs. Bostock's home, a large and rather grim-looking Victorian terrace house with big bay

2 nowter *Good-for-nothing.*
3 owt *Anything.*
4 tartar *An unexpectedly for-*
midable person.

windows on a long curving avenue off Halifax Road, and was joined on the step by Lucy Fryer.

Mrs. Bostock herself let them in and showed them into a large and shabbily comfortable drawing-room furnished mostly with a varied assortment of easy chairs and settees, and more books than Albert had ever seen at one time outside the public library. He was introduced to a thin, distinguished-looking pipe-smoking man who turned out to be Mr. Bostock, and then the members of the drama group began to arrive.

There were only seven speaking parts in the play, but several people who would be responsible for backstage production turned up too, and soon the room was full of men and women whose common characteristic seemed to be that they all talked at the top of their voices. Albert was bewildered, and then smitten with acute embarrassment when Mrs. Bostock, standing on the hearthrug, clapped her hands together and saying, "Listen, everybody; I'd like you all to meet our new recruit," directed all eyes to him.

"I'm trying to talk Mr. Royston into playing the policeman in *Son of the House* and I want you all to be nice to him because he isn't completely sold on the idea yet."

"But my dear Effie," said a stocky young man in a tweed jacket and yellow shirt, "you're a genius. You really are. Where on earth did you find him?" And Albert stood there feeling very uncomfortable while everybody looked at him as though he were an antique which Mrs. Bostock had uncovered in an obscure shop and was now presenting for their admiration.

"Mr. Royston is the assistant manager in Moorend Grocery," Mrs. Bostock told them. "I took one look at him and knew he was our man."

To Albert's relief attention turned from him and he was able for a time to sit in his corner and watch what went on without being called upon to do or say anything. But not for long. A first group-reading of the play was started upon and Albert followed the action in his copy, amazed at the way the actors let themselves go in their parts, delivering the most embarrassing lines without the least sign of self-consciousness. "'You know I love you,'" the young man in the yellow shirt said to a pretty dark girl sitting next to Albert. "'*Do* you love me?'" she replied. Albert blushed.

At the entrance of the policeman a silence fell upon the room and Mrs. Bostock, still directing operations from the hearthrug, said, "Now, Mr. Royston, this is where you come in."

Oh, it was terrible. His heart thumped sickeningly. He found his place, put his forefinger under the line, swallowed thickly, and said in a faint voice:

"Is one of you gentlemen the owner of that car standing outside?'"

"Weak," Mrs. Bostock said. "Come now, Mr. Royston, a little more authority. Can't you imagine the impact of your entrance? . . ."

"Just imagine it, Alice," Albert said, getting up out of his chair with the book in his hand. "Here's this rotter of a bloke, who's had one too many an' been drivin' like mad an' hit somebody an' left 'em in the road. He's scared out of his wits an' now he's telling his brother an' pleadin' with him to help him, when the maid comes in and says there's a policeman come—and I walk in.

"'Is one of you gentlemen the owner of that car standing outside?' An' this 'ere young chap nearly passes out with fright, thinkin' they're on to him. And really, y'see, all I'm doin' is pinchin' him for parking without lights. Just imagine it. It's . . . it's one of the dramatic climaxes of the play."

"It's ever so thrilling, Albert," Alice said. "Did you say it like that tonight?"

"What?"

"Is one of you gentlemen the owner of that car outside?'"

"Well, happen not quite like that. It's not so bad when there's only you listening to me, but it sort o' puts you off with all them la-di-da fellers there. You're scared to death you'll drop an aitch or say a word wrong. . . . It'll be easier when I'm a bit more used to it."

"You're really taking it on, then?"

"Well," Albert said, scratching his head, "I don't seem to have much option, somehow. She's a very persuasive woman, that Mrs. Bostock. Besides," he went on, "it sort of gets you, you know. If you know what I mean."

Alice smiled. "I know what you mean. You do it, Albert. You show them."

Albert looked at her and in a moment a slow grin spread across his face. "I think I will, Alice," he said. "I think I will."

Once committed, Albert sank himself heart and soul into the perfecting of his part. Attendance at Mrs. Bostock's house on Monday evenings opened up a new vista of life to him. It was his first contact with the artistic temperament and he soon realized that very often the amount of temperament varied in inverse ratio to the amount of talent. He was fascinated.

"You've never met anybody like 'em," he said to Alice one night. "They shake hands to feel how long the claws are an' put their arms round one another so's it's easier to slip the knife in."

"Oh, surely, Albert," said Alice, a person of sweetness and light, "they're not as bad as all that."

"No," he admitted; "some of 'em's all right; but there's one or two proper devils." He shook his hand. "They're certainly not sort o' folk I've been used to. Three quarters of 'em don't even work for t'Co-op."

"How is it coming along?" Alice asked.

"Pretty fair. We're trying it out on the stage next week, with all the actions an' everything."

On the night of the dress rehearsal Alice answered a knock on the door to find a policeman on the step.

"Does Albert Royston live here?" a gruff official voice asked.

Alice was startled. "Well, he does," she said, "but he's not in just now."

She opened the door a little wider and the light fell across the man's face. Her husband stepped toward her, laughing.

"You silly fool, Albert," Alice said indulgently. "You gave me a shock."

Albert was still chuckling as he walked through into the living room. "Well, how do I look?"

"You look marvellous," Alice said. "But you've never come through the streets like that, have you? You could get into trouble."

"It's all right," Albert told her. "I had me mac[5] on over the uniform and the helmet in a bag. I just had to give you a preview like. An' Mrs. Bostock says could you put a little tuck in the tunic: summat they can take out before it goes back. It's a bit on the roomy side."

"It must have been made for a giant," Alice said as she fussed about behind him, examining the tunic. "Ooh, Albert, but isn't it getting exciting! I can't wait for the night."

"Well, like it or lump it," Albert said, "there's only another week."

He was at the hall early on the night of the play and made up and dressed in the police constable's uniform by the end of the first act. As the second act began he found himself alone in the dressing room. He looked into the mirror and squared the helmet on his head. He certainly looked the part all right. It would be a bit of a lark to go out in the street and pinch somebody for speeding or something. He narrowed his eyes, looking fiercely at himself, and spoke his opening line in a guttural undertone.

Well, this was it. No good looking in the book. If he didn't know the part now he never would. Out there the second act was under way, the players doing their very best, revelling in a hobby they loved, giving entertainment to all those people; and in return the audience was thrilling to every twist and climax of the plot, and not letting one witty

5 mac *Short for macintosh, a raincoat.*

phrase, one humorous exchange go by without a laugh. A good audience, Mrs. Bostock had said: the sort of audience all actors, professional or amateur, loved: at one with the players, receptive, responsive, appreciative. And soon its eyes would be on him.

He was suddenly seized by an appalling attack of stage fright. His stomach was empty, a hollow void of fear. He put his head in his hands. He couldn't do it. How could he ever have imagined he could? He couldn't face all those people. His mouth was dry and when he tried to bring his lines to memory he found nothing but a blank.

A knock on the door made him look up. He felt panic grip him now. Had he missed his entrance? Had he ruined the performance for everybody by cringing here like a frightened child? The knock was repeated and Mrs. Bostock's voice said from outside, "Are you there, Mr. Royston?"

Albert took his script in his hand and opened the door. She smiled brightly up at him. "Everything all right?" She gave him an appraising look. "You look wonderful. You're not on for a little while yet but I should come and stand in the wings and get the feel of the action. You look a bit pale about the gills. What's wrong—stage fright?"

"It's all a bit new to me," Albert said feebly.

"Of course it is. But you know your lines perfectly and once you're out there you'll forget your nervousness. Just remember the audience is on your side."

They went up the narrow steps to the level of the stage. The voices of the actors became more distinct. He caught the tail-end of a line he recognized. There already? Recurrent fear gripped his stomach.

He looked out on to the brightly lit stage, at the actors moving about, talking, and across to where the girl who was acting as prompter sat with an open script on her knee. "Shirley hasn't had a thing to do so far," Mrs. Bostock murmured. "The whole thing's gone like a dream." She took the script from Albert's hands and found the place for him. "Here we are. Now you just follow the action in there and relax, take it easy. You'll be on and off so quick you'll hardly know you've left the wings."

"I'm all right now," Albert told her.

He realized to his own surprise that he was; and he became increasingly so as the action of the play absorbed him, so that he began to feel himself part of it and no longer a frightened amateur shivering in the wings.

Two pages to go. The younger son was telling his brother about the accident. The row was just beginning and at the very height of it he would make his entrance. He began to feel excited. What was it Mrs. Bostock had said? "From the second you step on you dominate the stage. Your entrance is like a thunder-clap." By shots! He realized vaguely that Mrs. Bostock had left his side, but he didn't care now. He felt a supreme confidence. He was ready. He'd show them. By shots he would!

One page. "'You've been rotten all your life, Paul,'" the elder brother was saying. "'I've never cherished any illusions about you, but this, this is more than even I dreamed you were capable of.'"

"'I know you hate me, Tom. I've always known it. But if only for father's sake, you must help me now. You know what it will do to him if he finds out. He couldn't stand it in his condition.'"

"'You swine. You utter swine . . .'"

The girl who was the maid appeared at his side. She gave him a quick smile. No nerves about her. She'd been on and off the stage all evening, living the part. Albert stared out, fascinated. Not until this moment had he known the true thrill of acting, of submerging one's own personality in that of another.

"'Where are you going?'"

"'I'm going to find that man you knocked down and get him to a hospital. And you're coming with me.'"

"'But it's too late, Tom. It was hours

ago. Someone's sure to have found him by now. Perhaps the police . . .'"

Any minute now. They were working up to his entrance. *Like a thunder-clap.* Albert braced his shoulders and touched his helmet. He glanced down at the script and quickly turned a page. He had lost his place. Panic smote him like a blow. They were still talking, though, so he must be all right. And anyway the maid gave him his cue and she was still by his side. Then suddenly she was no longer at his side. She had gone. He fumbled with his script. Surely . . . not so far . . .

He felt Mrs. Bostock at his elbow. He turned to her in stupid surprise.

"But," he said, "they've . . . they've——"

She nodded. "Yes. They've skipped three pages. They've missed your part right out."

He was already at home when Alice returned.

"Whatever happened, Albert?" she said anxiously. "You weren't ill, were you?"

He told her. "I went and got changed straight away," he said, "and came home."

"Well, isn't that a shame."

"Oh, they just got carried away," Albert said. "One of 'em lost his place and skipped and the other had to follow him. They did it so quick nobody could do owt about it." He smiled as he began to take off his shoes. "Looks as though I'll never know whether I'd've stood up to it or not," he said.

He never did anything of the kind again.

A long time after, he was able to face with equanimity his wife's request, in the presence of acquaintances, that he should tell them about his "acting career," and say, "No, you tell 'em, Alice. You tell it best." And the genuine smile on his honest face during the recounting of the story of the unspoken lines, which never failed to provoke shouts of laughter, always deceived the listeners. So that never for one moment did they guess just how cruel, how grievous a disappointment it had been to him at the time.

For Discussion

1. The point of the story is indicated by the title. At first glance we may think it is called "The Actor" because Albert takes part in an amateur theatrical production. But in what other, and more important, sense is he an actor?

2. At first, Albert pretends to be uninterested in being in a play. What signs do you see that he is in fact interested? Why does he feel that he has to pretend otherwise?

3. Why does Alice encourage him to take the part in the play? What does she know about him that most people don't know?

4. Among other things, this story is a study in the subtleties of the English class system. How are the other members of the dramatic society different from Albert? How does his speech contrast with theirs? Is Albert aware of the difference?

5. Albert never gets to appear on the stage. What are the full implications of the author's comment, "He never did anything of the kind again"?

6. Albert's life cannot be called tragic. He has a good wife, a good job, and shows no signs of being discontented. What does the author think is sad about Albert's life? In what way can Albert be said to stand for a large number of people?

This story, which takes place in modern Dublin, presents a strange conflict of wills between a man and a racing pigeon. The fact that the hero's adversary is only a bird gives the story a comic tone. Yet the stakes are serious: the effects of the struggle on both Larry and the pigeon, Brian Boru, are far from comic.

Sean O'Faolain

The End of a Good Man

Men who go into competition with the world are broken into fragments by the world, and it is such men we love to analyze. But men who do not go into competition with the world remain intact, and these men we cannot analyze. They are always contented men, with modest ambitions. Larry Dunne was that kind of man. All that there is to say about him, therefore, is that he bred pigeons and was happy.

And yet, this unconditional lump of reality, this unrefracted thought in the mind of God, suddenly did fall into fragments. He fell for the same reason as Adam. For when God was saying, "Orchards for Adam," and "Finance for J. P. Morgan," and "Politics for Teddy Roosevelt," and "Pigeons for Larry

Dunne," He must have added (*sotto voce*),[1] "*But one pigeon he must never control.*" And it was to that one pigeon, that one ambition, that Larry Dunne gave his heart. The pigeon's name was Brian Boru.[2] Larry got him on his thirty-fifth birthday from his father.

Any evening that summer you could have met Larry at the pigeon club—it sat every night under the canal bridge on the towpath —and you might have guessed in what direction his heart was already moving by the way he talked endlessly without ever mentioning the fatal bird. You might have heard him, towering over the rest of the club, talking of his runts, tumblers, pouters, homers, racers, without ever mentioning

---

1   sotto voce   *Under the breath.*
2   Brian Boru   *The pigeon derived his name from one of the legendary heroes of Ireland.*

Brian Boru; you might have heard how he had a jacobin, and nearly had a scandaroon;[3] how "pigeons, mind you, must never be washed, only sprayed with rain water. And what's more, pigeons should be sprayed from the shoulders down—never the head, unless you want them to die of meningitis." What a scoundrel the man in Saint Rita's Terrace was, a low fellow who kept budgerigars[4] and had once actually said that pigeons were mere riffraff. How his father had stolen a sacred pigeon out of an Indian temple, when he was in Rangoon with the Royal Irish, and how the rajah chased him into the jungle for two miles trying to catch him. "And what's more, you should never dry a pigeon, unless, to be sure, you wrapped him up in warm flannel—which isn't the same thing." And anyway, what were budgerigars, only pups off parrots? "They are not even called budgerigars! They call them budgies—as if anyone would ever dare to call a pigeon a pidgy! Doesn't it show yeh?"

But whatever he spoke of, or whomever he spoke to, you might notice that he never spoke to one little runt of a man who always listened to him with a sly, sneering smile on his face. That was the club member whose Michael Collins the Second[5] had beaten Larry's Brian Boru in every race since the season began—beaten the bird that had laid its beak on Larry's heart.

Nobody knew the history of this Brian Boru. Larry's father swore he was the great-grandson of the Indian rajah's sacred pigeon, but that, of course, was a tall yarn. Whatever its pedigree, the bird was a marvel. Such speed! Such direction! Such a homer! A bird that had only one flaw! Time and again, when there was a race, Larry had seen that faint speck of joy come into the sky over the flat counties and the checkered market gardens where he lived, each time half an hour, at the very least, ahead of every other bird in the team; and on one occasion as much as fifty-eight minutes ahead of them, and that in the teeth of a thirty-mile gale.

For while other birds had to follow the guiding shore line, or the railway line that dodged the hills, Brian came sailing over mountaintop and moor like an arrow from the bow. Time and again, after greeting him with an adoring shout, Larry had gone tearing back down the lane to his tumble-down cottage, roaring to his da[6] to get out the decoys, and to light the primus stove for some new concoction whose smell was to tempt Brian Boru down to his loft. Back then to the bridge, waving to the sky, calling the bird by name as it came nearer and nearer to the parapet on which stood the club's timepiece—a clock with a glass front on which there was a blue-and-green painting of a waterfall. (A bird was not officially home until its owner had tipped the waterfall with its beak.)

But . . . time and again the one flaw told. Brian Boru would circle, and Brian Boru would sink, and inevitably Brian Boru would rise again. After about thirty minutes of this he would come down to the telegraph pole over Larry's back yard, and stay there until some slow coach[7] like Michael Collins the Second had walked off with the race. The bird so loved the air that it could not settle down.

"Oh!" Larry had been heard to moan, as he looked up at the telegraph pole. "Isn't it a sign? Isn't it a symbol? Isn't that poor Ireland all over again? First in the race. Fast as the lightning. But she won't settle down! That bird has too much spirit—he's a highflier—and aren't we the same? Always up in the air. Can't come down to earth." And then he would beseech the bird, as it looked down at him over its prima-donna chest with a bleary eye, rather like an old damp-nosed judge falling asleep on his bench: "O Brian Boru! Yeh sweet limb o' the divil, will you come down? Look! I've custards for yeh. I have yer loft lined with the sweetest straw." And he would start clucking and chortling at it. "Coordle-coordle-coordle, Brian Boru-u-u-yu." Or:

---

3 runts, tumblers, pouters, homers, racers . . . jacobin . . . scandaroon *Types of pigeons.*
4 budgerigars *Type of parakeet.*

5 Michael Collins the Second *A pigeon named after the famous Irish patriot.*
6 da *Short for dad.*

7 slow coach *Slang: a slow person or thing.*

"Tchook, tchuc, thc, thc, thc, thc. Ychook, thc, thc . . . oh, but I'll tchook you if I lay me hands on you, you criminal type from British India! Brian, my *darling,* aren't you *going* to come *down* to me?"

Brian would snuggle his beak on his chest, or make a contemptuous noise like a snore.

Then, that night at the bridge—for on race nights Larry simply had to talk about Brian Boru:

"It's not fair," Larry would protest. "The rules should be altered. That bird is not being given his due. That bird is suffering an injustice. Sure, it's only plain, honest reason. The bird is first home in every race —will any member of the club deny it?"

"No, Larry!" they would reply, appeasingly. "No! He's a grand bird, we all admit it, but a bird who won't settle is no good. And, for another thing, as we're sick and tired of telling you, supposing two birds come into sight at one and the same time, who the blazes is going to tell which one of them is first past the winning post—if there's going to be no winning post?"

"Ah!" Larry would roar. "But sure this bird is home hours before any of your so-called pigeons—cripples, I call them." And then, true to his happy, lighthearted nature, he could not help laughing and making a joke of it. Six feet two, and as innocent as a child. "Did I call them cripples? Cripples is too good for them. The one half of ye must be breeding yeer birds from a cross between penguins and pelicans!"

At which he would recover something of his natural good humor again, and go off chortling—a chortle that would die as he remembered what began it.

As the season approached its end the bird got fat, and Larry got thin; but the bird retained its speed, and Larry became slow-moving and sullen. Those who had always known him for a gay fellow shook their heads sadly over it. He still entered Brian for the races; but each Saturday, now, he

would barely stroll to the bridge when the regular two hours were passed since the birds had been released down the country. And when he saw the familiar speck in the sky he would actually turn his back on it.

It was the Easter Monday race that brought things to a head. That day a passing stranger said to him, as Brian Boru came into sight, "Whose bird is that?"

Larry, leaning with his back and two elbows on the parapet, gave an idle glance over his shoulder at the sky.

"Him? He's my bird. But—eh—he's not in the race, you know. He's what you might call a gentleman pigeon. He's doing it for fun. That bird, sir, could win any race he wanted to. But the way it is with him, he couldn't be bothered. Pride is what's wrong with that bird, sir. Pride! Pride, they say, made the angels fall. Maybe it did. I wish something would make that fellow fall."

Whereupon, Larry, as if a new understanding of the nature of pigeons had suddenly been vouchsafed to him, turned and gave the circling speck a terrible look. It was the look of a man struck by rejected love. Just at that moment it was that the man who owned Michael Collins the Second said the fatal word, as they all remembered and often recounted long after. He was a shrimp of a creature, a Tom Thumb of a man, who worked as a boots[8] in a hotel and bred his pigeons out of his tips. Seeing that look of misery in Larry's face he laughed and said, "Why don't you breed budgerigars, Larry? At least you could take them out of their cage and kiss 'em." The row of pigeon fanciers, staring up at the sky, chuckled. They did not see the look of hate in Larry's face, or notice the way he slouched away home to his cabin.

There, as he was at his tea, he suddenly heard the clatter of wings like tearing silk and, looking up through his cabin window, he saw his bird in its loft among the custards and dainties, and now and again it glanced

8 boots *Shoeshine boy.*

indifferently towards the cabin door. Pushing aside his cup, Larry said to his father—the old man recorded it when there was no use in recording it—"I wish to God, Da, you never gave me that pigeon. That bird isn't human. He despises me." And he put his head between his hands.

Later in the night, while the drizzle of rain fell on him, and the red reflections of the city illuminated the sky, he stood outside until his hair was pricked with the dew of the drizzle, talking now to himself, now to Brian; and though his father kept coming to the door, telling him not to be behaving like a child of two, Larry would not stir. He was like a boy hanging about under the window of his beloved.

"Is it the way you're faulting me?" he whispered. "Is there something you think I ought to do? But what is there I can do? I can't alter the rules, and you won't come down! I know it's a dishonor. It's a dishonor for both of us. I know that, Brian my darling, just as well as you know it. But I don't think it's my fault. I brought you up well. I did my best for you. I swear to God above this night I'd lay down my life for you. But, bar flying up in the air myself and bringing you down, what *can* I do?"

From the loft no reply, except the deep breathing of sleep.

Once more he entered the bird. Once more the pigeon scorned the earth. Once more the boots mentioned budgerigars, and this time he added that canaries can at least sing. Once more, Michael Collins won the race. That finished it. Larry went home, and on the following Monday he sold every bird, box, loft, packet of food, and medicine bottle that he possessed. With the money he bought an old Smith and Wesson, thirty-two bore, and five rounds of ammunition from a former pal of the I.R.A.[9] Then, for the last time, he entered the bird, saw it come, as always, first of the team up against the clouds

that floated like bridesmaids over the hedgerows; saw through the veils of the sun how Brian swerved, and circled, and sank . . . and rose again; and did so his usual number of times before making for the inaccessible perch on the telegraph pole. While the dozen heads along the bridge shook their commiseration, Larry gripped his revolver in his pocket, and waited for the boots to laugh. The boots laughed. At that Larry's body took on the old fighting slouch; he pulled his hat savagely down over one eye; he buttoned his coat across his chest; he became the old down-looking gunman he had been fifteen years ago when he was in the I.R.A. Then with a roll of his shoulders like a militiaman, a trick learned from his soldier da, he looked at the boots between the shoulder blades, put on the final bit of the gunman's manner—the ominously casual strolling gait—and walked quietly down the lane. There he found Brian on the pole.

"Brian," he whispered, but without hope, "will you come down to me now?"

The bird rose and flew away, circled and came back again.

"So yeh won't come down?" whispered Larry out of the corner of his mouth. The bird looked haughtily over the lane roofs, as if contemplating another circle of flight. Before it could stir the shot cracked. With one head-sinking tumble it fell with a plop to the ground. Larry stooped, lifted the hot, twitching body in his palms, gave it one agonized look, and pelted back to the bridge, roaring like a maniac.

"By the Lord Almighty!" they said, when they saw him coming, screeching, with the bird in his palms. "Brian Boru is after winning at last!"

Shouldering their cluster right and left, Larry snapped the beak to the glass of the clock, displayed the celluloid ring on the stiff ankle, and shouted, pale as the clouds, "Has he won?"

It was only then that they saw the blood

oozing down between his trembling fingers; but before they could tell him what they thought of him they saw the mad look in his eyes, and the way his hand stole to his pocket.

"Well?" yelled Larry at the boots. "Has he won? Or has he not won? Or maybe you'll say there's a rule that a dead bird can't win a race?"

"He's w-w-won, all right," trembled the boots.

"Gimme his prize!" said Larry.

In fear they gave it to him. It was a new dovecot, painted a lovely green. (*Eau de canal,*[10] the boots called it afterwards, being the sarcastic brute he was.) Larry took the dovecot, and with the reddening beak hang-ing from his fist he slouched away. On Monday he sold the dovecot, had the bird stuffed and put in the window of his lane cabin for the world to see.

You never see Larry Dunne at the canal bridge now. He walks moodily by himself along the towpaths, idly flickering a little twig against the hedges: or he sits with his father at the other side of the fire, learning off bits from his favorite book, *Who's Who,* or he sits gazing into the dancing devils of flame. The sky outside is lurid with the lights of Dublin. In the little curtained window, the pigeon looks with two glassy eyes out over the damp market gardens and the heavy, odorous night fields at the bloody sky.

For Discussion

1 What kind of young man is Larry Dunne? What is the difference between his behavior when he is alone and when he is among his friends? Is he a simple man? How does he change during the story?

2 It was a commonplace of medieval thought that Fortune was like a wheel, and that whatever was exalted would have to be cast down as the wheel turned. The only way to escape the destructive cycle of Fortune was never to place yourself in a position from which you might fall, or in which you might fail. Does this apply to Larry Dunne? Is Brian Boru the only reason for his despair?

3 What does Larry mean when he says of Brian Boru, "Isn't it a sign? Isn't it a symbol? Isn't that poor Ireland all over again?" What are the qualities of Ireland that Larry sees in the bird? Does the bird reflect any of the qualities of Larry himself?

4 What irony is there in Larry's solution to his problem? Why does he have the pigeon stuffed and mounted? Does Larry enjoy his misery? Is it possible that he created his own grief in the form of Brian Boru?

5 The author says that Larry fell for the same reason that Adam fell. What does he mean? We have already mentioned the Fall and the Garden of Eden in discussing two earlier stories in this section, "The Ring" and "Like a Bad Dream." Why do you suppose it is so easy to see analogies between the Bible story and so many things that happen in the modern world? To put the question another way: why do writers refer to this story so often, either directly or indirectly?

10 Eau de canal *French: "canal water." The boots implies that the dovecot was the same color as the water in the canal.*

One of the most quoted remarks of modern times is that of the English historian Lord Acton: "All power corrupts, but absolute power corrupts absolutely." This story by a contemporary Polish writer seems to be an illustration of Lord Acton's formula. The story is both grim and comic. It takes a very real fact of life in the twentieth century and pushes it just a bit beyond reality.

Julian Kawalec

I Kill Myself

Today I shall destroy the Zeta bomb. I shall do it this evening, when I begin my tour of duty in the army laboratory. Today I have achieved the capacity for sacrifice; I realized that when I looked at the slender, mournful boughs of the trees; I can't say why it was just at the moment when I noticed the trees.

I am walking along an avenue in the park. I feel a keen rawness in the air. People go past me. They pay no attention to me. They don't know that I, a homely-looking man in a gray raincoat, with big ears and a mole on the cheek, am capable of a great self-sacrifice; that this evening I shall turn the key in the door of an iron safe, open it, and take out something which looks like a large goose egg. That's the Zeta bomb. The distance between the contact pin and the critical point of the bomb is three millimeters. That is the distance to which Professor Lombard set the contact pin when he solicitously laid the Zeta in its plush case.

The Zeta rests like a child in swaddling clothes; today I shall destroy that steel child, for today I have achieved the capacity to make this great sacrifice of myself.

I must do it, I must free humanity from the terrible nightmare and that powerful mite. Why should a tiny steel pin have power of life and death over people? . . . So long as it doesn't touch the critical point, the sun will go on shining; when it does touch, night will fall, all men will die, and the birds will drop like meteors. By the force of its explosion the Zeta bomb exceeds the most powerful hydrogen bomb a billion times. If it were to explode, the result would not be death, for death is an equal partner with life —one can argue with it, one can quarrel and be reconciled with it. In comparison with the consequences of an explosion of Zeta, death is something anodyne. The term "death" doesn't apply to the effects of that. One must create a new word for it.

I'm walking along the park avenues, waiting for the evening. When evening comes, I shall destroy Professor Lombard's "iron child." I shall unscrew the contact pin; I shall throw the bomb into a marsh, and the pin into a river some five kilometers distant from the marsh. The Zeta and the pin will never meet again. And if they don't meet, the world will continue to exist. I shall burn the documents giving the sketches and specifications of the bomb, and tread the ashes into the ground. Professor Lombard will not live long enough to give birth to a second "iron child."

I shall destroy the Zeta bomb. I shall do it for the sake of the trees, the animals, the birds, the people, the insects. I shall do it for my own sake, and for the sake of that young man with black hair who is sitting on a bench hidden among the trees, waiting for a girl; for you, gnarled elm, and for your inhabitant the woodpecker, and for you, black worm corkscrewing through the earth.

In the midst of all these people and trees I feel an enormous and oppressive loneliness. I cannot tell anyone what I'm planning to do. I'm afraid they might stop me from destroying the bomb. But after all, great sacrifice demands great loneliness. If I talk about it, I'm sharing it with others, reducing its greatness. But the feeling of loneliness doesn't weaken my determination.

The sky withdraws from the far end of the avenue, a sign that evening will soon be coming on. I leave the park. Today I shall walk to the laboratory. I take a road which shows up white among the small houses and crisscrossed fallow land. On my left someone is singing; on my right a gentle breeze is noisily tousling withered branches. After a moment the singing and the sound of the wind both stop. All is still.

Beyond a small pine wood I come to the first control barrier. They shine a beam of light toward me. They've recognized me. The guards know the senior laboratory assistant very well; he's a quiet sort and docile, with large ears and a mole on the cheek. I pass the first control barrier; the road is as smooth as a table top; the army laboratory has good roads leading to it. In a clump of leafy trees I come to the second control barrier. They pick me out with three beams of light; as they did so a single bird woke up in a tree and began to twitter. They scrutinize me closely, though they know I'm the senior laboratory assistant and initiated into all the secrets. Beyond the second control barrier the road passes underground. Now I'm walking along a lighted tunnel. The side walls of the tunnel have innumerable little windows, through which guards poke their heads. One must walk steadily and calmly along the tunnel; the best thing is to whistle.

In a small hall, brilliantly lit, I show my identity papers, then I enter a narrow corridor. A tall guard opens an iron door for me. Now I'm in the anteroom of the laboratory. I am alone. I set to work. I bend over the secret drawer which contains the keys; it is known only to Professor Lombard, the commander-in-chief, and myself.

I pick up the key. In the third room of the laboratory I disconnect the alarm signal fixed to the iron safe. I open a drawer and take the Zeta bomb out of its plush case. Zeta is cold and slippery. I could destroy it here, in the laboratory; I could thaw it out; but that would take time, and the three junior laboratory assistants will be arriving in a few minutes. I conceal the bomb and the sketches in the broad pocket of my light raincoat, which I hang over my arm. I telephone to Professor Lombard, using a one-figure number known only to me and the commander-in-chief. I tell him I've forgotten to bring important reagents from the store and I must go for them myself at once.

In a minute or two I am on my way. I am not detained at the control points. The commander of the guard has been informed that it is a question of getting important reagents swiftly.

I have passed the last control barrier. Now there are no more lights. I turn off the main road. I'm going across flat, soft ground, in the direction of an alder grove.

Surely this must be a sown field. It is night. Cold. I put on my raincoat. I have it, I have the bomb; with every step I take I feel it knocking against my ribs. Now and again I put my hand into the raincoat pocket to make sure it's there. It is, it is. I touch it with my hand. It is cold, slippery. Professor Lombard polished it, smoothed it. He gave it the gleam of a monstrous distorting mirror. Under my forefinger I feel the tiny head of the contact pin. All I have to do is to slip back the safety catch, press that little head, and then only invisible, inchoate fragments will be left of everything. However, the words "visible" and "invisible" wouldn't have any meaning whatever then. But that will never happen. Quite soon now I shall throw the Zeta bomb into the marsh. I shall throw it with all my strength, so that it flies into the very middle, where the mud is thinnest, where it will sink most easily and swiftly. I shall throw the contact pin into the river. Who will ever find a pin only a little thicker than a needle?

And then? Then I must go into hiding. I must find a good hiding place, for they are sure to search for me. I dare say the whole of the police force, the special military departments and forces, and the secret service will all be called in to search for me. I can already see, already hear, the orders being issued, the instructions intercrossing; how they'll be shouting, how they'll be whispering, all to find out where I am. But the great sacrifice to which I have dedicated myself cares nothing for such things. The great sacrifice must even require such things. And yet the great sacrifice doesn't require that after I've destroyed the bomb I should voluntarily and even frivolously put myself in the hands of those who have produced it. No, I cannot give them that pleasure. I cannot do anything which would give those wicked people the least satisfaction. And so, after I've destroyed Professor Lombard's "iron child," I must conceal myself thoroughly. The people, for whom I am making this great sacrifice, will not defend me. It will be a long time before they even learn of my exploit, before they have any realization of its benefits. They will stop to consider the matter; they will discuss, doubt, suspect; they will pluck up courage and succumb to cowardice; and maybe they will be ready to come to my defense only when it's too late. So I must seek out a good hiding place. But if they come upon my tracks, if I hear their steps, the clatter of belts hung about with weapons, the rustle of uniforms, and the snorting of highly sensitive, perfectly trained dogs, shall I leave my hiding place with my hands up? Does my self-sacrifice call for putting up a valiant resistance or for valiant renunciation of resistance? For valiant resistance, for resistance. But my sacrifice connotes prudent resistance, which in certain circumstances demands that I should hide from the enemy, should deceive the enemy. So I shall not go out to meet the police with my hands up. Rather, the moment they see me I shall spring at the throat of the nearest policeman. If I had a revolver I could kill several before I died. If I had a machine gun I could mow down several dozen from my hiding place.

The ground over which I'm now walking is no longer even and soft; it is hard and crowded with little tussocks. So it must be quite close to the alder grove. I think I see a dark patch in front. Yes, that surely is the alder grove. The marsh lies just beyond it. I am coming across more and more of those little tussocks. My steps are inevitably becoming broken, and short. At times my feet slip farther down than I expect. Then my body is subjected to an involuntary jolt. Then Zeta strikes more violently against my ribs. It reminds me more insistently of its presence. I swiftly thrust my hand into my raincoat pocket. It's there, it's there. It's not so cold now as it was, it's rather warmer. Its shape also isn't so ugly. But it's a monster threatening something which cannot be called death or silence, or by any word from a modern dictionary. It's a tiny, sleeping monster.

The dark patch grows blacker. Now the alder grove is very close. All around is still.

Now I can hear the gentle murmur of the trees. I am in the alder grove. I'm walking along a narrow path. The trees surround me with a friendly air; they're whispering something to me. The Zeta bomb must be destroyed so that the alders can live. Beyond the alder grove the ground turns soft again. But it's not the softness of a sown field, it's the springy softness of India rubber. I am conscious of the marsh; I can hear it. It too has its voice. The voice of the marsh is like the heavy breathing of a dying man. I can still go on for the time being; my feet are not sinking in yet; I know I shall go on safely as far as the first clump of tall spear grass. So now only minutes are left. The ground is getting softer and softer. Now I am at the spot, by a clump of spear grass. I hurriedly thrust my hand into my raincoat pocket. The bomb is warm. I hold its warm, smooth metal a long time in my palm. Then I cautiously take Zeta out of my pocket. Now it is lying on my palm. And so, in a moment *that* will be happening. In a moment the world will be freed from multitudinous death. But the world knows nothing about it. The world is quiet, indifferent, and sluggish. Is it possible that such a great deed can be accomplished in such great silence? I put the thumb and forefinger of my right hand on the safety catch. But just as I do so I hear a loud rustling. I seize the safety catch between my fingers and release it. I'm being pursued. No, it's only the wind running over the reeds.... But if it were indeed a pursuit, if dogs picking up my trail began to bark at the edge of the marsh, if the first policemen were to put in an appearance ... after all, I could threaten them with the bomb. I could shout to them: "Halt. I've got the Zeta bomb in my hand. With the safety catch released. The contact pin is one millimeter away from the critical point. If you advance a single step I shall press the pin. And don't try shooting at me, for if I fall the bomb will be given a violent jolt and

it will explode. You'll perish!" But I wouldn't be the only one to perish. And not only would they perish. Millions of innocent people would perish. Such reasoning is not worthy of a man who has decided to sacrifice himself. And yet, the police will not move one step if I threaten them with the bomb. They're cowards. So nothing will happen to the world. My courage, which should accompany my sacrifice, will not suffer either, for I shall threaten the police, not because they're afraid, but because they're in the service of those who produce the bomb, those I hate. So that threat and that hatred should be included in the program of sacrifice. I cling to this thought; I consider it fine and pure, for I can hold the makers of the Zeta bomb, and their assistants, under threat, I can do as I like with them. That's a wise sacrifice. I can command them to march to a hollow between hills and leave them there, and starve them. I can send Professor Lombard there, and even the chief of staff himself. I'm grateful to that rustle in the reeds. It has brought about a judicious change in my thinking.

I shan't destroy the Zeta bomb today. Pity I didn't bring the plush box also when I brought it away, I'd have had something in which to keep it. I shall keep Zeta and devote it to the service of the good. I'm astonished that I could ever have forgotten the great significance of the bomb in this kind of service.

Blind self-sacrifice made me regard it only as the source of a great evil. Prudence, which I now associate with the desire for sacrifice, makes it possible for me to consider Zeta from various aspects. With Zeta's aid I can set the world free from Zeta. By using it as a threat, I can order the laboratories in which it was to have serial production to be destroyed. I can render Professor Lombard harmless, and all the experts on the bomb, and its guards. I can do this if I screw the contact pin to a distance of one millimeter from the critical point. The threat of its explosion will compel them to submit and be absolutely obedient to me. With Zeta in my possession I can destroy every wicked man. With Zeta I can do much, I can do almost everything. Why do I say "almost"? I'm in a position not only to achieve general reforms, but to break into the life of every man on this earth and arbitrarily change it. If I wish, the wealthiest of merchants will hand over his store to me. If I wish, Mrs. Emilia will forsake the husband she loves, will bow to me and go wandering about the world. If I wish, the daughter of the chief of staff will present herself naked to me. If I give the order, the Nestor[1] of science will shave off his beard and climb a tree in the city park in broad daylight. I imagine the scene and laugh: the Nestor of science climbing to the top of the tree with the agility of a monkey. I already see people coming from all over the world and bowing to me and handing me all sorts of articles and titles. One gives me a sumptuous villa at the seaside; another proposes that I should accept a doctorate of all sciences; a third humbly explains that kingship is the finest form of government and that I am highly suited to be king, for I have a fine bearing and profound intelligence. Someone tells me I have very handsome ears.

I try to cast out these thoughts. For I am to serve the good. I must set about the destruction of evil. That's why I'm keeping Zeta. In order to destroy evil I must divide the people into wicked and good.

I can do that: I shall be the supreme judge. But why the future tense? I am the supreme judge. There is no one higher than I. I touch Zeta. I stroke it. How beautiful it has become, how smooth and pleasant it is, how brilliantly it shines. I press Zeta to my heart, I kiss it. What am I saying, what am I doing? But why ask? I'm doing and performing that which ought to be done; all this is included within my enlarged, human program of sacrifice. I cannot hestitate—I should be ridiculous if I hesitated. I am Caesar, Napoleon, Alexander the Great; I am the supreme judge, I am God, I surpass God. I shout: "I am God." The trees already know; they bow down to the ground. The human beings don't know it yet. I hurry back to the city by the shortest route. To judgment. I shall judge. All human beings are wicked; they must all be destroyed. I alone am good. I ALONE AM GOOD, FOR I POSSESS ZETA.

Harry Stevens/TRANSLATOR

For Discussion

1 Is this story believable? Would any modern nation which had a Zeta bomb allow it to be so easily stolen by a single man? Does this matter at all for the purpose of this story?

2 To whom is the narrator of the story talking? Is he mad or sane?

3 How does the narrator's purpose change after he has the bomb in his possession? What important decision does he make after he gets out into the countryside?

4 Science has not developed a bomb as powerful as Zeta. Do you think that a nation which had the necessary scientific knowledge would go ahead and develop it? If a nation did develop such a bomb, what public justification would it give?

5 The Zeta bomb is only fiction, invented for the purposes of this story. But what real things in our world is it like?

6 Can you think of any examples from the history of men or organizations which began with highly idealistic purposes, then changed after they achieved power?

1 Nestor *The oldest and wisest of the Greek generals who fought at Troy.*

Australian
Bark painting
Australian News and Information Bureau

Unit Three Fables & Legends

About a hundred years ago some writers and critics began to talk about "Art for Art's sake." This concept represented a sharp break with the past, for throughout the centuries writers and readers had taken it for granted that literature did not exist *solely* for itself, but had some religious, or moral, or political purpose. Of course, all artists wanted to make their work beautiful in some sense; to give it a shape or form that would be delightful or interesting. At the same time, writers felt that their work was *saying* something about life. And indeed the doctrine of Art for Art's sake has found more takers among critics than among writers, most of whom still go on thinking that they have something to say.

Exactly *how* poems or plays or stories say something about life is a complicated question. Literature may explain, or praise, or condemn, or explore the mysteries of the universe and of human behavior; or it may combine all of these purposes. It is comparatively easy to see the general purpose of some books. Milton's epic *Paradise Lost* is about the Creation, the Garden of Eden, the Fall of Adam and Eve. It is a complex theological argument in the form of a poem, but Milton knew what his purpose was: to "justify the ways of God to men." With other works it is harder to find a moral; or, if we attempt to state a moral, we find ourselves greatly oversimplifying the literature. What messages can we find in Shakespeare's plays? Yet surely Shakespeare would have been surprised to hear that all he was doing was making marvelous constructions of words which ask us to *believe* nothing.

In other words, for centuries writers intended their work to have some sort of *didactic* or teaching function; but this is very different from saying that art exists primarily as something through which we hunt for messages or formulas by which to live. One kind of literature, however, has always had a frankly didactic purpose: the fable.

The fable is one of the oldest kinds of literature, though not as old as some kinds of religious literature such as the hymn or the myth. Fables appear in the oral traditions of all peoples, as a way of embodying simple wisdom, such as *"Pride goes before a fall."* Since primitive people live very close to Nature and to the world of animals, fables are often about animals, but not always. Usually they are quite short. Often, but not always, they begin or end by stating clearly the moral for which they exist. Sometimes, however, the moral is left unstated, though the meaning is clear.

Another very early form of literature is the legend, a story about a people's past, often about a heroic figure, such as a king. Before a story takes on the true stature of a legend it has to be told and retold thousands of times until it becomes part of a people's general culture. For thousands of years men made no distinction between legends and history, if we take history to mean something for which we have evidence. People simply believed traditional stories without wondering about whether or not they were "true." Many legends are in fact based on historical events. Homer's epic tales about the Trojan war, for example, were not history in our sense of the word, but there had really been a Trojan war and certain legends had grown up about it. Even rather modern history, such as the lives of Washington and Lincoln, are often treated in a legendary way.

Most modern literature no longer has the surface appearance of the fable, the myth, or the legend. Modern literature tends to be more complex and to find subtle or ironic ways to disguise its didactic, heroic, or religious purposes. However, it would be hard to find any writing, no matter how sophisticated, which does not have its roots in these earliest forms of literature.

Almost all cultures—African, American Indian, Asian —have animal fables. The ones with which we are most familiar were gathered together or given shape by the legendary Greek writer Aesop. None of Aesop's original versions of the fables have been preserved; we know them through versions written centuries later by the Roman poet Phaedrus. About fifteen centuries after the time of Phaedrus the French poet La Fontaine rewrote the fables in polished French verse. His versions of the fables contain a sharpness all his own. La Fontaine's wit brought the traditional stories far from their beginnings as the folktales of preliterate peoples.

Jean de La Fontaine

The Fox and the Crow

A crow, perched debonairly on a branch,
  Was holding a cheese he'd found—by
    chance.
Along came a fox. He sniffed that cheese,
  And he spoke to its owner in words
    like these:

"Good morning, good morning, dear
  Brother Crow!
  My, you look fine! I've never seen
    you so—
So—*handsome*. Yes! I mean every word
  of it!
  And your lovely voice! Won't you
    sing a bit?"

The crow was enchanted—he could see
  no choice
  But give the fox a sample of his voice.
He opened his beak, and—cheese, good-
  bye!
  The fox grabbed it up without batting
    an eye.

Said the fox: "As a payment for what
  you've lost
  I'll give you a lesson worth twice the
    cost:
Flattery's a game for two, my dear,
  One to talk—and another to hear."

George Kearns/TRANSLATOR

For Discussion

1 In a sentence, state the moral of this story. Does it apply any less today than it did in the times of Aesop, Phaedrus, or La Fontaine?

2 Why is the crow a good choice for the fox's victim? Would a lark or a robin serve as effectively? An owl? Why not? What characteristics of the crow make his surrender to flattery so funny?

3 Animal fables, of course, are not about animals, but people. What kinds of people is La Fontaine satirizing?

Death has been portrayed in literature not just as a state or condition, but as a legendary or mythic creature. In the art of the Middle Ages, we often find Death pictured as a skeleton wearing a shroud and carrying a scythe. Here the great German poet Goethe uses the old folktale of the Erl-King, a ghastly crowned figure visible only to the victim he entices to his dark kingdom. The speaker in the third, fifth, and seventh stanzas is the Erl-King himself.

Johann Wolfgang von Goethe

The Erl-King

O who rides by night thro' the woodland
   so wild?
It is the fond father embracing his child;
And close the boy nestles within his
   loved arm,
To hold himself fast, and to keep himself
   warm.
"O father, see yonder! see yonder!" he
   says;
"My boy, upon what dost thou fearfully
   gaze?"
"O 'tis the Erl-King with his crown and
   his shroud."
"No, my son, it is but a dark wreath of
   the cloud."

"O come and go with me, thou loveliest
   child;
By many a gay sport shall thy time be
   beguiled;
My mother keeps for thee full many a
   fair toy,
And many a fine flower shall she pluck
   for my boy."

"O father, my father, and did you not
   hear
The Erl-King whisper so low in my ear?"
"Be still, my heart's darling—my child,
   be at ease;
It was but the wild blast as it sung thro'
   the trees."

"O wilt thou go with me, thou loveliest
boy?
My daughter shall tend thee with care
and with joy;
She shall bear thee so lightly thro' wet
and thro' wild,
And press thee, and kiss thee, and sing
to my child."

"O father, my father, and saw you not
plain
The Erl-King's pale daughter glide past
thro' the rain?"
"O yes, my loved treasure, I knew it full
soon;
It was the gray willow that danced to
the moon."

"O come and go with me, no longer
delay,
Or else, silly child, I will drag thee
away."
"O father! O father! now, now, keep
your hold,
The Erl-King has seized me—his grasp
is so cold!"

Sore trembled the father; he spurr'd thro'
the wild,
Clasping close to his bosom his shuddering child;
He reaches his dwelling in doubt and
dread
But, clasp'd to his bosom, the infant was
dead.

Sir Walter Scott/TRANSLATOR

For Discussion

1 Why doesn't the father hear the Erl-King's
voice? Does he suspect that something
is wrong? How does he show his suspicion? How does he try to defeat the
power of the Erl-King?

2 What are the three arguments the Erl-
King gives to the child? What does the
last of these arguments show about the
true nature of the Erl-King?

3 How does the physical setting of the
poem add dramatic power?

4 Describe the Erl-King in the poem. Is
he proud? Does he abuse his power?
What attitude toward death does the
poem contain?

5 What stories still told to children are
similar to the legend of the Erl-King?

Every once in a while some educators, librarians, and child psychologists raise the question as to whether or not some of the most famous nursery rhymes and fairy tales should be told to children. They argue that these tales are really violent, bloody, and horrible and may have an adverse effect on young minds. Red Riding Hood and her Grandmother are eaten by the Wolf, then the Wolf is hacked up with an ax. Hansel and Gretel only narrowly escape from the Witch's oven.

Of course every argument has two sides, and there are other educators, librarians, and child psychologists who say that this is silly, that children need fantasy tales, that these stories are a vital part of our heritage, and so forth.

Familiarity often makes it difficult to see things as they are. In the case of many fairy tales, we have come to think of them as merely pretty and amusing stories. They are not. Many of these tales were not originally written for children: they are an expression of the mind of the "folk" and reflect a world full of fears and terrors, even if they usually work out to a happy ending. This becomes clear as soon as we look, not at the familiar "Jack and the Beanstalk," but at the less familiar folktale "The Robber-Bridegroom."

The Brothers Grimm

The Robber-Bridegroom

There was once a miller who had a pretty daughter; and when she was grown up, he thought to himself, "If a seemly man should come to ask her for his wife, I will give her to him that she may be taken care of." Now it so happened that one did come, who seemed to be very rich, and behaved very well; and as the miller saw no reason to find fault with him, he said he should have his daughter. Yet the maiden did not love him quite so well as a bride ought to love her bridegroom, but, on the other hand, soon began to feel a kind of inward shuddering whenever she saw or thought of him.

One day he said to her, "Why do you not come and see my home, since you are to be my bride?" "I do not know where your house is," said the girl. "'Tis out there," said her bridegroom, "yonder in the dark green wood." Then she began to try and avoid going, and said, "But I cannot find the way thither." "Well, but you must come and see me next Sunday," said the bridegroom; "I have asked some guests to meet you, and that you may find your way through the wood, I will strew ashes for you along the path."

When Sunday came and the maiden was to go out, she felt very much troubled, and took care to put on two pockets, and filled them with peas and beans. She soon came to the wood, and found her path strewed with ashes; so she followed the track, and at every step threw a pea on the right and a bean on the left side of the road; and thus she journeyed on the whole day till she came to a house which stood in the middle of the dark wood. She saw no one within, and all was quite still, till on a sudden she heard a voice cry,

> "Turn again, bonny bride!
>   Turn again home!
> Haste from the robber's den,
>   Haste away home!"

She looked around, and saw a little bird sitting in a cage that hung over the door; and he flapped his wings, and again she heard him cry,

> "Turn again, bonny bride!
>   Turn again home!
> Haste from the robber's den,
>   Haste away home!"

However, the bride went in, and roamed along from one room to another, and so over all the house; but it was quite empty, and not a soul could she see. At last she came to a room where a very, very old woman was sitting. "Pray, can you tell me, my good woman," said she, "if my bridegroom lives here?" "Ah! my dear child!" said the old woman, "you are come to fall into the trap laid for you: your wedding can only be with Death, for the robber will surely take away your life; if I do not save you, you are lost!" So she hid the bride behind a large cask, and then said to her, "Do not stir or move yourself at all, lest some harm should befall you; and when the robbers are asleep we will run off; I have long wished to get away."

She had hardly done this when the robbers came in, and brought another young maiden with them that had been ensnared like the bride. Then they began to feast and drink, and were deaf to her shrieks and groans: and they gave her some wine to drink, three glasses, one of white, one of red, and one of yellow; upon which she fainted and fell down dead. Now the bride began

to grow very uneasy behind the cask, and thought that she too must die in her turn. Then the one that was to be her bridegroom saw that there was a gold ring on the little finger of the maiden they had murdered; and as he tried to snatch it off, it flew up in the air and fell down again behind the cask just in the bride's lap. So he took a light and searched about all round the room for it, but could not find any thing; and another of the robbers said, "Have you looked behind the large cask yet?" "Pshaw!" said the old woman, "come, sit still and eat your supper now, and leave the ring alone till tomorrow; it won't run away, I'll warrant."

So the robbers gave up the search, and went on with their eating and drinking; but the old woman dropped a sleeping-draught into their wine, and they laid themselves down and slept, and snored roundly. And when the bride heard this, she stepped out from behind the cask; and as she was forced to walk over the sleepers, who were lying about on the floor, she trembled lest she should awaken some of them. But heaven aided her, so that she soon got through her danger; and the old woman went upstairs with her, and they both ran away from the murderous den. The ashes that had been strewed were now all blown away, but the peas and beans had taken root and were springing up, and showed her the way by the light of the moon. So they walked the whole night, and in the morning reached the mill, when the bride told her father all that had happened to her.

As soon as the day arrived when the wedding was to take place, the bridegroom came; and the miller gave orders that all his friends and relations should be asked to the feast. And as they were all sitting at table, one of them proposed that each of the guests should tell some tale. Then the bridegroom said to the bride, when it came to her turn, "Well, my dear, do you know nothing? come, tell us some story." "Yes," answered she, "I can tell you a dream that I dreamt. I once thought I was going through a wood, and went on and on till I came to a house where there was not a soul to be seen, but a bird in a cage that cried out twice,

> 'Turn again, bonny bride!
>   Turn again home!
> Haste from the robber's den,
>   Haste away home!'

—I only dreamt that, my love. Then I went through all the rooms, which were quite empty, until I came to a room where there sat a very old woman; and I said to her, 'Does my bridegroom live here?' but she answered, 'Ah! my dear child! you have fallen into a murderer's snare; your bridegroom will surely kill you';—I only dreamt that, my love. But she hid me behind a large cask;

and hardly had she done this, when the robbers came in, dragging a young woman along with them; then they gave her three kinds of wine to drink, white, red, and yellow, till she fell dead upon the ground;—I only dreamt that, my love. After they had done this, one of the robbers saw that there was a gold ring on her little finger, and snatched at it; but it flew up to the ceiling, and then fell behind the great cask just where I was, and into my lap; and here is the ring!" At these words she brought out the ring and showed it to the guests.

When the robber saw all this, and heard what she said, he grew as pale as the ashes with fright, and wanted to run off; but the guests held him fast and gave him up to justice, so that he and all his gang met with the due reward of their wickedness.

For Discussion

1 How deep is the characterization in this story? What do we know about the bride? The robber-bridegroom? The old woman? As you read the story, did you have any desire to know more about the characters?

2 What about the plot? In what ways is it filled with improbable events?

3 Most readers will recognize that this is a fairy tale, and will accept the plot and and characters as appropriate to this type of story. But what would happen if the balance were upset? That is, suppose the characters were made more realistic, more complex. What, then, would happen to the plot? Would it still be acceptable?

4 Some readers might describe this tale as a scary fantasy with a happy ending. Can you see anything deeper in it? In spite of its improbability, does it project any fears or fantasies which are common to us all?

S. Y. Agnon was born in Poland in 1888 and settled in Palestine in 1908, long before it became the modern nation of Israel. For material, Agnon drew upon the life of the Jewish people, using their folklore for stories, parables, fables, and proverbs.

The "Fable of the Goat" is an original modern story, but it might just as well be a version of a tale thousands of years old. It carries with it both the humor and the suffering of the Jewish people and their longing to return to the Promised Land.

S. Y. Agnon
The Fable of the Goat

The tale is told of an old man who groaned from his heart. The doctors were sent for, and they advised him to drink goat's milk. He went out and bought a she-goat and brought her into his home. Not many days passed before the goat disappeared. They went out to search for her but did not find her. She was not in the yard and not in the garden, not on the roof of the House of Study and not by the spring, not in the hills and not in the fields. She tarried several days and then returned by herself; and when she returned, her udder was full of a great deal of milk, the taste of which was as the taste of Eden. Not just once, but many times she disappeared from the house. They would go out in search for her and would not find her until she returned by herself with her udder full of milk that was sweeter than honey and whose taste was the taste of Eden.

One time the old man said to his son, "My son, I desire to know where she goes and whence she brings this milk which is sweet to my palate and a balm to all my bones."

His son said to him, "Father, I have a plan."

He said to him, "What is it?"

The son got up and brought a length of cord. He tied it to the goat's tail.

His father said to him, "What are you doing, my son?"

He said to him, "I am tying a cord to the goat's tail, so that when I feel a pull on it I will know that she has decided to leave, and I can catch the end of the cord and follow her on her way."

The old man nodded his head and said to him, "My son, if your heart is wise, my heart too will rejoice."

The youth tied the cord to the goat's tail and minded it carefully. When the goat set off, he held the cord in his hand and did not let it slacken until the goat was well on her way and he was following her. He was dragged along behind her until he came to a cave. The goat went into the cave, and the youth followed her, holding the cord. They walked thus for an hour or two, or maybe even a day or two. The goat wagged her tail and bleated, and the cave came to an end.

When they emerged from the cave, the youth saw lofty mountains, and hills full of the choicest fruit, and a fountain of living waters that flowed down from the mountains; and the wind wafted all manner of perfumes. The goat climbed up a tree by clutching at the ribbed leaves. Carob fruits full of honey dropped from the tree, and she ate of the carobs and drank of the garden's fountain.

The youth stood and called to the wayfarers: "I adjure you, good people, tell me where I am, and what is the name of this place?"

They answered him, "You are in the Land of Israel, and you are close by Safed."

The youth lifted up his eyes to the heavens and said, "Blessed be the Omnipresent, blessed be He who has brought me to the Land of Israel." He kissed the soil and sat down under the tree.

He said, "Until the day breathe and the shadows flee away, I shall sit on the hill under this tree. Then I shall go home and bring my father and mother to the Land of Israel." As he was sitting thus and feasting his eyes on the holiness of the Land of Israel, he heard a voice proclaiming:

"Come, let us go out to greet the Sabbath Queen."

And he saw men like angels, wrapped in white shawls, with boughs of myrtle in their hands, and all the houses were lit with a great many candles. He perceived that the eve of Sabbath would arrive with the darkening, and that he would not be able to return. He uprooted a reed and dipped it in gallnuts, from which the ink for the writing of Torah scrolls is made. He took a piece of paper and wrote a letter to his father:

"From the ends of the earth I lift up my voice in song to tell you that I have come in peace to the Land of Israel. Here I sit, close by Safed, the holy city, and I imbibe its sanctity. Do not inquire how I arrived here but hold onto this cord which is tied to the goat's tail and follow the footsteps of the goat; then your journey will be secure, and you will enter the Land of Israel."

The youth rolled up the note and placed it in the goat's ear. He said to himself: When she arrives at Father's house, Father will pat her on the head, and she will flick her ears. The note will fall out, Father will pick it up and read what is written on it. Then he will take up the cord and follow the goat to the Land of Israel.

The goat returned to the old man, but she did not flick her ears, and the note did not fall. When the old man saw that the goat had returned without his son, he clapped his hands to his head and began to cry and weep and wail, "My son, my son, where are you? My son, would that I might die in your stead, my son, my son!"

So he went, weeping and mourning over his son, for he said, "An evil beast has devoured him, my son is assuredly rent in pieces!"

And he refused to be comforted, saying, "I will go down to my grave in mourning for my son."

And whenever he saw the goat, he would say, "Woe to the father who banished his son, and woe to her who drove him from the world!"

The old man's mind would not be at peace until he sent for the butcher to slaughter the goat. The butcher came and slaughtered the goat. As they were skinning her, the note fell out of her ear. The old man picked up the note and said, "My son's handwriting!"

When he had read all that his son had written, he clapped his hands to his head and cried, "*Vay! Vay!* Woe to the man who robs himself of his own good fortune, and woe to the man who requites good with evil!"

He mourned over the goat many days and refused to be comforted, saying, "Woe to me, for I could have gone up to the Land of Israel in one bound, and now I must suffer out my days in this exile!"

Since that time the mouth of the cave has been hidden from the eye, and there is no longer a short way. And that youth, if he has not died, shall bear fruit in his old age, full of sap and richness, calm and peaceful in the Land of the Living.

Barney Rubin/TRANSLATOR

For Discussion

1 What did the old man do that was wrong?
2 La Fontaine's "The Fox and the Crow" ended with a clear statement of its moral. Agnon's fable does not. If you had to supply a moral for it, what would that moral be? There is no single answer to this question which is "right" to the exclusion of other possible answers.
3 How does this fable attempt to explain anything about history?

Twentieth-century writers have found it difficult to come forth with the easy and well-defined morals of traditional tellers of fables, such as Aesop and La Fontaine. They portray a world in which it becomes presumptuous for man to say that he knows what is truth and what is not. Life is often seen as basically absurd, and man's task in living is somehow to accept this absurdity and live with it, or live in spite of it.

No writer has captured this aspect of the modern temperament more brilliantly than the Austrian writer Franz Kafka. The particular flavor of Kafka's style comes from the fact that he wrote about a puzzling, bewildering, irrational world, but wrote about it with the utmost clarity and exactness. Things are so clearly presented in Kafka, that his confused heroes, and the reader, are constantly tricked into thinking that reason and logic can get them somewhere. When they find that they are controlled by forces beyond reason, they experience a kind of frustration described by a modern word drawn from the writer's name: *Kafka-esque*.

Franz Kafka

My Destination

I gave orders for my horse to be brought round from the stable. The servant did not understand me. I myself went to the stable, saddled my horse and mounted. In the distance I heard a bugle call, I asked him what this meant. He knew nothing and had heard nothing. At the gate he stopped me, asking: "Where are you riding to, master?" "I don't know," I said, "only away from here, away from here. Always away from here, only by doing so can I reach my destination." "And so you know your destination?" he asked. "Yes," I answered, "didn't I say so? Away-From-Here, that is my destination." "You have no provisions with you," he said. "I need none," I said, "the journey is so long that I must die of hunger if I don't get anything on the way. No provisions can save me. For it is, fortunately, a truly immense journey."

For Discussion

1 Where is the master going? Where is "Away-From-Here"?

Here is an etching of the famous fable, "The Hare and the Tortoise." It is representative of the type of fable in which animals have human characteristics and are used to expose a basic truth.

Jean Baptiste Oudry
Le Lievre et La Tortue
Prints Division
The New York Public Library
Astor, Lenox and Tilden Foundations

The Artist's View

Fables can be divided into two groups: those which enforce a truth, usually by having animals represent human beings, and those which are legendary stories of supernatural happenings.

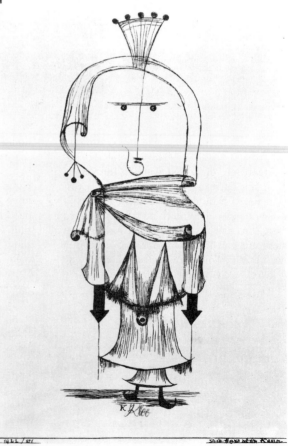

In this lithograph, the artist has imaginatively depicted a witch, a familiar supernatural being that is often an important character in many fables.

Paul Klee
The Witch with the Comb
Collection, The Museum
of Modern Art, New York

This is another supernatural being, a griffin. It is fabled that this creature was sacred to the sun and guarded hidden treasures.

Martin Schongauer
The Griffin
National Gallery of Art,
    Washington, D.C.
Rosenwald Collection

King Arthur is the central character in a famous legend. The English and French stories about him were merged into a tale of knights, magicians, and chivalry.

Nicolas Bataille, probably
Christian Heroes (Nine Heroes tapestry)
The Metropolitan Museum of Art,
The Cloisters Collection,
    Munsey Fund, 1932.

Romulus and Remus, twins who were raised by a she-wolf, were the legendary founders of Rome. They quarreled over the site, and Romulus slew Remus, thus becoming the first king of Rome.

Alexander Calder
Romulus and Remus
The Solomon R. Guggenheim
    Museum, New York

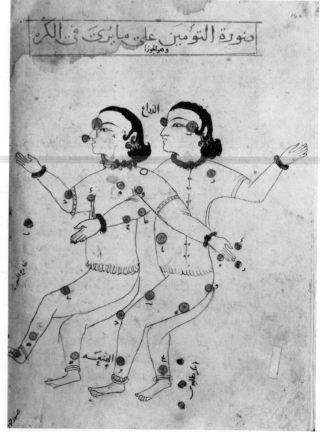

Some legends are explanations for mysteries which primitive people, without the scientific knowledge and technology of today, could not explain. Some dealt with why the stars are in the sky and how they got there. Here is an illustration from the tenth century of the constellation of Gemini.

Illustration from *The Book of the Fixed Stars* by 'Abd ar- Rahman al-Sufi
Constellation of Gemini, the Twins
The Metropolitan Museum of Art, Rogers Fund, 1913

125

To many who could not believe that a good God could create evil, Satan, or Lucifer, was an explanation for the evil in the world.

from John Milton's *Paradise Lost*
Lucifer
The Pierpont Morgan Library

The Greeks developed a whole mythology around gods and events that explained the mysteries of life. Orpheus was one of the figures which populated this other world.

Jacques Lipchitz
The Joy of Orpheus
Marlborough-Gerson Gallery, Inc.

Julio Cortázar, a native of Argentina, is one of the more experimental young writers of Latin America. A few years ago a very successful movie, *Blow Up*, was made from one of his stories.

As soon as we have read six words of this piece, we

know that we are in the world of fable: "A man sold cries and words...." But this fable is closer to Kafka than to Aesop. We pass through an anecdote, but never emerge into an easy

moral. Modern writers like Cortázar seem to be saying that the simple, comforting formulas of folk wisdom no longer apply; that life appears to make narrative sense, but does not quite.

Julio Cortázar

Story With No Moral

A man sold cries and words, and he got along all right although he was always running into people who argued about his prices and demanded discounts. The man almost always gave in, and that way he was able to sell a lot of cries to street vendors, a few sighs which ladies on annuities usually bought, and words for fence posters, wall placards, slogans, letterheads, business cards, and used jokes.

The man realized finally that the hour had come and he requested an audience with the dictator of the country, who resembled all his colleagues and received him surrounded by generals, secretaries, and cups of coffee.

"I've come to sell you your last words," the man said. "They are very important because they'll never come out right for you when the moment comes, and on the other

hand it would be suitable for you to say them at the critical moment so as in retrospect to shape easily an historical destiny."

"Translate what he's saying," the dictator ordered his interpreter.

"He's speaking Argentine, your Excellency."

"In Argentine? And how come I don't understand it?"

"You have understood very well," the man said. "I repeat, I've come to sell you your final words."

The dictator got to his feet as is the practice under these circumstances, and repressing a shiver ordered that they arrest the man and put him in the special dungeons which always exist in those administrative circles.

"It's a pity," said the man while they were leading him off. "In reality you would want to say your final words when the moment arrives, and it would be necessary to say them so as to shape in retrospect, and easily, an historical destiny. What I was going to sell you was what you yourself would want to say, so there's no cheating involved. But as you refuse to do business, you're not going to learn these words beforehand and when the moment arrives when they want to spring out for the first time, naturally you won't be able to say them."

"Why should I not be able to say them if they're what I would have wanted to say anyway?" demanded the dictator, already standing in front of another cup of coffee.

"Because fear will not let you," the man said sadly. "Since there will be a noose around your neck, you'll be in a shirt and shaking in terror and with the cold, your teeth chattering, and you won't be able to articulate a word. The hangman and his assistants, among whom there will be several of these gentlemen, will wait a couple of minutes for decorum's sake, but when your mouth brings forth only a moan interrupted by hiccups and appeals for a pardon (because that, sure, you'll articulate without trouble), they will come to the end of their patience and they'll hang you."

Highly indignant, the assistants and the generals in particular crowded around the dictator to beg that he have the fellow shot immediately. But the dictator, who was pale-as-death, jostled all of them out the door and shut himself up with the man so as to buy his last words.

The generals and the secretaries in the meantime, humiliated in the extreme by the treatment they had received, plotted an uprising, and the following morning seized the dictator while he was eating grapes in his favorite pavilion. So that he should not be able to say his last words, they shot him then and there, eating grapes. Afterwards they set about to find the man, who had disappeared from the presidential palace, and it didn't take them long to find him since he was walking through the market selling routines to the comedians. Putting him in an armored car they carried him off to the fortress where they tortured him to make him reveal what the dictator's last words would have been. As they could not wring a confession from him, they killed him by kicking him to death.

The street vendors who had bought street cries went on crying them on streetcorners, and one of these cries served much later as the sacred writ and password for the counterrevolution which finished off the generals and the secretaries. Some of them, before their death, thought confusedly that really the whole thing had been a stupid chain of confusions, and that words and cries were things which, strictly speaking, could be sold but could not be bought, however absurd that would seem to be.

And they kept on rotting, the whole lot of them, the dictator, the man, and the generals and the secretaries, but from time to time on streetcorners, the cries could be heard.

Paul Blackborn/TRANSLATOR

For Discussion

1. What do you think the author is saying with his title, "Story With No Moral"?
2. Each of the characters in this fable could draw a different moral from his experience, and that is why the story itself has no moral. What moral might the dictator have drawn? The generals and secretaries who overthrew him as he was eating grapes? The man who sold words and cries? The people of Argentina?

Friedrick Karl Gotsch
Charles Chaplin
Collection, The Museum of Modern Art, New York
Gift of J. B. Neumann

Unit Four Drama

Conflict and imitation are the fundamentals of drama. Not action itself, but the *imitation* of an action makes a play. In all ages and in all cultures, men have devised ways of representing action: ritual dances, verse tragedies, slapstick comedies, television plays, operas, puppet shows, street theater. It is not a particular kind of building which makes a theater: it can happen anyplace—a street, a field, a garage, a backyard, a cellar, a classroom. Wherever one or more people stand in front of some other people (who become the audience) and pretend to be something they are not—that's theater.

The theater is often called a place of illusion. More accurately, we should say that it is a place where we are willing to *pretend* that there is an illusion. This is an important distinction, for as soon as we really have an illusion, mistake theater for reality, we no longer have theater at all. In a theater the audience knows that it is an audience, the actors know that they are actors. But for a couple of hours, as we sit in a theater, we are willing to pretend that we are watching something happening tomorrow or two thousand years ago, that we are in Rome one minute and in Egypt the next.

American and European drama has its roots in both Greek and Christian religious ceremonies, and through them extends back into primitive rituals. The ancient Greeks gathered in the woods around a statue of the god Dionysius for ceremonies which included songs and dances. From these ceremonies grew the forms of classical Greek tragedy and comedy. Centuries later, at Eastertime, Christians presented little dramatizations of Bible stories. These in time became the mystery and morality plays that entertained and instructed audiences gathered in the marketplaces of medieval towns.

The forms of drama are many. They may or may not employ any of the following: language, dancing, music, costumes, masks, scenery, or pantomime. A play may be as short as a television commerical, some of which contain an amazing amount of drama within the space of a minute. Or, like the classical Greek trilogies and the Passion Play at Oberammergau, a play may take almost a whole day to perform. One thing remains common to all plays and to all theaters—they aim to satisfy man's need to cry, laugh, shudder at the spectacle of himself.

In the following unit there appear to be three plays. In fact there are no plays in this book at all, only the *scripts* for plays. Here is the difference between drama and all other forms of literature: that is, a play is meant to be "acted out" even if the theater happens only to be the mind of the reader. It is convenient to read plays for the simple reason that even if you live in New York or London or Paris, it is impossible to walk out any evening and find a production of any particular play. The day is coming near when we may read classic plays less than we do today; we will be able to go to the library and take out a video tape of an actual production and play it at home, just as we take out a book to read whenever we wish to.

Some plays read better than others. Of the three plays in the following section, two should be fairly easy to visualize from the printed page: *Galileo* and *The Jewels of the Shrine*. In each of these plays the characters move and speak in a more or less realistic setting which you can imagine without much difficulty. The third play, *The Dwarf Trees*, is certainly easy to read, but the effect of a production in the traditional Japanese theater will be far from the experience of American readers. Unless one has had the rare opportunity of seeing Japanese actors in performance, it is hard to imagine a stylized production with its elaborate costumes, dancing, gestures, and half-sung, half-spoken dialogue.

Sometimes it is hard to judge the merits of a play just from reading it. Often, the play we thought dull in a book turns to magic in the theater; and the play that enchanted us on the stage looks very thin in print. The same play can be brilliant in one production and boring in the next. The "ideal" production the reader stages in his own mind may be more exciting than any he is likely to see in a theater. Reading a play requires an active, creative participation on the part of the reader. For an hour or two his imagination becomes the stage, and he is in turn actor, actress, choreographer, designer and director.

All his life Brecht was involved in political controversy. He has been criticized sharply for his shrewdness in always finding a way to survive, to save his own neck, to watch out for himself in spite of all the dangers of a political life. But Brecht believed that part of an artist's job was to be "cunning," to find ways in which to serve the truth even if he had to find strange subterfuges. Though Brecht himself made many compromises in order to stay alive in difficult times, he wrote, in *Galileo*, a strong criticism of a man who made compromises not unlike his own.

Galileo appears to be a historical drama, but it is important to recognize that it is not really about the past but about the present. Perhaps a better way to put it would be to say that writers have always used history for their own purposes without giving much attention to historical accuracy. For playwrights, history is a form of raw material from which they can mine universal truths. So if we want to find out about Roman history, for example, we should go to historians, not to Shakespeare's *Julius Caesar* or his *Antony and Cleopatra*. Likewise, Brecht's *Galileo* has more to do with

the moral problems of the scientist in the atomic age than it has to do with the real problems of the historical Galileo. As the noted critic Harold Clurman wrote about a production of the play, "*Galileo* is entirely contemporary in view of the events of our atomic age and in relation to certain problems of conscience."

For this reason there is no need for us to know much about the real Galileo in order to read Brecht's play. Most of the necessary information is given in the play itself. Galileo was the greatest Italian mathematician and scientist of his time (1564–1642). Among his contributions to science were his discovery of the law of falling bodies and his invention of the thermometer. But the great controversy of Galileo's life came about because of the newly invented telescope.

Some time before Galileo, another scientist, Copernicus, had declared that the earth revolves around the sun. This does not seem like a revolutionary statement today, but in the sixteenth century it was an idea which completely upset man's concept of the universe and his place in it. Everyone thought that

the earth was the center of the universe and that the sun revolved around it. This signified to men of that time that Man was the most important creature in the universe. But if the earth was just another planet revolving around the sun— what did that mean for Man's central position in the universe? However, there was no way for scientists to check out the Copernican theory and so no one paid much attention to it for a while.

Then, as we will see in the first scene of Brecht's play, Galileo heard about the recently invented telescope. He became immediately excited by the idea and began to build telescopes for himself. With his new scientific equipment he was able to check out the movement of the moon, stars, and sun and to develop evidence which supported Copernicus's theory. Galileo understood that his discoveries would upset so many established ideas of truth that they were likely to get him into trouble. For years he remained silent. His fears were justified, for when he finally published his findings he found himself summoned before the courts (many courts were part of the Church in those days) and accused of heresy. His trial went on for four years. By then Galileo was an old man of seventy, and his spirit was broken. In order to save what he could of his life he decided to agree to say that the truth as he saw it was not the truth after all. Galileo made a public declaration that the earth does not move. According to legend, as soon as he made his declaration he muttered under his breath, "But it *does* move!'

For Brecht, Galileo stands for any man who tries to have a new idea accepted by the establishment. Most of the discoveries and ideas which we take for granted today met with opposition and prejudice when they were new. As Brecht wrote: "Rulers have an intense dislike for significant changes. They would like to see everything remain the same—for a thousand years if possible. They would love it if the sun and moon stood still."

Bertolt Brecht

Galileo

Characters

GALILEO GALILEI
ANDREA SARTI   *two actors: boy and man*
MRS. SARTI
LUDOVICO MARSILI
PRIULI, THE CURATOR
SAGREDO   *Galileo's friend*
VIRGINIA GALILEI
TWO SENATORS
MATTI   *an iron founder*
PHILOSOPHER   *later, Rector of the University*

ELDERLY LADY
YOUNG LADY
FEDERZONI   *assistant to Galileo*
MATHEMATICIAN
LORD CHAMBERLAIN
FAT PRELATE
TWO SCHOLARS
TWO MONKS
INFURIATED MONK
OLD CARDINAL
ATTENDANT MONK

CHRISTOPHER CLAVIUS
FULGANZIO, THE LITTLE MONK
TWO SECRETARIES
CARDINAL BELLARMIN
CARDINAL BARBERINI   *later, Pope Urban VIII*
CARDINAL INQUISITOR
YOUNG GIRL
HER FRIEND
GIUSEPPE
BALLAD SINGER
HIS WIFE
REVELLER
A LOUD VOICE
INFORMER
TOWN CRIER

OFFICIAL
PEASANT
CUSTOMS OFFICER
BOY
SENATORS, OFFICIALS, PROFESSORS, ARTISANS, LADIES, GUESTS, CHILDREN

There are two wordless roles: The DOGE *in Scene II and* PRINCE COSIMO DE' MEDICI *in Scene IV. The ballad of Scene IX is filled out by a pantomime: among the individuals in the pantomimic crowd are three extras (including the* "KING OF HUNGARY"), COBBLER'S BOY, THREE CHILDREN, PEASANT WOMAN, MONK, RICH COUPLE, DWARF, BEGGAR, *and* GIRL.

Scene 1

In the year sixteen hundred and nine
Science' light began to shine.
At Padua City, in a modest house,
Galileo Galilei set out to prove
The sun is still, the earth is on the move.

Galileo's scantily furnished study. Morning.
GALILEO *is washing himself. A barefooted boy,* ANDREA, *son of his housekeeper,* MRS. SARTI, *enters with a big astronomical model.*

GALILEO   Where did you get that thing?

ANDREA   The coachman brought it.

GALILEO   Who sent it?

ANDREA   It said "From the Court of Naples" on the box.

GALILEO   I don't want their stupid presents. Illuminated manuscripts, a statue of Hercules the size of an elephant—they never send money.

ANDREA   But isn't this an astronomical instrument, Mr. Galilei?

GALILEO   That is an antique too. An expensive toy.

ANDREA   What's it for?

GALILEO   It's a map of the sky according to the wise men of ancient Greece. Bosh! We'll try and sell it to the university. They still teach it there.

ANDREA   How does it work, Mr. Galilei?

GALILEO   It's complicated.

ANDREA   I think I could understand it.

GALILEO   [*interested*] Maybe. Let's begin at the beginning. Description!

ANDREA   There are metal rings, a lot of them.

GALILEO   How many?

ANDREA   Eight.

GALILEO   Correct. And?

ANDREA   There are words painted on the bands.

GALILEO   What words?

ANDREA   The names of stars.

GALILEO   Such as?

ANDREA   Here is a band with the sun on it and on the inside band is the moon.

GALILEO   Those metal bands represent crystal globes, eight of them.

ANDREA   Crystal?

GALILEO Like huge soap bubbles one inside the other and the stars are supposed to be tacked onto them. Spin the band with the sun on it. [ANDREA *does so*] You see the fixed ball in the middle?

ANDREA Yes.

GALILEO That's the earth. For two thousand years man has chosen to believe that the sun and all the host of stars revolve about him. Well. The Pope, the cardinals, the princes, the scholars, captains, merchants, housewives, have pictured themselves squatting in the middle of an affair like that.

ANDREA Locked up inside?

GALILEO [*triumphant*] Ah!

ANDREA It's like a cage.

GALILEO So you sensed that. [*Standing near the model*] I like to think the ships began it.

ANDREA Why?

GALILEO They used to hug the coasts and then all of a sudden they left the coasts and spread over the oceans. A new age was coming. I was onto it years ago. I was a young man, in Siena. There was a group of masons arguing. They had to raise a block of granite. It was hot. To help matters, one of them wanted to try a new arrangement of ropes. After five minutes' discussion, out went a method which had been employed for a thousand years. The millennium of faith is ended, said I, this is the millennium of doubt. And we are pulling out of that contraption. The sayings of the wise men won't wash any more. Everybody, at last, is getting nosy. I predict that in our time astronomy will become the gossip of the market place and the sons of fishwives will pack the schools.

ANDREA You're off again, Mr. Galilei. Give me the towel. [*He wipes some soap from Galileo's back*]

GALILEO By that time, with any luck, they will be learning that the earth rolls round the sun, and that their mothers, the captains, the scholars, the princes, and the Pope are rolling with it.

ANDREA That turning-around business is no good. I can see with my own eyes that the sun comes up one place in the morning and goes down in a different place in the evening. It doesn't stand still—I can see it move.

GALILEO You see nothing, all you do is gawk. Gawking is not seeing. [*He puts the iron washstand in the middle of the room*] Now—that's the sun. Sit down. [ANDREA *sits on a chair.* GALILEO *stands behind him*] Where is the sun, on your right or on your left?

ANDREA Left.

GALILEO And how will it get to the right?

ANDREA By your putting it there, of course.

GALILEO Of course? [*He picks* ANDREA *up, chair and all, and carries him round to the other side of the washstand*] Now where is the sun?

ANDREA On the right.

GALILEO And did it move?

ANDREA I did.

GALILEO Wrong. Stupid! The chair moved.

ANDREA But I was on it.

GALILEO Of course. The chair is the earth, and you're sitting on it.

MRS. SARTI, *who has come in with a glass of milk and a roll, has been watching.*

MRS. SARTI What are you doing with my son, Mr. Galilei?

ANDREA Now, mother, you don't understand.

MRS. SARTI You understand, don't you? Last night he tried to tell me that the earth goes round the sun. You'll soon have him saying that two times two is five.

GALILEO [*eating his breakfast*] Apparently we are on the threshold of a new era, Mrs. Sarti.

MRS. SARTI Well, I hope we can pay the milkman in this new era. A young gentleman is here to take private lessons and he is well-dressed and don't you frighten him away like you did the others. Wasting your time with Andrea! [*To* ANDREA] How many times have I told you not to wheedle free lessons out of Mr. Galilei? [*She goes*]

GALILEO So you thought enough of the turning-around business to tell your mother about it.

ANDREA Just to surprise her.

GALILEO Andrea, I wouldn't talk about our ideas outside.

ANDREA Why not?

GALILEO Certain of the authorities won't like it.

ANDREA Why not, if it's the truth?

GALILEO [*laughs*] Because we are like the worms who are little and have dim eyes and can hardly see the stars at all, and the new astronomy is a framework of guesses or very little more—yet.

MRS. SARTI *shows in* LUDOVICO MARSILI, *a presentable young man.*

GALILEO This house is like a market place. [*Pointing to the model*] Move that out of the way! Put it down there!

LUDOVICO *does so.*

LUDOVICO Good morning, sir. My name is Ludovico Marsili.

GALILEO [*reading a letter of recommendation he has brought*] You came by way of Holland and your family lives in the Campagna? Private lessons, thirty scudi a month.

LUDOVICO That's all right, of course, sir.

GALILEO What is your subject?

LUDOVICO Horses.

GALILEO Aha.

LUDOVICO I don't understand science, sir.

GALILEO Aha.

LUDOVICO They showed me an instrument like that in Amsterdam. You'll pardon me, sir, but it didn't make sense to me at all.

GALILEO It's out of date now.

ANDREA *goes.*

LUDOVICO You'll have to be patient with me, sir. Nothing in science makes sense to me.

GALILEO Aha.

LUDOVICO I saw a brand-new instrument in Amsterdam. A tube affair. "See things five times as large as life!" It had two lenses, one at each end, one lens bulged and the other was like that. [*Gesture*] Any normal person would think that different lenses cancel each other out. They didn't! I just stood and looked a fool.

GALILEO I don't quite follow you. What does one see enlarged?

LUDOVICO Church steeples, pigeons, boats. Anything at a distance.

GALILEO Did you yourself—see things enlarged?

LUDOVICO Yes, sir.

GALILEO And the tube had two lenses? Was it like this? [*He has been making a sketch*]

LUDOVICO *nods.*

GALILEO A recent invention?

LUDOVICO It must be. They only started peddling it on the streets a few days before I left Holland.

GALILEO [*starts to scribble calculations on the sketch; almost friendly*] Why do you bother your head with science? Why don't you just breed horses?

Enter MRS. SARTI. GALILEO *doesn't see her. She listens to the following.*

LUDOVICO My mother is set on the idea that science is necessary nowadays for conversation.

GALILEO Aha. You'll find Latin or philosophy easier. [MRS. SARTI *catches his eye*] I'll see you on Tuesday afternoon.

LUDOVICO I shall look forward to it, sir.

GALILEO Good morning. [*He goes to the window and shouts into the street*] Andrea! Hey, Redhead, Redhead!

MRS. SARTI The curator of the museum is here to see you.

GALILEO Don't look at me like that. I took him, didn't I?

MRS. SARTI I caught your eye in time.

GALILEO Show the curator in.

She goes. He scribbles something on a new sheet of paper. The CURATOR *comes in.*

CURATOR Good morning, Mr. Galilei.

GALILEO Lend me a scudo. [*He takes it and goes to the window, wrapping the coin in the paper on which he has been scribbling*] Redhead, run to the spectacle-maker and bring me two lenses; here are the measurements. [*He throws the paper out the window. During the following scene* GALILEO *studies his sketch of the lenses*]

CURATOR Mr. Galilei, I have come to return your petition for an honorarium. Unfortunately I am unable to recommend your request.

GALILEO My good sir, how can I make ends meet on five hundred scudi?

CURATOR What about your private students?

GALILEO If I spend all my time with students, when am I to study? My particular science is on the threshold of important discoveries. [*He throws a manuscript on the table*] Here are my findings on the laws of falling bodies. That should be worth two hundred scudi.

CURATOR I am sure that any paper of yours is of infinite worth, Mr. Galilei. . . .

GALILEO I was limiting it to two hundred scudi.

CURATOR [*cool*] Mr. Galilei, if you want money and leisure, go to Florence. I have no doubt Prince Cosimo de' Medici will be glad to subsidize you, but eventually you will be forbidden to think—in the name of the Inquisition. [GALILEO *says nothing*] Now let us not make a mountain out of a molehill. You are happy here in the Republic of Venice but you need money. Well, that's human, Mr. Galilei. May I suggest a simple solution? You remember that chart you made for the army to extract cube roots without any knowledge of mathematics? Now that was practical!

GALILEO Bosh!

CURATOR Don't say bosh about something that astounded the Chamber of Commerce. Our city elders are businessmen. Why don't you invent something useful that will bring them a little profit?

GALILEO [*playing with the sketch of the lenses; suddenly*] I see. Mr. Priuli, I may have something for you.

CURATOR You don't say so.

GALILEO It's not quite there yet, but . . .

CURATOR You've never let me down yet, Galilei.

GALILEO You are always an inspiration to me, Priuli.

CURATOR You are a great man: a discontented man, but I've always said you are a great man.

GALILEO [*tartly*] My discontent, Priuli, is for the most part with myself. I am forty-six years of age and have achieved nothing which satisfies me.

CURATOR I won't disturb you any further.

GALILEO Thank you. Good morning.

CURATOR Good morning. And thank you.

He goes. GALILEO *sighs.* ANDREA *returns, bringing lenses.*

ANDREA One scudo was not enough. I had to leave my cap with him before he'd let me take them away.

GALILEO We'll get it back someday. Give them to me. [*He takes the lenses over to the window, holding them in the relation they would have in a telescope*]

ANDREA What are those for?

GALILEO Something for the Senate. With any luck, they will rake in two hundred scudi. Take a look!

ANDREA   My, things look close! I can read the copper letters on the bell in the Campanile. And the washerwomen by the river, I can see their washboards!

GALILEO   Get out of the way. [*Looking through the lenses himself*]   Aha!

Scene 2

No one's virtue is complete:
Great Galileo liked to eat.
You will not resent, we hope,
The truth about his telescope.

The Great Arsenal of Venice, overlooking the harbor full of ships. SENATORS *and* OFFICIALS *on one side,* GALILEO, *his daughter* VIRGINIA, *and his friend* SAGREDO, *on the other side. They are dressed in formal, festive clothes.* VIRGINIA *is fourteen and charming. She carries a velvet cushion on which lies a brand-new telescope. Behind* GALILEO *are some* ARTISANS *from the Arsenal. There are onlookers,* LUDOVICO *among them.*

CURATOR   [*announcing*]   Senators, Artisans of the Great Arsenal of Venice; Mr. Galileo Galilei, professor of mathematics at your University of Padua.

GALILEO *steps forward and starts to speak.*

GALILEO   Members of the High Senate! Gentlemen: I have great pleasure, as director of this institute, in presenting for your approval and acceptance an entirely new instrument originating from this our Great Arsenal of the Republic of Venice. As professor of mathematics at your University of Padua, your obedient servant has always counted it his privilege to offer you such discoveries and inventions as might prove lucrative to the manufacturers and merchants of our Venetian Republic. Thus, in all humility, I tender you this, my optical tube, or telescope, constructed, I assure you, on the most scientific and Christian principles, the product of seventeen years' patient research at your University of Padua.

GALILEO *steps back. The* SENATORS *applaud.*

SAGREDO   [*aside to* GALILEO]   Now you will be able to pay your bills.

GALILEO   Yes. It will make money for them. But you realize that it is more than a money-making gadget? I turned it on the moon last night . . .

CURATOR   [*in his best chamber-of-commerce manner*]   Gentlemen: Our Republic is to be congratulated not only because this new acquisition will be one more feather in the cap of Venetian culture—[*polite applause*]—not only because our own Mr. Galilei has generously handed this fresh product of his teeming brain entirely over to you, allowing you to manufacture as many of these highly salable articles as you please—[*considerable applause*]—but, Gentlemen of the Senate, has it occurred to you that—with the help of this remarkable new instrument—the battle fleet of the enemy will be visible to us a full two hours before we are visible to him? [*Tremendous applause*]

GALILEO   [*aside to* SAGREDO]   We have been held up three generations for lack of a thing like this. I want to go home.

SAGREDO   What about the moon?

GALILEO   Well, for one thing, it doesn't give off its own light.

CURATOR   [*continuing his oration*]   And now, Your Excellency, and Members of the Senate, Mr. Galilei entreats you to accept the instrument from the hands of his charming daughter Virginia.

Polite applause. He beckons to VIRGINIA, *who steps forward and presents the telescope to the* DOGE.

CURATOR [*during this*] Mr. Galilei gives his invention entirely into your hands, Gentlemen, enjoining you to construct as many of these instruments as you may please.

More applause. The SENATORS *gather round the telescope, examining it, and looking through it.*

GALILEO [*aside to* SAGREDO] Do you know what the Milky Way is made of?

SAGREDO No.

GALILEO I do.

CURATOR [*interrupting*] Congratulations, Mr. Galilei. Your extra five hundred scudi a year are safe.

GALILEO Pardon? What? Of course, the *five hundred* scudi! Yes!

A prosperous man is standing beside the CURATOR.

CURATOR Mr. Galilei, Mr. Matti of Florence.

MATTI You're opening new fields, Mr. Galilei. We could do with you at Florence.

CURATOR Now, Mr. Matti, leave something to us poor Venetians.

MATTI It is a pity that a great republic has to seek an excuse to pay its great men their right and proper dues.

CURATOR Even a great man has to have an incentive. [*He joins the* SENATORS *at the telescope*]

MATTI I am an iron founder.

GALILEO Iron founder!

MATTI With factories at Pisa and Florence. I wanted to talk to you about a machine you designed for a friend of mine in Padua.

GALILEO I'll put you onto someone to copy it for you, I am not going to have the time. How are things in Florence?

They wander away.

FIRST SENATOR [*peering*] Extraordinary! They're having their lunch on that frigate. Lobsters! I'm hungry!

Laughter.

SECOND SENATOR Oh, good heavens, look at her! I must tell my wife to stop bathing on the roof. When can I buy one of these things?

Laughter. VIRGINIA *has spotted* LUDOVICO *among the onlookers and drags him to* GALILEO.

VIRGINIA [*to* LUDOVICO] Did I do it nicely?

LUDOVICO I thought so.

VIRGINIA Here's Ludovico to congratulate you, father.

LUDOVICO [*embarrassed*] Congratulations, sir.

GALILEO I improved it.

LUDOVICO Yes, sir. I am beginning to understand science.

GALILEO *is surrounded.*

VIRGINIA Isn't father a great man?

LUDOVICO Yes.

VIRGINIA Isn't that new thing father made pretty?

LUDOVICO Yes, a pretty red. Where I saw it first it was covered in green.

VIRGINIA What was?

LUDOVICO Never mind. [*A short pause*] Have you ever been to Holland?

They go. All Venice is congratulating GALILEO, *who wants to go home.*

Scene 3

January ten, sixteen ten:
Galileo Galilei abolishes heaven.

Galileo's study at Padua. It is night. GALILEO *and* SAGREDO *at a telescope.*

SAGREDO [*softly*] The edge of the crescent is jagged. All along the dark part, near the shiny crescent, bright particles of light keep coming up, one after the other, and growing larger and merging with the bright crescent.

GALILEO How do you explain those spots of light?

SAGREDO It can't be true . . .

GALILEO It *is* true: they are high mountains.

SAGREDO On a star?

GALILEO Yes. The shining particles are mountain peaks catching the first rays of the rising sun while the slopes of the mountains are still dark, and what you see is the sunlight moving down from the peaks into the valleys.

SAGREDO But this gives the lie to all the astronomy that's been taught for the last two thousand years.

GALILEO Yes. What you are seeing now has been seen by no other man besides myself.

SAGREDO But the moon can't be an earth with mountains and valleys like our own any more than the earth can be a star.

GALILEO The moon *is* an earth with mountains and valleys, and the earth *is* a star. As the moon appears to us, so we appear to the moon. From the moon, the earth looks something like a crescent, sometimes like a half globe, sometimes a full globe, and sometimes it is not visible at all.

SAGREDO Galileo, this is frightening.

An urgent knocking on the door.

GALILEO I've discovered something else, something even more astonishing.

More knocking. GALILEO *opens the door and the* CURATOR *comes in.*

CURATOR There it is—your "miraculous optical tube." Do you know that this invention he so picturesquely termed "the fruit of seventeen years' research" will be on sale tomorrow for two scudi apiece at every street corner in Venice? A shipload of them has just arrived from Holland.

SAGREDO Oh, dear!

GALILEO *turns his back and adjusts the telescope.*

CURATOR When I think of the poor gentlemen of the Senate who believed they were getting an invention they could monopolize for their own profit. . . . Why, when they took their first look through the glass, it was only by the merest chance that they didn't see a peddler, seven times enlarged, selling tubes exactly like it at the corner of the street.

SAGREDO Mr. Priuli, with the help of this instrument, Mr. Galilei has made discoveries that will revolutionize our concept of the universe.

CURATOR Mr. Galilei provided the city with a first-rate water pump and the irrigation works he designed function splendidly. How was I to expect this?

GALILEO [*still at the telescope*] Not so fast, Priuli. I may be on the track of a very large gadget. Certain of the stars appear to have regular movements. If there were a clock in the sky, it could be seen from anywhere. That might be useful for your shipowners.

CURATOR I won't listen to you. I listened to you before, and as a reward for my friendship you have made me the laughingstock of the town. You can laugh—you got your money. But let me tell you this: you've destroyed my faith in a lot of things, Mr. Galilei. I'm disgusted with the world. That's all I have to say. [*He storms out*]

GALILEO [*embarrassed*] Businessmen bore me, they suffer so. Did you see the frightened look in his eyes when he caught sight of a world not created solely for the purpose of doing business?

SAGREDO Did you know that telescopes had been made in Holland?

GALILEO I'd heard about it. But the one I made for the Senators was twice as good as any Dutchman's. Besides, I needed the money. How can I work, with the tax collector on the doorstep? And my poor daughter will never acquire a husband unless she has a dowry, she's not too bright. And I like to buy books—all kinds of books. Why not? And what about my appetite? I don't think well unless I eat well. Can I help it if I get my best ideas over a good meal and a bottle of wine? They don't pay me as much as they pay the butcher's boy. If only I could have five years to do nothing but research! Come on. I am going to show you something else.

SAGREDO I don't know that I want to look again.

GALILEO This is one of the brighter nebulae of the Milky Way. What do you see?

SAGREDO But it's made up of stars—countless stars.

GALILEO Countless worlds.

SAGREDO [hesitating] What about the theory that the earth revolves round the sun? Have you run across anything about that?

GALILEO No. But I noticed something on Tuesday that might prove a step towards even that. Where's Jupiter? There are four lesser stars near Jupiter. I happened on them on Monday but didn't take any particular note of their position. On Tuesday I looked again. I could have sworn they had moved. They have changed again. Tell me what you see.

SAGREDO I only see three.

GALILEO Where's the fourth? Let's get the charts and settle down to work.

They work and the lights dim. The lights go up again. It is near dawn.

GALILEO The only place the fourth can be is round at the back of the larger star where we cannot see it. This means there are small stars revolving around a big star. Where are the crystal shells now, that the stars are supposed to be fixed to?

SAGREDO Jupiter can't be attached to anything: there are other stars revolving round it.

GALILEO There is no support in the heavens. [SAGREDO laughs awkwardly] Don't stand there looking at me as if it weren't true.

SAGREDO I suppose it is true. I'm afraid.

GALILEO Why?

SAGREDO What do you think is going to happen to you for saying that there is another sun around which other earths revolve? And that there are only stars and no difference between earth and heaven? Where is God then?

GALILEO What do you mean?

SAGREDO God? Where is God?

GALILEO [angrily] Not there! Any more than He'd be here—if creatures from the moon came down to look for Him!

SAGREDO Then where is He?

GALILEO I'm not a theologian: I'm a mathematician.

SAGREDO You are a human being! [Almost shouting] Where is God in your system of the universe?

GALILEO Within ourselves. Or—nowhere.

SAGREDO Ten years ago a man was burned at the stake for saying that.

GALILEO Giordano Bruno was an idiot: he spoke too soon. He would never have been condemned if he could have backed up what he said with proof.

SAGREDO [incredulously] Do you really believe proof will make any difference?

GALILEO I believe in the human race. The only people that can't be reasoned with are the dead. Human beings are intelligent.

SAGREDO Intelligent—or merely shrewd?

GALILEO I know they call a donkey a horse when they want to sell it, and a horse a donkey when they want to buy it. But is that the whole story? Aren't they susceptible to truth as well? [He fishes a small pebble out of his pocket] If anybody were to drop a stone—[drops the pebble]—and tell them that it didn't fall, do you think they would keep quiet? The evidence of your own eyes is a very seductive thing. Sooner or later everybody must succumb to it.

SAGREDO Galileo, I am helpless when you talk.

A church bell has been ringing for some time, calling people to mass. Enter VIRGINIA, *muffled up for mass, carrying a candle, protected from the wind by a globe.*

VIRGINIA   Oh, father, you promised to go to bed tonight, and it's five o'clock again.

GALILEO   Why are you up at this hour?

VIRGINIA   I'm going to mass with Mrs. Sarti. Ludovico is going too. How was the night, father?

GALILEO   Bright.

VIRGINIA   What did you find through the tube?

GALILEO   Only some little specks by the side of a star. I must draw attention to them somehow. I think I'll name them after the Prince of Florence. Why not call them the Medicean planets? By the way, we may move to Florence. I've written to His Highness, asking if he can use me as Court Mathematician.

VIRGINIA   Oh, father, we'll be at the court!

SAGREDO   [*amazed*] Galileo!

GALILEO   My dear Sagredo, I must have leisure. My only worry is that His Highness after all may not take me. I'm not accustomed to writing formal letters to great personages. Here, do you think this is the right sort of thing?

SAGREDO   [*reads*] "Whose sole desire is to reside in Your Highness' presence—the rising sun of our great age." Cosimo de' Medici is a boy of nine.

GALILEO   The only way a man like me can land a good job is by crawling on his stomach. Your father, my dear, is going to take his share of the pleasures of life in exchange for all his hard work, and about time too. I have no patience, Sagredo, with a man who doesn't use his brains to fill his belly. Run along to mass now.

VIRGINIA *goes.*

SAGREDO   Galileo, do not go to Florence.

GALILEO   Why not?

SAGREDO   The monks are in power there.

GALILEO   Going to mass is a small price to pay for a full belly. And there are many famous scholars at the court of Florence.

SAGREDO   Court monkeys.

GALILEO   I shall enjoy taking them by the scruff of the neck and making them look through the telescope.

SAGREDO   Galileo, you are traveling the road to disaster. You are suspicious and skeptical in science, but in politics you are as naïve as your daughter! How can people in power leave a man at large who tells the truth, even if it be the truth about the distant stars? Can you see the Pope scribbling a note in his diary: "Tenth of January, 1610, Heaven abolished"? A moment ago, when you were at the telescope, I saw you tied to the stake, and when you said you believed in proof, I smelt burning flesh!

GALILEO   I am going to Florence.

Before the next scene, a curtain with the following legend on it is lowered:

> *By setting the name of Medici in the sky, I am bestowing immortality upon the stars. I commend myself to you as your most faithful and devoted servant, whose sole desire is to reside in Your Highness' presence, the rising sun of our great age.*
> —Galileo Galilei

Scene 4

Galileo's house at Florence. Well-appointed. GALILEO *is demonstrating his telescope to* PRINCE COSIMO DE' MEDICI, *a boy of nine, accompanied by his* LORD CHAMBERLAIN, LADIES *and* GENTLEMEN *of the court, and an assortment of university* PROFESSORS. *With* GALILEO *are* ANDREA *and* FEDERZONI, *the new assistant (an old man).* MRS. SARTI *stands by. Before the scene opens, the voice of the* PHILOSOPHER *can be heard.*

VOICE OF THE PHILOSOPHER Quaedam miracula universi. Orbes mystice canorae, arcus crystallini, circulatio corporum coelestium. Cyclorum epicyclorumque intoxicatio, integritas tabulae chordarum et architectura elata globorum coelestium.

GALILEO Shall we speak in everyday language? My colleague Mr. Federzoni does not understand Latin.

PHILOSOPHER Is it necessary that he should?

GALILEO Yes.

PHILOSOPHER Forgive me. I thought he was your mechanic.

ANDREA Mr. Federzoni is a mechanic and a scholar.

PHILOSOPHER Thank you, young man. If Mr. Federzoni insists . . .

GALILEO I insist.

PHILOSOPHER It will not be as clear, but it's your house. Your Highness . . . [*The* PRINCE *is ineffectually trying to establish contact with* ANDREA] I was about to recall to Mr. Galilei some of the wonders of the universe as they are set down for us in the Divine Classics. [*The* LADIES *"ah"*] Remind him of the "mystically musical spheres, the crystal arches, the circulation of the heavenly bodies——"

ELDERLY LADY Perfect poise!

PHILOSOPHER "—the intoxication of the cycles and epicycles, the integrity of the tables of chords, and the enraptured architecture of the celestial globes."

ELDERLY LADY What diction!

PHILOSOPHER May I pose the question: Why should we go out of our way to look for things that can only strike a discord in the ineffable harmony?

The LADIES *applaud.*

FEDERZONI Take a look through here—you'll be interested.

ANDREA Sit down here, please.

The PROFFESSORS *laugh.*

MATHEMATICIAN Mr. Galilei, nobody doubts that your brain child—or is it your adopted brain child?—is brilliantly contrived.

GALILEO Your Highness, one can see the four stars as large as life, you know.

The PRINCE *looks to the* ELDERLY LADY *for guidance.*

MATHEMATICIAN Ah. But has it occurred to you that an eyeglass through which one sees such phenomena might not be a too reliable eyeglass?

GALILEO How is that?

MATHEMATICIAN If one could be sure you would keep your temper, Mr. Galilei, I could suggest that what one sees in the eyeglass and what is in the heavens are two entirely different things.

GALILEO [*quietly*] You are suggesting fraud?

MATHEMATICIAN No! How could I, in the presence of His Highness?

ELDERLY LADY The gentlemen are just wondering if Your Highness' stars are really, really there!

Pause.

YOUNG LADY [*trying to be helpful*] Can one see the claws on the Great Bear?

GALILEO And everything on Taurus the Bull.

FEDERZONI Are you going to look through it or not?

MATHEMATICIAN With the greatest of pleasure.

Pause. Nobody goes near the telescope. All of a sudden the boy ANDREA *turns and marches pale and erect past them through the whole length of the room. The* GUESTS *follow with their eyes.*

MRS. SARTI [*as he passes her*] What is the matter with you?

ANDREA [*shocked*] They are wicked.

PHILOSOPHER Your Highness, it is a delicate matter and I had no intention of bringing it up, but Mr. Galilei was about to demonstrate the impossible. His new stars would have broken the outer crystal sphere—which we know of on the authority of Aristotle.[1] I am sorry.

MATHEMATICIAN The last word.

FEDERZONI He had no telescope.

MATHEMATICIAN Quite.

GALILEO [*keeping his temper*] "Truth is the daughter of Time, not of Authority." Gentlemen, the sum of our knowledge is pitiful. It has been my singular good fortune to find a new instrument which brings a small patch of the universe a little bit closer. It is at your disposal.

PHILOSOPHER Where is all this leading?

GALILEO Are we, as scholars, concerned with where the truth might lead us?

PHILOSOPHER Mr. Galilei, the truth might lead us anywhere!

GALILEO I can only beg you to look through my eyeglass.

MATHEMATICIAN [*wild*] If I understand Mr. Galilei correctly, he is asking us to discard the teachings of two thousand years.

GALILEO For two thousand years we have been looking at the sky and didn't see the four moons of Jupiter, and there they were all the time. Why defend shaken teachings? You should be doing the shaking. [*The* PRINCE *is sleepy*] Your Highness! My work in the Great Arsenal of Venice brought me in daily contact with sailors, carpenters, and so on. These men are unread. They depend on the evidence of their senses. But they taught me many new ways of doing things. The question is whether these gentlemen here want to be found out as fools by men who might not have had the advantages of a classical education but who are not afraid to use their eyes. I tell you that our dockyards are stirring with that same high curiosity which was the true glory of ancient Greece.

Pause.

PHILOSOPHER I have no doubt Mr. Galilei's theories will arouse the enthusiasm of the dockyards.

CHAMBERLAIN Your Highness, I find to my amazement that this highly informative discussion has exceeded the time we had allowed for it. May I remind Your Highness that the State Ball begins in three-quarters of an hour?

The COURT *bows low.*

ELDERLY LADY We would really have liked to look through your eyeglass, Mr. Galilei, wouldn't we, Your Highness?

The PRINCE *bows politely and is led to the door.* GALILEO *follows the* PRINCE, CHAMBERLAIN, *and* LADIES *toward the exit. The* PROFESSORS *remain at the telescope.*

GALILEO [*almost servile*] All anybody has to do is look through the telescope, Your Highness.

MRS. SARTI *takes a plate with candies to the* PRINCE *as he is walking out.*

MRS. SARTI A piece of homemade candy, Your Highness?

ELDERLY LADY Not now. Thank you. It is too soon before His Highness' supper.

PHILOSOPHER Wouldn't I like to take that thing to pieces.

MATHEMATICIAN Ingenious contraption. It must be quite difficult to keep clean. [*He rubs the lens with his handkerchief and looks at the handkerchief*]

FEDERZONI We did not paint the Medicean stars on the lens.

ELDERLY LADY [*to the* PRINCE, *who has whispered something to her*] No, no, no, there is nothing the matter with your stars!

CHAMBERLAIN [*across the stage to* GALILEO] His Highness will of course seek the opinion of the greatest living authority: Christopher Clavius, Chief Astronomer to the Papal College in Rome.

1 Aristotle *The Greek philosopher and scientist whose word on many subjects was considered as "law" for centuries. Aristotle had stated that the heavens were enclosed by a crystal sphere.*

Scene 5

*Things take indeed a wondrous turn
When learned men do stoop to learn.
Clavius, we are pleased to say,
Upheld Galileo Galilei.*

A burst of laughter is heard and the curtains reveal a hall in the Collegium Romanum. HIGH CHURCHMEN, MONKS, *and* SCHOLARS *standing about talking and laughing.* GALILEO *by himself in a corner.*

FAT PRELATE [*shaking with laughter*] Hopeless! Hopeless! Hopeless! Will you tell me something people won't believe?

A SCHOLAR Yes, that you don't love your stomach!

FAT PRELATE They'd believe that. They only do not believe what's good for them. They doubt the devil, but fill them up with some fiddle-de-dee about the earth rolling like a marble in the gutter and they swallow it hook, line, and sinker. Sancta simplicitas!²

He laughs until the tears run down his cheeks. The others laugh with him. A group has formed whose members boisterously begin to pretend they are standing on a rolling globe.

A MONK It's rolling fast, I'm dizzy. May I hold onto you, Professor? [*He sways dizzily and clings to one of the scholars for support*]

THE SCHOLAR Old Mother Earth's been at the bottle again. Whoa!

MONK Hey! Hey! We're slipping off! Help!

SECOND SCHOLAR Look! There's Venus! Hold me, lads. Whee!

SECOND MONK Don't, don't hurl us off onto the moon. There are nasty sharp mountain peaks on the moon, brethren!

VARIOUSLY Hold tight! Hold tight! Don't look down! Hold tight! It'll make you giddy!

FAT PRELATE And we cannot have giddy people in Holy Rome.

They rock with laughter. An INFURIATED MONK *comes out from a large door at the rear holding a Bible in his hand and pointing out a page with his finger.*

INFURIATED MONK What does the Bible say —"Sun, stand thou still on Gideon and thou, moon, in the valley of Ajalon." Can the sun come to a standstill if it doesn't ever move? Does the Bible lie?

FAT PRELATE How did Christopher Clavius, the greatest astronomer we have, get mixed up in an investigation of this kind?

INFURIATED MONK He's in there with his eye glued to that diabolical instrument.

FAT PRELATE [*to* GALILEO, *who has been playing with his pebble and has dropped it*] Mr. Galilei, something dropped down.

GALILEO Monsignor, are you sure it didn't drop up?

INFURIATED MONK As astronomers we are aware that there are phenomena which are beyond us, but man can't expect to understand everything!

Enter a very old CARDINAL *leaning on a* MONK *for support. Others move aside.*

OLD CARDINAL Aren't they out yet? Can't they reach a decision on that paltry matter? Christopher Clavius ought to know his astronomy after all these years. I am informed that Mr. Galilei transfers mankind from the center of the universe to somewhere on the outskirts. Mr. Galilei is therefore an enemy of mankind and must be dealt with as such. Is it conceivable that God would trust this most precious fruit of His labor to a minor, frolicking star? Would He have sent His Son to such a place? How can there be people with such twisted minds that they believe what they're told by the slave of a multiplication table?

2 Sancta simplicitas! *Latin:
"Holy simplicity!"*

FAT PRELATE [*quietly to* CARDINAL] The gentleman is over there.

OLD CARDINAL So you are the man. You know my eyes are not what they were, but I can see you bear a striking resemblance to the man we burned. What was his name?

MONK Your Eminence must avoid excitement the doctor said . . .

OLD CARDINAL [*disregarding him*] So you have degraded the earth despite the fact that you live by her and receive everything from her. I won't have it! I won't have it! I won't be a nobody on an inconsequential star briefly twirling hither and thither. I tread the earth, and the earth is firm beneath my feet, and there is no motion to the earth, and the earth is the center of all things, and I am the center of the earth, and the eye of the Creator is upon me. About me revolve, affixed to their crystal shells, the lesser lights of the stars and the great light of the sun, created to give light upon me that God might see me—Man, God's greatest effort, the center of creation. "In the image of God created He him." Immortal . . . [*His strength fails him and he catches for the* MONK *for support*]

MONK You mustn't overtax your strength, Your Eminence.

At this moment the door at the rear opens and CHRISTOPHER CLAVIUS *enters followed by his* ASTRONOMERS. *He strides hastily across the hall, looking neither to right nor left. As he goes by we hear him say——*

CLAVIUS He is right.

Deadly silence. All turn to GALILEO.

OLD CARDINAL What is it? Have they reached a decision?

No one speaks.

MONK It is time that Your Eminence went home.

The hall is emptying fast. One little MONK *who had entered with* CLAVIUS *speaks to* GALILEO.

LITTLE MONK Mr. Galilei, I heard Father Clavius say: "Now it's for the theologians to set the heavens right again." You have won.

Before the next scene, a curtain with the following legend on it is lowered:

As these new astronomical charts enable us to determine longitudes at sea and so make it possible to reach the new continents by the shortest routes, we would beseech Your Excellency to aid us in reaching Mr. Galilei, mathematician to the Court of Florence, who is now in Rome . . .

—From a letter written by a member of the Genoa Chamber of Commerce and Navigation to the Papal Legation.

Scene 6

When Galileo was in Rome
A Cardinal asked him to his home.
He wined and dined him as his guest
And only made one small request.

Cardinal Bellarmin's house in Rome. Music is heard and the chatter of many guests. Two SECRETARIES *are at the rear of the stage at a desk.* GALILEO, *his daughter* VIRGINIA, *now twenty-one, and* LUDOVICO MARSILI, *who has become her fiancé, are just arriving. A few* GUESTS, *standing near the entrance with masks in their hands, nudge each other and are suddenly silent.* GALILEO *looks at them. They applaud him politely and bow.*

VIRGINIA Oh, father! I'm so happy. I won't dance with anyone but you, Ludovico.

GALILEO [*to a* SECRETARY] I was to wait here for His Eminence.

FIRST SECRETARY His Eminence will be with you in a few minutes.

VIRGINIA Do I look proper?

LUDOVICO You are showing some lace.

GALILEO *puts his arms around their shoulders.*

GALILEO [*quoting mischievously*]
Fret not, daughter, if perchance
You attract a wanton glance.
The eyes that catch a trembling lace
Will guess the heartbeat's quickened pace.
Lovely woman still may be
Careless with felicity.

VIRGINIA [*to* GALILEO] Feel my heart.

GALILEO [*to* LUDOVICO] It's thumping.

VIRGINIA I hope I always say the right thing.

LUDOVICO She's afraid she's going to let us down.

VIRGINIA Oh, I want to look beautiful.

GALILEO You'd better. If you don't they'll start saying all over again that the earth doesn't turn.

LUDOVICO [*laughing*] It *doesn't* turn, sir.

GALILEO *laughs.*

GALILEO Go and enjoy yourselves. [*He speaks to one of the* SECRETARIES] A large fete?

FIRST SECRETARY Two hundred and fifty guests, Mr. Galilei. We have represented here this evening most of the great families of Italy, the Orsinis, the Villanis, the Nuccolis, the Soldanieris, the Canes, the Lecchis, the Estes, the Colombinis, the . . .

VIRGINIA *comes running back.*

VIRGINIA Oh, father, I didn't tell you: you're famous.

GALILEO Why?

VIRGINIA The hairdresser in the Via Vittorio kept four other ladies waiting and took me first. [*Exit*]

GALILEO [*at the stairway, leaning over the well*] Rome!

Enter CARDINAL BELLARMIN, *wearing the mask of a lamb, and* CARDINAL BARBERINI, *wearing the mask of a dove.*

SECRETARIES Their Eminences, Cardinals Bellarmin and Barberini.

The CARDINALS *lower their masks.*

GALILEO [*to* BELLARMIN] Your Eminence.

BELLARMIN Mr. Galilei, Cardinal Barberini.

GALILEO Your Eminence.

BARBERINI So you are the father of that lovely child!

BELLARMIN Who is inordinately proud of being her father's daughter.

They laugh.

BARBERINI [*points his finger at* GALILEO] "The sun riseth and setteth and returneth to its place," saith the Bible. What saith Galilei?

GALILEO Appearances are notoriously deceptive, Your Eminence. Once, when I was so high, I was standing on a ship that was pulling away from the shore and I shouted, "The shore is moving!" I know now that it was the ship which was moving.

BARBERINI [*laughs*] You can't catch that man. I tell you, Bellarmin, his moons around Jupiter are hard nuts to crack. Unfortunately for me I happened to glance at a few papers on astronomy once. It is harder to get rid of than the itch.

BELLARMIN Let's move with the times. If it makes navigation easier for sailors to use new charts based on a new hypothesis, let them have them. We only have to scotch doctrines that contradict Holy Writ.

He leans over the balustrade of the well and acknowledges various GUESTS.

BARBERINI But Bellarmin, you haven't caught onto this fellow. The scriptures don't satisfy him. Copernicus does.

GALILEO   Copernicus? "He that withholdeth corn, the people shall curse him." Book of Proverbs.

BARBERINI   "A prudent man concealeth knowledge." Also Book of Proverbs.

GALILEO   "Where no oxen are, the crib is clean: but much increase is by the strength of the ox."

BARBERINI   "He that ruleth his spirit is better than he that taketh a city."

GALILEO   "But a broken spirit drieth the bones." [*Pause*] "Doth not wisdom cry?"

BARBERINI   "Can one go upon hot coals and his feet not be burned?" Welcome to Rome, friend Galileo. You recall the legend of our city's origin? Two small boys found sustenance and refuge with a she-wolf and from that day we have paid the price for the she-wolf's milk. But the place is not bad. We have everything for your pleasure—from a scholarly dispute with Bellarmin to ladies of high degree. Look at that woman flaunting herself. No? He wants a weighty discussion! All right! [*To* GALILEO] You people speak in terms of circles and ellipses and regular velocities—simple movements that the human mind can grasp—very convenient —but suppose Almighty God had taken it into His head to make the stars move like that—[*he describes an irregular motion with his fingers through the air*]— then where would you be?

GALILEO   My good man—the Almighty would have endowed us with brains like that— [*repeats the movement*]—so that we could grasp the movements—[*repeats the movement*]—like that. I believe in the brain.

BARBERINI   I consider the brain inadequate. He doesn't answer. He is too polite to tell me he considers *my* brain inadequate. What is one to do with him? Butter wouldn't melt in his mouth. All he wants to do is to prove that God made a few

boners in astronomy. God didn't study His astronomy hard enough before He composed Holy Writ. [*To the* SECRETARIES] Don't take anything down. This is a scientific discussion among friends.

BELLARMIN   [*to* GALILEO] Does it not appear more probable—even to you—that the Creator knows more about His work than the created?

GALILEO   In his blindness man is liable to misread not only the sky but also the Bible.

BELLARMIN   The interpretation of the Bible is a matter for the ministers of God. [GALILEO *remains silent*] At last you are quiet. [*He gestures to the* SECRETARIES. *They start writing*] Tonight the Holy Office has decided that the theory according to which the earth goes around the sun is foolish, absurd, and a heresy. I am charged, Mr. Galilei, with cautioning you to abandon these teachings [*To the* FIRST SECRETARY] Would you repeat that?

FIRST SECRETARY   [*reading*] "His Eminence, Cardinal Bellarmin, to the aforesaid Galilei: 'The Holy Office has resolved that the theory according to which the earth goes around the sun is foolish, absurd, and a heresy. I am charged, Mr. Galilei, with cautioning you to abandon these teachings.' "

GALILEO   [*rocking on his base*] But the facts!

BARBERINI   [*consoling*] Your findings have been ratified by the Papal Observatory, Galilei. That should be most flattering to you . . .

BELLARMIN   [*cutting in*] The Holy Office formulated the decree without going into details.

GALILEO   [*to* BARBERINI] Do you realize, the future of all scientific research is——

BELLARMIN   [*cutting in*] Completely assured, Mr. Galilei. It is not given to man to know the truth: it is granted to him to seek after the truth. Science is the legitimate and beloved daughter of the Church. She must have confidence in the Church.

GALILEO [infuriated] I would not try confidence by whistling her too often.

BARBERINI [quickly] Be careful what you're doing——you'll be throwing out the baby with the bath water, friend Galilei. [Serious] We need you more than you need us.

BELLARMIN Well, it is time we introduced our distinquished friend to our guests. The whole country talks of him!

BARBERINI Let us replace our masks, Bellarmin. Poor Galilei hasn't got one. [He laughs]

They take GALILEO out.

FIRST SECRETARY Did you get his last sentence?

SECOND SECRETARY Yes. Do you have what he said about believing in the brain?

Another cardinal—the INQUISITOR—enters.

INQUISITOR Did the conference take place?

The FIRST SECRETARY hands him the papers and the INQUISITOR dismisses the SECRETARIES. They go. The INQUISITOR sits down and starts to read the transcription. Two or three YOUNG LADIES skitter across the stage; they see the INQUISITOR and curtsy as they go.

YOUNG GIRL Who was that?

HER FRIEND The Cardinal Inquisitor.

They giggle and go. Enter VIRGINIA. She curtsies as she goes. The INQUISITOR stops her.

INQUISITOR Good evening, my child. Beautiful night. May I congratulate you on your betrothal? Your young man comes from a fine family. Are you staying with us here in Rome?

VIRGINIA Not now, Your Eminence. I must go home to prepare for the wedding.

INQUISITOR Ah. You are accompanying your father to Florence. That should please

him. Science must be cold comfort in a home. Your youth and warmth will keep him down to earth. It is easy to get lost up there. [He gestures to the sky]

VIRGINIA He doesn't talk to me about the stars, Your Eminence.

INQUISITOR No. [He laughs] They don't eat fish in the fisherman's house. I can tell you something about astronomy. My child, it seems that God has blessed our modern astronomers with imaginations. It is quite alarming! Do you know that the earth—which we old fogies supposed to be so large—has shrunk to something no bigger than a walnut, and the new universe has grown so vast that prelates—and even cardinals—look like ants. Why, God Almighty might lose sight of a Pope! I wonder if I know your Father Confessor.

VIRGINIA Father Christopherus, from Saint Ursula's at Florence, Your Eminence.

INQUISITOR My dear child, your father will need you. Not so much now perhaps, but one of these days. You are pure, and there is strength in purity. Greatness is sometimes, indeed often, too heavy a burden for those to whom God has granted it. What man is so great that he has no place in a prayer? But I am keeping you, my dear. Your fiancé will be jealous of me, and I am afraid your father will never forgive me for holding forth on astronomy. Go to your dancing and remember me to Father Christopherus.

VIRGINIA kisses his ring and runs off. The INQUISITOR resumes his reading.

Scene 7

Galileo, feeling grim,
A young monk came to visit him.
The monk was born of common folk.
It was of science that they spoke.

Garden of the Florentine Ambassador in Rome. Distant hum of a great city. GALILEO *and the* LITTLE MONK *of Scene V are talking.*

GALILEO Let's hear it. That robe you're wearing gives you the right to say whatever you want to say. Let's hear it.

LITTLE MONK I have studied physics, Mr. Galilei.

GALILEO That might help us if it enabled you to admit that two and two are four.

LITTLE MONK Mr. Galilei, I have spent four sleepless nights trying to reconcile the decree that I have read with the moons of Jupiter that I have seen. This morning I decided to come to see you after I had said mass.

GALILEO To tell me that Jupiter has no moons?

LITTLE MONK No, I found out that I think the decree a wise decree. It has shocked me into realizing that free research has its dangers. I have had to decide to give up astronomy. However, I felt the impulse to confide in you some of the motives which have impelled even a passionate physicist to abandon his work.

GALILEO Your motives are familiar to me.

LITTLE MONK You mean, of course, the special powers invested in certain commissions of the Holy Office? But there is something else. I would like to talk to you about my family. I do not come from the great city. My parents are peasants in the Campagna, who know about the cultivation of the olive tree, and not much about anything else. Too often these days when I am trying to concentrate on tracking down the moons of Jupiter, I see my parents. I see them sitting by the fire with my sister, eating their curded cheese. I see the beams of the ceiling above them, which the smoke of centuries has blackened, and I can see the veins stand out on their toil-worn hands, and the little spoons in their hands. They scrape a living, and underlying their poverty there is a sort of order. There are routines. The routine of scrubbing the floors, the routine of the seasons in the olive orchard, the routine of paying taxes. The troubles that come to them are recurrent troubles. My father did not get his poor bent back all at once, but little by little, year by year, in the olive orchard. . . . They draw the strength they need to sweat with their loaded baskets up the stony paths, to bear children, even to eat, from the sight of the trees greening each year anew, from the reproachful face of the soil, which is never satisfied, and from the little church and Bible texts they hear there on Sunday. They have been told that God relies upon them and that the pageant of the world has been written around them that they may be tested in the important or unimportant parts handed out to them. How could they take it, were I to tell them that they are on a lump of stone ceaselessly spinning in empty space, circling around a second-rate star? What, then, would be the use of their patience, their acceptance of misery? What comfort, then, the Holy Scriptures, which have mercifully explained their crucifixion? The Holy Scriptures would then be proved full of mistakes. No, I see them begin to look frightened. I see them slowly put their spoons down on the table. They would feel cheated. "There is no eye watching over us, after all," they would say. "We have to start out on our own, at our time of life. Nobody has planned a part for us beyond this wretched one on a worthless star. There is no meaning in our misery. Hunger is just not having eaten. It is no test of strength. Effort is just stooping and carrying. It is not a virtue." Can you understand that I read into the decree of the Holy Office a noble, motherly pity and a great goodness of the soul?

GALILEO [*embarrassed*] Hm, well at least you have found out that it is not a question of the satellites of Jupiter, but of the peasants of the Campagna! And don't try to break me down by the halo of beauty that radiates from old age. How does a pearl develop in an oyster? A jagged grain of sand makes its way into the oyster shell and makes its life unbearable. The oyster exudes slime to cover the grain of sand and the slime eventually hardens into a pearl. The oyster nearly dies in the process. [Never mind] the pearl, give me the healthy oyster! And virtues are not exclusive to misery. If your parents were prosperous and happy, they might develop the virtues of happiness and prosperity. Today the virtues of exhaustion are caused by the exhausted land. For that, my new water pumps could work more wonders than their ridiculous superhuman efforts. Be fruitful and multiply: for war will cut down the population, and our fields are barren! [*A pause*] Shall I lie to your people?

LITTLE MONK We must be silent from the highest of motives: the inward peace of less fortunate souls.

GALILEO My dear man, as a bonus for not meddling with your parents' peace, the authorities are tendering me, on a silver platter, persecution-free, my share of the fat sweated from your parents, who, as you know, were made in God's image. Should I condone this decree, my motives might not be disinterested: easy life, no persecution and so on.

LITTLE MONK Mr. Galilei, I am a priest.

GALILEO You are also a physicist. How can new machinery be evolved to domesticate the river water if we physicists are forbidden to study, discuss, and pool our findings about the greatest machinery of all, the machinery of the heavenly bodies? Can I reconcile my findings on the paths of falling bodies with the current belief in the tracks of witches on broomsticks? [*A pause*] I am sorry—I shouldn't have said that.

LITTLE MONK You don't think that the truth, if it is the truth, would make its way without us?

GALILEO No! No! No! As much of the truth gets through as we push through. You talk about the Campagna peasants as if they were the moss on their huts. Naturally, if they don't get a move on and learn to think for themselves, the most efficient of irrigation systems cannot help them. I can see their divine patience, but where is their divine fury?

LITTLE MONK [*helpless*] They are old!

GALILEO *stands for a moment, beaten; he cannot meet the Little Monk's eyes. He takes a manuscript from the table and throws it violently on the ground.*

LITTLE MONK What is that?

GALILEO Here is writ what draws the ocean when it ebbs and flows. Let it lie there. Thou shalt not read. [*The* LITTLE MONK *has picked up the manuscript*] Already! An apple of the tree of knowledge, he can't wait, he wolfs it down. He will rot in hell for all eternity. Look at him, where are his manners? Sometimes I think I would let them imprison me in a place a thousand feet beneath the earth, where no light could reach me, if in exchange I could find out what stuff that is: "Light." The bad thing is that, when I find something, I have to boast about it like a lover or a drunkard or a traitor. That is a hopeless vice and leads to the abyss. I wonder how long I shall be content to discuss it with my dog!

LITTLE MONK [*immersed in the manuscript*] I don't understand this sentence.

GALILEO I'll explain it to you, I'll explain it to you.

They are sitting on the floor.

Scene 8

Eight long years with tongue in cheek
Of what he knew he did not speak.
Then temptation grew too great
And Galileo challenged fate.

Galileo's house in Florence again. GALILEO *is supervising his assistants—*ANDREA, FEDER-ZONI, *and the* LITTLE MONK*—who are about to prepare an experiment.* MRS. SARTI *and* VIRGINIA *are at a long table sewing bridal linen. There is a new telescope, larger than the old one. At the moment it is covered with a cloth.*

ANDREA [*looking up a schedule*] Thursday. Afternoon. Floating bodies again. Ice, bowl of water, scales, and it says here an iron needle. Aristotle.

VIRGINIA Ludovico likes to entertain. We must take care to be neat. His mother notices every stitch. She doesn't approve of father's books.

MRS. SARTI That's all a thing of the past. He hasn't published a book for years.

VIRGINIA That's true. Oh, Sarti, it's fun sewing a trousseau.

MRS. SARTI Virginia, I want to talk to you. You are very young, and you have no mother, and your father is putting those pieces of ice in water, and marriage is too serious a business to go into blind. Now you should go to see a real astronomer from the university and have him cast your horoscope so you know where you stand. [VIRGINIA *giggles*] What's the matter?

VIRGINIA I've been already.

MRS. SARTI Tell Sarti.

VIRGINIA I have to be careful for three months now because the sun is in Capricorn, but after that I get a favorable ascendant, and I can undertake a journey if I am careful of Uranus, as I'm a Scorpion.

MRS. SARTI What about Ludovico?

VIRGINIA He's a Leo, the astronomer said. Leos are sensual. [*Giggles*]

There is a knock at the door, it opens. Enter the RECTOR OF THE UNIVERSITY, *the philosopher of Scene IV, bringing a book.*

RECTOR [*to* VIRGINIA] This is about the burning issue of the moment. He may want to glance over it. My faculty would appreciate his comments. No, don't disturb him now, my dear. Every minute one takes of your father's time is stolen from Italy. [*He goes*]

VIRGINIA Federzoni! The rector of the university brought this.

FEDERZONI *takes it.*

GALILEO What's it about?

FEDERZONI [*spelling*] D-e m-a-c-u-l-i-s i-n s-o-l-e.

ANDREA Oh, it's on the sun spots!

ANDREA *comes to one side, and the* LITTLE MONK *the other, to look at the book.*

ANDREA A new one!

FEDERZONI *resentfully puts the book into their hands and continues with the preparation of the experiment.*

ANDREA Listen to this dedication. [*Quotes*] "To the greatest living authority on physics, Galileo Galilei." I read Fabricius' paper the other day. Fabricius says the spots are clusters of planets between us and the sun.

LITTLE MONK Doubtful.

GALILEO [*noncommittal*] Yes?

ANDREA Paris and Prague hold that they are vapors from the sun. Federzoni doubts that.

FEDERZONI Me? You leave me out. I said "hm," that was all. And don't discuss new things before me. I can't read the material, it's in Latin. [*He drops the scales and stands trembling with fury*] Tell me, can I doubt anything?

GALILEO *walks over and picks up the scales silently. Pause.*

LITTLE MONK   There is happiness in doubting, I wonder why.

ANDREA   Aren't we going to take this up?

GALILEO   At the moment we are investigating floating bodies.

ANDREA   Mother has baskets full of letters from all over Europe asking his opinion.

FEDERZONI   The question is whether you can afford to remain silent.

GALILEO   I cannot afford to be smoked on a wood fire like a ham.

ANDREA   [*surprised*]   Ah. You think the sun spots may have something to do with that again?   [GALILEO *does not answer*] Well, we stick to fiddling about with bits of ice in water. That can't hurt you.

GALILEO   Correct. Our thesis!

ANDREA   All things that are lighter than water float, and all things that are heavier sink.

GALILEO   Aristotle says——

LITTLE MONK   [*reading out of a book, translating*]   "A broad and flat disk of ice, although heavier than water, still floats, because it is unable to divide the water."

GALILEO   Well. Now I push the ice below the surface. I take away the pressure of my hands. What happens?

Pause.

LITTLE MONK   It rises to the surface.

GALILEO   Correct. It seems to be able to divide the water as it's coming up, doesn't it?

LITTLE MONK   Could it be lighter than water after all?

GALILEO   Aha!

ANDREA   Then all things that are lighter than water float, and all things that are heavier sink. Q.E.D.[3]

GALILEO   Not at all. Hand me that iron needle. Heavier than water?   [*They all nod*]   A piece of paper.   [*He places the needle on a piece of paper and floats it on the surface of the water. Pause*]   Do not be hasty with your conclusion. [*Pause*] What happens?

FEDERZONI   The paper has sunk, the needle is floating.   [*They laugh*]

VIRGINIA   What's the matter?

MRS. SARTI   Every time I hear them laugh it sends shivers down my spine.

There is a knocking at the outer door.

MRS. SARTI   Who's that at the door?

Enter LUDOVICO. VIRGINIA *runs to him. They embrace.* LUDOVICO *is followed by a* SERVANT *with baggage.*

MRS. SARTI   Well!

VIRGINIA   Oh! Why didn't you write that you were coming?

LUDOVICO   I decided on the spur of the moment. I was over inspecting our vineyards at Bucciole. I couldn't keep away.

GALILEO   Who's that?

LITTLE MONK   Miss Virginia's intended. What's the matter with your eyes?

GALILEO   [*blinking*]   Oh, yes, it's Ludovico, so it is. Well! Sarti, get a jug of that Sicilian wine, the old kind. We celebrate.

Everybody sits down. MRS. SARTI *has left, followed by* LUDOVICO's *servant.*

GALILEO   Well, Ludovico, old man. How are the horses?

LUDOVICO   The horses are fine.

GALILEO   Fine.

LUDOVICO   But those vineyards need a firm hand.   [*To* VIRGINIA]   You look pale. Country life will suit you. Mother's planning on September.

VIRGINIA   I suppose I oughtn't, but stay here, I've got something to show you.

LUDOVICO   What?

VIRGINIA   Never mind. I won't be ten minutes. [*She runs out*]

LUDOVICO   How's life these days, sir?

GALILEO   Dull. How was the journey?

LUDOVICO   Dull. Before I forget, mother sends her congratulations on your ad-

---

3 Q.E.D.   *Abbreviation of the Latin phrase* quod erat demonstrandum, *meaning "which was the thing to be proved."*

mirable tact over the latest rumblings of science.

GALILEO Thank her from me.

LUDOVICO Christopher Clavius had all Rome on its ears. He said he was afraid that the turning-around business might crop up again on account of these spots on the sun.

ANDREA Clavius is on the same track! [*To* LUDOVICO] My mother's baskets are full of letters from all over Europe asking Mr. Galilei's opinion.

GALILEO I am engaged in investigating the habits of floating bodies. Any harm in that?

MRS. SARTI *re-enters, followed by the* SERVANT. *They bring wine and glasses on a tray.*

GALILEO [*hands out the wine*] What news from the Holy City, apart from the prospect of my sins?

LUDOVICO The Holy Father is on his deathbed. Hadn't you heard?

LITTLE MONK My goodness! What about the succession?

LUDOVICO All the talk is of Barberini.

GALILEO Barberini?

ANDREA Mr. Galilei knows Barberini.

LITTLE MONK Cardinal Barberini is a mathematician.

FEDERZONI A scientist in the chair of Peter!

Pause.

GALILEO [*cheering up enormously*] This means change. We might live to see the day, Federzoni, when we don't have to whisper that two and two are four. [*To* LUDOVICO] I like this wine. Don't you, Ludovico?

LUDOVICO I like it.

GALILEO I know the hill where it is grown. The slope is steep and stony, the grape almost blue. I am fond of this wine.

LUDOVICO Yes, sir.

GALILEO There are shadows in this wine. It is almost sweet but just stops short. . . . Andrea, clear that stuff away, ice, bowl,

and needle. . . . I cherish the consolations of the flesh. I have no patience with cowards who call them weaknesses. I say there is a certain achievement in enjoying things.

The PUPILS *get up and go to the experiment table.*

LITTLE MONK What are we to do?

FEDERZONI He is starting on the sun.

They begin with clearing up.

ANDREA [*singing in a low voice*]
The Bible proves the earth stands still,
The Pope, he swears with tears:
The earth stands still. To prove it so
He takes it by the ears.

LUDOVICO What's the excitement?

MRS. SARTI You're not going to start those hellish goings-on again, Mr. Galilei?

ANDREA
And gentlefolk, they say so too.
Each learned doctor proves
(If you grease his palm): The earth stands still.
And yet—and yet it moves.

GALILEO Barberini is in the ascendant, so your mother is uneasy, and you're sent to investigate me. Correct me if I am wrong, Ludovico. Clavius is right: these spots on the sun interest me.

ANDREA We might find out that the sun also revolves. How would you like that, Ludovico?

GALILEO Do you like my wine, Ludovico?

LUDOVICO I told you I did, sir.

GALILEO You really like it?

LUDOVICO I like it.

GALILEO Tell me, Ludovico, would you consider going so far as to accept a man's wine or his daughter without insisting that he drop his profession? I have no wish to intrude, but have the moons of Jupiter affected Virginia's [figure]?

MRS. SARTI That isn't funny, it's just vulgar. I am going for Virginia.

LUDOVICO [*keeps her back*] Marriages in families such as mine are not arranged on a basis of [physical] attraction alone.

GALILEO Did they keep you back from marrying my daughter for eight years because I was on probation?

LUDOVICO My future wife must take her place in the family pew.

GALILEO You mean, if the daughter of a bad man sat in your family pew, your peasants might stop paying the rent?

LUDOVICO In a sort of way.

GALILEO When I was your age, the only person I allowed to rap me on the knuckles was my girl.

LUDOVICO My mother was assured that you had undertaken not to get mixed up in this turning-around business again, sir.

GALILEO We had a conservative Pope then.

MRS. SARTI Had! His Holiness is not dead yet!

GALILEO [*with relish*] Pretty nearly.

MRS. SARTI That man will weigh a chip of ice fifty times, but when it comes to something that's convenient, he believes it blindly. "Is His Holiness dead?" "Pretty nearly!"

LUDOVICO You will find, sir, if His Holiness passes away, the new Pope, whoever he turns out to be, will respect the convictions held by the solid families of the country.

GALILEO [*to* ANDREA] That remains to be seen. Andrea, get out the screen. We'll throw the image of the sun on our screen to save our eyes.

LITTLE MONK I thought you'd been working at it. Do you know when I guessed it? When you didn't recognize Mr. Marsili.

MRS. SARTI If my son has to go to hell for sticking to you, that's my affair, but you have no right to trample on your daughter's happiness.

LUDOVICO [*to his* SERVANT] Giuseppe, take my baggage back to the coach, will you?

MRS. SARTI This will kill her. [*She runs out, still clutching the jug*]

LUDOVICO [*politely*] Mr. Galilei, if we Marsilis were to countenance teachings frowned on by the church, it would unsettle our peasants. Bear in mind: these poor people in their brute state get everything upside down. They are nothing but animals. They will never comprehend the finer points of astronomy. Why, two months ago a rumor went around, an apple had been found on a pear tree, and they left their work in the fields to discuss it.

GALILEO [*interested*] Did they?

LUDOVICO I have seen the day when my poor mother has had to have a dog whipped before their eyes to remind them to keep their place. Oh, you may have seen the waving corn from the window of your comfortable coach. You have, no doubt, nibbled our olives, and absentmindedly eaten our cheese, but you can have no idea how much responsibility that sort of thing entails.

GALILEO Young man, I do not eat my cheese absentmindedly. [*To* ANDREA] Are we ready?

ANDREA Yes, sir.

GALILEO [*leaves* LUDOVICO *and adjusts the mirror*] You would not confine your whippings to dogs to remind your peasants to keep their places, would you, Marsili?

LUDOVICO [*after a pause*] Mr. Galilei, you have a wonderful brain, it's a pity.

LITTLE MONK [*astonished*] He threatened you.

GALILEO Yes. And he threatened you too. We might unsettle his peasants. Your sister, Fulganzio, who works the lever of the olive press, might laugh out loud if she heard the sun is not a gilded coat of arms but a lever too. The earth turns because the sun turns it.

ANDREA That could interest his steward too and even his moneylender—and the seaport towns . . .

FEDERZONI None of them speak Latin.

GALILEO   I might write in plain language. The work we do is exacting. Who would go through the strain for less than the population at large!

LUDOVICO   I see you have made your decision. It was inevitable. You will always be a slave of your passions. Excuse me to Virginia. I think it's as well I don't see her now.

GALILEO   The dowry is at your disposal at any time.

LUDOVICO   Good afternoon. [*He goes, followed by the* SERVANT]

ANDREA   Exit Ludovico. [Good-bye to] all Marsilis, Villanis, Orsinis, Canes, Nuccolis, Soldanieris . . .[4]

FEDERZONI   . . . who ordered the earth stand still because their castles might be shaken loose if it revolves . . .

LITTLE MONK   . . . and who only kiss the Pope's feet as long as he uses them to trample on the people. God made the physical world, God made the human brain. God will allow physics.

ANDREA   They will try to stop us.

GALILEO   Thus we enter the observation of these spots on the sun in which we are interested, at our own risk, not counting on protection from a problematical new Pope . . .

ANDREA   . . . but with great likelihood of dispelling Fabricius' vapors, and the shadows of Paris and Prague, and of establishing the rotation of the sun . . .

GALILEO   . . . and with *some* likelihood of establishing the rotation of the sun. My intention is not to prove that I was right but to find out *whether* I was right. "Abandon hope all ye who enter—an observation." Before assuming these phenomena are spots, which would suit us, let us first set about proving that they are not—fried fish. We crawl by inches. What we find today we will wipe from the blackboard tomorrow and reject it—unless it shows up again the day after tomorrow. And if we find anything which

would suit us, that thing we will eye with particular distrust. In fact, we will approach this observing of the sun with the implacable determination to prove that the earth stands still, and only if hopelessly defeated in this pious undertaking can we allow ourselves to wonder if we may not have been right all the time: the earth revolves. Take the cloth off the telescope and turn it on the sun.

Quietly they start work. When the coruscating image of the sun is focused on the screen, VIRGINIA *enters hurriedly, her wedding dress on, her hair disheveled,* MRS. SARTI *with her, carrying her wedding veil. The two women realize what has happened.* VIRGINIA *faints.* ANDREA, LITTLE MONK, *and* GALILEO *rush to her.* FEDERZONI *continues working.*

Scene 9

On April Fools' Day, thirty two,
Of science there was much ado.
People had learned from Galilei:
They used his teaching in their way.

Around the corner from the market place a BALLAD SINGER *and his* WIFE, *who is costumed to represent the earth in a skeleton globe made of thin bands of brass, are holding the attention of a sprinkling of representative citizens, some in masquerade, who were on their way to see the carnival procession. From the market place the noise of an impatient crowd.*

BALLAD SINGER   [*accompanied by his* WIFE *on the guitar*]
When the Almighty made the universe
He made the earth and then he made the sun.
Then round the earth he bade the sun to turn—
That's in the Bible, Genesis, Chapter One.
And from that time all beings here below

---

4   Marsilis, Villanis, Orsinis, Canes, Nuccolis, Soldanieris
Noble Italian families.

Were in obedient circles meant to go:
　Around the pope the cardinals
　Around the cardinals the bishops
　Around the bishops the secretaries
　Around the secretaries the aldermen
　Around the aldermen the craftsmen
　Around the craftsmen the servants
　Around the servants the dogs, the chickens,
　　and the beggars.

*A conspicuous reveller—henceforth called
the* SPINNER—*has slowly caught on and is ex-
hibiting his idea of spinning around. He does
not lose dignity, he faints with mock grace.*

BALLAD SINGER
Up stood the learned Galileo
Glanced briefly at the sun
And said: "Almighty God was wrong
In Genesis, Chapter One!"
　Now that was rash, my friends, it is no
　　matter small:
　For heresy will spread today like foul dis-
　　eases.
　Change Holy Writ, forsooth? What will be
　　left at all?
　Why: each of us would say and do just
　　what he pleases!

Three wretched EXTRAS, *employed by the
Chamber of Commerce, enter. Two of them,
in ragged costumes, moodily bear a litter with
a mock throne. The third sits on the throne.
He wears sacking, a false beard, a prop
crown, he carries a prop orb and sceptre, and
around his chest the inscription "*THE KING OF
HUNGARY.*" The litter has a card with "No. 4"
written on it. The litter bearers dump him
down and listen to the* BALLAD SINGER.

BALLAD SINGER
Good people, what will come to pass
If Galileo's teachings spread?
No altar boy will serve the mass
No servant girl will make the bed.
　Now that is grave, my friends, it is no
　　matter small:

For independent spirit spreads like foul
　diseases!
(Yet life is sweet and man is weak and
　after all—
How nice it is, for a little change, to do
　just as one pleases!)

The BALLAD SINGER *takes over the guitar. His*
WIFE *dances around him, illustrating the motion of the earth. A* COBBLER'S BOY *with a pair
of resplendent lacquered boots hung over his
shoulder has been jumping up and down in
mock excitement. There are three more children, dressed as grownups, among the spectators, two together and a single one with
mother. The* COBBLER'S BOY *takes the three*
CHILDREN *in hand, forms a chain and leads it,
moving to the music, in and out among the
spectators, "whipping" the chain so that the
last child bumps into people. On the way
past a* PEASANT WOMAN, *he steals an egg
from her basket. She gestures to him to return it. As he passes her again he quietly
breaks the egg over her head. The* KING OF
HUNGARY *ceremoniously hands his orb to one
of his bearers, marches down with mock dignity, and chastises the* COBBLER'S BOY. *The
parents remove the three* CHILDREN. *The un-
seemliness subsides.*

BALLAD SINGER
The carpenters take wood and build
Their houses—not the church's pews.
And members of the cobblers' guild
Now boldly walk the streets—in shoes.
The tenant kicks the noble lord
Quite off the land he owned—like that!
The milk his wife once gave the priest
Now makes (at last!) her children fat.
　Ts, ts, ts, ts, my friends, this is no matter
　　small:
　For independent spirit spreads like foul
　　diseases.
　People must keep their place, some down
　　and some on top!
　(Though it is nice, for a little change, to
　　do just as one pleases!)

The COBBLER'S BOY *has put on the lacquered boots he was carrying. He struts off. The* BALLAD SINGER *takes over the guitar again. His* WIFE *dances around him in increased tempo. A* MONK *has been standing near a* RICH COUPLE, *who are in subdued, costly clothes, without masks; shocked at the song, he now leaves. A* DWARF *in the costume of an astronomer turns his telescope on the departing* MONK, *thus drawing attention to the* RICH COUPLE. *In imitation of the* COBBLER'S BOY, *the* SPINNER *forms a chain of grownups. They move to the music, in and out, and between the* RICH COUPLE. *The* SPINNER *changes the gentleman's bonnet for the ragged hat of a beggar. The* GENTLEMAN *decides to take this in good part, and a* GIRL *is emboldened to take his dagger. The* GENTLEMAN *is miffed, throws the beggar's hat back. The* BEGGAR *discards the gentleman's bonnet and drops it on the ground. The* KING OF HUNGARY *has walked from his throne, taken an egg from the* PEASANT WOMAN, *and paid for it. He now ceremoniously breaks it over the gentleman's head as he is bending down to pick up his bonnet. The* GENTLEMAN *conducts the* LADY *away from the scene. The* KING OF HUNGARY, *about to resume his throne, finds one of the* CHILDREN *sitting on it. The* GENTLEMAN *returns to retrieve his dagger. Merriment. The* BALLAD SINGER *wanders off. This is part of his routine. His* WIFE *sings to the* SPINNER.

WIFE
Now speaking for myself I feel
That I could also do with a change.
You know, for me—[*turning to a reveller*]—
    you have appeal
Maybe tonight we could arrange . . .

The DWARF-ASTRONOMER *has been amusing the people by focusing his telescope on her legs. The* BALLAD SINGER *has returned.*

BALLAD SINGER
No, no, no, no, no, stop, Galileo, stop!
For independent spirit spreads like foul diseases.

People must keep their place, some down and
    some on top!
(Though it is nice, for a little change, to do
    just as one pleases!)

The SPECTATORS *stand embarrassed. A* GIRL *laughs loudly.*

BALLAD SINGER AND HIS WIFE
Good people who have trouble here below
In serving cruel lords and gentle Jesus
Who bids you turn the other cheek just so . . .
    (*With mimicry.*)
While they prepare to strike the second blow:
Obedience will never cure your woe
So each of you wake up and do just as he
    pleases!

The BALLAD SINGER *and his* WIFE *hurriedly start to try to sell pamphlets to the spectators.*

BALLAD SINGER   Read all about the earth going round the sun, two centesimi only. As proved by the great Galileo. Two centesimi only. Written by a local scholar. Understandable to one and all. Buy one for your friends, your children and your Aunty Rosa, two centesimi only. Abbreviated but complete. Fully illustrated with pictures of the planets, including Venus, two centesimi only.

During the speech of the BALLAD SINGER *we hear the carnival procession approaching, followed by laughter. A* REVELLER *rushes in.*

REVELLER   The procession!

The litter bearers speedily joggle out the KING OF HUNGARY. *The* SPECTATORS *turn and look at the first float of the procession, which now makes its appearance. It bears a gigantic figure of* GALILEO, *holding in one hand an open Bible with the pages crossed out. The other hand points to the Bible, and the head mechanically turns from side to side as if to say "No! No!"*

A LOUD VOICE   Galileo, the Bible-killer!

The laughter from the market place becomes uproarious. The MONK *comes flying from the market place followed by delighted* CHILDREN.

Scene 10

The depths are hot, the heights are chill,
The streets are loud, the court is still.

Antechamber and staircase in the Medicean
palace in Florence. GALILEO, *with a book un-*
der his arm, waits with his daughter VIRGINIA
to be admitted to the presence of the PRINCE.

VIRGINIA   They are a long time.

GALILEO   Yes.

VIRGINIA   Who is that funny-looking man?
[*She indicates the* INFORMER, *who has
entered casually and seated himself in
the background, taking no apparent
notice of* GALILEO]

GALILEO   I don't know.

VIRGINIA   It's not the first time I have seen
him around. He gives me the creeps.

GALILEO   Nonsense. We're in Florence, not
among robbers in the mountains of Cor-
sica.

VIRGINIA   Here comes the Rector.

The RECTOR *comes down the stairs.*

GALILEO   Gaffone is a bore. He attaches himself to you.

The RECTOR *passes, scarcely nodding.*

GALILEO   My eyes are bad today. Did he
acknowledge us?

VIRGINIA   Barely. [*Pause*] What's in your
book? Will they say it's heretical?

GALILEO   You hang around church too much.
And getting up at dawn and scurrying to
mass is ruining your skin. You pray for
me, don't you?

A MAN *comes down the stairs.*

VIRGINIA   Here's Mr. Matti. You designed a
machine for his iron foundries.

MATTI   How were the squabs, Mr. Galilei?
[*Low*] My brother and I had a good
laugh the other day. He picked up a racy
pamphlet against the Bible somewhere.
It quoted you.

GALILEO   The squabs, Matti, were wonderful,
thank you again. Pamphlets I know
nothing about. The Bible and Homer are
my favorite reading.

MATTI   No necessity to be cautious with me,
Mr. Galilei. I am on your side. I am not
a man who knows about the motions of
the stars, but you have championed the
freedom to teach new things. Take that
mechanical cultivator they have in Germany which you described to me. I can
tell you, it will never be used in this
country. The same circles that are ham-
pering you now will forbid the physicians
at Bologna to cut up corpses for research.
Do you know, they have such things as
money markets in Amsterdam and in
London? Schools for business, too. Regular papers with news. Here we are not
even free to make money. I have a stake
in your career. They are against iron
foundries because they say the gathering
of so many workers in one place fosters
immorality! If they ever try anything, Mr.
Galilei, remember you have friends in all
walks of life, including an iron founder.
Good luck to you.   [*He goes*]

GALILEO   Good man, but need he be so affec-
tionate in public? His voice carries. They
will always claim me as their spiritual
leader, particularly in places where it
doesn't help me at all. I have written a
book about the mechanics of the firma-
ment, that is all. What they do or don't
do with it is not my concern.

VIRGINIA   [*loud*] If people only knew how
you disagreed with those goings-on all
over the country last All Fools' day.

GALILEO   Yes. Offer honey to a bear, and
lose your arm if the beast is hungry.

VIRGINIA   [*low*] Did the Prince ask you to
come here today?

GALILEO   I sent word I was coming. He will
want the book, he has paid for it. My
health hasn't been any too good lately. I
may accept Sagredo's invitation to stay
with him in Padua for a few weeks.

VIRGINIA You couldn't manage without your books.

GALILEO Sagredo has an excellent library.

VIRGINIA We haven't had this month's salary yet——

GALILEO Yes. [*The* CARDINAL INQUISITOR *passes down the staircase. He bows deeply in answer to Galileo's bow*] What is he doing in Florence? If they try to do anything to me, the new Pope will meet with them with an iron NO. And the Prince is my pupil, he would never have me extradited.

VIRGINIA Psst. The Lord Chamberlain.

The LORD CHAMBERLAIN *comes down the stairs.*

LORD CHAMBERLAIN His Highness had hoped to find time for you, Mr. Galilei. Unfortunately, he has to leave immediately to judge the parade at the Riding Academy. On what business did you wish to see His Highness?

GALILEO I wanted to present my book to His Highness.

LORD CHAMBERLAIN How are your eyes today?

GALILEO So, so. With His Highness' permission, I am dedicating the book . . .

LORD CHAMBERLAIN Your eyes are a matter of great concern to His Highness. Could it be that you have been looking too long and too often through your marvelous tube? [*He leaves without accepting the book*]

VIRGINIA [*greatly agitated*] Father, I am afraid.

GALILEO He didn't take the book, did he? [*Low and resolute*] Keep a straight face. We are not going home, but to the house of the lens-grinder. There is a coach and horses in his backyard. Keep your eyes to the front, don't look back at that man.

They start. The LORD CHAMBERLAIN *comes back.*

LORD CHAMBERLAIN Oh, Mr. Galilei, His Highness has just charged me to inform you that the Florentine court is no longer in a position to oppose the request of the Holy Inquisition to interrogate you in Rome.

Scene 11

The Pope

A chamber in the Vatican. The POPE, URBAN VIII—*formerly Cardinal Barberini—is giving audience to the* CARDINAL INQUISITOR. *The trampling and shuffling of many feet is heard throughout the scene from the adjoining corridors. During the scene the* POPE *is being robed for the conclave he is about to attend: at the beginning of the scene he is plainly Barberini, but as the scene proceeds he is more and more obscured by grandiose vestments.*

POPE No! No! No!

INQUISITOR [*referring to the owners of the shuffling feet*] Doctors of all chairs from the universities, representatives of the special orders of the Church, representatives of the clergy as a whole, who have come believing with childlike faith in the word of God as set forth in the Scriptures, who have come to hear Your Holiness confirm their faith: and Your Holiness is really going to tell them that the Bible can no longer be regarded as the alphabet of truth?

POPE I will not set myself up against the multiplication table. No!

INQUISITOR Ah, that is what these people say, that it is the multiplication table. Their cry is, "The figures compel us," but where do these figures come from? Plainly they come from doubt. These men doubt everything. Can society stand on doubt and not on faith? "Thou are my

160

master, but I doubt whether it is for the best." "This is my neighbor's house and my neighbor's wife, but why shouldn't they belong to me?" After the plague, after the new war, after the unparalleled disaster of the Reformation, your dwindling flock look to their shepherd, and now the mathematicians turn their tubes on the sky and announce to the world that you have not the best advice about the heavens either—up to now your only uncontested sphere of influence. This Galilei started meddling in machines at an early age. Now that men in ships are venturing on the great oceans—I am not against that of course—they are putting their faith in a brass bowl they call a compass and not in Almighty God.

POPE This man is the greatest physicist of our time. He is the light of Italy, and not just any muddlehead.

INQUISITOR Would we have had to arrest him otherwise? This bad man knows what he is doing, not writing his books in Latin, but in the jargon of the market place.

POPE [*occupied with the shuffling feet*] That was not in the best of taste. [*A pause*] These shuffling feet are making me nervous.

INQUISITOR May they be more telling than my words, Your Holiness. Shall all these go from you with doubt in their hearts?

POPE This man has friends. What about Versailles?[5] What about the Viennese court? They will call Holy Church a cesspool for defunct ideas. Keep your hands off him.

INQUISITOR In practice it will never get far. He is a man of the flesh. He would soften at once.

POPE He has more enjoyment in him than any man I ever saw. He loves eating and drinking and thinking. To excess. He indulges in thinking-bouts! He cannot say no to an old wine or a new thought. [*Furious*] I do not want a condemna-

tion of physical facts. I do not want to hear battle cries: Church, Church, Church! Reason, Reason, Reason! [*Pause*] These shuffling feet are intolerable. Has the whole world come to my door?

INQUISITOR Not the whole world, Your Holiness. A select gathering of the faithful.

Pause.

POPE [*exhausted*] It is clearly understood: he is not to be tortured. [*Pause*] At the very most, he may be shown the instruments.

INQUISITOR That will be adequate, Your Holiness. Mr. Galilei understands machinery.

The eyes of BARBERINI *look helplessly at the* CARDINAL INQUISITOR *from under the completely assembled panoply of* POPE URBAN VIII.

Scene 12

June twenty second, sixteen thirty three,
A momentous date for you and me.
Of all the days that was the one
An age of reason could have begun.

Again the garden of the Florentine AMBASSADOR *at Rome, where Galileo's assistants wait the news of the trial. The* LITTLE MONK *and* FEDERZONI *are attempting to concentrate on a game of chess.* VIRGINIA *kneels in a corner, praying and counting her beads.*

LITTLE MONK The Pope didn't even grant him an audience.

FEDERZONI No more scientific discussions.

ANDREA The "Discorsi"[6] will never be finished. The sum of his findings. They will kill him.

5 Versailles *The French court. Brecht was either in error or was making some sort of joke here, because the French court did not in fact move to Versailles until* many years after the time of the play.
6 "Discorsi" The Discourses, Galileo's great book in which he set forth his discoveries.

FEDERZONI [*stealing a glance at him*] Do you really think so?

ANDREA He will never recant.

Silence.

LITTLE MONK You know when you lie awake at night how your mind fastens on to something irrelevant. Last night I kept thinking: if only they would let him take his little stone in with him, the appeal-to-reason-pebble that he always carries in his pocket.

FEDERZONI In the room *they'll* take him to, he won't have a pocket.

ANDREA But he will not recant.

LITTLE MONK How can they beat the truth out of a man who gave his sight in order to see?

FEDERZONI Maybe they can't.

Silence.

ANDREA [*speaking about* VIRGINIA] She is praying that he will recant.

FEDERZONI Leave her alone. She doesn't know whether she's on her head or on her heels since they got hold of her. They brought her Father Confessor from Florence.

The INFORMER *of Scene X enters.*

INFORMER Mr. Galilei will be here soon. He may need a bed.

FEDERZONI Have they let him out?

INFORMER Mr. Galilei is expected to recant at five o'clock. The big bell of Saint Marcus will be rung and the complete text of his recantation publicly announced.

ANDREA I don't believe it.

INFORMER Mr. Galilei will be brought to the garden gate at the back of the house, to avoid the crowds collecting in the streets. [*He goes*]

Silence.

ANDREA The moon is an earth because the light of the moon is not her own. Jupiter is a fixed star, and four moons turn around Jupiter, therefore we are not shut in by crystal shells. The sun is the pivot of our world, therefore the earth is not the center. The earth moves, spinning about the sun. And he showed us. You can't make a man unsee what he has seen.

Silence.

FEDERZONI Five o'clock is one minute.

VIRGINIA *prays louder.*

ANDREA Listen all of you, they are murdering the truth.

He stops up his ears with his fingers. The two other pupils do the same. FEDERZONI *goes over to the* LITTLE MONK, *and all of them stand absolutely still in cramped positions. Nothing happens. No bell sounds. After a silence, filled with the murmur of* VIRGINIA's *prayers,* FEDERZONI *runs to the wall to look at the clock. He turns around, his expression changed. He shakes his head. They drop their hands.*

FEDERZONI No. No bell. It is three minutes after.

LITTLE MONK He hasn't.

ANDREA He held true. It is all right, it is all right.

LITTLE MONK He did not recant.

FEDERZONI No.

They embrace each other, they are delirious with joy.

ANDREA So force cannot accomplish everything. What has been seen can't be unseen. Man is constant in the face of death.

FEDERZONI June 22, 1633: dawn of the age of reason. I wouldn't have wanted to go on living if he had recanted.

LITTLE MONK I didn't say anything, but I was in agony. O ye of little faith!

ANDREA I was sure.

FEDERZONI It would have turned our morning to night.

ANDREA It would have been as if the mountain had turned to water.

LITTLE MONK [*kneeling down, crying*] O God, I thank Thee.

ANDREA Beaten humanity can lift its head. A man has stood up and said No.

At this moment the bell of Saint Marcus begins to toll. They stand like statues. VIRGINIA *stands up.*

VIRGINIA The bell of Saint Marcus. He is not damned.

From the street one hears the TOWN CRIER *reading* GALILEO's *recantation.*

TOWN CRIER I, Galileo Galilei, Teacher of Mathematics and Physics, do hereby publicly renounce my teaching that the earth moves. I forswear this teaching with a sincere heart and unfeigned faith and detest and curse this and all other errors and heresies repugnant to the Holy Scriptures.

The lights dim; when they come up again the bell of Saint Marcus is petering out. VIRGINIA *has gone but the* SCHOLARS *are still there waiting.*

ANDREA [*loud*] The mountain did turn to water.

GALILEO *has entered quietly and unnoticed. He is changed, almost unrecognizable. He has heard* ANDREA. *He waits some seconds by the door for somebody to greet him. Nobody does. They retreat from him. He goes slowly and, because of his bad sight, uncertainly, to the front of the stage, where he finds a chair and sits down.*

ANDREA I can't look at him. Tell him to go away.

FEDERZONI Steady.

ANDREA [*hysterically*] He saved his big gut.

FEDERZONI Get him a glass of water.

The LITTLE MONK *fetches a glass of water for* ANDREA. *Nobody acknowledges the presence of* GALILEO, *who sits silently on his chair listening to the voice of the* TOWN CRIER, *now in another street.*

ANDREA I can walk. Just help me a bit.

They help him to the door.

ANDREA [*in the door*] "Unhappy is the land that breeds no hero."

GALILEO No, Andrea: "Unhappy is the land that needs a hero."

Before the next scene, a curtain with the following legend on it is lowered:

> You can plainly see that if a horse were to fall from a height of three or four feet, it could break its bones, whereas a dog would not suffer injury. The same applies to a cat from a height of as much as eight or ten feet, to a grasshopper from the top of a tower, and to an ant falling down from the moon. Nature could not allow a horse to become as big as twenty horses nor a giant as big as ten men, unless she were to change the proportions of all its members, particularly the bones. Thus the common assumption that great and small structures are equally tough is obviously wrong.
>
> —From the "Discorsi"

Scene 13

1633–1642
Galileo Galilei remains a prisoner of the Inquisition until his death.

A country house near Florence. A large room simply furnished. There is a huge table, a leather chair, a globe of the world on a stand, and a narrow bed. A portion of the adjoining anteroom is visible, and the front door, which opens into it. An OFFICIAL *of the Inquisition sits on guard in the anteroom. In the large room,* GALILEO *is quietly experimenting with a bent wooden rail and a small ball of wood. He is still vigorous but almost blind. After a while there is a knocking at the outside door. The* OFFICIAL *opens it to a peasant who brings a plucked goose.* VIRGINIA *comes from the kitchen. She is past forty.*

PEASANT [*handing the goose to* VIRGINIA] I was told to deliver this here.

VIRGINIA I didn't order a goose.

PEASANT I was told to say it's from someone who was passing through.

VIRGINIA *takes the goose, surprised. The* OFFICIAL *takes it from her and examines it suspicuously. Then, reassured, he hands it back to her. The* PEASANT *goes.* VIRGINIA *brings the goose in to* GALILEO.

VIRGINIA Somebody who was passing through sent you something.

GALILEO What is it?

VIRGINIA Can't you see it?

GALILEO No. [*He walks over*] A goose. Any name?

VIRGINIA No.

GALILEO [*weighing the goose*] Solid.

VIRGINIA [*cautiously*] Will you eat the liver, if I have it cooked with a little apple?

GALILEO I had my dinner. Are you under orders to finish me off with food?

VIRGINIA It's not rich. And what is wrong with your eyes again? You should be able to see it.

GALILEO You were standing in the light.

VIRGINIA I was not. You haven't been writing again?

GALILEO [*sneering*] What do you think?

VIRGINIA *takes the goose out into the anteroom and speaks to the* OFFICIAL.

VIRGINIA You had better ask Monsignor Carpula to send the doctor. Father couldn't see this goose across the room. Don't look at me like that. He has not been writing. He dictates everything to me, as you know.

OFFICIAL Yes?

VIRGINIA He abides by the rules. My father's repentance is sincere. I keep an eye on him. [*She hands him the goose*] Tell the cook to fry the liver with an apple and an onion. [*She goes back into the large room*] And you have no business to be doing that with those eyes of yours, father.

GALILEO You may read me some Horace.

VIRGINIA We should go on with your weekly letter to the Archbishop. Monsignor Carpula, to whom we owe so much, was all smiles the other day because the Archbishop had expressed his pleasure at your collaboration.

GALILEO Where were we?

VIRGINIA [*sits down to take his dictation*] Paragraph four.

GALILEO Read what you have.

VIRGINIA "The position of the Church in the matter of the unrest at Genoa. I agree with Cardinal Spoletti in the matter of the unrest among the Venetian rope-makers . . ."

GALILEO Yes. [*Dictates*] I agree with Cardinal Spoletti in the matter of the unrest among the Venetian rope-makers: it is better to distribute good, nourishing food in the name of charity than to pay them more for their bell ropes. It being surely better to strengthen their faith than to encourage their acquisitiveness. St. Paul says: Charity never faileth. . . . How is that?

VIRGINIA It's beautiful, father.

GALILEO It couldn't be taken as irony?

VIRGINIA No. The Archbishop will like it. It's so practical.

GALILEO I trust your judgment. Read it over slowly.

VIRGINIA "The position of the Church in the matter of the unrest——"

There is a knocking at the outside door. VIRGINIA *goes into the anteroom. The* OFFICIAL *opens the door. It is* ANDREA.

ANDREA   Good evening. I am sorry to call so late, I'm on my way to Holland. I was asked to look him up. Can I go in?

VIRGINIA   I don't know whether he will see you. You never came.

ANDREA   Ask him.

GALILEO *recognizes the voice. He sits motionless.* VIRGINIA *comes in to* GALILEO.

GALILEO   Is that Andrea?

VIRGINIA   Yes. [*Pause*] I will send him away.

GALILEO   Show him in.

VIRGINIA *shows* ANDREA *in.* VIRGINIA *sits,* ANDREA *remains standing.*

ANDREA   [*cool*] Have you been keeping well, Mr. Galilei?

GALILEO   Sit down. What are you doing these days? What are you working on? I heard it was something about hydraulics in Milan.

ANDREA   As he knew I was passing through, Fabricius of Amsterdam asked me to visit you and inquire about your health.

Pause.

GALILEO   I am very well.

ANDREA   [*formally*] I am glad I can report you are in good health.

GALILEO   Fabricius will be glad to hear it. And you might inform him that, on account of the depth of my repentance, I live in comparative comfort.

ANDREA   Yes, we understand that the Church is more than pleased with you. Your complete acceptance has had its effect. Not one paper expounding a new thesis has made its appearance in Italy since your submission.

Pause.

GALILEO   Unfortunately there are countries not under the wing of the Church. Would you not say the erroneous, condemned theories are still taught—there?

ANDREA   [*relentless*] Things are almost at a standstill.

GALILEO   Are they? [*Pause*] Nothing from Descartes in Paris?

ANDREA   Yes. On receiving the news of your recantation, he shelved his treatise on the nature of light.

GALILEO   I sometimes worry about my assistants, whom I led into error. Have they benefited by my example?

ANDREA   In order to work I have to go to Holland.

GALILEO   Yes.

ANDREA   Federzoni is grinding lenses again, back in some shop.

GALILEO   He can't read the books.

ANDREA   Fulganzio, our little monk, has abandoned research and is resting in peace in the Church.

GALILEO   So. [*Pause*] My superiors are looking forward to my spiritual recovery. I am progressing as well as can be expected.

VIRGINIA   You are doing well, father.

GALILEO   Virginia, leave the room.

VIRGINIA *rises uncertainly and goes out.*

VIRGINIA   [*to the* OFFICIAL] He was his pupil, so now he is his enemy. Help me in the kitchen.

She leaves the anteroom with the OFFICIAL.

ANDREA   May I go now, sir?

GALILEO   I do not know why you came, Sarti. To unsettle me? I have to be prudent.

ANDREA   I'll be on my way.

GALILEO   As it is, I have relapses. I completed the "Discorsi."

ANDREA   You completed what?

GALILEO   My "Discorsi."

ANDREA   How?

GALILEO   I am allowed pen and paper. My superiors are intelligent men. They know the habits of a lifetime cannot be broken abruptly. But they protect me from any unpleasant consequences: they lock my pages away as I dictate them. And I should know better than to risk my comfort. I wrote the "Discorsi" out again during the night. The manuscript is in the globe. My vanity has up to now prevented me from destroying it. If you consider taking it, you will shoulder the entire risk. You will say it was pirated from the original in the hands of the Holy Office.

ANDREA, *as in a trance, has gone to the globe. He lifts the upper half and gets the book. He turns the pages as if wanting to devour them. In the background the opening sentences of the "Discorsi" appear:*

My purpose is to set forth a very new science dealing with a very ancient subject—motion. . . . and I have discovered by experiment some properties of it which are worth knowing. . . .

GALILEO   I had to employ my time somehow.

The text disappears.

ANDREA   Two new sciences! This will be the foundation stone of a new physics.

GALILEO   Yes. Put it under your coat.

ANDREA   And we thought you had deserted. [*In a low voice*]   Mr. Galilei, how can I begin to express my shame. Mine has been the loudest voice against you.

GALILEO   That would seem to have been proper. I taught you science and I decried the truth.

ANDREA   Did you? I think not. Everything is changed!

GALILEO   What is changed?

ANDREA   You shielded the truth from the oppressor. Now I see! In your dealings with the Inquisition you used the same superb common sense you brought to physics.

GALILEO   Oh!

ANDREA   We lost our heads. With the crowd at the street corners we said: "He will die, he will never surrender!" You came back: "I surrendered but I am alive." We cried: "Your hands are stained!" You say: "Better stained than empty."

GALILEO   "Better stained than empty." It sounds realistic. Sounds like me.

ANDREA   And I of all people should have known. I was twelve when you sold another man's telescope to the Venetian Senate, and saw you put it to immortal use. Your friends were baffled when you bowed to the Prince of Florence: science gained a wider audience. You always laughed at heroics. "People who suffer bore me," you said. "Misfortunes are due mainly to miscalculations." And: "If there are obstacles, the shortest line between two points may be the crooked line."

GALILEO   It makes a picture.

ANDREA   And when you stooped to recant in 1633, I should have understood that you were again about your business.

GALILEO   My business being?

ANDREA   Science. The study of the properties of motion, mother of the machines which will themselves change the ugly face of the earth.

GALILEO   Aha!

ANDREA   You gained time to write a book that only you could write. Had you burned at the stake in a blaze of glory they would have won.

GALILEO   They have won. And there is no such thing as a scientific work that only one man can write.

ANDREA   Then why did you recant, tell me that!

GALILEO   I recanted because I was afraid of physical pain.

ANDREA   No!

GALILEO   They showed me the instruments.

ANDREA   It was not a plan?

GALILEO   It was not.

Pause.

ANDREA   But you have contributed. Science has only one commandment: contribution. And you have contributed more than any man for a hundred years.

GALILEO   Have I? Then welcome to my gutter, dear colleague in science and brother in treason: I sold out, you are a buyer. The first sight of the book! His mouth watered and his scoldings were drowned.

Blessed be our bargaining, whitewashing, death-fearing community!

ANDREA   The fear of death is human.

GALILEO   Even the Church will teach you that to be weak is not human. It is just evil.

ANDREA   The Church, yes! But science is not concerned with our weaknesses.

GALILEO   No? My dear Sarti, in spite of my present convictions, I may be able to give you a few pointers as to the concerns of your chosen profession.   [*Enter* VIRGINIA *with a platter*]   In my spare time, I happen to have gone over this case. I have spare time. Even a man who sells wool, however good he is at buying wool cheap and selling it dear, must be concerned with the standing of the wool trade. The practice of science would seem to call for valor. She trades in knowledge, which is the product of doubt. And this new art of doubt has enchanted the public. The plight of the multitude is old as the rocks, and is believed to be basic as the rocks. But now they have learned to doubt. They snatched the telescopes out of our hands and had them trained on their tormentors: prince, official, public moralist. The mechanism of the heavens was clearer, the mechanism of their courts was still murky. The battle to measure the heavens is won by doubt; by credulity the Roman housewife's battle for milk will always be lost. Word is passed down that this is of no concern to the scientist, who is told he will only release such of his findings as do not disturb the peace, that is, the peace of mind of the well-to-do. Threats and bribes fill the air. Can the scientist hold out on the numbers? For what reason do you labor? I take it that the intent of science is to ease human existence. If you give way to coercion, science can be crippled, and your new machines may simply suggest new drudgeries. Should you, then, in time, discover all there is to be discovered, your progress must become a progress away from the bulk of humanity. The gulf might even grow so wide that the sound of your cheering at some new achievement would be echoed by a universal howl of horror. As a scientist I had an almost unique opportunity. In my day astronomy emerged into the market place. At that particular time, had one man put up a fight, it could have had wide repercussions. I have come to believe that I was never in real danger; for some years I was as strong as the authorities, and I surrendered my knowledge to the powers that be, to use it, no, not *use* it, *abuse* it, as it suits their ends. I have betrayed my profession. Any man who does what I have done must not be tolerated in the ranks of science.

VIRGINIA, *who has stood motionless, puts the platter on the table.*

VIRGINIA   You are accepted in the ranks of the faithful, father.

GALILEO [*sees her*]   Correct. [*He goes over to the table*]   I have to eat now.

VIRGINIA   We lock up at eight.

ANDREA   I am glad I came. [*He extends his hand.* GALILEO *ignores it and goes over to his meal*]

GALILEO [*examining the plate; to* ANDREA]   Somebody who knows me sent me a goose. I still enjoying eating.

ANDREA   And your opinion is now that the "new age" was an illusion?

GALILEO   Well. This age of ours turned out to be . . . spattered with blood. Maybe new ages [must be spattered with blood]. Take care of yourself.

ANDREA   Yes. [*Unable to go*]   With reference to your evaluation of the author in question—I do not know the answer. But I cannot think that your savage analysis is the last word.

GALILEO   Thank you, sir.

OFFICIAL *knocks at the door.*

VIRGINIA [*showing* ANDREA *out*] I don't like visitors from the past, they excite him.

She lets him out. The OFFICIAL *closes the iron door.* VIRGINIA *returns.*

GALILEO [*eating*] Did you try and think who sent the goose?

VIRGINIA Not Andrea.

GALILEO Maybe not. I gave Redhead his first lesson; when he held out his hand, I had to remind myself he is teaching now. How is the sky tonight?

VIRGINIA [*at the window*] Bright.

GALILEO *continues eating.*

Scene 14

The great book o'er the border went
And, good folk, that was the end.
But we hope you'll keep in mind
You and I were left behind.

Before a little Italian customs house early in the morning. ANDREA *sits upon one of his traveling trunks at the barrier and reads Galileo's book. The window of a small house is still lit, and a big grotesque shadow, like an old witch and her cauldron, falls upon the house wall beyond. Barefoot* CHILDREN *in rags see it and point to the little house.*

CHILDREN [*singing*]
One, two, three, four, five, six,
Old Marina is a witch.
At night, on a broomstick she sits
And on the church steeple she spits.

CUSTOMS OFFICER [*to* ANDREA] Why are you making this journey?

ANDREA I am a scholar.

CUSTOMS OFFICER [*to his* CLERK] Put down under "Reason for Leaving the Country": Scholar. [*He points to the baggage*]

Books! Anything dangerous in these books?

ANDREA What is dangerous?

CUSTOMS OFFICER Religion. Politics.

ANDREA These are nothing but mathematical formulas.

CUSTOMS OFFICER What's that?

ANDREA Figures.

CUSTOMS OFFICER Oh, figures. No harm in figures. Just wait a minute, sir, we will soon have your papers stamped. [*He exits with* CLERK]

Meanwhile, a little council of war among the CHILDREN *has taken place.* ANDREA *quietly watches. One of the* BOYS, *pushed forward by the others, creeps up to the little house from which the shadow comes, and takes the jug of milk on the doorstep.*

ANDREA [*quietly*] What are you doing with that milk?

BOY [*stopping in mid-movement*] She is a witch.

The other CHILDREN *run away behind the customs house. One of them shouts, "Run, Paolo!"*

ANDREA Hmm! And because she is a witch she mustn't have milk. Is that the idea?

BOY Yes.

ANDREA And how do you know she is a witch?

BOY [*points to shadow on house wall*] Look!

ANDREA Oh! I see.

BOY And she rides on a broomstick at night —and she bewitches the coachman's horses. My cousin Luigi looked through the hole in the stable roof, that the snow storm made, and heard the horses coughing something terrible.

ANDREA Oh! How big was the hole in the stable roof?

BOY Luigi didn't tell. Why?

ANDREA I was asking because maybe the horses got sick because it was cold in the stable. You had better ask Luigi how big that hole is.

BOY   You are not going to say Old Marina isn't a witch, because you can't.

ANDREA   No, I can't say she isn't a witch. I haven't looked into it. A man can't know about a thing he hasn't looked into, or can he?

BOY   No! But THAT! [*He points to the shadow*] She is stirring hellbroth.

ANDREA   Let's see. Do you want to take a look? I can lift you up.

BOY   You lift me to the window, mister! [*He takes a slingshot out of his pocket*] I can really bash her from there.

ANDREA   Hadn't we better make sure she is a witch before we shoot? I'll hold that.

The BOY *puts the milk jug down and follows him reluctantly to the window.* ANDREA *lifts the boy up so that he can look in.*

ANDREA   What do you see?

BOY   [*slowly*]   Just an old girl cooking porridge.

ANDREA   Oh! Nothing to it then. Now look at her shadow, Paolo.

The BOY *looks over his shoulder and back and compares the reality and the shadow.*

BOY   The big thing is a soup ladle.

ANDREA   Ah! A ladle! You see, I would have

taken it for a broomstick, but I haven't looked into the matter as you have, Paolo. Here is your sling.

CUSTOMS OFFICER   [*returning with the* CLERK *and handing* ANDREA *his papers*]   All present and correct. Good luck, sir.

ANDREA *goes, reading Galileo's book. The* CLERK *starts to bring his baggage after him. The barrier rises.* ANDREA *passes through, still reading the book. The* BOY *kicks over the milk jug.*

BOY   [*shouting after* ANDREA]   She *is* a witch! She *is* a witch!

ANDREA   You saw with your own eyes: think it over!

The BOY *joins the others. They sing:*

One, two, three, four, five, six,
Old Marina is a witch.
At night, on a broomstick she sits
And on the church steeple she spits.

The CUSTOMS OFFICERS *laugh.* ANDREA *goes.*

> May you now guard science' light,
> Kindle it and use it right,
> Lest it be a flame to fall
> Downward to consume us all.

For Discussion

SCENE 1

The play begins in 1609 when Galileo was already a mature scientist of forty-six. The rest of the play will cover the remaining thirty-two years of his life. The final scene presumably takes place some time after his death. In its fourteen short scenes, the play moves swiftly, forming an epic drama which involves important ideas in the development of European history and culture.

1   This first scene is short but supplies a great deal of information about Galileo himself and suggests the major themes of

the play. A novelist, if he wishes, may be more leisurely; he can take his time getting around to the main action and his principal characters. A playwright does not have the luxury of such leisurely development: the audience is sitting in the theater and he must capture their interest at once.

Usually the first moments of a play are given over to an *exposition*. That is, the playwright sketches very quickly the kind of information we need to follow the rest of the story: who the main characters are, where they are, and what their situation is as the play begins.

What do we find out about Galileo in this opening scene? Make a list of the things Brecht tells us about him: his profession, his financial condition, his personality, his interests, and so forth.

2 The play begins as the boy Andrea brings in an astrological instrument, a three-dimensional map of the sky. Why does Galileo immediately call it an "antique"?

3 Galileo gives Andrea a lesson in astronomy. Is he a good teacher? What methods of instruction does he use?

4 What are the serious implications of Galileo's colloquial remark, "Everybody, at last, is getting nosy"? What happens to any society when people get "nosy"?

5 The full implications of some things that happen in this first scene will only come out as the play progresses. Here some of the dialogue is a *foreshadowing* of later events. From what you know about Galileo's life, what are the implications of the following exchange:

GALILEO   *Andrea, I wouldn't talk about our ideas outside.*

ANDREA   *Why not?*

GALILEO   *Certain of the authorities won't like it.*

ANDREA   *Why not, if it's the truth?*

6 In the middle of the scene Galileo meets a young man who has come to study with him. As is so often the case, the teacher learns from the student. What important information does Ludovico bring from Holland?

7 Brecht makes no attempt at realism in this scene: less than five minutes pass from the time Galileo first hears about the "new instrument" to the time he has assembled the materials and constructed his first crude telescope. Why is this extreme shortening of time justified in a play?

8 How should the actor playing Galileo read the last word of the scene, "Aha!"?

SCENE 2

1 Galileo is divided between his interest in pure science and his need to survive in a commercial society. As Brecht says in the little poem at the beginning of the scene:

No one's virtue is complete:
Great Galileo liked to eat.

This scene takes place only about a year after Scene 1, yet Galileo tells the Venetians that his telescope is "the product of seventeen years' patient research." What information is he withholding from them? Why does he lie to them?

2 Why are the Venetian officials excited about the telescope? How do they expect to make money out of it?

3 How is Galileo's interest in the telescope different from that of the Venetians?

4 What is the implication of Ludovico's final line, "Have you ever been to Holland?"

SCENE 3

1 This scene takes place shortly after Scene 2. Galileo's lie is discovered: he did not exactly invent the telescope. In fact, the telescope is only a tool for more important work. What is Galileo's real contribution to science, something which goes beyond the invention of the telescope?

2 How does Galileo react when the Curator tells him that his deception has been discovered? Does he have a guilty conscience? How does he justify his behavior?

3 What else is Galileo interested in besides science?

SCENE 4

This scene takes place not too long after Scene 3. Galileo has moved to Florence and is under the patronage of the young Prince Cosimo De' Medici.

1 Why are the Philosopher and his way of thinking ridiculous? On what does the Philosopher base his knowledge? What is the answer to his question: "Why should we go out of our way to look for things

that can only strike a discord in the ineffable harmony?"

2 What is the significance of the stage direction, *Nobody goes near the telescope*"?

3 Galileo suggests that illiterate sailors and carpenters are wiser than the learned Philosopher and the Mathematician. Why?

4 Do you find it believable that people refuse to look at something which might change their ideas?

SCENE 5

1 What is illogical about the Old Cardinal's argument: "I am informed that Mr. Galilei transfers mankind from the center of the universe to somewhere on the outskirts. Mr. Galilei is therefore an enemy of mankind . . ."?

2 Why is Clavius's testimony so important?

3 What is the significance of the quotation which is written on a curtain at the end of the scene?

SCENE 6

1 The little poem at the beginning of the scene tells us that a Cardinal asked Galileo "one small request." What is ironic about this? What was the "small request"?

2 In what dilemma does Galileo find himself at the end of this scene?

SCENE 7

Galileo is, in a sense, being bribed to keep silent about his discoveries. The truth about the stars and the sun would upset too many established ideas.

1 In the years since Galileo's time it has become clear that there was never any real conflict between his ideas and the claims of any religion. Today his basic ideas are accepted by all thinking people, religious and nonreligious. Why then was there such opposition to his concepts during his own lifetime?

2 How does the Little Monk of this scene contrast with the great Cardinals of Scene 6?

3 The Little Monk is himself a scientist, and he has no scientific argument with Galileo. Why then does he want to give up his work as a scientist? What is the basis of his argument?

4 After the Little Monk picks up Galileo's manuscript and glances at it, Galileo exclaims, "An apple of the tree of knowledge. . . ." What is the allusion? What is the implication for the Little Monk?

5 When the Little Monk enters at the beginning of the scene he has a plan. How has his plan been frustrated by the end of the scene? Why did this happen?

SCENE 8

1 This scene takes place eight years after Galileo has been silenced by the Holy Office, as we saw in Scene 6. How has he spent those eight years? Has he prospered? What has happened to his reputation in Europe?

2 In Scene 4 the Philosopher argued that Galileo's ideas were wrong because they contradicted the ideas of the Greek philosopher Aristotle, who had lived about two thousand years before. Now, in Scene 8, Galileo still has to contend with the writings of Aristotle. What does his experiment with water, ice, and needle show?

3 How has Galileo's family life become mixed up with his life as a pure scientist?

4 Ludovico has been long engaged to Galileo's daughter, Virginia, but he refuses to marry her. Why? How is this another example of the illogical effects of science on economics and politics?

5 Cardinal Barberini, from Scene 6, now appears about to become the new Pope. Why does Galileo rejoice at this news?

SCENE 9

1 The Ballad Singer says that Galileo claimed that "Almighty God was wrong / In Genesis, Chapter One!" Did Galileo ever make such a claim?

2 Brecht, throughout the play, more than suggests that very few people are interested in Truth for its own sake. Rather, they look at Truth to see whether it can harm or promote their own financial or political positions. In this April Fool's Day scene, the common people have got hold of a somewhat distorted idea of Galileo's discoveries. What is their interpretation? How does Galileo's teaching turn out to have political consequences?

3 Discuss: if the authorities had never suppressed Galileo's ideas, this scene would never have taken place.

4 What does this scene suggest about the attempts of governments to suppress the truth?

SCENE 10

1 After many years of silence, Galileo can no longer restrain himself from publishing his book about astronomy. At the end of Scene 7 he said, "I wonder how long I shall be content to discuss it with my dog!" How has Galileo's book become a symbol of forces in which he had no particular interest? Consider both the April Fool's Day scene (Scene 9) and his conversation with the industrialist, Matti, in Scene 10.

2 What reception does Galileo expect to receive from the Prince? What actually happens?

3 What support does Galileo still expect from the new Pope?

4 What threat is suggested by the final speech of the Lord Chamberlain?

SCENE 11

1 Is the new Pope presented as a reasonable man? Does he understand Galileo? Does he like him as a person?

2 It is suggested that Galileo might have been better off if he had published his book in Latin rather than in Italian, the language of the common people. Why?

3 Why does the Pope want to avoid a conflict between the Church and Reason?

4 At the end of the scene the Pope changes his mind to this extent: he will not allow Galileo to be tortured, but he will allow the Inquisitor to "show" the instruments of torture. What kinds of pressure is the Pope under?

SCENE 12

1 We first met Andrea at the beginning of the play when he was a little boy. Now he is a grown man, Galileo's leading student. What expectations does he have for Galileo? How does Galileo disappoint him? What is the implication of Andrea's line, "He saved his big gut"?

2 The exchange at the end of this scene between Andrea and Galileo is one of the most famous passages of modern drama. In one sense Galileo is talking to Andrea, but in another sense the playwright is talking directly to his audience. What do you think Brecht means by " 'Unhappy is the land that needs a hero' "?

3 The legend printed on the curtain at the end of this scene is a quotation from Galileo's scientific writings. It appears to be a flat scientific statement. In fact it is highly ironic as placed here in the play. How has Galileo's own behavior shown that the "assumption that great and small structures are equally tough is obviously wrong"? How can this scientific statement be figuratively applied to his life or spirit?

SCENE 13

There remains another scene after this one, but this is the last time we are to see Galileo. We can assume that he is near the end of his life.

1 Galileo has been a prisoner for years, but not the usual kind of "prisoner" we think of. What conditions does he live in? Why has he been allowed such special considerations? How has he used his opportunities?

2 What assumptions must we make about Virginia's engagement to Ludovico?

3 In the conversation between Andrea and Galileo, Brecht brings about a startling reversal of our expectations. In earlier scenes, Science was always treated as a noble and valuable search for the Truth. Andrea still thinks of it that way, but Galileo has more complex thoughts on the subject. In his long speech toward the end of the scene, what doubts does he have about Science? What does he think is the true purpose of Science? How, in Galileo's opinion, does Science often lose sight of its most important purposes?

4 In the introduction to the play we said that Brecht was not really writing a historical drama, but a play about our own times, and that he was profoundly stirred by the invention of the atom bomb. How does this scene relate to the role of Science in the twentieth century?

5 Does Galileo see himself as a hero? What is he ashamed of?

6 The final visual picture we have of Galileo is that of a man eating heartily. How does his zest for food relate symbolically to the rest of his life?

SCENE 14

1 We first met Andrea when he was a boy of twelve. What kind of man has he become? What meaningful contrast is there between Andrea's ideas and the mentality of the children in this scene?

2 What is ironic—especially in the light of what we know in the twentieth century—about the Customs Officer's remark, "Oh, figures. No harm in figures"?

3 Galileo does not appear in this scene. In what sense, however, is he present?

4 In one sense this scene suggests the triumph of Galileo and of Truth. But the little poem at the end undercuts any sentimentality we may have about the "glory of Science." What does it mean?

Brecht's *Galileo* appears to be a straightforward play written in simple language. The simplicity of its surface, however, masks a complicated series of values and judgments. No character in Brecht's play is wholly evil and none is wholly good; there are no villains and no heroes. If Galileo himself looks like a hero at the beginning of the play, we soon find that the author has pulled the rug from beneath some of our assumptions; for Galileo turns out to be human after all, a man capable of fear, willing to make compromises, ready to sacrifice the truth in order to save his skin. Likewise, Brecht plays games with our assumptions about the glories of science and technological progress.

The following play by a Nigerian writer is much simpler, much more direct. It may remind you of a folktale or fable. The good people and bad people are clearly distinguished from each other. Values are firmly established: the author clearly disapproves of the greedy grandsons and their lack of respect for an older member of their family. The play is a bit like a morality play and is constructed very much like *Cinderella*: the grandsons are like the wicked stepsisters, and the grandfather is like Cinderella herself. The proud are made humble, and a person who is badly treated is rewarded in the end.

An authority on African literature has said that the primary theme in modern African writing is the conflict between the old (tribal) and the new (urbanized) way of living. This conflict of values is often dramatized in terms of a conflict between generations. Both of these themes are clearly seen in *The Jewels of the Shrine*.

James Ene Henshaw

The Jewels of the Shrine

Characters

OKORIE *an old man*
AROB
OJIMA } *Okorie's grandsons*
BASSI *a woman*
A STRANGER

SCENE: *An imaginary village close to a town in Nigeria. All the scenes of this play take place in* OKORIE's *mud-walled house. The time is the present.*

Scene 1

The hall in OKORIE's *house. There are three doors. One leads directly into* OKORIE's *room. The two others are on either side of the hall. Of these, one leads to his grandsons' apartment, whilst the other acts as a general exit.*

The chief items of furniture consist of a wide bamboo bed, on which is spread a mat; a wooden chair, a low table, and a few odds and ends, including three hoes.

OKORIE, *an old man of about eighty years of age, with scanty grey hair, and dressed in the way his village folk do, is sitting at the edge of the bed. He holds a stout, rough walking-stick and a horn filled with palm wine.*

On the wooden chair near the bed sits a STRANGER, *a man of about forty-five years of age. He, too, occasionally sips wine from a calabash cup. It is evening. The room is rather dark, and a cloth-in-oil lantern hangs from a hook on the wall.*

OKORIE   Believe me, Stranger, in my days things were different. It was a happy thing to become an old man, because young people were taught to respect elderly men.

STRANGER   [*sipping his wine*]   Here in the village you should be happier. In the town where I come from, a boy of ten riding a hired bicycle will knock down a man of fifty years without any feeling of pity.

OKORIE   Bicycle. That is why I have not been to town for ten years. Town people seem to enjoy rushing about doing nothing. It kills them.

STRANGER   You are lucky that you have your grandchildren to help you. Many people in town have no one to help them.

OKORIE   Look at me, Stranger, and tell me if these shabby clothes and this dirty beard show that I have good grandchildren.

Believe me, Stranger, in my younger days things were different. Old men were happy. When they died, they were buried with honour. But in my case, Stranger, my old age has been unhappy. And my only fear now is that when I die, my grandsons will not accord me the honour due to my age. It will be a disgrace to me.

STRANGER   I will now go on my way, Okorie. May God help you.

OKORIE   I need help, Stranger, for although I have two grandsons, I am lonely and unhappy because they do not love or care for me. They tell me that I am from an older world. Farewell, Stranger. If you call again and I am alive, I will welcome you back.

Exit STRANGER. BASSI, *a beautiful woman of about thirty years, enters.*

BASSI   Who was that man, Grandfather?

OKORIE   He was a stranger.

BASSI   I do not trust strangers. They may appear honest when the lights are on. But as soon as there is darkness, they creep back as thieves. [OKORIE *smiles and drinks his wine.* BASSI *points to him*] What has happened, Grandfather? When I left you this afternoon, you were old, your mind was worried, and your eyes were swollen. Where now are the care, the sorrow, the tears in your eyes? You never smiled before, but now——

OKORIE   The stranger has brought happiness back into my life. He has given me hope again.

BASSI   But don't they preach in town that it is only God who gives hope? Every other thing gives despair.

OKORIE   Perhaps that stranger was God. Don't the preachers say that God moves like a stranger?

BASSI   God moves in strange ways.

OKORIE   Yes, I believe it, because since that stranger came, I have felt younger again. You know, woman, when I worshipped at our forefathers' shrine, I was happy. I knew what it was all about. It was my life. Then the preachers came, and I abandoned the beliefs of our fathers. The old ways did not leave me; the new ways did not wholly accept me. I was therefore unhappy. But soon I felt the wings of God carrying me high. And with my loving and helpful son, I thought that my old age would be as happy as that of my father before me. But death played me a trick. My son died and I was left to the mercy of his two sons. Once more unhappiness gripped my life. With all their education my grandsons lacked one thing—respect for age. But today the stranger who came here has once more brought happiness to me. Let me tell you this——

BASSI It is enough, Grandfather. Long talks make you tired. Come, your food is now ready.

OKORIE [*happily*] Woman, I cannot eat. When happiness fills your heart, you cannot eat.

Two voices are heard outside, laughing and swearing.

BASSI Your grandchildren are coming back.

OKORIE Don't call them my grandchildren. I am alone in this world.

Door flings open. Two young men, about eighteen and twenty, enter the room. They are in shirt and trousers.

AROB By our forefathers, Grandfather, you are still awake!

BASSI Why should he not keep awake if he likes?

AROB But Grandfather usually goes to bed before the earliest chicken thinks of it.

OJIMA Our good grandfather might be thinking of his youthful days, when all young men were fond of farming and all young women loved the kitchen.

BASSI Shame on both of you for talking to an old man like that. When you grow old, your own children will laugh and jeer at you. Come, Grandfather, and take your food.

OKORIE *stands up with difficulty and limps with the aid of his stick through the exit, followed by* BASSI, *who casts a reproachful look on the two men before she leaves.*

AROB I wonder what Grandfather and the woman were talking about.

OJIMA It must be the usual thing. We are bad boys. We have no regard for the memory of our father, and so on.

AROB Our father left his responsibility to us. Nature had arranged that he should bury Grandfather before thinking of himself.

OJIMA But would Grandfather listen to Nature when it comes to the matter of death? Everybody in his generation, including all his wives, have died. But Grandfather has made a bet with death. And it seems that he will win.

OKORIE [*calling from offstage*] Bassi! Bassi! Where is that woman?

OJIMA The old man is coming. Let us hide ourselves. [*Both rush under the bed*]

OKORIE [*comes in, limping on his stick as usual*] Bassi, where are you? Haven't I told that girl never——

BASSI [*entering*] Don't shout so. It's not good for you.

OKORIE Where are the two people?

BASSI You mean your grandsons?

OKORIE My, my, well, call them what you like.

BASSI They are not here. They must have gone into their room.

OKORIE Bassi, I have a secret for you. [*He narrows his eyes*] A big secret. [*His hands tremble*] Can you keep a secret?

BASSI Of course I can.

OKORIE [*rubbing his forehead*] You can, what can you? What did I say?

BASSI [*holding him and leading him to sit on the bed*] You are excited. You know that whenever you are excited, you begin to forget things.

OKORIE That is not my fault. It is old age. Well, but what was I saying?

BASSI You asked me if I could keep a secret.

OKORIE Yes, yes, a great secret. You know, Bassi, I have been an unhappy man.

BASSI I have heard it all before.

OKORIE Listen, woman. My dear son died and left me to the mercy of his two sons. They are the worst grandsons in the land. They have sold all that their father left. They do not care for me. Now when I die, what will they do to me? Don't you think that they will abandon me in disgrace? An old man has a right to be properly cared for. And when he dies, he has a right to a good burial. But my grandchildren do not think of these things.

BASSI See how you tremble, Grandfather! I have told you not to think of such things.

OKORIE Why should I not? But sh! . . . I hear a voice.

BASSI It's only your ears deceiving you, Grandfather.

OKORIE It is not my ears, woman. I know when old age hums in my ears and tired nerves ring bells in my head, but I know also when I hear a human voice.

BASSI Go on, Grandfather; there is no one.

OKORIE Now, listen. You saw the stranger that came here. He gave me hope. But wait, look around, Bassi. Make sure that no one is listening to us.

BASSI No one, Grandfather.

OKORIE Open the door and look.

BASSI [opens the exit door] No one.

OKORIE Look into that corner.

BASSI [looks] There is no one.

OKORIE Look under the bed.

BASSI [irritably] I won't, Grandfather. There is no need; I have told you that there is nobody in the house.

OKORIE [pitiably] I have forgotten what I was talking about.

BASSI [calmly] You have a secret from the stranger.

OKORIE Yes, the stranger told me something. Have you ever heard of the "Jewels of the Shrine"?

BASSI Real jewels?

OKORIE Yes. Among the beads which my father got from the early white men, were real jewels. When war broke out and a great fever invaded all our lands, my father made a sacrifice in the village shrine. He promised that if this village were spared, he would offer his costly jewels to the shrine. Death roamed through all the other villages, but not one person in this village died of the fever. My father kept his promise. In a big ceremony the jewels were placed on our shrine. But it was not for long. Some said they were stolen. But the stranger who came here knew where they were. He said that they were buried somewhere near the big oak tree on our farm. I must go out and dig for them immediately. They can be sold for fifty pounds these days.

BASSI But, Grandfather, it will kill you to go out in this cold and darkness. You must get someone to do it for you. You cannot lift a hoe.

OKORIE [infuriated] So, you believe I am too old to lift a hoe. You, you, oh, I . . .

BASSI [coaxing him] There now, young man, no temper. If you wish, I myself will dig up the whole farm for you.

OKORIE Every bit of it?

BASSI Yes.

OKORIE And hand over to me all that you will find?

BASSI Yes.

OKORIE And you will not tell my grandsons?

BASSI No, Grandfather, I will not.

OKORIE Swear, woman, swear by our fathers' shrine.

BASSI I swear.

OKORIE [relaxing] Now life is becoming worthwhile. Tell no one about it, woman. Begin digging tomorrow morning. Dig inch by inch until you bring out the jewels of our forefathers' shrine.

BASSI I am tired, Grandfather. I must sleep now. Good night.

OKORIE [*with feeling*] Good night. God and our fathers' spirits keep you. When dangerous bats alight on the roofs of wicked men, let them not trouble you in your sleep. When far-seeing owls hoot the menace of future days, let their evil prophecies keep off your path. [BASSI *leaves.* OKORIE, *standing up and trembling, moves to a corner and brings out a small hoe. Struggling with his senile joints, he tries to imitate a young man digging*]

Oh, who said I was old? After all, I am only eighty years. And I feel younger than most young men. Let me see how I can dig. [*He tries to dig again*] Ah! I feel aches all over my hip. Maybe the soil here is too hard. [*He listens*] How I keep on thinking that I hear people whispering in this room! I must rest now.

Carrying the hoe with him, he goes into his room. AROB *and* OJIMA *crawl out from under the bed.*

AROB [*stretching his hip*] My hip, oh my hip!

OJIMA My legs!

AROB So there is a treasure in our farm! We must waste no time; we must begin digging soon.

OJIMA Soon? We must begin tonight—now. The old man has taken one hoe. [*Pointing to the corner*] There are two over there. [*They fetch two hoes from among the heap of things in a corner of the room*] If we can only get the jewels, we can go and live in town and let the old man manage as he can. Let's move now.

As they are about to go out, each holding a hoe, OKORIE *comes out with his own hoe. For a moment the three stare at each other in silence and surprise.*

AROB Now, Grandfather, where are you going with a hoe at this time of night?

OJIMA [*impudently*] Yes, Grandfather, what is the idea?

OKORIE I should ask you; this is my house. Why are you creeping about like thieves?

AROB All right, Grandfather, we are going back to bed.

OKORIE What are you doing with hoes? You were never fond of farming.

OJIMA We intend to go to the farm early in the morning.

OKORIE But the harvest is over. When everybody in the village was digging out the crops, you were going around the town with your hands in your pockets. Now you say you are going to the farm.

OJIMA Digging is good for the health, Grandfather.

OKORIE [*re-entering his room*] Good night.

AROB and **OJIMA** Good night, Grandfather.

They return to their room. After a short time AROB *and* OJIMA *come out, each holding a hoe, and tiptoe out through the exit. Then, gently,* OKORIE *too comes out on his toes, and placing the hoe on his shoulder, warily leaves the hall.*

Curtain.

Scene 2

The same, the following morning.

BASSI [*knocking at* OKORIE's *door; she is holding a hoe*] Grandfather, wake up. I am going to the farm.

OKORIE [*opening the door*] Good morning. Where are you going so early in the morning?

BASSI I am going to dig up the farm. You remember the treasure, don't you?

OKORIE Do you expect to find a treasure whilst you sleep at night? You should have dug at night, woman. Treasures are never found in the day.

BASSI   But you told me to dig in the morning, Grandfather.

OKORIE   My grandsons were in this room somewhere. They heard what I told you about the Jewels of the Shrine.

BASSI   They could not have heard us. I looked everywhere. The stranger must have told them.

OKORIE   [rubbing his forehead]   What stranger?

BASSI   The stranger who told you about the treasure in the farm.

OKORIE   So it was a stranger who told me! Oh, yes, a stranger! [He begins to dream]   Ah, I remember him now. He was a great man. His face shone like the sun. It was like the face of God.

BASSI   You are dreaming, Grandfather. Wake up! I must go to the farm quickly.

OKORIE   Yes, woman, I remember the jewels in the farm. But you are too late.

BASSI   [excitedly]   Late? Have your grandsons discovered the treasure?

OKORIE   They have not, but I have discovered it myself.

BASSI   [amazed]   You? [OKORIE nods his head with a smile on his face]   Do you mean to say that you are now a rich man?

OKORIE   By our fathers' shrine, I am.

BASSI   So you went and worked at night. You should not have done it, even to forestall your grandchildren.

OKORIE   My grandsons would never have found it.

BASSI   But you said that they heard us talking of the treasure.

OKORIE   You see, I suspected that my grandsons were in this room. So I told you that the treasure was in the farm, but in actual fact it was in the little garden behind this house, where the village shrine used to be. My grandsons travelled half a mile to the farm last night for nothing.

BASSI   Then I am glad I did not waste my time.

OKORIE   [with delight]   How my grandsons must have toiled in the night!   [He is overcome with laughter]   My grandsons, they thought I would die in disgrace, a pauper, unheard of. No, not now.   [Then boldly]   But those wicked children must change, or when I die, I shall not leave a penny for them.

BASSI   Oh, Grandfather, to think you are a rich man!

OKORIE   I shall send you to buy me new clothes. My grandsons will not know me again. Ha—ha—ha—ha!

OKORIE and BASSI leave. AROB and OJIMA crawl out from under the bed, where for a second time they have hidden. They look rough, their feet dirty with sand and leaves. Each comes out with his hoe.

AROB   So the old man fooled us.

OJIMA   Well, he is now a rich man, and we must treat him with care.

AROB   We have no choice. He says that unless we change, he will not leave a penny to us.

A knock at the door.

AROB and OJIMA   Come in.

OKORIE   [comes in, and seeing them so rough and dirty, bursts out laughing; the others look surprised]   Look how dirty you are, with hoes and all. "Gentlemen" like you should not touch hoes. You should wear white gloves and live in towns. But see, you look like two pigs. Ha—ha—ha—ha—ha! Oh what grandsons! How stupid they look! Ha—ha—ha! [AROB and OJIMA are dumbfounded]   I saw both of you a short while ago under the bed. I hope you now know that I have got the Jewels of the Shrine.

AROB   We, too, have something to tell you, Grandfather.

OKORIE   Yes, yes, "gentlemen." Come, tell me. [He begins to move away]   You must hurry up. I am going to town to buy myself some new clothes and a pair of shoes.

AROB New clothes?

OJIMA And shoes?

OKORIE Yes, grandsons, it is never too late to wear new clothes.

AROB Let us go and buy them for you. It is too hard for you to——

OKORIE If God does not think that I am yet old enough to be in the grave, I do not think I am too old to go to the market in town. I need some clothes and a comb to comb my beard. In am happy, grandchildren, very happy. [AROB *and* OJIMA *are dumbfounded*] Now, "gentlemen," why don't you get drunk and shout at me as before? [*Growing bolder*] Why not laugh at me as if I were nobody? You young puppies, I am now somebody, somebody. What is somebody? [*Rubbing his forehead as usual*]

AROB [*to* OJIMA] He has forgotten again.

OKORIE Who has forgotten what?

OJIMA You have forgotten nothing. You are a good man, Grandfather, and we like you.

OKORIE [*shouting excitedly*] Bassi! Bassi! Bassi! Where is that silly woman? Bassi, come and hear this. My grandchildren like me; I am now a good man. Ha—ha—ha—ha!

He limps into his room. AROB *and* OJIMA *look at each other. It is obvious to them that the old man has all the cards now.*

AROB What has come over the old man?

OJIMA Have you not heard that when people have money, it scratches them on the brain? That is what has happened to our grandfather now.

AROB He does not believe that we like him. How can we convince him?

OJIMA You know what he likes most: someone to scratch his back. When he comes out, you will scratch his back, and I will use his big fan to fan at him.

AROB Great idea. [*Okorie coughs from the room*] He is coming now.

OKORIE [*comes in*] I am so tired.

AROB You said you were going to the market, Grandfather.

OKORIE You do well to remind me. I have sent Bassi to buy the things I want.

OJIMA Grandfather, you look really tired. Lie down here. [OKORIE *lies down and uncovers his back*] Grandfather, from now on, I shall give you all your breakfast and your midday meals.

AROB [*jealously*] By our forefathers' shrine, Grandfather, I shall take care of your dinner and supply you with wine and clothing.

OKORIE God bless you, little sons. That is how it should have been all the time. An old man has a right to live comfortably in his last days.

OJIMA Grandfather, it is a very long time since we scratched your back.

AROB Yes, it is a long time. We have not done it since we were infants. We want to do it now. It will remind us of our younger days, when it was a pleasure to scratch your back.

OKORIE Scratch my back? Ha—ha—ha—ha. Oh, go on, go on; by our fathers' shrine you are now good men. I wonder what has happened to you.

OJIMA It's you, Grandfather. You are such a nice man. As a younger man you must have looked very well. But in your old age you look simply wonderful.

AROB That is right, Grandfather, and let us tell you again. Do not waste a penny of yours any more. We will keep you happy and satisfied to the last hour of your life.

OKORIE *appears pleased.* AROB *now begins to pick at, and scratch,* OKORIE'S *back.* OJIMA *kneels near the bed and begins to fan the old man. After a while a slow snore is heard. Then, as* AROB *warms up to his task,* OKORIE *jumps up.*

OKORIE Oh, that one hurts. Gently, children, gently.

He relaxes and soon begins to snore again. OJIMA *and* AROB *gradually stand up.*

AROB   The old fogy is asleep.

OJIMA   That was clever of us. I am sure he believes us now.

They leave. OKORIE *opens an eye and peeps at them. Then he smiles and closes it again.* BASSI *enters, bringing some new clothes, a pair of shoes, a comb and brush, a tin of face powder, etc. She pushes* OKORIE.

BASSI   Wake up, Grandfather.

OKORIE   [*opening his eyes*] Who told you that I was asleep? Oh! you have brought the things. It is so long since I had a change of clothes. Go on, woman, and call those grandsons of mine. They must help me to put on my new clothes and shoes.

BASSI *leaves.* OKORIE *begins to comb his hair and beard, which have not been touched for a long time.* BASSI *re-enters with* AROB *and* OJIMA. *Helped by his grandsons and* BASSI, OKORIE *puts on his new clothes and shoes. He then sits on the bed and poses majestically like a chief.*

Curtain.

Scene 3

The same, a few months later. OKORIE *is lying on the bed. He is well dressed and looks happy, but it is easily seen that he is nearing his end. There is a knock at the door.* OKORIE *turns and looks at the door but cannot speak loudly. Another knock; the door opens, and the* STRANGER *enters.*

OKORIE   Welcome back, Stranger. You have come in time. Sit down. I will tell you of my will.

Door opens slowly. BASSI *walks in.*

BASSI   [*to* STRANGER] How is he?

STRANGER   Just holding on.

BASSI   Did he say anything?

STRANGER   He says that he wants to tell me about his will. Call his grandsons.

BASSI *leaves.*

OKORIE   Stranger.

STRANGER   Yes, Grandfather.

OKORIE   Do you remember what I told you about my fears in life?

STRANGER   You were afraid your last days would be miserable and that you would not have a decent burial.

OKORIE   Now, Stranger, all that is past. Don't you see how happy I am? I have been very well cared for since I saw you last. My grandchildren have done everything for me, and I am sure they will bury me with great ceremony and rejoicing. I want you to be here when I am making my will. Bend to my ears; I will whisper something to you. [STRANGER *bends for a moment.* OKORIE *whispers. Then he speaks aloud*] Is that clear, Stranger?

STRANGER   It is clear.

OKORIE   Will you remember?

STRANGER   I will.

OKORIE   Do you promise?

STRANGER   I promise.

OKORIE   [*relaxing on his pillow*] There now. My end will be more cheerful than I ever expected.

A knock.

STRANGER   Come in.

AROB, OJIMA, *and* BASSI *enter. The two men appear as sad as possible. They are surprised to meet the* STRANGER, *and stare at him for a moment.*

OKORIE   [*with effort*] This man may be a stranger to you, but not to me. He is my friend. Arob, look how sad you are! Ojima, how tight your lips are with sorrow! Barely a short while ago you would not have cared whether I lived or died.

AROB   Don't speak like that, Grandfather.

OKORIE   Why should I not? Remember, these are my last words on earth.

OJIMA   You torture us, Grandfather.

OKORIE   Since my son, your father, died, you have tortured me. But now you have changed, and it is good to forgive you both.

STRANGER   You wanted to make a will.

OKORIE   Will? Yes, will. Where is Bassi? Has that woman run away already?

BASSI   [*standing above the bed*]   No, Grandfather, I am here.

OKORIE   Now there is my family complete.

STRANGER   The will, Grandfather, the will.

OKORIE   Oh, the will; the will is made.

AROB   Made? Where is it?

OKORIE   It is written out on paper.

AROB *and* OJIMA *together:*

AROB   Written?

OJIMA   What?

OKORIE   [*coolly*]   Yes, someone wrote it for me soon after I had discovered the treasure.

AROB   Where is it, Grandfather?

OJIMA   Are you going to show us, Grandfather?

OKORIE   Yes, I will. Why not? But not now, not until I am dead.

AROB *and* OJIMA   What?

OKORIE   Listen here. The will is in a small box buried somewhere. The box also contains all my wealth. These are my wishes. Make my burial the best you can. Spend as much as is required, for you will be compensated. Do not forget that I am the oldest man in this village. An old man has a right to be decently buried. Remember, it was only after I had discovered the Jewels of the Shrine that you began to take good care of me. You should, by carrying out all my last wishes, atone for all those years when you left me poor, destitute, and miserable.

[*To the* STRANGER, *in broken phrases*]   Two weeks after my death, Stranger, you will come and unearth the box of my treasure. Open it in the presence of my grandsons.

Read out the division of the property, and share it among them. Bassi, you have nothing. You have a good husband and a family. No reward or treasure is greater than a good marriage and a happy home. Stranger, I have told you where the box containing the will is buried. That is all. May God . . .

AROB *and* OJIMA   [*rushing to him*]   Grandfather, Grandfather——

STRANGER   Leave him in peace.   [BASSI, *giving out a scream, rushes from the room*] I must go now. Don't forget his will. Unless you bury him with great honour, you may not touch his property.

He leaves.

Curtain.

Scene 4

All in this scene are dressed in black. AROB, OJIMA, *and* BASSI *are sitting around the table. There is one extra chair. The bed is still there, but the mat is taken off, leaving it bare. The hoe with which* OKORIE *dug out the treasure is lying on the bed as a sort of memorial.*

AROB   Thank God, today is here at last. When I get my own share, I will go and live in town.

OJIMA   If only that foolish stranger would turn up! Why a stranger should come into this house and——

BASSI   Remember, he was your grandfather's friend.

OJIMA   At last, poor Grandfather is gone. I wonder if he knew that we only played up just to get something from his will.

AROB   Well, it didn't matter to him. He believed us, and that is why he has left his property to us. A few months ago he would rather have thrown it all into the sea.

OJIMA Who could have thought, considering the way we treated him, that the old man had such a kindly heart!

There is a knock. All stand. STRANGER *enters from Grandfather's room. He is grim, dressed in black, and carries a small wooden box under his arm.*

AROB Stranger, how did you come out from Grandfather's room?

STRANGER Let us not waste time on questions. This box was buried in the floor of your grandfather's room. [*He places the box on the table;* AROB *and* OJIMA *crowd together.* STRANGER *speaks sternly*] Give me room, please. Your grandfather always wanted you to crowd around him. But no one would, until he was about to die. Step back, please.

Both AROB *and* OJIMA *step back.* OJIMA *accidentally steps on* AROB.

AROB [*to* OJIMA] Don't you step on me!

OJIMA [*querulously*] Don't you shout at me!

STRANGER *looks at both.*

AROB When I sat day and night watching Grandfather in his illness, you were away in town, dancing and getting drunk. Now you want to be the first to grab at everything.

OJIMA You liar! It was I who took care of him.

AROB You only took care of him when you knew that he had come to some wealth.

BASSI Why can't both of you——

AROB [*very sharply*] Keep out of this, woman. That pretender [*pointing to* OJIMA] wants to bring trouble today.

OJIMA I, a pretender? What of you, who began to scratch the old man's back simply to get his money?

AROB How dare you insult me like that!

He throws out a blow. OJIMA *parries. They fight and roll on the floor. The* STRANGER *looks on.*

BASSI Stranger, stop them.

STRANGER [*calmly looking at them*] Don't interfere, woman. The mills of God, the preachers tell us, grind slowly.

BASSI I don't know anything about the mills of God. Stop them, or they will kill themselves.

STRANGER [*clapping his hands*] Are you ready to proceed with your grandfather's will, or should I wait till you are ready? [*They stop fighting and stand up, panting*] Before I open this box, I want to know if all your Grandfather's wishes have been kept. Was he buried with honour?

AROB Yes, the greatest burial any old man has had in this village.

OJIMA You may well answer, but I spent more money than you did.

AROB No, you did not. I called the drummers and the dancers.

OJIMA I arranged for the shooting of guns.

AROB I paid for the wine for the visitors and the mourners.

OJIMA I——

STRANGER Please, brothers, wait. I ask you again, Was the old man respectably buried?

BASSI I can swear to that. His grandsons have sold practically all they have in order to give him a grand burial.

STRANGER That is good. I shall now open the box.

There is silence. He opens the box and brings out a piece of paper.

AROB [*in alarm*] Where are the jewels, the money, the treasure?

STRANGER Sh! Listen. This is the will. Perhaps it will tell us where to find everything. Listen to this.

AROB But you cannot read. Give it to me.

OJIMA Give it to me.

STRANGER I can read. I am a schoolteacher.

AROB Did you write this will for Grandfather?

STRANGER Questions are useless at this time. I did not.

AROB Stop talking, man. Read it.

STRANGER [*reading*] Now, my grandsons, now that I have been respectably and honourably buried, as all grandsons should do to their grandfathers, I can tell you a few things.

First of all, I have discovered no treasure at all. There was never anything like the "Jewels of the Shrine." [AROB *makes a sound as if something had caught him in the throat.* OJIMA *sneezes violently*] There was no treasure hidden in the farm or anywhere else. I have had nothing in life, so I can only leave you nothing. The house which you now live in was my own. But I sold it some months ago and got a little money for what I needed. That money was my "Jewels of the Shrine." The house belongs now to the stranger who is reading this will to you. He shall take possession of this house two days after the will has been read. Hurry up, therefore, and pack out of this house. You young puppies, do you think I never knew that you had no love for me, and that you were only playing up in order to get the money which you believed I had acquired?

When I was a child, one of my first duties was to respect people who were older than myself. But you have thrown away our traditional love and respect for the elderly person. I shall make you pay for it. Shame on you, young men, who believe that because you can read and write, you need not respect old age as your forefathers did! Shame on healthy young men like you, who let the land go to waste because they will not dirty their hands with work!

OJIMA [*furiously*] Stop it, Stranger, stop it, or I will kill you! I am undone. I have not got a penny left. I have used all I had to feed him and to bury him. But now I have not even got a roof to stay under. You confounded Stranger, how dare you buy this house?

STRANGER Do you insult me in my own house?

AROB [*miserably*] The old cheat! He cheated us to the last. To think that I scratched his back only to be treated like this! We are now poorer than he had ever been.

OJIMA It is a pity. It is a pity.

STRANGER What is a pity?

OJIMA It is a pity we cannot dig him up again.

Suddenly a hoarse, unearthly laugh is heard from somewhere. Everybody looks in a different direction. They listen. And then again . . .

VOICE Ha—ha—ha—ha! [*They all look up*] Ha—ha—ha—ha! [*The voice is unmistably Grandfather* OKORIE's *voice. Seized with terror, everybody except* BASSI *runs in confusion out of the room, stumbling over the table, box, and everything. As they run away, the voice continues*] Ha—ha—ha—ha! [BASSI, *though frightened, boldly stands her ground. She is very curious to know whether someone has been playing them a trick. The voice grows louder*] Ha—ha—ha—ha! [BASSI, *too, is terrorised, and runs in alarm off the stage*] Ha—ha—ha—ha!!!

Curtain.

For Discussion

1 What is the theme of "Jewels of the Shrine"? Is it a common theme?

2 In a morality-type play, the characters are never really fully developed. The author intends them to appear as types rather than as fully developed individuals. Do you feel that there is a fully developed character in "Jewels of the Shrine?" If you feel the characters are types, what does each stand for?

3 What role does the Stranger play in "Jewels of the Shrine"?

4 It is obvious that Okorie represents the forces of good which ultimately triumph over evil. But is he completely good? Examine his methods. Do they appear to be justified under the circumstances?

5 In one sense, "Jewels of the Shrine" has something to say about the conflict between generations. This conflict is obviously not confined to Nigeria. How widespread is this conflict in the United States today? Is some conflict inevitable? Can it be healthy? Explain as fully as you can.

The No (or Noh) plays of Japan reach back to the fourteenth and fifteenth centuries. The No theater is one of the most formal and traditional of arts; the secrets and techniques of the actors are passed down through generations of a family; in 600 years there have been very few changes in the plays or in the way they are produced. There is little scenery, but the costumes are elaborate and brilliantly colored; and the actors, all of whom are men, wear wooden masks when they portray women or supernatural beings. There is no attempt at realism; an orchestra of drums and flutes sits on the stage, and the actors sing and dance as they recite their lines.

The stories have become traditional, and the excitement of the performance comes from the skill and grace with which the actors carry out their roles. A Japanese audience watching *The Dwarf Trees* will not be surprised to find that a poor wandering priest is the Emperor of Japan in disguise. The play emphasizes the ancient values of Japanese society: loyalty, sacrifice, and gratitude.

Seami

The Dwarf Trees

Characters

THE EMPEROR OF JAPAN *disguised as a wandering priest*
TSUNEYO *a poor man*
TSUNEYO'S WIFE
THE MINISTER OF STATE *and other followers of the* EMPEROR

Scene 1

The play takes place in winter: a landscape in a lonely country district. The stage is bare, except for a small hut at the right. A road winds past the hut and leads to the left. It is snowing.

At the beginning, the stage is empty. Then a traveler enters. We can see from his gestures that he is suffering from the cold and that he is lost. The traveler is the EMPEROR OF JAPAN, *disguised as a poor wandering priest.*

EMPEROR   I can no longer tell where I have come from, nor where I am going. I am a holy man, wandering through the world, with no home of my own. How cold it is! With this snow falling, I can no longer see the path. I must seek shelter. [*He sees* TSUNEYO'S *house, goes to it, and knocks at the door*]   Is there anyone in this house?

TSUNEYO'S WIFE   [*opening the door only a crack*]   Who is there?

EMPEROR   I am a poor pilgrim, and I am lost. Pray, let me stay here for the night.

WIFE   It is a small thing you ask. But the master of the house, my husband, is away. Only he can invite you in under his roof.

EMPEROR   Then I shall wait for his return.

WIFE   That must be as you please. I will go to the turn of the path and watch for him. When he comes I will tell him that you are here.

Enter TSUNEYO *on the other side of the stage, making the gestures of one who shakes snow from his clothes.*

TSUNEYO   [*to himself*]   Ah! How the snow falls! Long ago when I lived in the City and served in the forces of the Emperor, how I loved to see it. The snow that falls now is the same that I saw then. But I am old, watching it, and my hair is frost-white.   [*He sees his wife coming toward him*]   What is this? Why are you waiting here in the cold in the midst of this snowstorm?

WIFE   A pilgrim has come to our door asking for a night's lodging. When I told him you were not in the house he asked if he might wait until you returned. That is why I am here.

TSUNEYO   Where is this pilgrim now?

WIFE   [*leading him back towards the hut where the EMPEROR is standing*]   Here he stands!

EMPEROR   [*bowing*]   I am he. Though it is not yet night, how can I find my way in this great storm of snow? I beg you to give me shelter for the night.

TSUNEYO   It is not a great thing that you ask, but I cannot receive you. My house is too poor, and I have no lodging fit for you.

EMPEROR   No, no. I do not care how poor your house is. Allow me to stay here for one night only.

TSUNEYO   I would be glad to ask you to stay, but there is scarcely enough room for my wife and myself. How can we give you lodging? The village of Yamamoto lies only a few miles down the road. You will find a good inn there. You had better start, before night comes down upon you.

EMPEROR   Then you are determined to turn me away?

TSUNEYO   I am sorry, sir, but I cannot invite you to stay in my house. It is too poor for visitors.

EMPEROR   [*turning away*]   Much good it did me to wait for him! I must go my way.   [*He continues out along the path*]

WIFE   Husband, we live here in poverty and ruin because in some former life we did not obey the laws of Heaven. If we turn this pilgrim out into the storm it will surely bring us ill fortune in our next life. If it is by any means possible for us to shelter him here, please let him stay!

TSUNEYO   [*moved by her plea*]   If that is how you feel, wife, why did you not speak before? He cannot have gone far in this great storm. I shall go after him and bring him back.   [*He starts out after the EMPEROR, calling*]   Traveler! Traveler! Hear me! We will give you lodging! Come back!   [*There is no answer*]   The snow is falling so thick that he cannot hear me. What a sad plight he is in! Snow covers the path by which he came and new snow covers the path by which he must go.   [*He follows the EMPEROR, and calls again*]   Traveler! Come back! We will give you shelter!   [*He peers into the distance*]   Look! Look! There he is—he has heard me. He is standing still and shaking the snow from his clothes. Now he is returning.

The EMPEROR enters again.

TSUNEYO   Welcome, pilgrim. I was wrong to turn you from my door. Though my house is poor and small, my wife and I rejoice to give you lodging. Come, enter.   [*He opens the door of the hut. The EMPEROR goes in, and TSUNEYO follows him*]

Scene 2

The interior of TSUNEYO's *hut.*

TSUNEYO [*to his* WIFE] Listen. We have given this traveler lodging, but we have set no food before him. Is there nothing we can give him?

WIFE We have only a little boiled grain. It is a poor dish, but we can give it to him if he will accept it.

TSUNEYO I will tell him. [*To the* EMPEROR] I have given you lodging, traveler, but I have set no food before you. It happens that we have nothing to offer but a little boiled grain. It is coarse food, but pray eat it if you can.

EMPEROR Coarse food? Not at all! Please give it to me. I shall eat it with pleasure.

TSUNEYO [*to his* WIFE] He says he will take some. Hurry and give it to him.

WIFE I will do so.

TSUNEYO [*to himself*] Long ago when I lived in the City, I never tasted such coarse food as this boiled grain. I read about it in poems and songs about poor peasants. But now my whole life is changed. Now I no longer live in the world. I have retired to this lonely place, and this simple food is all I have.

Oh, that I might sleep
And see in my dreams
Good times that have passed away.
Such dreams would be a comfort.
But through my battered walls
Cold winds from the woods
Blow sleep away, and with it
All dreams and remembrances.

As TSUNEYO *sings this song, three beautiful miniature trees—each about two feet high—are carried out and set down on the opposite side of the stage.*

TSUNEYO How cold it is! As the night passes, each hour the frost grows keener. Traveler, we have no fuel to light a fire with so that you might sit and warm yourself. Ah, I have thought of something! I have three dwarf trees. I shall cut them down and make a fire of them.

EMPEROR [*surprised*] Have you indeed dwarf trees?

TSUNEYO Yes, years ago I served the Emperor (though I never had the good fortune to see him) and took part in the affairs of the world. In those days I was prosperous and I had a fine collection of trees. But then trouble came upon me. I lost my fancy for raising these beautiful trees and gave them all away. But three of them I kept—plum, cherry, and pine. I brought them with me, and planted them here in this wilderness. Come. [*He leads the* EMPEROR *outside the hut to where the three dwarf trees stand*] Look, there they are, covered with snow. They are precious to me, yet for this night's entertainment, I shall gladly cut them down and set them on fire.

EMPEROR No, no, you must not do that. I thank you for your kindness, but these trees are all that remain to you of the days when you were prosperous and lived in the City. You need these trees for your pleasure. It is unthinkable that they should be burned.

TSUNEYO My life is like a dead tree.
It shoots forth no blossoms.

WIFE These shrubs, the remains of a former life,
Are profitless toys. Pilgrim.
We gladly burn them to keep you warm.

TSUNEYO [*He leaves the hut and walks across the stage to where the dwarf trees stand*] I cannot, cannot! Oh, beautiful trees, must I destroy you? You, plum tree, were always the first to send forth your blossoms in the Spring and scent the cold air with flowers. You first shall fall. [*He cuts down the plum tree*] Now you, pine tree, whom the wind wraps in mist. Now you shall burn like the beacon by a palace gate guarding a king. [*He cuts down the pine tree*] Cherry tree, each Spring your blossoms were always the last to come forth. I thought you a lonely tree, and I raised you tenderly. Now I am more lonely than you, and you shall blossom only in flames. [*He cuts down the cherry tree*] Come, let us build our fire. [*Carrying the trees, he returns to the hut*]

Scene 3

Inside the hut. A fire is burning.

EMPEROR Now that we have a good fire we can forget the cold.

TSUNEYO If you had not stopped to ask us for shelter, my wife and I would now have no fire to sit by.

EMPEROR There is something I must ask you. I would like to know to what family my host belongs, and something of his history.

TSUNEYO I am not of high birth. My family has no famous name.

EMPEROR Say what you will, I cannot believe that you are a common peasant. Bad luck is not something to be ashamed of. And, after all, your fortune may change. Do not be ashamed to tell me your name.

TSUNEYO Indeed, I have no reason to conceal it. Know then, that I am Tsuneyo, Lord of Sano, and that I have sunk to such evil days.

EMPEROR How did it happen, sir, that you fell upon such misery?

TSUNEYO My relatives stole my land from me. They tricked me and left me to become what I now am.

EMPEROR Why do you not go up to the Capital and lay your case before the Emperor?

TSUNEYO It is said that the Emperor cannot be seen. Moreover, they say that he is absent, making a lengthy pilgrimage.

EMPEROR You are right, I have heard it also.

TSUNEYO I shall go to the City only if the Emperor is in danger and needs my help. Look, here upon the wall my tall spear hangs ready. Here is my armor hanging beside it. And my horse is tied outside. If at any time there comes news from the City that my Master is in danger,

Rusty though they be,
I shall gird this armor on
And take down this tall spear.
Lean-ribbed though he be,
I shall mount my horse and ride,
Neck by neck with the swiftest,
To enlist in the Emperor's service.

And when the battle begins,
Though the enemy be many,
Yet I shall be the first
To break through their ranks,
Choose one, fight with him, and die.
But here in this wilderness
Another fate awaits me.
Worn out with hunger
I die, useless. Oh, despair, despair!

He buries his face in his hands and his voice sinks.

EMPEROR Take courage. You shall not end so. [*Rising*] Now it is light. The storm has ended and I must continue my journey. If I live, I shall return to visit you one day.

TSUNEYO We cannot let you go so soon. At first we were ashamed that you should see the misery of our dwelling.

WIFE Now we ask you to stay with us awhile.

EMPEROR Thank you. Do you think that if it were only my own desire I were following, that I would go forth into the snow?

TSUNEYO After the storm even a clear sky is cold, and tonight——

WIFE Stay with us one more day.

EMPEROR My heart remains, but I must leave you.

TSUNEYO *and* WIFE   Then, farewell.

EMPEROR   [*bowing*]   Farewell.

TSUNEYO *and* WIFE   Come back to us again.

EMPEROR   If one day you should change your mind and come back up to the City, perhaps we shall meet. I am only a humble priest, yet I may be of some help to you. I may be able to bring you before the presence of the Emperor. Do not give up hope. Now I must go my way, though I am sad to leave you.

TSUNEYO   We are sad to lose you from our sight.

They bow in farewell.

Scene 4

Six months later. TSUNEYO *is standing outside his hut. His gestures show that he is watching a large number of travelers passing by him on the road.*

TSUNEYO   [*calling out to the passers-by*]   Hi, you travelers! Is it true that there is a war? Are they raising an army and marching to Kamakura? [*He nods his head as if the unseen travelers answer him. To himself*] So it is true. Barons and Knights from all the Counties of the East are riding to Kamakura to defend the Emperor. What a fine sight it is. They are wearing silver breastplates decorated with bright tassels; their swords and daggers have hilts of gold. Their horses are sleek and well-fed. Even the grooms and pack horses are magnificently appareled.

I am an old warrior. I have nothing left but a rusting sword and broken armor. My horse, too, is old and thin. Yet I cannot stand and watch this army go to the aid of My Lord, the Emperor. I shall join them with horse, sword, and armor that no longer seem worthy of the name.

He goes into the hut and takes down his sword and armor from the wall. He goes outside again and pantomimes the untethering of his horse. He buckles on his armor. Then, as he speaks the following words, he walks across the stage slowly as if proceeding on a journey, miming the action of leading his horse.

TSUNEYO   Let them laugh at me when they see me! I am not a worse man than any of them. Had I a steed to match my heart... [*Gesture of cracking a whip*] Come on, you laggard! Come on, we are falling behind!

He goes out, still leading his horse.

Scene 5

The throne room in the palace of the EMPEROR. *The* EMPEROR *is seated, wearing magnificent robes. He claps his hands, and the* MINISTER OF STATE *appears before him.*

MINISTER   I stand before you.

EMPEROR   Have all the armies arrived?

MINISTER   They have all arrived, my Lord.

EMPEROR   Somewhere among them there will be a Knight in broken armor, carrying a broken sword and leading an old horse whose thin ribs show through its flesh. Find him, and bring him to me.

MINISTER   [*bowing*]   I tremble and obey. [*He goes out.*]

TSUNEYO *enters at the other side of the stage. The* MINISTER OF STATE *approaches him.*

MINISTER   [*to* TSUNEYO]   I must speak with you.

TSUNEYO   What is it?

MINISTER   You are to appear immediately before my Lord.

TSUNEYO   I do not know your lord. Who is he?

MINISTER   The Emperor of Japan!

TSUNEYO   Is it I you are asking to appear before the Emperor?

MINISTER   Yes, you indeed.

TSUNEYO   It cannot be. You have mistaken me for another man.

MINISTER   No, it is you I want. I was told to bring the poorest-looking of all the soldiers. Come at once.

TSUNEYO   The poorest of all the Emperor's soldiers?

MINISTER   Yes, truly.

TSUNEYO   Then I am surely the man you seek. Tell your Lord that I obey.

MINISTER   Follow me.

TSUNEYO   I understand. Too well I understand. One of my enemies has called me a traitor and I am being led before the throne to be executed. Well, there is no help for it. Take me to the Emperor.

He follows the MINISTER *across the stage to where the* EMPEROR *sits. There are several richly dressed warriors and courtiers standing at the* EMPEROR'S *side. When they see* TSUNEYO *they point their fingers at him and burst out laughing. The* EMPEROR *raises his hand for silence.* TSUNEYO *bows before the throne.*

TSUNEYO   My Lord, I have come.

EMPEROR   Gentlemen, I bid you to bow to this man, Tsuneyo, Lord of Sano!

Somewhat bewildered, all the courtiers bow to TSUNEYO.

EMPEROR   [*to* TSUNEYO]   Tsuneyo, have you forgotten the wandering priest whom you once sheltered in a snowstorm? I see you have been true to the words you spoke that night: "If at any time there came news from the City that my Master is in danger,

Rusty though they be,
I shall gird this armor on
And take down this tall spear.
Lean-ribbed though he be,

I shall mount my horse and ride,
Neck by neck with the swiftest,
To enlist in the Emperor's service."

Tsuneyo, those were not empty words—you have come truly and bravely. Know that this levy of armies was made for only one purpose: to test you and see whether you spoke true or false.

Now I shall hear the pleas of all the faithful warriors who have obeyed my summons. And first, in the case of Tsuneyo I make judgement: To him shall be returned his lawful estate—all the land of Sano. Above all else one thing shall not be forgotten: that in the great snowstorm he cut down his dwarf trees, his treasures, and burned them to keep me warm. And now in gratitude for those three trees—plum, cherry, and pine—I grant him three new estates. One in Kaga, where plums grow; one in Etchū, famous for its cherry trees; one in the pine-covered hills of Kōzuke. He shall hold them forever and leave them to his heirs.   [*Handing a scroll to* TSUNEYO]   In testimony whereof we give this title deed by our own hand, signed and sealed.

TSUNEYO   [*his voice choked with emotion*]   My lord . . .   [*He takes the title deeds and bows three times to the* EMPEROR. *Addressing the courtiers*]   Look, you barons! You laughed at me. Now let your laughter turn to envy.

EMPEROR   [*rises from his throne, comes downstage and addresses the audience*]:

Then the warriors took leave of the Emperor
And went their homeward ways.
And among them went Tsuneyo,
Joy breaking upon his brow,
Riding now on a splendid steed.
He returned to the lands torn from him,
Now once again his own.

For Discussion

1 What is the central characteristic of Tsuneyo's personality? Is it possible that the very things which win him back his title and possessions may have been the cause of his falling into poverty and ruin in the first place?

2 Does Tsuneyo have any plan to avenge the wrong done to him? How does his wife explain the miserable conditions under which they are forced to live?

3 In a sentence or two, try to define the moral of *The Dwarf Trees*. How is this play like a fable? Can you think of any other fable or fairy tales which present the same lesson?

4 The Japanese dwarf trees are called *bonsai*. In recent years the oriental art of growing *bonsai* has become a favorite hobby of Americans. As an extension of your reading (this isn't necessary in order to understand the play), do some light research on the growing of *bonsai*. What kind of temperament is necessary to a gardener who would be successful in growing dwarf trees? Does the growing of dwarf trees indicate some sort of special attitude toward time on the part of the Japanese?

5 Why is Tsuneyo's destruction of the dwarf trees looked upon as a heroic sacrifice? Why would it be different from, say, an American who had to sacrifice his rose bushes?

6 The traditional setting of the No play is extremely simple. A square platform covered by a roof represents a palace, a house, a roadway, or a battlefield. Devise your own production of *The Dwarf Trees*. How much of the traditional staging would you employ? What overall effect would your production try to convey to an audience?

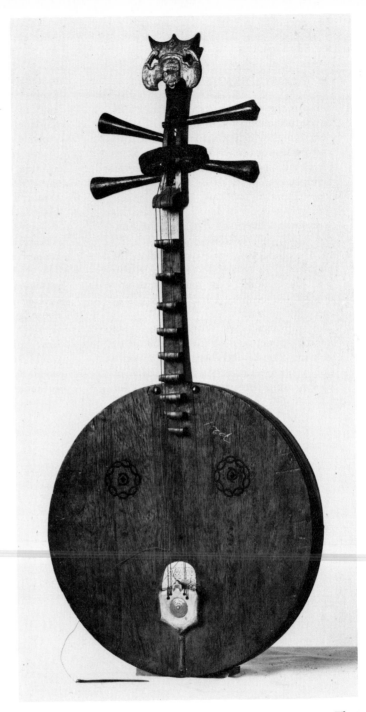

Siamese or Thai
Sung (moon guitar)
The Metropolitan Museum of Art,
The Crosby Brown Collection of Musical Instruments, 1889

Unit Five Poetry

The best poetry is about the whole of life. Whatever you are concerned with, poetry is concerned with too.

Of course, not every poem appeals to every reader. Nor should it. Part of the fun of reading is giving in to enthusiasms, and you can't be equally enthusiastic about everything. Any reader has the right to find one poet exciting and another poet boring. And remember that most of the poetry that gets written *is* boring. When an editor selects poems for a book like this, he tries to choose what he finds interesting or lively, but he is making his selections from perhaps less than one percent of the available material. Also, no two editors have exactly the same taste; nor do any two readers. The best poems in this book will be the ones that make *each reader* see and feel something that is fresh and new.

One of the poet's most important devices is *compression*. He packs a great deal into few words in order to intensify his vision and give it greater power. Look, for example, at García Lorca's poem "Gypsy Funeral" (page 204). The material for this poem could have been expanded into a novel: where the gypsy girl was born, how she lived, whom she loved, how she died. Lorca might have told us of his own meetings with the girl, repeated long conversations, reported the attitudes of the "nice" people of Spain toward the gypsy way of life, and so forth. Instead, he wrote a funeral lament in fifteen lines. As an experience, it is complete in itself. If you find it exciting it is because García Lorca has compressed whole lifetimes of feeling into these few lines.

194

Another natural part of poetry is *metaphor,* ways of telling about one thing in terms of another. Comparing things, placing them side by side, invites the reader to see and feel things in a fresh, surprising way. For example, we see the sun in the sky day after day. But do we really *see* it? How much more vivid and precise the sun becomes when Stephen Crane writes: "The red sun was pasted in the sky like a wafer." A good metaphor is not merely pretty or clever; it is not a description plastered across an idea. A good metaphor *becomes* the ideas it expresses; it is so vital to the idea that it would be impossible to express the idea without it. In "My Fiftieth Year" (page 226), Yeats says, "My body of a sudden blazed." Literally this makes no sense; the poet's body did not shine, was not actually on fire. But Yeats *felt* as if he were blazing, and this choice of metaphor precisely conveys his feeling to the reader.

Then, too, a poem is nothing if it has no *music,* a sound which catches the thought and holds it perfectly together. The music of poetry comes from common speech intensified by rhythm or rhyme or by other means of repeating sounds. Rhyme, of course, is not essential to poetry: classical Japanese, Greek, and Latin poetry never used rhyme. The rhythms of a poem may be strong and regular, as in Burns's "A Red, Red Rose" (page 197); or they may be closer to the rhythms of everyday speech, as in Pablo Neruda's "The Horses" (page 214). Each poem must find its own voice, its own music. Of course, since many of the poems in this section were written in other languages, the English translations can hope only to suggest the sounds and rhythms of the original poems.

Compression, metaphor, music—these forces operate to give a successful poem its unity and its uniqueness. Poetry is hard to define, yet large numbers of people across the centuries have agreed that there is such an experience as being in the presence of great poetry. Tastes change in poetry as in all things, but to a remarkable extent men have been able to agree upon who the greatest of the poets are.

Poems about Love

Ravished by all that to the eyes is fair

Michelangelo Buonarroti would have won fame if he had never done anything but write poetry. As it is, his work as a painter, sculptor, and architect overshadows his poetry. For every reader who knows his poems there are thousands of people who know his Pietà and David, and his vast paintings for the Sistine Chapel in the Vatican at Rome. In both his poetry and his sculpture Michelangelo's genius avoided the smooth and the easy to move toward more powerful, direct, sometimes rough statements. Other poets of his time tended to spin words into delicate and complex sonnets. A contemporary critic said to Michelangelo's fellow poets: "He says things and you say words."

"Ravished by all that to the eyes is fair" is part of one of the great traditions of Renaissance love poetry, a tradition Michelangelo shared with two of the greatest of Italian poets, Petrarch and Dante. The poet aspires to a heavenly or divine love, but while he lives within his earthly body he can never know the experience of divine love directly. Therefore his love for his earthly lady becomes a kind of brilliant foreshadowing of a purer love beyond. The light of heaven comes to him through his lady's eyes.

Ravished by all that to the eyes is fair,
Yet hungry for the joys that truly bless,
My soul can find no stair
To mount to heaven, save earth's loveliness.
For from the stars above   5
Descends a glorious light
That lifts our longing to their highest height
And bears the name of love.
Nor is there aught can move
A gentle heart, or purge or make it wise,
But beauty and the starlight of her eyes.

Michelangelo
George Santayana/TRANSLATOR

The River Merchant's Wife: a Letter

The dramatic poem "The River Merchant's Wife" takes the form of a letter from a young bride, still in her teens, to her husband, who is absent on business. The story of their childhood friendship, their early marriage, and their separation is sketched in a few lines, as the poem moves effortlessly through time and space. The translation suggests the formality with which a Chinese wife addresses her husband, yet the formal tone does not hide her affection.

Chinese poetry is difficult to translate into English because the grammars of the two languages operate in very different ways. Here the translator uses standard English but manages to suggest the quality of the Chinese original by using short, direct sentences and a large number of simple, one-syllable words.

While my hair was still cut straight
    across my forehead
I played about the front gate, pulling
    flowers.
You came by on bamboo stilts, playing
    horse,
You walked about my seat, playing with
    blue plums.
And we went on living in the village of
    Chokan: **5**
Two small people, without dislike or
    suspicion.

At fourteen I married My Lord you.
I never laughed, being bashful.
Lowering my head, I looked at the wall.
Called to, a thousand times, I never
    looked back.   **10**

At fifteen I stopped scowling,
I desired my dust to be mingled with
    yours

Forever and forever and forever.
Why should I climb the look out?

At sixteen you departed,   **15**
You went into far Ku-to-yen, by the river
    of swirling eddies,
And you have been gone five months.
The monkeys make sorrowful noise over-
    head.

Li Po

Ezra Pound/TRANSLATOR

Hep-Cat Chung

Hep-Cat Chung is not from one of Confucius's philosophical works, but rather from a collection of ancient Chinese songs which he put together. It was translated by the same man who translated "The River Merchant's Wife"—the American poet Ezra Pound. Another great poet, T. S. Eliot, called Pound "the inventor of Chinese poetry for our time," for Pound was able to bring to Chinese poetry a new life in English in a way that other translators, most of whom knew more Chinese than Pound, were not.

Some forty years separate these two translations, and Pound's approach to each is entirely different. For "Hep-Cat Chung" Pound attempted a translation into a kind of "American" rather than standard English. He uses slang and twitchy, syncopated jive rhythms. One of the dangers of using slang in literature is that it gets out of date: the expression *hep-cat* (a young man who is hip or "with it," often associated with jazz musicians) has already become a period piece.

Hep-Cat Chung, 'ware my town,
don't break my willows down.
The trees don't matter.
but father's tongue, mother's tongue
    Have a heart, Chung,
            it's awful.

Hep-Cat Chung, don't jump my wall
nor strip my mulberry boughs,
The boughs don't matter
But my brothers' clatter!
    Have a heart, Chung,
              it's awful.

Hep-Cat Chung, that is *my* garden wall,
Don't break my sandalwood tree.
The tree don't matter
But the subsequent chatter!
    Have a heart, Chung,
              it's awful.

Confucius
Ezra Pound/TRANSLATOR

'But I can get a hair-dye
And set such colour there,
Brown, or black, or carrot,
That young men in despair   10
May love me for myself alone
And not my yellow hair.'

'I heard an old religious man
But yesternight declare
That he had found a text to prove   15
That only God, my dear,
Could love you for yourself alone
And not your yellow hair.'

William Butler Yeats

For Anne Gregory

People often say that they want to be loved "just for themselves" rather than for their fame, or their wealth, or their beauty. But aren't one's qualities a part of one's "self"? This is the question that Yeats playfully asks in "For Anne Gregory." Anne Gregory was the daughter of a friend of the poet's. She appears to have been complaining because people were praising her beautiful hair rather than herself. Although the poem is light—after all, Anne's problem is not a very serious one—it is written in a mock-serious tone, as if some weighty point were being discussed. In fact, it does touch upon a serious philosophical question: the difference that exists between human and divine love.

Yeats (1865–1939) was the greatest poet of modern Ireland. He was awarded the Nobel Prize for Literature in 1923.

'Never shall a young man,
Thrown into despair
By those great honey-coloured
Ramparts at your ear,
Love you for yourself alone   5
And not your yellow hair.'

A Red, Red Rose

Few English lyric poems are simpler, or more popular, than Robert Burns's "A Red, Red Rose." The poet mentions only a few universal, elemental things: rose, music, ocean, rocks, time. This simplicity and directness gives the poem its feeling of burning sincerity.

Notice how Burns suggests the speech of his native Scotland with the use of a few dialect words and contractions.

O my luve is like a red, red rose,
  That's newly sprung in June.
O my luve is like the melodie,
  That's sweetly played in tune.

As fair art thou, my bonny lass,   5
  So deep in luve am I,
And I will luve thee still, my dear,
  Till a' the seas gang dry.

Till a' the seas gang dry, my dear,
  And the rocks melt wi' the sun!   10
And I will luve thee still, my dear,
  While the sands o' life shall run.

And fare thee weel, my only luve,
   And fare thee weel a while!
And I will come again, my luve,   15
   Tho' it were ten thousand mile!

Robert Burns

Pine Tree and Palm Tree

The German poet Heine, separated from his beloved, expressed his feelings in this little fable about two unhappy trees.

There is a touch of tender comedy in the idea of two trees in love with each other. In spite of the comedy, the poem conveys a genuine feeling of longing. Heine often introduced a bit of irony into his verse to counteract what otherwise would be a sentimental thought.

A pine tree stands on a Northern slope,
   Alone, where the cold winds blow.
Sleeping, he is wrapped in a white
   Blanket of ice and snow.

And there he dreams of a palm tree   5
   That weeps, sad and alone,
On a golden shore, where other winds
   Across the scorched sands moan.

Heinrich Heine

Sonnet 29

Shakespeare's sonnets are one of literature's most lasting monuments in praise of love. Sonnet 29 begins with the poet being weighed down by the frustrations of age, ambition, and envy. The poem turns on the words "Haply I think on thee" and changes to a mood of exaltation and serenity.

When, in disgrace with fortune and
   men's eyes,
I all alone beweep my outcast state,
And trouble deaf heaven with my bootless cries,
And look upon myself, and curse my fate,
Wishing me like to one more rich in
   hope,   **5**
Featured like him, like him with friends
   possessed,
Desiring this man's art and that man's
   scope,
With what I most enjoy contented least;
Yet in these thoughts myself almost despising,
Haply I think on thee—and then my
   state,   **10**
Like to the lark at break of day arising
From sullen earth, sings hymns at heaven's gate;
For thy sweet love remembered such
   wealth brings
That then I scorn to change my state
   with kings.

William Shakespeare

Sestina

The masterpiece of the great Italian poet Dante Alighieri is *The Divine Comedy*, a long poem telling of a journey from Hell to Purgatory and finally to Heaven. The following sestina is one of Dante's shorter poems. In it he tells of his passion for a lady who coldly refuses to return his love. He has traveled up into the hills in order to forget her, but distance does not lessen his suffering. The word *stone* in this poem has a special meaning: the lady's name was Pietra, which means "stone" in Italian. Dante sees her name as a reflection of the hardness of her heart.

The sestina is an elaborate verse form seldom used in English. Notice that each stanza contains six lines ending in the same six words: *shade, grass, green, stone, hill, lady.* The word ending the last line of each stanza also ends the first line of the next stanza, and so on. At the end, all six of these key words are used within a special three-line stanza, which gives a feeling of finality and intensity to the ending of the poem.

To the dim light and the large circle of
    shade
I have clomb,[1] and to the whitening of
    the hills
There where we see no color in the grass.
Natheless[2] my longing loses not its green,
It has so taken root in the hard stone 5
Which talks and hears as though it were
    a lady.

Utterly frozen is this youthful lady
Even as the snow that lies within the
    shade;
For she is no more moved than is a stone
By the sweet season which makes warm
    the hills   10
And alters them afresh from white to
    green,
Covering their sides again with flowers
    and grass.

When on her hair she sets a crown of
    grass
The thought has no more room for other
    lady;
Because she weaves the yellow with the
    green   15
So well that Love sits down there in the
    shade—
Love who has shut me in among low hills
Faster than between walls of granite-
    stone.

She is more bright than is a precious
    stone;
The wound she gives may not be heal'd
    with grass: 20

I therefore have fled far o'er plains and
    hills
For refuge from so dangerous a lady;
But from her sunshine nothing can give
    shade—
Not any hill, nor wall, nor summer-green.

A while ago, I saw her dress'd in green—
So fair, she might have waken'd in a
    stone
This love which I do feel even for her
    shade;
And therefore, as one woos a graceful
    lady,
I wooed her in a field that was all grass
Girdled about with very lofty hills.   30

Yet shall the streams turn back and climb
    the hills
Before Love's flame in this damp wood
    and green
Burn, as it burns within a youthful lady,
For my sake, who would sleep away in
    stone
My life, or feed like beasts upon the
    grass,   35
Only to see her garments cast a shade.

How dark soe'er[3] the hills throw out their
    shade,
Under her summer-green the beautiful
    lady
Covers it, like a stone cover'd in grass.

Dante Alighieri

This Living Hand

    Within the span of his brief life—he died in 1821 at the age of twenty-five—John Keats wrote a relatively small number of intense poems which have placed him among the greatest of the English Romantic poets. Keats never published "This Living Hand": it was found among his papers after his death. It

1 clomb *Climbed.*
2 Natheless *Nevertheless.*
3 How dark soe'er *However dark.*

200

is addressed to Fanny Brawne, a girl with whom Keats had a tortured love affair. Written during his final illness, the poem shows a full awareness by Keats of his approaching death.

The theme of this poem is similar to that of Dante's "Sestina": the poet is complaining that the woman he loves does not return his love. Beyond the fact that they share this common theme, the two poems are very different. Dante has cooled and distanced his experience, made it almost impersonal, by weaving it into an elaborate formal structure. Keats, in this poem, has almost abandoned "art" as if to say "My experience at this moment is so intense that I do not have time to stop for a stanza form or rhyme."

the seeds from which his later poems grew. Yeats's poetry seemed to advance in brilliance until his death. He was awarded the Nobel prize for literature in 1923.

In modern psychological jargon, both this poem and the preceding one by Keats might be called wish-fulfillment fantasies. Keats in "This Living Hand" is imagining how his beloved will feel after he is dead; that then she will feel sorry for the way she has treated him. Yeats, too, is imagining what his beloved will think and feel sometime in the future. Their love affair seems to have ended, and the poet is saying something like: "You may not love me now, but some day—when you are old—you will understand how much I loved you."

This living hand, now warm and capable
Of earnest grasping, would, if it were
    cold
And in the icy silence of the tomb,
So haunt thy days and chill thy dreaming
    nights
That thou wouldst wish thy own heart
    dry of blood   5
So in my veins red life might stream
    again,
And thou be conscience-calmed—see
    here it is—I hold it towards you.

John Keats

When You Are Old

Yeats was the greatest poet of modern Ireland. This poem, one of Yeat's earlier works, foreshadows those he wrote in the twentieth century. The imagination, the style, and the theme—the passing of time and love—are

When you are old and grey and full of
    sleep,
And nodding by the fire, take down this
    book,
And slowly read, and dream of the soft
    look
Your eyes had once, and of their shadows
    deep;

How many loved your moments of glad
    grace,   5
And loved your beauty with false love or
    true,
But one man loved the pilgrim soul in
    you,
And loved the sorrows of your changing
    face;

And bending down beside the glowing
    bars,
Murmur, a little sadly, how Love fled
And paced upon the mountains overhead
And hid his face among a crowd of stars.

William Butler Yeats

For Discussion

RAVISHED BY ALL THAT TO THE EYES IS FAIR

1 The peculiar beauty of this poem partly arises from its mixture of satisfaction and dissatisfaction. What are the sources of the poet's satisfaction? What are the sources of his dissatisfaction or unfulfilled longing?

2 Is this attitude toward love common in our own time? How, in your opinion, would the typical modern love poem differ from this?

3 In the headnote to this poem we quoted a contemporary of Michelangelo's to the effect that while other poets say "words," Michelangleo says "things." Does this statement make any sense to you in light of the poem printed here? Discuss.

THE RIVER MERCHANT'S WIFE

1 The art of translation requires great precision and is much more than a matter of looking up words in a dictionary. The translator of this poem originally wrote that the girl wore her hair in "bangs." His English wife said that "bangs" was an exclusively American term; she suggested the English term for the same kind of haircut, "fringe." Since each word was woven into a non-Chinese culture, the poet finally settled for the phrase "While my hair was still cut straight across my forehead." Do you agree that this is better than either "bangs" or "fringe"? If so, why?

2 How does the young wife change from the time when her hair was "still cut straight" until the time when she writes this letter? How long has she known her husband? How old was she when she married? How old is she as she writes the letter? What details does the poet use to suggest the stages of her maturity?

3 Why has the husband gone away?

4 What are some of the sharp pictorial images the poem suggests? Are there any parts of the poem which are vague?

5 Often the things a person notices reveal how he feels. How does Li Po use nature to suggest the young wife's emotions? How does she describe each of the following: the mosses, the river, the butterflies, the noise of the monkeys? What is the emotional meaning of each of these images?

HEP-CAT CHUNG

1 Is the young girl who is speaking in love with Chung, or at least very much interested in him? What is her problem?

2 Do you think it was a mistake for the translator to put this traditional Chinese poem into modern American colloquial language? Has he been successful in suggesting the tone of voice of an American teen-age girl?

3 Could this translation be set to music more easily than "The River Merchant's Wife"? If so, why?

4 This translation is obviously a very free one. Do you think it's more important for a translator of poetry to bring his original to life by whatever means? Or to stick to a word-for-word dictionary translation?

FOR ANNE GREGORY

1 The poem is a dialogue between two speakers. Identify each. How can the reader tell their relationship? Their relative ages?

2 Explain the last three lines of the poem. Is the poet being ironic? Is the girl's yellow hair really a problem, or is it probably an asset? Do you think the poet really heard "an old religious man" make the statement in the last stanza, or is it probably his own invention?

3 In the final stanza the poet presents the girl with a paradox: without her yellow

hair, only God can love her; with it, young men will never love her for herself alone. Is the meaning of the poem only restricted to Anne Gregory's problem? Suggest some general applications.

A RED, RED ROSE

1 Could this poem be set to music easily? How would the appropriate music for this poem differ from the appropriate music you would use for "Hep-Cat Chung"?

2 Is the lover in this poem more interested in the way he feels, or in the person who creates the feeling in him?

3 In the first two lines, does the speaker mean that his sweetheart resembles a rose? Or that the love he has for her resembles a rose? Do roses in bloom last very long? Is the speaker aware of the implications of his comparison? Does it matter to the poem?

4 Would the poem be improved or spoiled if the dialect words were changed to standard English?

5 Note that many words and phrases are repeated throughout the poem. What is the effect of this repetition? In most writing, too much repetition is considered a fault. Why is it justified here?

PINE TREE AND PALM TREE

1 If this poem is a fable, does it have a moral? If so, what is it? If not, what effect does the absence of a moral give?

2 Why has Heine chosen two trees which are native to different climates? Would the poem have the same meaning if both trees were either palms or pines?

3 Describe a human situation comparable to that of the trees. What common truth about life and love forms the basis of this poem? How does the poet give this common truth a fresh and unusual expression?

SONNET 29

1 As soon as the poet turns from his miseries to the thought of his beloved, he thinks of the lark arising. Why is this image appropriate? What is meant by "sullen earth"? To what state of mind of the poet's does it correspond?

2 Most sonnets are divided into two sections, one of eight lines and one of six. The thought in the final six lines usually contrasts with the thought in the first part. Does Shakespeare make such use of the sonnet form in this poem? How?

3 How does the poem show a process of self-discovery? The sonnet begins with one state of mind and ends with another. Is the change logical? Is it convincing?

SESTINA

1 Writers often take a painful experience and transform it into something beautiful. In your opinion, has Dante done this in this sestina? What is the essential emotion of the poem?

2 Study the use of the color green in the poem. What does it symbolize? With what does it contrast?

3 Using the letters *a* through *f*, make a diagram of the rhyme scheme of this poem. Find the complete pattern with which the words move from one stanza to the next.

THIS LIVING HAND

1 Paraphrase the poem. In your own words, what is the heart of the message Keats is sending to the woman he loves?

2 Why does the poet believe that after his death the woman he loves will have a bad conscience?

3 The hand in the poem is a metaphor for something larger. When the poet says "I hold it towards you" he is talking about his hand, but also about something more than his hand. What is he holding out toward the girl he loves?

4 The last line of the poem is shorter than the first seven lines. It breaks off abruptly. Can you imagine this last line being fol-

lowed by a gesture? What would it be? What other effect do you feel from this abrupt line?

WHEN YOU ARE OLD

1 Why does the poet say that taking down his book from a shelf is going to make the lady "Murmur, a little sadly"?
2 He says that many people have loved the lady he is addressing, but that his love was different from all others. How was it different?
3 Why has Love "hid his face"?
4 The poet is obviously still in love with the woman he is addressing, and suggests that he will always love her, even when she is old. Where do you find traces of regret or bitterness in the poem?

Poems about Death

THREE POEMS

Rider's Song

In "Rider's Song" the speaker sees death ahead on the road to Córdoba, but with wild acceptance he goes on toward his destiny instead of attempting an escape. "Gypsy Funeral" is a lament as well as a tribute to the beauty of the dead gypsy girl. In "The Balcony" the poet expresses his intense love of life by asking that, after his death, the doors to the balcony be left open so that the life of the world may continue to enter his room.

Córdoba.
Distant. Alone.
Black my pony, big the moon,
Olives in my saddlebag.
I know the roads, and yet   5
I shall not get to Córdoba.

Across the plain, beneath the wind,
Black my pony, red the moon,
Death stands and watches as I come,
Watches from the towers of Córdoba.

Ay! How long the road goes on!
Ay! How brave my pony is!
Ay! Death lies in wait for me
Before I get to Córdoba.

Córdoba.   15
Distant. Alone.

Federico García Lorca

Gypsy Funeral

Ay! you fierce gypsy!
Yayay! fierce gypsy girl!

There were no "nice" girls
at your funeral.

204

None of those who wear 5
white mantillas on fair days,
and cut off their beautiful curls
to toss at Christ's coffin.
Those at your funeral
were sinister people who carry 10
their hearts in their heads.
They followed your body
crying through the streets.

Ay! you fierce gypsy!
Yayay! fierce gypsy girl! 15

Federico García Lorca

The Balcony

And if I die
leave the balcony open!

A small boy eating an orange
(can be seen from my balcony).

They are harvesting the wheat 5
(you can hear from my balcony).

If I die
leave the balcony open!

Federico García Lorca
George Kearns/TRANSLATOR

When I Have Fears

In "This Living Hand" (page 199) we saw
a love poem by Keats in which his fear of an
early death intensified his sense of life. Here,
in one of the most famous sonnets in English,
Keats was more explicit about his forebodings
that life would not give him space enough in
which to fulfill his genius.

It would be difficult to describe the mood
of the last line of this sonnet. It combines

personal despair with a kind of acceptance of
a larger order in the universe. The poet seems
to say, "Although I am sad to think I shall
never achieve Love and Fame, what, in fact,
do they mean in the light of Eternity?"

When I have fears that I may cease to be
Before my pen has gleaned my teeming
brain,
Before high-pilèd books, in charact'ry,
Hold like rich garners the full ripened
grain;
When I behold, upon the night's starred
face, 5
Huge cloudy symbols of a high romance,
And think that I may never live to trace
Their shadows, with the magic hand of
chance;
And when I feel, fair creature of an hour!
That I shall never look upon thee more,
Never have relish in the faery power
Of unreflecting love!—then on the shore
Of the wide world I stand alone, and
think
Till Love and Fame to nothingness do
sink.

John Keats

Heraclitus

Hearing of the death of another poet, his
friend Heraclitus, Callimachus wrote this simple, polished poem. In it he insists, as men
have insisted in all ages, that his friend will
live on in memory. The "nightingales" are
Heraclitus's poems, the reason for which he
will be remembered.

Much of the dramatic effect of this epitaph
comes from the sharp contrast between two
images: "ashes" and "nightingales."

They told me, Heraclitus, they told me
you were dead;
They brought me bitter news to hear and
bitter tears to shed.

I wept as I remember'd how often you
    and I
Had tired the sun with talking and sent
    him down the sky.

And now that thou art lying, my dear old
    Carian[1] guest,   5
A handful of grey ashes, long, long ago
    at rest,
Still are thy pleasant voices, thy nightin-
    gales, awake,
For Death, he taketh all away, but them
    he cannot take.

Callimachus
William Barnstone/TRANSLATOR

On the Burial of His Brother

Catullus was one of the leading lyric poets of Rome's Augustan Age. When his brother died in Asia Minor, far from Rome, the poet made the long journey to his brother's burial place, bearing symbolic gifts as a final tribute.

This verse was written in Latin during the first century B.C. In its brevity and polished grace it is typical of the poems the ancient Greeks and Romans composed in memory of the dead. Sometimes they were actually inscribed on monuments, sometimes not. The brief, polished epitaph is one of the great traditions of lyric poetry. For other examples see "Heraclitus" (page 205), "Elegy For J.F.K." (page 206), and "Inscription For the Grave of a Dog" (page 218).

By ways remote and distant waters sped,
    Brother, to thy sad graveside am I
    come,
That I may give the last gift to the dead,
    And vainly parley with thine ashes
    dumb;
Since She who now bestows and now
    denies   5

Hath ta'en thee, hopeless brother,
    from mine eyes.
But lo! these gifts, the heirlooms of past
    years,
    Are made sad things to grace thy cof-
    fin-shell;
Take them, all drenchèd with a brother's
    tears,
    and, brother, for all time, hail and
    farewell.   10

Gaius Valerius Catullus
Aubrey Beardsley/TRANSLATOR

Elegy for J. F. K.

The assassination of President John F. Kennedy was one of the most shocking events of recent history. This short poem, which captures the stoical spirit of the ancient Romans, was a reaction to Kennedy's death by one of the greatest modern poets in English. Auden's tightly controlled poem suggests through its brevity and thoughtfulness that we must draw a line to grief on such an occasion. The poem suggests a state of shock, but at the same time the need to move beyond shock toward finding some meaning in what seems to be a meaningless act.

When President Kennedy died, newspapers, magazines, and books were filled with millions of words about his death and its implications. Auden's short poem seems to stand in sharp contrast to this vast outpouring of language. The poem appears to say, "The details do not matter. There is very little to say about such a death which has any real meaning. The meaning now depends upon us and how we act in the future."

The word *elegy* suggests a lament for the dead, and indeed, the poem begins with a "cry." However, there is no increase to the outpouring of emotion as the poem continues. Rather, it moves from being a cry and turns toward stillness, toward a quiet philosophical statement. This movement from agitation to

---

1 Carian *A person from Caria, an ancient division of southwest Asia Minor.*

acceptance is similar to that in Keats's sonnet "When I Have Fears."

Why *then*, why *there*,
Why *thus*, we cry, did he die?
The heavens are silent.

What he was, he was:
What he is fated to become   5
Depends on us.

Remembering his death,
How we choose to live
Will decide its meaning.

When a just man dies,   10
Lamentation and praise,
Sorrow and joy, are one.

W. H. Auden

For Discussion

THREE POEMS

1 "Rider's Song" suggests a story, but who the rider is, why he is riding toward Córdoba, and what kind of death awaits him, these are left deliberately vague. Would the poem be improved if these "story" elements were more clearly defined? Or would it then become a different kind of poem?

2 In "Gypsy Funeral" what does the poet mean by "nice" girls? What is his attitude toward them? The poem contrasts two ways of life. What are they? Which way does the poet prefer? What does he mean by "people who carry/their hearts in their heads"?

3 In Spanish houses most rooms open onto balconies that overlook the street or countryside. Although "The Balcony" concerns death, the effect it produces is of an intense relish for life. How do the details— a boy eating an orange and the sound of the harvesters—contribute to the poem?

WHEN I HAVE FEARS

1 In this poem, what concept does Keats have of a rich and full life? In your opinion, is it a valid concept?

2 Describe the main image contained in the first four lines. The key words are *gleaned, garners,* and *grain.*

3 What is the central image of the last three lines? Does the contrast between the opening and closing images add to the effectiveness of the poem?

4 What, in this poem, is Keats's attitude toward life and death?

HERACLITUS

1 A lyric poem might be defined as one that tells more about how the poet feels about a subject than it does about the subject itself. Does this definition fit "Heraclitus"? If so, how?

2 In a paragraph, support or attack the following proposition: when Callimachus says that Heraclitus will be immortal, he is also suggesting his own victory over time and death.

ON THE BURIAL OF HIS BROTHER

1 Who is meant by "She who now bestows and now denies"? Does this suggest that the poem is more than a personal lament and has philosophical implication?

2 What sort of tributes and gifts might be meant by "heirlooms of past years"? What effect is gained by leaving the gifts unspecified?

3 What is the effect of the final three words of the poem? Is there an element of surprise in seeing these two words placed side by side? Why is the very end of the poem a good position for the phrase "hail and farewell"?

ELEGY FOR J.F.K.

1 What are the implications of the line "The heavens are silent"? If the heavens will not answer these questions, who will?

2 In what way does the future of the dead president—either of his reputation or of the things he stood for—depend on us? Who does the poet mean by "us"?

3 The final stanza brings forth two pairs of contrasts or contradictions, "Lamentation and praise" and "Sorrow and joy." How are these contradictions resolved?

4 Why should there be any "joy" in thinking about such a tragic event as the assassination of a president?

Poems about Nature

SIX JAPANESE HAIKU

Japanese haiku poetry has become increasingly popular among English-speaking people. The form is a strict one: in Japanese the haiku always contains exactly seventeen syllables. The syllables are divided into three lines: five in the first, seven in the second, and five in the third. (In translations of Japanese haiku and in haiku composed in English, a few syllables more or less do not matter. The 5–7–5 syllable pattern does not suit the structure of English.)

A traditional haiku is based on a sharp impression of nature: tree, mountain, animal, insect, pond, snow, and so forth. It usually contains a contrast of opposites: small against large (as in "The Great Statue of Buddha"); silence against sound (as in "By the Old Pond"); hot against cold (as in "Heat"); or presence against absence (as in "Cherry Trees").

It is interesting to see the way a haiku operates in Japanese. Here is one of the six poems transliterated from the Japanese word for word into our Western alphabet. There is a literal English translation beneath each word. The poem is "The New Moon":

Mikazuki   / wa
Three-day-moon / as-for
   soru   / zo / samusa
   be-curved / ! / cold /
    saekaeru
    is-very-strong

The single word which makes up the last line has five syllables because each of the vowels is pronounced separately. (For a more detailed description of how haiku are written and what they mean, see Harold G. Henderson's *An Introduction to Haiku*, which is available as a paperback.)

Cherry Trees

They blossom, and then
   we gaze, and then the blooms
     scatter, and then . . .

Onitsura

The Great Statue of Buddha

Out from the hollow
   of Great Buddha's nose—
     comes a swallow.

Issa

The New Moon

Just three days old,
   the moon, and it's all warped and bent!
     How keen the cold!

Issa

Autumn

On a withered branch
   a crow has settled—
     autumn nightfall.

Bashō

By the Old Pond

Old pond—
   and a frog-jump-in
     water-sound.

Bashō

1 boon *Gift.*

Heat

The summer river:
   although there is a bridge, my horse
     goes through the water.

Shiki

Harold G. Henderson/TRANSLATOR

The world is too much with us

In this sonnet, Wordsworth complains of modern man's separation from natural things. Too often, he says, we give up our natural heritage to pursue material things which are temporary and worthless.

Proteus and Triton are figures from Greek myth. Proteus was the Old Man of the Sea; he tended the herds that belonged to the King of the Sea, Poseidon. Triton was Poseidon's son, a merman (half man, half fish) who lived in the sea and carried a trumpet made from a conch shell.

The world is too much with us; late and
    soon,
Getting and spending, we lay waste our
    powers:
Little we see in Nature that is ours;
We have given our hearts away, a sordid
    boon![1]
The Sea that bares her bosom to the
    moon;   5
The winds that will be howling at all
    hours
And are up-gathered now like sleeping
    flowers;
For this, for everything, we are out of
    tune;
It moves us not.—Great God! I'd rather
    be
A pagan suckled in a creed outworn;   10

So might I, standing on this pleasant lea,
Have glimpses that would make me less
  forlorn;
Have sight of Proteus rising from the sea;
Or hear old Triton blow his wreathèd
  horn.

William Wordsworth

Song

In Robert Browning's play *Pippa Passes*, the child Pippa roams the countryside, pleased with the world and with all humanity. Older people, caught up in greed, envy, and passion, watch Pippa as she goes by. Her shining innocence reforms them. This is the song she sings as she goes along.

In any work of literature, each statement must be looked at in its context. It would be unfair to say that Browning's own philosophy of life can be summed up by the words "All's right with the world!" In fact, Browning saw much that was wrong with the world. A song such as this is a momentary lyrical expression of a way of feeling, not a pronouncement about the whole of life.

The year's at the spring
And day's at the morn;
Morning's at seven;
The hillside's dew-pearled;
The lark's on the wing;   5
The snail's on the thorn:
God's in his heaven—
All's right with the world!

Robert Browning

June Nights

The poet often finds himself reflected in the natural world. Earth, sky, or sea becomes a mirror of his own emotions and attitudes. When Shakespeare's Hamlet describes the world as "an unweeded garden that grows to seed," he tells us more about his own mind than he does about the world itself. In "June Nights" Victor Hugo evokes the sights and sounds of a summer night in the country. The poet's own inner peace is transferred to the surrounding landscape. "June Nights" is simpler, more lyrical than most of his verse. The poem produces a sense of the mixture of day and night, light and dark.

In summer, when the daylight's gone, the
  fields,
Covered with blossoms, scent the air for
  miles around.
We sleep, but in a half sleep of transparent dreams,
Eyes shut, ears half opened to the summer's sound.

Pure are the stars, then; and the dark is
  sweet: 5
A faint half daylight stains the eternal
  dome,
And gentle dawn, waiting for her hour to
  come,
All night below the sky's edge seems to
  roam.

Victor Hugo
George Kearns/TRANSLATOR

Cold Up North

This ancient Chinese poem makes a sharp contrast with Hugo's "June Nights." In Hugo's poem everything is hazy and things merge into each other in a dreamlike way: sound and silence, light and dark, sleep and wakefulness. In this Chinese poem everything is sharp and distinct. There is beauty in this Chinese landscape, but it is not a warm, powerful beauty which overwhelms the mind. Rather, one has the impression that the beauty has been wrested from Nature by the poet's imagination. Notice the upward motion of the poem, which begins with a lowering black sky and ends with "rainbows of jade."

Li Ho first became famous when he was a child. When two high officials in the government heard a rumor about a seven-year-old boy who could write poetry, they found it hard to believe. The officials came to Li Ho's house and asked the boy to write them a poem. Without hestitation, he picked up a brush and wrote a poem called "The Tall Official Carriage Comes on a Visit." The officials were astonished.

> One quarter lowers black while three
>   turn purple,
> Ice vaults the Yellow River, fish and
>   dragons die.

Tree-bark three feet thick splits into patterns,
Chariots of a ton or more travel on the flood.

Frost-flowers on the grass, big as silver pieces,   **5**
No brandished blade could penetrate this sombre sky.
Whirling in a raging sea the flying icefloes roar,
Soundless hang mountain waterfalls, rainbows of jade.

Li Ho

J. D. Frodsham/TRANSLATOR

For Discussion

SIX JAPANESE HAIKU
1 Identify the pairs of opposites in each of the haiku. Explain how each part of the pair intensifies the other.
2 Each haiku is in itself an image. Describe the picture formed by each. What do all six poems have in common?
3 Attempt writing some haiku of your own, using objects familiar to you. Writers of modern haiku do not limit themselves to nature in the sense of trees, ponds, animals. They include anything that stirs their imaginations: a jet plane, a necktie, a piece of wrapping paper, the fragmented image on a TV screen, and so forth.

THE WORLD IS TOO MUCH WITH US
1 Is the speaker of the poem angry? Why? With whom and with what is he disturbed? What has made him "forlorn"?
2 What is meant by "we are out of tune"?
3 Is the way of life the poet advocates possible in the modern world?

4 Does the poet literally wish to see Proteus rising from the sea and to hear Triton's horn? What is he really asking for? Why does he mention these two mythical figures here?
5 Wordsworth is comparing modern beliefs with those of the ancient Greeks. What, as he sees it, is the essential difference?

SONG
1 What is the design of the poem? How does it move from the particular to the general? How do the first six lines prepare for the last two?
2 What is the rhyme scheme of the poem?
3 In a brief essay, defend or disagree with this proposition: the philosophy of life expressed in this poem is too simple.

JUNE NIGHTS
1 What effect is made by the repetition of the word *half?* How does it combine with the words *faint* and *transparent?*
2 How many of the senses are appealed to in this poem?

3 Here the poet has used the summer night to suggest that his own spirit mingles peacefully with Nature. Suppose you wanted to write a poem about a summer night in which the speaker was tormented, angry, or unhappy. What aspects of nature might then be emphasized?

4 Where in the poem do you find an example of personification (that is, something which is not human being referred to as if it were a person)?

COLD UP NORTH

1 The winter landscape described in this poem must have been very far into the northern part of China, where the cold is extremely powerful. What details show the sheer power of the cold?

2 Why does the fact that "dragons die" make the poem more intense? How would the poem be different if we were only told that the fish are being killed by the cold?

3 What implication must we draw from the fact that "Chariots of a ton or more" can cross the river?

4 Where do you find sharp visual contrasts in the poem? For example: motion and stillness? sound and silence?

5 In which details do you feel that the poet has almost forced beauty upon this winter landscape?

Poems about Animals

The Horses

In the nature poems on the preceding pages, we saw that poets often used Nature as a reflection of their own moods and attitudes. This is also true, perhaps even more so, in poems about animals.

"The Horses" gives a brilliantly sharp picture of a group of horses, but it is primarily about the speaker's mood, which changes as the vision of the horses takes on a personal, almost spiritual meaning.

Pablo Neruda is generally recognized as the most widely read and most influential of Latin American poets. His work somewhat resembles the poetry of Walt Whitman: it is usually written in long, cadenced unrhymed lines, contains an encyclopedic zest for all aspects of creation, and displays a wide sympathy for the common man. He has been awarded the Noble Prize in Literature.

From my window I saw the horses.

It was in Berlin, one winter. The light
was without light, there was no sky in
    the sky.

The air was white like fresh bread.

From my window I saw a kind of circus-
    ring,   **5**
a ring bitten in snow by the teeth of
    winter.

Suddenly, led out by a man,
ten horses walked out into the snow.

They scarcely shook or moved as they
    came out,
like fire, but to my eyes they filled the
    world,   **10**
which had been empty before. Perfect,
    flaming,
they were like ten gods with great, clean
    hooves,
their manes were like a dream of salt-
    spumed waves.
Their rumps were round as worlds or
    oranges.

Their color was honey, amber, fire.   **15**

Their necks were like towers
carved out of stone in pride.
And energy, like a prisoner,
looked out from their furious eyes.

And there in the silence, in the middle of
    the day,   **20**

one dirty, disorganized winter,
those intense horses became blood,
became rhythm, became the vibrant
    treasure of life.

I looked at them, looked, and revived!
I hadn't known it, but this was the foun-
    tain,   25
the golden dance, the sky, the fire that
    lived in beauty!

I have forgotten that dark winter in
    Berlin.

I shall never forget the light from those
    horses.

Pablo Neruda

George Kearns/TRANSLATOR

THREE POEMS

    These three short poems, translated from Spanish, do not obey all of the "rules" of the haiku, but it is clear that they are haiku-like in spirit.

The Peacock

Peacock, great shining,
you pass through the democratic
barnyard like a procession.

José Juan Tablada

The Monkey

The little monkey looks at me . . .
He wants to tell me
something he's forgotten!

José Juan Tablada

Flying Fish

One blow from the sun's gold
splinters the glass of the sea.

José Juan Tablada

George Kearns/TRANSLATOR

Snake

    The next two poems are about encounters between a human and a snake. The snake is one animal which most people do *not* find charming. Each of these two poems shows the poet's ability to wrest something beautiful and interesting out of a subject which does not appear at all "poetic."

    In the first poem, Emily Dickinson never uses the word *snake*. In fact she did not even call the poem "Snake," for she seldom gave titles to any of her poems. The reader must decipher the subject from the indirect description.

A narrow fellow in the grass
Occasionally rides;
You may have met him—did you not?
His notice instant is.

The grass divides as with a comb,   5
A spotted shaft is seen;
And then it closes at your feet
And opens further on.

He likes a boggy acre,
A floor too cool for corn,   10
Yet when a boy, and barefoot,
I more than once, at noon,

Have passed, I thought, a whiplash
Unbraiding in the sun—
When stooping to secure it,   15
It wrinkled, and was gone.

Several of nature's people
I know, and they know me;

I feel for them a transport
Of cordiality;   20

But never met this fellow,
Attended or alone,
Without a tighter breathing,
And zero at the bone.

Emily Dickinson

Snake

In "Snake" Lawrence describes his encounter with a poisonous snake as much more than a casual meeting of man and animal. The poem begins quietly in a garden in Sicily, and then builds in power and turns into a solemn, primitive ceremony as, in the sudden meeting, the snake becomes "one of the lords / Of life," "a king in exile."

Lawrence was as much a prophet as a writer. The message he preached in his novels and poems is that modern man has become too abstract, too intellectual. Civilized men, as Lawrence saw it, have begun to live only with their minds; they have lost touch with their feelings and with their more primitive instincts. In this poem Lawrence uses a personal experience to dramatize the conflict between "thought" and "instinct."

A snake came to my water-trough
On a hot, hot day, and I in pajamas for
    the heat,
To drink there.

In the deep, strange-scented shade of the
    great dark carob-tree[1]
I came down the steps with my pitcher
And must wait, must stand and wait, for
    there he was at the trough before
    me.

He reached down from a fissure in the
    earth-wall in the gloom
And trailed his yellow-brown slackness
    soft-bellied down, over the edge of
    the stone trough

And rested his throat upon the stone
    bottom,
And where the water had dripped from
    the tap, in a small clearness,   10
He sipped with his straight mouth,
Softly drank through his straight gums,
    into his slack long body,
Silently.

Someone was before me at my water-
    trough,
And I, like a second comer, waiting.   15

He lifted his head from his drinking, as
    cattle do,
And looked at me vaguely, as drinking
    cattle do,
And flickered his two-forked tongue from
    his lips, and mused a moment,
And stooped and drank a little more,
Being earth brown, earth golden from the
    burning burning bowels of the earth
On the day of Sicilian July, with Etna[2]
    smoking.

The voice of my education said to me
He must be killed,
For in Sicily the black, black snakes are
    innocent, the gold are venomous.

And voices in me said, If you were a man
You would take a stick and break him
    now, and finish him off.

But I must confess how I liked him,
How glad I was he had come like a guest
    in quiet, to drink at my water-
    trough
And depart peaceful, pacified, and thank-
    less,
Into the burning bowels of this earth.

Was it cowardice, that I dared not kill
    him?
Was it perversity, that I longed to talk to
    him?
Was it humility, to feel so honored?
I felt so honored.

1 carob-tree *A tree with red flowers that grows in the Mediterranean area.*

2 Etna *Mt. Aetna, a volcano in Sicily.*

And yet those voices: 35
*If you were not afraid, you would kill
    him!*

And truly I was afraid, I was most afraid,
But even so, honored still more
That he should seek my hospitality
From out the dark door of the secret
    earth.   40

He drank enough
And lifted his head, dreamily, as one
    who has drunken,
And flickered his tongue like a forked
    night on the air, so black,
Seeming to lick his lips,
And looked around like a god, unseeing,
    into the air,   45
And slowly turned his head,
And slowly, very slowly, as if thrice
    adream,
Proceeded to draw his slow length curv-
    ing round
And climb again the broken bank of my
    wall-face.

And as he put his head into that dread-
    ful hole,   50
And as he slowly drew up, snake-easing
    his shoulders, and entered farther,
A sort of horror, a sort of protest against
    his withdrawing into that horrid
    black hole,
Deliberately going into the blackness,
    and slowly drawing himself after,
Overcame me now his back was turned.
I looked round, I put down my pitcher,
I picked up a clumsy log
And threw it at the water-trough with a
    clatter.

I think it did not hit him,
But suddenly that part of him that was
    left behind convulsed in undignified
    haste,
Writhed like lightning, and was gone
Into the black hole, the earth-lipped fis-
    sure in the wall-front,

At which, in the intense still noon, I
    stared with fascination.

And immediately I regretted it.
I thought how paltry, how vulgar, what
    a mean act!
I despised myself and the voices of my
    accursed human education.   65

And I thought of the albatross,[3]
And I wished he would come back, my
    snake.

For he seemed to me again like a king,
Like a king in exile, uncrowned in the
    underworld,
Now due to be crowned again.   70

And so, I missed my chance with one of
    the lords
Of life.

And I have something to expiate;
A pettiness.

D. H. Lawrence

The Albatross

Most people enjoy zoos, but many do not,
for they find it painful to see creatures taken
away from freedom and penned in cages.
Here Charles Baudelaire, one of the greatest
of the French poets, describes the capture of
a majestic bird by the crew of a ship. Deprived of its power to fly, the bird becomes
a ludicrous freak.

Baudelaire's first version of this poem consisted only of the first three stanzas. Years
later, he added the final lines in which he
compares the captured bird to poets (including himself) and the jeering sailors to society.

Sometimes the sailors, to amuse them-
    selves,
Capture an albatross, one of those huge
    seabirds

---

3   albatross   *A reference to
Coleridge's* Rime of the Ancient
Mariner, *in which a curse was*   *put upon the narrator for killing
an albatross.*

That tirelessly follow a ship on its voyage,
Making slow beautiful circles above the
    mast.

Once they take the bird out of their nets,
This giant of the air, his pride destroyed,
Hobbles pathetically on the wooden deck,
    his wings
Hanging down heavily, useless as oars, at
    his side.

How funny the poor helpless creature
    seems—
He who a moment ago was flying lordly
    through space!   **10**
The sailors tease him. One sticks a pipe
    in his beak.
Another imitates the bird's walking, and
    laughs.

The Poet is like that wild creature of the
    clouds:
He sails through storms, higher than ar-
    rows and the reach of stones.
On earth he is an exile, laughed at by the
    crowd.   **15**
His wings are no good to him. It's hard
    to walk.

Charles Baudelaire
George Kearns/TRANSLATOR

Inscription for the Grave of a Dog

The Greek poet Simonides of Ceos was the master of the epitaph—that is, the short lyric poem written as a tribute to the dead. This verse on the death of a dog shows Simonides's best qualities: it is dignified without being pompous, and it conveys sincere emotion without being sentimental.

The dog's capacity for loyalty has made him a favorite companion of man. The poem is a moving tribute to the hunting dog who had been the poet's companion on many expeditions.

    Beneath this mound, my hound, my faith-
        ful huntress,
    Rest by a hearth whose flames forever
        burn.
    The hills around recall your barking
        valor;
    The beasts we hunted fear, still, your
        return.

Simonides

FIVE JAPANESE HAIKU

These five brief poems give delicate in-sights into animal life familiar to the Japanese. These haiku about animals appear to be simpler and more direct than the six nature haiku printed earlier (page 210). (For com-ments on the haiku itself, see page 209.) Because these are simpler it is harder to say exactly what are the "opposites" in them.

"The Monkey's Raincoat" contrasts the shivering of the animal with his ordinary high spirits. In "The Mournful Chirping" a new interpretation of the cricket's song occurs to the poet. "The Whale" is a study in motion: up and down. "In the House" contrasts free-dom with captivity, stillness with motion. In "The Snake" the contrast is based on presence and absence.

The Monkey's Raincoat

The first cold showers pour.
    Even the monkey seems to want
      a little coat of straw.

Bashō

The Mournful Chirping

Eaten by the cat!
  Perhaps the cricket's widow
    may be wailing that!

Kikaku

The Whale

A whale!
  Down it goes, and more and more
    up goes its tail!

Buson

In the House

At the butterflies
  the caged bird gazes, envying—
    just watch its eyes!

Issa

The Snake

A snake! Though it passes,
  eyes that had glared at me
    stay in the grasses.

Kyoshi

Harold G. Henderson/TRANSLATOR

For Discussion

THE HORSES

1 The poet never states his own feelings directly except to tell us that he "revived." And yet his subjective feelings are clearly expressed in his description of Nature. Moreover, his feelings change in the course of the poem. What details toward the end of the poem clearly show his changed mood?
2 What kind of horses is he describing?
3 How do the horses become a symbol of something beyond the horses themselves?
4 The poem is being written many years after the event described. Why does this gap in time make the poem more intense?
5 What are the implications of the last two lines? What is the important distinction between what he has forgotten and what he remembers?

THREE POEMS

1 Why is the peacock set apart from the "democratic / barnyard"? What is witty about describing a barnyard as "democratic" anyway? Which word suggests the movement of the peacock?
2 Of all animals the members of the ape family, especially monkeys and chimpanzees, fascinate humans because they seem to be so near (and yet so far) from what we are. How does Tablada's "The Monkey" suggest both the similarities and the differences between men and monkeys?
3 The flying fish is native to the Caribbean and South Atlantic. It is a broad, flat fish which appears to fly as it leaps out of the water and skims in the air just above the surface. In "Flying Fish" what does the poet mean by "One blow from the sun's gold"?

SNAKE (page 215)

1 What are the synonyms for *snake* used in the poem? Do these ways of describing the snake make it more loathsome? Or do they make it less·alarming?

2 What does the word *barefoot* contribute to the poem? How does it increase the sensation described?

3 Discuss the last phrase in the poem, "zero at the bone." What does it mean?

SNAKE (page 216)

1 When the speaker sees the golden snake his first thought is: "The voice of my education said to me / He must be killed" (lines 22–23). What kind of "education" does he mean? What comment does the poem make about this kind of education?

2 Why does the speaker feel "honored" by the visit from the snake? How do his true feelings conflict with what he has been taught he *ought* to feel?

3 Did the speaker follow his education or his instinct?

4 How did he feel after he had thrown the log at the snake? Why?

THE ALBATROSS

1 Why do the sailors trap the albatross? How does the poet criticize them without stating his disapproval directly?

2 Why is the albatross a good choice of bird in this poem? Why would the penguin be a poor one?

3 Is the comparison in the last stanza a good one? Is this what a poet should be— someone who sails high in the air but is out of place among ordinary people on earth? Is there a suggestion that Baudelaire is dramatizing himself or feeling sorry for himself?

4 In your opinion, would the poem be better if Baudelaire had left it as he first wrote it—that is, without the last stanza?

INSCRIPTION FOR THE GRAVE OF A DOG

1 What qualities of the dog does the poet praise in this epitaph? What kind of a "future life" does the poet project for the dog? Why is it appropriate?

2 Does the poet reveal his feelings for the dog? How? What are they?

FIVE JAPANESE HAIKU

1 Compare the haiku "The Snake" with Emily Dickinson's and D. H. Lawrence's poems about the same animal.

2 Write some haiku on two or three animals you have observed. Try to include not only exact observation but also an element of surprise.

Poems of Delights

Song of the Soul

By definition, a mystical experience cannot be explained by logic, nor communicated directly. The mystic, such as San Juan de la Cruz, claims to have had a personal spiritual experience. He has to reach for metaphors if he wishes even to approximate his experience in words. "Song of the Soul" attempts to communicate a spiritual joy which can never be fully communicated.

San Juan spent much of his life either in prison or in exile in the desert. There he passed through what he called "the dark night of the soul," a state of depression or spiritual deprivation. Darkness and light became the chief symbols of his poetry: darkness represented the condition of the soul when deprived of Divine Grace; light represented the mystical presence of God. In this poem the speaker is the soul itself. The refrain at the end of each verse refers to its "dark night." Here, however, it is not light, but water ("the eternal spring") which refers to the Divine Spirit.

The poem might be paraphrased as follows: Although my mind is dark, and I cannot understand it intellectually, I know that the healing waters of God are at hand. Although I cannot see it clearly, I sense its presence.

> How well I know that spring that runs
>   and overflows:
>   although it's night.
>
> Spring that's eternal, hidden,
>   and yet how well I know from where
>   it flows,
>   although it's night.   **5**

I do not know its source: it has none;
    everything else springs from it,
    although it's night.

I know that nothing else can be so lovely,
    and that the earth and heavens drink
        its beauty,   **10**
    although it's night.

How well I know it's deep and bottom-
    less,
    so deep no one can cross it,
    although it's night.

So clear it is, and never shadowed;   **15**
    all light, I know, comes from it,
    although it's night.

So rich are its brimming waters
    that it gives life to hell and heaven
        and every people,
    although it's night.   **20**

And the stream whose source was in this
    spring,
    I know how powerful it is,
    although it's night.

And from these two a third stream rises,
    but the first two are not greater,   **25**
    although it's night.

And that eternal spring is hidden
    within this living bread to give us life,
    although it's night.

Here it is crying out to every creature
    to drink these waters, although it's
    dark,
    because it's night.

The living waters of the spring that I
    desire
    I clearly see within this bread of life,
    although it's night.   **35**

San Juan de la Cruz
George Kearns/TRANSLATOR

A Prayer to Go to Paradise with the Donkeys

Francis Jammes lived a simple life in the Basque region of France. "A Prayer to Go to Paradise With the Donkeys is typical of his mature work, for Jammes usually celebrated simple religious emotions and country life in plain language. The poem conveys a great sense of delight springing from humility and simplicity.

When I must come to you, O my God, I
    pray
It be some dusty-roaded holiday,
And even as in my travels here below,
I beg to choose by what road I shall go
To Paradise, where the clear stars shine
    by day.   **5**
I'll take my walking-stick and go my way,
And to my friends the donkeys I shall
    say,
'I am Francis Jammes, and I'm going to
    Paradise,
For there is no hell in the land of the
    loving God.'
And I'll say to them: 'Come, sweet
    friends of the blue skies,   **10**
Poor creatures who with a flap of the
    ears or a nod
Of the head shake off the buffets, the
    bees, the flies . . .'

Let me come with these donkeys, Lord,
    into your land,
These beasts who bow their heads so
    gently, and stand
With their small feet joined together in
    a fashion   **15**
Utterly gentle, asking your compassion.
I shall arrive, followed by their thousands
    of ears,
Followed by those with baskets at their
    flanks,

By those who lug the carts of mounte-
banks[1]
Or loads of feather-dusters and kitchen-
wares,   20
By those with humps of battered water-
cans,
By bottle-shaped she-asses who halt and
stumble,
By those tricked out in little pantaloons
To cover their wet, blue galls where
flies assemble
In whirling swarms, making a drunken
hum.   25
Dear God, let it be with these donkeys
that I come,
And let it be that angels lead us in peace
To leafy streams where cherries tremble
in air,
Sleek as the laughing flesh of girls; and
there
In that haven of souls let it be that, lean-
ing above   30
Your divine waters, I shall resemble these
donkeys,
Whose humble and sweet poverty will
appear
Clear in the clearness of your eternal
love.

Francis Jammes

Richard Wilbur/TRANSLATOR

On First Looking into Chapman's Homer

It is not necessary to travel widely in order
to experience the thrill of discovery. John
Keats, sitting at home reading a book, experienced such a sense of discovery that it made
him reach for an extraordinary comparison to
an early explorer of the New World. Keats
could not read Greek, and so he could not
read Homer in the original; but Chapman's
English translation suddenly revealed a "new
world."

Keats's sonnet is one of the most famous in
English. It also contains one of the most fa-
mous literary "boners": it was Balboa, not
Cortez, who discovered the Pacific Ocean.
However, this does not in any way mar the
beauty of the sonnet.

Much have I travell'd in the realms of
gold,
And many goodly states and kingdoms
seen;
Round many western islands have I
been
Which bards in fealty to Apollo[1] hold.
Oft one of wide expanse had I been told
That deep-brow'd Homer ruled as his
demesne:
Yet did I never breathe its pure serene
Till I heard Chapman speak out loud and
bold.

Then felt I like some watcher of the skies
When a new planet swims into his
ken;   10
Or like stout Cortez when with eagle eyes
He stared at the Pacific—and all his
men
Look'd at each other with a wild sur-
mise—
Silent, upon a peak in Darien.[2]

John Keats

Pirate Jenny

"Pirate Jenny" is a song from Brecht's
Three Penny Opera, for which Kurt Weill
wrote one of the great scores of the musical
theater.

Jenny is a pirate only in her imagination.
In fact, she is a maid in a cheap commercial
hotel. The customers she waits on give her
little respect, and she returns their scorn with
hatred. In her song she displays one of her
daydreams: that some day she will have
power in a world in which she now has to

---

1 mountebanks *Persons who
sell quack medicines from a
platform.*

1 Apollo *In Greek mythology
the god of sunlight, prophecy,
and music and poetry.*

2 Darien *Colony settled by
Spaniards on the west shore of
the Isthmus of Darien (later the
Isthmus of Panama).*

slave for a living. She seems to take enormous pleasure in working out the details of her fantasy.

Like so much of Brecht's writing, "Pirate Jenny" shows sympathy for the underdog, but Brecht's sympathy is never sentimental. The song suggests that Jenny has been dehumanized by her experience and that she would like to repay her oppressors with violence.

Gentlemen, you see me washing glasses
  in the bar
And making up the beds for you to sleep
  in,
And sometimes you tip me and I say
  thanks,
And you see me wearing rags around this
  crummy hotel,
And you have no idea who you're talking
  to.   5
  But one evening a cry will be heard
    from the harbor
  And they'll say: Did you hear that
    shout?
  And they'll see me laughing as I wash
    the glasses,
  And they'll say: What's she got to
    laugh about?

      And a ship with eight sails
      And fifty guns
      Will sail up to the dock.

And they'll say: Go on washing your
  glasses, girl!
And they'll give me a little tip and I'll
  say thanks,
And go upstairs to make the beds, the
  beds   15
That none of them will sleep in that
  night.
And they still won't have any idea who
  I am.
  And on that night they'll hear a noise
    from the harbor,

And they'll ask: Did you hear that
  awful roar?
And they'll see me looking out the
  window,   20
And they'll say: What's she laughing
  for?

      And the ship with eight sails
      And fifty guns
      Will bomb the city.

Yes, gentlemen, then you'll all stop
  laughing,   25
As the walls of the city tumble down
And the bombs crush everything to dust.
But this one crummy hotel will be safe,
And they'll say: Does someone important
  live here?
  And all night long they'll be shrieking
    in the hotel,   30
  And they'll say: Why is this place be-
    ing spared?
  And when they see me walking out
    the door in the morning
  They'll say: Is *that* who was living
    there?

      And the ship with eight sails
      And fifty guns   35
      Will send up its flags.

And towards noon a hundred men will
  come ashore
And march through the shadows
And drag everyone they find out into the
  street
And put them in chains and bring them
  to me,   40
And ask: Which ones shall we kill?
  And on that noon the harbor will be
    hushed,
  As they ask me which should be the
    first to go.
  And you'll hear me say out loud: *All
    of them!*
And as each head falls I'll shout: *Bravo!*

And the ship with eight sails
And fifty guns
Will take me away.

Bertolt Brecht

George Kearns/TRANSLATOR

Street Cries

To the alert eye and ear, everyday life can be a source of excitement and delight. Sarojini Naidu's "Street Cries" reflects the poet's pleasure in the sights and sounds of a village in India. The poem's structure follows the rhythm of the day: the first stanza takes place at dawn, the second at noon, the last at evening.

When dawn's first cymbals beat upon the
  sky,
Rousing the world to labor's various cry,
To tend the flock, to bind the mellowing
  grain,
From ardent toil to forge a little gain,
And fasting men go forth on hurrying
  feet,   5
Buy bread, buy bread, rings down the
  eager street.

When the earth falters and the waters
  swoon
With the implacable radiance of noon,
And in dim shelters koels[1] hush their
  notes,
And the faint, thirsting blood in languid
  throats   10
Craves liquid succor from the cruel heat,
Buy fruit, buy fruit, steals down the pant-
  ing street.

When twilight twinkling o'er the gay
  bazaars,
Unfurls a sudden canopy of stars,
When lutes are strung and fragrant
  torches lit   15

On white roof terraces where lovers sit
Drinking together of life's poignant sweet,
Buy flowers, buy flowers, floats down the
  singing street.

Sarojini Naidu

Jazz Fantasia

In "Jazz Fantasia" Carl Sandburg communicates his pleasure in one of the true American contributions to culture—jazz.

Sandburg tries to go beyond a mere description of jazz music. He attempts to turn the poem itself into an imitation of the music by putting the sounds and the rhythms into the verse. He evokes the beat, the sounds, and the images that the sounds suggest.

Drum on your drums, batter on your banjoes, sob on the long cool winding saxophones.
Go to it, O jazzmen.

Sling your knuckles on the bottoms of the happy tin pans, let your trombones ooze, and go husha-husha-hush with the slippery sand-paper.

Moan like an autumn wind high in the lonesome treetops, moan soft like you wanted somebody terrible, cry like a racing car slipping away from a motorcycle cop, bang-bang! you jazzmen, bang altogether drums, traps, banjoes, horns, tin cans—make two people fight on top of a stairway and scratch each other's eyes in a clinch tumbling down the stairs.

Can the rough stuff . . . now a Mississippi steamboat pushes up the night river with a hoo-hoo-hoo-oo . . . and the green lanterns calling to the high soft stars . . . a red moon rides on the humps of the low river hills . . . go to it, O jazzmen.

Carl Sandburg

---

1 koels *Cuckoos of a kind
usually found in India.*

My fiftieth year had come and gone

Sometimes happiness seems to come to us for no apparent reason. Such a moment of illumination is described in "My Fiftieth Year" by the great Irish poet Yeats.

At first, Yeats emphasizes his age and his loneliness. The shop itself is an ordinary, everyday place. Notice the sharp contrast between the first and second stanzas: the dull background of the first stanza makes the blaze of happiness stand out more sharply in the second.

My fiftieth year had come and gone,
I sat, a solitary man,
In a crowded London shop,
An open book and empty cup
On the marble table-top.   5

While on the shop and street I gazed
My body of a sudden blazed;
And twenty minutes more or less
It seemed, so great my happiness,
That I was blessèd and could bless.   10

William Butler Yeats

For Discussion

A PRAYER TO GO TO PARADISE WITH THE DONKEYS

1 Why does the poet want to be associated with the donkeys rather than with anything rich, proud, or famous?

2 How are the donkeys treated on earth? Does the poet feel compassion for them? How might this compassion be extended to other human beings?

3 How does this poem relate to the biblical saying that it is harder for a rich man to get into heaven than for a camel to pass through the eye of a needle?

4 Does the poet seem like a happy man?

ON FIRST LOOKING INTO CHAPMAN'S HOMER

1 The metaphor which stands at the center of this poem is that of travel and exploration: intellectual adventure is compared to the physical adventures of sailors and explorers. With this central metaphor in mind, what does the poet mean when he says that he has "travell'd in the realms of gold"?

PIRATE JENNY

1 Where do Jenny's illusions of grandeur first become apparent?

2 What are the implications of her statement that "they still won't have any idea who I am"? Who does she think she is?

3 Why, in Jenny's fantasy, is "this one crummy hotel" spared from the bombs of the pirate ships?

4 How does the horror of Jenny's dream increase with each stanza? Where is the climax? At which point does she appear to reach the height of pleasure in her daydream?

5 Do you think many people have power fantasies like Jenny's? What causes them?

STREET CRIES

1 What is the climate of the town described in this poem? Is this an industrial town? What sort of people are described? What are their occupations?

2 Does the poet seem completely satisfied with the life of his town? Is there any suggestion of social protest?

JAZZ FANTASIA

1 *Diction* refers to the kinds of words a writer chooses. How is the diction of

"Jazz Fantasia" different from that of most of the poems in this book? Do you expect to find the following phrases in something called poetry: "Sling your knuckles," "Can the rough stuff," "in a clinch"? Are they justified in this poem?

MY FIFTIETH YEAR

1 What does the poet do to cause this blaze of happiness? Could it be because he was gazing at the shop and street rather than at his book?

2 The speaker of the poem tells us that he is over fifty years of age. Is the meaning of the poem understandable only to older people?

3 Why does the speaker say that his *body* "blazed" rather than his mind? Explain carefully the last line of the poem.

Poems of Regrets

To Himself

Literature is often very bleak or dark as it probes into the tragic side of man's nature. Yet even the most tragic literature usually tries to wring some possibility of hope or meaning out of misfortune. See, for example, Villon's "Ballad of the Hanged Men" (page 228). There, though the speaker is already dead and his body is hanging from the gallows, the spirit of the executed man still has some hope. The final prayer holds out the possibility of mercy and forgiveness. "To Himself" by the Italian poet Leopardi, however, suggests a personal despair which refuses to be comforted. The loss of all hope and illusion is, in fact, the subject of the poem.

And now be still forever,
My weary heart. For the last deception's
    over,
That I thought would last forever. Gone.
    I know
Our delusions are finished,
Not only the hope, but also the desire.
Now rest forever. You have throbbed
Enough. All your motions
Have come to nothing, not even the earth
Is worth your sighs. Life
Is bitter and boring; the rest nothing;
The world is dirt.
Be calm forever. Beat
Your last despairing beat. All fate has
    given us—
People like us—is to die. So:
Despise yourself, nature, the brutish
    power   15
Which, hidden, orders this common
    doom,
And makes everything, everything empty.

Giacomo Leopardi
George Kearns/TRANSLATOR

Ballad of the Hanged Men

In this ballad François Villon speaks as if he were one of a group of six criminals who have died by hanging. He looks back on a life that has gone astray and sincerely begs pardon from both man and God.

Sometimes the term *ballad* refers to a simple story poem, often one which can be sung. Villon's ballad, however, follows an elaborate and strict form developed by troubadours in the Middle Ages. The last line of each stanza serves as a refrain; that is, each last line is the same, or has only very slight variations. The last six lines are always called an "envoi," or "address." In them the poet usually speaks to the prince who is his protector, or to the lady he loves. Here, most appropriate for this poem, it is not an earthly but a heavenly Prince whom the poet addresses in the final lines.

Brother men that after us shall be,
 Let not your hearts be hard to us:
If you take pity on our misery,
 God shall in time to you be piteous.
 Look at us six that hang here thus,
Observe the flesh we so much cherished,
How it is eaten by the birds, and perished—
 Dust and ashes starting to take its place.
Mock not at us that now so feeble be,
 But pray God pardon us out of His grace. **10**

Listen, we pray you, and look not in scorn,
 Though it is just that we are cast to die:
For neither you nor any man is born
 Who keeps his wisdom with him constantly.
 Be you then merciful and cry **15**
To Mary's Son that is all piteous
That He with mercy take our stain from us,
 And save us from Hell's fiery place.
We are but dead: let no soul now deny
 To pray God pardon us out of His grace. **20**

We are washed clean by rain down from the skies;

The sun has scorched us black and bare;
Ravens and crows have pecked our eyes
 And feathered their nests with our beards and hair.
 Hanging, tossing here and there, 25
This way and that, at the wind's will,
Not for a moment is my body still—
 And the birds are busy about my face.
Live not as we! Fare not as we fare!
 Pray God pardon us out of His grace!

ENVOI

Prince Jesus, Master of all, to Thee
We pray Hell gain no mastery
 Upon us, and that we avoid that place.
Brother men, that after us shall be,
 Pray God pardon us out of His grace.

François Villon
George Kearns/TRANSLATOR

Taking Leave of a Friend

China is a vast country, and at the time "Taking Leave of a Friend" was written, over a thousand years ago, there was no means of rapid transportation. One traveled by foot, by horseback, or by riverboat. Therefore, when two friends parted to go off to different sections of the country, it meant that they might not see each other again for many years. The parting of friends became a standard theme for classical Chinese poetry. Here, Li Po supplies a vivid, fresh picture for this familiar emotion.

The last two lines of this poem are a good example of the way Chinese poetry often presents emotions through specific images. Although the poet does not state it directly, we can tell that the two friends are already too far away from each other to speak: they can only bow. The sharp sound of the horses' neighing is really an extension of the voices of the two friends themselves.

> Blue mountains to the north of the walls,
> White river winding about them;
> Here we must make separation
> And go out through a thousand miles of
>   dead grass.
>
> Mind like a floating wide cloud,   5
> Sunset like the parting of old acquaint-
>   ances
> Who bow over their clasped hands at a
>   distance.
> Our horses neigh to each other
>   As we are departing.

Li Po
Ezra Pound/TRANSLATOR

My Heart's in the Highlands

Another familiar theme in literature is that of the person who becomes nostalgic for his native land after he has gone to live in the "big city" or in another country. Here, Robert Burns sings of his longing for his native Scotland.

In "My Heart's in the Highlands," unlike his "A Red, Red Rose" (page 197), Burns uses no Scots dialect words. The lilt of a Scottish tune, however, can still be heard. Burns did, in fact, write many of his poems to fit traditional Scottish tunes.

> Farewell to the Highlands, farewell to
>   the North,
> The birthplace of valor, the country of
>   worth;
> Wherever I wander, wherever I rove,
> The hills of the Highlands forever I love.

> My heart's in the Highlands, my heart
>   is not here;   5
> My heart's in the Highlands, a-chasing
>   the deer;
> A-chasing the wild deer, and following
>   the roe,
> My heart's in the Highlands wherever
>   I go.

> Farewell to the mountains, high-covered
>   with snow;
> Farewell to the straths and green valleys
>   below;   10
> Farewell to the forests and wild-hanging
>   woods,
> Farewell to the torrents and loud-pouring
>   floods.

> My heart's in the Highlands, my heart
>   is not here;
> My heart's in the Highlands, a-chasing
>   the deer;
> A-chasing the wild deer, and following
>   the roe,   15
> My heart's in the Highlands wherever
>   I go.

Robert Burns

Candles

No poet has treated the passing of time more poignantly than the Greek poet Cavafy. In poem after poem he mourns the disappearance of youth and the oncoming of age.

About two thousand years ago Alexandria, after the collapse of the Greek city-states, had become a great center of Greek culture. In his imagination, Cavafy often seemed to dwell more in the vanished past than he did in the present. His own Alexandria—the Alexandria of the twentieth century—appears in his poems as only a shadow of its past. One sees the city through his eyes as a place crumbling beneath poverty and commerce, where only with difficulty can a few fleeting moments of happiness be found.

The days of our future stand before us
like a row of little lighted candles—
golden, warm, and lively little candles.

The days gone by remain behind us,
a mournful line of burnt-out candles;   5
the nearest ones are still smoking,
cold candles, melted and bent.

I do not want to look at them; their form
    saddens me,
and it saddens me to recall their first
    light.
I look ahead at my lighted candles.

I do not want to turn back, lest I see and
    shudder—
how quickly the somber line lengthens,
how quickly the burnt-out candles mul-
    tiply.

C. P. Cavafy

Rae Dalven/TRANSLATOR

TWO POEMS

We have already seen a poem by Li Ho in
the group of nature poems (page 211). After
a promising youth, Li Ho was unable to find
a position in the Chinese Civil Service and
spent the rest of his life wandering in exile
and poverty. His isolation and disappointment became the principal theme of his
poetry. Sometimes he expressed his loneliness
and exile indirectly, but in these two poems
he makes no attempt to hide his feelings.

Chinese poetry in English translation often
appears to be more simple than it really is.
To the Chinese student many of the references are related to Chinese history and to
other Chinese poems in ways which few
Americans can ever appreciate. In a scholarly
edition of Li Ho's poems the footnotes to
"Lament of the Brazen Camels" are longer
than the poem itself. However, as in the case

of so many poems in translation, we can still
appreciate the poetry on the level available
to us.

The bronze camels described in the poem
stood for centuries on the Street of the Brazen
Camels in the Chinese city of Lo-Yang.

Lament of the Brazen Camels

At the end of the third month, out of of-
    fice and poor,
I went to my eastern neighbour in search
    of flowers.
Who was it wrote a farewell song to
    spring?
The brazen camels lament on the banks
    of the Lo.

South of the bridge are many riders on
    horseback,   5
The northern mountain is girdled with
    ancient graves.
While men are quaffing cups of wine,
The camels sit and mourn ten million
    springs.

Useless to toil away in this life of ours,
It's only a wind-blown candle in a bowl.
Tired of seeing peach-trees smile again,
The brazen camels weep as night comes
    on.

Li Ho

The Capital

Out of my gate I galloped, full of hope—
But now my heart is lonely in Ch'ang-an.
Since I have no one to confide in
I chant a poem alone with the autumn
    wind.

Li Ho

J. D. Frodsham/TRANSLATOR

For Discussion

TO HIMSELF

1 What is Leopardi looking forward to when he tells his heart to "be still forever" and "Be calm forever"?

2 The poem appears to have been written shortly after some personal misfortune, for the poet says "the last deception's over." Does he tell us what "the last deception" is?

3 Is the poet saying that all men should feel the way he does at the time he is writing the poem? Or does he put himself into a special group?

4 Whom does he mean when he says "our," "us," and "you"?

5 According to the poem, what is the cause of the darkness and emptiness which the poet finds in his life?

BALLAD OF THE HANGED MEN

1 Does the speaker blame society for his death by hanging? Does he admit the guilt of himself and of his companions? What reason does he give for their execution?

2 Does the poet identify himself and his fellow criminals with the rest of humanity?

3 What kind of redemption do these criminals look forward to? Why do they think they deserve it?

4 The poem vividly describes the medieval practice of allowing the bodies of executed victims to remain hanging in a public place as a warning to others. Does Villon show either approval or disapproval of this practice? Or does he take it for granted? Does it seem like a barbaric practice to you? Or is it a contribution to social order?

TAKING LEAVE OF A FRIEND

1 Does the poem present a series of sharp pictures? What is meant by "a thousand miles of dead grass"?

2 How is nature used to express the feelings of the poet?

3 Sentimentality has been described as a display of more emotion than a situation calls for. In your opinion, is this poem sentimental, or does the poet suggest a deeper emotion than he actually displays? Explain your answer.

MY HEART'S IN THE HIGHLANDS

1 How is this poem related to the longing for a specific place? Do the specific references make the poem any less universal?

2 What features of his homeland does the poet miss the most? What does this show about his background and about the kind of man he is?

CANDLES

1 For what are the candles a symbol?

2 How are the candles of the future different from the candles of the past?

3 Are all the candles of the past the same, or does the poet make a distinction among them?

4 Although the poet says that he does not want to look back at the past but intends to "look ahead at my lighted candles," where, in fact, does he seem most to be looking? Which image from this poem makes the strongest impression on your mind?

TWO POEMS

1 Obviously the bronze camels can neither lament nor weep. What is the poet doing by ascribing human emotions to them?

2 What symbol does "Lament of the Brazen Camels" share with Cavafy's poem (page 230)? Why is it an appropriate choice in both cases?

3 Does "The Capital" seem too simple to you? Do you prefer a very simple poem like this to those which are more complicated or difficult? (There is no reason, of course, why you can't enjoy both.)

Poems about War

The Nefarious War

One of the greatest of the classic Chinese poets, Li Po, lived during the Sung period. In "The Nefarious War" he protests the slaughter that men do in the name of an ideal.

Li Po lived many years after Bunno, the author of the "Song of the Bowmen of Shu" on page 234. Yet the war he describes here might be the same war as in Bunno's poem. The whole history of China may be viewed as a struggle between the Good Emperors (or the "benign sovereigns," as this translation calls them), who worked for peace, order, and justice, and those who allowed their people to suffer under disorder and war.

Last year we fought by the head-stream
of the So-kan,
This year we are fighting on the Tsung-ho
road.
We have washed our armor in the waves
of the Chiao-chi lake,

We have pastured our horses on Tien-
shan's snowy slopes.
The long, long war goes on ten thousand
miles from home,   5
Our three armies are worn and grown
old.

The barbarian does man-slaughter for
plowing;
On his yellow sand-plains nothing has
been seen but blanched skulls and
bones.
Where the Chin emperor built the walls
against the Tartars,
There the defenders of Han are burning
beacon fires.   10
The beacon fires burn and never go out,
There is no end to war!—

In the battlefield men grapple each other
and die;
The horses of the vanquished utter la-
mentable cries to heaven,

233

While ravens and kites peck at human
    entrails,   15
Carry them up in their flight, and hang
    them on the branches of dead trees.
So, men are scattered and smeared over
    the desert grass,
And the generals have accomplished
    nothing.

Oh, nefarious war! I see why arms
Were so seldom used by the benign
    sovereigns.   20

Li Po

Shigeyoshi Obata/TRANSLATOR

The Inscription at Thermopylae

When Xerxes invaded Greece with his
Persian army (480 B.C.), Leonidas and three
hundred men from Sparta successfully held
off the attack for three days in the narrow
mountain pass at Thermopylae. All of the
Spartans died, but their heroic stand saved
Greece. This inscription for a monument was
written as a tribute to their courage and
loyalty.

Traveler, if you get to Sparta, say:
Here, obedient to their command, we lie.

Anonymous

Song of the Bowmen of Shu

One theme runs through most of these
poems on the subject of war: that war is evil
and unproductive. The Chinese poet Bunno,
who lived thousands of years ago, writes of
two emotions familiar to all soldiers: boredom
and discontent with the "brass hats."

The bowmen (archers) of Shu were waging
an endless campaign against invading Mongol
forces. The horses of the generals become a
symbol of the foot soldiers themselves—well
trained but tired.

Here we are, picking the first fern-shoots
And saying: When shall we get back to
    our country?
Here we are because we have the Ken-
    nin for our foemen,
We have no comfort because of these
    Mongols.
We grub the soft fern-shoots,   5
When anyone says "Return," the others
    are full of sorrow.
Sorrowful minds, sorrow is strong, we are
    hungry and thirsty.
Our defence is not yet made sure, no one
    can let his friend return.
We grub the old fern-stalks.
We say: Will we be let to go back in
    October?   10
There is no ease in royal affairs, we have
    no comfort.
Our sorrow is bitter, but we would not
    return to our country.
What flower has come into blossom?
Whose chariot? The General's.
Horses, his horses even, are tired. They
    were strong.   15
We have no rest, three battles a month.
By heaven, his horses are tired.
The generals are on them, the soldiers are
    by them.
The horses are well trained, the generals
    have ivory arrows and quivers orna-
    mented with fish-skin.
The enemy is swift, we must be careful.
When we set out, the willows were
    drooping with spring,
We come back in the snow,
We go slowly, we are hungry and thirsty,
Our mind is full of sorrow, who will know
    of our grief?

Bunno

Ezra Pound/TRANSLATOR

With the Army at the North Frontier

This short poem, "With the Army at the North Frontier," by the Chinese poet Li I, has something of the same effect as a haiku: in one sharply drawn symbol it presents a moment of revelation. The cold, hardship, and violence of war are placed in contrast to a moment of tender beauty as the moon rises above the desert.

The size of the army—three hundred thousand soldiers—is probably exaggerated by the poet. The exaggeration, however, produces a moment of poetic truth: a vast number of men united by a single emotion.

> It snowed soon after the cold sea wind came;
> The flutes blew all the time, and the roads were hard.
> There were three hundred thousand soldiers on the desert.
> Suddenly they all turned and looked at the moon.

Li I

Robert Payne/TRANSLATOR

The Sleeper of the Valley

From earliest times, poets have lamented the deaths of young men in battle. In "The Sleeper of the Valley," Arthur Rimbaud makes the violent death of a soldier more poignant by placing it within a quiet, beautiful countryside.

From the time he was fifteen years old, Arthur Rimbaud vigorously rebelled against authority of all kinds and kept running away from school and from home. His earlier poems, such as "The Sleeper of the Valley," are more or less conventional, but his later prose poems are among the most original ever written, both in imagery and in language.

> There's a green hollow where a river sings
> Silvering the torn grass in its glittering flight,
> And where the sun from the proud mountain flings
> Fire—and the little valley brims with light.
>
> A soldier young, with open mouth, bare head,   5
> Sleeps with his neck in dewy watercress,
> Under the sky and on the grass his bed,
> Pale in the deep green and the light's excess.
>
> He sleeps amid the iris and his smile
> Is like a sick child's slumbering for a while.   10
> Nature, in thy warm lap his chilled limbs hide!
>
> The perfume does not thrill him from his rest.
> He sleeps in sunshine, hand upon his breast,
> Tranquil—with two red holes in his right side.

Arthur Rimbaud

Ludwig Lewisohn/TRANSLATOR

Mambru

"Mambru" is a modern Mexican poem, but its setting and period are really timeless. Mambru could be any young man going off to war, and the narrator could be any young woman waiting for him.

Compare this poem with Jacques Prévert's "In the Flower Shop" (page 238). Notice

236

how both poets have omitted almost all punctuation marks and have run their sentences together. This poetic license is taken for expressive effect: both poets attempt to imitate the flow of thought through a person's mind. Real time—clock time—stops in these two poems, and psychological time is revealed.

he did not come to say goodbye
I did not see him
Mambru went off to the war
what sorrow what sorrow what pain
I don't know when he'll return   5
All I remember is his purple cape
his hair slowly disappearing in the distance
behind his young page
younger than him if that's possible
it was on a cold afternoon   10
the sun was shining
was it only I who felt cold?
days went by, days,
he went off in silence
his father said goodbye to him on the
     drawbridge   15
the memory of him, of his face, becomes
     more imprecise
if he comes back at Easter
what sorrow what sorrow what joy
or on Trinity Sunday
then Easter came   20
and Trinity Sunday came
then Trinity Sunday was over
what sorrow what sorrow what fury
Mambru has not returned
high above the tower   25
the wind seemed to be singing
I climbed up into the tower
what sorrow what sorrow what height
do re me do re fa
to see if he were coming   30
until this sad afternoon
when I saw coming down the road
his glorious clothes all torn
his slow defeated step
there comes his page   35
what sorrow what sorrow what clothes

do re me do re fa
what news will he bring
then I remembered
he never came to say goodbye   40
I did not see him.

Francisco Cervantes

George Kearns/TRANSLATOR

An Irish Airman Foresees His Death

The Irish flyer in this poem served in the Royal Air Force during the First World War. These were the years when the Irish people were engaged in a bitter struggle for independence from England. It is for this reason that the speaker of the poem, the pilot, declares, "Those that I guard I do not love." Why then does a man risk his life for a cause he does not believe in? Can danger itself give meaning to life? In the poem, the airman resolves this problem in a dramatic way. The Kiltartan Cross referred to in the poem is the airman's native village in Ireland.

I know that I shall meet my fate
Somewhere among the clouds above;
Those that I fight I do not hate,
Those that I guard I do not love;
My country is Kiltartan Cross,   5
My countrymen Kiltartan's poor,
No likely end could bring them loss
Or leave them happier than before.
Nor law, nor duty bade me fight,
Nor public men, nor cheering crowds,
A lonely impulse of delight
Drove to this tumult in the clouds;
I balanced all, brought all to mind,
The years to come seemed waste of breath,
A waste of breath the years behind   15
In balance with this life, this death.

William Butler Yeats

For Discussion

THE NEFARIOUS WAR

1 Compare this poem with "Song of the Bowmen of Shu." Both poems present war as a wasteful, inglorious activity. Which poem is the angrier?
2 Compare the attitude toward war in this poem with that in "The Inscription at Thermopylae" (page 234).
3 Who are the "we" in this poem?
4 Would the point of this poem still be clear without the last two lines?

SONG OF THE BOWMEN OF SHU

1 How does the poet show the passage of time? How does the reader know that this has been a long campaign? What sort of war is this? Is it a war which has decisive moments?
2 What do the bowmen long for most? What is their attitude toward the war they are fighting? Toward their own leaders?
3 What is meant by the line "What flower has come into blossom?" Why is it ironic?

WITH THE ARMY AT THE NORTH FRONTIER

1 There are several contrasts or "opposites" in this poem. Identify as many as possible.
2 What attitude toward war is implied by this poem? How is the attitude communicated?

THE SLEEPER OF THE VALLEY

1 What line tells the reader that the young sleeper has been killed in battle? Is it a surprise?
2 What is the season of the year? How can you tell? What is meant by the "perfume" in line 12?

3 Identify the elements that are contrasted in the final line.

MAMBRU

1 Who is the speaker of the poem? What is the relation between the speaker and Mambru?
2 Is this poem being spoken at a single moment in time, or over a long period of time? Explain.
3 The poem is a modern version of the ballad, but the traditional ballad form—the four-line stanza and so forth—is missing. Nevertheless, there is a refrain, a repeated songlike element. Where do you find this refrain in the poem?
4 What is the situation at the very end of the poem—that is, after Mambru comes back from the war? What are the implications of "he never came to say good-bye"?

AN IRISH AIRMAN FORESEES HIS DEATH

1 What is the airman's attitude toward the enemy? Is it any different from his attitude toward those on whose side he is fighting? What will be the effect of victory on the pilot's own people, "Kiltartan's poor"? What effect will defeat have on them?
2 Discuss the airman's attitude toward his own past and future. What motive drives him to the "tumult in the clouds"?
3 What effect does the poet obtain by repeating the phrase "Waste of breath" and the word "balance"?
4 There are two ideas of "death" in the poem: one expressed in the title and the other in the last line. Discuss the difference between these two meanings. Try to define exactly what the airman means by "this life, this death" in the final line.

Poems on the Conduct of Life

In the Flower Shop

In "In the Flower Shop" Prévert stretches out a moment in time as if in a slow-motion film. The punctuation of the translation exactly reproduces the punctuation of Prévert's original in French.

A man goes into a flower shop
and picks out some flowers
the girl in the flower shop wraps them up
the man puts his hand in his pocket
to get some money   5
money to pay for the flowers
but all of a sudden, at the same time,
he puts his hand to his heart
and falls down

At the same time that he falls down   10
the money starts to roll on the floor
and the flowers fall down

at the same time that the man falls
and the money is rolling on the floor
and the girl in the flower shop stands
     there   15
with the money rolling around
and the flowers getting ruined
and the man dying
it's obviously all very sad
and she ought to do something   20
the girl in the flower shop,
but she doesn't know what to do
she doesn't know where to begin
there are so many things to do
with this man dying   25
and these flowers spoiling
and this money
this money rolling around
this money that won't stop rolling.

Jacques Prévert
George Kearns/TRANSLATOR

238

TWO POEMS

The title of the first of these two poems by the Greek poet Cavafy is a reference to another poem, *The Divine Comedy* of Dante. The Italian words mean "who made . . . the Great Refusal," by which Dante describes a pope who had resigned from office, thereby (as Dante saw it) shirking his responsibility. For another poem by Cavafy see page 230).

Chi...Fece Il Gran Rifuto

To certain people there comes a day
when they must say the great Yes or the
    great No.
He who has the Yes ready within him
reveals himself at once, and saying it he
    crosses over

to the path of honor and his own convic-
    tion.   5
He who refuses does not repent. Should
    he be asked again,
he would say No again. And yet that
    No—
the right No—crushes him for the rest of
    his life.

C. P. Cavafy

As Much As You Can

And if you cannot make your life as you
    want it,
at least try this
as much as you can: do not disgrace it
in the crowding contact with the world,
in the many movements and all the talk.

Do not disgrace it by taking it,
dragging it around often and exposing it
to the daily folly
of relationships and associations,
till it becomes like an alien burdensome
        life.   10

C. P. Cavafy
Rae Dalven/TRANSLATOR

Dreaming in the Shanghai Restaurant

In this poem the English writer D. J. Enright portrays a man who has created a life which is harmonious and peaceful. The Chinese gentleman and his family are sharply described. The real interest of the poem, however, is in the speaker himself. He tells us very little about himself, but just enough to suggest that he lacks the peaceful family life he admires as he observes the Chinese gentleman.

I would like to be that elderly Chinese
    gentleman.
He wears a gold watch with a gold brace-
    let,
But a shirt without sleeves or tie.
He has good-luck moles on his face, but
    is not disfigured with fortune.
His wife resembles him, but is still a
    handsome woman,   5
She has never bound her feet or her
    belly.
Some of the party are his children, it
    seems,
And some his grandchildren;
No generation appears to intimidate an-
    other.
He is interested in people, without want-
    ing to convert them or pervert them.
He eats with gusto, but not with lust;
And he drinks, but is not drunk.

He is content with his age, which has always suited him.

When he discusses a dish with the pretty waitress,

It is the dish he discusses, not the waitress.　15

The tablecloth is not so clean as to show indifference,

Not so dirty as to signify a lack of manners.

He proposes to pay the bill but knows he will not be allowed to.

He walks to the door, like a man who doesn't fret about being respected, since he is;

A daughter or grand-daughter opens the door for him,　20

And he thanks her.

It has been a satisfying evening. Tomorrow

Will be a satisfying morning. In between he will sleep satisfactorily.

I guess that for him it is peace in his time.

It would be agreeable to be this Chinese gentleman.　25

D. J. Enright

Life Is a Dream

The speaker of "Life Is a Dream" is Segismundo. He has lived since childhood in a prison in the wilderness, unaware that he is a prince. Suddenly, he is taken out of his chains, brought to a castle, told that he is a prince, and given rich robes to wear. Then, just as suddenly, he finds himself back in his prison, in chains and rags. In this speech he wonders if everything that happened to him was only a dream. Possibly, he decides, for life itself is only a dream.

Calderón de la Barca's play *Life Is a Dream* (*La vida es sueño*, 1635) holds a position in Spanish literature similar to that held by *Hamlet* in English literature. To Spanish-speaking people this speech of Segismundo's is as famous as Hamlet's "To be or not to be" is to us.

How strange—a world where life itself's a dream!

Experience has taught me that the man who lives

Dreams, and goes on dreaming 'till he wakes.

The king is only dreaming he's a king:

He goes on making laws with an imagined power,　5

Until the winds have carried off his praises

(Which were only borrowed) and Death turns him to ashes.

Why, then, do men wish power? Since they know

That they must wake up to a dream of death?

The rich man's only dreaming that he's rich—　10

And it's a dream that brings him care and worry.

The poor man's only dreaming that he's hungry.

The man who has luck dreams; the man of action

Dreams; and those who harm the lives of others dream.

So in this whole wide world everyone's dreaming,　15

Whatever he is: but no one understands it.

Right now I dream I'm lying here in chains:

A while ago I dreamed that I enjoyed

A life more pleasing. And what is life? Frenzy!

What is life? Illusion! Shadow! Fiction!　20

The good in life is little. Life is a dream,

And dreams themselves are only parts of dreams.

Pedro Calderón de la Barca

On His Blindness

There are two references to the Bible in "On His Blindness." The word *talent* refers to the parable of the talents (Matthew 25:15–30), in which a servant was condemned for burying his talent (a coin) in the earth rather than putting it to use. Milton puns on the word *talent*, using it both in the sense of the Biblical coin and in the modern sense of *talent*—that is, "skill" or "ability." The second biblical reference is "his mild yoke." Jesus said (Matthew 11:29–30), "My yoke is easy."

> When I consider how my light is spent
> Ere half my days, in this dark world and
>   wide,
> And that one talent which is death to
>   hide
> Lodged with me useless, though my soul
>   more bent
> To serve therewith my Maker, and
>   present   5
> My true account, lest He returning chide;
> "Doth God exact day labor, light denied?"
> I fondly ask. But Patience, to prevent
> That murmur, soon replies, "God doth
>   not need
> Either man's work or his own gifts. Who
>   best   10
> Bear his mild yoke, they serve him best.
>   His state
> Is kingly: thousands at his bidding speed,
> And post o'er land and ocean without
>   rest;
> They also serve who only stand and
>   wait."

John Milton

Hamlet

In "Hamlet," Pasternak compares himself to Shakespeare's Hamlet—a man suffering from his own indecision and from a sense of isolation from the world. He also compares his suffering to that of Jesus in the Garden of Gethsemane.

> The plaudits slowly die away.
> Again I come upon the stage.
> I strain to hear in dying echoes
> The fate that waits our present age.
>
> Through thousands of binoculars   5
> The night of darkness stares at me.
> If possible, O Abba, Father,
> Then take away this cup from me.
>
> I love Thy stern design, and I am
> Content to act this role of woe.   10
> But there's another play on stage;
> Then spare me now, and let me go.
>
> The acts and parts are planned with care;
> The end, foredoomed. I stand alone.
> The Pharisees[1] exult. How hard   15
> This life, and long my way of stone.

Boris Pasternak

Eugene M. Kayden/TRANSLATOR

Tomorrow

The subject of the sonnet "Tomorrow" is man's refusal to accept the grace of God. Lope de Vega makes this abstract idea dramatic by presenting a sharp visual image— Christ standing outside the gate like a beggar in the cold. The final lines are a debate between the poet's soul and his guardian angel.

> What had I, Lord, to offer, that with
>   such care
> You sought my friendship? and for my
>   sake did wait,
> Covered with dew, standing outside my
>   gate
> Passing the long, black nights of Winter
>   there?

1 Pharisees *Those persons marked by hypocritical censorious self-righteousness.*

Strange was my madness, that I did not
   greet   5
Your blest approach. Heaven to me is
   lost
If with ingratitude's unkindly frost
I've chilled the bleeding wounds upon
   your feet!

Often my guardian angel gently cried:
"Soul, from thy window look, and thou
   shalt see   10
How He persists to call and wait for
   thee."
And often, to that angel's voice of sorrow,
"Tomorrow He may enter," I replied;
Then, when tomorrow came, said, "No—
   tomorrow!"

Lope de Vega

Bangkok

Bangkok, capital of Thailand, is an ancient city famous for the beauty of its Buddhist temples. The modern Canadian poet F. R. Scott describes his experience during a visit to one of these temples.

The subject of "Bangkok" is a conflict of cultures within an individual. Conditioned to one way of life and to one faith, the poet finds it impossible to give himself to another kind of experience.

Deep in the brown bosom
Where all the temples rose
I wandered in a land
That I had never owned
With millions all around.   5

I had been here before
But never to this place
Which seemed so nearly home
Yet was so far away
I was not here at all.   10

There was a central mound
That took away my breath
So steep it was and round
So sudden by my side
So Asia all beyond.   15

And when I came inside
I had to walk barefoot
For this was holy ground
Where I was being taught
To worship on a mat.   20

A great white wind arose
And shakes of temple bells
Descended from the eaves
To make this gold and brown
One continent of love.   25

And only my own lack
Of love within the core
Sealed up my temple door
Made it too hard to break
And forced me to turn back.   30

F. R. Scott

Indian Reservation: Caughnawaga

A. M. Klein describes a visit to an Indian reservation in his native Canada. He contrasts his boyhood ideas about the noble, graceful Indian to the reality he sees before him. These pale Indians are no longer vital or exciting; they are "fauna in a museum." Their own culture is dead, preserved on a reservation as an amusement for tourists ("the pious prosperous ghosts") who come to buy baskets, blankets, and other relics of the past.

"Indian Reservation: Caughnawaga" is not a difficult poem if read with close attention. Like much modern poetry (like poetry of all ages, for that matter), it contains some phrases which are so compressed in meaning that the reader must "decipher" them. The structure of the poem is as follows: the first two stanzas present the speaker's romantic, boyhood ideas about Indians; the second two stanzas present the reality he finds on a modern Indian reservation; in the last stanza he reflects on the meaning of his experience.

Where are the braves, the faces like autumn fruit,
who stared at the child from the coloured frontispiece?
And the monosyllabic chief who spoke with his throat?
Where are the tribes, the feathered bestiaries?—
Rank Aesop's animals erect and red,   5
with fur on their names to make all live things kin—
Chief Running Deer, Black Bear, Old Buffalo Head?

Childhood, that wished me Indian, hoped that
one afterschool I'd leave the classroom chalk,
the varnish smell, the watered dust of the street,   10
to join the clean outdoors and the Iroquois track.
Childhood; but always,—as on a calendar,—
there stood that chief, with arms akimbo, waiting
the runaway mascot paddling to his shore.

With what strange moccasin stealth that scene is changed!   15
With French names, without paint, in overalls,
their bronze, like their nobility expunged,—
the men.   Beneath their alimentary shawls
sit like black tents their squaws; while for the tourist's

brown pennies scattered at the old church door,   20
the ragged papooses jump, and bite the dust.

Their past is sold in a shop: the beaded shoes,
the sweetgrass basket, the curio Indian,
burnt wood and gaudy cloth and inch-canoes—
trophies and scalpings for a traveller's den.   25
Sometimes, it's true, they dance, but for a bribe;
after a deal don the bedraggled feather
and welcome a white mayor to the tribe.

This is a grassy ghetto, and no home.
And these are fauna in a museum kept.
The better hunters have prevailed.   The game,
losing its blood, now makes these grounds its crypt.
The animals pale, the shine of the fur is lost,
bleached are their living bones.   About them watch
as through a mist, the pious prosperous ghosts.   35

A. M. Klein

𝕿he Window

A successful poem must be more than a vehicle for a message about morality, politics, or anything else.   It is the sound, the images, the play of language which make the poem. Yet the poet is concerned with the conduct of life: How should I think about the world? How should I behave?

"The Window" is a good example of the way in which a poet turns such concerns into a work of art.   A man closes a window.   The poet dramatizes this simple, common action, making it a symbol for a way of life.

244

Jaime Torres Bodet (1902–   ), one of Mexico's most distinguished writers, has served as his country's Minister of Education.

You closed the window. And it was the
    world,
the world that wanted to enter, all at
    once,
the world that gave that great shout,
that great, deep, rough cry
you did not want to hear—and now
will never call to you again as it called
    today,
asking your mercy!

The whole of life was in that cry:
the wind, the sea, the land
with its poles and its tropics,   10
the unreachable skies,
the ripened grain in the resounding
    wheat field,
the thick heat above the wine presses,
dawn on the mountains, shadowy woods,
parched lips stuck together longing for
cool water condensed in pools,
and all pleasures, all sufferings,
all loves, all hates,
were in this day, anxiously
asking your mercy . . .   20

But you were afraid of life.
And you remained alone,
behind the closed and silent window,
not understanding that the world calls to
    a man
only once that way, and with that kind
    of cry,   25
with that great, rough, hoarse cry!

Jaime Torres Bodet

Stopping by Woods on a Snowy Evening

Robert Frost's "Stopping by Woods on a Snowy Evening" is one of the finest lyrics in the English language. Simple and direct, it communicates the emotion of a moment with precision and grace. The reader's imagination, however, is invited to go beyond the surface anecdotes—a man stopping to watch snow fall in a dark wood—and consider the poem on other levels.

The rhyme scheme of Frost's poem binds the four stanzas together: the final sound of the third line in each stanza becomes the main rhyme of the next stanza.

Whose woods these are I think I know.
His house is in the village though;
He will not see me stopping here
To watch his woods fill up with snow.

My little horse must think it queer   5
To stop without a farmhouse near
Between the woods and frozen lake
The darkest evening of the year.

He gives his harness bells a shake
To ask if there is some mistake.   10
The only other sound's the sweep
Of easy wind and downy flake.

The woods are lovely, dark and deep.
But I have promises to keep,
And miles to go before I sleep,   15
And miles to go before I sleep.

Robert Frost

The Words of Buddha

Buddha was the great Indian religious leader whose teachings have so profoundly influenced the world, especially the Orient, through the spread of Buddhism. "The Words of Buddha," by the young Mexican poet Pacheco, is a meditation on Buddha's statement that everything which appears to be solid and permanent is in reality changing, burning, on fire.

In most writing we try to avoid repeating the same word too often. We seek for pronouns, synonyms, or other substitutes. Here the poet has repeated the words *flame, fire,* and *burn* some seventeen times within seventeen lines. What might be considered bad writing in prose becomes an effective poetic device, turning the "words of Buddha" into an illusion of vivid reality.

> The whole world is on fire: the visible
> burns and the eye, in flames, asks questions.
> The fire of hatred burns.
>   Usury burns.
> Birth and the Fall are burning.   5
>   Pain burns.
> Weeping and suffering
>   also burn.

> The weight of sorrow is a flame,
>   anguish
>   is a bonfire   10
> in which
>   everything burns:
> Flames,
>   the flames burn,
> flames burn,   15
>   world and fire, see
> (how sad) the leaf in the wind of the
>   bonfire.

Juan Emilio Pacheco

George Kearns/TRANSLATOR

For Discussion

IN THE FLOWER SHOP
1 Why is there virtually no punctuation in this poem? Does the poet leave out punctuation just to be different? Or does it relate to the meaning of the poem? Does it suggest the workings of the girl's mind?
2 Why does the girl appear paralyzed, not knowing "where to begin"?
3 Where should the girl's attention be? Where is it?
4 Is this poem an attack on materialism? If so, how?

TWO POEMS
1 Popular moralists often say, in one form or another, that we should always think positively, that we should avoid negative thinking. Cavafy's "Chi Fece . . . Il Gran Rifiuto" takes us into a deeper level of experience than such a simple statement. According to this poem, who has the easier path in life, the man who says Yes or the man who says No? Notice that sometimes a No can be "right." Is there a suggestion that sometimes it might even be heroic to say No?

2 What might be an example of "the right No"? That is, when might it be more honorable to say No to something, even though your No might crush you for the rest of your life?
3 In "As Much As You Can" Cavafy suggests that you are lucky if you can "make your life as you want it." But many people are not so lucky. According to the poem, what control over their own lives then remains?

DREAMING IN THE SHANGHAI RESTAURANT
1 What does the word *dreaming* in the title refer to? Who is dreaming? About what?
2 How could a person be "disfigured with fortune"?
3 The secret of the Chinese gentleman's happiness seems to lie in balance and moderation. What are some specific examples of balance or moderation in the poem?
4 What is the attitude of the speaker of the poem toward the Chinese gentleman and his family?
5 Do you agree that "It would be agreeable to this Chinese gentleman"? Why, or why not?

6   Is it possible to "be" someone else? To what extent can one model one's life on someone else's life?

LIFE IS A DREAM

1   The speaker, Segismundo, is in prison, bound with chains. Why would the thought that "life is a dream" be comforting to him?
2   Does he limit his idea that "life is a dream" only to people who are poor or suffering?
3   Explain: "And dreams themselves are only parts of dreams." What two meanings of the word *dream* are involved?
4   In a short essay, tell why you agree or disagree with the philosophy put forth in this speech.

ON HIS BLINDNESS

1   Half of this sonnet is a question and half is its answer. Who states the question? Who gives the answer?
2   What does Milton think God expects of him? What is the "one talent" he names? Why would it be "death" to hide one's talent?
3   What is the human problem Milton faces in this poem? How does the last line of the poem suggest a solution?

HAMLET

1   What view of the future does the poem give? What will be the poet's own part in the future? Is he a man of action?
2   Where does the poet switch from comparing himself to Hamlet to comparing himself to Christ? Who were the Pharisees? Who are the Pharisees of the modern world? Why do they jeer at the poet? Compare this with the last stanza of Baudelaire's "The Albatross" (page 217).
3   What causes the speaker's suffering? What resolution of this suffering does he see for himself?
4   How is this poem like Milton's "On His Blindness" (page 241)?

TOMORROW

1   What concept of God is given in this poem?
2   What kind of person is the speaker of the poem? In spite of the fact that he knows that he is wrong, he continues to refuse the grace of God. Is this believable?
3   How is the speaker of this poem like the speaker of F. R. Scott's "Bangkok" (page 242)?

BANGKOK

1   What words describe the interior of the temple? What is the meaning of the word *love* as used in this poem? What kind of love does the poet mean?
2   In the second stanza, what does the poet mean when he says, "I had been here before / But never to this place"? How is this possible?
3   What is the reason he gives for not being able to join the "continent of love" he finds inside the temple?
4   In line 27, what does the word *temple* refer to?

INDIAN RESERVATION: CAUGHNAWAGA

1   What does this poem say about the way in which the Indian has been treated by the white man?
2   Who is "the child" in the first stanza? What is ironic about the phrase "to make all live things kin"?
3   The second stanza presents the writer's childhood fantasy. Explain the phrase "Childhood, that wished me Indian."
4   Much of the population of Canada is of French ancestry. The Indians have dropped their tribal names for modern French ones. Explain line 17, "their bronze, like their nobility expunged."
5   The phrase "alimentary shawls" (line 18) is particularly compressed. The shawls are alimentary (food-giving, nourishing) because the Indians live by selling them to tourists. What is the irony of the phrase

"bite the dust" (line 21)? Explain the meaning of "inch-canoes."

6 What is meant by a "grassy ghetto"? Who are "the better hunters"? Who are "the game" and "The animals"? In what sense are the white tourists, the "prosperous ghosts," pious?

THE WINDOW

1 Who is the "you" in the poem?
2 Tell in your own words what the closing of the window stands for.
3 The window is the most obvious symbol in the poem, but there are others. Identify some of them and discuss their use.
4 We have suggested that a poem should never be reduced to a "message." As an experiment, try to write out the message in this poem. Then compare the message with the poem itself. What does the poem have which your message does not?

STOPPING BY WOODS ON A SNOWY EVENING

1 How does the rhyme scheme of the last stanza differ from the others? What is the effect produced?

2 Repetition gives emphasis. Why is the last line repeated? What effect does it give? Would it be fair to say that the line has a slightly different meaning each time? If so, how does it change?
3 Does the poem present a sharp, clear picture?
4 Explain in your own words the meaning or meanings you find in the last stanza. What temptation is the speaker offered? Why does he refuse it?

THE WORDS OF BUDDHA

1 The point of the poem is clearly stated in the opening words. Then the poet goes on to give some examples of a few specific things which are "on fire." These few things are meant to suggest everything in the universe. Do they? Or, in your opinion, should more specific things have been named?
2 How do you know that the poem is talking about a spiritual rather than a physical fire?
3 Which two words in the poem most clearly show the author's personal reaction to this burning universe?

Poems of Comedy and Satire

THREE SATIRICAL EPIGRAMS

The range of satire is wide: from good-natured laughter at human foibles to bitter attacks on greed and stupidity. The satirist usually presents himself as a man of common sense. He hopes to correct society by laughing at it and by appealing to the laughter of other sensible people.

One of the earliest satirists was the Roman poet Martial, who lived in the first century. He supported himself by writing short clever poems for pay. If a wealthy man wanted to be flattered, Marital would write a flattering poem. If a man wanted to attack an enemy, he could hire Marital to write a poem in which his enemy's weaknesses were brought to light. These satirical squibs would then be circulated throughout Rome.

A Hinted Wish

You told me, Maro, whilst you live
You'd not a single penny give,
But that, whene'er you chanced to die,
You'd leave a handsome legacy:
You must be mad beyond redress,   5
If my next wish you cannot guess!

Martial
Samuel Johnson/TRANSLATOR

248

Bought Locks

The golden hair that Gulla wears
    Is hers: who would have thought it?
She swears 'tis hers, and true she swears,
    For I know where she bought it.

Martial

*Sir John Harrington/*TRANSLATOR

A Stingy Host

Varus invited me to dinner.
There was a lot of expensive furniture,
But not much food.
There was gold all over the table,
But no meat.   5
My *eyes* were filled all right,
But not my stomach.
Please! Take some of that gold away
And just give me something to eat!

Martial

*George Kearns/*TRANSLATOR

Spring Blossom

"Spring Blossom," by a modern African writer, is similar to Martial's "Bought Locks." Note that this poem is constructed very much like the epigrams of Martial: it begins with something which looks like a compliment, then turns into an insult.

Shall I compare thee,
Fair creature of an hour,
To a spring blossom,
Bursting forth in lovely splendour?
Or yet shall I,   5
Thou apple of my eye,
Compare thy charms
To the silvery moon on a summer's eve?

No, I won't—go wash off thy disgusting
    makeup.

Ernest Attah

A New Freedom

Like Auden's "The Unknown Citizen," "A New Freedom" by Jacques Prévert is an attack on regimentation. The tone, however, is entirely different. Auden takes a certain kind of logic and pushes it to absurd lengths. Prévert ignores logic and simply turns the world upside down.

For another poem by Jacques Prévert, see "In the Flower Shop" (page 238).

I put my cap inside the cage,
put the bird on my head, and went out.
"Well!
Are we no longer saluting?"
asked the Commanding Officer.   5
"No,
We are no longer saluting,"
answered the bird.
"Ah! Good!
Excuse me, I didn't know we had stopped
    saluting,"   10
said the Commanding Officer.
"That's perfectly all right, everybody
    makes mistakes,"
said the bird.

Jacques Prévert

*George Kearns/*TRANSLATOR

Anxiety of a Young Girl to Get Married

A young girl of ancient China, plucking plums from a tree, becomes more and more concerned as the plums disappear and no one comes to ask for her hand. Centuries have passed, but some girls still worry about whether or not they will ever receive a proposal of marriage.

Most of the other satirical poems in this section are attacks on human foibles. "Anxiety of a Young Girl to Get Married" is much too good-natured to be called an attack. The light tone of the poem assures the reader that the girl really has little to worry about.

> Ripe, the plums fall from the bough;
> Only seven-tenths left there now!
> Ye whose hearts on me are set,
> Now the time is fortunate!
>
> Ripe, the plums fall from the bough;   5
> Only three-tenths left there now!
> Ye who wish my love to gain
> Will not now apply in vain!
>
> No more plums upon the bough!
> All are in my basket now!   10
> Ye who me with ardor seek,
> Need the word but freely speak!

Anonymous

James Legge/TRANSLATOR

Richard Cory

The object of satire in "Richard Cory" is not Richard Cory but ourselves, to the extent that we think that money means happiness. The "we" of this poem are Richard Cory's fellow townspeople. Of Richard Cory we know little: that he was rich; that he had beautiful clothes and manners; that for all his aristocratic surface he did not have the inner strength to face life. The townspeople are satirized for their willingness to accept Richard Cory's glittering surface as "everything," and to debase themselves before him.

> Whenever Richard Cory went downtown,
>   We people on the pavement looked at him:

> He was a gentleman from sole to crown,
>   Clean favored, and imperially slim.
>
> And he was always quietly arrayed,   5
>   And he was always human when he talked;
> But still he fluttered pulses when he said,
>   "Good-morning," and he glittered when he walked.
>
> And he was rich—yes, richer than a king—
>   And admirably schooled in every grace: 10
> In fine, we thought that he was everything
>   To make us wish that we were in his place.
>
> So on we worked, and waited for the light,
>   And went without the meat, and cursed the bread;
> And Richard Cory, one calm summer night,   15
>   Went home and put a bullet through his head.

Edwin Arlington Robinson

The Unknown Citizen

"The Unknown Citizen" is deadly serious in its intent. Auden satirizes a mechanical attitude toward man which is a very real force in the modern world. More and more in recent years people feel that they are being turned into numbers.

Notice the use of capital letters for satirical effect. Ordinarily such words as *press, health card, installment plan, greater community,* and *modern man* would be written with small letters. The capitals show that these ideas have become institutionalized. They have come to have an importance of their own which overshadows the importance of the individual.

He was found by the Bureau of Statistics
to be
One against whom there was no official
complaint,
And all the reports on his conduct agree
That, in the modern sense of an old-
fashioned word, he was a saint,
For in everything he did he served the
Greater Community.   5
Except for the war till the day he retired
He worked in the factory and never got
fired,
But satisfied his employers, Fudge Motors
Inc.
Yet he wasn't a scab or odd in his views,
For his Union reports that he paid his
dues,   10
(Our report on his Union shows it was
sound)
And our Social Psychology workers found
That he was popular with his mates and
liked a drink.
The Press are convinced that he bought
a paper every day
And that his reactions to poetry were
normal in every way.   15
Policies taken out in his name prove that
he was fully insured,

And his Health Card shows he was once
in hospital but left it cured.
Both Producers Research and High-Grade
Living declare
He was fully sensible to the advantages
of the Installment Plan
And had everything necessary to the
Modern Man,   20
A gramophone, a radio, a car, and a
frigidaire.
Our researchers into public opinion are
content
That he held the proper opinions for the
time of year.
When there was peace, he was for peace;
when there was war, he went.
He was married and added five children
to the population,   25
Which our Eugenists say was the right
number for a parent of his generation,
And our teachers report that he never interfered with their education.
Was he free? Was he happy? The
question is absurd:
Had anything been wrong, we certainly
should have heard.

W. H. Auden

For Discussion

THREE SATIRICAL EPIGRAMS

1 What common human fault does Martial attack in "A Hinted Wish"? What is the relation of Maro to the speaker of the poem? What is the speaker's "next wish"?

2 Making fun of women has always been a favorite sport of satirists. Women may not think it amusing to be portrayed as vain and flighty, but then most satirists are men. What "feminine" characteristic is attacked in "Bought Locks"? In our

own time might some men be laughed at in the same way?

3 What is the point of attack in "A Stingy Host"? What kind of person is Varus?

4 How do these three poems appeal to the common sense of the reader?

SPRING BLOSSOM

1 What is the meaning of the title, "Spring Blossom"?

2 The satirist often takes a stand in favor of what he thinks is "natural" as opposed to what is false or unnatural. Here the poet is addressing his girlfriend. How is she

different from a "spring blossom" and from "the silvery moon on a summer's eve"?

3 Do you think the comment in the last line is fair or unfair? Is the tone too harsh, or is it justified?

A NEW FREEDOM

1 In a narrow sense this poem might be taken as an attack on military discipline. But how might it be applied to a much broader subject?

2 Notice the matter-of-fact way in which the speaker tells his story. It's almost as if he were recounting a perfectly ordinary experience. Does this add to the humor of the poem?

3 The soldier in the poem is obviously happy with his "new freedom." But what about the Commanding Officer? He accepts the bird's statement very readily. Is there a suggestion here that even those "in charge" in society would like more freedom if they saw an opportunity for it?

ANXIETY OF A YOUNG GIRL
TO GET MARRIED

1 What is the season of the year? How is it related to the theme of the poem?

2 Of what is the plum tree a symbol in the young girl's mind?

3 Where is the humor in this poem? Is the situation funny from the girl's point of view? Why then should it be amusing to the reader?

RICHARD CORY

1 Does the last line of the poem come as a surprise? Why? Has it been prepared for in any way?

2 The reason why Richard Cory kills himself is not given. Why isn't it important to the meaning of the poem?

3 Irony is saying one thing and meaning something else. In what ways are the following words and phrases ironic: *crown, imperially, arrayed, he was always human when he talked, glittered,* and *one calm summer night?*

THE UNKNOWN CITIZEN

1 Who is the speaker of this poem? What is his attitude toward a good and full life? What lines show this attitude? By implication, what is Auden's own concept of the things most important to man? How does he communicate it?

2 Why, in the poem, has *saint* become an "old-fashioned word"?

3 List examples of irony in this poem. In what sense is the whole poem—which pretends to be a genuine document—ironic?

African and Indian Songs and Ceremonies

All That Dances

The following eight poems (which are also songs, ceremonies, rituals) are very different from the rest of the literature in this book. These poems were not "written"; they have no "authors." They are traditional ceremonial songs gathered from African and American Indian tribes.

Most of the poems we read are meant to be complete experiences in themselves; that is, the *words* of the poem *are* the poem. These African and Indian songs are not complete experiences in the same sense. Here the words are only a part of the entire experience. The words are accompanied by singing and dancing, and the ceremony—dance, music, words, costume, symbol—has a religious meaning. It is woven into the life or culture of the tribe.

The poem below is from the Gabon Pygmy tribe in Africa. It is obviously meant to be sung as an accompaniment to a dance in which the dancer imitates the movements of the fish, the bird, and the monkey. The song and dance celebrate the idea that all things are sacred. As the philosopher Ernst Cassirer has said, to primitive man "Life is felt as an unbroken continuous whole."

The fish does . . . HÍP
The bird does . . . VISS
The marmot does . . . GNAN

I throw myself to the left,
I turn myself to the right,   5
I act the fish,
Which darts in the water, which darts
Which twists about, which leaps—
All lives, all dances, & all is loud.

The fish does . . . HIP   10
The bird does . . . VISS
The marmot does . . . GNAN

The bird flies away,
It flies, flies, flies,
Goes, returns, passes,   15
Climbs, soars & drops.
I act the bird—
All lives, all dances, & all is loud.

The fish does . . . HIP
The bird does . . . VISS   20
The marmot does . . . GNAN

The monkey from branch to branch,
Runs, bounds & leaps,
With his wife, with his brat,
His mouth full, his tail in the air,   25
There goes the monkey! There goes the
    Monkey!
All lives, all dances, & all is loud.

from
The Night Chant

The following Navaho Indian chant is part
of a very complex nine-day ceremony intended to heal the sick. On the ninth night
the chanting goes on without interruption
from sunset until dawn. The ceremony is
conducted by a *shaman,* a man who combines
the functions of priest and doctor. An anthropologist described the ceremony as he
witnessed it around the turn of the century:

The patient and shaman are in the west,
facing the east, and the priest prays a long
prayer to each god, which the patient then
repeats after him, sentence by sentence. . . .
While it is being said, the dancer keeps up a
constant motion, bending and straightening
the left knee and swaying the head from side
to side.

In this section of The Night Chant the
prayer is addressed to a male divinity who is
asked to "take away your spell for me." The
"Tsegihi" mentioned in the first line is the
dwelling of the gods.

In Tsegihi
In the house made of the dawn
In the house made of evening twilight
In the house made of dark cloud
In the house made of rain & mist, of
    pollen, of grasshoppers   5
Where the dark mist curtains the door-
    way
The path to which is on the rainbow
Where the zigzag lightning stands high
    on top
Where the he-rain stands high on top

O male divinity   10
With your moccasins of dark cloud, come
    to us
With your mind enveloped in dark cloud,
    come to us
With the dark thunder above you, come
    to us soaring
With the shapen cloud at your feet,
    come to us soaring
With the far darkness made of the dark
    cloud over your head, come to us
    soaring   15
With the far darkness made of the rain &
    mist over your head, come to us
    soaring
With the zigzag lightning flung out high
    over your head
With the rainbow hanging high over your
    head, come to us soaring
With the far darkness made of the rain &
    the mist on the ends of your wings,
    come to us soaring
With the far darkness of the dark cloud
    on the ends of your wings, come to
    us soaring   20
With the zigzag lightning, with the rain-
    bow high on the ends of your wings,
    come to us soaring

With the near darkness made of the dark
    cloud of the rain & the mist, come
    to us
With the darkness on the earth, come
    to us

With these I wish the foam floating on
    the flowing water over the roots of
    the great corn
I have made your sacrifice   25
I have prepared a smoke for you
My feet restore for me
My limbs restore, my body restore, my
    mind restore, my voice restore for me
Today, take out your spell for me

Today, take away your spell for me   30
Away from me you have taken it
Far off from me it is taken
Far off you have done it

Happily I recover
Happily I become cool   35

My eyes regain their power, my head
    cools, my limbs regain their strength,
    I hear again

Happily the spell is taken off for me
Happily I walk, impervious to pain I
    walk, light within I walk, joyous I
    walk

Abundant dark clouds I desire
An abundance of vegetation I desire
An abundance of pollen, abundant dew,
    I desire

Happily may fair white corn come with
    you to the ends of the earth
Happily may fair yellow corn, fair blue
    corn, fair corn of all kinds, plants of
    all kinds, goods of all kinds, jewels
    of all kinds, come with you to the
    ends of the earth

With these before you, happily may they
    come with you

With these behind, below, above, around
    you, happily may they come with
    you   45
Thus you accomplish your tasks

Happily the old men will regard you
Happily the old women will regard you
The young men & the young women will
    regard you
The children will regard you   50
The chiefs will regard you

Happily as they scatter in different direc-
    tions they will regard you
Happily as they approach their homes
    they will regard you

May their roads home be on the trail of
    peace
Happily may they all return   55

In beauty I walk
With beauty before me I walk
With beauty behind me I walk
With beauty above me I walk
With beauty above & about me I walk
It is finished in beauty
It is finished in beauty

Death Song

    This song was collected by the anthropolo-
gist Frances Densmore from a Papago Indian
named Owl Woman, who had received it
from the spirit of a dead man named José
Gomez. Miss Densmore writes:

*The spirits first revealed themselves to Owl
Woman when she was in extreme grief over
the death of her husband and other relatives.
This was 30 or 40 years prior to the recording of her songs in 1920. The spirits took
her to the spirit land in the evening and
brought her back in the early dawn, escorting
her along a road. . . . When the spirits had
taken her many times, they decided that she
should be taught certain songs for the cure*

of sickness caused by the spirits. . . . She has now received hundreds of these songs, so many that she cannot remember them all. It is possible for her to treat the sick without singing, but she prefers to have songs.

In the great night my heart will go out
Toward me the darkness comes rattling
In the great night my heart will go out

Lamentation

This song of the Owl Sacred Pack of the Fox Indians is a lamentation for the dead. The owl and the manitou are both animals and divinities. As in the poems above, we see a universe in which man, animal, and nature exist very closely together and in which "all things are sacred."

It is he, it is he,
The person with the spirit of an owl
It is he, it is he,
The person with the spirit of an owl
It is he, it is he   5

All the manitous are weeping
Because I go around weeping
Because I go around weeping
All the manitous are weeping

The sky will weep   10
The sky
At the end of the earth
The sky will weep

The String Game

This song was collected in 1875 from the Bushman tribe in Africa. It was said to have been sung by a man named Xaattin after the death of a friend of his who was a magician. This friend had "died from the effects of a shot he had received when going about, by night, in the form of a lion." The breaking of the string, of course, is symbolic of the friend's death.

These were people
Who broke the string for me.
    Therefore
This place became like this for me,
On account of it.   5
Because the string broke for me,
    Therefore
The place does not feel to me
As the place used to feel to me,
    On account of it.   10
The place feels as if it stood open before me,
Because the string has broken for me.
    Therefore
The place does not feel pleasant to me
    Because of it.   15

A Song of Changes

This song of the Gabon Pygmy tribe in Africa accompanies the offering of gifts to the spirits to appease their anger.

The light becomes dark.
The night, & again the night,
The day with hunger tomorrow.
The Maker is angry with us.
The Old Ones have passed away,   5
Their bones are far off, below.
Their spirits are wandering—
Where are their spirits wandering?
Perhaps the passing wind knows.
Their bones are far off, below.   10
Are they below, the spirits? Are they here?
Do they see the offerings set out?
Tomorrow is empty & naked
For the Maker is no more there,
Is no more the host seated at the hearth.

Where the Wind Is Blowing

This song was collected by the anthropologist Frances Densmore from a man named Teal Duck, a member of the Teton Sioux tribe. Teal Duck said that he received it from an elk in a dream. Each line in the translation represents a single word in the original Sioux version.

```
where
the wind
is blowing
the wind
is roaring                    5
I stand
westward
the wind
is blowing
the wind                      10
is roaring
I stand
```

The Splendor of the Heavens

This prose poem, a sort of fable, was collected from the Eskimos by the great Scandinavian explorer Knud Rasmussen.

Two men came to a hole in the sky. One asked the other to lift him up. If only he would do so, then he in turn would lend him a hand.

His companion lifted him up, but hardly was he up when he shouted aloud for joy, forgot his companion & ran into heaven.

The other could just manage to peep in over the edge of the hole; it was full of feathers inside. But so beautiful was it in heaven that a man who looked in over the edge forgot everything, forgot his companion whom he had promised to help up & simply ran off into all the splendor of heaven.

Concrete Poems

The next six works represent the experimental modern school of "concrete" poetry. In a concrete poem the visual arrangement of the words or letters on the page becomes all-important. The poem becomes a kind of picture or object to be looked at, and the choice of typography and the spacing of the print makes the poem. Most of these concrete poems are playful, and none of them is intended to be profound.

O

Gloria

The first poem, "Gloria," is by a Czechoslovakian poet and maker of collages, Ladislav Novak. The lettering used is of the kind which is usually carved into stone monuments. The poet has taken the simple word *gloria* ("glory" or "praise") and attempted to express the feeling of glory, praise, or exaltation by lifting a single letter as if toward heaven.

GL   RIA

Brancusi

The second poem is a tribute by Jiri Kolar, also a Czechoslovakian, to the great Romanian sculptor Constantin Brancusi. Kolar has typed out the sculptor's name over and over again and then cut the writing into the shape of Brancusi's most famous statue, *Bird in Flight*.

brancusi
brancusi
brancusi
brancusi
brancusi

film

Ernst Jandl is a translator and teacher who lives in Vienna. His poem "film" looks like a strip of film, with each line representing a frame. He describes the poem as follows:

The poem is a film. There are two actors, i and l. The action starts in line 5 and ends in the 5th line from the bottom. i is alone, changes position three times, and disappears; l appears disappears; i appears disappears; both appear together changing position, like dancing; then i disappears for a long time, which, after stunning l, makes l restless, then immobile, like resignation; when at last i reappears the dancelike jumping about and out of the picture and back again is resumed for a longer stretch than the first time. This state is final. It is the happy ending to the film.

```
film
film
film
film
fi m
f im
fi m
f im
f  m
fl m
f im
f  m
flim
film
flim
film
f lm
f lm
fl m
f lm
fl m
f  m
f lm
fl m
f  m
f lm
f  m
fl m
f lm
fl m
fl m
fl m
fl m
fl m
film
film
film
film
film
film
film
f  m
film
f  m
film
film
film
film
film
film
film
film
```

Silencio

Eugen Gomringer was born in Bolivia and now lives in Switzerland where he is an art director, poet, and publisher. His poem "Silencio" (the Spanish word for "silence") speaks (or is silent) for itself.

silencio silencio silencio
silencio silencio silencio
silencio   silencio
silencio silencio silencio
silencio silencio silencio

rendering the legible illegible

Claus Bemer was born in Germany, where he is active in the theater as a director, actor, and translator. His poem "rendering the legible illegible" actually performs the action it mentions in the first line.

rendering the legible illegible
rendering the il**legible**
rend**e**t**ia**gi**b**h**e**
i**e**h**e**g**i**b**l**g

full

void

full

full

void

full

full

full

full-void

Pedro Xisto is a Brazilian lawyer, writer, and
diplomat who has represented his country in
Canada, the United States, and Japan. His
poem in the original is made up of the two
Portuguese words *cheio* and *vazio*. He has
translated the poem into English especially
for this volume. Mr. Xisto says, in a letter
to the editor, "My best line would be that
blank one. The blank is both a conclusion
and an opening. Open to you."

Suzuki Harunobu
Girl with Lantern on Balcony at Night
The Metropolitan Museum of Art,
Fletcher Fund, 1929

Unit Six
A Diversity of Cultures

Culture means more than art and literature, more than the refinement of taste. The culture of a race or nation includes all of its beliefs, its language, social forms, and material goods. The culture of the United States includes our houses and public buildings, the songs we hear, the patterns of logic and intuition that make up the way we think—in short, everything that goes to shape our collective behavior.

Travel in the modern world is faster and less expensive than it has ever been before. More than ever, men and women of differing cultures come in contact with each other. The following selections look at what happens when two cultures meet. What kinds of conflicts arise? How are they resolved? Are they always resolved happily? Or do they sometimes have tragic results? These stories and essays suggest that there is no simple formula which will unite men of many faiths, languages, and customs. Only a wide and sympathetic understanding, free of prejudice and based on knowledge, can help men of different traditions to live together harmoniously.

The stories and articles in this unit often recognize an unpleasant fact: that the world we live in is not a world of complete harmony. The brotherhood of man is an ideal, but not always a reality. The loyalty of men to their own culture brings about clashes when one group comes in contact with another. Sometimes, as in "The Wizard" and "The Oyster," one way of life is sacrificed to another.

In Gerald Durrell's "The Fon's Beef," two cultures meet with happy results. There is no conflict because all the people involved—the author and his wife and the African Fon—treat each other with respect and goodwill.

In other selections, two cultures come together less fortunately. "Dance of the Streets" (page 314) gives an African poet's impressions of New York City, and the impressions are not flattering: things which New Yorkers take for granted seem strange and at times inhuman to the eye of a visitor from another culture. In Doris Lessing's "No Witchcraft For Sale" we find a racial situation which prevents people from completely communicating with each other. Albert Camus's classic story "The Guest" shows a man of goodwill who is helpless as he becomes caught in the crossfire of history.

Relations between men of different cultures have become an important theme in modern literature because they form an important problem of the modern world. Writers are often concerned with this question: must the world be dominated by one superculture, or will it be possible for many peoples, each with its unique culture, to live together in peace and mutual respect?

"No Witchcraft For Sale" takes place against a background of South Africa's official policy of *apartheid*, separation of the races.

Such a policy creates a situation of mistrust which even the goodwill of individual citizens cannot completely erase.

Doris Lessing
No Witchcraft for Sale

The Farquars had been childless for years when little Teddy was born; and they were touched by the pleasure of their servants, who brought presents of fowls and eggs and flowers to the homestead when they came to rejoice over the baby, exclaiming with delight over his downy golden head and his blue eyes. They congratulated Mrs. Farquar as if she had achieved a very great thing, and she felt that she had—her smile for the lingering, admiring natives was warm and grateful.

Later, when Teddy had his first haircut, Gideon the cook picked up the soft gold tufts from the ground, and held them reverently in his hand. Then he smiled at the little boy and said: "Little Yellow Head." That became the native name for the child. Gideon and Teddy were great friends from the first. When Gideon had finished his work, he would lift Teddy on his shoulders to the shade of a big tree, and play with him there, forming curious little toys from twigs and leaves and grass, or shaping animals from wetted soil. When Teddy learned to walk it was often Gideon who crouched before him, clucking encouragement, finally catching him when he fell, tossing him up in the air till they both became breathless with laughter. Mrs. Farquar was fond of the old cook because of his love for her child.

There was no second baby; and one day Gideon said: "Ah, missus, missus, the Lord above sent this one; Little Yellow Head is the most good thing we have in our house." Because of that "we" Mrs. Farquar felt a warm impulse towards her cook; and at the end of the month she raised his wages. He had been with her now for several years; he was one of the few natives who had his wife and children in the compound and never wanted to go home to his kraal,[1] which was some hundreds of miles away. Sometimes a small piccanin who had been born the same time as Teddy, could be seen peering from the edge of the brush, staring in awe at the little white boy with his miraculous fair hair and Northern blue eyes. The two little children would gaze at each other with a wide, interested gaze, and once Teddy put out his hand curiously to touch the black child's cheeks and hair.

Gideon, who was watching, shook his head wonderingly, and said: "Ah, missus, these are both children, and one will grow up to be a baas,[2] and one will be a servant"; and Mrs. Farquar smiled and said sadly, "Yes, Gideon, I was thinking the same." She sighed. "It is God's will," said Gideon, who was a mission boy. The Farquars were very religious people; and this shared feeling about God bound servant and masters even closer together.

Teddy was about six years old when he was given a scooter, and discovered the intoxications of speed. All day he would fly around the homestead, in and out of flowerbeds, scattering squawking chickens and irritated dogs, finishing with a wide dizzying arc into the kitchen door. There he would cry: "Gideon, look at me!" And Gideon would laugh and say: "Very clever, Little Yellow Head." Gideon's youngest son, who was now a herdsboy, came especially up from the compound to see the scooter. He was afraid to come near it, but Teddy showed off in front of him. "Piccanin," shouted Teddy, "get out of my way!" And he raced in circles around the black child until he was frightened, and fled back to the bush.

"Why did you frighten him?" asked Gideon, gravely reproachful.

Teddy said defiantly: "He's only a black boy," and laughed. Then, when Gideon turned away from him without speaking, his face fell. Very soon he slipped into the house and found an orange and brought it to Gideon, saying: "This is for you." He could not bring himself to say he was sorry; but he could not bear to lose Gideon's affection either. Gideon took the orange unwillingly and sighed. "Soon you will be going away to school, Little Yellow Head," he said wonderingly, "and then you will be grown up." He shook his head gently and said, "And that is how our lives go." He seemed to be putting a distance between himself and Teddy, not because of resentment, but in the way a person accepts something inevitable. The baby had lain in his arms and smiled up into his face: the tiny boy had swung from his shoulders and played with him by the hour. Now Gideon would not let his flesh touch the flesh of the white child. He was kind, but there was a grave formality in his voice that made Teddy pout and sulk away. Also, it made him into a man: with Gideon he was polite, and carried himself formally, and if he came into the kitchen to ask for something, it was in the way a white man uses towards a servant, expecting to be obeyed.

But on the day that Teddy came staggering into the kitchen with his fists to his eyes, shrieking with pain, Gideon dropped the pot full of hot soup that he was holding, rushed to the child, and forced aside his fingers. "A snake!" he exclaimed. Teddy had been on his scooter, and had come to a rest with his foot on the side of a big tub of plants. A tree-snake, hanging by its tail from the roof, had spat full into his eyes. Mrs. Farquar came running when she heard the commotion. "He'll go blind," she sobbed, holding Teddy close against her. "Gideon, he'll go blind!" Already the eyes, with perhaps half an hour's sight left in them, were swollen up to the size of fists: Teddy's small white face was distorted by great purple oozing protuberances. Gideon said: "Wait a minute, missus, I'll get some medicine." He ran off into the bush.

Mrs. Farquar lifted the child into the house and bathed his eyes with permanganate. She had scarcely heard Gideon's

1 kraal *A native village in southern Africa.*
2 baas *Master, boss. A form of address.*

words; but when she saw that her remedies had no effect at all, and remembered how she had seen natives with no sight in their eyes, because of the spitting of a snake, she began to look for the return of her cook, remembering what she heard of the efficacy of native herbs. She stood by the window, holding the terrified, sobbing little boy in her arms, and peered helplessly into the bush. It was not more than a few minutes before she saw Gideon come bounding back, and in his hand he held a plant.

"Do not be afraid, missus," said Gideon, "this will cure Little Yellow Head's eyes." He stripped the leaves from the plant, leaving a small white fleshy root. Without even washing it, he put the root in his mouth, chewed it vigorously, and then held the spittle there while he took the child forcibly from Mrs. Farquar. He gripped Teddy down between his knees, and pressed the balls of his thumbs into the swollen eyes, so that the child screamed and Mrs. Farquar cried out in protest: "Gideon, Gideon!" But Gideon took no notice. He knelt over the writhing child, pushing back the puffy lids till chinks of eyeball showed, and then he spat hard, again and again, into first one eye, and then the other. He finally lifted Teddy gently into his mother's arms, and said: "His eyes will get better." But Mrs. Farquar was weeping with terror, and she could hardly thank him: it was impossible to believe that Teddy could keep his sight. In a couple of hours the swellings were gone: the eyes were inflamed and tender but Teddy could see. Mr. and Mrs. Farquar went to Gideon in the kitchen and thanked him over and over again. They felt helpless because of their gratitude: it seemed they could do nothing to express it. They gave Gideon presents for his wife and children, and a big increase in wages, but these things could not pay for Teddy's now completely cured eyes. Mrs. Farquar said: "Gideon, God chose you as an instrument for His goodness," and Gideon said: "Yes, missus, God is very good."

Now, when such a thing happens on a farm, it cannot be long before everyone hears of it. Mr. and Mrs. Farquar told their neighbors and the story was discussed from one end of the district to the other. The bush is full of secrets. No one can live in Africa, or at least on the veld,[3] without learning very soon that there is an ancient wisdom of leaf and soil and season—and, too, perhaps most important of all, of the darker tracts of the human mind—which is the black man's heritage. Up and down the district people were telling anecdotes, reminding each other of things that had happened to them.

"But I saw it myself, I tell you. It was a puff-adder. The kaffir's[4] arm was swollen to the elbow, like a great shiny black bladder. He was groggy after a half a minute. He was dying. Then suddenly a kaffir walked out of the bush with his hands full of green stuff. He smeared something on the place, and next day my boy was back at work, and all you could see was two small punctures in the skin."

This was the kind of tale they told. And, as always, with a certain amount of exasperation, because while all of them knew that in the bush of Africa are waiting valuable drugs locked in bark, in simple-looking leaves, in roots, it was impossible to ever get the truth about them from the natives themselves.

The story eventually reached town; and perhaps it was at a sundowner party, or some such function, that a doctor, who happened to be there, challenged it. "Nonsense," he said. "These things get exaggerated in the telling. We are always checking up on this kind of story, and we draw a blank every time."

Anyway, one morning there arrived a strange car at the homestead, and out stepped one of the workers from the laboratory in town, with cases full of test-tubes and chemicals.

Mr. and Mrs. Farquar were flustered and pleased and flattered. They asked the scientist to lunch, and they told the story all over

3 veld A grassland, especially of southern Africa, usually with scattered shrubs or trees.

4 kaffir A member of a group of southern African Bantu-speaking peoples.

again, for the hundredth time. Little Teddy was there too, his blue eyes sparkling with health, to prove the truth of it. The scientist explained how humanity might benefit if this new drug could be offered for sale; and the Farquars were even more pleased: they were kind, simple people, who liked to think of something good coming about because of them. But when the scientist began talking of the money that might result, their manner showed discomfort. Their feelings over the miracle (that was how they thought of it) were so strong and deep and religious, that it was distasteful to them to think of money. The scientist, seeing their faces, went back to his first point, which was the advancement of humanity. He was perhaps a trifle perfunctory: it was not the first time he had come salting the tail of a fabulous bush-secret.

Eventually, when the meal was over, the Farquars called Gideon into their living-room and explained to him that this baas, here, was a Big Doctor from the Big City, and he had come all that way to see Gideon. At this Gideon seemed afraid; he did not understand; and Mrs. Farquar explained quickly that it was because of the wonderful thing he had done with Teddy's eyes that the Big Baas had come.

Gideon looked from Mrs. Farquar to Mr. Farquar, and then at the little boy, who was showing great importance because of the occasion. At last he said grudgingly: "The Big Baas want to know what medicine I used?" He spoke incredulously, as if he could not believe his old friends could so betray him. Mr. Farquar began explaining how a useful medicine could be made out of the root, and how it could be put on sale, and how thousands of people, black and white, up and down the continent of Africa, could be saved by the medicine when that spitting snake filled their eyes with poison. Gideon listened, his eyes bent on the ground, the skin of his forehead puckering in discomfort. When Mr. Farquar had finished he did not reply. The scientist, who all this

time had been leaning back in a big chair, sipping his coffee and smiling with sceptical good-humor, chipped in and explained all over again, in different words, about the making of drugs and the progress of science. Also, he offered Gideon a present.

There was silence after this further explanation, and then Gideon remarked indifferently that he could not remember the root. His face was sullen and hostile, even when he looked at the Farquars, whom he usually treated like old friends. They were beginning to feel annoyed; and this feeling annulled the guilt that had been sprung into life by Gideon's accusing manner. They were beginning to feel that he was unreasonable. But it was at that moment that they all realized he would never give in. The magical drug would remain where it was, unknown and useless except for the tiny scattering of Africans who had the knowledge, natives who might be digging a ditch for the municipality in a ragged shirt and a pair of patched shorts, but who were still born to healing, hereditary healers, being the nephews or sons of the old witch doctors whose ugly masks and bits of bone and all the uncouth properties of magic were the outward signs of real power and wisdom.

The Farquars might tread on that plant fifty times a day as they passed from house to garden, from cow kraal to mealie field,[5] but they would never know it.

But they went on persuading and arguing, with all the force of their exasperation; and Gideon continued to say that he could not remember, or that there was no such root, or that it was the wrong season of the year, or that it wasn't the root itself, but the spit from his mouth that had cured Teddy's eyes. He said all these things one after another, and seemed not to care they were contradictory. He was rude and stubborn. The Farquars could hardly recognise their gentle, lovable old servant in this ignorant, perversely obstinate African, standing there in front of them with lowered eyes, his hands twitching his

5   mealie field   *African: "a field of Indian corn."*

cook's apron, repeating over and over whichever one of the stupid refusals that first entered his head.

And suddenly he appeared to give in. He lifted his head, gave a long, blank angry look at the circle of whites, who seemed to him like a circle of yelping dogs pressing around him, and said: "I will show you the root."

They walked single file away from the homestead down a kaffir path. It was a blazing December afternoon, with the sky full of hot rain-clouds. Everything was hot: the sun was like a bronze tray whirling overhead, there was a heat shimmer over the fields, the soil was scorching underfoot, the dusty wind blew gritty and thick and warm in their faces. It was a terrible day, fit only for reclining on a verandah with iced drinks, which is where they would normally have been at that hour.

From time to time, remembering that on the day of the snake it had taken ten minutes to find the root, someone asked: "Is it much further, Gideon?" And Gideon would answer over his shoulder with angry politeness: "I'm looking for the root, baas." And indeed, he would frequently bend sideways and trail his hand among the grasses with a gesture that was insulting in its perfunctoriness. He walked them through the bush along unknown paths for two hours, in that melting destroying heat, so that the sweat trickled coldly down them and their heads ached. They were all quite silent: the Farquars because they were angry, the scientist because he was being proved right again; there was no such plant. His was a tactful silence.

At last, six miles from the house, Gideon suddenly decided they had had enough; or perhaps his anger evaporated at that moment. He picked up, without an attempt at looking anything but casual, a handful of blue flowers from the grass, flowers that had been growing plentifully all down the paths they had come.

He handed them to the scientist without looking at him, and marched off by himself on the way home; leaving them to follow him if they chose.

When they got back to the house, the scientist went to the kitchen to thank Gideon: he was being very polite, even though there was an amused look in his eyes. Gideon was not there. Throwing the flowers casually into the back of his car, the eminent visitor departed on his way back to his laboratory.

Gideon was back in his kitchen in time to prepare dinner, but he was sulking. He spoke to Mr. Farquar like an unwilling servant. It was days before they liked each other again.

The Farquars made enquiries about the root from their labourers. Sometimes they were answered with distrustful stares. Sometimes the natives said: "We do not know. We have never heard of the root." One, the cattle boy, who had been with them a long time, and had grown to trust them a little, said: "Ask your boy in the kitchen. Now, there's a doctor for you. He's the son of a famous medicine man who used to be in these parts, and there's nothing he cannot cure." Then he added politely: "Of course, he's not as good as the white man's doctor, we know that, but he's good for us."

After some time, when the soreness had gone from between the Farquars and Gideon, they began to joke: "When are you going to show us the snake-root, Gideon?" And he would laugh and shake his head, saying, a little uncomfortably: "But I did show you, missus, have you forgotten?"

Much later, Teddy, as a schoolboy, would come into the kitchen and say: "You old rascal, Gideon! Do you remember that time you tricked us all by making us walk miles all over the veld for nothing? It was so far my father had to carry me!"

And Gideon would double up with polite laughter. After much laughing, he would suddenly straighten himself up, wipe his old eyes, and look sadly at Teddy, who was grinning mischievously at him across the kitchen: "Ah, Little Yellow Head, how you have grown! Soon you will be grown up with a farm of your own . . ."

For Discussion

1 Are the Farquars decent people? What is their attitude toward their African servants? Would it be fair or unfair to call them racists?

2 How does Teddy's treatment of Gideon's little boy reflect the society in which the two boys live? Where has six-year-old Teddy picked up his attitudes?

3 Why does Gideon change from a "gentle, lovable old servant" to an "ignorant, perversely obstinate African" when asked to share his medical secret with the white man? What role is Gideon playing? Why?

4 Do the Farquars really understand Gideon?

5 In your opinion was Gideon right or wrong in hiding his secret from the white world? Why did he do it?

6 At the end of the story, in his final conversation with Teddy, what familiar role is Gideon playing?

Since 1830 Algeria, on the Northern coast of Africa, had been a French colony. The native Arabs had suffered economic and racial discrimination at the hands of the *colons*—the French Algerians. After the Second World War the Arabs began to fight for their independence. Incidents of terror- ism were common. The French, who had no intention of abandoning a rich colony, retaliated with equal measures of cruelty. For years, French and Arab citizens died in bombings and raids. The struggle for independence spread and brought terror even to the streets of Paris. It is against this background of civil war and terror that "The Guest" takes place.

In this story Albert Camus writes of the tragic divisions within his native country and of one man's attempt to remove himself from the conflict.

Albert Camus
The Guest

The schoolteacher watched the two men climb toward his place. One was on horseback, the other on foot. They hadn't yet reached the steep grade leading to his hillside school. They were making slow progress in the snow and over the stones of the immense stretch of high, desolate plateau. From time to time the horse stumbled. Its hoofs couldn't yet be heard where the schoolteacher was standing, but he could see the steamy breath coming from its nostrils. At least one of the men knew the region. They were following the trail that had disappeared several days before under the dirty white blanket of snow. The schoolteacher calculated that they would not reach the top of the hill for another half hour. It was cold. He went into the schoolhouse to get his sweater.

He crossed the empty, frigid schoolroom. On the blackboard, the four rivers of France, traced with chalk of four different colors, had been flowing toward their estuaries for the past three days. Heavy snows had come in mid-October after eight months of drought, and without the transition of rain, and his twenty or so pupils, who lived in the villages scattered over the plateau, had been staying home. They had to wait for better weather. Daru now heated only the single room that constituted his lodging. It adjoined the classroom and also gave onto the plateau, to the east. One of his windows, like the classroom's, opened to the south. On that side, the schoolhouse was only a few kilometers from where the plateau began to slope toward the south. In clear weather you could see the violet mass of the mountain range with its opening to the desert.

Feeling a little warmer, Daru returned to the window from which he had first noticed the two men. He could no longer see them. This meant that they had begun to come up the steep rise. The sky was less overcast; the snow had stopped falling during the night. The morning had risen with a murky light that scarcely grew brighter as the clouds lifted. Now, at two in the afternoon, it seemed as if the day were just beginning. Yet this was better than the three previous days, when the heavy snow was falling in unrelieved darkness and the shifting winds rattled the double door of the classroom. Daru had then waited out the storm, spending long hours in his room and leaving it only to go down into the lean-to in order to feed the chickens and get some coal. Fortunately, the delivery truck from Tadjid, the nearest village to the north, had brought his supplies two days before the tempest. The truck would return in forty-eight hours.

Actually he had enough to sit out a siege. His small room was cluttered with bags of wheat which the authorities had left with him for distribution to those of his pupils whose families were victims of the drought. Misfortune had struck all the families, since they were all poor. Daru planned to give out a daily ration to the children. He knew that they had gone without food during these bad days. Perhaps one of the fathers or one of the big brothers would come before dark and he could let them have the wheat. They simply had to be carried over to the next harvest. There was no alternative. Shiploads of wheat were now arriving from France, and the worst was over. But it would be hard to forget that famine, those ragged ghosts drifting in the sunlight, the plateau burned month after month, the earth literally scorched and gradually shriveling up, every stone splintering into dust underfoot. The sheep had died then by the thousands; also a few men here and there, sometimes without anyone's knowing.

Witnessing such poverty, this man who lived like a monk in his remote schoolhouse, content with the little he had and with his rugged life, had felt like a lord with his whitewashed walls, narrow cot, crude bookshelves, his well, and his modest weekly supply of food and water. Then suddenly the snow, without warning, without the relief of rain. The region was like that, cruel to live in even had it not been for its people, who did not make things easier either. But Daru was born here. Anywhere else he felt like an exile.

He went outside and crossed the terrace. The two men were now halfway up the slope. He recognized the one on horseback—it was Balducci, an old gendarme. Daru had known him for a long time. Balducci was leading an Arab at the end of a rope. The man was walking behind him, his hands tied and his head bowed. The gendarme waved a greeting to which Daru didn't respond, totally absorbed as he was in looking at the Arab. The prisoner was dressed in a loose, faded overgarment called a *djellabah;* he had sandals on his feet but he also wore heavy, raw-wool socks; his head was covered with a *chèche,* a narrow, short scarf twisted into a turban. The two men were approaching. Balducci had reined in his animal so as not to pull too hard on the rope, thus avoiding hurting the Arab. The group was advancing slowly.

When they were within earshot, Balducci shouted, "Did the three kilometers from El Ameur in one hour!" Daru didn't answer. He stood there, short and square in his thick sweater, and watched them climb. Not once did the Arab raise his head.

"Hello," said Daru when they reached the terrace. "Come in and warm up." Balducci dismounted with difficulty; he didn't let go of the rope. He smiled at the schoolteacher from under his bristling mustache. His small dark eyes, deep-set under his tanned forehead, and his mouth surrounded by wrinkles, made him look stern and determined. Daru took the bridle, led the horse to the shed, and returned to the two men who were now waiting for him in the schoolhouse. He took them to his room. "I'm going to heat the classroom," he said. "We'll be more comfortable there."

When he entered his room again, Balducci was on the couch. He had undone the rope which had tied him to the Arab. The Arab was now squatting near the stove. His hands still bound, the *chèche* pushed back on his head, he was looking in the direction of the window. Daru noticed at first only his enormous lips, full, smooth, almost Negroid. He noticed that his nose was thin. His eyes were black and feverish. The raised *chèche* uncovered a stubborn brow, and the man's whole face, weathered and somewhat discolored with the cold, had an anxious and rebellious look, which struck Daru when the Arab, turning his face toward him, looked him straight in the eyes. "Go into the other room," the schoolteacher said. "I'll make you some mint tea."

"Thanks," said Balducci. "What a job I've got! Can't wait to retire." And addressing his prisoner in Arabic: "Come along, you." The Arab got up and, holding his tied-up wrists in front of him, slowly walked to the classroom.

With the tea Daru brought a chair. But Balducci had enthroned himself in the front on a pupil's table, and the Arab was squatting against the teacher's platform facing the stove, which was between the desk and the window. Offering the glass of tea to the prisoner, Daru hesitated when he saw his bound hands. "Could you perhaps untie him?"

"Sure," said Balducci. "That was only for the trip." And he started to get to his feet. But Daru placed the glass on the floor and knelt down beside the Arab; without saying anything the Arab watched him with his feverish eyes as he untied his hands. He rubbed his freed swollen wrists against each other, lifted the glass of tea, and drank the scalding liquid in eager little sips.

"Well," said Daru to the gendarme, "where will you be going now?"

Balducci withdrew his mustache from the tea. "We stay here, son."

"Odd schoolchildren! Are you staying the night?"

"No. I'm going back to El Ameur. And you will hand over this fellow at Tinguit. The police there know he's on his way."

Balducci looked at Daru with a friendly little smile.

"What kind of story is this?" said the schoolteacher. "Are you pulling my leg?"

"No, son. Those are the orders."

"Orders? But I'm not . . ." Daru hesitated; he didn't want to offend the old Corsican. "I mean, that's not my occupation."

"How's that? . . . You know that doesn't mean anything nowadays. In wartime people are called upon to do all kinds of jobs."

"Then I'll wait for a declaration of war."

Balducci nodded.

"All right. But these are the orders and they concern you too. It appears that things are brewing. There's talk of a coming revolt. We are, so to speak, mobilized."

Daru continued to look determined.

"Listen, son," said Balducci, "I like you a lot, you must know that. There are only about a dozen of us in El Ameur to patrol the territory of the entire department—that's not many, small though the department is, and I have to get back there. They told me to hand this 'zebra' over to you and return in a hurry. Back there he couldn't be guarded safely. His village was up in arms, they wanted to get him out. So you must take him to Tinguit. Do it in the daytime. It's only about twenty kilometers from here; that shouldn't strain a vigorous fellow like you. After that you can forget the whole thing. You can then come back to your kids and to your serene life."

They heard the horse snorting and stamping the ground on the other side of the wall. Daru looked out the window. The weather was certainly clearing, and it was lighter now over the snow-covered plateau. When all the snow had melted, the sun would dominate again and scorch the fields of stone once more. For days the unchanging sky would keep shedding its dry light over the desolate expanse, where there was nothing to suggest the existence of man.

Turning to Balducci, Daru said, "But tell me, what has he done?" And before the gendarme opened his mouth to answer, he asked, "Does he speak French?"

"A little. We looked for him for a month, but they were hiding him. He killed his cousin."

"Is he against us?"

"I don't think so. But you can't be sure."

"Why did he kill him?"

"A family squabble, I think. It seemed one owed some grain to the other. It's not clear. In short, he killed his cousin with a blow of the billhook. You know, like a sheep, *zic!*"

Balducci made the gesture of striking with a blade across his throat, and the Arab, his attention attracted, looked at him uneasily. Daru felt a sudden wrath against this man, against all men and their sordid malice, their endless hatreds, their lust for blood.

But the kettle was purring on the stove. He served Balducci more tea, hesitated, then served the Arab a second time; again the prisoner drank avidly. His raised arms drew the *djellabah* half open, and the schoolteacher noticed his chest, thin and muscular.

"Thanks, son," Balducci said. "And now I'm off."

He got up and went over to the Arab, taking a small rope from his pocket.

"What are you doing?" Daru asked bluntly.

Balducci, nonplused, showed him the rope.

"You don't need to do it."

The old gendarme hesitated.

"All right, have it your way. I suppose you're armed?"

"I have my hunting gun."

"Where?"

"In my trunk."

"You ought to keep it near your bed."

"Why? I have nothing to fear."

"You're mad, son! If they stage a rebellion, no one will be safe—we'll all be in the same boat."

"I'll defend myself. I'll have time to see them coming."

Balducci began to laugh, then suddenly the mustache again covered his white teeth.

"You'll have time, you say? Fine. And I say you have always been a little cracked. But that's why I like you; my son was like that."

At the same time he pulled out his revolver and placed it on the desk.

"Keep it, I don't need two weapons from here to El Ameur."

The revolver sparkled against the black paint of the table. When the gendarme turned toward him, the schoolteacher smelled the odor of leather and horses.

"Listen, Balducci," Daru said suddenly, "all this disgusts me, and worst of all this specimen of yours. But I won't hand him over. I'll fight, yes, if it's necessary. But not that."

The old gendarme stood in front of him and looked at him severely.

"You are acting like a fool," he said slowly. "I don't like it either. You don't get used to putting a rope on a man, even after years of doing it, and you're even, yes, ashamed. But you can't let them do as they please."

"I won't hand him over," Daru repeated.

"It's an order, son, and I'm telling you this again."

"I understand. Repeat to them what I've said to you: I won't hand him over."

Balducci made an apparent effort to weigh the matter. He looked at the Arab and at Daru. At last he came to a decision.

"No, I won't tell them anything. If you want to stand against us, do as you please; I'll not denounce you. I have an order to deliver the prisoner; I'm doing so. Now you'll sign this paper for me."

"There's no need to do that. I'll not deny that you left him with me."

"Don't be difficult with me. I know you'll tell the truth. You are known here, and you are a man. But you must sign, that's the rule."

Daru opened his drawer, took out a small, square bottle of purple ink, the red wooden penholder with the "sergeant-major" penpoint that he used for tracing models of penmanship, and he signed. The gendarme folded the paper carefully and put it into his billfold. Then he moved toward the door.

"I'll see you off," Daru said.

"No," said Balducci. "It's no use being polite. You have offended me."

He looked at the Arab, motionless in the same spot, sniffed with vexation, and turned away toward the door. "Good-by, son," he said. The door slammed behind him. Balducci suddenly loomed outside the window and then disappeared. His footsteps were muffled by the snow. The horse stirred on the other side of the wall and the chickens fluttered in fright. A moment later Balducci passed again in front of the window, pulling the horse by the bridle. He walked toward the slope without turning around and disappeared from sight with the horse following him. A large stone could be heard softly bouncing down.

Daru returned to the prisoner, who hadn't stirred, never taking his eyes off him. "Wait," the schoolteacher said in Arabic and went toward the adjoining room. As he was crossing the threshold, he thought of something, went to the desk, picked up the revolver and stuck it in his pocket. Then, without looking back, he went into his room.

For some time he remained stretched out on his couch, watching the sky gradually close in, and listening to the silence. It was this silence that had disturbed him during the first days here, after the war. He had asked for a position in the little town at the bottom of the foothills that separate the desert from the high plateau. It is there that the rock walls, green and black to the north, pink and lavender to the south, mark the frontier of eternal summer. He had instead been given a position farther north, on the plateau itself. At first the solitude and the stillness had been hard for him on this barren land inhabited only by stones. Here and there furrows suggested cultivation, but they had been dug only to locate a certain kind of stone good for construction. People plowed here only to harvest rocks. Occasionally the thin soil blown into the hollows would be scraped up to enrich the earth of meager village gardens. But that was all—nothing but stones covering three quarters of the region. Towns sprang up here, flourished, then disappeared; men passed through, loved one another or were at each other's throats, then died. In this desolation, neither he nor his guest mattered. And yet, Daru knew that outside this desert neither he nor the other could really have lived.

He got up. No noise came from the classroom. He was amazed at the frank joy that came over him at the mere thought that the Arab might have fled and that he would be alone again, with no decision to make. But the prisoner was there. He had merely stretched out between the stove and the desk. His eyes were open, and he was staring at the ceiling. In this position, his thick lips were particularly noticeable; they gave him a sullen look.

"Come," Daru said. The Arab got up and followed him. In his room the schoolteacher pointed to a chair near the table at the window. The Arab sat down without taking his eyes off Daru.

"Are you hungry?"

"Yes," the prisoner said.

Daru set two places. He took flour and oil, kneaded a flat cake in a plate, and lighted the butane stove. While the cake was frying, he went to the shed for some cheese, eggs, dates, and condensed milk. When the cake was done, he put it on the windowsill to cool, heated some condensed milk diluted with water and, lastly, began to beat up the eggs for an omelette. His arm brushed against the revolver stuck in his right pocket. He put the bowl down, went into the classroom, and put the revolver in his desk drawer. He came back to the room. Night was falling. He turned on the light, and served the Arab. "Eat," he said. The Arab broke off a piece of the flat cake, lifted it avidly to his mouth, but stopped short.

"And you?" he said.

"After you. Then I'll eat."

The thick lips opened slightly. The Arab hesitated, then bit into the cake without further ado.

The meal over, the Arab looked at the schoolteacher. "Are you . . . the judge?"

"No, I'm keeping you until tomorrow."

"Why do you sit down to eat with me?"

"I'm hungry."

The Arab fell silent. Daru got up and left the room. He brought back a folding bed from the shed, set it up between the table and the stove, perpendicular to his own bed. From a large suitcase in the corner, serving as a shelf for school folders, he took two blankets and spread them on the camp bed. This done, he felt at loose ends, and sat down on his bed. There was nothing more to do or to prepare. He had to look at this man. He gazed at him, trying to imagine that face transported with rage. He was unable to. He saw only his gloomy yet shining eyes and the coarse mouth.

"Why did you kill him?" he asked in a voice whose hostile tone surprised him.

The Arab lowered his eyes.

"He ran away. I ran after him."

He looked up at Daru again and his eyes bore an expression of miserable questioning. "Now what will they do to me?"

"Are you afraid?"

The Arab stiffened, and looked away.

"Are you sorry?"

The Arab looked at him openmouthed. Obviously he did not understand. Daru was becoming irritated. At the same time he felt clumsy and ill at ease, with his big body wedged between the two beds.

"Lie down there," he said impatiently. "That's your bed."

The Arab did not move. He called out to Daru:

"Listen!"

The schoolteacher looked at him.

"Is the gendarme coming back tomorrow?"

"I don't know."

"Are you coming with us?"

"I don't know. Why?"

The prisoner got up and stretched out on top of the blankets, his feet toward the window. The light from the electric bulb shone straight into his eyes and he closed them at once.

"Why?" Daru repeated, standing beside the bed.

The Arab opened his eyes under the blinding light and looked at him, trying hard not to blink.

"Come with us," he said.

In the middle of the night Daru was still awake. He had lain down on his bed after undressing completely—he was used to sleeping naked. But now when he realized that he had no clothes on him, he was uneasy. He did not feel safe and was tempted to dress again. Then he shrugged the matter off; after all, he had been through such things before, and if attacked he could break his adversary in two. He observed the Arab from his bed, lying there on his back, still motionless, with his eyes closed against the harsh light. When Daru put out the light, the darkness seemed to thicken all at once. The night grew vivid in the window, the starless sky stirring gently. The schoolteacher could soon distinguish the stretched-out body in front of him. The Arab remained motionless, but his eyes seemed open now. A light wind prowled around the schoolhouse. It would probably chase away the clouds and the sun would return tomorrow.

The wind increased during the night. The hens fluttered a bit and then quieted down. The Arab turned over on his side with his back to Daru. Daru thought he heard him moan. He kept listening to that breathing, so close to him, and brooded, unable to fall asleep. This presence, here in the room where he had been sleeping alone for a long year, disturbed him. But it disturbed him also because it imposed on him a certain kind of brotherhood he knew well—but which he rejected in the present circumstances—the brotherhood of men sharing the same room, such as soldiers or prisoners, when they begin to feel a strange bond. Having shed their armor with their civilian clothes, they are able to gather every evening, despite their differences, in the ancient community of hope and exhaustion. But Daru shook himself; he didn't like such foolish musings, and he had to get some sleep.

Still later, however, when the Arab stirred about almost imperceptibly, the schoolteacher was still awake. When the prisoner moved a second time, he stiffened, on the alert. The Arab slowly raised himself on his arms, almost with the motion of a sleepwalker. Sitting up on his bed, he waited, motionless, without turning his head toward Daru, as if he were listening with all his attention. Daru did not move, though it had just occurred to him that the revolver was still in his desk drawer. It would be better to act right away. Yet he continued to observe the prisoner, who, with the same smooth and soundless motion lowered his feet to the floor, waited again, then began slowly to stand up. Daru was going to call out to him, when the Arab began to walk, in a natural but uncannily silent way. He went toward the back door leading into the shed. He lifted the latch with precaution and went out, pulling the door behind him, without shutting it. Daru had not stirred. "He's escaping," he merely thought. "Good riddance!" Yet he kept his ear cocked. The hens were not fluttering— he must therefore be on the plateau. A faint sound of water reached him, and he didn't understand what it was until the Arab again stood framed in the doorway, closed the door carefully, and came back to bed without a sound. Then Daru turned his back to him and fell asleep. Later, in his deep sleep, he seemed to hear stealthy steps around the schoolhouse. "I'm dreaming, I'm dreaming!" he repeated to himself. And he went on sleeping.

When he awoke, the sky was clear; the loosely fitting window let in a stream of cold and pure air. The Arab was asleep, curled up under the blankets now, his mouth open, completely relaxed. But when Daru shook him, he jumped with terror, staring wildly at Daru without recognizing him and with such an expression of panic that the schoolteacher drew back. "Don't be afraid. It's me. You must get up and have something to eat." The Arab nodded his head and said yes. He was calm again but his expression was vacant and listless.

The coffee was ready. They drank it, both seated on the folding bed and munching their pieces of flat cake. Then Daru led the Arab to the shed and showed him the faucet where he washed. He went back into the room, folded up the blankets and the bed, made his own bed, and put the room in order. Then he went out onto the terrace through the classroom. The sun was already rising in the blue sky; a soft and radiant light was bathing the barren plateau. On the slope the snow was melting here and there. The stones were about to reappear. Crouched on the edge of the plateau, the schoolteacher contemplated the arid expanse. He thought of Balducci. He had hurt the man's feelings, he had sent him off brusquely, seeming indifferent to his predicament. He could still hear the tone of the gendarme's good-by, and, without knowing the reason for it, he felt strangely hollow and vulnerable. At that moment, from the other side of the schoolhouse, he heard the prisoner cough. Daru listened to him almost despite himself, and then, furious, he flung a pebble, sending it whistling through the air before it sank into the snow. The stupid crime the man had committed revolted him, but to hand him over was dishonorable—the mere thought of it made him fume with indignation. And he cursed both his own people who had sent him this Arab and the Arab himself who had had the nerve to kill but had not known how to escape. Daru got up, walked in a circle over the terrace, stood stock-still for a moment, then went back to the schoolhouse.

The Arab, bending over the cement floor of the shed, was washing his teeth with two fingers. Daru looked at him, then said, "Come." He returned to his room, walking ahead of the prisoner. He put on a hunting jacket over his sweater and pulled on his walking shoes. He stood up and waited for the Arab to get into his *chèche* and sandals. They walked into the classroom and the schoolteacher pointed to the exit. "Go," he said. The other didn't move. "I'm coming with you," said Daru. The Arab went out. Daru returned to his room, where he made a package of pieces of rusk, some dates, and sugar. Back in the classroom, before leaving, he hesitated a second in front of his desk, then crossed the school threshold and locked the door.

"We go this way," he said, and started out eastward, followed by the prisoner. When they were but a short distance from the schoolhouse, he thought he heard a slight sound behind him. He retraced his steps and inspected the grounds around the building; there was no one there. The Arab watched him without seeming to understand. "Let's go," Daru said.

They walked for an hour then rested beside a jagged limestone. The snow was melting ever faster, with the sun sucking up the puddles at once and rapidly clearing the plateau, which gradually dried and vibrated like the air itself. When they resumed walking, the newly bared ground rang under their feet. Now and then a bird rent the air in front of them with a joyful cry. Daru drank in the fresh morning radiance with deep breaths. A kind of exaltation rose in him before the familiar vast expanse, almost all of it yellow now under the vault of blue sky. They walked another hour, descending toward the south. They reached a sort of flat-topped elevation covered with crumbling rock. From there the plateau sloped eastward, toward a low plain with a few sparse trees. To the south it sloped toward masses of rock, which gave the landscape a chaotic look.

Daru scanned both directions. There was nothing but the sky on the horizon—there was no sign of man. He turned to the Arab, who was staring at him blankly. Daru held out the parcel to him. "Take it," he said, "they're dates, bread, and sugar—they'll last you for two days. Here are a thousand francs too." The Arab took the parcel and the money; he held them at chest level, as if he didn't know what to do with what had just been given him. "Now look," the schoolteacher said, pointing east, "that's the way to Tinguit. It's a two hours' walk. The administration and the police are at Tinguit—they're expecting you." The Arab looked in the direction in which Daru was pointing, still holding the parcel and the money against his chest. Daru took him by the arm and turned him, not gently, toward the south. At the foot of the elevation on which they were standing, the faint markings of a path could be discerned. "That's the trail across the plateau. In a day's distance from here you'll find pasturelands and the first nomads. They'll welcome you and give you shelter, as is their custom."

The Arab had now turned toward Daru, his face expressing a sort of panic. "Listen," he said.

Daru shook his head, "No, don't speak. I'm going to leave you now." He turned away, took two long strides in the direction of the school, looked around hesitantly at the motionless Arab, and started off again. For a few minutes he heard nothing but his own footsteps against the cold earth, and he did not turn his head. A moment later, however, he turned around. The Arab was still standing there, on the crest of the hill, his arms hanging at his sides now, and he was looking at the schoolteacher. Daru felt a lump in his throat. But he swore, waved his arm with impatience, and started off again. After walking some distance, he again stopped and looked. There was no one on the hill now.

Daru hesitated. The sun was quite high in the sky and was beginning to beat down on his head. He retraced his steps, at first somewhat uncertainly, then with determination. By the time he reached the little hill his body was streaming with sweat. He climbed it as fast as he could and stopped, out of breath, at the top. The fields of rock to the south were clearly outlined against the blue sky, but on the plain to the east a heat-haze was already rising. And in that light haze, Daru, with heavy heart, made out the Arab walking slowly along the road to prison.

A little later, standing in front of the classroom window, the schoolteacher was watching the clear light rise over the whole plateau, but he hardly saw it. Behind him on the blackboard, across the winding French rivers, stretched the words clumsily written with chalk, which he had just read: "You handed over our brother. You will pay for this." Daru looked at the sky, the plateau, and beyond, at the invisible regions stretching all the way to the sea. In this vast land he had so loved, he was alone.

Justin O'Brien/TRANSLATOR

For Discussion

1 Often it is simpler to think in terms of abstractions rather than make a sincere effort to understand the complications that exist within another man or another group. Which of the two men, Daru or Balducci, thinks of the Arab as an abstraction? Which tries to deal with the Arab as a man?

2 The Arab is a murderer. Does this create a difficult test for Daru?

3 Daru gives the Arab his choice of freedom or prison. Is Daru avoiding his own responsibility? What is Daru's responsibility? Is it to Balducci? To the French government that pays his wages? To the Arab? To himself? Does he take the easy way out?

4 Given his choice of freedom, the Arab takes the road that leads to prison. Why?

5 Is Daru a hero? If so, what kind of hero is he?

6 What does the message on the blackboard indicate? Who wrote it? What is Daru's fate? Explain the final sentence of the story.

In some cultures young girls are considered to be women at an earlier age than in our culture. It is an important event and is celebrated with much ceremony and ritual.

Naiche, Apache chief
Skin-painting of sacred girls' puberty ceremony
Courtesy of the Oklahoma Historical Society

The Artist's View

People of all cultures are interested in the same things: themselves, their community, government, religion, and survival, to name some. It is the different ways that things are done, the different ideas that people believe in, and the different ways things take form, that lend diversity to cultures. Sometimes this diversity may bring about a conflict.

In all cultures creativity is a necessary outlet for emotions. Depending on the type of civilization, this creativity takes various forms. Here it emerges as a somewhat primitive figure.

Caribbean, Dominican Republic
Figure
Courtesy of The Museum of Primitive Art, New York

Communities have developed in all cultures. The social structure of the community varies from culture to culture. In this print of an early Oriental town, the artist has shown many levels of society, from the fishermen, to the traders, to the wealthy citizens.

Bry
Indiae Orientalis
Rare Book Division
The New York Public Library
Astor, Lenox and Tilden Foundations

As communities grow, they develop a need for leadership and government. This is a statue of an important person in a Mesopotamian town that existed 2,000 years before Christ was born.

Mespotamia, Diorite
Seated figure of Gudea
The Metropolitan Museum of Art, Harris Brisbane Dick Fund, 1959

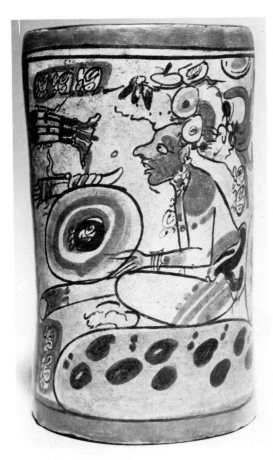

Here is a Mayan dignitary painted about 500 to 800 years after Christ was born. Although the cultures of this dignitary and the preceding one varied greatly in time and type, both men probably performed much the same role.

Mayan
Classic cylinder vase
Photograph by André Emmerich

All cultures have a religion of some type that fulfills a basic human need. Throughout the ages, paintings and statues of a religious nature, such as this statue of the Mexican god Macuilxochitl, have been a favorite of artists.

Mexico: Mixteca-Puebla
Macuilxochitl
Courtesy of The Museum of Primitive Art, New York

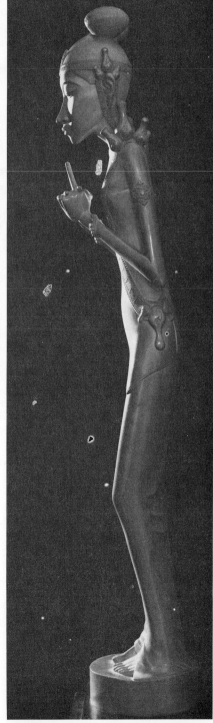

Ritual and ceremony play a large part in some religions. This African casque mask was part of a ceremony, one probably concerning good luck in battle or war.

Bapulde, Congo, Africa
Casque Mask
Courtesy of the American Museum
  of Natural History

Peace, the cherished goal of most cultures, is represented here by a Balinese priest.

Indonesian
Peace
Courtesy of the United Nations

"The Fon's Beef" is an account of a visit to the remote African kingdom of Bafut by the author and his wife, Jacquie. Gerald Durrell is a zoologist, and the purpose of his visit was to gather live animals for study. His style is relaxed, and he never misses an opportunity to find humor in his experiences. The humor, however, is never exaggerated, for Durrell describes the customs of Bafut with respect and fascination. Not the least of Bafut's wonders was the remarkable man who was its *fon*, or "chief."

Gerald Durrell

The Fon's Beef

We drove on through the green, gold, and white grassland, under a blue sky veined with fine wisps of wind-woven white cloud, like frail twists of sheep's wool blowing across the sky. Everything in this landscape seemed to be the work of the wind. The great outcrops of grey rocks were carved and ribbed by it into fantastic shapes; the long grass was curved over into frozen waves by it; the small trees had been bent, carunculated, and distorted by it. And the whole landscape throbbed and sang with the wind, hissing softly in the grass, making the small trees creak and whine, hooting and blaring round the towering cornices of rock.

Towards the end of the day the sky became pale gold. Then, as the sun sank behind the farthest rim of mountains, the world was enveloped in the cool green twilight, and in the dusk the truck roared round the last bend and drew up at the hub of Bafut, the compound of the Fon. To the left lay the vast courtyard, and behind it the clusters of huts in which lived the Fon's wives and children. Dominating them all was the great hut in which dwelt the spirit of his father, and a great many other lesser spirits, looming like a monstrous time-blackened beehive against the jade night sky. To the right of the road, perched on top of a tall bank, was the Fon's rest house, like a two-story Italian villa, stone-built and with a neatly tiled roof. It was shoebox-shaped, and both lower and upper stories were surrounded by wide verandas, festooned with bougainvillaea covered with pink and brick-red flowers.

Wearily we climbed out of the truck and supervised the unloading of the animals and their installation on the top-story veranda. Then the rest of the equipment was unloaded and stored, and while we made vague attempts to wash some of the red dust off our bodies, Phillip seized the remains of his bedding and his box full of cooking utensils and food and marched off to the kitchen quarters in a stiff, brisk way, like a military patrol going to quell a small but irritating insurrection. By the time we had fed the animals he had reappeared with an astonishingly good meal, and having eaten it we fell into bed and slept like the dead.

The next morning, in the cool dawn light, we went to pay our respects to our host, the Fon. We made our way across the great courtyard and plunged into the maze of tiny squares and alleyways formed by the huts of the Fon's wives. Presently we found ourselves in a small courtyard shaded by an immense guava tree, and there was the Fon's own villa, small, neat, stone- and tile-built, with a wide veranda along one side. And there, at the top of the steps that ran up to the veranda, stood my friend the Fon of Bafut.

He stood there, tall and slender, wearing a plain white robe embroidered with blue. On his head was a small skullcap in the same colours. His face was split by the joyous, mischievous grin I knew so well, and he was holding out one enormous slender hand in greeting.

"My friend, *iseeya*," I called, hurrying up the stairs to him.

"Welcome, welcome. You done come. Welcome," he exclaimed, seizing my hand in his huge palm and draping a long arm round my shoulders and patting me affectionately.

"You well, my friend?" I asked, peering up into his face.

"I well, I well," he said, grinning.

It seemed to me to be an understatement: he looked positively blooming. He had been well into his seventies when I had last met him, eight years before, and he appeared to have weathered the intervening years better than I had. I introduced Jacquie, and was quietly amused by the contrast. The Fon, six feet three inches, and appearing taller because of his robes, towered beamingly over Jacquie's five feet one inch, and her hand was as lost as a child's would have been in the depths of his great dusky paw.

"Come, we go for inside," he said, and holding our hands led us into his villa.

The interior was as I remembered it, a cool, pleasant room with leopard skins on the floor, and wooden sofas, beautifully carved, piled high with cushions. We sat down, and one of the Fon's wives came forward carrying a tray with glasses and drinks on it. The Fon splashed scotch into three glasses with a liberal hand, and passed them round, beaming at us. I surveyed the four inches of neat spirit in the bottom of my glass and sighed. I could see that the Fon had not, in my absence, joined the temperance movement, whatever else he had done.

"Chirri-ho!" said the Fon, and downed half the contents of his glass at a gulp. Jacquie and I sipped ours more sedately.

"My friend," I said, "I happy too much I see you again."

"Wah! Happy?" said the Fon. "I get happy for see you. When dey done tell me you come for Cameroon again I get happy too much."

I sipped my drink cautiously. "Some man done tell me that you get angry for me because I done write dat book about dis happy time we done have together before. So I de fear for come back to Bafut," I said.

The Fon scowled. "Which kind of man tell you dis ting?" he inquired furiously.

"Some European done tell me."

"Ah! European," said the Fon, shrugging, as if surprised that I should believe anything told to me by a white person. "Na lies dis."

"Good," I said, greatly relieved. "If I think you get angry for me, my heart no go be happy."

288

"No, no, I no get angry for you," said the Fon, splashing another large measure of scotch into my glass before I could stop him. "Dis book you done write . . . I like um foine. You done make my name go for all de world. Every kind of people 'e know my name. Na foine ting dis."

Once again I realized I had underestimated the Fon's abilities. He had obviously realized that any publicity is better than none. "Look um," he went on, "plenty plenty people come here for Bafut, all different different people, dey all show me dis your book 'e get my name for inside. Na foine ting dis."

"Yes, na fine thing," I agreed, rather shaken. I had had no idea that I had unwittingly turned the Fon into a sort of literary lion.

"Dat time I done go for Nigeria," he said, holding the bottle of scotch up to the light pensively. "Dat time I done go for Lagos to meet dat Queen woman, all dis European dere 'e get dis your book. Plenty, plenty people dey ask me for write dis ma name for inside dis your book."

I gazed at him open-mouthed; the idea of the Fon in Lagos sitting and autographing copies of my book rendered me speechless.

"Did you like the Queen?" asked Jacquie.

"Wah! Like? I like um too much. Na foine woman dat. Na small, small woman, same same for you. But 'e get power, time no dere. Wah! Dat woman get power *plenty.*"

"Did you like Nigeria?" I asked.

"I no like," said the Fon firmly. " 'E hot too much. Sun, sun, sun, I shweat, I shweat. But dis Queen woman she get plenty power. She walker walker she never shweat. Na foine woman dis."

He chuckled reminiscently, and absent-mindedly poured us all out another drink.

"I done give dis Queen," he went on, "dis teeth for elephant. You savvay um?"

"Yes, I savvay um," I said, remembering the magnificent carved tusk the Cameroons

had presented to Her Majesty. "I done give dis teeth for all dis people of Cameroon," he explained. "Dis Queen she sit for some chair an' I go softly softly for give her dis teeth. She take um. Den all dis European dere day say it no be good ting for show your [back] for dis Queen woman, so all de people walker walker backwards. I walker walker backwards. Wah! Na step dere, eh? I de fear I de fall, but I walker walker softly and I never fall . . . but I de fear too much."

He chuckled over the memory of himself backing down the steps in front of the Queen until his eyes filled with tears.

"Nigeria no be good place," he said, "hot too much. I shweat."

At the mention of sweat I saw his eyes fasten pensively on the whisky bottle, so I rose hurriedly to my feet and said that we really ought to be going as we had a lot of unpacking to do.

The Fon walked out into the sunlit courtyard with us, and, holding our hands, peered earnestly down into our faces. "For evening time you go come back," he said, "we go drink, eh?"

"Yes, for evening time we go come," I assured him.

He beamed down at Jacquie. "For evening time I go show you what kind of happy time we get for Bafut," he said.

"Good," said Jacquie, smiling bravely.

The Fon waved his hands in elegant dismissal, and then turned and made his way back into his villa, while we trudged our way back to the rest house.

"I don't think I could face any breakfast after that scotch," said Jacquie.

"But that wasn't drinking," I protested. "That was just a sort of mild *apéritif* to start the day. You wait until tonight."

"Tonight I shan't drink. I'll leave it to you two," said Jacquie firmly. "I shall have one drink and that's all."

After breakfast, while we were attending to the animals, I happened to glance over the veranda rail and noticed on the road below a small group of men approaching the house. When they drew nearer I saw that each of them was carrying either a raffia basket or a calabash with the neck stuffed with green leaves. I could hardly believe that they were bringing animals as soon as this, for generally it takes up to a week for the news to get around and for the hunters to start bringing stuff in. But as I watched them with bated breath they turned off the road and started to climb the long flight of steps up to the veranda, chattering and laughing among themselves. Then, when they reached the top step, they fell silent, and carefully laid their offerings on the ground.

"*Iseeya*, my friends," I said.

"Morning, Masa," they chorused, grinning.

"Na whatee all dis ting?"

"Na beef, sah," they chorused.

"But how you savvay dat I done come for Bafut for buy beef?" I asked, greatly puzzled.

"Eh, Masa, de Fon 'e done tell us," said one of the hunters.

"Good Lord, if the Fon's been spreading the news before we arrived we'll be inundated in next to no time," said Jacquie.

"We're pretty well inundated now," I said, surveying the group of containers at my feet, "and we haven't even unpacked the cages yet. Oh well, I suppose we'll manage. Let's see what they've got." . . .

After dinner we armed ourselves with a bottle of whisky and an abundant supply of cigarettes and, taking our pressure lamp, made our way to the Fon's house. The air was warm and drowsy, full of the scents of wood smoke and sun-baked earth. Crickets tinkled and trilled in the grass verges of the road, and in the gloomy fruit trees around the Fon's great courtyard we could hear the fruit bats honking and flapping their wings among the branches. In the courtyard a group of the Fon's children were standing in a circle clapping their hands and chanting in some sort of game, and away through the

trees in the distance a small drum throbbed like an irregular heartbeat. We made our way through the maze of wives' huts, each lit by the red glow of a cooking fire, each redolent with the smell of roasting yams, frying plantain, stewing meat, or the sharp, pungent smell of dried salt fish. We came presently to the Fon's villa and he was waiting on the steps to greet us, looming large in the gloom, his robe swishing as he shook our hands.

"Welcome, welcome," he said, beaming. "Come, we go for inside."

"I done bring some whisky for make our heart happy," I said, flourishing the bottle as we entered the house.

"Wah! Good, good," said the Fon, chuckling. "Dis whisky na foine ting for make man happy."

He was wearing a wonderful scarlet and yellow robe that glowed like a tiger skin in the soft lamplight, and on one slender wrist was a thick, beautifully carved ivory bracelet. We sat down and waited in silence while the solemn ritual of the pouring of the first drink was observed. Then, when each of us was clutching a tumbler half full of neat whisky, the Fon turned to us, giving his wide, mischievous grin.

"Chirri-*ho!*" he said, raising his glass. "Tonight we go have happy time."

And so began what we were to refer to later as the Evening of the Hangover.

As the level in the whisky bottle fell, the Fon told us once again about his trip to Nigeria, how hot it had been and how much he had "shweated." His praise for the Queen knew no bounds for, as he pointed out, here was he in his own country feeling the heat and yet the Queen did twice the amount of work that he had done and always managed to look cool and charming. I found his lavish and perfectly genuine praise rather extraordinary, for the Fon belonged to a society where women are considered to be nothing more than rather useful beasts of burden.

"You like musica?" inquired the Fon of

Jacquie, the subject of the Nigerian tour now being exhausted.

"Yes," said Jacquie, "I like it very much."

The Fon beamed at her. "You remember dis my musica?" he asked me.

"Yes, I remember. You get musica time no dere, my friend."

The Fon gave a prolonged crow of amusement. "You done write about dis my musica inside dis your book, eh?"

"Yes, that's right."

"And," said the Fon, coming to the point, "you done write about dis dancing an' dis happy time we done have, eh?"

"Yes. All dis dance we done do na fine one."

"You like we go show dis your wife what kind of dance we get here for Bafut?" he inquired, pointing a long forefinger at me.

"Yes, I like too much."

"Foine, foine . . . Come, we go for dancing house," he said, rising to his feet majestically, and stifling a belch with one slender hand. Two of his wives, who had been sitting quietly in the background, rushed forward and seized the tray of drinks and scuttled ahead of us as the Fon led us out of his house and across the compound towards his dancing house.

The dancing house was a great square building, not unlike the average village hall, but with an earth floor and very few and very small windows. At one end of the building was a line of wickerwork armchairs, which constituted a sort of royal enclosure, and on the wall above these were framed photographs of various members of the royal family. As we entered the dancing hall the assembled wives, about forty or fifty of them, uttered the usual greeting, a strange, shrill ululation, caused by yelling loudly and clapping their hands rapidly over their mouths at the same time. The noise was deafening. All the petty councillors there in their brilliant robes clapped their hands as well, and thus added to the general turmoil. Nearly deafened by this greeting, Jacquie and I were

installed in two chairs, one on each side of the Fon. The table of drinks was placed in front of us, and the Fon, leaning back in his chair, surveyed us both with a wide and happy grin.

"Now we go have happy time," he said, and leaning forward poured out half a tumblerful of scotch each from the depths of a virgin bottle that had just been broached.

"Chirri-ho," said the Fon.

"Chin-chin," I said absent-mindedly.

"Na whatee dat?" inquired the Fon interestedly.

"What?" I asked, puzzled.

"Dis ting you say."

"Oh, you mean chin-chin?"

"Yes, yes, dis one."

"It's something you say when you drink."

"Na same same for chirri-ho?" asked the Fon, intrigued.

"Yes, na same same."

He sat silent for a moment, his lips moving, obviously comparing the respective merits of the two toasts. Then he raised his glass again.

"Shin-shin," said the Fon.

"Chirri-ho!" I responded, and the Fon lay back in his chair and went off into a paroxysm of mirth.

By now the band had arrived. It consisted of four youths and two of the Fon's wives, and the instruments consisted of three drums, two flutes, and a calabash filled with dried maize that gave off a pleasant rustling noise similar to a marimba [sic]. They got themselves organized in the corner of the dancing house, and then gave a few experimental rolls on the drums, watching the Fon expectantly. The Fon, having recovered from the joke, barked out an imperious order, and two of his wives placed a small table in the centre of the dance floor and put a pressure lamp on it. The drums gave another expectant roll.

"My friend," said the Fon, "you remember when you done come for Bafut before you done teach me European dance, eh?"

"Yes," I said, "I remember."

It had been at one of the Fon's parties that, having partaken liberally of the Fon's hospitality, I had proceeded to show him, his councillors, and his wives how to do the conga. It had been a riotous success, but I had supposed that in the eight years that had passed the Fon would have forgotten about it.

"I go show you," said the Fon, his eyes gleaming. He barked out another order and about twenty of his wives shuffled out onto the dance floor and formed a circle round the table, each one holding firmly to the waist of the one in front. Then they assumed a strange crouching position, rather like runners at the start of a race, and waited.

"What are they going to do?" whispered Jacquie.

I watched them with an unholy glee. "I do believe," I said dreamily, "that he's been making them dance the conga ever since I left, and we're now going to have a demonstration."

The Fon lifted a large hand and the band launched itself with enthusiasm into a Bafut tune that had the unmistakable conga rhythm. The Fon's wives, still in their strange crouching position, proceeded to circle round the lamp, kicking their black legs out on the sixth beat, their brows furrowed with concentration. The effect was delightful.

"My friend," I said, touched by the demonstration, "dis na fine ting you do."

"Wonderful," agreed Jacquie enthusiastically. "They dance very fine."

"Dis na de dance you done teach me," explained the Fon.

"Yes, I remember."

He turned to Jacquie, chuckling. "Dis man your husband 'e get plenty power. We dance, we dance, we drink. . . . Wah! We done have happy time." The band came to an uneven halt, and the Fon's wives, smiling shyly at our clapping, raised themselves from their crouching position and returned to their former places along the wall. The Fon

barked an order, and a large calabash of palm wine was brought in and distributed among the dancers, each getting her share poured into her cupped hands. Stimulated by this sight, the Fon filled all our glasses up again.

"Yes," he went on, reminiscently, "dis man your husband get plenty power for dance and drink."

"I no get power now," I said. "I be old man now."

"No, no, my friend," said the Fon laughing. "I be old, you be young."

"You look more young now den for the other time I done come to Bafut," I said, and really meant it.

"That's because you've got plenty wives," said Jacquie.

"Wah! No!" said the Fon, shocked. "Dis ma wives tire me too much."

He glared moodily at the array of females standing along the wall, and sipped his drink. "Dis ma wife dey humbug me too much," he went on.

"My husband says I humbug him," said Jacquie.

"Your husband catch lucky. 'E only get one wife, I get plenty," said the Fon, "an' dey de humbug me time no dere."

"But wives are very useful," said Jacquie.

The Fon regarded her sceptically.

"If you don't have wives you can't have babies. Men can't have babies," said Jacquie practically.

The Fon was so overcome with mirth at this remark I thought he might have a stroke. He lay back in his chair and laughed until he cried. Presently he sat up, wiping his eyes, still shaking with gusts of laughter. "Dis woman your wife get brain," he said, still chuckling, and poured Jacquie out an extra-large scotch to celebrate her intelligence. "You be good wife for me," he said, patting her on the head affectionately. "Shin-shin."

The band members now returned, wiping their mouths from some mysterious errand outside the dancing house and, apparently well fortified, launched themselves into one of my favourite Bafut tunes, the butterfly dance. It was a pleasant, lilting little tune, and the Fon's wives now took the floor and did the delightful dance that accompanied it. They danced in a row with minute but complicated hand and foot movements, and then the two that formed the head of the line joined hands, while the one at the farther end of the line whirled up and then fell backwards, to be caught and thrown upright again by the two with linked hands. As the dance progressed and the music got faster and faster the one representing the butterfly whirled more and more rapidly, and the ones with linked hands catapulted her upright again with more and more enthusiasm. Then, when the dance reached its feverish climax, the Fon rose majestically to his feet, amid screams of delight from the audience, and joined the end of the row of dancing wives. He started to whirl down the line, his scarlet and yellow robe turning into a blur of colour, loudly singing the words of the song.

"I dance, I dance, and no one can stop me," he carolled merrily, "but I must take care not to fall to the ground like the butterfly."

He went whirling down the line of wives like a top, his voice booming out above theirs.

"I hope . . . they don't drop him," I said to Jacquie, eyeing the two short, fat wives who, with linked hands, were waiting rather nervously at the head of the line to receive their lord and master.

The Fon performed one last mighty gyration and hurled himself backwards at his wives, who caught him neatly enough, but reeled under the shock. As the Fon landed he spread his arms wide so that for a moment his wives were invisible under the flowing sleeves of his robes and he lay there looking very like a gigantic multicoloured butterfly. He beamed at us, lolling across his wives' arms, his skullcap slightly askew, and then his wives with an effort bounced him back to his

feet again. Grinning and panting, he made his way back to us and hurled himself into his chair.

"My friend, na fine dance dis," I said in admiration, "you get power time no dere."

"Yes," agreed Jacquie, who had also been impressed by this display, "you get plenty power."

"Na good dance dis, na foine one," said the Fon, chuckling and automatically pouring us all out another drink.

"You get another dance here for Bafut I like too much," I said, "dis one where you dance with dat beer-beer for horse."

"Ah, yes, yes, I savvay um," said the Fon. "Dat one where we go dance with dis tail for horshe."

"That's right. Sometime, my friend, you go show dis dance for my wife?"

"Yes, yes, my friend," he said. He leaned forward and gave an order and a wife scuttled out of the dancing hall. The Fon turned and smiled at Jacquie. "Small time dey go bring dis tail for horshe an' den we go dance," he said.

Presently the wife returned, carrying a large bundle of white, silky horses' tails, each about two feet long, fixed in beautifully made handles woven out of leather thongs. The Fon's tail was a particularly long and luxuriant one, and the thongs that had been used to make the handle were dyed blue, red, and gold. The Fon swished it experimentally through the air with languid, graceful movements of his wrist, and the hair rippled and floated like a cloud of smoke before him. Some twenty of the Fon's wives, each armed with their switches, went onto the floor and formed a circle. The Fon walked over and stood in the centre of the circle; he gave a wave of his horse's tail, the band struck up, and the dance was on.

Of all the Bafut dances this horsetail dance was undoubtedly the most sensuous and beautiful. The rhythm was peculiar, the small drums keeping up a sharp, staccato beat, while beneath them the big drums rumbled and muttered and the bamboo flutes squeaked and twittered with a tune that seemed to have nothing to do with the drums and yet merged with it perfectly. To this tune the Fon's wives gyrated slowly in a clockwise direction, their feet performing minute but formalized steps, while they waved the horses' tails gently to and fro across their faces. The Fon, meanwhile, danced round the inside of the circle in a counter-clockwise direction, bobbing, stamping, and twisting in a curiously stiff, unjointed sort of way, while his hand with incredibly supple wrist movements kept his horse's tail weaving through the air in a series of lovely and complicated movements. The effect was odd and almost indescribable; one minute the dancers resembled a bed of white seaweed, moved and rippled by sea movement, and the next minute the Fon would stamp and twist, stiff-legged, like some strange bird with white plumes, absorbed in a ritual dance of courtship among his circle of hens. Watching this slow pavan and the graceful movements of the tails had a curious sort of hypnotic effect, so that even when the dance ended with a roll of drums you could still see the white tails weaving and merging before your eyes.

The Fon moved gracefully across the floor towards us, twirling his horse's tail negligently, and sank into his seat. He beamed breathlessly at Jacquie. "You like dis ma dance?" he asked.

"It was *beautiful*," she said. "I liked it very much."

"Good, good," said the Fon, well pleased. He leaned forward and inspected the whisky bottle hopefully, but it was obviously empty. Tactfully I refrained from mentioning that I had some more over at the rest house. The Fon surveyed the bottle gloomily. "Whisky done finish," he pointed out.

"Yes," I said unhelpfully.

"Well," said the Fon, undaunted, "we go drink gin."

My heart sank, for I had hoped that we could now move on to something innocuous like beer to quell the effects of so much neat alcohol. The Fon roared at one of his wives and she ran off and soon reappeared with a bottle of gin and one of bitters. The Fon's idea of gin-drinking was to pour about half a tumblerful and then colour it a deep brown with bitters. The result was guaranteed to slay an elephant at twenty paces. Jacquie, on seeing this cocktail the Fon concocted for me, hastily begged to be excused, saying that she couldn't drink gin on doctor's orders. The Fon, though obviously having the lowest possible opinion of a medical man who could even suggest such a thing, accepted with good grace.

The band started up again and everyone poured onto the floor and started to dance, singly and in couples. As the rhythm of the tune allowed it, Jacquie and I got up and did a swift foxtrot round the floor, the Fon roaring encouragement and his wives hooting with pleasure.

"Foine, foine," shouted the Fon as we swept past.

"Thank you, my friend," I shouted back, steering Jacquie carefully through what looked like a flower bed of councillors in their multicoloured robes.

"I do wish you wouldn't tread on my feet," said Jacquie plaintively.

"Sorry. My compass bearings are never at their best at this hour of night."

"So I notice," said Jacquie acidly.

"Why don't you dance with the Fon?" I inquired.

"I did think of it, but I wasn't sure whether it was the right thing for a mere woman to ask him."

"I think he'd be tickled pink. Ask him for the next dance," I suggested.

"What can we dance?" asked Jacquie.

"Teach him something he can add to his Latin American repertoire," I said. "How about a rumba?"

"I think a samba would be easier to learn at this hour of night," said Jacquie. So when the dance ended we made our way back to where the Fon was sitting, topping up my glass.

"My friend," I said, "you remember dis European dance I done teach you when I done come for Bafut before?"

"Yes, yes, na foine one," he replied, beaming.

"Well, my wife like to dance with you and teach you other European dance. You agree?"

"Wah!" bellowed the Fon in delight. "Foine, foine. Dis your wife go teach me. Foine, foine, I agree."

Eventually we discovered a tune that the band could play that had a vague samba rhythm, and Jacquie and the Fon rose to their feet, watched breathlessly by everyone in the room.

The contrast between the Fon's six foot three and Jacquie's five foot one made me choke over my drink as they took the floor. Very rapidly Jacquie showed him the simple, basic steps of the samba, and to my surprise the Fon mastered them without trouble. Then he seized Jacquie in his arms and they were off. The delightful thing from my point of view was that as he clasped Jacquie tightly to his bosom she was almost completely hidden by his flowing robes, so at some points in the dance she could not be seen at all and it looked as though the Fon, having mysteriously grown another pair of feet, were dancing round by himself. There was something else about the dance that struck me as curious, but I could not think what it was for some time. Then I suddenly realized that Jacquie was leading the Fon. They sambaed past, both grinning at me, obviously enjoying themselves.

"You dance fine, my friend," I shouted. "My wife done teach you fine."

"Yes, yes," roared the Fon over the top of Jacquie's head. "Na foine dance dis. Your wife na good wife for me."

Eventually, after half an hour's dancing, they returned to their chairs, hot and exhausted. The Fon took a large gulp of neat gin to restore himself, and then leaned across to me.

"Dis your wife na foine," he said in a hoarse whisper, presumably thinking that praise might turn Jacquie's head. "She dance foine. She done teach me foine. I go give her mimbo. Special mimbo I go give her."

I turned to Jacquie who, unaware of her fate, was sitting fanning herself. "You've certainly made a hit with our host," I said.

"He's a dear old boy," said Jacquie, "and he dances awfully well. Did you see how he picked up that samba in next to no time?"

"Yes," I said, "and he was so delighted with your teaching that he's going to reward you."

Jacquie looked at me supiciously. "How's he going to reward me?" she asked.

"You're now going to receive a calabash of special mimbo—palm wine."

"Oh . . . and I can't stand the stuff," said Jacquie in horror.

"Never mind. Take a glassful, taste it, tell him it's the finest you've ever had, and then ask if he will allow you to share it with his wives."

Five calabashes were brought, each with the neck plugged with green leaves, and the Fon solemnly tasted them all before making up his mind which was the best vintage. Then a glass was filled and passed to Jacquie. Summoning up all her social graces, she took a mouthful, rolled it round her mouth, swallowed, and allowed a look of intense satisfaction to appear on her face. "This is very fine mimbo," she proclaimed in delighted astonishment, with the air of one who has just been presented with a glass of Napoleon brandy. The Fon beamed. Jacquie took another sip, as he watched her closely. An even more delighted expression appeared on her face. "This is the best mimbo I've ever tasted," said Jacquie.

"Ha! Good!" said the Fon. "Dis na foine mimbo. Na fresh one."

"Will you let your wives drink with me?" asked Jacquie.

"Yes, yes," said the Fon with a lordly wave of his hand, and so the wives shuffled forward, grinning shyly, and Jacquie hastily poured the remains of the mimbo into their pink palms.

At this point, the level of the gin bottle having fallen alarmingly, I suddenly glanced at my watch and saw, with horror, that in two and a half hours it would be dawn. So, pleading heavy work on the morrow, I broke up the party. The Fon insisted on accompanying us to the foot of the steps that led up to the rest house, preceded by the band. Here he embraced us fondly.

"Good night, my friend," he said, shaking my hand.

"Good night," I replied. "Thank you. You done give us happy time."

"Yes," said Jacquie. "Thank you very much."

"Wah!" said the Fon, patting her on the head. "We done dance foine. You be good wife for me, eh?"

We watched him as he wended his way across the great courtyard, tall and graceful in his robes, the boy trotting beside him carrying the lamp that cast a pool of golden light about him. They disappeared into the tangle of huts, and the twittering of the flutes and the bang of the drums became fainter and died away, until all we could hear was the calls of crickets and tree frogs and the faint honking cries of the fruit bats. Somewhere in the distance the first cock crowed, huskily and sleepily, as we crept under our mosquito nets.

For Discussion

1 Reread the first paragraph. Does the author have a good eye and a good memory for details? Does he use any clichés? Are there any places where he appears to be straining for an effect? Or does his purpose seem to be to allow the reader to share his experience?

2 Do you think that if you had ever passed through this same African landscape you would be able to describe it as well? Why or why not?

3 Is the author good at describing the way the Fon speaks? After you become familiar with his brand of English do you begin to hear its intonations? Obviously the Fon does not speak "standard" English. But does he have any trouble in making himself understood? Point to some places where you find his English particularly expressive or charming.

4 What kind of society does the author find in Bafut? Are some of the tensions of our own society missing? Why?

5 At the time of the Durrells visit the Fon must have been about eighty years old. How does his behavior differ from what we expect to find in someone of that age? What qualities has he been able to keep which most older people lose?

6 How would you describe the attitude of the author toward the Fon? Does he seem genuinely to consider him a friend? How have these two men, Durrell and the Fon, been able to bridge the extreme cultural gap between them?

Tagore was equally at home in India and in England. During his long life he acted as a kind of cultural go-between for Eastern and Western cultures, interpreting each for the other.

Tagore also translated a great deal of Indian literature, including his own poetry, into English.

In this essay Tagore talks about some of the differences between East and West, and also about the forces which prevent human understanding and creative development.

Rabindranath Tagore

East and West

I

It is not always a profound interest in man that carries travelers nowadays to distant lands. More often it is the facility for rapid movement. For lack of time and for the sake of convenience we generalize and crush our human facts into the packages within the steel trunks that hold our traveler's reports.

Our knowledge of our own countrymen and our feelings about them have slowly and unconsciously grown out of innumerable facts which are full of contradictions and subject to incessant change. They have the elusive mystery and fluidity of life. We cannot define to ourselves what we are as a whole, because we know too much; because our knowledge is more than knowledge. It is an immediate consciousness of personality, any evaluation of which carries some emotion, joy or sorrow, shame or exaltation. But in a foreign land we try to find our compensation for the meagerness of our data by the compactness of the generalizaton which our imperfect sympathy itself helps us to form. When a stranger from the West travels in the Eastern world he takes the facts that displease him and readily makes use of them for his rigid conclusions, fixed upon the unchallengeable authority of his personal experience. It is like a man who has his own boat for crossing his village stream, but, on being compelled to wade across some strange watercourse, draws angry comparisons as he goes from every patch of mud and every pebble which his feet encounter.

Our mind has faculties which are universal, but its habits are insular. There are men who become impatient and angry at the least discomfort when their habits are incommoded. In their idea of the next world they probably conjure up the ghosts of their slippers and dressing-gowns, and expect the latchkey that opens their lodging-house door on earth to fit their front door in the other world. As travelers they are a failure; for they have grown too accustomed to their mental easy-chairs, and in their intellectual nature love home comforts, which are of local make, more than the realities of life, which, like earth itself, are full of ups and downs, yet are one in their rounded completeness.

The modern age has brought the geography of the earth near to us, but made it difficult for us to come into touch with man. We go to strange lands and observe; we do not live there. We hardly meet men: but only specimens of knowledge. We are in haste to seek for general types and overlook individuals.

When we fall into the habit of neglecting to use the understanding that comes of sympathy in our travels, our knowledge of foreign people grows insensitive, and therefore easily becomes both unjust and cruel in its character, and also selfish and contemptuous in its application. Such has, too often, been the case with regard to the meeting of Western people in our days with others for whom they do not recognize any obligation of kinship.

It has been admitted that the dealings between different races of men are not merely between individuals; that our mutual understanding is either aided, or else obstructed, by the general emanations forming the social atmosphere. These emanations are our collective ideas and collective feelings, generated according to special historical circumstances.

For instance, the caste-idea is a collective idea in India. When we approach an Indian who is under the influence of this collective idea, he is no longer a pure individual with his conscience fully awake to the judging of the value of a human being. He is more or less a passive medium for giving expression to the sentiment of a whole community.

It is evident that the caste-idea is not creative; it is merely institutional. It adjusts human beings according to some mechanical arrangement. It emphasizes the negative side of the individual—his separateness. It hurts the complete truth in man.

In the West, also, the people have a certain collective idea that obscures their humanity. Let me try to explain what I feel about it.

II

Lately I went to visit some battlefields of France which had been devastated by war. The awful calm of desolation, which still bore wrinkles of pain—death-struggles stiffened into ugly ridges—brought before my mind the vision of a huge demon, which had no shape, no meaning, yet had two arms that could strike and break and tear, a gaping mouth that could devour, and bulging brains that could conspire and plan. It was a purpose, which had a living body, but no complete humanity to temper it. Because it was passion—belonging to life, and yet not having the wholeness of life—it was the most terrible of life's enemies.

Something of the same sense of oppression in a different degree, the same desolation in a different aspect, is produced in my mind when I realize the effect of the West upon Eastern life—the West which, in its relation to us, is all plan and purpose incarnate, without any superfluous humanity.

I feel the contrast very strongly in Japan. In that country the old world presents itself with some ideal of perfection, in which man has his varied opportunities of self-revelation in art, in ceremonial, in religious faith, and in customs expressing the poetry of social relationship. There one feels that deep delight of hospitality which life offers to life. And side by side, in the same soil, stands the modern world, which is stupendously big and powerful, but inhospitable. It has no simple-hearted welcome for man. It is living; yet the incompleteness of life's ideal within it cannot but hurt humanity.

The wriggling tentacles of a cold-blooded utilitarianism, with which the West has grasped all the easily yielding succulent portions of the East, are causing pain and indignation throughout the Eastern countries. The West comes to us, not with the imagination and sympathy that create and unite, but with a shock of passion—passion for power and wealth. This passion is a mere force, which has in it the principle of separation, of conflict.

I have been fortunate in coming into close touch with individual men and women of the Western countries, and have felt with them their sorrows and shared their aspirations. I have known that they seek the same God, who is my God—even those who deny Him. I feel certain that, if the great light of culture be extinct in Europe, our horizon in the East will mourn in darkness. It does not hurt my pride to acknowledge that, in the present age, Western humanity has received its mission to be the teacher of the world; that her science, through the mastery of laws of nature, is to liberate human souls from the dark dungeon of matter. For this very reason I have realized all the more strongly, on the other hand, that the dominant collective idea in the Western countries is not creative. It is ready to enslave or kill individuals, to drug a great people with soul-killing poison, darkening their whole future with the black mist of stupefaction, and emasculating entire races of men to the utmost degree of helplessness. It is wholly wanting in spiritual power to blend and harmonize; it lacks the sense of the great personality of man.

The most significant fact of modern days is this, that the West has met the East. Such a momentous meeting of humanity, in order to be fruitful, must have in its heart some great emotional idea, generous and creative.

There can be no doubt that God's choice has fallen upon the knights-errant of the West for the service of the present age; arms and armor have been given to them; but have they yet realized in their hearts the single-minded loyalty to their cause which can resist all temptations of bribery from the devil? The world to-day is offered to the West. She will destroy it, if she does not use it for a great creation of man. The materials for such a creation are in the hands of science; but the creative genius is in Man's spiritual ideal.

III

When I was young, a stranger from Europe came to Bengal. He chose his lodging among the people of the country, shared with them their frugal diet, and freely offered them his service. He found employment in the houses of the rich, teaching them French and German, and the money thus earned he spent to help poor students in buying books. This meant for him hours of walking in the mid-day heat of a tropical summer; for, intent upon exercising the utmost economy, he refused to hire conveyances. He was pitiless in his exaction from himself of his resources, in money, time, and strength, to the point of privation; and all this for the sake of a people who were obscure, to whom he was not born, yet whom he dearly loved. He did not come to us with a professional mission of teaching sectarian creeds; he had not in his nature the least trace of that self-sufficiency of goodness, which humiliates by gifts the victims of its insolent benevolence. Though he did not know our language, he took every occasion to frequent our meetings and ceremonies; yet he was always afraid of intrusion, and tenderly anxious lest he might offend us by his ignorance of our customs. At last, under the continual strain of work in an alien climate and surroundings, his health broke down. He died, and was cremated at our burning ground, according to his express desire.

The attitude of his mind, the manner of his living, the object of his life, his modesty, his unstinted self-sacrifice for a people who had not even the power to give publicity to any benefaction bestowed upon them, were so utterly unlike anything we were accustomed to associate with the Europeans in India, that it gave rise in our mind to a feeling of love bordering upon awe.

We all have a realm, a private paradise, in our mind, where dwell deathless memories of persons who brought some divine light to our life's experience, who may not be known to others, and whose names have no place in the pages of history. Let me confess to you that this man lives as one of those immortals in the paradise of my individual life.

He came from Sweden, his name was Hammargren. What was most remarkable in the event of his coming to us in Bengal was the fact that in his own country he had chanced to read some works of my great countryman, Ram Mohan Roy, and felt an immense veneration for his genius and his character. Ram Mohan Roy lived in the beginning of the last century, and it is no exaggeration when I describe him as one of the immortal personalities of modern time. This young Swede had the unusual gift of a far-sighted intellect and sympathy, which enabled him even from his distance of space and in spite of racial differences, to realize the greatness of Ram Mohan Roy. It moved him so deeply that he resolved to go to the country which produced this great man, and offer her his service. He was poor, and he had to wait some time in England before he could earn his passage money to India. There he came at last, and in reckless generosity of love utterly spent himself to the last breath of his life, away from home and kindred and all the inheritances of his motherland. His stay among us was too short to produce any outward result. He failed even to achieve during his life what he had in mind, which was to found by the help of his scanty earnings a library as a memorial to Ram Mohan Roy, and thus to leave behind him a visible symbol of his devotion. But what I prize most in this European youth, who left no record of his life behind him, is not the memory of any service of goodwill, but the precious gift of respect which he offered to a people who are fallen upon evil times, and whom it is so easy to ignore or to humiliate. For the first time in the modern days this obscure individual from Sweden brought to our country the chivalrous courtesy of the West, a greeting of human fellowship.

The coincidence came to me with a great and delightful surprise when the Nobel prize was offered to me from Sweden. As a recognition of individual merit it was of great value to me, no doubt; but it was the acknowledgment of the East as a collaborator with the Western continents, in contributing its riches to the common stock of civilization, which had the chief significance for the present age. It meant joining hands in comradeship by the two great hemispheres of the human world across the sea.

For Discussion

1 After India gained its independence from England the caste system was legally abolished. However, law is one thing and tradition another, and the caste system persists in spite of official disapproval. In this essay Tagore clearly expresses his disapproval of the caste system. What reasons does he give for opposing it?

2 What does Tagore admire in Western culture?

3 What aspects of the West does Tagore fear the most? Of what does he disapprove strongly?

4 In the first two sections of the essay Tagore sets forth some general propositions about the relationship between East and West and about the uses of power. In the third section he tells a story; he gives a biographical sketch of his young friend Hammargren. This young Swede's life becomes for Tagore a symbol of what the relation between East and West should be. What qualities in Hammargren does he admire? How does Hammargren's behavior in India serve as an example for the West?

Members of minority groups and immigrants from other countries often find themselves with divided loyalties. How much of their own culture must they hide? How much of the mainstream culture may they adopt without losing their true selves?

"The Oyster" concerns an Indian student, Gopal, who has been raised as a Hindu. He has come to live and study in Paris. He is torn between his own heritage and the temptations of Western civilization. To eat or not to eat an oyster or a chicken—to one who is not a Hindu it may seem a trivial matter. Yet Gopal's choice may determine the direction the rest of his life will take.

Rumer Godden

The Oyster

"To travel is to broaden the mind." Tooni, Gopal's sister-in-law, had told him that, but, thought Gopal, the mind can become so broad that it suddenly becomes a wild prairie in which it cannot hope to find its way.

"When in Rome, do as the Romans do."

"To thine own self be true . . ."

Which?

Tooni loved axioms; she had taught Gopal these two as well, she had "instilled them," murmured Gopal. Gopal earnestly intended to believe everything he was told, he knew that Tooni was sensible and wise, but now, suddenly, in this restaurant in Paris his mind had become a howling wilderness. "When in Rome . . ." "To thine own self . . ." Which? He was not old enough to see that by his travels and experiences, he was taking the only possible first step to reconcile these conflicts, by beginning to find out what he was himself.

Gopal was a sweet, naïve, young Indian student, almost breathless with goodwill; yet he was dignified. René Desmoulins, the witty, dark, French, senior-year student, reading English at the University, had seen the dignity and especially marked Gopal out, though he was twenty-three to Gopal's nineteen. Everyone was kind to the young Indian. Gopal was charming to look at; his body was tall and slim and balanced, his teeth and eyes were beautiful and his face was so quick and ingenuous that it showed every shade of feeling; they teased him about that but now he suddenly knew he was not as ingenuous as they, or he, had thought; he had come across something in himself that was stronger than his will or his desire to please. "Aaugh!" shuddered Gopal.

Up to this evening, that should have been the most delightful of all, everything had been delightful. "Delightful" was Gopal's word. "London is delightful," he wrote home. "The College is delightful, Professor William Morgan is delightful and so is Mrs. Morgan and the little Morgans, but perhaps," he added with pain, for he had to admit that the Morgan children were rough and spoilt, "perhaps not *as* delightful if you see them for a very long time. . . . The Hostel is delightful. . . . I find my work delightful." He had planned to write home that Paris was delightful. "We went to a famous French restaurant in the Rue Perpignan"; he had meant to write, "it is called the *Chez Perpignan*. It is de——" Now tears made his dark eyes bright; he could not write that; it was not delightful at all.

Through his tears he seemed to see far beyond the white starched tablecloth marked "Perpignan" in a red cotton laundry-mark, beyond the plates and glasses, the exciting bottle of wine of which he had asked to inspect the label after the waiter had shown it to René. He saw beyond the single scarlet carnation in the vase on the table, beyond everything in the restaurant that had thrilled him as they came in; the dark-brown walls with their famous old theatre posters—"French printed in French" Gopal had exclaimed as if he had not really believed that French could be printed—the serving-table where a flame burnt under a silver dish and a smell rose into the air mingling with other strange and, to him, piquant smells, of hot china plates, starch, coffee, toast, old wine-spills, food and clothes. He saw, beyond them all, the low tables spread for dinner at home, one of the dinners that he had always thought most ordinary, old-fashioned and dull, prepared by his mother and Tooni. Gopal's

family lived in Bengal; they were Brahmin Hindus and his mother kept the household to orthodox ways in spite of all he and his elder brother could do; now Gopal saw her orthodox food: the flat brass platters of rice, the pile of *luchis*—flaky, puffed, pale-gold biscuits—the vegetable fritters fried crisp, the great bowl of lentil purée and the small accompanying bowls of relishes, shredded coconut or fried onion, or spinach or chillis in tomato sauce or chutney, all to be put on the rice. He saw fruit piled on banana leaves, the bowl of fresh curd, the milk or orange or bael-fruit juice in the silver drinking tumblers; no meat, nor fish, not even eggs were eaten in that house, "we shall not take life," said his mother. Gopal looked down at his plate in the Perpignan and shuddered.

He had come to Europe with shining intentions, eager, anxious to do as the Romans did, as the English, the French, as Romans everywhere. "There will be things you will not be able to stomach," he had been warned; so far he had stomached everything. His elder brother Jai had been before him and had come back utterly accustomed to everything Western; when Jai and Tooni went out to dinner they had Western dishes; they ate meat, even beef, but not in their own home; "Not while I live," said his mother, and she had told Gopal, "You are not the same as Jai. You are not as coarse."

"Oh I am, Mother," Gopal had pleaded. "I am just as coarse," but now another shudder shook him.

"Are you cold, Gopal-ji?" asked René. Gopal had taught René the endearment, he had thrilled to hear him use it and even now he managed to smile, though in truth even his lips were cold. "I am not at all cold," lied Gopal, "this is . . . delightful."

If it had been the cold that upset him it would have been nothing; all Indians were supposed to feel the cold. Gopal did not mind the lack of sun, the grey rain, though several things were very strange to him; the perpetual wearing of shoes, for instance, made his feet ache but he had liked his feet to ache; he had been proud of them when they ached, he felt they were growing wise. Now he wriggled his toes in his shoes under the table and would have given anything to be sitting with bare sunwarmed feet, and a feeling that he had not had all this time abroad welled up in him; he felt sick, sick for home.

He saw his own family front door, with the family shoes dropped down in a row at the entrance; he saw the hall, empty of everything but a rickety hat-rack that never had a hat hung on it; how could it? They wore no hats. He thought how he would come in, drop off his shoes on the step, and go to the tap to wash and take off his shirt, calling out to his mother and Tooni in a lordly way, "Isn't there anything to eat in this house?" His mother, who never knew a joke when she heard one, would begin to shoo the maid-servant and Tooni about and hurry them and presently Tooni would bring him a few sweets in a saucer to keep him quiet.

"O Soul, be patient, thou shalt find
a little matter mend all this,"

Tooni would say, and she would add, "That is by Robert Bridges. Bridges was once Poet Laureate of England." Tooni was always anxious to improve her little brother-in-law.

In Europe Gopal had eaten everything. "Roast lamb, kidneysontoast, baconandsausage," murmured Gopal, and when René, who, being a Frenchman, had a proper feeling for food, had talked of the food they would eat in Paris Gopal had not flinched though some of it sounded rather startling to him; "Rather *bare*," he had written to Tooni. "Imagine suckling-pig, Tooni," he had written, "and René says it is laid out *whole* on the dish; *tête de veau*, and that is calf's head with its eyes and its brain all there. He says we shall have steak, rare, I don't know what that means but I shall find out, and oysters, I shall eat oysters. What

are oysters? I shall find out. I shall come back more Parisian than Paris!"

René, the dazzling, elderly René, had asked Gopal home with him to Paris for the vacation. "It is a delightful *compliment*," Gopal wrote, "and, let me tell you, there are not many he would ask but he asked me!"

René, with his brilliance, his terse quick wit, his good looks, his ruthlessness and his foreignness, was venerated by the students and a little feared by the masters which made him all the more popular and, when he was kind to Gopal, Gopal was completely dazzled. "You are too good to me," he gasped and, shyly, "You must love me very much." René had the grace not to laugh at him. "You do not know *how* delightful he is!" wrote Gopal to his mother, and to Tooni he wrote, "René is like Hamlet, only humorous; like Byron, only good." He looked at these two comparisons and their qualifications; they seemed to come out null and void and he tried again. "He is like Jesus Christ," he wrote reverently, "only very, very sophisticated." For René, Gopal would have made one of those pilgrimages sometimes made by the devout in India when, at every step, the pilgrim measures his length in the dust.

On that thought Gopal realized how much he missed the dust. What a funny thing to miss, he thought, but he missed the dust. He wriggled his toes uncomfortably in his shoes and thought he could even smell the dust of his own great Bengal town. It seemed to rise in his nostrils as he looked out of the restaurant window; across the Paris twilight and its multitudinous lights, he seemed to see the small oil-flares of the orange-sellers' booths on a certain narrow pavement near his home. He heard the car horns, not Paris horns but the continuous horns of the Sikh taxi-drivers; he heard bicycle-rickshaw bells, the shuffling feet and the pattering noise as a flock of goats was driven by and he wanted to go home, past the white oleander bushes by the gate, past the rows of shoes, up to his own small room where on moonlight nights the shadow of the fig-tree and the bars of his barred window were thrown together on the whitewashed wall. How many nights had he lain on his bed and watched the shadow-leaves move, stir gently in the heat, as he had wondered about going away far over the sea to travel in Europe, in England and, yes, in France? And now in France he thought, as he had never thought he could think, of that small room at home and the tears stung his eyes again.

René saw the tears and was concerned. Under the terseness and the sophistication René was simple and young and kind. "What is it, Gopal-ji?" he asked.

"I . . . swallowed . . . something hot," said Gopal.

"But you are used to hot things."

"Yes, chillis," said Gopal and laughed but it was not safe to think of such homely things as chillis; they made him see a string of them, scarlet, in the kitchen. He saw the kitchen; and his mother's housekeeping, which had often seemed to him old-fashioned and super-stitious, now seemed as simple and pure as a prayer; as . . . as uncruel, he thought. His mother rose at five and woke the children so that they could make their morning ritual to the sun; many and many a time had she gently pulled him, Gopal, sleepy and warm and lazy, from his bed. She saw that the house was cleaned, then did the accounts and then, still early, sent Jai, as the eldest son, to market with the list of household things to buy and the careful allowance of money (few Indian women shopped in the market). When Jai came back, with a coolie boy carry-ing a basket on his head, the basket had a load of vegetables, pale-green lettuce and lady's-fingers perhaps, or glossy, purple au-bergines, beans, the pearly paleness of Indian corn still in its sheaf. The basket held coco-nut too, ghee-butter and the inevitable pot of curd made fresh that day. The kitchen was very clean; no one was allowed to go there in shoes or in their street clothes. Before

Gopal and Jai ate they washed and changed or took off their shirts; the women ate apart, even the go-ahead Tooni. All was modesty, cleanliness, quiet, and it did no hurt, thought Gopal shuddering. All of it had an inner meaning so that it was not . . . not just of earth, he thought. Once a month was house-hold day when the pots and pans and sweep-ing brushes were consecrated; first they were cleaned, the brass scoured with wood-ash until it shone pale gold, the silver made bright, the brushes and dusting-cloths washed, cupboards turned out, everything washed again in running water and dried in the sun; then prayers were said for the household tools, and marigold flowers and jessamine were put on the shelves. I used to think it was stupid, thought Gopal, I teased my mother and called her ignorant to believe in such things but they made it all different; quite different.

"Gopal, what *is* the matter?" asked René and he laid his hand on Gopal's.

In India it is usual for young men who are friends to hold hands; for René to take Gopal's hand would have filled him with pride half an hour ago; now he flinched, and the intelligent René felt him flinch and took his own hand away and looked at Gopal closely. "Explain what it is," suggested René gently, but Gopal shook his head. He could not explain; how could he tell René that, for the first time, he saw not what the world did to Gopal but what he, Gopal, did to the world.

Last night he had found out what *rare* steak is; he had cut the meat red and eaten it, only thinking of the redness going in to him and wondering if he could get it down, could "stomach" it; now, suddenly, every-thing was in reverse. René had ordered the famous oysters and Gopal had looked so doubtfully at the plate of grey-brown shells and the strange, glutinous, greenish objects in each, that René had laughed. "Pepper one, squeeze a little lemon on it and let it slide down your throat," said René. He showed Gopal and Gopal had copied him but, when Gopal squeezed the lemon juice on his oyster, he had seen the oyster shrink.

"But . . . but it's alive ! ! !"

"Of course it's alive. It would be dangerous to eat it otherwise. If they served you a dead oyster," René had said gravely, "I should have to take it out and show it to a policeman." Seeing Gopal's face, he said, "Don't worry, it will die as soon as it touches you."

"Auhaugh!" said Gopal.

René had laughed. Now, remembering that, Gopal seethed with rage; his ears were burning, his cheeks and his heart. The plate with the oysters seemed to swim in front of him. Centuries of civilization, of learning, of culture, to culminate in this!

"What *is* the matter?"

"You are a barbarian," said Gopal in a low, burning voice. He trembled to speak like this to René but he spoke. "Your ancestors were running about in blue skins," said Gopal, "when mine had religion, a way of life." For a moment he stopped; René, in a blue skin, would look like Krishna; Krishna, the Hindu God, often had a blue skin, he played the flute and was the God of Love and had many amiable peccadilloes, but Gopal hardened his heart against René, even in his most lovable aspects. It was this learning, this culture, this barbarism, that he had come all this way to share. I want to go home, thought Gopal. I want to go home.

"You all think we Indians should study your customs, why don't you study ours?" he cried to René. "We could teach you a thing or two! Why should we have to Westernize? Why don't you Easternize? It would do you a lot of good, let me tell you that. You are cruel," cried Gopal. "You are not even honest. In England they teach children, 'Little Lamb, who made thee?' and give them the roast lamb for lunch, lamb with mint sauce. Yes! you eat lamb and little pigs and birds. You are cruel. Cruel and barbarous and

greedy and . . ." he broke off, trying to think of the world he wanted; it meant "too much," ah yes! a dozen dozen, thought Gopal and hurled the word at René. "You are *gross!*" he cried, and stopped. Though he was sitting down even his legs were trembling. The effort had left him weak. "You are gross," he said in a whisper.

"You are perfectly right," said René. He put another oyster down his throat but there was something so mild, so tempered in his reply that Gopal was checked.

"These are things," said René when he had finished the oyster, "that a man has to arrange for himself."

It was not only a small rebuke, it was a suggestion made as Tooni would have made it, but of course Tooni was not as subtle and delicate as René, the same René who was now preparing to eat the last oyster on his plate; and he had a dozen, thought Gopal, when I had ordered only six! Subtle, delicate René, who was gross and delicate, fastidious and greedy, ruthless and mild. Gopal shook his head in despair.

"Travel broadens the mind." Then if it is broad, thought Gopal, it has to include all sorts of things; he looked at René's hand, putting pepper and squeezing the lemon, that clever, cruel hand. The world, when it was opened out, was not delightful; no, not delightful at all, thought Gopal. It had a bitter taste; he did not like it.

"When in Rome, do as the Romans do." René was a Roman of Romans; now, with grace and elegance, he slid the oyster down his throat and smiled at Gopal. René agreed that he was not delightful; he was content not to be; no, not content, thought Gopal, looking at him; he knows that he cannot hope to be, all of him, delightful. And if René can't, thought Gopal in despair, who can? Excepting . . . Well, it is easy if you stay in one place, like your mother's kitchen, but if you go into Rome?

He thought of that steak, *rare*; he had

eaten it and now in his mind there was a vision of the sacred bull that came every day to their house to be fed; he saw its soft, confident nose, its noble face and the eyes lustrous with thick, soft eye lashes; its cream dewlap swung like a fold of heavy velvet and it wore a cap worked in blue and white beads on its hump; Gopal had saved up to buy that cap with his own money.

"To thine own self . . ." Tooni seemed very far away. Gopal turned away his head.

At that moment, René having beckoned, the waiter came and took the plate of oysters away.

"Now what shall we eat?" asked René, and he asked, "Have you ever tasted *vol-au-vent?*"

"How strange! It sounds like hitting balls at tennis," said Gopal, beginning to revive.

"It isn't tennis, it's chicken," said René. "Would you like to try it?"

"Chicken . . . ?" The word seemed to hang in the balance, then Gopal asked, "Is it new? Is it exciting?"

"Well." René could not say *vol-au-vent* was exciting. "You may like it."

"Nothing venture, nothing win," said Gopal, and René gave the order to the waiter.

"This is delightful," said Gopal.

For Discussion

1 "When in Rome, do as the Romans do" and "This above all: to thine own self be true" are two mottos which contradict each other. Yet Gopal attempts to reconcile the two within himself. Does he accomplish this? How do these two mottos reflect the conflict in the story?

2 Gilbert Highet, an American scholar, has written that Westerners have a difficult time understanding Eastern cultures because the Eastern traditions represent a much more mature civilization. Does this story support Highet's remark? How?

3 Is Gopal right in calling René a barbarian? Why is eating oysters so repulsive to Gopal?

4 What do you learn about everyday Indian life in this story? Is it appealing? Hurried? Ambitious? As reflected in this story, how does the Indian way of life differ from your own? Are there any aspects of it you would like to adopt?

5 Is Gopal's final choice (eating *vol-au-vent*) a victory or a defeat? Heroism or cowardice? How would you evaluate Gopal's action?

Within the boundaries of a single nation there can be conflicts between cultures, and sometimes one culture can be completely wiped out by the ruthlessness of the other. The Soviet Union is a vast country welded together from peoples of many races. After the Revolution of 1917 there continued to be small civil wars in Russia until finally the ruling Bolsheviks came into complete control of the country. Boris Pasternak's novel *Dr. Zhivago* presents a picture of the savage methods used by the Bolsheviks to stamp out all rivals. This same conflict is sharply portrayed in "The Wizard."

The forces led by the shrewd divisional commander represent the "regular" army, the Communist government. The forces led by Batko Gonchar are irregular guerilla forces from the Ukraine. The conflict is cultural as well as political: the divisional commander is a "new" man. He has no time for the "superstitious" faith that Batko Gonchar's men have in their wizard. Yet he promises them: "Your customs will not be disturbed in any manner." The simple faith of Batko Gonchar's men is touching, and the final scene of the story, in which their faith is put to the test, is one of great power.

Alexander Stepanovich Yakovlev

The Wizard

At night the three deputies finally arrived. They were young mouzhiks,[1] with bristling mustaches, stalwart as stallions, slow-going, with craftiness in their eyes, calculating, and very sparing of speech. They looked over every man on the staff inquisitively, yet sought to conceal their inquisitiveness—their sidelong glances, like the glances of thieves, seeming to frisk one and making not only an individual uneasy but breeding general uneasiness. They wore, all three of them, short gray overcoats of Ukrainian cut and towering shakoes with crowns of raspberry-hued velvet. The oldest of the three had gold braid running around the crown of his shako. It was he, the oldest one, who opened the parley.

"Greetings, once again! There, you have called us, and we have come to see you."

As for the other two, they simply doffed their shakoes, bowed, and muttered: "Greetings!"

"Sit down, comrades, I beg of you," the divisional commander invited them amiably and, standing up, indicated by sweeping gestures the broad benches running along the walls. Cheerful, animated, wide awake, he opened his silver cigarette-case and held it out to them—opened it with an air as if it were no mere cigarette-case but his own heart, brimming over with love for these sturdy lads with bristling mustaches.

"I'm ever so happy to welcome such worthy knights as yourselves, my dear comrades.

1 mouzhiks *Ukrainian peasants.*

I've been looking a long while for some means of combining with you. It hurts me very much that we're wasting our strength, even though we're fighting for the very same cause. We ought to join forces, comrades."

He spoke rather emotionally, with so much sincerity that the deputies exchanged glances of suspicion, and because of this exchange the commander caught on that they did not believe him. Whereupon he began to speak plainly, his sincerity no longer assumed. He put the proposition baldly:

"Let's join forces, then! State your terms."

The deputies were silent for a while. Again they exchanged glances. It was the oldest who began speaking, and this time in Russian, dropping his Ukrainian *mova*, his native dialect:

"Well, our terms are——"

The doughty men of Batko Gonchar (Dad Potter) would join the Red Division if they could retain the same command and the same customs which they enjoyed right now. That was point one. And the second point was that the Reds supply them with machine-guns, rifles and cartridges without delay.

"Comrades!" the division commander exclaimed, and this time his sincerity was staggering. "We find your terms quite satisfactory. Your commanders will remain in their posts. Your customs will not be interfered with in any manner. Your basic conditions are accepted——"

The deputies exchanged looks, as if they were asking one another: "Should we believe him, or shouldn't we?"

"Let's work out the details," said the commander, and signalled to his clerk, who had been huddling in a corner of the hut. The clerk hastily placed pencils and a sheet of blank paper on the table.

Toward morning the terms were worked out, and toward evening the detachment of Batko Gonchar, in full force, was entering the settlement of Peredbrody (Forenenst-the-Fords), where it was solemnly met by the Red division. The commander of that division and his full staff—all of them on horseback—were lined up on the square next to the church, awaiting their welcome guests. The fighters had ranged themselves in close ranks, stretching far into the wide main street of the settlement, where behind the wattle-fences one could glimpse the white walls of clay-daubed huts and dense greenery. The staff officers astride their horses were softly laughing among themselves. They were discussing the ease with which the unification had been put through.

"I told them: 'We'll let you have the stuff,' but they wouldn't believe me," the divisional commander was saying. " 'We'll let you have the stuff,' but they wouldn't believe me," he repeated, raising his voice. "However, I'm not the sort to let grass grow under my feet —all that was needed was to start the parley rolling."

The commander of the regiment twirled his mustache with a devil-may-care gesture of his left hand and said, smiling slyly, flatteringly:

"You're a wizard, Comrade Leader!"

The divisional commander winked his left eye and returned the other's smile condescendingly.

A hurdy-gurdy broke out far down the street, followed by thunderous hurrahing, and Batko Gonchar's detachment hove into view at the edge of the square. The staff officers ceased smiling. The division band blared forth the *Welcome!* song. A field-cart appeared next, drawn by a white horse, its mane loose and fluffed up and its tail unbound. It was on this cart that the hurdy-gurdy, adorned with lots of bright ribbons, was enthroned. A lanky, gaunt yokel, kneeling before it, was busily turning its curved handle. The hurdy-gurdy, piercingly squealing, was grinding out the *Russian March*. At a distance of ten paces from this hurdy-gurdy a troika[2] was rolling along, all in ribbons and jingle-bells. The magnificent horses —dappled grays—were prancing at a walk. The driver, walrus-mustached, square-shouldered, in red shirt and sleeveless jacket of

2 troika *A Russian vehicle drawn by three horses abreast. Also a team for such a vehicle.*

corduroy reaching to the knees, was standing as he guided the team. His round velvet cap was adorned with a multitude of peacock feathers. The troika-drawn tarantass, a sort of half-covered wagon, was draped with priceless rugs and, squatting like an idol upon them, was a husky man in a thick blue overcoat of Ukrainian cut, with gold braid splashed all over it. On coming up to the staff officers, he condescendingly saluted. The commander of the Red division gave his mount the merest flick of his quirt and rode up to the man, since he had recognized in him the celebrated partisan Batko Gonchar. The troika halted. The music stopped.

"Greetings to you, dear comrade!" the commander of the division called out.

Batko Gonchar smiled condescendingly.

"And greetings from me to you," he boomed in a bass.

This was followed by general hurrahing. The divisional band again blared forth the *Welcome!*

Batko's staff—a score of mounted men, in such colorful and motley costumes that they could have joined any masquerade right off—halted alongside the staff of the division. The field-carts again crawled off in a ribbon; the partisans were seated in these carts in twos and threes, each dressed to suit his own taste, they sat with legs dangling peacefully over the sides, so that one could hardly believe that these were warriors, and only the rifles sticking out higgledy-piggledy on all sides, and the occasional machine-guns looking like swine with their snouts turned up to the sky, indicated that the carts were coming not from some fair but from bloody battlefields.

The band was playing deafeningly. The field-carts rolled along. The commander of the division was conversing with Gonchar. Suddenly two columns of field-carts drew closer together, just as though two long ropes had been tightened and knotted, and the Red warriors, as well as the whole staff of the Red division, and all the others there, beheld a strange sight: bringing up the rear of the field-carts, riding a bay stallion, came an old man, all aglitter, like the sun. All of the ancient's apparel, and his conical hat in particular, was studded with tiny mirrors. With his left hand the old man was guiding his horse, while in his outstretched right he was holding a big white cage with a black rooster. Flanking the old man, as well as before and behind him, rode other columns of field-carts. Batko Gonchar was the first to set an example: before any of the others he lifted his cap to the old man. His staff officers immediately bared their heads as well. The commander of the Red division, just to be on the safe side, saluted the old man and all his staff did likewise. And only after this, bending toward Gonchar, did the divisional commander ask:

"And what rank does he hold among you?"

Batko Gonchar tugged at the left tip of his mustache with his right hand.

"Why, that's our wizard," said he in a bass.

"How come he isn't with your staff, then?"

"When you're working at your wizardry you've got to be alone—with the fiends," Gonchar answered soberly.

Oho-ho! The divisional commander had, of course, been right in his reckoning: the detachment of Batko Gonchar was a wonder-working force, surmounting all obstacles. These lads, boisterous at their bivouacs, evaporating like water in their retreats—they were magnificent in battles. Within three days the settlements and small towns of Smota, Moyachna, and Ozery were taken. There was a break-through at the front, and the Polacks were skedaddling in a north-westerly direction. The victory at Ozery was celebrated triumphantly. Batka sent an ukase[3] throughout the district, the beginning of which sounded like a Czar's manifesto and the end of it like a proclamation:

"And next I command all priests and prelates, as well as all deacons, to say masses for six days running in all the churches in celebration of our victories, and to ring all bells

3 ukase *A proclamation by a Russian emperor or government having the force of law.*

both day and night. All hail to a free Ukraine!"

That's how the ukase-proclamation of Batko Gonchar wound up. And, sure enough, in all the churches, near and far, the bells began to peal; and for two days and nights did they peal, since Batko's couriers had not overlooked a single church.

But in the staff of the division (where the celebration had also been a riotous one) Batko Gonchar's ukase had aroused both laughter and indignation.

"Why, he's belittling our strength, the Devil take him!" said the divisional commander to his chief of staff. "I don't know how to act. Should I go and explain things to him? He may resent it, like as not, and break away. Suppose I'll have to put up with it."

"Well, as they say, a little evil for a great good," answered the chief of staff. "We'll put up with this for a while."

"Gonchar told me that he always plays things safe—he just goes along with what his wizard predicts."

"What the Devil!" the chief of staff guffawed.

"That wizard looked at me rather crossly, somehow, last time I visited Gonchar," said the divisional commander with concern.

"Likely enough, he may sense how we feel and start giving us trouble."

"Oh, now, come!" The divisional commander smiled slyly. "For every spell of his we'll find a counter-spell."

"It's odd, though. Did you notice—he was riding in the very thick of the men when we were closing in on Ozery."

"How else? All the partisans are convinced that neither bullet nor saber can touch a wizard. Being behind him is like being behind an iron wall."

And, each steaming up the other, they began discussing this weird staff of Batko Gonchar's and his wizard.

"He won't take a step without this wizard. And everything works out as if it were all figured out black and white. Just what *is* going on?"

"Simple coincidence."

"Now and then I'm overcome by an odd feeling: 'But suppose it should suddenly turn out that this wizard does possess some sort of inner power?'"

"Now, now, now! That's absolute superstition."

"I'm convinced that sooner or later he'll pull some dirty trick on us."

"We'll find some means against his mischief."

"Yes, but just what means?"

"Oh, we'll see when the time comes. As long as he's of any good to us we can stand him. We'll settle accounts later."

"It'll be dangerous. All the partisans are for him, body and soul."

"Well, aren't we used to dangerous situations?"

This discussion took place the day before the detachment was to advance against Brody—and toward evening a courier from Batko Gonchar came to the divisional commander with a secret dispatch. After reading it the commander swore furiously and expertly.

"What is it?" asked the chief of staff.

"Gonchar refuses to attack."

"What reason does he give?"

"He refuses—and that's that. And he doesn't give any reasons. I'll have to go to him immediately."

Gonchar was in the next settlement, carousing with three of his cronies when the commander arrived to see him.

"Comrade Gonchar, what's the matter with you?" the divisional commander asked before they were through shaking hands.

Gonchar, who only the moment before had been laughing his head off over something, suddenly glowered and his face grew stubborn.

"We're not fighting!" said he in a low, mysterious voice.

"Why, what's up?"

"We're not fighting," Gonchar repeated with a shake of his head.

The divisional commander tensed, ready to oppose this stubborn fellow, but at once checked himself and asked in a voice as low as the other's and also somewhat mysterious:

"Tell me—have you received word of any sort, then?"

"No, it's not a matter of any word, but the wizard says we'll get licked. We've got to wait two weeks."

"Two weeks! What do you mean, two weeks?" the divisional commander shouted, flaring up. "How can one let such a thing happen? Have you gone daft, or what, you old devil?"

"Sh! Don't say anything!" Gonchar warned, lowering his voice still more, and shook a thick forefinger before the commander's nose. "He'll find out!"

"Let him! But you, now, Comrade Gonchar—can it be you yourself don't understand that we can't stand still? Why, this will be the death of us!"

"I understand, but the brotherhood wouldn't stir, even if I wished them to advance. They heed the wizard more than they do me."

"Well, you call the brethren together and we'll talk to them, and to the wizard too."

Five minutes later a trumpet was blaring out on the square, summoning the worthy knights to gather. The evening was already far advanced, and the entire settlement with its white huts and green gardens was plunged in darkness, except for a few small windows glimmering here and there. The sound of voices and the clatter of steps rang out sharply in the quiet street. Two big heaps of straw were burning on the square: the flames rose seven feet high, casting a bright light not only on the white enclosure of the church but on the dark, restless throng and the boughs of the nearest trees.

Strong lads rolled a field-cart out of a nearby yard. Gonchar scrambled up on the cart and, as the talk died out among the thronged men, cleared his throat and kept twiddling his mustache with both hands.

"Comrades, the commander wants to talk to you," said he, when all voices on the square had died away. "He wants to keep on fighting——"

"It isn't a matter of my wanting to!" the divisional commander called out, scrambling up on the cart. "But we *must* go on. The enemy is crushed. The enemy is on the run. We must pursue him without a letup, so as not to give him a chance to recover——"

"We don't want to go!" a high tenor piped up in the throng.

And immediately all the square, from one side of it to the other, echoed as one man:

"We don't want to go!"

And there was an unbroken surge, and a soughing as if of the wind.

"But why don't you?"

"Grandfather bids us not to go!" individual voices called out. "Grandfather!"—"There, he's coming himself!"—"Grandfather!"

Within the heart of the throng, beyond the dark ranks, something sparkled. The men parted; fell silent. The flames for a moment sank, then soared still higher—someone had tossed in new sheaves of straw. Through the clear spaces between the two closed rows of the partisans came the wizard. His tall cap and his clothing, ornamented with small mirrors, were all aglitter. The light lent a purple tint to everything. In one hand, outstretched before him, the wizard was bearing the black rooster in its white cage, and kept mumbling:

"Grym, glym, telepe. . . ."

The crowd seemed to have died; no one spoke or as much as coughed; only, somewhere far down the street, a male voice was singing. Mumbling gibberish, the wizard came up to the field-cart near which Gonchar, his staff officers and the divisional commander were grouped. He looked point-blank at the commander and asked:

"What are you raising a ruckus for?"

His gray goatee was thrust out belligerently, his yellow, rather watery eyes were flashing angrily, his cheeks were sunken—it was the first time the commander had seen the wizard so close at hand. He was malevolent and, at the same time, pitiful. His mirrors tinkled faintly.

"What are you raising a ruckus for?" the wizard repeated grimly.

"We must go after the enemy," the commander answered with an ingratiating smile.

"We're not fighting, we're not fighting," the wizard answered quietly.

And he shook his head, and reflections from his mirror-trimmed hat spattered in all directions.

"But why? Why?" the commander asked.

He understood that the question was useless, and he was becoming irritated, yet was trying to keep his temper.

"We're not fighting," repeated the wizard mulishly.

"How come you know that we're not fighting, Grandfather?" the commander asked in a rasping voice.

"I know everything," said the wizard, quietly and slowly.

"He knows everything," voices sprang up in the ranks. "Even a bullet wouldn't harm him!"

A barely perceptible smile flitted across the commander's face.

"Comrades!" he cried out, once more leaping up on the field-cart. "If that's how things stand then, of course, there's nothing to be done here. But the trouble, comrades, is that my fighters won't believe me. Those devils don't believe in wizards of any kind. When I inform them tomorrow that we must wait two weeks, at Grandfather's bidding, they'll laugh and jeer at me. I want Grandfather himself to prove to them his extraordinary power to work miracles."

He paused for a moment, as if groping for the words he needed.

"Yes—let him!" voices in the crowd called out.

"All of you know, comrades, that neither bullet nor saber can harm your Grandfather——"

"Right! Neither one nor the other!"

"Very well, then. I ask Grandfather to prove his wonder-working powers tomorrow. Let my lads convince themselves that neither bullet nor saber can harm Grandfather!"

And he fell silent. He had the air of a gambler who has played a trump card and is anxious to see whether or not it will be beaten. The crowd was now deathly still. A minute passed in strained silence.

"Well, now, Grandfather, can we have a demonstration?"

His voice could be heard clearly throughout the square. The wizard, who had been standing absolutely motionless, nodded.

"We can," he answered.

The crowd sighed in relief and began to hum. The commander held out his left hand and declared solemnly:

"Thanks, Grandfather! You will convince my comrades that fighting is out, as you say."

Out in the field, beyond the settlement, there was a green knoll, and the road snaked over it in a gray ribbon. The wizard in his glittering garments and glittering hat took his stand on this road; Batko Gonchar's men gathered in the field to the right, and those of the regular division were in the field to the left. The commander himself picked the spot where the machine-guns were to be placed. As they were being brought up, one of the partisans called out:

"No need for machine-guns! Make the test with a rifle——"

"Isn't it all one what bullets are used?" the commander asked calmly. "What's the odds if they fly out of a rifle or a machine-gun?"

"Right! Nothing will harm him anyway!" certain voices agreed.

The two machine-guns were placed side by side. The commander chose the best machine-gunners and instructed them in a low voice:

"Aim at the belly—below the mirrors. You, Tarassov, take care of the right side—and you of the left."

The commander's face was thoughtful. The wizard kept jerking aloft the white cage with the black rooster. The partisans and the Army men were tense and silent. Gonchar, three sheets in the wind, who was also hanging around the spot, said in a thick, melancholy bass:

"Nothing will harm him——"

"Well, now, can we start?" asked the commander.

"Go ahead!"

The commander himself inspected the sights. The wizard was glittering above the sights of both machine-guns—just right. The commander stepped back two paces, looked about him. All—both his men and the partisans—were watching him closely.

"Fire!" he commanded.

The machine-guns broke into their choppy chuckling in unison. And fell silent. The wizard slowly crumpled to the ground.

"Got him!" came the cries from right and left. "Sawed him right in half!"

The commander looked over his shoulder at Gonchar. Gonchar twirled his right mustache with his left hand and got out in a thick bass:

"You must have a charmed bullet, little brother——"

"Yes—charmed," the commander answered with a laugh. "There, don't you know that I'm something of a wizard myself?"

Bernard Guilbert Guerney/TRANSLATOR

For Discussion

1 What is the chief difference between Batko Gonchar and the divisional commander? Who is more concerned with military victory? Are the two men from the same cultural background?

2 What does the presence of the wizard tell about the men who believe in him? What do the various parts of the wizard's costume represent? What might the black rooster in the white cage symbolize?

3 Many people have pet superstitions: a rabbit's foot, a four-leaf clover, a broken mirror. These same people often belong to churches which preach against such superstitions. Does Batko Gonchar display a similar contradiction when he commands priests and prelates to celebrate his victories with masses? How, if he believes in the wizard, can he still be a Christian?

4 The official position of the Soviet government is against all religious and superstitious beliefs. With which character in this story would a good Soviet citizen presumably sympathize the most? With whom do you find yourself sympathizing?

5 How did the divisional commander destroy the wizard? Was the wizard a fool for submitting to the test? Did he believe in his own powers?

6 Do you think that Batko Gonchar and his men should have been allowed to keep their own customs and superstitions? Or was the divisional commander right in trying to force them into the "mainstream" of Soviet culture?

314

Miss Ismaili, an African poet, wrote this poem after a visit to New York City. At first it appears to be a series of disconnected fragments, but the fragments come together to form a mosaic picture of the city. Miss Ismaili has very sharp eyes and ears. Her poem includes tag lines taken from signs, ads, popular songs, and the fragmentary remarks one might hear if one walked around in New York City.

Rashidah Bint Rashin Ibn Ismaili

Dance of the Streets

I walked down the street but people were
    there
They stopped and looked with vacacious
    stares
I backed away and bumped into a bus
Ran down the other way, a policeman's
    stick
Box cars trapped me in threatening to
    fall   5
Windows with people half dressed all
    nude
Books, records, churches and liquors
Perfumes and the stench of dog dung
Balloons and polluted air
Fumes of carbon-dioxidized oxygen   10
Hair sprays and deodorant
No litter baskets and dogs water
Fire hydrants, and heavenly coffee
Flowers intertwine in Atlas' hair
Nipponese geishas and Stouffer's   15

St. Moritz and Charles of the Ritz
Central park outing, little old ladies
Feeding the pigeons, people prohibited
People not allowed on the grass
Dogs and squirrels and birds frolic   20
Baseball calls, cat calls, bird calls
Nature calls, the Eye is watching the
    sparrow
Downtown traffic going uptown
Doormen doorbells, red lights green lights
Uniformed drivers blue frocked dog
    walkers   25
No hellos only so long dears
Circular and beautiful and uncompre-
    hended
Useless and needless, helpers and func-
    tionless
Sirens and boats, swans and fish
Houses upon houses upon people   30
Talk and smoke rats and cats

The devil look no vacancies here
No help wanted no pets here
Keep going no loitering . . .
Virtuousness is godlessness emptiness . . .
Fires in the summer water in the winter
Snow capped faucets leaking in the
    buckets
Who you gonna marry Buck Jones
Neck bones on sale red ripe watermelon
Cotton and corn, potatoes and tomatoes
Rocks and socks on blocks of lava
No more auction sales marshal here
Peace and Blessings guns and Amen
Meandering on Friday noon
Cloudy and cool in June   45
Moon, spoon, croon, loon boon coon
Goons are flying
Everywhere a crack quack
Poppies are growing on the purple
    shadows
The fly, beware it creeps along the wall
Someone's been sleeping in my bed
Here's the girl who broke my chair
Fee, fie fo fum I hear the blood of mo-
    tors run
Run Joe as fast as you can
Lord, how come I here   55
I would rather be a beggar in the house
My father has a great big Cadillac

Two mansions and four yachts
I'm gonna go where dem chilly winds
    don blow
Honey baby come let us put our two
    hearts together   60
Fly with me lets fly to the moon
Hey stop, I want to get off
This ain't the way to Podunk
Sometimes I feel like a motherless child
How come I gotta die   65
Follow my lead in the need of prayer
I need someone to watch over me
Sharpies fraudies and Blackberries
Run for your life, the blue coats are
    coming
We shall not be moved   70
We are not scared and
We ain't bowing down no more
Well that's how it goes
Please don't talk about me when I'm
    gone
I need money honey any body   75
Help me oh well that's how it goes
Love me love me as if I was a baby
Small and a little not taking too much
    space
Hold me till the cows come
Home sweet home   80
Love and joy come to you and yours
This is it the beginning of the End.

For Discussion

1   The poem is essentially a harsh condemna-
    of New York City and certain aspects
    of its social system. Point to two or three
    examples of social criticism in the poem.

2   Any visitor to New York must be struck
    by the extraordinary contrast between
    great riches and luxury on the one hand
    and extreme poverty and misery on the
    other. How does the poem reflect this
    contrast?

3   Another contrast to be seen on the streets
    of New York, or the streets of almost any
    large city, is between beauty and ugliness.
    Where do you find this in the poem?

4   There are many voices speaking in this
    poem. Which ones indicate that a long-
    ing, suffering humanity exists on the
    streets in the city?

5   What are the implications of the last line?
    Within the terms of the poem, how is
    New York "the beginning of the End"?

Marc Chagall
Grandfather's House. Plate from: **Mein Leben** series.
Collection, The Museum of Modern Art, New York

Unit Seven Personal Experience

In "Childhood in an Indian Village" (page 319) Wilfred Pelletier makes a passing remark which gives an important insight into writing:

These kinds of things are very important to me and that is why I am talking about them and, probably, exploring while I'm talking, now.

There are three important points in this sentence; two of them are ideas with which most of us are familiar. Those two are, first, that good writing is about something important to the writer; and second, that writing is merely a way of talking to people. The third point which Pelletier makes is one which many people overlook: that good writing is always an act of exploration.

Many inexperienced writers assume that they should have all their ideas on hand and organized before they begin to write. The act of writing itself becomes rather mechanical, a kind of fleshing out of already existing ideas. Such writing may be clear, but it will also be lifeless. Of course, every good writer has a general idea of what his topic is and what he wants to say about it. But he discovers things about himself and about his subject *as he writes.* Good writing is always an encounter with experience; there is always a sense of surprise and discovery which gives life to the prose.

At first glance there should be nothing easier to write about than your own experience. It would seem that all you have to do is put down what happened to you and what you think about it. But in fact, such writing sounds easier than it is. Most of us know where we were born, where we went to school, where we were last Saturday night, and so forth. But does such a list of facts or events make up a life? What is the real experience behind the facts? What is the *point* of it all?

To form an image of oneself, to have a meaningful point of view toward one's own experience, requires an act of the imagination as bold and creative as does the writing of fiction. In one case we seem to be dealing with "reality" and in the other with "imagination." Yet as we approach the act of serious writing, we find that what is real and what is imagined become hard to distinguish.

To see things clearly, to see them freshly, to see them for what they are—these are difficult things to do. For one thing, we must struggle against all the clichés, all the stale formulas with which experience is encrusted. Suppose, for example, that in your city a lot of older buildings are being torn down and replaced by modern glass and steel structures. All around you you hear people saying, "Did you see the beautiful new buildings down-

town?" The newspapers are filled with articles about the grand openings of these "beautiful" buildings. It becomes easy for you to assume that the buildings are what people say they are. Your own experience becomes confused or blanked out. Are the buildings really beautiful? What do you *see* when you look at them? What do you really think as opposed to what you are told you ought to think?

In each of the following essays a writer sets out to encounter some aspect of his own experience. Some of these essays are about adventures such as Hemingway's travels in Africa and Thor Heyerdahl's dangerous voyage on the *Kon-Tiki.* Those by Pelletier, Laye, and Colette are based upon memories of their childhoods. As you read each of these pieces, see if you agree that it has a liveliness to it which springs from the fact that each writer has had a genuine *encounter* with his own experience. He has looked at life with a fresh, clear vision. He has avoided seeing things in terms of stale categories. And this sense of freshness and discovery is communicated in the writing itself.

Pelletier writes with the same fascinating "double vision" to be found in another autobiographical essay, Camara Laye's "The Snake and the Crocodile" (page 338). Each of these authors, one Canadian Indian and one African, has lived in two cultures: each was raised in a tribal society and later became educated in a "mainstream" society, one in France and the other in Canada.

Pelletier writes in a direct style, just as if he were talking to the reader. This simplicity of style lends a sincerity and urgency to his message. In this article he is not addressing his fellow Indians, but Western civilization in general. He looks back on his Indian childhood not so much for its own sake, but to find in it values for the whole of society.

Wilfred Pelletier

Childhood in an Indian Village

Going back as far as I can remember as a child in an Indian community, I had no sense of knowing about the other people around me except that we were all somehow equal: the class structure in the community was horizontal. There was only one class. Nobody was interested in getting on top of anybody else.

You could see it in our games. Nobody organized them. There weren't any competitive sports. But we were involved in lots of activity (I was not like I am now; I was in pretty good shape at that time) and we were organized, but not in the sense that there were ways of finding out who had won and who had lost. We played ball like everyone else, but no one kept score. In fact, you would stay up at bat until you hit the ball. If somebody happened to walk by on the street, an old guy, we'd tease him and bug him to come over and try to hit the ball, and he would come over and he'd swing away. If they threw us out on first, we'd stay on first anyway. We ran to second, and they would throw us out there, and sometimes we'd get thrown out all the way around.

We had a number of other games we used to play. There was one where we used to try and hit each other between two lines with a ball. It didn't really make any difference if you got hit or whether you stayed in the centre and tried to hit the other guy or not. But it was very, very difficult to hit these guys. I remember standing between these two lines, and all of a sudden the guys would take off, and you could be two or three feet from them, and you would have to throw the ball at them, and you just couldn't hit those guys. They were really terrific.

It was later on in life that I began to realize that what we were really doing was playing. Very much like animals play. When you observe the bear, the adult, the male and female are always playing with the cubs. The otters do the same thing. None of the kind of play we had was really structured and organized. That came after the recreation directors from the outside world came in and told us that we had a problem in the community, that we were not organized, and they were going to introduce some.

They introduced them all right, and the tremendous competitiveness that went with them. It's not as bad on Manitoulin Island, where I'm from, as it is a lot of other places where competitiveness is rolling in. I'm glad I can remember that as a kid I was able to become involved with a community with others and nobody was competing. Even if we did formally compete in the games we did, no one was a winner though someone may have won. It was only the moment. If you beat someone by pulling a bow and arrow and shooting the arrow further, it only meant that you shot the arrow further at that moment. That's all it lasted. It didn't mean you were better in any way whatsoever. It just meant that at that particular time the arrow went further; maybe it was just the way you let the bow go. These kinds of things are very important to me and that is why I am talking about them and, probably, exploring while I'm talking, now. When I get the opportunity to listen to myself I try to explore those kinds of things that I can remember as a child.

One of the very important things was the relationship we had with our families. We didn't always live at home. We lived wherever we happened to be at that particular time when it got dark. If you were two or three miles away from home, then that is where you slept. People would feed you even if they didn't know who you were. We'd spend an evening, perhaps, with an old couple, and they would tell us stories. Most of these stories were legends, and they were told to us mostly in the wintertime. In the summer people would generally take us out and we would do a number of things which in some way would allow us to learn about life and what it was all about: that is, by talking about some particular person and demonstrating what that person did. At no time, in all the years I spent there, do I ever remember anyone teaching us anything.

I have been to numerous communities across Canada and I still do not find where Indians teach. All young children were allowed to grow, to develop, to learn. They didn't teach you that this was mommy, daddy, desk, ash-tray, house, etc. We learned about these things by listening to the words adults spoke, what they said when they were talking, and built our own kind of relationship with the article. If you observe your children now you will see a child turn a chair over, cover it with a blanket and use it for a house. He can relate many ways to a chair. As we get older we have only one relationship and that is to stick our rear ends on that chair. It's for no other purpose, and, in fact, we tell our kids that that is what it is, and it belongs in a corner and don't move it out of there.

These things I remember very well. We were brought up to have a different relationship to a house and to all the things that surrounded us. That is, the values that adults placed on things in the community did not necessarily carry over into their child and lead him to place the same values on them. Children discovered the values of these things on their own, and developed their own particular relationship to them.

This is very closely related to the religion of the community, which centered entirely on man. One of the practiced ethics of the community was non-interference. No one interfered with us, and this way of living still exists today. If you go to an Indian home the kids don't come up and bug you while you are talking to someone else. They might come and stand by you quietly, just as an adult might. If you observe Indians some-place, they will stand quietly, and only when they are acknowledged, will they speak. If they get into a group session, they will act the same way. They will sit and listen to people talk, and when they get the opportunity they will speak, but they won't cut you off or interfere. There are some who do this now, but not very many. Most of them will just wait. The whole background in the educational system was that of observing and feeling. This is how they learned.

It was a very different kind of learning situation that we were in as children. In fact, all of the things we did related to our way of life. Everything had to fit into the whole; we didn't learn things in parts. As an example: if we watched someone running an outboard motor, we would learn everything that was involved in working that motor. If someone taught someone here to do that, after he was finished he might add a safety program on top of it. This would be an additional thing. The way Indians learned it, they built in a safety program while they were learning through their observations and because their very lives depended on their doing it right.

And just as we didn't separate our learning from our way of life, we didn't separate our work from it either. The older women, for example, who used to work all day at what-ever—tanning hides, etc., didn't really think of it as work. It was a way of life. That's the real difference between the kind of society we have now where we equate these kinds of things with work and yet will go out and play sports and enjoy it and the kind of soci-ety I'm talking about. Here we go and work and use maybe half or a quarter of the energy we spend playing sports, but we call it work and we feel differently about it alto-gether. These are the kinds of differences

that exist. Indian people who had a way of life and who felt it was their way of life didn't call it work. It was part of the way they provided for their families; and they "worked" very hard.

One of the reasons, of course, why they didn't call it "work" was that they didn't have any kind of a vertical structure in the community. In these communities what existed was a sharing of power. In spite of what everybody says, we really didn't have chiefs, that is, people who were bosses. We had medicine men, who were wise men. The rest were leaders in particular ways. They weren't leaders as we look at them today. It was a different kind of leadership in that the person who was leader had special abilities, say in fishing or hunting. He took the lead-ership that day, and then discarded the lead-ership when he was finished with the job. He had power only for the time he wanted to do something. That power came in all forms of all the things he did in the community, so that he used power only for the things he wanted to do, and then he immediately shed it so that someone else could pick it up and it could change hands several times in the community in a day or a week or whatever.

Only in times of war and disaster was a vertical structure used. The war chief would designate various jobs to various people and use that vertical structure. This was only in times of danger. Otherwise, it was horizon-tal. My grandfather one time told me this, although it didn't sink in until just a few years ago, that to have power is destructive. You'll be destructive if you have power be-cause if people don't join you, then you will destroy them. I forgot this and dug around for power and began to lose friends. I was making decisions for people even with the background I have. Now I have such a prob-lem fighting this thing off, because people are always putting me in a position where I have power. They say I am director of the Insti-tute of Indian Studies. This is not true. I'm just at Rochdale College. Where I am everyone makes up their own minds in terms of what they want to do, and they do those things, and if I can be of assistance, then I assist. I've got my own thing that I hope to do. One of the things that I'm interested in is the kind of lives that the young Indian people now at Rochdale live—what is happening to them in the city.

The city has special problems for them as it had for me. For many of them were raised in Indian homes, where the attitude is that no child ever should be rejected. In an Indian home, if a child's face is dirty or his diaper is wet, he is picked up by anyone. The mother or father or whoever comes into the house. He is never rejected. And they don't stick children in cribs, where they can only look in one direction—up. The child generally sits or stands (often tied in), so he can relate to the world in all directions. And children are fed whenever they are hungry. They are never allowed to be in want. Whatever is wanted is given to them. If a child wants to play with something, it is always placed in his hand. No one would think of putting a rattle slightly out of reach, so he would try to grab it and be aggressive. No one would think of feeding the baby only at set times. What follows this approach in terms of attitudes and way of life is immense. The child's nature is very strongly influenced in the first four or five years. The children become very non-competitive. They have no need to compete.

The whole situation changes, however, when they go out into the world, where the attitudes and values are totally different. A world, further, in which their values are not acceptable. Where for many of us as children we were not even permitted to speak our own language. Of course, we still tried to speak our own language, but we were punished for it. Four or five years ago they were still stripping the kids of their clothes up around Kenora and beating them for speaking their own language. It is probably still happening in many other institutions today. I was punished several times for speaking Indian not only on the school grounds but off the school grounds and on the street, and I lived across from the school. Almost in front of my own door my first language was forbidden me, and yet when I went into the house my parents spoke Indian.

Our language is so important to us as a people. Our language and our language structure related to our whole way of life. How beautiful that picture language is where they only tell you the beginning and the end, and you fill in everything, and they allow you to feel how you want to feel. Here we manipulate and twist things around and get you to hate a guy. The Indian doesn't do that. He'll just say that some guy got into an accident, and he won't give you any details. From there on you just explore as far as you want to. You'll say: "What happened?" and he'll tell you a little more. "Did he go through the windshield?" "Yep!" He only answers questions. All of the in-between you fill in for yourself as you see it. We are losing that feeling when we lose our language at school. We are taught English, not Indian, as our first language. And that changes our relationship with our parents. All of a sudden we begin saying to our parents "you're stupid." We have begun to equate literacy with learning, and this is the first step down. It is we who are going down and not our parents, and because of that separation we are going down lower and lower on the rung because it is we who are rejecting our parents; they are not rejecting us. The parents know that, but they are unable to do anything about it. And we take on the values, and the history of somebody else.

And part of the reason our parents say so little is that that's their way. They don't teach like white people; they let their children make their own decisions. The closest they ever got to formal teaching was to tell us stories. Let me give you an example. We had been out picking blueberries one time, and while sitting around this guy told us this story. The idea was that he wanted to get us to wash up—to wash our feet because we had been tramping through this brush all day long. He talked about a warrior who really had a beautiful body. He was very well built, and he used to grease himself and take care of his body. One day this warrior was out, and he ran into a group of other people whom he had never seen before. They started to chase him. He had no problem because he was in such good shape. He was fooling around and playing with them because he was such a good runner. He ran over hills and over rocks, teasing them. Then he ran into another group. The first group gave up the chase. But now he had to run away from this other group, and he was fooling around doing the same thing with them. All of a sudden he ran into a third group. He ran real hard and all of a sudden he fell. He tried to get up and he couldn't. He spoke to his feet and said "What's wrong with you? I'm going to get killed if you don't get up and get going." They said: "That's alright. You can comb your hair and grease your body and look after your legs and arms but you never did anything for us. You never washed us or cleaned us or greased us or nothing." He promised to take better care of the feet if they would get up and run, and so they did.

This is one of the stories we were told, and we went up and washed our feet right away and then went to bed. Maybe this happens among other ethnic groups, I don't know, but this is the kind of learning we had. I will never forget the kinds of things we learned, because to me it all belongs to me. It isn't something that someone says is so; it's mine. I'd want to go hunting, and the guys would know I couldn't get across the stream because it was flooded, but they wouldn't say anything. They'd let me go, and I'll tell them I'd see them later where the rocks are, and they'd say O.K. knowing all this time I couldn't get through. But they wouldn't tell me that. They'd let me experience it. And

I'm grateful to these people for allowing me to have this kind of exploration/learning situation. Secondly, of course, the fact is that maybe I could have gotten across where they couldn't, discovered something different, a method that was new. I think this kind of learning situation is one of the really important things that Indians have today and which could contribute to the society we have today. That is, a learning situation *for people*, instead of teaching or information giving.

All these things—the various ways Indian life differed from that in our present society —I didn't learn until after I left the reserve community later on in life. Then I could understand how very differently structured the two communities are. While it didn't have a vertical structure, our community was very highly structured. So highly structured that there wasn't anything that could happen that somebody could almost immediately, in some way, solve, whatever problem arose. Without any given signals or the appearance of any communication whatsoever (there were no telephones) the most complex social action used to happen. If somebody died in that community, nobody ever said we should dig a grave. The grave was dug, the box was made, everything was set up . . . the one who baked pies baked pies. Everyone did something in that community, and if you tried to find out who organized it, you couldn't.

It's exactly the same way today. You cannot find out who organizes these things. In 1964 Prime Minister Pearson came up to the reserve. We had a cocktail party in the hall, and at the same time there was a big buffet organized for him. This was organized by a woman from Toronto. She went up there and set this whole thing up. He had been coming there every year. This was his riding. Every year they turned out a beautiful meal for him, and he never knew who to thank because it was just all of a sudden there; it was done. The people just got together.

There was no foreman or boss. There was no vertical structure, and it just happened. You should have been there in '64. It was chaotic. There were no knives, no desserts, nobody had cut up the heads of lettuce that were all over, because this woman came there and gave orders, and the people wouldn't do anything until she told them what to do. She got so busy that she couldn't tell everybody what to do, and she had four or five turkeys all over the town in different people's ovens, and that's where they sat. They had to go and tell the women to bring the turkeys down because they wouldn't do it on their own. There was someone in charge. Had there not been anyone in charge it would have gone off fine. It was a real mess. This is the difference. Here you organize, and you know those kinds of structures, and they mean something to you. You instinctively behave in certain ways to those things.

But it's more than that too. As I see it, organization comes out of a need for immediate order—say in war. When it develops this way so that people say let's organize, and they get together and create a vertical structure, and place somebody up at the top and then it becomes a power group, and from there on it filters on down until after a while you have somebody running that organization, two or three people or maybe eventually just one, and all the rest of the people get suppressed, pushed down, and held down by that very thing they formally sought. You give power to someone and suppress others.

I don't know if a different kind of structural organization can exist today. I know some people are trying to make a different one— some people in Rochdale College and I suspect in many places where people are getting together and trying to live communally. I remember as a child a different kind of organization existing, and I have come to call it now "community consciousness." That community can exist and function and solve all its problems without any kinds of signals, like a school of fish. All of a sudden you see them move; they shift altogether. That is exactly the way most Indian communities function. And yet we have the Department of Indian Affairs coming and telling us we have no organization. The local priest or minister will come and tell us we have to be organized. The Recreation Department will come along and say there's no organization in this community. And when they come it's like shooting a goose in a flock of geese. When you hit him you disrupt the pattern. So every time somebody comes into the community they disrupt the pattern. Every time you remove a resource person from the community you disrupt the pattern. You break it up, and they have to reorganize. But in a lot of communities this is very hard to do, and some of them have been too hurt to make it. Indian resource people begin to drop out of sight and white organizers take over, making it even more difficult for Indian people to function. I know that in one community where there are 740 people (about two-thirds of them children) there are 18 organizations. There are three churches that all have two or three organizations, and there is also a community development officer who has a number of organizations behind him, and they are in such conflict that the community cannot function. It's just sitting there, with people at each other's throats. The people who come in can't understand that if a guy is sitting under a tree and doing nothing but observing the stars or the clouds in the daytime or the birds flying, he is running through a recreational pattern and at the same time he is learning. These are all parts of a whole. Most Indian people deal with wholeness. It is much different than the way we deal with things where we segment them and deal with them only in parts.

It is also very difficult to know what to do now—now that the organizers have come in. The dependency is so great and government and outside resources have created this dependency. They have removed most of the human resource and certainly all the economic base from most Indian communities and there is very little left. Yet the Indian relationship to that dependency is much different from ours in this society. Indians may receive welfare, but most of them feel it is a right. They don't look down on people who are on welfare. Drawing welfare doesn't change the nature of the person. In the same way, if they walk into a room that is messy they don't say the woman is sloppy. They say the room is sloppy. A lot of them don't paint their houses. That is because they don't have the same relationship to that house that we in this society do. Clothes don't make the man. Relationships are built on something that is not materialistic. The same thing applies to money. If you observe your children when they have money, they want to get rid of it right away. How long do children stay mad at one another? A moment. All of these behaviour patterns that you observe in children are very much related to adult Indians. Your history books say that when the white men first came here they noted that the Indians were very child-like. That is very true in many ways. But if you look at it, how beautiful to be child-like and yet be mature. Here we say that you mustn't show feelings. I don't agree with that. If a man can cry, then he has feelings. Indians cry all the time. We get together and sing songs, and we cry in these songs. But this society is very machine-like, and so we begin to act like machines and then we become machines.

Because of this approach Indians don't really want to fight for their rights. They really don't want to get into the society at all. In this way they are probably different from the black people on this continent who are a much larger group, and have no choice but to fight for their rights. When they get these rights, what they are doing in essence is moving into society. When they do get in, they might make the changes they want in terms of their cultural background or how they look at things, or whatever, and these

changes may give them the freedom to practice or do those things they want to do.

But the Indians have fundamentally rejected society as it now is. The Indians are expert at making all programs that the Indian Affairs Branch has ever come up with a failure by withdrawing. The Indians embrace everything that comes into a community. If you want to build a church, that's fine. We'll help you build that church, etc. Then once they see that they can't relate to that church in any way, they withdraw and the thing falls apart. If you want to build a road, they'll help you build one, with the result that some reserves have roads running all over the place, but nobody uses them. The Branch has a history of complete failure. The Indians have always rejected it. We have a society here where we must win. For everything you do you must end up fighting— fighting for your rights, good against evil, war against poverty, the fight for peace. The whole base of the western culture has an enemy concept. What would happen if you remove the enemy? How then do you defeat somebody who is on your side? I suspect that if you remove the enemy the culture might collapse. The Indian can't fight on your terms. For a start he doesn't even have the numbers, much less the inclination. So he withdraws. And he pays a certain price. He suffers poverty in many ways.

But maybe the future is with the Indian. Marshall McLuhan[1] says that the only people living in the 21st century are the Indians, the Eskimos, some French people and the Japanese. All the rest, because they deal with history, live in the 19th century because they deal with the past and not the present. The pan-Indian movement, with the Native American Church, recognizes this and there are various Indian cultures that are moving closer and closer together. It's a spontaneous thing that just happened. It's just growing and there isn't anyone who is heading it up. It's a movement. And it's made me much more hopeful.

1 Marshall McLuhan *A Canadian educator who has written about the effects of media on society.*

For Discussion

1 The title of the essay, "Childhood in an Indian Village," might lead the reader to think he is about to read a detailed description of the author's youth. He does give some details, but the point of his article is not merely a description of his past. He says little or nothing, for example, about food, or clothes, or music, and so forth. The details are carefully chosen to make one main point. In your own words, what is this main point? What is the greatest value the author finds in the traditional Indian way of life?

2 The author obviously likes the idea that in the Indian society of his childhood "Nobody was interested in getting on top of anybody else." Do you think it possible for a large nation to exist without a competitive spirit? What are some of the advantages and disadvantages of competition?

3 How does the author feel about the kind of "help" which outsiders have tried to give the Indians? What has it done to the Indians? How have they tried to preserve their own ways?

4 Compare this essay with the poem "Indian Reservation: Caughnawaga" (page 242). Both pieces are by Canadians, one white and the other Indian, and both are about the effect of "civilization" on tribal life. On what points do both writers agree?

5 Discuss the style of this essay. Is it organized and unified? Does the plain language and general informality support the author's argument?

Colette was the pen name of the great French novelist who was baptized Sidonie Gabrielle Colette.

When she was still young, Colette left her country home and went to Paris where she lived most of her life.

Although the little country girl became in time a sophisticated Parisian, she never lost touch with her simple, provincial background. She almost made a cult of memory and childhood and was able to evoke in writing her extraordinary understanding of animals and natural things. A critic has said of Colette, "She has a distinctive feeling for the no-man's-land in personal experience, which lies between the senses and the emotions." Colette's gift for supersensitive understanding of other people and of the world of nature seems to have been partly inherited from her mother, Sido.

These two memories of Sido —a strong, independent woman—are written with a great affection, but without a trace of sentimentality.

Colette

Two Memories of Sido

I. The Time Came . . .

The time came when all her strength left her. She was amazed beyond measure and would not believe it. Whenever I arrived from Paris to see her, as soon as we were alone in the afternoon in her little house, she had always some sin to confess to me. On one occasion she turned up the hem of her dress, rolled her stocking down over her shin, and displayed a purple bruise, the skin nearly broken.

"Just look at that!"

"What on earth have you done to yourself this time, Mother?"

She opened wide eyes, full of innocence and embarrassment.

"You wouldn't believe it, but I fell downstairs!"

"How do you mean—'fell'?"

"Just what I said. I fell, for no reason. I was going downstairs and I fell. I can't understand it."

"Were you going down too quickly?"

"Too quickly? What do you call too quickly? I was going down quickly. Have I time to go downstairs majestically like the Sun King? And if that were all . . . But look at this!"

On her pretty arm, still so young above the faded hand, was a scald forming a large blister.

"Oh goodness! Whatever's that!"

"My footwarmer."

"The old copper footwarmer? The one that holds five quarts?"

"That's the one. Can I trust anything, when that footwarmer has known me for forty years? I can't imagine what possessed it, it was boiling fast, I went to take it off the fire, and crack, something gave in my wrist. I was lucky to get nothing worse than the blister. But what a thing to happen! After that I let the cupboard alone. . . ."

She broke off, blushing furiously.

"What cupboard?" I demanded severely.

My mother fenced, tossing her head as though I were trying to put her on a lead.

"Oh, nothing! No cupboard at all!"

"Mother! I shall get cross!"

"Since I've said, 'I let the cupboard alone,' can't you do the same for my sake? The cupboard hasn't moved from its place, has it? So, shut up about it!"

The cupboard was a massive object of old walnut, almost as broad as it was high, with no carving save the circular hole made by a Prussian bullet that had entered by the right-hand door and passed out through the back panel.

"Do you want it moved from the landing, Mother?"

An expression like that of a young she-cat, false and glittery, appeared on her wrinkled face.

"I? No, it seems to me all right there—let it stay where it is!"

All the same, my doctor brother and I agreed that we must be on the watch. He saw my mother every day, since she had followed him and lived in the same village, and he looked after her with a passionate devotion which he hid. She fought against all her ills with amazing elasticity, forgot them, baffled them, inflicted on them signal if temporary defeats, recovered, during entire days, her vanished strength; and the sound of her battles, whenever I spent a few days with her, could be heard all over the house till I was irresistibly reminded of a terrier tackling a rat.

At 5:00 in the morning I would be awakened by the clank of a full bucket being set down in the kitchen sink immediately opposite my room.

"What are you doing with that bucket, Mother? Couldn't you wait until Josephine arrives?"

And out I hurried. But the fire was already blazing, fed with dry wood. The milk was boiling on the blue-tiled charcoal stove. Nearby, a bar of chocolate was melting in a little water for my breakfast, and, seated squarely in her cane armchair, my mother was grinding the fragrant coffee which she roasted herself. The morning hours were always kind to her. She wore their rosy colors in her cheeks. Flushed with a brief return to health, she would gaze at the rising sun, while the church bell rang for early Mass, and rejoice at having tasted, while we still slept, so many forbidden fruits.

The forbidden fruits were the overheavy bucket drawn up from the well, the firewood split with a billhook on an oaken block, the spade, the mattock, and above all the double steps propped against the gable window of the woodhouse. There were the climbing vine whose shoots she trained up to the gable windows of the attic, the flowery spikes of the too-tall lilacs, the dizzy cat that had to be rescued from the ridge of the roof. All the accomplices of her old existence as a plump and sturdy little woman, all the minor rustic divinities who once obeyed her and made her so proud of doing without servants, now assumed the appearance and position of adversaries. But they reckoned without that love of combat which my mother was to keep till the end of her life. At seventy-one, dawn still found her undaunted, if not always undamaged. Burnt by the fire, cut with the pruning knife, soaked by melting snow or spilled water, she had always managed to enjoy her best moments of independence before the earliest risers had opened their shutters. She was able to tell us of the cats' awakening, of what was going on in the nests, of news gleaned, together with the morning's milk and the warm loaf, from the milkmaid and the baker's girl, the record in fact of the birth of a new day.

It was not until one morning when I found the kitchen unwarmed, and the blue enamel saucepan hanging on the wall, that I felt my mother's end to be near. Her illness knew many respites, during which the fire flared up again on the hearth, and the smell of fresh bread and melting chocolate stole under the door together with the cat's impatient paw. These respites were periods of unexpected alarms. My mother and the big walnut cupboard were discovered together in a heap at the foot of the stairs, she having determined to transport it in secret from the upper landing to the ground floor. Whereupon my elder brother insisted that my mother should keep still and that an old servant should sleep in the little house. But how could an old servant prevail against a vital energy so youthful and mischievous that it contrived to tempt and lead astray a body already half fettered by death? My brother, returning before sunrise from attending a distant patient, one day caught my mother red-handed in the most wanton of crimes. Dressed in her nightgown, but wearing heavy gardening sabots,[1] her little gray septuagenarian's plait of hair turning up like a scorpion's tail on the nape of her neck, one foot firmly planted on the crosspiece of the beech trestle, her back bent in the attitude of the expert jobber, my mother, rejuvenated by an indescribable expression of guilty enjoyment, in defiance of all her promises and of the freezing morning dew, was sawing logs in her own yard.

II. "Sir, you ask me . . ."

"Sir,

"*You ask me to come and spend a week with you, which means I would be near my daughter, whom I adore. You who live with her know how rarely I see her, how much her presence delights me, and I'm touched that you should ask me to come and see her. All the same I'm not going to accept your kind invitation, for the time being at any rate.*

The reason is that my pink cactus is probably going to flower. It's a very rare plant I've been given, and I'm told that in our climate it flowers only once every four years. Now, I am already a very old woman, and if I went away when my pink cactus is about to flower, I am certain I shouldn't see it flower again.

"So I beg you, sir, to accept my sincere thanks and my regrets, together with my kind regards."

This note, signed *"Sidonie Colette, née Landoy,"* was written by my mother to one of my husbands, the second. A year later she died, at the age of seventy-seven.

Whenever I feel myself inferior to everything about me, threatened by my own mediocrity, frightened by the discovery that a muscle is losing its strength, a desire its power, or a pain the keen edge of its bite, I can still hold up my head and say to myself: "I am the daughter of the woman who wrote that letter—that letter and so many more that I have kept. This one tells me in ten lines that at the age of seventy-six she was planning journeys and undertaking them, but that waiting for the possible bursting into bloom of a tropical flower held everything up and silenced even her heart, made for love. I am the daughter of a woman who, in a mean, close-fisted, confined little place, opened her village home to stray cats, tramps, and pregnant servant girls. I am the daughter of a woman who many a time, when she was in despair at not having enough money for others, ran through the wind-whipped snow to cry from door to door, at the houses of the rich, that a child had just been born in a poverty-stricken home to parents whose feeble, empty hands had no swaddling clothes for it. Let me not forget that I am the daughter of a woman who bent her head, trembling, between the blades of a cactus, her wrinkled face full of ecstasy over the promise of a flower, a woman who herself never ceased to flower, untiringly, during three quarters of a century."

1 sabots *Wooden shoes worn in various European countries.*

For Discussion

1 The affection of a daughter for a mother is, of course, a common human experience. Has Colette written about this experience in a way which seems fresh and alive? Does she make you think of Sido just as "my mother"? Or does she make the reader see Sido as a unique person?

2 As a good daughter, Colette felt it necessary to worry about her mother's health and safety. She had to object to some of the things the old lady wanted to do. But now, as she writes about Sido, her attitude is one of admiration. Where do you find evidence that Colette admired the independent spirit of her mother?

3 Colette was a master at observing specific details, especially about domestic life, gardens, and animals. Point out some closely observed details in these essays. Are they things which a stale or routine eye might never have noticed?

4 Sido's children tried to persuade her not to do things like sawing wood on a freezing morning. Why did she refuse to obey them? Do you think the old lady was right in going on with her own way of life, even when her actions may have been dangerous?

5 What is remarkable about the letter which Sido wrote to Colette's husband? What lesson does Colette herself draw from it?

Albert Schweitzer was one of the most remarkable men of this century. After a brilliant career as a student, he became very successful. Well known as a musician, Schweitzer was also the head of the Theological College at the University of Strasbourg. At the age of thirty he turned his back on success, studied medicine, and left Europe for French Equatorial Africa, where he founded a missionary hospital. Of course, in time his fame became greater than if he had remained in Europe. The legend of the self-sacrificing jungle doctor who preached respect for all living things spread across the world. Schweitzer occasionally left his African hospital to raise funds in Europe and in America by giving concerts and by lecturing.

This account of personal experience is different from the others in this unit, because "The Renunciation of Thought" has little to do with any external adventure, with childhood memories, or with the description of society. Rather, Schweitzer writes about his spiritual and philosophical experiences. He stands up for truth and reason, although he sees that his position places him in opposition to the spirit of his own times.

Albert Schweitzer

The Renunciation of Thought

With the spirit of the age I am in complete disagreement, because it is filled with disdain for thinking. That such is its attitude is to some extent explicable by the fact that thought has never yet reached the goal which it must set before itself. Time after time it was convinced that it had clearly established a world-view which was in accordance with knowledge and ethically satisfactory. But time after time the truth came out that it had not succeeded.

But today, in addition to that neglect of thought, there is also prevalent a mistrust of it. The organized political, social, and religious associations of our time are at work to induce individual man not to arrive at his convictions by his own thinking but to take as his own such convictions as they keep ready-made for him. Any man who thinks for himself and at the same time is spiritually free is to the associations something inconvenient and even uncanny. He does not offer sufficient guarantee that he will merge himself in their organizations in the way they wish. All corporate bodies look today for their strength not so much to the spiritual worth of the ideas they represent and to that of the people who belong to them, as to the attainment of the highest possible degree of unity and exclusiveness. It is here that they expect to find their strongest power for offense and defense.

Hence the spirit of the age rejoices, instead of lamenting, that thinking seems to be unequal to its task, and gives it no credit for what, in spite of imperfections, it has already accomplished. It refuses to admit, what is nevertheless the fact, that all spiritual progress up to today has come about through the achievements of thought, or to reflect that thinking may still be able in the future to accomplish what it has not succeeded in accomplishing as yet. Of such considerations the spirit of the age takes no account. Its only concern is to discredit individual thinking in every possible way, dealing with such thought according to the saying: "Whosoever hath not, from him shall be taken away even that which he hath."

Thus, his whole life long, modern man is exposed to influences which are bent on robbing him of all confidence in his own thinking. The spirit of spiritual dependence to which he is called on to surrender is in everything that he hears or reads; it is the people whom he meets every day; it is in the parties and associations which have claimed him as their own; it pervades all the circumstances of his life.

From every side and in the most varied ways it is dinned into him that the truth and convictions which he needs for life must be taken by him from the associations which have rights over him. The spirit of the age never lets him come to himself. Over and over again convictions are forced upon him in the same way as, by means of the electric advertisements which flare in the streets of every large town, any company which has sufficient capital to get itself securely established, exercises pressure on him at every step he takes to induce him to buy their boot polish or their soup tablets.

By the spirit of the age, then, the man of today is forced into skepticism about his own thinking, in order to make him receptive to truth which comes to him from authority. To all this constant influence he cannot make the resistance that is desirable because he is an overworked and distracted being without power to concentrate. Moreover, the manifold material trammels which are his lot work upon his mentality in such a way that he comes at last to believe himself unqualified even to make any claim to thoughts of his own.

His self-confidence is also diminished through the pressure exercised upon him by the huge and daily increasing mass of Knowledge. He is no longer in a position to take in all the new discoveries that are constantly announced; he has to accept them as fact although he does not understand them. This being his relation to scientific truth he is tempted to acquiesce in the idea that in matters of thought also his judgment cannot be trusted.

Thus do the circumstances of the age do their best to deliver us up to the spirit of the age.

The seed of skepticism has germinated. In fact, modern man has no longer any spiritual self-confidence at all. Behind a self-confident exterior he conceals a great inward lack of confidence. In spite of his great capacity in material matters he is an altogether stunted being, because he makes no use of his capacity for thinking. It will ever remain incomprehensible that our generation, which has shown itself so great by its achievements in discovery and invention, could fall so low spiritually as to give up thinking.

Renunciation of thinking is a declaration of spiritual bankruptcy. Where there is no longer a conviction that men can get to know the truth by their own thinking, skepticism begins. Those who work to make our age skeptical in this way, do so in the expectation that, as a result of renouncing all hope of self-discovered truth men will end by accepting as truth what is forced upon them with authority and by propaganda.

But their calculations are wrong. No one who opens the sluices to let a flood of skepticism pour itself over the land must expect to be able to bring it back within its proper bounds. Of those who let themselves get too disheartened to try any longer to discover truth by their own thinking, only a few find a substitute for it in truth taken from others. The mass of people remain skeptical. They lose all feeling for truth, and all sense of need for it as well, finding themselves quite comfortable in a life without thought, driven now here, now there, from one opinion to another.

But the acceptance of authoritative truth, even if that truth has both spiritual and ethical content, does not bring skepticism to an end; it merely covers it up. Man's unnatural condition of not believing that any truth is discoverable by himself, continues, and produces its natural results. The city of truth cannot be built on the swampy ground of skepticism. Our spiritual life is rotten throughout because it is permeated through and through with skepticism; in consequence, we live in a world which in every respect is full of falsehood. We are not far from shipwreck on the rock of wanting to have even truth organized.

Truth taken over by a skepticism which has become believing has not the spiritual qualities of that which originated in thinking. It has been externalized and rendered torpid. It does obtain influence over a man, but it is not capable of uniting itself with him to the very marrow of his being. Living truth is that alone which has its origin in thinking.

Just as a tree bears year after year the same fruit and yet fruit which is each year new, so must all permanently valuable ideas be continually born again in thought. But our age is bent on trying to make the barren tree of skepticism fruitful by tying fruits of truth on its branches.

It is only by confidence in our ability to reach truth by our own individual thinking, that we are capable of accepting truth from outside. Unfettered thought, provided it be deep, never degenerates into subjectivity. With its own ideas it stirs those within itself which enjoy any traditional credit for being true, and exerts itself to be able to possess them as knowledge.

Not less strong than the will to truth must be the will to sincerity. Only an age which can show the courage of sincerity can possess truth which works as a spiritual force within it.

Sincerity is the foundation of the spiritual life.

With its depreciation of thinking our generation has lost its feeling for sincerity and with it that for truth as well. It can therefore be helped only by its being brought once more on to the road of thinking.

Because I have this certainty I oppose the spirit of the age, and take upon myself with confidence the responsibility of taking my part in the rekindling of the fire of thought.

For Discussion

1 Why is Schweitzer in disagreement with "the spirit of the age"?
2 Does he believe that thinking or reasoning is a perfect way of arriving at truth? What failures of "thought" does he recognize?

3 Comment on the following sentence taken from the second paragraph: "Any man who thinks for himself and at the same time is spiritually free is to the associations [that is, the organized political, social, and religious associations] something inconvenient and even uncanny." Why is individual freedom and independence inconvenient to what Schweitzer calls "asso-

ciations" and what we might today term "the Establishment"? Can you think of any examples drawn from your own experience which might support this statement?

4 What does Schweitzer think about modern advertising? Do you agree?

5 In the sixth paragraph from the end, Schweitzer uses an extended metaphor to explain his ideas: "Just as a tree bears year after year. . . ." Explain this metaphor in detail. In your opinion does the metaphor help the reader understand what the author is saying? If so, why?

6 What arguments might one give in opposition to Schweitzer's? Are there any areas of modern experience which might be happier if there were less "thinking"? What else does Man have to go on other than "thought"?

As more than one potential writer has discovered, writing is not an easy task. It is simply a difficult activity to begin and a difficult activity to conclude successfully. In this essay, Jean Cocteau, the French poet, novelist, dramatist, and film writer, comments on the difficulties of the writer's craft and explains the qualities of writing which are most important to him.

Jean Cocteau

On My Style

I am neither cheerful nor sad. But I can be completely the one or completely the other to excess. In conversation, if I am in good form, I forget the sorrows behind me, a pain I am suffering from, forget myself, so greatly do words intoxicate me and sweep ideas along with them. They come to me far better than in solitude and, often, to write an article is torture, whereas I can speak it without effort. This frenzy of speech gives an impression of a facility that I do not possess. For as soon as I hold myself in check, this facility gives way to arduous labour, the climbing of a hill that seems to me precipitous and interminable. Added to which is a superstitious fear of getting going, being always afraid of starting on the wrong tack. This induces a kind of laziness and is akin to what the psychiatrists call "the agony of the act." The white paper, the ink, the pen alarm me.

I know that they are in league against my will to write. If I succeed in conquering them, then the engine warms up, the work drives me and my mind functions. But it is essential that I should interfere as little as possible; that I should almost doze over it. The slightest consciousness of this process stops it. And if I want to get it going again, I have to wait until the machinery chooses, and not try to persuade it by some trick. That is why I do not use tables, which intimidate me and look too inviting. I write at any hour, on my knee. With drawing it is the same. I know very well how to fake a line, but that's not the real thing, and I only give birth to the true line when it so wishes.

My dreams are nearly always criticisms of my actions, so severe and so accurate that they could be a lesson to me. But unfortunately they caricature the very structure of my soul and discourage me rather than giving me the means to battle with myself. For no one knows his own weaknesses better than I, and if I happen to read some article attacking me, I feel that I could strike closer to the mark, that the steel would bury itself up to the hilt and there would be nothing left for me to do but fold up, hang out my tongue and fall on my knees in the arena.

One must not confuse intelligence, so adept at duping its man, with that other organ, seated we know not where, which informs us —irrevocably—of our limitations. No one can scale them. The effort would be seen through. It would further emphasize the narrow space accorded to our movements. It is through the power to revolve within this space that talent proves itself. Only thus can we progress. And each progress can only be of a moral kind, since each one of our ventures takes us unawares. We can count on nothing but integrity. Every trick leads to another. A blunder is preferable. The anonymous public boos at it, but forgives us. Tricks give themselves away with the blank expression of a woman who once loved but loves no longer.

That is why I took pains not to waste my strength at school. I correct carelessly, let a thousand faults pass, am lazy about rereading my work and only reread the idea. So long as what's to be said is said, it's all one to me.

All the same I have my method. This consists in being quick, hard, economical in words, in unrhyming my prose, in taking aim regardless of style and hitting the bull's-eye at whatever cost.

Rereading my work in proper perspective I am ashamed only of the trimmings. They harm us, because they distract from us. The public loves them; it is blinded by them and ignores the rest. I have heard Charles Chaplin deplore having left in his film *The Gold Rush* that dance of the bread rolls for which every spectator congratulates him. To him it is only a blot that catches the eye. I have also heard him say (on the subject of decorative style) that after a film he "shakes the tree." One must only keep, he added, what sticks to the branches.

Often the decoration is not of one's own volition. It is the result of a certain balance. For the public such balance has a superficial charm which consoles them for not properly appreciating the basic matter. This is the case with Picasso. This complete artist is made up of a man and a woman. In him terrible domestic scenes take place. Never was so much crockery smashed. In the end the man is always right and slams the door. But there remains of the woman an elegance, an organic gentleness, a kind of luxuriousness which gives an excuse to those who are afraid of strength and cannot follow the man beyond the threshold.

For Discussion

1 According to Cocteau, what is the difference between his ability to speak and his ability to write? Why does he feel that writing is harder?

2 Cocteau maintains that he is aware of his limitations as a writer. He then goes on to say: "It is through the power to revolve within this space that talent proves itself." What does he mean by that statement? What does he seem to be saying about what *talent* means to him?

3 Cocteau says about his style ". . . my method . . . consists in being quick, hard, economical in words, in unrhyming my

prose, in taking aim regardless of style and hitting the bull's-eye at whatever cost." Cite examples of these qualities from this essay.

4 Cocteau maintains that when he rereads what he has written, he is ashamed only of the "trimmings." What does he mean by "trimmings"? What "trimmings" have you encountered in a recent book or film? Would the book or film have been improved if they had been removed? Explain and offer examples.

338

Africa is a land of contradictions. A few minutes' drive from great modern cities there are villages where life remains pretty much as it was centuries ago. Many Africans find themselves with divided loyalties: they are torn between their traditional tribal beliefs and the technological methods that go with economic progress.

Camara Laye has lived in both worlds, as he tells in this essay. He grew up as a member of an African tribe. Later he studied engineering in Paris. The fascination of his autobiography, *The Dark Child*, comes from the fact that it was written by a man with a "modern" mind who looks back on his own childhood and bears witness to mysterious events that he can neither explain nor deny.

Camara Laye

The Snake and the Crocodile

I

I was a little boy playing around my father's hut. How old would I have been at that time? I cannot remember exactly. I must still have been very young: five, maybe six years old. My mother was in the workshop with my father, and I could just hear their familiar voices above the noise of the anvil and the conversation of the customers.

Suddenly I stopped playing, my whole attention fixed on a snake that was creeping around the hut. After a moment I went over to him. I had taken in my hand a reed that was lying in the yard—there were always some lying around; they used to get broken off the fence of plaited reeds that marked the boundary of our concession[1]—and I thrust it into his mouth. The snake did not try to get away; he was beginning to enjoy our little game; he was slowly swallowing the reed; he was devouring it, I thought, as if it were some delicious prey, his eyes glittering with voluptuous bliss; and inch by inch his head was drawing nearer to my hand. At last the reed was almost entirely swallowed, and the snake's jaws were terribly close to my fingers.

I was laughing. I had not the slightest fear, and I feel sure that the snake would not have hesitated much longer before burying his fangs in my fingers if, at that moment, Damany, one of the apprentices, had not come out of the workshop. He called my father, and almost at once I felt myself lifted off my feet: I was safe in the arms of one of my father's friends.

Around me there was a great commotion. My mother was shouting hardest of all, and

1 concession *The area within an African village that belongs to one family.*

she gave me a few sharp slaps. I wept, more upset by the sudden uproar than by the blows. A little later, when I was somewhat calmer and the shouting had ceased, my mother solemnly warned me never to play that game again. I promised, although the game still didn't seem dangerous to me.

My father's hut was near the workshop, and I often played beneath the veranda that ran around the outside. It was his private hut, and like all our huts built of mud bricks that had been pounded and moulded with water; it was round, and proudly helmeted with thatch. It was entered by a rectangular doorway. Inside, a tiny window let in a thin shaft of daylight. On the right was the bed, made of beaten earth like the bricks, and spread with a simple wickerwork mat on which lay a pillow stuffed with kapok. At the rear, right under the window where the light was strongest, were the toolboxes. On the left were the *boubous* and the prayer-rugs.[2] At the head of the bed, hanging over the pillow and watching over my father's slumber, stood a row of pots that contained extracts from plants and the bark of trees. These pots all had metal lids and were profusely and curiously garlanded; it did not take long to discover that they were the most important things in the hut; they contained magic charms—those mysterious liquids that keep the evil spirits at bay, and, if smeared on the body, make it invulnerable to every kind of black magic. My father, before going to bed, never failed to smear his body with a little of each liquid, first one, then another, for each charm had its own particular property: but exactly *what* property I did not know: I had left my father's house much too soon.

From the veranda under which I played I could keep an eye on the workshop opposite, and the adults for their part could keep an eye on me. This workshop was the main building in our concession, and my father was generally to be found there, looking after the work, forging the most important item him-

self, or repairing delicate mechanisms; there he received his friends and his customers, and the place resounded with noise from morning to night. Moreover, everyone who entered or left our concession had to cross the workshop. There was a perpetual coming and going, though no one seemed to be in any particular hurry; each had his bit of gossip; each lingered at the forge to watch. Sometimes I came near the door, but I rarely went in; everyone there frightened me, and I would run away as soon as anyone tried to touch me. It was not until very much later that I got into the habit of crouching in a corner of the workshop to watch the fire blazing in the forge.

My private domain at that time was the veranda that encircled my father's hut, my mother's hut, and the orange tree that grew in the middle of the concession.

As soon as you crossed the workshop and went through the door at the back, you would see the orange tree. Compared with the giants of our native forests, the tree was not very big, but its mass of glossy leaves cast a dense shade that kept the heat at bay. When it was in flower a heady perfume pervaded the entire concession. When the fruit first appeared we were only allowed to look: we had to wait patiently until it was ripe. Then my father, who as head of the family—and a very large family it was—governed the concession, gave the order to pick the fruit. The men who did the picking brought their baskets one by one to my father, who portioned them out among the people who lived in the concession and among his neighbors and customers. After that we were permitted to help ourselves from the baskets and we were allowed as much as we liked! My father was open-handed; in fact, a lavish giver. Any visitor, no matter who he was, shared our meals; since I could never keep up with the speed at which such guests ate I might have remained forever hungry if my mother had not taken the precaution of putting my share aside.

2 boubous . . . prayer-rugs *Like many west Africans, Laye's family is Moslem. The* boubou *is the long, loose garment worn* *by Moslem men during prayers. Each Moslem has his own prayer-rug upon which he kneels.*

"Sit here," she would say, "and eat, for your father's mad."

She did not look upon such guests with a kindly eye. There were too many for her liking, all bent on filling their bellies at her expense. My father, for his part, ate very little; he was an extremely temperate man.

We lived beside a railroad. The trains skirted the reed fence of the concession so closely that sparks thrown off from the locomotive set fire to it every now and then which had to be quickly extinguished so that the whole concession would not go up in smoke. These alarms, frightening yet exciting, made me aware of the passing trains. And even where there were no trains—for in those days the railroad was dependent on a most irregular water traffic—much of my time was spent watching the iron rails. They glistened cruelly in a light which nothing in that place could relieve. Baking since dawn, the roadbed was so hot that oil which dropped from the locomotives evaporated immediately, leaving no trace. Was it the oven-like heat or the smell of oil—for the smell remained in spite of everying—which attracted the snakes? I do not know. But often I came upon them crawling in that hot roadbed. It would have been fatal if they had gotten into the concession.

Ever since the day when I had been forbidden by my mother to play with snakes I ran to her as soon as I saw one.

"There's a snake!" I would cry.

"What? Another?"

And she would come running to see what sort of snake it was. If it was just a snake like any other snake—actually they were all quite different—she would immediately beat it to death; and, like all the women of our country, she would work herself into a frenzy, beating the snake to a pulp. The men contented themselves with a single hard blow, neatly struck.

One day, however, I noticed a little black snake with a strikingly marked body. He was proceeding slowly in the direction of the workshop. I ran to warn my mother, as usual. But as soon as she saw the black snake she said to me gravely:

"My son, this one must not be killed: he is not like other snakes, and he will not harm you; you must never interfere with him."

Everyone in our concession knew that this snake must not be killed—everyone except myself, and, I suppose, my little playmates, who were still ignorant children.

"This snake," my mother added, "is your father's guiding spirit."

I gazed dumbfounded at the little snake. He was proceeding calmly toward the workshop, gracefully, very sure of himself, and almost as if conscious of his immunity; his body, black and brilliant, glittered in the harsh light of the sun. When he reached the worshop, I noticed for the first time a small hole in the wall, cut out level with the ground. The snake disappeared through this hole.

"Look," said my mother, "the snake is going to pay your father a visit."

Although I was familiar with the supernatural, this sight filled me with such astonishment that I was struck dumb. What business would a snake have with my father? And why this particular snake? No one was to kill him because he was my father's guiding spirit! At any rate, that was the explanation my mother had given me. But what exactly *was* a "guiding spirit"? What were these guiding spirits that I encountered almost everywhere, forbidding one thing, commanding another to be done? I could not understand it at all, though their presences surrounded me as I grew to manhood. There were good spirits, and there were evil ones; and more evil than good ones, it seemed. And how was I to know that this snake was harmless? He was a snake like the others: black, to be sure, with extraordinary markings—but for all that a snake. I was completely perplexed, but I did not question my mother: I had decided that I must ask my father about it, as if this were a mystery to be discussed only between men, a mystery in which women had no part. I decided to wait until evening to speak to him.

Immediately after the evening meal, when the palavers were over, my father bade his friends farewell and sat under the veranda of his hut; I seated myself near him. I began questioning him in a dilatory manner, as all children do, regarding every subject under the sun. Actually I was no more talkative than on other evenings. Only this evening I withheld what troubled me, waiting for the opportunity when—my face betraying nothing—I might ask the question which had worried me so deeply from the moment when I first saw the black snake going toward the workshop. Finally, unable to restrain myself any longer, I asked:

"My father, what is that little snake that comes to visit you?"

"What snake do you mean?"

"Why, the little black snake that my mother forbids us to kill."

"Ah!" he said.

He gazed at me for a long while. He seemed to be considering whether to answer or not. Perhaps he was thinking about how old I was, perhaps he was wondering if it was not a little too soon to confide such a secret to a twelve-year-old boy. Then suddenly he made up his mind.

"That snake," he said, "is the guiding spirit of our race. Can you understand that?"

"Yes," I answered, although I did not understand very well.

"That snake," he went on, "has always been with us; he has always made himself known to one of us. In our time, it is to me that he has made himself known."

"Yes," I said.

And I said it with all my heart, for it seemed obvious to me that the snake could have made himself known to no one but my father. Was not my father the head man in our concession? Was it not my father who had authority over all the blacksmiths in our

district? Was he not the most skilled? Was he not, after all, my father?

"How did he make himself known?" I asked.

"First of all, he made himself known in the semblance of a dream. He appeared to me several times in sleep and told me the day on which he would appear to me in reality: he gave me the precise time and place. But when I really saw him for the first time, I was filled with fear. I took him for a snake like any other snake, and I had to keep myself under control or I would have tried to kill him. When he saw that I did not receive him kindly, he turned away and departed the way he had come. And there I stood, watching him depart, wondering all the time if I should not simply have killed him there and then; but a power greater than I stayed my hand and prevented me from pursuing him. I stood watching him disappear. And even then, at that very moment, I could easily have overtaken him; a few swift strides would have been enough; but I was struck motionless by a kind of paralysis. Such was my first encounter with the little black snake."

He was silent a moment, then went on:

"The following night, I saw the snake again in my dream. 'I came as I foretold,' he said, 'but thou didst not receive me kindly; nay, rather I did perceive that thou didst intend to receive me unkindly: I did read it thus in thine eyes. Wherefore dost thou reject me? Lo, I am the guiding spirit of thy race, and it is even as the guiding spirit of thy race that I make myself known to thee, as to the most worthy. Therefore forbear to look with fear upon me, and beware that thou dost not reject me, for behold, I bring thee good fortune.' After that, I received the snake kindly when he made himself known to me a second time; I received him without fear, I received him with loving kindness, and he brought me nothing but good."

My father again was silent for a moment, then he said:

"You can see for yourself that I am not

more gifted than other men, that I have nothing which other men have not also, and even that I have less than others, since I give everything away, and would even give away the last thing I had, the shirt on my back. Nevertheless I am better known. My name is on everyone's tongue, and it is I who have authority over all the blacksmiths in the five cantons. If these things are so, it is by virtue of this snake alone, who is the guiding spirit of our race. It is to this snake I owe everything; it is he who gives me warning of all that is to happen. Thus I am never surprised, when I awake, to see this or that person waiting for me outside my workshop: I already know that he will be there. No more am I surprised when this or that motorcycle or bicycle breaks down, or when an accident happens to a clock: because I have had foreknowledge of what would come to pass. Everything is transmitted to me in the course of the night, together with an account of all the work I shall have to perform, so that from the start, without having to cast about in my mind, I know how to repair whatever is brought to me. These things have established my renown as a craftsman. But all this—let it never be forgotten—I owe to the snake, I owe it to the guiding spirit of our race."

He was silent; and then I understood why, when my father came back from a walk he would enter the workshop and say to the apprentices: "During my absence, this or that person has been here, he was dressed in such and such a way, he came from such and such a place and he brought with him such and such a piece of work to be done." And all marveled at this curious knowledge. When I raised my eyes, I saw that my father was watching me.

"I have told you all these things, little one, because you are my son, the eldest of my sons, and because I have nothing to hide from you. There is a certain form of behavior to observe, and certain ways of acting in order that the guiding spirit of our race

may approach you also. I, your father, was observing that form of behavior which persuades our guiding spirit to visit us. Oh, perhaps not consciously: but nevertheless it is true that if you desire the guiding spirit of our race to visit you one day, if you desire to inherit it in your turn, you will have to conduct yourself in the selfsame manner; from now on, it will be necessary for you to be more and more in my company."

He gazed at me with burning eyes, then suddenly he heaved a sigh.

"I fear, I very much fear, little one, that you are not often enough in my company. You are all day at school, and one day you will depart from that school for a greater one. You will leave me, little one. . . ."

And again he heaved a sigh. I saw that his heart was heavy within him. The hurricane-lamp hanging on the veranda cast a harsh glare on his face. He suddenly seemed to me an old man.

"Father!" I cried.

"Son . . ." he whispered.

And I was no longer sure whether I ought to continue to attend school or whether I ought to remain in the workshop: I felt unutterably confused.

"Go now," said my father.

I went to my mother's hut. The night was full of sparkling stars; an owl was hooting nearby. Ah! what was the right path for me? Did I know yet where that path lay? My perplexity was boundless as the sky, and mine was a sky, alas, without any stars. . . . I entered my mother's hut, which at that time was mine also, and went to bed at once. But sleep did not come and I tossed restlessly on my bed.

"What's the matter with you?" asked my mother.

"Nothing."

No. I couldn't find anything to say.

"Why don't you go to sleep?" my mother continued.

"I don't know."

"Go to sleep!" she said.

"Yes," I said.

"Sleep . . . Nothing can resist sleep," she said sadly.

Why did she, too, appear so sad? Had she divined my distress? Anything that concerned me she sensed very deeply. I was trying to sleep, but I shut my eyes and lay still in vain: the image of my father under the hurricane-lamp would not leave me: my father who had suddenly seemed so old and who was so young, so lively—younger and livelier than the rest of us, a man no one could outrun, who was swifter of limb than any of us. . . . "Father! . . . Father! . . . !" I kept repeating. "What must I do if I am to do the right thing?" And I wept silently and fell asleep still weeping.

After that we never mentioned the little black snake again: my father had spoken to me about him for the first and last time. But from that time on, as soon as I saw the little snake, I would run and sit in the workshop. I would watch him glide through the little hole in the wall. As if informed of his presence, my father at that very instant would turn his eyes to the hole and smile. The snake would go straight to him, opening his jaws. When he was within reach my father would stroke him and the snake would accept the caress with a quivering of his whole body. I never saw the little snake attempt to do the slightest harm to my father. That caress and the answering tremor—but I ought to say: that appealing caress and that answering tremor—threw me each time into an inexpressible confusion. I imagined I know not what mysterious conversations: the hand inquired and the tremor replied. . . .

Yes. It was like a conversation. Would I too converse that way some day? No. I would continue to attend school. Yet I should have liked so much to place my hand, my own hand, on that snake, and to understand and listen to that tremor too; but I did not know whether the snake would have accepted my hand, and I felt now that he would have nothing to tell me. I was afraid that he would never have anything to tell me.

When my father felt that he had stroked the snake enough he left him alone. Then the snake coiled himself under the edge of one of the sheepskins on which my father, facing his anvil, was seated.

II

Of all the different kinds of work my father engaged in, none fascinated me so much as his skill with gold. No other occupation was so noble, no other needed such a delicate touch. And then, every time he worked in gold it was like a festival—indeed it *was* a festival—that broke the monotony of ordinary working days.

So, if a woman, accompanied by a go-between, crossed the threshold of the workshop, I followed her in at once. I knew what she wanted: she had brought some gold, and had come to ask my father to transform it into a trinket. She had collected it in the placers of Siguiri[3] where, crouching over the river for months on end, she had patiently extracted grains of gold from the mud.

These women never came alone. They knew my father had other things to do than make trinkets. And even when he had the time, they knew they were not the first to ask a favor of him, and that, consequently, they would not be served before others.

Generally they required the trinket for a certain date, for the festival of Ramadan or the Tabaski[4] or some other family ceremony or dance.

Therefore, to enhance their chances of being served quickly and to more easily persuade my father to interrupt the work before him, they used to request the services of an official praise-singer, a go-between, arranging in advance the fee they were to pay him for his good offices.

The go-between installed himself in the workshop, tuned up his *cora*, which is our harp, and began to sing my father's praises.

3 placers of Siguiri *Places where gold is washed from the river at Siguiri, a town in what is now the Republic of Guinea.*

4 Ramadan . . . Tabaski *The Ramadan is the ninth month of the Mohammedan calendar, a period of fasting. The Tabaski is a Moslem religious holiday.*

This was always a great event for me. I heard recalled the lofty deeds of my father's ancestors and their names from the earliest times. As the couplets were reeled off it was like watching the growth of a great genealogical tree that spread its branches far and wide and flourished its boughs and twigs before my mind's eye. The harp played an accompaniment to this vast utterance of names, expanding it with notes that were now soft, now shrill.

I could sense my father's vanity being inflamed, and I already knew that after having sipped this milk-and-honey he would lend a favorable ear to the woman's request. But I was not alone in my knowledge. The woman also had seen my father's eyes gleaming with contented pride. She held out her grains of gold as if the whole matter were settled. My father took up his scales and weighed the gold.

"What sort of trinket do you want?" he would ask.

"I want . . ."

And then the woman would not know any longer exactly what she wanted because desire kept making her change her mind, and because she would have liked all the trinkets at once. But it would have taken a pile of gold much larger than she had brought to satisfy her whim, and from then on her chief purpose in life was to get hold of it as soon as she could.

"When do you want it?"

Always the answer was that the trinket was needed for an occasion in the near future.

"So! You are in that much of a hurry? Where do you think I shall find the time?"

"I am in a great hurry, I assure you."

"I have never seen a woman eager to deck herself out who wasn't in a great hurry! Good! I shall arrange my time to suit you. Are you satisfied?"

He would take the clay pot that was kept specially for smelting gold, and would pour the grains into it. He would then cover the gold with powdered charcoal, a charcoal he prepared by using plant juices of exceptional purity. Finally, he would place a large lump of the same kind of charcoal over the pot.

As soon as she saw that the work had been duly undertaken, the woman, now quite satisfied, would return to her household tasks, leaving her go-between to carry on with the praise-singing which had already proved so advantageous.

At a sign from my father the apprentices began working two sheepskin bellows. The skins were on the floor, on opposite sides of the forge, connected to it by earthen pipes. While the work was in progress the apprentices sat in front of the bellows with crossed legs. That is, the younger of the two sat, for the elder was sometimes allowed to assist. But the younger—this time it was Sidafa—was only permitted to work the bellows and watch while waiting his turn for promotion to less rudimentary tasks. First one and then the other worked hard at the bellows: the flame in the forge rose higher and became a living thing, a genie implacable and full of life.

Then my father lifted the clay pot with his long tongs and placed it on the flame.

Immediately all activity in the workshop almost came to a halt. During the whole time that the gold was being smelted, neither copper nor aluminum could be worked nearby, lest some particle of these base metals fall into the container which held the gold. Only steel could be worked on such occasions, but the men, whose task that was, hurried to finish what they were doing, or left it abruptly to join the apprentices gathered around the forge. There were so many, and they crowded so around my father, that I, the smallest person present, had to come near the forge in order not to lose track of what was going on.

If he felt he had inadequate working space, my father had the apprentices stand well away from him. He merely raised his hand in a simple gesture: at that particular moment he never uttered a word, and no one else would: no one was allowed to utter a word. Even the go-between's voice was no longer raised in song. The silence was broken only by the panting of the bellows and the faint hissing of the gold. But if my father never actually spoke, I know that he was forming words in his mind. I could tell from his lips, which kept moving, while, bending over the pot, he stirred the gold and charcoal with a bit of wood that kept bursting into flame and had constantly to be replaced by a fresh one.

What words did my father utter? I do not know. At least I am not certain what they were. No one ever told me. But could they have been anything but incantations? On these occasions was he not invoking the genies of fire and gold, of fire and wind, of wind blown by the blastpipes of the forge, of fire born of wind, of gold married to fire? Was it not their assistance, their friendship, their espousal that he besought? Yes. Almost certainly he was invoking these genies, all of whom are equally indispensable for smelting gold.

The operation going on before my eyes was certainly the smelting of gold, yet something more than that: a magical operation that the guiding spirits could regard with favor or disfavor. That is why, all around my father, there was absolute silence and anxious expectancy. Though only a child, I knew there could be no craft greater than the goldsmith's. I expected a ceremony; I had come to be present at a ceremony; and it actually was one, though very protracted. I was still too young to understand why, but I had an inkling as I watched the almost religious concentration of those who followed the mixing process in the clay pot.

When finally the gold began to melt I could have shouted aloud—and perhaps we all would have if we had not been forbidden to make a sound. I trembled, and so did everyone else watching my father stir the mixture—it was still a heavy paste—in which the charcoal was gradually consumed. The next

stage followed swiftly. The gold now had the fluidity of water. The genies had smiled on the operation!

"Bring me the brick!" my father would order, thus lifting the ban that until then had silenced us.

The brick, which an apprentice would place beside the fire, was hollowed out, generously greased with Galam butter. My father would take the pot off the fire and tilt it carefully, while I would watch the gold flow into the brick, flow like liquid fire. True, it was only a very sparse trickle of fire, but how vivid, how brilliant! As the gold flowed into the brick, the grease sputtered and flamed and emitted a thick smoke that caught in the throat and stung the eyes, leaving us all weeping and coughing.

But there were times when it seemed to me that my father ought to turn this task over to one of his assistants. They were experienced, had assisted him hundreds of times, and could certainly have performed the work well. But my father's lips moved and those inaudible, secret words, those incantations he addressed to one we could not see or hear, was the essential part. Calling on the genies of fire, of wind, of gold and exorcising the evil spirits —this was a knowledge he alone possessed.

By now the gold had been cooled in the hollow of the brick, and my father began to hammer and stretch it. This was the moment when his work as a goldsmith really began. I noticed that before embarking on it he never failed to stroke the little snake stealthily as it lay coiled up under the sheepskin. I can only assume that this was his way of gathering strength for what remained to be done, the most trying part of his task.

But was it not extraordinary and miraculous that on these occasions the little black snake was always coiled under the sheepskin? He was not always there. He did not visit my father every day. But he was always present whenever there was gold to be worked. His presence was no surprise to *me*. After that evening when my father had spoken of the guiding spirit of his race I was no longer astonished. The snake was there intentionally. He knew what the future held. Did he tell my father? I think that he most certainly did. Did he tell him everything? I have another reason for believing firmly that he did.

The craftsman who works in gold must first of all purify himself. Great respecter of ceremony as he was, it would have been impossible for my father to ignore these rules. Now, I never saw him make these preparations. I saw him address himself to his work without any apparent preliminaries. From that moment it was obvious that, forewarned in a dream by his black guiding spirit of the task which awaited him in the morning, my father must have prepared for it as soon as he arose, entering his workshop in a state of purity, his body smeared with the secret potions hidden in his numerous pots of magical substances; or perhaps he always came into his workshop in a state of ritual purity. I am not trying to make him out a better man than he was—he was a man and had his share of human frailties—but he was always uncompromising in his respect for ritual observance.

The woman for whom the trinket was being made, and who had come often to see how the work was progressing, would arrive for the final time, not wanting to miss a moment of this spectacle—as marvelous to her as to us—when the gold wire, which my father had succeeded in drawing out from the mass of molten gold and charcoal, was transformed into a trinket.

There she would be. Her eyes would devour the fragile gold wire, following it in its tranquil and regular spiral around the little slab of metal which supported it. My father would catch a glimpse of her and I would see him slowly beginning to smile. Her avid attention delighted him.

"Are you trembling?" he would ask.

"Am I trembling?"

And we would all burst out laughing at her. For she would be trembling! She would be trembling with covetousness for the spiral pyramid in which my father would be inserting, among the convolutions, tiny grains of gold. When he had finally finished by crowning the pyramid with a heavier grain, she would dance in delight.

No one—no one at all—would be more enchanted than she as my father slowly turned the trinket back and forth between his fingers to display its perfection. Not even the praise-singer whose business it was to register excitement would be more excited than she. Throughout this metamorphosis he did not stop speaking faster and ever faster, increasing his tempo, accelerating his praises and flatteries as the trinket took shape, shouting to the skies my father's skill.

For the praise-singer took a curious part— I should say rather that it was direct and effective—in the work. He was drunk with the joy of creation. He shouted aloud in joy. He plucked his *cora* like a man inspired. He sweated as if he were the trinket-maker, as if he were my father, as if the trinket were his creation. He was no longer a hired censer-bearer,[5] a man whose services anyone could rent. He was a man who created his song out of some deep inner necessity. And when my father, after having soldered the large grain of gold that crowned the summit, held out his work to be admired, the praise-singer would no longer be able to contain himself. He would begin to intone the *douga*, the great chant which is sung only for celebrated men and which is danced for them alone.

But the *douga* is a formidable chant, a provocative chant, a chant which the praise-singer dared not sing, and which the man for whom it is sung dared not dance before certain precautions had been taken. My father had taken them as soon as he woke, since he had been warned in a dream. The praise-singer had taken them when he concluded his arrangements with the woman. Like my father he had smeared his body with magic substances and had made himself invulnerable to the evil genies whom the *douga* in-

5 censer-bearer *A censer is a receptacle in which incense is burned during religious cere-* monies. *"Censer-bearer" refers to the acolyte who carries the censer.*

evitably set free; these potions made him invulnerable also to rival praise-singers, perhaps jealous of him, who awaited only this song and the exaltation and loss of control which attended it, in order to begin casting their spells.

At the first notes of the *douga* my father would arise and emit a cry in which happiness and triumph were equally mingled; and brandishing in his right hand the hammer that was the symbol of his profession and in his left hand a ram's horn filled with magic substances, he would dance the glorious dance.

No sooner had he finished, than workmen and apprentices, friends and customers in their turn, not forgetting the woman for whom the trinket had been created, would flock around him, congratulating him, showering praises on him and complimenting the praise-singer at the same time. The latter found himself laden with gifts—almost his only means of support, for the praise-singer leads a wandering life after the fashion of the troubadours of old. Aglow with dancing and the praises he had received, my father would offer everyone cola nuts, that small change of Guinean courtesy.

Now all that remained to be done was to redden the trinket in a little water to which chlorine and sea salt had been added. I was at liberty to leave. The festival was over! But often as I came out of the workshop my mother would be in the court, pounding millet or rice, and she would call to me:

"Where have you been?" although she knew perfectly well where I had been.

"In the workshop."

"Of course. Your father was smelting gold. Gold! Always gold!"

And she would beat the millet or rice furiously with her pestle.

"Your father is ruining his health!"

"He danced the *douga*."

"The *douga*! The *douga* won't keep him from ruining his eyes. As for you, you would be better off playing in the courtyard instead

of breathing dust and smoke in the workshop."

My mother did not like my father to work in gold. She knew how dangerous it was: a trinket-maker empties his lungs blowing on the blow-pipe and his eyes suffer from the fire. Perhaps they suffer even more from the microscopic precision which the work requires. And even if there had been no such objections involved, my mother would scarcely have relished this work. She was suspicious of it, for gold cannot be smelted without the use of other metals, and my mother thought it was not entirely honest to put aside for one's own use the gold which the alloy had displaced. However, this was a custom generally known, and one which she herself had accepted when she took cotton to be woven and received back only a piece of cotton cloth half the weight of the original bundle.

III

I realize that my mother's authoritarian attitudes may appear surprising; generally the role of the African woman is thought to be a ridiculously humble one, and indeed there are parts of the continent where it is insignificant; but Africa is vast, with a diversity equal to its vastness. The woman's role in our country is one of fundamental independence, of great inner pride. We despise only those who allow themselves to be despised; and our women very seldom give cause for that. My father would never have dreamed of despising anyone, least of all my mother. He had the greatest respect for her too, and so did our friends and neighbors. That was due, I am sure, to my mother's character, which was impressive; it was due also to the strange powers she possessed.

I hesitate to say what these powers were, and I do not wish to describe them all. I know that what I say will be greeted with skeptical smiles. And today, now that I come to remember them, even I hardly know how I should regard them. They seem to be unbelievable; they *are* unbelievable. Nevertheless I can only tell you what I saw with my own eyes. How can I disown the testimony of my own eyes? Those unbelievable things. I saw them. I see them again as I saw them then. Are there not things around us, everywhere, which are inexplicable? In our country there were mysteries without number, and my mother was familiar with them all.

One day—it was toward evening—I saw some men request her to use her powers to get a horse on his feet after he had resisted all attempts to make him rise. He was out at pasture, but he was lying down, and his owner wanted to bring him back to the stable before nightfall. The horse obstinately refused to move, although there was no apparent reason why he should disobey. But his inclination was otherwise, though it might have been a magic spell that immobilized him. I heard the men telling my mother about it, and asking her help.

"Well, then, let's go and have a look at this horse," said my mother.

She called the eldest of my sisters and told her to look after the cooking of the evening meal, and then went off with the men. I followed her. When we arrived at the pasture, we saw the horse: he was lying in the grass, gazing at us unconcernedly. His owner tried again to make him get up and spoke to him in honeyed tones, but the horse remained deaf to all entreaty. His master raised a hand to strike him.

"Do not strike him," said my mother. "It won't do any good."

She went up to the horse and, lifting her own hand, declaimed in a solemn tone: "I command you, horse, rise up!"

And we all saw the horse get up at once and follow his master quietly away. I have told in very simple words, and very exact words, what I saw then, with my own eyes, and to my mind it is unbelievable; but the event was just as I have described it: the horse got up without any further delay and followed his master: if he had refused to follow him, my mother's intervention would once more have had its effect.

Where did these powers come from? Well, my mother was the next child born after my twin uncles in Tindican. Now, they say that twin brothers are wiser than other children, and are practically magicians. As for the child that follows them, and who receives the name *sayon*, that is, the younger brother of twins, he too is endowed with the gift of magic, and he is even considered to be more powerful and more mysterious than the twins in whose lives he plays a very important role.

I have given one example of my mother's supernatural powers; I could give many others, equally strange, equally mysterious. How many times I have seen her, at daybreak, walk a few steps into the yard and turn her head in one direction or another to shout at the top of her voice:

"If this business goes any further, I shall not hesitate to expose you. That's my final word!"

In the early morning her voice traveled far: it was intended to reach the ears of the witch-doctor, for whom the warning had been uttered. He understood that if he did not stop his nocturnal activities, my mother would denounce him in public; and this threat always worked: from then on, the witch-doctor kept quiet. My mother used to receive warning of these activities while she was asleep. We never wakened her, for fear of interrupting the course of the revelations that flowed through her dreams. This power was well known by our neighbors and by the whole community: no one ever doubted it.

Though my mother could see what evil was being hatched and could denounce the author of it, her power went no further. Even if she had wished, her power to cast spells did not allow her to do any evil on her own account. She was never suspect. If people made themselves pleasant to her, it was not at all out of fear. They were pleasant because they thought she deserved it, and because they respected her power to cast spells from which nothing was to be feared. On the contrary, much was to be hoped from them.

As well as this gift, or rather part-gift, of magic, my mother had other powers that she had inherited in the same way. At Tindican her father had been a skillful blacksmith and my mother possessed the usual powers of that caste from which the majority of soothsayers are drawn. It was in my mother that the spirit of her caste was most visibly—I was going to say ostensibly—manifested. I don't pretend that she was more faithful to it than my uncles were, but she alone demonstrated her fidelity. Finally, she had inherited, as a matter of course, my grandfather's totem which is the crocodile. This totem allowed all Damans to draw water from the Niger without running any danger of harm.

Normally, everyone draws water from the river. The Niger flows slowly and abundantly; it can be forded; and the crocodiles, which keep to the deep water upstream or downstream from where the water is drawn, are not to be feared. You can bathe quite freely on the banks of pale sand and do your washing there.

But when the water rises, the volume of the river is increased three-fold. The water is deep, and the crocodiles are dangerous. One can see their triangular heads breaking the surface. Everyone, therefore, keeps away from the river and instead draws water from the little streams.

My mother used to continue to draw water from the river. I watched her draw it from the place where the crocodiles were. Naturally I watched her from a distance, for my totem is not my mother's. And I had every reason to fear those voracious beasts; but my mother could draw water without fear, and no one warned her of the danger, because everyone knew that the danger did not exist for her. Whoever else had ventured to do what my mother used to do would inevitably have been knocked down by a blow from a powerful tail, seized in the terrible jaws and dragged into deep water. But the crocodiles could do no harm to my mother; and this privilege is quite understandable: the totem is identified with its possessor: this identification is absolute, and of such a nature that its possessor has the power to take on the form of the totem itself; it follows quite obviously that the totem cannot devour itself. My uncles at Tindican had the same prerogative.

I do not wish to say more, and I have told you only what I saw with my own eyes. These miracles—they were miracles indeed—I think about now as if they were the fabulous events of a far-off past. That past is, however, still quite near: it was only yesterday. But the world rolls on, the world changes, my own world perhaps more rapidly than anyone else's; so that it appears as if we are ceasing to be what we were, and that truly we are no longer what we were, and that we were not exactly ourselves even at the time when these miracles took place before our eyes. Yes, the world rolls on, the world changes; it rolls on and changes, and the proof of it is that my own totem—I too have my totem—is still unknown to me.

For Discussion

1 Could modern science explain the relationship between Camara Laye's father and the small black snake? Can you find any explanation of how the father knew about things he had not seen? Can you explain the snake's presence whenever the father worked with gold? Does the author convince you that these things really happened?

2 What kind of man was Camara Laye's father? What were his weaknesses and virtues?

3 In Shakespeare's *Hamlet* the hero says to his friend, "There are more things in heaven and earth, Horatio, than are dreamt of in your philosophy." Does this apply to "The Snake and the Crocodile"? Do you believe that there are areas of experience which can never be explained by science?

4 What is the significance of the railroad line which ran past the concession where Camara Laye grew up? Is this detail the author's way of expressing the side-by-side existence of the old world and the new? Explain.

5 Is the mother's relation to the crocodile easier to explain than the father's relation to the snake? How can you explain her other powers?

6 What does the author mean when he says that his own totem is still unknown to him? Can you offer any reasons why?

Occasionally you find yourself in a situation where the mere fact of living suddenly becomes an unexplainable joy. It may occur at the seashore, at a party, on a hunting trip, even in a sun-flooded kitchen, or while raking and burning leaves in the yard. The world, for a harmonious moment, seems bright, kind, and full of peace. The friends around us seem perfect friends. Then time intrudes, and the routine reality of life returns. The interlude fades into a warm memory. It is just such a warm moment in his own life which Ernest Hemingway writes about in this selection from *Green Hills of Africa*. Riding across Africa in an open car on a hunting expedition, he met a group of natives who may never have seen a car before. For a moment, Hemingway saw the untamed African landscape as a Garden of Eden, where brotherhood and peace and love and happiness prevailed.

Ernest Hemingway

African Encounter

By now there was no more road, only a cattle track, but we were coming to the edge of the plain. Then the plain was behind us and ahead there were big trees and we were entering a country the loveliest that I had seen in Africa. The grass was green and smooth, short as a meadow that had been mown and is newly grown, and the trees were big, high-trunked, and old with no undergrowth but only the smooth green of the turf like a deer park and we drove on through shade and patches of sunlight following a faint trail the Wanderobo pointed out. I could not believe we had suddenly come to any such wonderful country. It was a country to wake from, happy to have had the dream and, seeing if it would clown away, I reached up and touched the Wanderobo's ear. He jumped and Kamau snickered. M'Cola nudged me from the back seat and pointed and there, standing in an open space between the trees, his head up, staring at us, the bristles on his back erect, long, thick, white tusks up-curving, his eyes showing bright, was a very large wart-hog boar watching us from less than twenty yards. I motioned to Kamau to stop and we sat looking at him and he at us. I put the rifle up and sighted on his chest. He watched and did not move. Then I motioned to Kamau to throw in the clutch and we went on and made a curve to the right and left the wart-hog, who had never moved, nor showed any fright at seeing us.

352

I could see that Kamau was excited and, looking back, M'Cola nodded his head up and down in agreement. None of us had ever seen a wart-hog that would not bolt off, fast-trotting, tail in air. This was a virgin country, an unhunted pocket in the million miles of bloody Africa. I was ready to stop and make camp anywhere.

This was the finest country I had seen but we went on, winding along through the big trees over the softly rolling grass. Then ahead and to the right we saw the high stockade of a Masai village. It was a very large village and out of it came running long-legged, brown, smooth-moving men who all seemed to be of the same age and who wore their hair in a heavy clublike queue that swung against their shoulders as they ran. They came up to the car and surrounded it, all laughing and smiling and talking. They all were tall, their teeth were white and good, and their hair was stained a red brown and arranged in a looped fringe on their foreheads. They carried spears and they were very handsome and extremely jolly, not sullen, nor contemptuous like the northern Masai, and they wanted to know what we were going to do. The Wanderobo evidently said we were hunting kudu and were in a hurry. They had the car surrounded so we could not move. One said something and three or four others joined in and Kamau explained to me that they had seen two kudu bulls go along the trail in the afternoon.

"It can't be true," I said to myself. "It can't be."

I told Kamau to start and slowly we pushed through them, they all laughing and trying to stop the car, making it all but run over them. They were the tallest, best-built, handsomest people I had ever seen and the first truly light-hearted happy people I had seen in Africa. Finally, when we were moving, they started to run beside the car smiling and laughing and showing how easily they could run and then, as the going was better, up the smooth valley of a stream, it became a contest

and one after another dropped out of the running, waving and smiling as they left until there were only two still running with us, the finest runners of the lot, who kept pace easily with the car as they moved long-legged, smoothly, loosely, and with pride. They were running too, at the pace of a fast miler, and carrying their spears as well. Then we had to turn to the right and climb out of the putting-green smoothness of the valley into a rolling meadow and, as we slowed, climbing in first gear, the whole pack came up again, laughing and trying not to seem winded. We went through a little knot of brush and a small rabbit started out, zig-zagging wildly and all the Masai behind now in a mad sprint. They caught the rabbit and the tallest runner came up with him to the car and handed him to me. I held him and could feel the thumping of his heart through the soft, warm, furry body, and as I stroked him the Masai patted my arm. Holding him by the ears I handed him back. No, no, he was mine. He was a present. I handed him to M'Cola. 'Cola did not take him seriously and handed him to one of the Masai. We were moving and they were running again now. The Masai stooped and put the rabbit on the ground and as he ran free they all laughed. M'Cola shook his head. We were all very impressed by these Masai.

"Good Masai," M'Cola said, very moved. "Masai many cattle. Masai no kill to eat. Masai kill man."

The Wanderobo patted himself on the chest.

"Wanderobo—Masai," he said, very proudly, claiming kin. His ears were curled in the same way theirs were. Seeing them running and so damned handsome and so happy made us all happy. I had never seen such quick disinterested friendliness, nor such fine looking people.

"Good Masai," M'Cola repeated, nodding his head emphatically. "Good, good Masai." Only Garrick seemed impressed in a different way. For all his khaki clothes and his letter from B'wana Simba, I believe these Masai frightened him in a very old place. They were our friends, not his. They certainly were our friends though. They had that attitude that makes brothers, that unexpressed but instant and complete acceptance that you must be Masai wherever it is you come from. That attitude you only get from the best of the English, the best of the Hungarians and the very best Spaniards; the thing that used to be the most clear distinction of nobility when there was nobility. It is an ignorant attitude and the people who have it do not survive, but very few pleasanter things ever happen to you than the encountering of it.

So now there were only the two of them left again, running, and it was hard going and the machine was beating them. They were still running well and still loose and long but the machine was a cruel pacemaker. So I told Kamau to speed it up and get it over with because a sudden burst of speed was not the humiliation of a steady using. They sprinted, were beaten, laughed, and then we were leaning out, waving, and they stood leaning on their spears and waved. We were still great friends but now we were alone again and there was no track, only the general direction to follow around clumps of trees and along the run of this green valley.

For Discussion

1 The author describes how he aimed his rifle at the wart-hog, then decided not to shoot it. Why is this incident—his refusal to shoot the wart-hog—well placed early in this selection?

2 The author never states directly that the Masai are fast runners. How is this information conveyed to the reader? Does Hemingway himself completely understand the mystery of his brotherly relationship with the Masai?

3 What does Hemingway mean when he says that the Masai had a noble attitude that he has found in the "best" of the English, Hungarians, and Spaniards? What do you think he means here by "best"?

4 Why do the Masai seem to love the race? Does their competition with the car have any larger significance? Which seems to have the greater dignity—the man or the machine?

5 Why does Hemingway say in the last paragraph that he prefers to "speed it up and get it over with"? What are the opposites that momentarily come together in this paragraph?

6 Hemingway's style is famous for the absolute clarity with which he presents action and feelings in simple language. Judging from this selection, would you agree with this statement? In reading this account of Hemingway's experience, is there any point at which you do not clearly see and feel what is happening?

In April of 1947, Thor Heyerdahl, an anthropologist, together with five companions, set sail from Callao, Peru, upon a huge balsawood raft, the *Kon-Tiki*. Heyerdahl wanted to test his theory that the natives of Polynesia in the South Seas had originally come from South America, navigating unbelievable distances of the Pacific in primitive crafts. Heyerdahl's daring and ingenuity brought to light many facts about the sea that might otherwise have remained unknown. The voyage became one of the great adventures of modern times. Thor Heyerdahl writes about it with both the sensitivity of an artist and the curiosity and precision of a scientist.

The reader of this essay finds himself deeply involved with the six men on the lonely raft drifting with the currents and winds of the Pacific Ocean. This essay is Heyerdahl's original account of his voyage. It is preceded by a foreword by the editors of *Natural History*, the magazine in which it first appeared.

Thor Heyerdahl

Kon-Tiki

FOREWORD BY THE EDITORS

Authorities generally agree that the ancestors of the American Indians came from Asia by way of the Aleutian Islands or Bering Strait. The earliest of these people may have come as much as twenty thousand to forty thousand years ago. But up to fifteen hundred years ago the vast island domain of the Central Pacific known as Polynesia apparently remained uninhabited. There seem to have been two migrations into these islands, one perhaps around A.D. 500 and the other around A.D. 1000.

The question of where these Polynesian people came from has long occupied the attention of anthropologists. Obviously they must have come from either Asia or America. Almost all specialists in this field of science have considered it more likely that they came from Asia.

The present article is written by a man who, after several years of study including approximately a year in Polynesia, a year among the Indians of the Northwest Coast, and many months in South America, became convinced that the Polynesians came from the American side of the Pacific. So firmly did certain cultural similarities lead him to this theory that he resolved to duplicate this long voyage from Peru to Polynesia with the same primitive equipment that the Peruvians are known to have had prior to the first European contacts. The present article is the story of this voyage.

Neither the author nor the editor would have felt it within the scope of this article to present or evaluate the various complex arguments bearing on this migration riddle. The author has assembled his own arguments in a sizeable book, and there they will be judged by scholars on their own merit. Here we have opportunity to see, as if at firsthand, the actual problems that would have been met by a group of prehistoric Peruvians if they embarked or were cast adrift on one of their large rafts. As such, the voyage of Mr.

Heyerdahl and his five companions provides new information on one of the significant aspects of this question, and it can be considered one of the most enterprising expeditions of recent years.

Usually men who have embarked on an ocean raft in modern times have been shipwrecked sailors whose sole desire was to escape the perils of the open sea and reach the nearest coast. But this was not the case in April of last year, when the tugboat *Guardian Rio* towed a clumsy raft away from the sheltered docks of the Peruvian port of Callao and left it adrift well outside the harbor entrance. The six of us that were left aboard the raft were filled with one single hope— that the wind and current would push our primitive craft far away from the South American mainland and right into the wide-open span of the vast Pacific Ocean.

Our purpose was not to flee the Republic of Peru. Leading officials of many nations had bidden us hearty farewell at the dock as the Peruvian Navy tugged us to our point of departure. Nor did we possess any desire to establish a world record in hazardous ocean drift. Yet the betting went high at the docks when we left.

Some claimed that we would be picked up off the coast in a few days or would never be seen again. The nine logs of porous balsa wood upon which we floated were too fragile and would break asunder in the heavy coastal swells, or they would at least be waterlogged and sink underneath us far short of the halfway mark to Polynesia, whose nearest islands lay some four thousand miles from Peru. With a foot and a half of freeboard at the highest section of the bamboo deck, and with an open bamboo hut with thatched roof as our only shelter, we would be at the constant mercy of the waves and the weather and be lost in the first storm.

Others claimed that ropes were no good in the tropic sun and in the sea water and that the complete absence of nails, pegs, and wire in our raft would allow it to tear to pieces as soon as the constant movements of the logs started to chafe the hemp-rope lashings. And if a balsa-wood raft, against all the warnings of the experts, should prove to be seaworthy, it would still not be navigable with its clumsy, square sail and primitive steering oar. How, then, could we possibly expect to hit one of the tiny, far-flung islands? The distance ahead was twice the journey of Columbus and the clumsy raft not even comparable.

All these sinister but well-meant warnings were haunting my mind the first night after the last smoke of the tugboat had dissolved behind the horizon. When I was relieved from watch and tried to sleep, I realized how everything was in motion, not so much the pitching and rolling, as the restlessly undulating movement of the bamboo matting on which we lay on top of the great logs. Each time the stern was lifted by the seas, I saw dancing black hills of water, silhouetted against the stars as they chased along both sides of our raft, with whitecaps hissing at us as they passed. I listened to the squeaking and gnawing of a hundred ropes and the splashing and hammering of water everywhere. At regular intervals heavy seas thundered on board astern, but I noticed with comfort how the water, after whirling up to the waists of the two steersmen, instantly dwindled by falling between the open logs or over the sides of the raft. The seas fell in a pit before they could reach the unprotected bamboo hut lashed on deck a few feet from the stern. Therefore, we struggled to hold the stern to the weather and never let the seas in from the sides.

Gradually I felt happy and proud of our peculiar craft. But I could not quite get away from the complaining music of all the light and heavy ropes as everything aboard moved slowly up and down and even sideways as far as the ropes would permit.

What would the future bring us? How would the raft behave after a week, a month, or perhaps a year at sea?

I was not a sailor, and only one of my companions was experienced in handling an ordinary boat at sea. I had not been able, word by word, to answer the pessimistic warnings of naval authorities and other experts before we put out to sea. I was, nevertheless, firmly convinced that our raft could float across the ocean and bring us safely to some distant Polynesian shore. The secret of my stubborn confidence was that I felt certain that this same ocean route had been covered before by prehistoric men on the very same type of craft.

Already in 1937, after leaving the University of Oslo, I had made a zoological-ethnological survey on the lonely Marquesas Islands in the Southeast Pacific. What I found led me to suspect that an influence from early Central or South America had somehow preceded the present Polynesian culture in this area. It is well known that a number of striking similarities in the culture of South America and Polynesia have been noted. These include two of the important cultivated plants—the sweet potato and the bottle gourd—and many cultural features. The theory has therefore frequently been advanced —and again as frequently rejected—that there must have been a prehistoric contact between these two areas.

There can be no possibility of any land bridge having existed in human times, for a comparative study of the animal life of Polynesia proves its hoary isolation. The island people, when first discovered by Europeans, possessed good seagoing canoes, whereas the natives of Peru had only clumsy balsa rafts for their costal navigation. Because of this, it has usually been assumed by the few who believe there was a cultural transfer that the South American cultures were influenced by the island people rather than vice versa. This view has never been fully accepted and is even doubted by competent scholars of the present day. It is too obvious that some of the Peruvian constructions, artifacts, and food plants in question date from an earlier period in America than A.D. 500, which is commonly accepted, through comparative genealogy, as the approximate date when the first Polynesians spread into the East Pacific.

Thus I had found myself inescapably drawn toward the alternative theory to explain the striking parallels between Peru and Polynesia—namely, that an offshoot from the amazing cultures of early Peru drifted, intentionally or otherwise, into the Pacific.

I was instantly met by one killing argument: How could the Peruvians have covered the thousands of miles of intermediate ocean when their only means of navigation in prehistoric times was an open balsa raft?

To me, there was only one satisfactory answer, and that was to build such a balsa raft and see if it could survive this journey.

I selected five dependable men who volunteered to join me on the experimental voyage. One of them, Herman Watzinger, was a technical engineer, and he directed the building of the balsa raft, guided by detailed accounts and sketches left in the earliest records after the conquest of Peru. First we had to get into the heart of the Ecuadorian jungle to find present-day balsa trees that would match the dimensions of the prehistoric rafts. We cut down nine giant trees, and floated on them down a jungle river to the Pacific coast. With the blessings of the President of Peru and his Naval Minister, the prehistoric type of craft was built in the main naval harbor of Callao under our own supervision.

The nine balsa logs were lashed together side by side with many separate pieces of hemp rope. The bow of the raft took an organ-pipe design, with the longest log in the middle measuring forty-five feet and projecting beyond the others both in the front and in the stern. In the stern it supported a big chunk of balsa holding tholepins for the steering oar. Of the two-foot cross section of these logs, more than half was submerged in the water, but nine smaller cross beams of light balsa covered with bamboo lifted the highest portion of the deck (including the floor of the open hut upon which we slept) eighteen inches above the sea. The little plaited bamboo hut with thatched roof; two hardwood masts side by side, with a square sail; five centerboards two feet wide and six feet deep, inserted at irregular intervals between the logs; and a long wooden steering oar astern completed our replica of the colorful prehistoric craft.

We named our raft *Kon-Tiki* in honor of the mythical sun king who the Incas claim built the enormous stone constructions near Lake Titicaca[1] before he was defeated in war by local tribes. After the defeat, according to legend, he fled with his light-colored people down to the coast and then westward into the Pacific Ocean, never again to return to Peru. Throughout the Polynesian islands, Tiki is remembered as the mythical hero who was first in the line of aboriginal chiefs to settle the islands and to claim direct descent from the sun. The Peruvian prefix "Kon" means Sun.

The six of us went aboard on April 28 and were left at the mercy of the elements in the old Inca fishing grounds outside the port of Callao. Our ages ranged from twenty-five to thirty-two. Herman Watzinger, second-in-command, was in charge of testing and hydrographic and meteorologic measurements. Erik Hesselberg, an artist, was responsible for plotting our drift. Our radio operators were Knut Haugland and Torstein Raaby, both famous for their sabotage activities dur-

ing World War II (instrumental, respectively, in the important sabotage of the German Heavy-Water Plant and the battleship *Tirpitz*). Bengt Danielsson, lonely Swede on our Norwegian expedition, was an ethnologist from the University of Upsala who joined us in South America after an expedition in the jungles of Brazil.

Our voyage would carry us through a vast span of ocean that was very little known, since it was outside all the usual shipping lanes. We had therefore been requested to make continuous observations and transfer them via the amateur radio network to the United States Weather Bureau. But unless we should use the radio for calling help, it would not alter the primitive conditions of our experiment in any way.

The first weeks at sea were hard. One man was seasick for several days and confined to the hut; consequently, with the ocean breaking over us, two of us at a time constantly had to battle with the clumsy steering oar, trying to hold our stern against the short, racing seas of the Humboldt Current. We were soon caught by the offshore trade winds and were then only able to sail before the wind. We now realized that we had cut all our bridges and that there was no road back to the coast.

We had been at sea only a couple of days when an airplane flew out to bring us a last farewell. We never saw the plane (our horizons were narrowly fenced in with watery hills on all sides), nor did they see us, but we spoke to them for several hours with our little radio.

After the first weeks we came into calmer seas with long, rolling swells. The great blue ocean was dotted with whitecaps, and trade wind clouds drifted across the blue sky. We had soft days with swimming and rest, and we traveled along in comfort. Our drift turned from northwest to west as we left the green and cold Humboldt Current and entered the blue and increasingly warm South Equatorial Current. We made as much

1 Lake Titicaca *The highest large navigable lake in the world, it is located on the Peru-Bolivia boundary. It was in the center of early South American civilizations.*

progress as seventy-two miles in one day, with a daily average of forty-two miles for the entire voyage. The surface drift exceeded the current drift and occasionally blew us out of the main sweep of the central current.

We found little wearing on the ropes and learned the reason why. The balsa was too soft to chafe them. In case of friction, a rope would soon work itself into the waterlogged surface of the balsa logs and thus remain protected. It was more discomforting to observe that splinters cut from the surface of the logs had become waterlogged and sank when thrown overboard. It had been common opinion in Peru that the logs would be completely submerged before we sighted the islands.

Archaeologists no longer doubt that the prehistoric Peruvians used sails. Not only are there good historical descriptions of rafts equipped with sails, but centerboards of late pre-European date have been found. Our testings with centerboards clearly proved that they are useless on a raft if it is merely paddled or carried along by the current.

The first real excitement we ran into after entering the South Equatorial Current was the largest monster of the seas—the rare but famous whale shark. Accompanied by a shoal of pilot fish, this giant among all fishes slowly caught up with us from astern, and the water splashed around its enormous, white-speckled back as though on a small reef. The fish bumped into the steering oar and placed its huge, frog-like head, with tiny eyes and a five-foot mouth, right up against the raft. The whale shark has been measured to a length of forty-five feet and undoubtedly grows larger. We would never have dared such an estimate, but while the head appeared on one side of the raft, the tail simultaneously appeared on the other.

The whale shark kept us company for several hours, and the excitement on board was great, with everybody prepared with spears, hand harpoons, and motion picture camera.

The peaceful visit ended when the excited navigator ran his harpoon with all his strength down between his legs and into the cartilaginous head of the monster. During the terrific commotion the whale shark dived, broke the harpoon, snapped the rope, and disappeared.

Only at one other time were we visited by what we suspected to be whale sharks. It was during a fairly calm night when three immensely large and phosphorescent bodies swam in circles under us. But occasionally we ran into schools of whales. The huge, snorting animals rolled right up beside us without the slightest fear. They could have splintered our raft with a single blow of their mighty tails, but after an exhibition of their swimming ability, they left us behind.

Some six hundred miles southwest of the Galápagos[2] we were twice visited by giant sea turtles. One was under constant attack by a dozen furious dolphins which tried to snap at the turtle's neck and fins. After sighting the raft, the turtle made its way right up to our side but swam away as soon as it saw us. Three of our men, equipped with rope, pursued the turtle in a tiny, inflatable rubber float, but our visitor escaped while the bewildered dolphins concentrated all their attention on the bouncing little float.

Weather permitting, we often got into our rubber float, two or three at a time, and took a "vacation" from our sturdy log raft to study our craft from a distance. We could imagine the sight that early Peruvian seafarers must have had when they sailed their flotillas of rafts side by side along the coast—or into the ocean like Inca Tupac Yupanqui, who according to legend discovered some East Pacific islands before the Spanish Conquest. Particularly at night, we experienced an unforgettable sight. Nightblack seas, billowing on all sides, and twinkling stars formed our entire world.

The year 1947—A.D. or B.C.—what did it mean? We were at least alive. Time had little meaning; we were lost in the endless

2 Galápagos *An island group 600 miles west of the South American mainland.*

dark. Ahead of us *Kon-Tiki* rose and then sank between the seas. In moonlight there was an unbelievable atmosphere around the raft. The huge, wet logs fringed with seaweed, the square contour of the sail, the bushy jungle hut with a petrol lamp astern looked like something cut from a fairy tale rather than from reality . . . Now and then the raft would disappear entirely behind the black sea; then, with water pouring from the logs, it would rise high to be silhouetted against the stars.

Although we spent 101 days and nights drifting on our raft, we never sighted a ship or any floating debris left by mankind. If a ship had crossed our path during an average day at sea, it would have found us slowly dancing up and down over great rolling swells dotted with minor waves that were stirred up by the trade winds, which constantly blow from the New World into the island domain. A tanned and bearded man, devoid of clothing, would have been sighted at the stern of the raft, either desperately struggling with the ropes of a long steering oar or, if the wind were steady, sitting and dozing in the sun. Bengt would be found on his stomach in the doorway of the hut reading one of his seventy-three sociological books. Herman would be seen busily occupied anywhere, at the top of the mast, underneath the logs, or running around with instruments to measure wind and water. Knut and Torstein were always struggling with the weather-beaten radio sets, repairing damage and sending out reports at night to the amateur stations that could hear our signals. Erik was always mending sail and splicing rope and sketching fishes and bearded men alike. And each noon he grabbed his sextant and gazed at the sun to determine how far we had moved since the day before. As to myself, I was writing logs, collecting plankton for food experimentation, and fishing or filming.

The day started with a glorious sunrise over the sea, the cook being relieved by the last night watchman to collect the flying fish that had flown on board during the night. These were fried on a small primus stove and devoured at the edge of the raft after a quick morning dip in the sea. Extra flying fish were used as bait for the great colorful dolphin fish that followed the raft day in and day out across the ocean. Dolphins that we did not eat were used as bait for the great sharks that calmly swam around us day and night. When the sea was high, we could see them sideways as though through a perpendicular glass wall raised high above the level of the raft. Then the raft tipped up and let the water and the slowly moving sharks pass beneath us. They never seemed treacherous except when we cleaned fish, and they scented blood. Then they would wake up in a fury. Yet we never quite trusted them, and in one day we pulled aboard nine six- to ten-foot sharks just to dispose of their intimate company.

When we slid the sharks up onto our shallow and slippery logs, the remoras, clinging to the sharks' skin by suction, would jump off and attach themselves to the side of the raft; and the pilot fish, having lost their king and master, would find a substitute in *Kon-Tiki*, joining us in nice formation before the bow or between the centerboards. If a big blue shark passed, they would occasionally follow him away, but more than forty of them tailed us right across the ocean until our raft was shattered on the reef.

Although we carried our rations lashed to the logs beneath the bamboo deck, it was still of great importance to me to find out whether primitive man, accustomed to hardship as he was, would have been able to renew his supply of food and water on such a long-lasting drift. The answer was affirmative. After the fourth day at sea, there was not a single day throughout the journey when we were not accompanied by numbers of dolphin fish. They kept to the side of the raft or beneath us and could be fished, speared, or hooked whenever we desired. Edible barnacles and seaweeds grew all over the huge logs and could be picked like garden greens. And they often housed tiny, edible pelagic crabs or very small fishes. A dozen or more flying fish, often accompanied by baby squids, came aboard almost every night, sailing through the air in schools right above the surface if pursued by dolphins or sharks. Twice in mid-ocean on dark nights, a long snakelike fish with huge eyes and carnivorous jaws jumped right into our sleeping bags inside the bamboo hut and caused a great commotion. It was probably the *Gempylus*, which was seen this way by man for the first time, only a couple of skeletons having previously been found on South American shores. Soaked shark meat, delicious bonito, and yellow-fin tuna completed our seafood menu and made it clear enough that early, hardy raftsmen were not menaced by hunger.

We carried two hundred coconuts and samples of the Peruvian sweet potato and gourd, which were important food plants that the aborigines of Peru shared with those of Polynesia. Those not eaten en route were successfully planted upon our arrival on the islands, to prove that they could be carried on a raft without loss of germinating power. These prehistoric food plants could never have drifted across the ocean without the aid and care of human hands, and the aboriginal name for sweet potato was *Kumara*—both in Peru and on the Polynesian islands.

The early raftsmen along the dry South American coast carried their water supply in gourds or pottery containers and in huge canes of bamboo with the joints pierced out. Left in the shade underneath the bamboo deck, where they were constantly washed by the seas, we found that our plain Peruvian spring water was preserved for more than two months before the first samples began to rot. At that time we had already entered a part of the ocean where drizzles were frequent and rains occasional, and we were able to collect sufficient rain water for our daily needs. We consumed a ton of water on the journey,

along with more than ample rations, and the buoyancy of the balsa logs would have permitted us to double our water supply in easily stored bamboo canes under the deck. With the warm climate creating a demand for salt, we could mix up to 40 per cent of sea water with our drinking water without evil effects. Like our early predecessors and many sailors shipwrecked during the war, we found several simple methods of abstracting the thirst-quenching juice from raw fish, a supply that never ran short.

In this way, with the days full of testings and practical experiments, we found ourselves carried across the ocean bit by bit. By the forty-fifth day we had drifted from the seventy-eighth meridian to the one hundred-eighth and were exactly halfway to the first islands. During those days we were more than two thousand miles away from the nearest shore in any direction. When the ocean was smoothly rolling, we could leave our raft in the little float and row away into the blue space between eternal sea and sky. As we watched our grotesque craft growing smaller and smaller in the distance, an oppressive sense of loneliness came over us. It was as though we were suspended in space, like disembodied spirits. When we rowed back to our distant raft, we felt a strange feeling of relief and were happy to crawl on board our precious, weather-beaten logs and find shade from the glaring sun inside the bamboo hut. The now familiar scent of bamboo and thatched roof made us feel that we were back in our earthly home again, inside a jungle dwelling that was far away from the limitless sea.

We enjoyed our evening meals as the glorious sun sank into the sea before our bow, while sky and water became a dream of colors. Small, striped pilot fish would rush to the surface to snap at our crumbs, and they were occasionally followed by a lazy shark, like kittens by a bulldog.

As darkness came we would light our petrol lamp, and Erik would fetch his guitar.

Then merry song and music from the raft spread with the dim light over the nearest waves of a trackless, endless ocean. We would soon roll up on the bamboo matting inside the hut, leaving the watchman alone with the stars and the steering oar.

We hit two storms when we approached the end of the journey. The first lasted one day and the second five. With sail down and ropes shrieking, *Kon-Tiki* rode the breaking ocean like a duck. A raft in high seas with wet and slippery logs and no railing requires careful stepping. The second storm had just begun when Herman went overboard. When visible again, he was seen struggling behind the stern. He struck for the blade of the steering oar, but a strong wind pushed us ahead, and he missed. We could not turn our raft around to go back a single inch. There was no possibility of even stopping our stubborn craft in its reckless trek to the west. The airy float would blow like a feather ahead of the raft if put to sea in such a wind. We threw out a life belt, once, twice, but it blew right back on board. We became desperate as Herman, our best swimmer, was left farther and farther behind. With a line in one hand Knut leaped into the sea, and slowly the two friends worked their way toward each other. Thirty yards behind the raft they joined hands, and the four of us on board pulled them in.

We had a green parrot as ship's pet. It was a perfect sailor and a joyous companion, until a big sea stole it on the sixtieth day.

At the end of the third month, we were constantly visited by Polynesian frigate birds and boobies in increasing numbers. Then we sighted a rising cumulo-nimbus cloud, revealing the existence of some hidden, sun-baked isle beneath the western horizon. We steered for the clouds as best we could, and as the golden sun rose from the sea on the ninety-third day, the blue haze of land was outlined against a reddish sky. We were passing the tiny atoll of Pukapuka,[3] but wind and current would not permit us to turn around. We had

covered four thousand miles of ocean heading west, and yet we could not force ourselves four miles to the east to reach the island. More than ever was this a plain and unmistakable lesson, stressing the fact that in this ocean a drifting craft and a natural migration would inevitably be pushed to the west. And it was with strange feelings that we sat quietly down on our raft and saw the little, solid speck of land—the first and only for twelve weeks—slide away on our port stern. For a moment the wind carried a mild whiff of verdant tropical foliage and smoky native household odors, and we filled our salty lungs before the fata morgana—the mirage of our hopes—sank into the sea.

On the ninety-seventh day another island grew up out of the ocean, straight ahead of us in line with the bow. As we approached, we saw from the top of the mast that a roaring reef was twisted like a submerged snake all around the island, blocking the approach to the palm-clad beaches behind. All day long we struggled in the current alongside the island to keep clear of the boiling reef and yet be close enough to attempt a landfall wherever an opening might be seen.

Late in the afternoon we sighted the first natives on a beach, and we hoisted all our flags in joy. A great commotion was seen on the beach, and shortly after, the first Polynesians in small outrigger canoes slid through a passage in the reef and swarmed aboard the *Kon-Tiki*. A strong wind blew up, and our ocean raft struggled away from land as the sun went down in the sea. There was a desperate fight against the elements, in which we were assisted by all the friendly natives who were able to get out and join us in the open sea. As the dark night engulfed the island and the sea, a great campfire was lit on shore to show us the direction of the entrance through the reef. But the wind increased its grip, and won another battle. When the glare of the great fire dwindled like a spark in the distance and the roar of the reef was no longer heard, our excited native friends

3   Pukapuka   *Chief island of the Danger Islands, in the Manikiki Island group in the central Pacific Ocean.*

jumped into their canoes to return to their homes on Angatau for fear of drifting with some crazy strangers into the open sea. And we drifted farther into the heart of the Tuamotu, or Dangerous Archipelago.

One night an unusual motion of the raft awakened me, and I suspected land ahead. Next morning, our one hundred-first at sea, we were alarmed by the watchman on the top of the mast, who had sighted an enormous reef that spanned the entire horizon ahead of us. It was the treacherous twenty-mile reef of Raroia Atoll. With white spray shooting high into the air, the surf battered the endless reef in fury.

As we rode directly into this boiling inferno, we had three hours to prepare for all eventualities. We lowered the sail and threw out an improvised anchor on a long rope that kept sliding along the bottom. We carried valuable cargo into the hut and lashed it fast in watertight bags. We cut off all ropes holding the centerboards in position and pulled them up to get a shallow draft. With shoes on for the first time in one hundred days, we concentrated on the last order: Hang on—hang onto the raft whatever happens!

The first walls of thundering water broke down upon us from above as soon as our logs ran against the solid coral reef. Tons of crashing water tore up the deck, flattened the hut, broke the hardwood mast like a match, and splintered the steering oar and stern crossbeam, while we were thrown in and dragged out, thrown in and dragged out, by the furious ocean. During these minutes, when we cramped every existing muscle to withhold the deadly grasp of the passing seas, we made up for all the leisure of the average ocean day. I felt the last of my strength giving away when a wave larger than the others lifted Kon-Tiki free of the water and tossed us high up on the reef. Other waves pushed us closer to shore, until we could jump off the raft and wade the shallow coral reef to a tiny, uninhabited coconut island. Never did any tiny piece of land embody paradise so perfectly to me as this verdant, palm-clad isle with its white and shiny beach facing a crystal clear lagoon, calm as green glass.

A week later we were found by natives who had detected from another island six miles across the lagoon the drift wreckage and the light from our campfire. And about the same time Kon-Tiki was carried by high seas right across the solid reef and left becalmed inside the lagoon. The nine main logs that had carried us 4,300 miles across the ocean in 101 days were still intact, and after an unforgettable two-week Polynesian welcome party on lonely Raroia, our battered raft was towed to Tahiti by the French Government schooner Tamara, which was sent expressly to pick us up.

We shall never forget the welcome on these Polynesian islands.

From Tahiti the Kon-Tiki was carried as deck cargo back to the Norwegian Museum of Navigation in Oslo.

For Discussion

1 How is Thor Heyerdahl's voyage like the voyage of Christopher Columbus? How do they differ? Were the dangers equal? Which took the more courage? Why?

2 List some of the dangers over which the men on the raft had no control. What threats to safety did they eliminate?

3 What were some of the sea creatures that the Kon-Tiki met? Were the men on the raft terrified of these creatures? What was Heyerdahl's attitude toward the sharks that followed the raft?

4 Did the voyage of the *Kon-Tiki* prove Heyerdahl's theory about the origin of the natives of Polynesia? Upon what evidence does he connect Polynesia with South America?

5 How does Heyerdahl's writing differ from a strictly scientific report? Point to two or three passages which would not have been included in purely scientific writing.

6 Heyerdahl conveys a good deal of information in this article. Does he also convey a sense of intellectual and emotional excitement? How does he make this scientific experiment into a human story?

Ben Shahn
Man
Collection, The Museum of Modern Art, New York
Gift of Mr. and Mrs. E. Powis Jones

Unit Eight

No Man Is an Island

More than three hundred and fifty years ago John Donne wrote: "No man is an island, entire of itself. . . . Any man's death diminishes me, because I am involved in Mankind."

That each man on earth is involved with all of humanity is a constant theme of world literature. But whom are we referring to or what do we mean by "mankind" or by "humanity"? These words refer not only to those in our own town and in our own nation, but literally to every other man on the face of the earth. This broad concept of humanity refers not only to those who are living, but to the past and the future as well; and as we accept this concept we also accept a heavy responsibility.

Most people agree that there is something called "the brotherhood of man." It is easy to agree to a phrase, but harder to know what responsibilities go with it. In what emotions and actions does this brotherhood of man show itself? How is it neglected? How is it violated? How is it honored? The selections that follow examine these questions.

Some of the selections suggest ways in which men have been able to achieve brotherhood. The keynote for the unit is the biblical "Parable of the Good Samaritan." The point of the parable is that the Good Samaritan gives his aid to a total stranger, to a man with whom he has no ties of kinship, loyalty, or affection. The only thing the two have in common is that they are human beings. To the Samaritan, this fact justifies his generosity. Another parable, "The Legend of the King and the Peasant," has a similar message.

Here two men make human contact across the barriers of tradition, wealth, and social position.

Some of the selections in this unit discuss the obstacles that prevent men from coming together in brotherhood and cooperation—obstacles such as social or class distinctions, war, and money. Brecht's poem "A Working Man Asks Questions As He Reads" points out that history books often give us a strange idea of just what makes up humanity: they concentrate so intensely on the lives of leaders and of the wealthy and cultured classes that we almost forget that most "history" has happened to the common man. Brecht's poem is an ironic comment on the kind of thinking which seems to exclude the common man from "humanity." Thomas Hardy's poem "The Man He Killed" protests against the way war forces men of goodwill into acts of inhumanity. Leo Tolstoy's ironic story "A Talk Among Leisured People" demonstrates the power that money and position wield over humanitarian ideals.

Goethe, the great German poet, once wrote in a letter: "If you enquire what the people are like here, I must answer, 'The same as everywhere.'" But the Russian writer Dostoevski pointed out some of the difficulties in making the brotherhood of man into a reality: "Until you have become really, in actual fact, a brother to everyone, brotherhood will not come to pass. No sort of scientific teaching, no kind of common interest, will ever teach men to share property and privileges with equal consideration for all."

All these writers agree with Donne's proposition that "No man is an island." But most of them also share Dostoevski's pessimism about whether or not the majority of mankind will ever come to act as if all men are brothers.

It would be hard to find anyone who would openly deny that he has some responsibility to his neighbor. But, as "a certain lawyer" asked Jesus, "who is my neighbor?" Does the word *neighbor* mean my friend? My countryman? Or the unknown peasant suffering from famine on the other side of the globe? The parable with which Jesus answered the lawyer is a classic reply to that everrecurring question.

St. Luke

The Parable of the Good Samaritan

AND, BEHOLD, *a certain lawyer stood up, and tempted him, saying, Master, what shall I do to inherit eternal life?*

He said unto him, What is written in the law? How readest thou?

And he answering said, Thou shalt love the Lord thy God with all thy heart, and with all thy soul, and with all thy strength, and with all thy mind; and thy neighbor as thyself.

And he said unto him, Thou hast answered right: this do, and thou shalt live.

But he, willing to justify himself, said unto Jesus, And who is my neighbor?

And Jesus answering said:

A certain man went down from Jerusalem to Jericho, and fell among thieves, who stripped him of his raiment, and wounded him, and departed, leaving him half dead.

And by chance there came down a certain priest that way: and when he saw him, he passed by on the other side.

And likewise a Levite, when he was at the place, came and looked on him, and passed by on the other side.

But a certain Samaritan, as he journeyed, came where he was: and when he saw him, he had compassion on him; and went to him, and bound up his wounds, pouring in oil and wine, and set him on his own beast, and brought him to an inn, and took care of him.

And on the morrow when he departed, he took out two pence, and gave them to the host, and said unto him, Take care of him; and whatsoever thou spendest more, when I come again, I will repay thee.

Which now of these three, thinkest thou, was neighbor unto him that fell among the thieves?

And he said, He that showed mercy on him.

Then Jesus said unto him, Go and do thou likewise.

John Donne, a contemporary of Shakespeare's, is one of the major poets of the English language. Donne himself was seriously ill about the time he wrote "Meditation XVII," from which this famous passage is taken. He lies in bed and hears the church bell tolling for the dead. But for whom? His neighbor? Himself? The tolling bell reminds him that no earthly life is permanent, and this thought in turn leads him to reflect upon the oneness of humanity.

John Donne

The Tolling Bell

Perchance he for whom this Bell tolls, may be so ill, as that he knows not it tolls for him; And perchance I may think my self so much better than I am, as that they who are about me, and see my state, may have caused it to toll for me, and I know not that. The Church is Catholic, universal, so are all her Actions; All that she does, belongs to all. When she baptizes a child, that action concerns me; for that child is thereby connected to that Head which is my Head too, and engrafed into that body, whereof I am a member. And when she buries a Man, that action concerns me: All mankind is of one Author, and is one volume; when one Man dies, one Chapter is not torn out of the book, but translated into a better language; and every Chapter must be so translated; God employs several translators; some pieces are translated by age, some by sickness, some by war, some by justice; but God's hand is in every translation; and his hand shall bind up all our scattered leaves again, for that Library where every book shall lie open to one another. As therefore the Bell that rings to a Sermon, calls not upon the Preacher only, but upon the Congregation to come; so this Bell calls us all: but how much more me, who am brought so near the door by this sickness. The Bell doth toll for him that thinks it doth; and though it intermit again, yet from that minute that that occasion wrought upon him, he is united to God. Who casts not up his Eye to the Sun when it rises? But who takes off his Eye from a Comet when that breaks out? Who bends not his ear to any bell, which upon any occasion rings? But who can remove it from that bell, which is passing a piece of himself out of this world? No man is an island, entire of it self; every man is a piece of the Continent, a part of the main, if a Clod be washed away by the Sea, Europe is the less, as well as if a Promontory were, as well as if a Manor of thy friend's or of thine own were; any mans death diminishes me, because I am involved in Mankind; And therefore never send to know for whom the bell tolls; It tolls for thee.... Another man may be sick too, and sick to death, and this affliction may lie in his bowels, as gold in a Mine, and be of no use to him; but this bell, that tells me of his affliction, digs out, and applies that gold to me: if by this consideration of another danger, I take mine own into contemplation, and so secure my self, by making my recourse to my God, who is our only security.

For Discussion

1 What indication is there that Donne himself is seriously ill?
2 Explain the meaning of the word "Catholic" in the second sentence. Check the basic meaning in a good dictionary.
3 Donne uses three major metaphors to express his concept of the unity of mankind. What are they?
4 How does Donne compare the bell to the sun?

The following legend is taken from Saadi's *Gulistan* ("Rose Garden"), one of the masterpieces of Persian literature. The complete work contains poetry and prose and is a mixture of tales, songs, religious verse, and moral advice.

Saadi

The Legend of the King and the Peasant

A king, attended by his courtiers, was out on a hunting expedition in the midst of winter. They had got far from the hunting lodge, and the night was falling fast when they saw a peasant's house in the distance.

The king said, "Let us go there, where we may shelter ourselves for the night from this freezing wind."

One of the courtiers replied, "It would not become the dignity of a king to enter the cottage of a low peasant. Rather, let us pitch a tent here and light a fire."

The peasant saw what was happening. He came forth with all the refreshments he had on hand and laid them at the king's feet. He kissed the ground and said, "Nothing can destroy the lofty dignity of Your Majesty, not even entering my poor house. These gentlemen must be unwilling to see the condition of a poor peasant exalted."

The king was pleased with this speech, and, in spite of the objections of his courtiers, he passed into the peasant's cottage, where he spent the night. In the morning he bestowed a handsome cloak and many fine gifts upon his host.

I have heard that the peasant accompanied the king for some distance along the road, walking by the side of his horse and touching the king's stirrups. The peasant said:

"The state and pomp of the king suffered no degradation by being a guest in the house of a peasant. But the brim of the peasant's cap rose to a level with the sun when the shadow of such a monarch fell upon it."

For Discussion

1 From this short story, what can the reader deduce about Persian life in the thirteenth century?
2 How are the king and the peasant different from the courtiers? What do the king and the peasant have in common?
3 Do you know any people who would consider it degrading to go into the house of a poor person?
4 How does this legend exemplify the theme of this unit, "No Man Is an Island"?

FOUR POEMS

Here four poets reflect on aspects of the brotherhood of man: Hardy and Eliot against a background of war; Brecht in an ironic look at history; and the Chilean poet, Pablo Neruda, in the light of his own relationship with the poor.

The Man He Killed

"Had he and I but met
By some old ancient inn,
We should have sat us down to wet
Right many a nipperkin![1]

"But ranged as infantry,   5
And staring face to face,
I shot at him as he at me,
And killed him in his place.

"I shot him dead because—
Because he was my foe,   10
Just so—my foe of course he was;
That's clear enough; although

"He thought he'd 'list perhaps,
Off-hand like—just as I—
Was out of work—had sold his traps—
No other reason why.

"Yes; quaint and curious war is!
You shoot a fellow down
You'd treat if met where any bar is,
Or help to half-a-crown."   20

Thomas Hardy

A Working Man Asks Questions As He Reads

Who built the Seven Gates of Thebes?
In books you find only the names of
kings.

Did the kings carry those heavy blocks
of stone?
And Babylon, destroyed so often,
Who built it again so many times?   In
Lima,   5
That shining city of gold, where did the
workers live?
And after the Great Wall of China was
finished
What happened to the masons who made
it?   Rome
Is filled with triumphant arches.   Who
built them?
Over whom did the Caesars triumph?
Poets sing of Byzantium,   10
But did it have palaces for its workers?
Even in legendary Atlantis, as it sank in
the sea,
Drowning men screamed in the night for
their slaves.

Young Alexander conquered India.
All alone?   15
Caesar beat the Gauls.
He must have had a cook along, at least.
Philip of Spain wept as his fleet
Sank in the ocean.   Who else wept?
Frederick the Great won the Seven Year
War.   20
Were there any other winners?

Victories on every page.
Who cooked those victory banquets?

Every ten years another great man.
Who paid his expenses?   25

So many facts.
So many questions.

Bertolt Brecht

Unrecognized

I want to find out how much I don't
know,
and so sometimes I arrive someplace

---

1   nipperkin   *A quantity of
liquor contained in a vessel with
a capacity of a half pint or less.*

without warning, and I knock and they
    open the door,
and I go in and see the old photographs
    on the walls,
the dining room that belongs to this
    woman and man,   5
the chairs, the beds, the salt-cellars.
And then—only then—I understand
that here they have no idea who I am.
Then I go out and walk through un-
    known streets,
wondering how many men this street
    has devoured,   10
how many poor tantalizing women—
workers of all races—without enough to
    live on.

Pablo Neruda

George Kearns/TRANSLATOR

To the Indians Who Died in Africa

A man's destination is his own village,
His own fire, and his wife's cooking;
To sit in front of his own door at sunset

And see his grandson, and his neighbor's
    grandson
    Playing in the dust together.   5

Scarred but secure, he has many memories
Which return at the hour of conversa-
    tion,
(The warm or the cool hour, according
    to the climate)
Of foreign men, who fought in foreign
    places,
    Foreign to each other.   10

A man's destination is not his destiny,
Every country is home to one man
And exile to another. Where a man dies
    bravely
At one with his destiny, that soil is his.
    Let his village remember.   15

This was not your land, or ours: but a
    village in the Midlands,[1]
And one in the Five Rivers, may have
    the same graveyard.
Let those who go home tell the same
    story of you:
Of action with a common purpose, action
None the less fruitful if neither you nor
    we   20
Know, until the moment after death,
    What is the fruit of action.

T. S. Eliot

For Discussion

1 Hardy's "The Man He Killed" was written during the First World War when individual encounters between enemy soldiers were common. Today, long-range modern weapons make such individual encounters less frequent. Does this in any way make the poem less timely than when Hardy wrote it?

2 In Brecht's ironic poem, a working man has been reading history books. All the questions that come to his mind can be summed up with one larger question which is never directly stated. What is it?

3 Pablo Neruda, Chile's greatest poet, and winner of the Nobel Prize, is probably the most famous citizen of his country. In this poem he tells about going into poor neighborhoods where he will not be recognized as a celebrity. What is his

1 Midlands *The central counties of England.*

motive? How do the poor treat him? What feelings does he have for the common man?

4 Eliot's "To the Indians Who Died in Africa" was written during the Second World War. At that time India was still part of the British Empire, and Indian soldiers fought and died next to the British in many parts of the world. Both the Indians and the British were far from their native villages, their cultural and political differences forgotten as they came together for a common purpose. How is Eliot's poem a comment on Kipling's famous line "East is East and West is West, and never the twain shall meet"?

The loneliness of this railroad station symbolizes one major obstacle to a common brotherhood. Departure of friends or departure from home leaves many people alone and unable to reach out for new friends.

Giorgio de Chirico
Gare Montparnasse (The Melancholy of Departure)
Collection, The Museum of Modern Art, New York
Fractional gift of James Thrall Soby

The Artist's View

Each man is involved with every other man, yet there are many obstacles which prevent a man from becoming the brother of others.

To the artist, the bathrobe is a symbol of his identity. A person usually sees himself differently than others see him. This can become an obstacle which prevents one man from truly knowing another, from becoming another's brother.

James Dine
Self-Portrait
New York University Art Collection
Photograph by Charles Uht

This artist has emphasized the aloneness of man even in a crowd. Such large, impersonal masses of mankind are often a deterrent to brotherhood.

Lester Johnson
Man & Street
Courtesy of Martha Jackson
Gallery, Inc.

The result of man's isolation from man, or man bearing life's pressures alone, is seldom pleasant. Here the artist has expressed the feeling that overwhelms man when he bears too much alone.

Edvard Munch
The Cry
National Gallery of Art,
Washington, D.C.
Rosenwald Collection

Turning to the family in the times of his need and their need, man takes the first steps toward becoming involved with others.

Henry Moore
Family Group
Collection, The Museum of
   Modern Art, New York
A. Conger Goodyear Fund

Religion emphasizes love for mankind. Thus, any man who is truly religious must believe in and work for the brotherhood of man.

New Mexican
Virgin and Child
Index of American Design
National Gallery of Art

This painting can be viewed as capturing the spirit of John Donne's famous lines: "No man is an island, entire of itself. Any man's death diminishes me, because I am involved in Mankind."

Shalom of Safed
Noah's Ark
Collection, The Museum of
Modern Art, New York
Gift of the Jerome L. and
Jane Stern Foundation

This story appears to be just what its title describes. But in fact it is a very personal statement by the author. Tolstoy suffered greatly because he was never able completely to put his humanitarian beliefs into practice.

None of the wealthy people in this story is particularly cruel or selfish. Their conversation becomes Tolstoy's ironic comment on the distance between the ideals to which we pay lip service and those habits by which we really live.

Leo Tolstoy
A Talk Among Leisured People

Some guests assembled at a wealthy house one day happened to start a serious conversation about life.

They spoke of people present and absent, but failed to find anyone who was satisfied with his life.

Not only could no one boast of happiness, but not a single person considered that he was living as a Christian should do. All confessed that they were living worldly lives concerned only for themselves and their families, none of them thinking of their neighbors, still less of God.

"Then why do we live so?" exclaimed a youth. "Why do we do what we ourselves disapprove of? Have we no power to change our way of life? We ourselves admit that we are ruined by our luxury, our effeminacy, our riches, and above all by our pride—our separation from our fellow-men. To be noble and rich we have to deprive ourselves of all that gives man joy.

"Why do we live so? Why do we spoil our lives and all the good that God gives us? I don't want to live in that old way! I will abandon the studies I have begun—they would only bring me to the same tormenting life of which we are all now complaining. I will renounce my property and go to the country and live among the poor. I will work with them, will learn to labour with my hands, and if my education is of any use to the poor I will share it with them, not through institutions and books but directly by living with them in a brotherly way.

"Yes, I have made up my mind," he added, looking inquiringly at his father, who was also present.

"Your wish is a worthy one," said his father, "but thoughtless and ill-considered. It seems so easy to you only because you do not know life. There are many things that seem to us good, but the execution of what is good is complicated and difficult. New paths are made only by men who are thoroughly mature and have mastered all that is attainable by man. It seems to you easy to make new paths of life only because you do not yet understand life. It is an outcome of thoughtlessness and youthful pride. Your active life lies before you. You are now growing up and developing. Finish your education, make yourself thoroughly conversant with things, get on to your own feet, have firm convictions of your own, and then start a new life if you feel you have strength to do so. But for the present you should obey those who are guiding you for your own good, and not try to open up new paths of life."

The youth was silent and the older guests agreed with what the father had said.

"You are right," said a middle-aged married man, turning to the youth's father. "It is true that the lad, lacking experience of life, may blunder when seeking new paths of life and his decision cannot be a firm one. But you know we all agreed that our life is contrary to our conscience and does not give us happiness. So we cannot but recognize the justice of wishing to escape from it.

"The lad may mistake his fancy for a reasonable deduction, but I, who am no longer young, tell you for myself that as I listened to the talk this evening the same thought occurred to me. It is plain to me that the life I now live cannot give me peace of mind or happiness. Experience and reason alike show me that. Then what am I waiting for? We struggle from morning to night for our fam-

ilies, but it turns out that we and our families live ungodly lives and get more and more sunk in sins. We work for our families, but our families are no better off, because we are not doing the right thing for them. And so I often think that it would be better if I changed my whole way of life and did just what that young man proposed to do; ceased to bother about my wife and children and began to think about my soul. Not for nothing did Paul say: 'He that is married careth how he may please his wife, but he that is unmarried careth how he may please the Lord.'"

But before he had finished speaking his wife and all the women present began to attack him.

"You ought to have thought of that before," said an elderly woman. "You have put on the yoke, so you must draw your load. Like that, everyone will say he wishes to go off and save his soul when it seems hard to him to support and feed his family. That is false and cowardly. Of course it would be easy enough to save your own soul all by yourself. But to behave like that would be to run contrary to Christ's teaching. God bade us love others; but in that way you would in his name offend others. No. A married man has his definite obligations and he must not shirk them. It's different when your family are already on their own feet. Then you may do as you please for yourself, but no one has a right to force his family."

But the man who had spoken did not agree. "I don't want to abandon my family," he said. "All I say is that my family should not be brought up in a worldly fashion, nor brought up to live for their own pleasure, as we have just been saying, but should be brought up from their early days to become accustomed to privation, to labour, to the service of others, and above all to live a brotherly life with all men. And for that we must relinquish our riches and distinctions."

"There is no need to upset others while you yourself do not live a godly life," exclaimed his wife irritably. "You yourself lived for your own pleasure when you were young, then why do you want to torment your children and your family? Let them grow up quietly, and later on let them do as they please without coercion from you!"

Her husband was silent, but an elderly man who was there spoke up for him.

"Let us admit," said he, "that a married man, having accustomed his family to a certain comfort, cannot suddenly deprive them of it. It is true that if you have begun to educate your children it is better to finish it than to break up everything—especially as the children when grown up will choose the path they consider best for themselves. I agree that for a family man it is difficult and even impossible to change his way of life without sinning. But for us old men it is what God commands. Let me say for myself: I am now living without any obligations, and to tell the truth, simply for my belly. I eat, drink, rest, and am disgusting and revolting even to myself. So it is time for me to give up such a life, to give away my property, and at least before I die to live for a while as God bids a Christian live."

But the others did not agree with the old man. His niece and godchild was present, to all of whose children he had stood sponsor and gave presents on holidays. His son was also there. They both protested.

"No," said the son. "You worked in your time, and it is time for you to rest and not trouble yourself. You have lived for sixty years with certain habits and must not change them now. You would only torment yourself in vain."

"Yes, yes," confirmed his niece. "You would be in want and out of sorts, and would grumble and sin more than ever. God is merciful and will forgive all sinners—to say nothing of such a kind old uncle as you!"

"Yes, and why should you?" added another old man of the same age. "You and I have perhaps only a couple of days to live, so why should we start new ways?"

"What a strange thing!" exclaimed one of the visitors who had until now been silent. "What a strange thing! We all say that it would be good to live as God bids us and that we are living badly and suffer in body and soul, but as soon as it comes to practice it turns out that the children must not be upset and must be brought up not in godly fashion but in the old way. Young folk must not run counter to their parents' will and must live not in a godly fashion but in the old way. A married man must not upset his wife and children and must live not in a godly way but as of old. And there is no need for old men to begin anything: they are not accustomed to it and have only a couple of days left to live. So it seems that none of us may live rightly: we may only talk about it."

Aylmer Maude/TRANSLATOR

For Discussion

1 What about the youth's proposals to renounce his property and live among the poor? Are they practical? Does the question of practicality have anything to do with it?

2 The whole story builds toward the simple paradox in the last sentence. Is this final comment a just one?

3 Evaluate the arguments put forth by: (a) the youth's father; (b) the elderly woman; (c) the son and niece of the old man.

4 Write a continuation of the conversation between these wealthy people. Introduce yourself as one of the characters. What position would you take in the discussion?

5 This conversation would have taken place in Russia in the early years of this century or the last years of the nineteenth century. Do similar conversations take place in America today? Explain.

Biographies

S(HMUEL) Y(OSEF HALEVI) AGNON (1888–1970) was born in Poland but emigrated to what is now Israel in 1908. His first poems were published in 1903. When he first went to Israel, Agnon served as the first secretary of the Jewish court in Jaffa and as secretary of the National Jewish Council. He lectured on Hebrew literature in Germany. As a writer, Agnon stimulated a new interest in Jewish folklore, traditions, and laws. In 1966 he received the Nobel Prize for literature.

LEONID ANDREYEV (1871–1919) was a Russian writer. After graduating with a degree in law, he turned to writing, receiving aid and encouragement from Maxim Gorki. Among the best of his earlier works are *In the Fog* (1902) and *Thought* (1902), both dealing with sensational themes, and both written in a realistic manner. His subsequent works became increasingly complex and often strained in their quest for sensationalism and symbolism.

ERNEST ATTAH is a modern African writer.

W(YSTAN) H(UGH) AUDEN (1907–1973) was the acknowledged leader of the social movement in English poetry in the 1930s. He emigrated from England to the United States in 1939 and became an American citizen several years later. Prior to his death, he returned to England. He won the Pultizer Prize for poetry in 1948. Auden also wrote several plays.

STAN BARSTOW (1928–   ) is an English prose writer. At sixteen he started working as an engineer and eventually became a sales executive. In 1962 he abandoned a business career to become a full-time writer. Most of Barstow's works are novels, although he has written a few television plays and some short stories.

BASHŌ (1644–1694) was a Japanese poet and diarist. Until 1667 he was the companion to the son of the local lord. With him he studied verse writing. In 1667, Bashō moved to Edo (Tokyo) and continued writing haiku in the conventional comic manner. After his move to a recluse's hut in 1680, Bashō's haiku became more original. Many of his poems are a record of his pilgrimages. Zen Buddhism played a large part in his life and strongly influenced his writing.

CHARLES BAUDELAIRE (1821–1867), an important figure in the Symbolist school, was a French poet. His poetry, written at a crucial point in literary history, formed the bridge which led to modern poetry. Reflected in twentieth century poetry is his view of life and nature as morbid and evil. Art alone could transform life into something beautiful. Although his literary output was important to the later development of poetry, Baudelaire published only one volume, *Les Fleurs du mal*.

GIOVANNI BOCCACCIO (1313–1375) was an Italian prose writer and poet. His prolific output, including many works that were the first of their kind in Italian or European literature, entitles him to a place beside Petrarch as a founder of the Italian Renaissance. Toward the end of his life, he turned to scholarly works written in Latin, rejecting all vernacular writing as sinful. These Latin works were important in the growth of humanism.

HEINRICH BÖLL (1917–   ) is a German novelist and short-story writer. The religious and moral principles on which his critical attitude toward modern society is based are set forth in his *Letter to a Young Catholic* (1958). His best known novels are *And Did Not Say a Single Word* (1953), and *Billiards at Half-Past Nine* (1959). Among his more recent works, *Irish Journal* (1967), *Absent Without Leave* (1965), and *Children Are Civilians Too* (1970) have been widely acclaimed. In 1972 he won the Nobel Prize for literature.

BERTOLT BRECHT (1898–1956) was a German dramatist. A cynical and critical irony toward modern society may be found in all of his works. But not until *The Threepenny Opera* and *The Rise and Fall of the City of Mahagonny* did Brecht advocate Marxism in his plays. It was also at this time that he developed the technique of the "epic theater," a technique that was to dominate his later works. Later plays included several direct attacks on Nazism and several with historical settings: *Galileo* and *Mother Courage and Her Children*, to name but two.

CLAUS BREMER was born in Germany. His primary interest is the theater, where he is active as an actor, director, and translator.

ROBERT BROWNING (1812–1889) was a famous English poet. At first he failed as a poet and tried writing drama, also without success. In 1846 he married Elizabeth Barrett, one of the most famous poets of the time. They lived in Italy until her death in 1861. Browning continued to publish poetic volumes which sold badly. Not until fairly late in life did Browning come into his own. Some of his more famous works, notable for their insight into character, are: "Fra Lippo Lippi," "Andrea del Sarto," "Soliloquy in a Spanish Cloister," and "My Last Duchess."

BUNNO was a Chinese poet who lived about 3,000 years ago.

ROBERT BURNS (1759–1796), the son of a Scots farmer, was himself a farmer with little formal education. His success as a poet demonstrated that true talent could triumph over great odds, and that his native Scots dialect could be a vehicle for fine poetry.

Much of his poetry is about nature, love, patriotism, and peasant life. Burns's poetry moves with a conversational rhythm. He almost always wrote to an old tune for which he sought appropriate words.

BUSON (1716–1783) was a Japanese poet and painter. He is famous for his haiku poems and is ranked along with Bashō as one of the best producers of haiku.

PEDRO CALDERÓN DE LA BARCA (1600–1681), a dramatist, was one of the greatest literary figures of Spain. After graduating from the university, Calderón became a soldier. His writing career began in 1620. In 1651 he became a priest and from then on wrote only his *Autos Sacramentales* and command plays for the court. Calderón wrote in a typically Baroque manner, imposing symbols upon the work and making frequent use of metaphor. During his life, he wrote more than 120 plays and 90 shorter works. His plays range through various types, from comedies to dramas to historical plays, and through various themes, from conjugal honor to Henry VIII and Anne Boleyn.

CALLIMACHUS (c.305–c.240 B.C.) was a Greek poet renowned during his life and after as a master of the short poem. He is said to have been the head of the Alexandrian library.

ALBERT CAMUS (1913–1959) was born in Algeria. He grew up in poverty, attending public schools and working his way through the University of Algiers. He graduated in 1936, and then worked in the theater as an actor and as a director. In 1940 he joined the staff of *Paris-Soir*, a Parisian newspaper. He became active in the French Resistance during World War II by editing an underground paper, *Combat*. After the war, Camus produced the plays, novels, and essays on man's behavior that won him the Nobel Prize for literature in 1957. During his life, he worked ceaselessly for humanitarian causes. He spoke out against all forms of aggression and exploitation.

GAIUS VALERIUS CATULLUS (c.84–c.54 B.C.) is one of the world's great lyric poets. He was born to a wealthy Roman family. In 62 B.C. Catullus went to Rome where he became a leader in the literary and social circles. Among his friends were Cicero and Julius Caesar. Catullus also wrote epigrams ridiculing the Romans of his day.

C(ONSTANTINE) P(ETER) CAVAFY (1863–1933) was a Greek poet. His poetry falls into two main groups: narrative poems of events in the Greek past, written in an ironic tone; and personal poems, often about love, which are to the point and unsentimental.

FRANCISCO CERVANTES is a modern Mexican poet.

MIGUEL DE CERVANTES SAAVEDRA (1547–1616) was born in Spain. As a young man, he was a soldier who fought against the Moors. While trying to get back to Spain, he was captured by

Barbary pirates and held for five years. Finally returning to Spain, he eked out a living by writing plays and stories that had little success. Cervantes died before he could enjoy the fame or fortune that *Don Quixote*, one of the masterpieces of world literature, would have brought him.

ANTON CHEKHOV (1860–1904) was the son of a poverty-ridden shopkeeper in Russia. He attended medical school, but turned to writing, which he found to be a more congenial career. His main interest lay with the characters; and, perhaps more than any other Russian writer, Chekhov illustrates the comment that "a Russian story is always the story of the undoing of a life." He is famous for his plays, which include *The Cherry Orchard* and *The Three Sisters*, performed all over the world.

JEAN COCTEAU (1889–1963) was a French author who produced works in almost every genre—poems, novels, essays, films, dramas. Always in the forefront of every movement, Cocteau did much to advocate the work of several modern creators, among them Picasso in art and Stravinsky in music.

COLETTE (1873–1954) is the pen name of Sidonie Gabrielle Colette, a French novelist. At one time she was a music-hall dancer and mime. Her novels are mainly wry, piercing looks into the lives of women. One of her best-known works is *Gigi* (1954).

CONFUCIUS (551?–497? B.C.) was a Chinese political and ethical philosopher. Confucius's teachings expounded a worldly, rational philosophy, one which puts the emphasis on humanity, reverence for the ancient sages, and government by personal virtue. Although he was unable to achieve his personal ambitions, Confucius's many disciples carried on his teachings, somewhat more developed and altered, until Confucianism became the dominant philosophy in China.

JULIO CORTÁZAR (1914–   ) was born in Belgium, but grew up in Argentina. In 1951 he left Argentina because he was opposed to the dictatorship of Juan Perón. Although he has returned there periodically, Cortázar has made his home in Paris. As a novelist and short-story writer, Cortázar is an experimenter, playing with form, reality and illusion, and language. When *Hopscotch* appeared in 1966, he was hailed as the first great Latin American novelist.

YULI DANIEL (1925–   ) is a Russian Jew. On September 13, 1965 he was arrested by the Soviet government which claimed that his writings were sacrilegious in content and seditious in intent. He was eventually sentenced to five years imprisonment. Before the arrest and trial, Daniel was not a well-known writer. In the Soviet Union, he was known mainly as a verse translator. Under the pseudonym "Nikolai Arzhak" he published four of his stories abroad. It was for these four stories that Daniel was arrested.

DANTE ALIGHIERI (1265–1321) was an Italian poet. He was a member of the Guelph family and was active in the feud between the Black and White Guelphs. When the Black Guelphs gained control of Florence in 1301, Dante was sent on a mission to the Pope. While he was away, he was exiled, and he could never return to Florence. For a while he lived in Verona, and then settled in Ravenna. His best-known work is the epic *The Divine Comedy,* a view of man's temporal and eternal destiny.

EMILY DICKINSON (1830–1886) was an American poet. After graduating from Mount Holyoke Female Seminary, she became a recluse. She dressed only in white and retired to her room, coming downstairs only rarely. Although she wrote more than 2,000 poems, only a few were published during her lifetime. Most of her poems are very short, written in a terse, concrete style. Like Emerson, Emily Dickinson believed that the Divine Spirit was manifested in Nature.

ISAK DINESEN (1885–1962) is the pseudonym of Baroness Karen Blixen. She was born in Denmark, but moved to British East Africa with her husband in 1914. In 1931 she returned to Denmark. Her stories and novels are full of unexpected appearances, strange characters, and mysterious settings. Her accounts of life in Africa are sensitive, penetrating studies of a different culture. Characteristic stories may be found in *Seven Cothic Tales* and *Winter's Tales.*

JOHN DONNE (1572?–1631) was an English metaphysical poet. His early poems were witty love lyrics, but in 1615 he became a clergyman of the Church of England and his work then took on a religious tone. His elaborate images, intricate metaphors, and rough rhythms, although considered unpolished in his day, now place him in the ranks of the great.

GERALD DURRELL (1925–   ) is an English zoologist who usually writes about animals. His brother, Lawrence Durrell, is also an author. Gerald's books include *My Family and Other Animals* (1956), *A Zoo in My Luggage* (1960), and *The Whispering Land* (1961).

T(HOMAS) S(TEARNS) ELIOT (1888–1965) was born in St. Louis, Missouri. He went to Harvard and then to graduate schools in Europe. After finishing his schooling, Eliot settled in London and in 1927 became a British subject. His first volume of poems was published in 1917, but not until the publication of *The Waste Land* in 1922 did he achieve fame. Additional volumes of verse in 1930 and 1943 added to his reputation as a great poet. Besides influencing the form of modern poetry, as a critic, Eliot did much to change the taste of modern audiences by bringing attention to such poets as Dryden, Donne, and Dante.

D(ENNIS) J(OSEPH) ENRIGHT (1920–   ) is an English poet and essayist. His career as a professor has taken him to several countries: Egypt, Japan, Germany, Thailand, and Singapore. He has published numerous volumes of poems and literary criticism.

ROBERT FROST (1874–1963) was an American poet known for his poetry about New England life. After failing to be published in the United States, Frost went to England in 1912, where he remained for three years. During this time he published two books. Back in the United States, Frost's reputation began to grow and continued to increase with each book he published. Frost won the Pulitzer Prize in 1924, 1931, 1937, and 1943 for *New Hampshire, Collected Poems, A Further Range,* and *A Witness Tree.*

FEDERICO GARCÍA LORCA (1899–1936) is widely considered the greatest twentieth-century poet of the Spanish language. His best poems have roots in the traditional songs of Spain and were meant to be read aloud. García Lorca also wrote plays which have been performed in all parts of the world. His plays, like his poetry, reflect the themes of violence and death which are so much a part of the literature of Spain. García Lorca was brutally murdered during the Spanish Civil War.

RUMER GODDEN (1907–   ) is an English novelist. Two of her novels, *Black Narcissus* (1939) and *The River* (1946), have been made into movies. Other successful books include *The Battle of the Villa Fiorita* (1963) and *An Episode of Sparrows* (1955). Rumer Godden has also written several children's books.

JOHANN WOLFGANG VON GOETHE (1749–1832) is to German literature what Shakespeare is to the literature of England. He was the first German writer since Luther to gain the attention of a European public. From the age of twenty-one until his death Goethe wrote great lyric poetry. His presence at the court in Weimar made it a cultural center for European intellectuals.

EUGEN GOMRINGER is a Bolivian by birth but now lives in Switzerland. Gomringer is an art director, poet, and avant-garde publisher.

JACOB (1785–1863) and WILHELM (1786–1859) GRIMM were German scholars. Their most famous work is *Grimm's Fairy Tales.* They obtained the material for their tales by interviewing peasants. Both brothers also helped to forward the systematic study of German philology.

THOMAS HARDY (1840–1928) was an English poet and novelist. In 1873 he published his first successful novel, *Far From the Madding Crowd.* In his major novels, Hardy's characters struggle against their physical and social environment, their own character, and chance. They are always defeated by forces over which they have no control. Examples may be found in *Far From the Madding Crowd, Jude the Obscure, The Return of the Native, The Mayor of Casterbridge,* and *Tess of the D'Urbervilles.* Late in the 1800s Hardy abandoned the novel as a literary form and turned exclusively to poetry. His poetry appeared in a wide variety of forms, themes, and moods.

JOHANN PETER HEBEL (1760–1826) was a German writer. From 1808 to 1815, he edited *Hausfreund*, a magazine. Hebel's writings reflect his provincialism and his closeness to peasant life. Through humor, realism, and a belief in Christianity, he sought to educate the common people.

HEINRICH HEINE (1797–1826) was one of Germany's finest lyric poets. Although he loved the land and the people of Germany, his political views were in opposition to those of the conservative Prussian government; therefore he went to Paris in 1931 and lived there until his death. In Paris Heine was active as a journalist and critic, writing many works designed to better the relations between Germany and France. Most Americans know him through his more romantic works—his ballads and love songs.

ERNEST HEMINGWAY (1898–1961) was a Nobel-Prize-winning American novelist and short-story writer. Born in Oak Park, Illinois, he spent much of his life in Europe, Africa, and Cuba. His own experience and interests provided the backgrounds for his major writings: service as a lieutenant in the Italian army during World War I (*A Farewell to Arms*) and as a newspaper correspondent in the Spanish Civil War (*For Whom the Bell Tolls*); hunting (*The Snows of Kilimanjaro, The Short, Happy Life of Francis Macomber*); and fishing (*The Old Man and the Sea*). The central passion of his life was to write honestly and well.

O. HENRY (1862–1910) is the pen name of William Sydney Porter. He was born in Greensboro, North Carolina. He became a bank teller in 1891, but in 1896 he was indicted by the bank for embezzlement and he fled to South America. He returned because his wife was ill and was convicted and sentenced to a five-year term in jail. In the three years he served, Porter began to write, using the name O. Henry to conceal his identity. Famous for surprise endings, O. Henry's stories portray the whimsical fate that he felt prevailed in human experience.

JAMES ENE HENSHAW (1924–   ), a playwright, was born in Nigeria. He earned his medical degree at the National University of Ireland at Dublin. Although Henshaw has written several dramas, playwriting comes second to his medical career. His volume of plays is very popular in Africa, and in 1952 he won the Henry Carr Memorial Cup in the All-Nigerian Festival of the Arts.

THOR HEYERDAHL (1914–   ) is a Norwegian author, famous for *Kon-Tiki*. At the University of Oslo, he specialized in zoology and geography and then anthropology. In 1947 he led an expedition from Peru to Polynesia on a raft that was a replica of the prehistoric vessels which he thought first transported South American Indians to Polynesia. The success of the expedition revolutionized the theories about the settlement of Polynesia. In

1970 Heyerdahl led an expedition on the *Ra-2,* a papyrus reed boat which sailed from Morocco to Barbados in the West Indies. He claimed that the success of the voyage proved that the ancient Egyptians could have sailed to the New World.

VICTOR HUGO (1802–1885) was a French writer who led the Romantic movement in France. He played an active role in the political life of France, but had little real influence. He did, however, have a great impact on French literature. His poetry is an excellent example of Romanticism at its best. *Notre-Dame de Paris* and *Les Misérables,* two of Hugo's many novels, are his best-known works.

RASHIDAH BINT RASHIN IBN ISMAILI is a modern African poetess.

ISSA (1763–1827) was a Japanese writer of both poetry and prose. He is best known for his haiku.

W. W. JACOBS (1863–1943) was a popular English storyteller. His comic tales about sailors and rustics were collected in *Snug Harbor* (1931). "The Monkey's Paw," his most widely reprinted work, is a powerful horror story. It has been dramatized by L. N. Parker.

FRANCIS JAMMES (1868–1938) was a French poet and novelist. His early poems, written during the time of his friendship with André Gide, are mainly pastoral elegies. After 1905, when he was converted to Catholicism, Jammes's poems became more seriously religious.

ERNST JANDL (1925–   ) was born in Vienna, Austria, and has taught at grammar schools there since 1949. His first experiments with language began in the 1950s. Dr. Jandl began these experiments as a protest against traditional poetry, but they soon became an end in themselves. He has published several books.

SAN JUAN DE LA CRUZ (1542–1591) was a Spanish mystic and poet. In his efforts to reform Spain according to his beliefs, he antagonized the church hierarchy and was imprisoned. It was here that San Juan began his *Songs of the Soul,* a group of lyrical, mystical poems. San Juan escaped from prison and spent his last years in reform efforts and in writing volumes on mystical theology.

FRANZ KAFKA (1883–1924) was a Bohemian writer. His works focus on the problematic existence of modern man. In them, a world of absurdity and paradox, aimlessness and futility, and sometimes faint hope, is revealed under the surface of day-to-day existence. Kafka's most famous works are *The Trial* (1925), *The Metamorphosis* (1915), and *In the Penal Colony* (1919).

JULIAN KAWALEC (1916–   ) was born in Poland. He was the only child in the family who attended school. He graduated from the University of Krakow with a major in Polish philology.

After World War II, Kawalec became a journalist and free-lance writer. His first work appeared in 1954.

JOHN KEATS (1795–1821) is considered to be one of the best of the English Romantic poets. Between 1818 and 1819 he wrote some of the finest odes in English—"Ode to a Nightingale," "Ode on a Grecian Urn," "Ode to Psyche," "Ode on Melancholy," and "To Autumn." He also produced an astonishing number of other great poems, including "La Belle Dame sans Merci," "The Eve of St. Agnes," and "On First Looking into Chapman's Homer." Keats's skill in transmitting the experiences of the senses and in sustaining feeling are probably unsurpassed in English poetry. His life was cut short when he died of tuberculosis at the age of twenty-five.

KIKAKU (1661–1705) was one of the most famous of the "Ten Philosophers," students of Bashō. This Japanese master of the haiku was a known observer of the nature of things. Unlike most haiku writers, Kikaku was not as interested in the "other" world as he was in this world.

A(BRAHAM) M(OSES) KLEIN (1909–   ) is a Canadian poet and lawyer. He has published several volumes of verse, the first of which appeared in 1940. His poetic themes concentrate on the traditions, history, and folklore of the Jews. In 1951 Klein published *The Second Scroll*, a novel dealing with the Jewish condition. Klein enjoys a reputation as a literary scholar. He has published several chapters from a work of his entitled "A Commentary on James Joyce's *Ulysses*."

JIRI KOLAR (1914–   ) was born in Protivin, Czechoslovakia, and now lives in Prague. He began experimenting with language in the 1940s. Between 1941 and 1957, Kolar published seven volumes of poetry. Since that time he has published a volume of "evident poetry" and has collaborated on translations of T. S. Eliot, Samuel Beckett, and other writers. Kolar also makes collages, which have been exhibited in one-man shows throughout Europe.

JERZY KOSINSKI (1933–   ) was born in Poland, but came to the United States in 1957. In 1965 he became an American citizen. Under the pseudonym Joseph Novak, he has written a few books about Russia. In 1965 *The Painted Bird* was published. It is the story of a young boy in eastern Europe during World War II. Although Kosinski does not consider it an autobiography, he does say "every incident is true." The influence of Kosinski's early years in war-torn Europe is strongly evidenced in his writings, which include *Steps, Being There,* and *The Devil Tree*.

KYOSHI (1874–1959), a student of Shiki's (see page 394), became the head of one of the divisions of the "Shiki school." The division under Kyoshi published the magazine *Hototogisu* which Shiki had established. Kyoshi followed Shiki's directions closely and aimed for sincerity in his haiku.

JEAN DE LA FONTAINE (1621–1695) was a French author. A prolific writer of comedies, lyrics, elegies, ballads, and earthy tales, La Fontaine is best remembered for his translations of Aesop's fables. But La Fontaine was more than a translator; he gave his animals the characteristics of the Frenchmen of his time. This twist adds a sharpness to the fables.

D(AVID) H(ERBERT) LAWRENCE (1885–1930) was an English author who wrote successfully in several genres. During his life many of his works were misunderstood and banned as obscene. Disgusted with England, Lawrence and his wife traveled extensively throughout the world. Most of his poetry is written in free verse, dealing with animals and nature. His novels, among them *Women in Love, Sons and Lovers,* and *Lady Chatterley's Lover,* express his view that sex (the primitive subconscious) and nature are the only healing forces in the modern world. He also wrote short stories, such as "The Rocking-Horse Winner" and "The Prussian Officer," which many critics believe to be his best works.

CAMARA LAYE (1928–   ) is an African novelist. After successfully completing his schooling in Africa, Laye went to Paris, where he studied industrial education. It was during this time that he began writing. On his return to Africa, Laye worked for the Guinea Ministry of Youth.

GIACOMO LEOPARDI (1798–1837) was an Italian poet. Physically deformed and afflicted by a spinal disease, Leopardi wrote melancholy, pessimistic poems, expressing his belief in a nature hostile to man, a nature denying man any happiness. It is this pervading mood of pessimism that is the connective in his several volumes of poetry.

DORIS LESSING (1919–   ) is an English writer who has lived in Rhodesia for many years. She writes novels, short stories, and essays. Her belief in several causes, chiefly socialism, is reflected in her works. Her published works include *The Golden Notebook* (1962), *Briefing for Descent Into Hell* (1970), and *The Four-Gated City* (1970).

LI HO (791–817) was a classical Chinese poet. He became famous at a very early age, impressing even visiting officials with his poetic talent. After this promising beginning Li Ho failed the Chinese Civil Service examination and spent the rest of his life in exile and poverty.

LI I (?–827) was a Chinese poet who lived during the T'ang Empire. He was probably the most popular poet of that time. At one time, Li I was a government official. He later wandered around China, but returned to the capital to work in the Imperial Library.

LI PO (c.701–c.762 B.C.) was a Chinese poet. At the age of twenty-five he left his home and wandered through China, a type of "knight-errant." In 742 he was summoned to be the court poet. After three years, however, Li Po fell out of favor and left to continue his wandering. In 757 he entered the service of Prince Lin, who was trying to succeed to the throne. When Prince Lin failed, Li Po was banished. But on his way to exile, he was reprieved. His poetry reflects his wide range of interests and his many talents.

ST. LUKE is the patron saint of painters and physicians. The Bible states that he was a physician himself. He was the author of the Gospel of St. Luke and Acts of the Apostles in the New Testament.

FRANÇOISE MALLET-JORIS (1930–   ) is a Belgian-born French novelist. While still in her teens she wrote *The Illusionists* (1950), which like its sequel *The Red Room* (1953), shows the defensive cruelty and cynicism of those who would love. *The House of Lies* (1956) and *Café Celeste* (1958) use a Flemish realism of detail to expose tragedies of self-delusion. Other works include *The Favorite* (1961) and *Cordelia* (1954).

MARTIAL (40–104) is the shortened name of Marcus Valerius Martialis, a Latin writer of epigrams. His epigrams provide us with a picture of the life and manners in Rome during his time. As an entertaining and amusing man of letters, Martial was admitted to court. He was the friend of several emperors—Titus, Domitian, and Trajan—as well as with Pliny the Younger.

GUY DE MAUPASSANT (1850–1893) was born in Normandy. During his short career, Maupassant produced over 300 short stories and six novels. His two most famous stories, each of which has been reprinted hundreds of times, are "A Piece of String," and "The Necklace."

MICHELANGELO (1475–1564) was an Italian sculptor, architect, painter, and poet of the Renaissance. As an artist he was responsible for great works of art, such as the Pietà, the ceiling of the Sistine Chapel, and a statue of David. Although Michelangelo is less well known as a writer, over 200 of his poems survive. These poems are mainly sonnets which reveal Michelangelo's preoccupation with art. He was struggling to reconcile his sense of the beauty of the human form with his Christian awareness of sin. Michelangelo's work is now credited as being the inspiration for two stylistic movements—Mannerism and Baroque —and as responsible for the direction art took for 200 years after his death.

JOHN MILTON (1608–1674), a poet and prose writer, was one of the outstanding figures in English literature. During his youth, Milton attended the best schools in England. When he graduated from Cambridge, he was supported through five years of independent study and then sent on a European tour for two years. After his return to England, Milton's somewhat heretical Puritan beliefs caused him to become a very controversial figure. With the onset of his blindness and his loss of hope for England, Milton began the epic *Paradise Lost* in 1652. It was published in 1667. Milton's character was paradoxical—combining passion, pride, and sensuality with high idealism, strength, and discipline. This character can be seen in his works, a number of which deal with temptation. Such poems are "L'Allegro," "Il Penseroso," and "Samson Agonistes."

INDRO MONTANELLI (1909–   ) is a popular Italian novelist and story writer. "His Excellency" has been made into a widely acclaimed movie, *General Della Rovere*.

SAROJINI NAIDU (1879–1949) was an Indian poet who wrote in English. She was active in the social and political life of India. Her works exemplify the romantic phase of Indian poetry; they are light, sentimental verses.

PABLO NERUDA (1904–1973) is the pen name of Neftali Ricardo Reyes, a Chilean poet. After his first volume of poems appeared in 1924, Neruda was appointed by the government to various consular posts in Europe and Asia. He was also active in the politics of Chile when he returned from Europe. Neruda's earliest works are closest to modernism. Later in his career, Neruda tried to make every work reveal his experience; the result has been described as surrealistic. His most recent poems became the vehicle for his Communist rhetoric; he thought of himself as the "people's poet." In 1972 he won the Nobel Prize for poetry.

LADISLAV NOVAK (1925–   ), born in Turnov, Czechoslovakia, is a poet, painter, and teacher. His "alchemical collages" have been exhibited widely in Europe. Novak has also published a collection of his poems and is now working on several performance pieces and events.

SEAN O'FAOLAIN (1900–   ) is an Irish novelist, biographer, and literary critic. He has distinguished himself as one of the great modern story tellers and has given artistic expression to his country and its people. The comic and tragic come together in his romantic, unpredictable characters.

ONITSURA (1660–1738) is one of the most interesting and individual of all the Japanese haiku poets. He began writing haiku when he was eight. When he was fifteen, Onitsura studied haiku under Soin, a recognized master of the form. At the age of seventy-three he entered the priesthood and stopped writing haiku.

JUAN EMILIO PACHECO is a young Mexican poet.

BORIS PASTERNAK (1890–1960) is considered one of the greatest modern poets. In 1957 he was awarded the Nobel Prize for his novel *Doctor Zhivago;* but, because of pressures by the Soviet government, Pasternak had to refuse the award. *Doctor Zhivago* exposed the brutality and thoughtlessness of the Russian revolution; the Soviet government therefore refused to allow its publication in Russia. Pasternak's poetry has also displeased the

Soviet censors because of its very personal nature and incompatibility with the Soviet doctrine of socialism.

WILFRED PELLETIER is an Odawa Indian born on an island in the Canadian province of Ontario. He became Executive Director of the Canadian National Indian Council and later was at the Institute for Indian Studies at Rochdale College in Toronto.

JACQUES PRÉVERT (1900–   ) is a French poet and screenwriter. Prévert uses his lyricism for varying purposes—sometimes to produce a satirical tone and sometimes to evoke tenderness or wistful melancholy. In his volume of poetry *Paroles* (1946), he satirizes the conventional and praises the joys to be found in the senses.

ALEXANDER PUSHKIN (1799–1837) was a Russian poet, dramatist, novelist, and short-story writer. Several times, because of political indiscreetness, Pushkin was exiled to regions of Russia far from his home in St. Petersburg. Much of Pushkin's work had a great influence on later Russian literature. The character of Ivan Belkin, narrator of *Tales of Belkin,* is one of the models of a realistic depiction of character in Russian literature. Eugene Onegin, the hero of Pushkin's great novel in verse *Eugene Onegin,* is one of the original "superfluous men."

ARTHUR RIMBAUD (1854–1891) was a French poet. All of his poetry was written before he reached the age of twenty. The rest of his life was spent in Africa, where he was a gunrunner. Considered a leader of the symbolist movement in France, Rimbaud had a great influence on the young French poets who were his followers.

EDWIN ARLINGTON ROBINSON (1869–1935) was an American poet. His first poems, including "Richard Cory," were published in campus publications during the two years he spent at Harvard. His first books caused little stir, but Theodore Roosevelt was impressed with them and gave Robinson a post in the New York Customs House. In 1916 Robinson published *The Man Against the Sky,* a critical success, and in the 1920s was the most widely read poet in America. Robinson won the Pulitzer Prize for poetry three times during the 1920s.

SAADI (1184–1291) was a Persian poet. Saadi is honored as a Mohammedan saint, and his tomb is still visited. He wrote prose and verse in both Arabic and Persian. Some authorities credit him with being the first poet to write in Hindustani.

CARL SANDBURG (1878–1967) was born in Illinois. While attending Lombard College, Sandburg's first volume of poetry was published at the expense of one of his professors. His poetry is a celebration of the many facets of America. Sandburg's most famous collections of poems are *Cornhuskers* and *Chicago Poems.* He also wrote a massive biography of Abraham Lincoln and a collection of American folklore, among other prose works. During his life,

Sandburg received two Pulitzer Prizes—one for *Abraham Lincoln: The War Years* (1939), and a second for his *Complete Poems* (1950).

ALBERT SCHWEITZER (1875–1965) was a German of great talent and intelligence. He studied philosophy, music, theology, and medicine. Most of his life was spent at the medical mission he founded in Africa in 1913. His philosophy was based on a respect for all living things, and he believed that human resources should be developed to their fullest. Schweitzer wrote several books on his life and philosophy. He received the Nobel Prize in 1952.

F. R. SCOTT (1899–   ) is a Canadian poet. Although his poetry is often witty and amusing, much of it exhibits his great concern with social problems. During the 1920s, Scott was a member of the "Montreal school," a group of modern poets who were influenced by T. S. Eliot, and published several of his more experimental works in a volume of poetry by the "Montreal school" writers. Scott later became an editor of an experimental literary magazine, *Preview*.

SEAMI (1362–1444) was a Japanese playwright. Like many playwrights, including Shakespeare and Molière, he began as an actor. Together with his father, also an actor, he established the traditional Noh style of theater, fashioning it out of other forms of popular entertainments. Seami is credited with 240 plays, many of which are still performed by classical Japanese actors.

WILLIAM SHAKESPEARE (1564–1616) was born in the town of Stratford-on-Avon in England. During his life he wrote approximately 37 plays and a large amount of poetry, including a sequence of 154 sonnets. These works were all written in London, between 1591 and 1611. The success of Shakespeare's works is based on the author's ability to observe all phases of life and to unite this knowledge with his gift of poetry in order to form a work of art, which as Ben Johnson said, was "not of an age, but for all time."

SHIKI (1867–1902), a Japanese, began writing at the age of eleven. At sixteen he went to Tokyo and began the serious study of haiku. In his twenties, Shiki joined the staff of a newspaper and began to attract attention to himself with his articles on poetry. The "Shiki school" of haiku was formally recognized in 1895. Shiki had revolted against the artificiality of haiku and formed it into a more natural form of poetry.

SIMONIDES (c.506–c.467 B.C.) was a Greek poet. He is most famous for his epigrams, which were widely admired by later Greek and Roman writers.

JOSÉ JUAN TABLADA is a young poet of modern Mexico.

RABINDRANATH TAGORE (1861–1941) was born in Calcutta, India, and educated in Europe. He became a poet, composer, educator, story-writer, dramatist, and painter. He was knighted by

King George V in 1915, but later renounced his title as a protest against the British government. Tagore's work helped to shape the course of events that led to India's eventual independence. He published his first story, "The Beggar Woman," when he was sixteen, and he continued to write stories until his death. In these stories he attempted to dramatize the dominant ideas of the India of his time and to reveal the special beauty of the Indian landscape. He won the Nobel Prize for literature in 1913.

LEO TOLSTOY (1828–1910) was born into a family of Russian nobility. In his early period, Count Leo Tolstoy wrote *War and Peace* and *Anna Karenina*. After a philosophical crisis, Tolstoy evolved a new concept of life and a new attitude toward his writing. He became deeply concerned with the condition of the serfs in Russia, with land reform, with pacifism, and with the question of a Supreme Being—and he tried to carry his beliefs through into his own life. Tolstoy alienated his family by desiring to give away his property, by becoming a vegetarian, and by openly showing his sympathy for the peasants. From this point on, he wrote only to teach a moral lesson.

JAIME TORRES BODET (1902–   ) is one of Mexico's most distinguished writers. He has published poems, criticisms, and essays on philosophy and politics. He has also served as his country's Minister of Education.

LOPE DE VEGA (1562–1635) was a Spanish dramatist and poet. At great speed he wrote hundreds of plays—sacred, comic, and tragic. His lyrical poems, however, are also of great importance. His plays are robust and filled with love, abductions, and profanity. It was Lope de Vega who created the Spanish national drama.

GIOVANNI VERGA (1840–1922), a novelist and leader of the naturalistic school, was born in Italy. He is at his best when describing the environment with which he was most familiar—the land and people of Sicily.

FRANÇOIS VILLON (1431–?) was a French scholar and poet. During his life, he had several brushes with the law—for robbery and brawling. One fight ended in his opponent's death. He was sentenced to be hanged in 1462; however, the sentence was commuted in 1463, and he was banished from Paris. Villon's masterpiece is *Le Petit Testament*. In the nineteenth century Villon became popular as a romantic rogue-hero. Many incidents from his life appeared in the literary works of that time.

WILLIAM WORDSWORTH (1770–1850) was an English poet. He and Samuel Coleridge are credited with starting the romantic movement in 1798 with their joint publication of *Lyrical Ballads*. Although Wordsworth was not the first to write about nature, he was the first major poet to make it his central theme. His most famous poems include the "Lucy" poems, "The world is too much with us," "Tintern Abbey," and "Ode: Intimations of Immortality." In 1843 he was appointed poet laureate of England.

PEDRO XISTO, in addition to being a gifted writer, is an eminent Brazilian lawyer and diplomat. He has represented his country in Canada, the United States, and Japan.

ALEXANDER STEPANOVICH YAKOVLEV (1886–   ) was a Russian novelist and short-story writer. His works are chiefly about life in the Russian villages.

WILLIAM BUTLER YEATS (1865–1939) was a man of many talents. During his life he was a folklorist, playwright, pamphleteer, editor, experimenter in spiritualism, critic, and poet. It was his deep poetic feelings that seem to have prompted all his activity. Although he lived abroad a great deal of the time, Yeats deeply identified with his native Ireland. Active in the "Young Ireland" society, Yeats dreamed of establishing a native Irish poetry. His own poetry is melodic and romantic, with strong mystical overtones. In 1923 Yeats was awarded the Nobel Prize for literature.

Index